Collins
Complete
Spanish

HarperCollins Publishers
Westerhill Road
Bishopbriggs
Glasgow
G64 2QT
Great Britain

First Edition 2009

Reprint 10 9 8 7

© HarperCollins Publishers 2009

ISBN 978-0-00-729940-9

www.collins.co.uk

A catalogue record for this book is available
from the British Library

Typeset by Davidson Pre-Press, Glasgow

Printed in India by Gopsons Papers Ltd

Acknowledgements
We would like to thank those authors and
publishers who kindly gave permission
for copyright material to be used in the
Collins Word Web. We would also like to
thank Times Newspapers Ltd for providing
valuable data.

Come to Collins for comprehensive
dictionaries www.collinsdictionary.com,
and to buy our full range of products,
please visit www.collins.co.uk

SERIES EDITOR
Rob Scriven

MANAGING EDITOR
Gaëlle Amiot-Cadey

PROJECT CO-ORDINATOR
Genevieve Gerrard

BASED ON:
Collins Easy Learning Spanish Grammar
Collins Easy Learning Spanish Verbs
Collins Easy Learning Spanish Words

Contents

Note on trademarks

Foreword for language teachers

The *Easy Learning Complete Spanish* is designed to be used with both young and adult learners, as a group reference book to complement your course book during classes, or as a recommended text for self-study and homework/coursework.

The text specifically targets learners from *ab initio* to intermediate or GCSE level, and therefore its structural content and vocabulary have been matched to the relevant specifications up to and including Higher GCSE.

The approach aims to develop knowledge and understanding of grammar and your learners' ability to apply it by:

- defining parts of speech at the start of each major section with examples in English to clarify concepts
- minimizing the use of grammar terminology and providing clear explanations of terms both within the text and in the **Glossary**
- illustrating points with examples (and their translations) based on topics and contexts which are relevant to beginner and intermediate course content

The text helps you develop positive attitudes to grammar learning in your classes by:

- giving clear, easy-to-follow explanations
- prioritizing content according to relevant specifications for the levels
- sequencing points to reflect course content, e.g. verb tenses
- highlighting useful **Tips** to deal with common difficulties
- summarizing **Key points** at the end of sections to consolidate learning

In addition to fostering success and building a thorough foundation in Spanish grammar, the optional **Grammar Extra** sections will encourage and challenge your learners to further their studies to higher and advanced levels.

The blue pages in the middle section of the book contain **Verb Tables** and a **Verb Index** which students can use as a reference in their work.

Finally the **Vocabulary** section in the last part of the book provides thematic vocabulary lists which can either be used for self-study or as an additional teaching resource.

Introduction for students

Whether you are starting to learn Spanish for the very first time, brushing up on topics you have studied in class, or revising for your GCSE exams, the *Easy Learning Complete Spanish* is here to help. This easy-to-use guide takes you through all the basics you will need to speak and understand modern, everyday Spanish.

Newcomers can sometimes struggle with the technical terms they come across when they start to explore the grammar of a new language. The *Easy Learning Complete Spanish* explains how to get to grips with all the parts of speech you will need to know, using simple language and cutting out jargon.

The text is divided into sections, each dealing with a particular area of grammar. Each section can be studied individually, as numerous cross-references in the text guide you to relevant points in other sections of the book for further information.

Every major section begins with an explanation of the area of grammar covered on the following pages. For quick reference, these definitions are also collected together on pages viii–xii in a glossary of essential grammar terms.

> **What is a verb?**
> A **verb** is a 'doing' word which describes what someone or something does, what someone or something is, or what happens to them, for example, *be*, *sing*, *live*.

Each grammar point in the text is followed by simple examples of real Spanish, complete with English translations, helping you understand the rules. Underlining has been used in examples throughout the text to highlight the grammatical point being explained.

➤ In orders and instructions telling someone <u>TO DO</u> something, the pronoun joins onto the end of the verb to form one word.

    Ayúda<u>me</u>.   Help me.
    Acompá<u>ñanos</u>.   Come with us.

In Spanish, as with any foreign language, there are certain pitfalls which have to be avoided. **Tips** and **Information** notes throughout the text are useful reminders of the things that often trip learners up.

Key points sum up all the important facts about a particular area of grammar, to save you time when you are revising and help you focus on the main grammatical points.

If you think you would like to continue with your Spanish studies to a higher level, check out the **Grammar Extra** sections. These are intended for advanced students who are interested in knowing a little more about the structures they will come across beyond GCSE.

The blue pages in the middle of the book contain **Verb Tables**, where 120 important Spanish verbs (both regular and irregular) are conjugated in full. Examples show you how to use these verbs in a sentence. You can look up any common verbs in the **Verb Index** on pages 460–464 to find a cross-reference to a model verb.

Finally the **Vocabulary** section at the end of the book is divided into 50 topics, followed by a list of **supplementary vocabulary**.

Glossary of Grammar Terms

ABSTRACT NOUN a word used to refer to a quality, idea, feeling or experience, rather than a physical object, for example, *size, reason, happiness*. Compare with **concrete noun**.

ACTIVE a form of the verb that is used when the subject of the verb is the person or thing doing the action, for example, *I wrote a letter*. Compare with **passive**.

ADJECTIVE a 'describing' word that tells you more about a person or thing, such as their appearance, colour, size or other qualities, for example, *pretty, blue, big*.

ADVERB a word usually used with verbs, adjectives or other adverbs that gives more information about when, where, how or in what circumstances something happens or to what degree something is true, for example, *quickly, happily, now, extremely, very*.

AGREE (to) in the case of adjectives and pronouns, to have the correct word ending or form according to whether what is referred to is masculine, feminine, singular or plural; in the case of verbs, to have the form which goes with the person or thing carrying out the action.

APOSTROPHE s an ending ('s) added to a noun to show who or what someone or something belongs to, for example, *Danielle's dog, the doctor's wife, the book's cover*.

ARTICLE a word like *the, a* and *an*, which is used in front of a noun. See also **definite article, indefinite article**.

AUXILIARY VERB a verb such as *be, have* or *do* used with a main verb to form tenses, negatives and questions.

BASE FORM the form of the verb without any endings added to it, for example, *walk, have, be, go*.

CARDINAL NUMBER a number used in counting, for example, *one, seven, ninety*. Compare with **ordinal number**.

CLAUSE a group of words containing a verb.

COMPARATIVE an adjective or adverb with *-er* on the end of it or *more* or *less* in front of it that is used to compare people, things or actions, for example, *slower, less important, more carefully*.

COMPOUND NOUN a word for a living being, thing or idea, which is made up of two or more words, for example, *tin-opener, railway station*.

CONCRETE NOUN a word that refers to an object you can touch with your hand, rather than to a quality or idea, for example, *ball, map, apples*. Compare with **abstract noun**.

CONDITIONAL a verb form used to talk about things that would happen or would be true under certain conditions, for example, *I would help you if I could*. It is also used to say what you would like or need, for example, *Could you give me the bill?*

CONJUGATE (to) to give a verb different endings according to whether you are referring to *I, you, they* and so on, and according to whether you are referring to the present, past or future, for example, *I have, she had, they will have*.

CONJUGATION a group of verbs which have the same endings as each other or change according to the same pattern.

CONJUNCTION a word such as *and, because* or *but* that links two words or phrases of a similar type or two parts of a sentence, for example, *Diane and I have been friends for years; I left because I was bored.*

CONSONANT a letter that isn't a vowel, for example, *b, f, m, s, v* and so on. Compare with **vowel**.

CONTINUOUS TENSE a verb tense formed using *to be* and the *-ing* form of the main verb, for example, *They're swimming* (present continuous); *He was eating* (past continuous).

DEFINITE ARTICLE the word *the*. Compare with **indefinite article**.

DEMONSTRATIVE ADJECTIVE one of the words *this, that, these* and *those* used with a noun to refer to particular peope or things, for example, *this woman, that dog.*

DEMONSTRATIVE PRONOUN one of the words *this, that, these* and *those* used instead of a noun to point out people or things, for example, *That looks fun.*

DIRECT OBJECT a noun or pronoun used with verbs to show who or what is acted on by the verb. For example, in *He wrote a letter* and *He wrote me a letter, letter* is the direct object. Compare **indirect object**.

DIRECT OBJECT PRONOUN a word such as *me, him, us* and *them* which is used instead of a noun to stand in for the person or thing most directly affected by the action expressed by the verb. Compare with **indirect object pronoun**.

ENDING a form added to a verb, for example, *go → goes*, and to adjectives and nouns depending on whether they refer to masculine, feminine, singular or plural things.

EXCLAMATION a word, phrase or sentence that you use to show you are surprised, shocked, angry and so on, for example, *Wow!; How dare you!; What a surprise!*

FEMININE a form of noun, pronoun or adjective that is used to refer to a living being, thing or idea that is not classed as masculine.

FUTURE a verb tense used to talk about something that will happen or will be true.

GENDER whether a noun, pronoun or adjective is feminine or masculine.

GERUND a verb form in English ending in *-ing*, for example, *eating, sleeping.*

IMPERATIVE the form of a verb used when giving orders and instructions, for example, *Shut the door!; Sit down!; Don't go!; Let's eat.*

IMPERFECT one of the verb tenses used to talk about the past, especially in descriptions, and to say what was happening or used to happen, for example, *It was sunny at the weekend; We were living in Spain at the time; I used to walk to school.* Compare to **preterite**.

IMPERSONAL VERB a verb whose subject is *it*, but where the *it* does not refer to any specific thing, for example, *It's raining; It's 10 o'clock.*

INDEFINITE ADJECTIVE one of a small group of adjectives used to talk about people or things in a general way, without saying who or what they are, for example, *several, all, every.*

INDEFINITE ARTICLE the words *a* and *an*. Compare with **definite article**.

INDICATIVE ordinary verb forms that aren't subjunctive, such as the present, preterite or future. Compare with **subjunctive**.

INDEFINITE PRONOUN a small group of pronouns such as *everything, nobody* and *something*, which are used to refer to people or things in a general way, without saying exactly who or what they are.

INDIRECT OBJECT a noun or pronoun used with verbs to show who benefits or is harmed by an action. For example, in *I gave the carrot to the rabbit, the rabbit* is the indirect object and *the carrot* is the direct object. Compare with **direct object**.

INDIRECT OBJECT PRONOUN a pronoun used with verbs to show who benefits or is harmed by an action. For example, in *I gave him the carrot* and *I gave it to him, him* is the indirect object and the *carrot* and *it* are the direct objects. Compare with **direct object pronoun**.

INDIRECT QUESTION a question that is embedded in another question or instruction such as *Can you tell me what time it is?*; *Tell me why you did it*. Also used for reported speech such as *He asked me why I did it*.

INDIRECT SPEECH the words you use to report what someone has said when you aren't using their actual words, for example, *He said that he was going out*. Also called **reported speech**.

INFINITIVE a form of the verb that hasn't any endings added to it and doesn't relate to any particular tense. In English the infinitive is usually shown with *to*, as in *to speak, to eat*.

INTERROGATIVE ADJECTIVE a question word used with a noun, for example, *What instruments do you play?*; *Which shoes do you like?*

INTERROGATIVE PRONOUN one of the words *who, whose, whom, what* and *which* when they are used instead of a noun to ask questions, for example, *What's that?*; *Who's coming?*

INTRANSITIVE VERB a type of verb that does not take a direct object, for example, *to sleep, to rise, to swim*. Compare with **transitive verb**.

INVARIABLE used to describe a form which does not change.

IRREGULAR VERB a verb whose forms do not follow a general pattern. Compare with **regular verb**.

MASCULINE a form of noun, pronoun or adjective that is used to refer to a living being, thing or idea that is not classed as feminine.

NEGATIVE a question or statement which contains a word such as *not, never* or *nothing*, and is used to say that something is not happening, is not true or is absent, for example, *I never eat meat; Don't you love me?* Compare with **positive**.

NOUN a 'naming' word for a living being, thing or idea, for example, *woman, desk, happiness, Andrew*.

NOUN GROUP, NOUN PHRASE a word or group of words that acts as the subject or object of a verb, or as the object of a preposition, for example, *my older sister; the man next door; that big house on the corner*.

NUMBER used to say how many things you are referring to or where something comes in a sequence. See also **ordinal number** and **cardinal number**. Also the condition of being singular or plural.

OBJECT a noun or pronoun which refers to a person or thing that is affected by the action described by the verb. Compare with **direct object**, **indirect object** and **subject**.

OBJECT PRONOUN one of the set of pronouns including *me, him* and *them*, which are used instead of the noun as the object of a verb or preposition. Compare with **subject pronoun**.

ORDINAL NUMBER a number used to indicate where something comes in an order or sequence, for example, *first, fifth, sixteenth.* Compare with **cardinal number**.

PART OF SPEECH a word class, for example, *noun, verb, adjective, preposition, pronoun.*

PASSIVE a form of the verb that is used when the subject of the verb is the person or thing that is affected by the action, for example, *we were told.*

PAST PARTICIPLE a verb form which is used to form perfect and pluperfect tenses and passives, for example, *watched, swum.* Some past participles are also used as adjectives, for example, *a broken watch.*

PAST PERFECT see **pluperfect**.

PERFECT a verb form used to talk about what has or hasn't happened, for example, *I've broken my glasses; We haven't spoken about it.*

PERSON one of the three classes: the first person (*I, we*), the second person (*you* singular and *you* plural), and the third person (*he, she, it* and *they*).

PERSONAL PRONOUN one of the group of words including *I, you* and *they* which are used to refer to you, the people you are talking to, or the people or things you are talking about.

PLUPERFECT one of the verb tenses used to describe something that had happened or had been true at a point in the past, for example, *I'd forgotten to finish my homework.* Also called **past perfect**.

PLURAL the form of a word which is used to refer to more than one person or thing. Compare with **singular**.

POSITIVE a positive sentence or instruction is one that does not contain a negative word such as *not*. Compare with **negative**.

POSSESSIVE ADJECTIVE one of the words *my, your, his, her, its, our* or *their,* used with a noun to show who it belongs to.

POSSESSIVE PRONOUN one of the words *mine, yours, hers, his, ours* or *theirs,* used instead of a noun to show who something belongs to.

PREPOSITION is a word such as *at, for, with, into* or *from,* which is usually followed by a noun, pronoun or, in English, a word ending in *-ing.* Prepositions show how people and things relate to the rest of the sentence, for example, *She's at home; a tool for cutting grass; It's from David.*

PRESENT a verb form used to talk about what is true at the moment, what happens regularly, and what is happening now, for example, *I'm a student; I travel to college by train; I'm studying languages.*

PRESENT PARTICIPLE a verb form in English ending in *-ing,* for example, *eating, sleeping.*

PRETERITE a verb form used to talk about actions that were completed in the past in Spanish. It often corresponds to the ordinary past tense in English, for example, *I bought a new bike; Mary went to the shops on Friday; I typed two reports yesterday.*

PRONOUN a word which you use instead of a noun, when you do not need or want to name someone or something directly, for example, *it, you, none.*

PROPER NOUN the name of a person, place, organization or thing. Proper nouns are always written with a capital letter, for example, *Kevin, Glasgow, Europe, London Eye.*

QUESTION WORD a word such as *why, where, who, which* or *how* which is used to ask a question.

RADICAL-CHANGING VERBS in Spanish, verbs which change their stem or root in certain tenses and in certain persons.

REFLEXIVE PRONOUN a word ending in -self or -selves, such as myself or themselves, which refers back to the subject, for example, He hurt himself; Take care of yourself.

REFLEXIVE VERB a verb where the subject and object are the same, and where the action 'reflects back' on the subject. A reflexive verb is used with a reflexive pronoun such as myself, yourself, herself, for example, I washed myself; He shaved himself.

REGULAR VERB a verb whose forms follow a general pattern or the normal rules. Compare with **irregular verb**.

RELATIVE PRONOUN a word such as that, who or which, when it is used to link two parts of a sentence together.

REPORTED SPEECH see **indirect speech**.

SENTENCE a group of words which usually has a verb and a subject. In writing, a sentence begins with a capital and ends with a full stop, question mark or exclamation mark.

SIMPLE TENSE a verb tense in which the verb form is made up of one word, rather than being formed from to have and a past participle or to be and an -ing form; for example, She plays tennis; He wrote a book.

SINGULAR the form of a word which is used to refer to one person or thing. Compare with **plural**.

STEM the main part of a verb to which endings are added.

SUBJECT a noun or pronoun that refers to the person or thing doing the action or being in the state described by the verb, for example, My cat doesn't drink milk. Compare with **object**.

SUBJECT PRONOUN a word such as I, he, she and they which carries out the action described by the verb. Pronouns stand in for nouns when it is clear who is being talked about, for example, My brother isn't here at the moment. He'll be back in an hour. Compare with **object pronoun**.

SUBJUNCTIVE a verb form used in certain circumstances to indicate some sort of feeling, or to show doubt about whether something will happen or whether something is true. It is only used occasionally in modern English, for example, If I were you, I wouldn't bother; So be it.

SUPERLATIVE an adjective or adverb with -est on the end of it or most or least in front of it that is used to compare people, things or actions, for example, thinnest, most quickly, least interesting.

SYLLABLE consonant+vowel units that make up the sounds of a word, for example, ca-the-dral (3 syllables), im-po-ssi-ble (4 syllables).

TENSE the form of a verb which shows whether you are referring to the past, present or future.

TRANSITIVE VERB a type of verb that takes a direct object, for example, to spend, to raise, to waste. Compare with **intransitive verb**.

VERB a 'doing' word which describes what someone or something does, is, or what happens to them, for example, be, sing, live.

VOWEL one of the letters a, e, i, o or u. Compare with **consonant**.

Nouns

> **What is a noun?**
> A **noun** is a 'naming' word for a living being, thing or idea, for example, *woman*, *desk*, *happiness*, *Andrew*.

Using nouns

➤ In Spanish, all nouns are either <u>masculine</u> or <u>feminine</u>. This is called their <u>gender</u>. Even words for things have a gender.

➤ Whenever you are using a noun, you need to know whether it is masculine or feminine as this affects the form of other words used with it, such as:

- adjectives that describe it
- articles (such as **el** or **una**) that go before it

⇨ *For more information on **Articles** and **Adjectives**, see pages 10 and 19.*

➤ You can find information about gender by looking the word up in a dictionary. When you come across a new noun, always learn the word for *the* or *a* that goes with it to help you remember its gender.

- **el** or **un** before a noun tells you it is masculine
- **la** or **una** before a noun tells you it is feminine

➤ We refer to something as <u>singular</u> when we are talking about just one of them, and as <u>plural</u> when we are talking about more than one. The singular is the form of the noun you will usually find when you look a noun up in the dictionary. As in English, nouns in Spanish change their form in the plural.

➤ Adjectives, articles and pronouns are also affected by whether a noun is singular or plural.

> *Tip*
> Remember that you have to use the right word for *the*, *a* and so on according to the gender of the Spanish noun.

2 Nouns

Gender

1 Nouns referring to people

➤ Most nouns referring to men and boys are <u>masculine</u>.

<u>el</u> hombre	the man
<u>el</u> rey	the king

➤ Most nouns referring to women and girls are <u>feminine</u>.

<u>la</u> mujer	the woman
<u>la</u> reina	the queen

➤ When the same word is used to refer to either men/boys or women/girls, its gender usually changes depending on the sex of the person it refers to.

<u>el</u> estudiante	the (male) student
<u>la</u> estudiante	the (female) student
<u>el</u> belga	the Belgian (man)
<u>la</u> belga	the Belgian (woman)

Grammar Extra!

Some words for people have only <u>one</u> possible gender, whether they refer to a male or a female.

<u>la</u> persona	the (male *or* female) person
<u>la</u> víctima	the (male *or* female) victim

➤ In English, we can sometimes make a word masculine or feminine by changing the ending, for example, English<u>man</u> and English<u>woman</u> or prince and princ<u>ess</u>. In Spanish, very often the ending of a noun changes depending on whether it refers to a man or a woman.

<u>el</u> camarer<u>o</u>	the waiter
<u>la</u> camarer<u>a</u>	the waitress
<u>el</u> emplead<u>o</u>	the employee (*male*)
<u>la</u> emplead<u>a</u>	the employee (*female*)
<u>el</u> ingl<u>és</u>	the Englishman
<u>la</u> ingl<u>esa</u>	the Englishwoman

For further explanation of grammatical terms, please see pages viii-xii.

⟹ *For more information on **Masculine and feminine forms of words**, see page 5.*

2 | Nouns referring to animals

➤ In English we can choose between words like *bull* or *cow*, depending on the sex of the animal. In Spanish too there are sometimes separate words for male and female animals.

el toro	the bull
la vaca	the cow

➤ Sometimes, the same word with different endings is used for male and female animals.

el perro	the (male) dog
la perra	the (female) dog, bitch
el gato	the (male) cat
la gata	the (female) cat

➤ Words for other animals don't change according to the sex of the animal. Just learn the Spanish word with its gender, which is always the same.

el sapo	the toad
el hámster	the hamster
la cobaya	the guinea pig
la tortuga	the tortoise

3 | Nouns referring to things

➤ In English, we call all things – for example, *table, car, book, apple* – 'it'. In Spanish, however, things are either <u>masculine</u> or <u>feminine</u>. As things don't divide into sexes the way humans and animals do, there are no physical clues to help you with their gender in Spanish. Try to learn the gender as you learn the word.

➤ There are lots of rules to help you. Certain endings are usually found on masculine nouns, while other endings are usually found on feminine nouns.

4 Nouns

➤ The following ending is usually found on <u>masculine nouns</u>.

Masculine ending	Examples
-o	el libro the book el periódico the newspaper BUT: la mano the hand la foto the photo la moto the motorbike la radio the radio (*although in parts of Latin America, it is* el radio)

➤ The following types of word are also masculine.

- names of the days of the week and the months of the year

  Te veré el lunes.   I'll see you on Monday.

- the names of languages

  el inglés   English

  el español   Spanish

  Estudio el español.   I'm studying Spanish.

- the names of rivers, mountains and seas

  el Ebro   the Ebro

  el Everest   Everest

  el Atlántico   the Atlantic

➤ The following endings are usually found on <u>feminine nouns</u>.

Feminine ending	Examples
-a	la casa the house la cara the face BUT: el día the day el mapa the map el planeta the planet el tranvía the tram and many words ending in -ma (el problema the problem, el programa the programme, el sistema the system, el clima the climate)
-ción -sión	la lección the lesson la estación the station la expresión the expression
-dad -tad -tud	la ciudad the city la libertad freedom la multitud the crowd

For further explanation of grammatical terms, please see pages viii-xii.

Grammar Extra!

Some words have different meanings depending on whether they are masculine or feminine.

Masculine	Meaning	Feminine	Meaning
el capital	the capital (meaning *money*)	la capital	the capital (meaning *city*)
el cometa	the comet	la cometa	the kite
el cura	the priest	la cura	the cure
el guía	the guide (*man*)	la guía	the guidebook; the guide (*woman*)

Invirtieron mucho capital.	They invested a lot of capital.
Viven en la capital.	They live in the capital.

4   Masculine and feminine forms of words

➤ Like English, Spanish sometimes has very different words for males and females.

el hombre	the man
la mujer	the woman
el rey	the king
la reina	the queen

➤ Many Spanish words can be used to talk about men or women simply by changing the ending. For example, if the word for the male ends in -o, you can almost always make it feminine by changing the -o to -a.

el amigo	the (male) friend
la amiga	the (female) friend
el hermano	the brother
la hermana	the sister
el empleado	the (male) employee
la empleada	the (female) employee
el viudo	the widower
la viuda	the widow

ℹ Note that some words referring to people end in -a in the masculine as well as in the feminine. Only the article (el or la, un or una) can tell you what gender the noun is.

el dentista	the (male) dentist
la dentista	the (female) dentist
el deportista	the sportsman
la deportista	the sportswoman

Nouns

➤ Many masculine nouns ending in a consonant (any letter other than a vowel) become feminine by adding an -a.

el español	the Spanish man
la española	the Spanish woman
el profesor	the (male) teacher
la profesora	the (female) teacher

Tip

If the last vowel of the masculine word has an accent, this is dropped in the feminine form.

un inglés	an Englishman
una inglesa	an Englishwoman
un francés	a Frenchman
una francesa	a Frenchwoman

⇨ For more information about **Spelling** and **Stress**, see pages 196 and 200.

Key points

✔ The ending of a Spanish word often helps you work out its gender: for instance, if a word ends in -o, it is probably masculine; if it ends in -a, it is probably feminine.

✔ These endings generally mean that the noun is feminine: -ción, -sión, -dad, -tad, -tud

✔ Days of the week and months of the year are masculine. So are languages, mountains and seas.

✔ You can change the ending of some nouns from -o to -a to make a masculine noun feminine.

Forming plurals

1 Plurals ending in -s and -es

➤ In English we usually make nouns plural by adding an -s to the end (*garden* → *gardens; house* → *houses*), although we do have some nouns which are irregular and do not follow this pattern (*mouse* → *mice; child* → *children*).

> *Tip*
>
> Remember that you have to use **los** (for masculine nouns) or **las** (for feminine nouns) with plural nouns in Spanish. Any adjective that goes with the noun also has to agree with it, as does any pronoun that replaces it.
>
> ⇨ *For more information on* **Articles**, **Adjectives** *and* **Pronouns**, *see pages* 10, 19 *and* 41.

➤ To form the plural in Spanish, add **-s** to most nouns ending in a vowel (*a, e, i, o* or *u*) which doesn't have an accent.

el libro	the book
los libros	the books
el hombre	the man
los hombres	the men
la profesora	the (female) teacher
las profesoras	the (female) teachers

➤ Add **-es** to singular nouns ending in a consonant (any letter other than a vowel).

el profesor	the (male) teacher
los profesores	the (male/male and female) teachers
la ciudad	the town/city
las ciudades	the towns/cities

i Note that some foreign words (that is, words which have come from another language, such as English) ending in a consonant just add **-s**.

el jersey	the jersey
los jerseys	the jerseys

➤ Words ending in -s which have an unstressed final vowel do not change in the plural.

el paraguas	the umbrella
los paraguas	the umbrellas
el lunes	(on) Monday
los lunes	(on) Mondays

⇨ *For more information on* **Stress**, *see page 200.*

➤ Some singular nouns ending in an accented vowel add **-es** in the plural while other very common ones add **-s**.

el jabalí	the boar
los jabalíes	the boars
el café	the café
los cafés	the cafés
el sofá	the sofa
los sofás	the sofas

Grammar Extra!

When nouns are made up of two separate words, they are called <u>compound nouns</u>, for example, **el abrelatas** (meaning *the tin-opener*) and **el hombre rana** (meaning *the frogman*). Some of these nouns don't change in the plural, for example, **los abrelatas**, while others do, for example, **los hombres rana**. It is always best to check in a dictionary to see what the plural is.

---

2   Spelling changes with plurals ending in -es

➤ Singular nouns which end in an accented vowel and either **-n** or **-s** drop the accent in the plural.

la canción	the song
las canciones	the songs
el autobús	the bus
los autobuses	the buses

➤ Singular nouns of more than one syllable which end in **-en** and don't already have an accent, add one in the plural.

el examen	the exam
los exámenes	the exams

For further explanation of grammatical terms, please see pages viii-xii.

el joven	the youth
los **jóvenes**	young people

➤ Singular nouns ending in -z change to -c in the plural.

la luz	the light
las lu**ces**	the lights
la vez	the times
las ve**ces**	the times

⇨ *For further information on **Spelling** and **Stress**, see pages 196 and 200.*

3 Plural versus singular

➤ A few words relating to clothing that are plural in English can be singular in Spanish.

una braga	(a pair of) knickers
un slip	(a pair of) underpants
un pantalón	(a pair of) trousers

➤ A few common words behave differently in Spanish from the way they behave in English.

un mueble	a piece of furniture
unos muebles	some furniture
una noticia	a piece of news
unas noticias	some news
un consejo	a piece of advice
unos consejos	some advice

Key points

✔ Add -s to form the plural of a noun ending in an unaccented vowel.

✔ Add -es to form the plural of most nouns ending in a consonant.

✔ Drop the accent when adding plural -es to nouns ending in an accented vowel + -n or -s.

✔ Add an accent when adding plural -es to words of more than one syllable ending in -en.

✔ Change -z to -c when forming the plural of words like luz.

✔ A few common words are plural in English but not in Spanish.

Articles

What is an article?
In English, an **article** is one of the words *the*, *a*, and *an* which is given in front of a noun.

Different types of article

➤ There are two types of article:

- the <u>definite</u> article: *the* in English. This is used to identify a particular thing or person.

    I'm going to <u>the</u> supermarket.
    That's <u>the</u> woman I was talking to.

- the <u>indefinite</u> article: *a* or *an* in English, whose plural is *some* or *any* (or no word at all). This is used to refer to something unspecific, or that you do not really know about.

    Is there <u>a</u> supermarket near here?
    I need <u>a</u> day off.

For further explanation of grammatical terms, please see pages viii-xii.

The definite article: el, la, los and las

1 The basic rules

➤ In English, there is only <u>one</u> definite article: *the*. In Spanish, you have to choose between <u>four</u> definite articles: **el**, **la**, **los** and **las**. Which one you choose depends on the noun which follows.

➤ In Spanish, all nouns (including words for things) are either masculine or feminine – this is called their <u>gender</u>. And just as in English they can also be either singular or plural. You must bear this in mind when deciding which Spanish word to use for *the*.

➯ *For more information on **Nouns**, see page 1.*

➤ **el** is used before <u>masculine singular nouns</u>.

<u>el</u> niño	the boy
<u>el</u> periódico	the newspaper

➤ **la** is used before <u>feminine singular nouns</u>.

<u>la</u> niña	the girl
<u>la</u> revista	the magazine

> *Tip*
>
> To help you speak and write correct Spanish, always learn the <u>article</u> or the <u>gender</u> together with the noun when learning vocabulary. A good dictionary will also give you this information.

➤ **los** and **las** are used before <u>plural nouns</u>. **los** is used with masculine plural words, and **las** is used with feminine plural words.

<u>los</u> niños	the boys
<u>las</u> niñas	the girls
<u>los</u> periódicos	the newspapers
<u>las</u> revistas	the magazines

ℹ️ Note that you use **el** instead of **la** immediately before a feminine singular word beginning with **a** or **ha** when the stress falls on the beginning of the word. This is because **la** sounds wrong before the 'a' sound. <u>BUT</u> if you add an adjective in front of the noun, you use **la** instead, since the two 'a' sounds do not come next to each other.

<u>el</u> agua	the water
<u>el</u> hacha	the axe
<u>la</u> misma agua	the same water
<u>la</u> mejor hacha	the best axe

2   a and de with the definite article

➤ If a is followed by el, the two words become al.

al cine	to the cinema
al empleado	to the employee
al hospital	to the hospital
Vio al camarero	He saw the waiter.

➤ If de is followed by el, the two words become del.

del departamento	of/from the department
del autor	of/from the author
del presidente	of/from the president

3   Using the definite article

➤ el, la, los and las are often used in Spanish in the same way as the is used in English. However, there are some cases where the article is used in Spanish but not in English.

➤ The definite article IS used in Spanish:

- when talking about people, animals and things in a general way

Me gustan los animales.	I like animals.
Están subiendo los precios.	Prices are going up.
Me gusta el chocolate.	I like chocolate.
No me gusta el café.	I don't like coffee.
El azúcar es dulce.	Sugar is sweet.

- when talking about abstract qualities, for example, *time, hope, darkness, violence*

El tiempo es oro.	Time is money.
Admiro la sinceridad en la gente.	I admire honesty in people.

[i] Note that the definite article is NOT used in certain set phrases consisting of tener and a noun or after certain prepositions.

tener hambre	to be hungry	(*literally: to have hunger*)
sin duda	no doubt	(*literally: without doubt*)
con cuidado	carefully	(*literally: with care*)

*For more information on **Prepositions**, see page 178.*

- when talking about colours

  El azul es mi color favorito.   Blue is my favourite colour.

- when talking about parts of the body – you do not use *my, your, his* and so on as you would in English

  Tiene los ojos verdes.   He's got green eyes.

  No puedo mover las piernas.   I can't move my legs.

[*i*] Note that possession is often shown by a personal pronoun in Spanish.

  La cabeza me da vueltas.   My head is spinning.

  Lávate las manos.   Wash your hands.

➪ *For more information on* **Personal pronouns,** *see page 42.*

- when using someone's title – for example, *Doctor, Mr* – but talking ABOUT someone rather than to them

  El doctor Vidal no está.   Dr Vidal isn't here.

  El señor Pelayo vive aquí.   Mr Pelayo lives here.

- when talking about institutions, such as school or church

en el colegio	at school
en la universidad	at university
en la iglesia	at church
en el hospital	in hospital
en la cárcel	in prison

- when talking about meals, games or sports

  La cena es a las nueve.   Dinner is at nine o'clock.

  Me gusta el tenis.   I like tennis.

  No me gusta el ajedrez.   I don't like chess.

- when talking about days of the week and dates, where we use the preposition *on* in English

  Te veo el lunes.   I'll see you on Monday.

  Los lunes tenemos muchos deberes.   We have a lot of homework on Mondays.

  Nací el 17 de marzo.   I was born on 17 March.

- when talking about the time

  Es la una.   It's one o'clock.

  Son las tres.   It's three o'clock.

  Son las cuatro y media.   It's half past four.

- when talking about prices and rates

Cuesta dos euros <u>el</u> kilo.	It costs two euros a kilo.
20 euros <u>la</u> hora	20 euros an hour

Key points

✔ Before masculine singular nouns → use **el**.

✔ Before feminine singular nouns → use **la**.

✔ Before feminine singular nouns starting with stressed **a** or **ha** → use **el**.

✔ Before masculine plural nouns → use **los**.

✔ Before feminine plural nouns → use **las**.

✔ **a + el → al**

✔ **de + el → del**

✔ There are some important cases when you would use a definite article in Spanish when you wouldn't in English; for example, when talking about:
  • things in a general way
  • abstract qualities
  • colours
  • parts of the body
  • someone with a title in front of their name
  • institutions
  • meals, games or sports
  • the time, days of the week and dates (*using the preposition <u>on</u> in English*)
  • prices and rates

The indefinite article: un, una, unos and unas

1 The basic rules

➤ In English, the indefinite article is *a*, which changes to *an* when it comes before a vowel or a vowel sound, for example, *an apple*. In the plural, we use *some* or *any*.

➤ In Spanish, you have to choose between <u>four</u> indefinite articles: **un**, **una**, **unos** and **unas**. Which one you choose depends on the noun that follows.

➤ In Spanish, all nouns (including words for things) are either masculine or feminine – this is called their <u>gender</u>. And, just as in English, they can also be either singular or plural. You must bear this in mind when deciding which Spanish word to use for *a*.

⇨ *For more information on* **Nouns**, *see page 1.*

➤ **un** is used before <u>masculine singular nouns</u>.

un niño	a boy
un periódico	a newspaper

➤ **una** is used before <u>feminine singular nouns</u>.

una niña	a girl
una revista	a magazine

➤ **unos** is used before <u>masculine plural nouns</u>.

unos niños	some boys
unos periódicos	some newspapers

➤ **unas** is used before <u>feminine plural nouns</u>.

unas niñas	some girls
unas revistas	some magazines

[i] Note that you use **un** instead of **una** immediately before a feminine singular word beginning with **a** or **ha** when the stress falls on the beginning of the word. This is because **una** sounds wrong before the '*a*' sound.

un ave	a bird

2 Using the indefinite article

➤ The indefinite article is often used in Spanish in the same way as it is in English. However, there are some cases where the article is not used in Spanish but is in English, and vice versa.

16 Articles

➤ The indefinite article is <u>NOT</u> used in Spanish:
  - when you say what someone's job is

Es profesor.	He's a teacher.
Mi madre es enfermera.	My mother is a nurse.

  - after **tener**, **buscar**, or **llevar (puesto)** when you are only likely *to have*, *be looking for* or *be wearing* one of the items in question

No tengo coche.	I haven't got a car.
¿Llevaba sombrero?	Was he wearing a hat?

ℹ️ Note that when you use an adjective to describe the noun, you <u>DO</u> use an article in Spanish too.

Es <u>un</u> buen médico.	He's a good doctor.
Tiene <u>una</u> novia española.	He has a Spanish girlfriend.
Busca <u>un</u> piso pequeño.	He's looking for a little flat.

➤ The indefinite article is <u>NOT</u> used in Spanish with the words **otro**, **cierto**, **cien**, **mil**, **sin**, and **qué**.

otro libro	another book
cierta calle	a certain street
cien soldados	a hundred soldiers
mil años	a thousand years
sin casa	without a house
¡Qué sorpresa!	What a surprise!

➤ The indefinite article <u>IS</u> used in Spanish but <u>NOT</u> in English when an abstract noun, such as **inteligencia** (meaning *intelligence*) or **tiempo** (meaning *time*) has an adjective with it.

Posee <u>una</u> gran inteligencia.	He possesses great intelligence.

Key points
- ✔ Before masculine singular nouns → use **un**.
- ✔ Before feminine singular nouns → use **una**.
- ✔ Before feminine singular nouns starting with stressed a or ha → use **un**.
- ✔ Before masculine plural nouns → use **unos**.
- ✔ Before feminine plural nouns → use **unas**.
- ✔ You do not use an indefinite article in Spanish for saying what someone's job is.
- ✔ You do not use an indefinite article in Spanish with the words **otro**, **cierto**, **cien**, **mil**, **sin**, and **qué**.

The article lo

➤ Unlike the other Spanish articles, and articles in English, lo is <u>NOT</u> used with a noun.

➤ lo can be used with a masculine singular adjective or past participle (the -ado and -ido forms of regular verbs) to form a noun.

<u>Lo único</u> que no me gusta ...	The only thing I don't like ...
Esto es <u>lo importante</u>.	That's the important thing.
<u>Lo bueno</u> de eso es que ...	The good thing about it is that ...
Sentimos mucho <u>lo ocurrido.</u>	We are very sorry about what happened.

⇨ *For more information on the **Past participle**, see page 115.*

➤ lo is also used in a number of very common phrases:

- a lo mejor   maybe, perhaps
  <u>A lo mejor</u> ha salido.   Perhaps he's gone out.

- por lo menos   at least
  Hubo <u>por lo menos</u> cincuenta heridos.   At least fifty people were injured.

- por lo general   generally
  <u>Por lo general</u> me acuesto temprano.   I generally go to bed early.

➤ lo can also be used with que to make lo que (meaning *what*).

Vi <u>lo que</u> pasó.	I saw what happened.
<u>Lo que</u> más me gusta es nadar.	What I like best is swimming.

Grammar Extra!

lo can be used with de followed by a noun phrase to refer back to something the speaker and listener both know about.

<u>Lo de tu hermano</u> me preocupa mucho.	<u>That business with your brother</u> worries me a lot.
<u>Lo de ayer</u> es mejor que lo olvides.	It would be best to forget <u>what happened yesterday.</u>

lo can be used with an adjective followed by **que** to emphasize how big/small/beautiful and so on something is or was. The adjective must agree with the noun it describes.

No sabíamos <u>lo pequeña que</u> **era la casa.**	We didn't know <u>how small</u> the house was.
No te imaginas <u>lo simpáticos que</u> **son.**	You can't imagine <u>how nice</u> they are.

lo can also be used in a similar way with an adverb followed by **que**.

Sé <u>lo mucho que</u> **te gusta la música.**	I know <u>how much</u> you like music.

Key points

✔ **lo** is classed as an article in Spanish, but is not used with nouns.

✔ You can use **lo** with a masculine adjective or past participle to form a noun.

✔ You also use **lo** in a number of common phrases.

✔ **lo que** can be used to mean *what* in English.

Adjectives

> **What is an adjective?**
> An **adjective** is a 'describing' word that tells you more about a person or thing, such as their appearance, colour, size or other qualities, for example, *pretty*, *blue*, *big*.

Using adjectives

➤ Adjectives are words like *clever*, *expensive* and *silly* that tell you more about a noun (a living being, thing or idea). They can also tell you more about a pronoun, such as *he* or *they*. Adjectives are sometimes called 'describing words'. They can be used right next to a noun they are describing, or can be separated from the noun by a verb like *be*, *look*, *feel* and so on.

    a <u>clever</u> girl
    an <u>expensive</u> coat
    a <u>silly</u> idea
    He's just being <u>silly</u>.

⇨ *For more information on **Nouns** and **Pronouns**, see pages 1 and 41.*

➤ In English, the only time an adjective changes its form is when you are making a comparison.

    She's <u>cleverer</u> than her brother.
    That's the <u>silliest</u> idea I've ever heard!

➤ In Spanish, however, most adjectives <u>agree</u> with what they are describing. This means that their endings change depending on whether the person or thing you are referring to is masculine or feminine, singular or plural.

un chico <u>rubio</u>	a fair boy
una chica <u>rubia</u>	a fair girl
unos chicos <u>rubios</u>	some fair boys
unas chicas <u>rubias</u>	some fair girls

➤ In English adjectives come <u>BEFORE</u> the noun they describe, but in Spanish you usually put them <u>AFTER</u> it.

    una casa <u>blanca</u>   a <u>white</u> house

⇨ *For more information on **Word order with adjectives**, see page 24.*

Making adjectives agree

1 Forming feminine adjectives

➤ The form of the adjective shown in dictionaries is generally the masculine singular form. This means that you need to know how to change its form to make it agree with the person or thing it is describing.

➤ Adjectives ending in -o in the masculine change to -a for the feminine.

mi hermano <u>pequeño</u>	my little brother
mi hermana <u>pequeña</u>	my little sister

➤ Adjectives ending in any vowel other than -o (that is: *a, e, i* or *u*) or ending in a vowel with an accent on it do <u>NOT</u> change for the feminine.

el vestido <u>verde</u>	the green dress
la blusa <u>verde</u>	the green blouse
un pantalón <u>caqui</u>	some khaki trousers
una camisa <u>caqui</u>	a khaki shirt
un médico <u>iraquí</u>	an Iraqi doctor
una familia <u>iraquí</u>	an Iraqi family

➤ Adjectives ending in a consonant (any letter other than a vowel) do <u>NOT</u> change for the feminine except in the following cases:

- Adjectives of nationality or place ending in a consonant add -a for the feminine. If there is an accent on the final vowel in the masculine, they lose this in the feminine.

un periódico <u>inglés</u>	an English newspaper
una revista <u>inglesa</u>	an English magazine
el equipo <u>francés</u>	the French team
la cocina <u>francesa</u>	French cooking
el vino <u>español</u>	Spanish wine
la lengua <u>española</u>	the Spanish language

🛈 Note that these adjectives do not start with a capital letter in Spanish.

- Adjectives ending in -or in the masculine usually change to -ora for the feminine.

un niño <u>encantador</u>	a charming little boy
una niña <u>encantadora</u>	a charming little girl

For further explanation of grammatical terms, please see pages viii-xii.

[*i*] Note that a few adjectives ending in -**or** used in comparisons – such as **mejor** (meaning *better, best*), **peor** (meaning *worse, worst*), **mayor** (meaning *older, bigger*), **superior** (meaning *upper, top*), **inferior** (meaning *lower, inferior*) as well as **exterior** (meaning *outside, foreign*) and **posterior** (meaning *rear*) do not change in the feminine.

- Adjectives ending in -**án**, -**ón** and -**ín** in the masculine change to -**ana**, -**ona** and -**ina** (without an accent) in the feminine.

un gesto <u>burlón</u>	a mocking gesture
una sonrisa <u>burlona</u>	a mocking smile
un hombre <u>parlanchín</u>	a chatty man
una mujer <u>parlanchina</u>	a chatty woman

➤ Adjectives ending in a consonant but which do not fall into the above categories do <u>NOT</u> change in the feminine.

un chico <u>joven</u>	a young boy
una chica <u>joven</u>	a young girl
un final <u>feliz</u>	a happy ending
una infancia <u>feliz</u>	a happy childhood

2 Forming plural adjectives

➤ Adjectives ending in an unaccented vowel (*a, e, i, o* or *u*) in the singular add -**s** in the plural.

el <u>último</u> tren	the last train
los <u>últimos</u> trenes	the last trains
una casa <u>vieja</u>	an old house
unas casas <u>viejas</u>	some old houses
una chica muy <u>habladora</u>	a very chatty girl
unas chicas muy <u>habladoras</u>	some very chatty girls
una pintora <u>francesa</u>	a French (woman) painter
unas pintoras <u>francesas</u>	some French (women) painters
una mesa <u>verde</u>	a green table
unas mesas <u>verdes</u>	some green tables

➤ Adjectives ending in a consonant in the masculine or feminine singular add -**es** in the plural. If there is an accent on the <u>FINAL</u> syllable in the singular, they lose it in the plural.

un chico muy <u>hablador</u>	a very chatty boy
unos chicos muy <u>habladores</u>	some very chatty boys
un pintor <u>francés</u>	a French painter
unos pintores <u>franceses</u>	some French painters

un examen **fácil**	an easy exam
unos exámenes **fáciles**	some easy exams
la tendencia **actual**	the current trend
las tendencias **actuales**	the current trends

➤ **-z** at the end of a singular adjective changes to **-ces** in the plural.

un día **feliz**	a happy day
unos días **felices**	happy days

Tip

When an adjective describes a mixture of both masculine and feminine nouns, use the <u>masculine plural</u> form of the adjective.

El pan y la fruta son **baratos.**	Bread and fruit are cheap.

Grammar Extra!

Adjectives ending in an accented vowel in the singular add **-es** in the plural.

un médico **iraní**	an Iranian doctor
unos médicos **iraníes**	some Iranian doctors

---

3 Invariable adjectives

➤ A small number of adjectives do not change in the feminine or plural. They are called <u>invariable</u> because their form <u>NEVER</u> changes, no matter what they are describing. These adjectives are often made up of more than one word – for example **azul marino** (meaning *navy blue*) – or come from the names of things – for example **naranja** (meaning *orange*).

las chaquetas **azul marino**	navy-blue jackets
los vestidos **naranja**	orange dresses

4 Short forms for adjectives

➤ The following adjectives drop the final **-o** before a <u>masculine singular noun</u>.

bueno	→	buen	→	un **buen** libro	a good book
malo	→	mal	→	**mal** tiempo	bad weather
alguno	→	algún	→	**algún** libro	some book
ninguno	→	ningún	→	**ningún** hombre	no man
uno	→	un	→	**un** día	one day
primero	→	primer	→	el **primer** hijo	the first child
tercero	→	tercer	→	el **tercer** hijo	the third child

For further explanation of grammatical terms, please see pages viii-xii.

i Note that the adjectives **alguno** and **ninguno** add accents when they are shortened to become **algún** and **ningún**.

➤ **grande** (meaning *big, great*) is shortened to **gran** before a <u>singular noun</u>.

| un gran actor | a great actor |
| una gran sorpresa | a big surprise |

➤ **ciento** (meaning *a hundred*) changes to **cien** before all <u>plural nouns</u> as well as before **mil** (meaning *thousand*) and **millones** (meaning *millions*).

| cien años | a hundred years |
| cien millones | a hundred million |

i Note that you use the form **ciento** before other numbers.

| ciento tres | one hundred and three |

⇨ *For more information on **Numbers**, see page 206.*

Grammar Extra!

➤ **cualquiera** drops the final **a** before any noun.

| cualquier día | any day |
| a cualquier hora | any time |

Key points

✔ Most Spanish adjectives change their form according to whether the person or thing they are describing is masculine or feminine, singular or plural.

✔ In Spanish, adjectives usually go after the noun they describe.

✔ Don't forget to make adjectives agree with the person or thing they describe – they change for the feminine and plural forms:

un chico español
una chica española
unos chicos españoles
unas chicas españolas

✔ Some adjectives never change their form.

✔ Some adjectives drop the final -o before a masculine singular noun.

✔ **grande** and **ciento** also change before certain nouns.

Word order with adjectives

➤ When adjectives are used right beside the noun they are describing, they go BEFORE it in English. Spanish adjectives usually go AFTER the noun.

una corbata azul	a blue tie
una palabra española	a Spanish word
la página siguiente	the following page
la hora exacta	the precise time

➤ When you have two or more adjectives after the noun, you use y (meaning *and*) between the last two.

un hombre alto y delgado	a tall, slim man

➤ A number of types of Spanish adjectives go BEFORE the noun:

- demonstrative adjectives
este sombrero	this hat

- possessive adjectives (mi, tu, su and so on)
mi padre	my father

- numbers
tres días	three days

- interrogative adjectives
¿qué hombré?	which man?

- adjectives used in exclamations
¡Qué lástima!	What a pity!

- indefinite adjectives
cada día	every day

- shortened adjectives
mal tiempo	bad weather

➤ Some adjectives can go both <u>BEFORE</u> and <u>AFTER</u> the noun, but their meaning changes depending on where they go.

Adjective	Before Noun	Examples	After Noun	Examples
antiguo	former	un antiguo colega a former colleague	old, ancient	la historia antigua ancient history
diferente	various	diferentes idiomas various languages	different	personas diferentes different people
grande	great	un gran pintor a great painter	big	una casa grande a big house
medio	half	medio melón half a melon	average	la nota media the average mark
mismo	same	la misma respuesta the same answer	self, very, precisely	yo mismo myself eso mismo precisely that
nuevo	new	mi nuevo coche my new car (= new to me)	brand new	unos zapatos nuevos some (brand) new shoes
pobre	poor (= wretched)	esa pobre mujer that poor woman	poor (= not rich)	un país pobre a poor country
viejo	old (= long-standing)	un viejo amigo an old friend	old (= aged)	esas toallas viejas those old towels

Key points

✔ Most Spanish adjectives go after the noun.

✔ Certain types of adjectives in Spanish go before the noun.

✔ Some adjectives can go before or after the noun – the meaning changes according to the position in the sentence.

Comparatives and superlatives of adjectives

1   Making comparisons using comparative adjectives

> **What is a comparative adjective?**
> A **comparative adjective** in English is one with -er on the end of it or *more* or *less* in front of it, that is used to compare people or things, for example, *cleverer, less important, more beautiful*.

➤ In Spanish, to say something is *cheaper, more expensive* and so on, you use **más** (meaning *more*) before the adjective.

Esta bicicleta es <u>más barata</u>.	This bicycle is cheaper.
La verde es <u>más cara</u>.	The green one is more expensive.

➤ To say something is *less expensive, less beautiful* and so on, you use **menos** (meaning *less*) before the adjective.

La verde es <u>menos cara</u>.	The green one is less expensive.

➤ To introduce the person or thing you are making the comparison with, use **que** (meaning *than*).

Es <u>más</u> alto <u>que</u> mi hermano.	He's taller than my brother.
La otra bicicleta es <u>más</u> cara <u>que</u> ésta.	The other bicycle is more expensive than this one.
Esta bicicleta es <u>menos</u> cara <u>que</u> la otra.	This bicycle is less expensive than the other one.

Grammar Extra!

When *than* in English is followed by a verbal construction, use <u>de lo que</u> rather than **que** alone.

Está <u>más</u> cansada <u>de lo que</u> parece.	She is more tired than she seems.

---

2   Making comparisons using superlative adjectives

> **What is a superlative adjective?**
> A **superlative adjective** in English is one with -est on the end of it or *most* or *least* in front of it, that is used to compare people or things, for example, *thinnest, most beautiful, least interesting*.

➤ In Spanish, to say something is *the cheapest*, *the most expensive* and so on, you use el/la/los/las (+ noun) + más + adjective.

el caballo más viejo	the oldest horse
la casa más pequeña	the smallest house
los hoteles más baratos	the cheapest hotels
las manzanas más caras	the most expensive apples
¿Quién es el más alto?	Who's the tallest?

➤ To say something is *the least expensive*, *the least intelligent* and so on, you use el/la/los/las (+ noun) + menos + adjective.

el hombre menos simpático	the least likeable man
la niña menos habladora	the least talkative girl
los cuadros menos bonitos	the least attractive paintings
las empleadas menos trabajadoras	the least hardworking (female) employees
¿Quién es el menos trabajador?	Who's the least hardworking?

> *Tip*
>
> In phrases like *the cleverest girl in the school* and *the tallest man in the world*, you use de to translate *in*.
>
> el hombre más alto del mundo — the tallest man in the world

3 Irregular comparatives and superlatives

➤ Just as English has some irregular comparative and superlative forms – *better* instead of '*more good*', and *worst* instead of '*most bad*' – Spanish also has a few irregular forms.

Adjective	Meaning	Comparative	Meaning	Superlative	Meaning
bueno	good	mejor	better	el mejor	the best
malo	bad	peor	worse	el peor	the worst
grande	big	mayor	older	el mayor	the oldest
pequeño	small	menor	younger	el menor	the youngest

Éste es mejor que el otro.	This one is better than the other one.
Es el mejor de todos.	It's the best of the lot.
Hoy me siento peor.	I feel worse today.
la peor alumna de la clase	the worst student in the class

[i] Note that **mejor, peor, mayor** and **menor** don't change their endings in the feminine. In the plural, they become **mejores, peores, mayores** and **menores**. Don't forget to use **el, la, los** or **las** as appropriate, depending on whether the person or thing described is masculine or feminine, singular or plural.

Tip

más grande and **más pequeño** are used mainly to talk about the actual size of something.

Este plato es <u>más grande</u> que aquél.	This plate is bigger than that one.
Mi casa es <u>más pequeña</u> que la tuya.	My house is smaller than yours.

mayor and **menor** are used mainly to talk about age.

mis hermanos <u>mayores</u>	my older brothers
la hija <u>menor</u>	the youngest daughter

---

4 **Other ways of making comparisons**

➤ To say *as ... as* (for example, *as pretty as, not as pretty as*) you use **tan ... como** in Spanish.

Pedro es <u>tan</u> alto <u>como</u> Miguel.	Pedro is as tall as Miguel.
No es <u>tan</u> guapa <u>como</u> su madre.	She isn't as pretty as her mother.
No es <u>tan</u> grande <u>como</u> yo creía.	It isn't as big as I thought.

Grammar Extra!

You use **tanto** with a noun rather than **tan** with an adjective in some expressions. This is because in Spanish you would use a noun where in English we would use an adjective.

Pablo tiene <u>tanto</u> miedo <u>como</u> yo.	Pablo is as frightened as I am.
Yo no tengo <u>tanta</u> hambre <u>como</u> tú.	I'm not as hungry as you are.

➤ To make an adjective stronger, you can use **muy** (meaning *very*).

Este libro es <u>muy</u> interesante.	This book is very interesting.

For further explanation of grammatical terms, please see pages viii-xii.

Grammar Extra!

For even more emphasis, you can add **-ísimo** (meaning *really, extremely*) to the end of an adjective. Take off the final vowel if the adjective already ends in one. For example, **delgado** (meaning *thin*) becomes **delgadísimo** (meaning *really thin*).

Se ha comprado un coche <u>carísimo</u>.	He's bought himself a really expensive car.
Está <u>delgadísima</u>.	She's looking really thin.

If you add **-ísimo**, you need to take off any other accent. For example, **fácil** (meaning *easy*) becomes **facilísimo** (meaning *extremely easy*) and **rápido** (meaning *fast*) becomes **rapidísimo** (meaning *extremely fast*).

Es <u>facilísimo</u> de hacer.	It's really easy to make.
un coche <u>rapidísimo</u>	an extremely fast car

When the adjective ends in **-co**, **-go** or **-z**, spelling changes are required to keep the same sound. For example, **rico** (meaning *rich*) becomes **riquísimo** (meaning *extremely rich*) and **feroz** (meaning *fierce*) becomes **ferocísimo** (meaning *extremely fierce*).

Se hizo <u>riquísimo</u>.	He became extremely rich.
un tigre <u>ferocísimo</u>	an extremely fierce tiger

⇨ *For more information on **Spelling** and **Stress**, see pages 196 and 200.*

Key points

✔ Comparative adjectives in Spanish are formed by:
- **más** + adjective + **que**
- **menos** + adjective + **que**

✔ Superlative adjectives in Spanish are formed by:
- **el/la/los/las** + **más** + adjective
- **el/la/los/las** + **menos** + adjective

✔ There are a few irregular comparative and superlative forms in Spanish.

✔ You can use **tan ... como** to say *as ... as*.

✔ To make an adjective stronger, use **muy**.

Demonstrative adjectives

> **What is a demonstrative adjective?**
> A **demonstrative adjective** is one of the words *this*, *that*, *these* and *those* used
> with a noun in English to point out a particular thing or person, for example,
> *this* woman, *that* dog.

1 Using demonstrative adjectives

➤ Just as in English, Spanish demonstrative adjectives go <u>BEFORE</u> the noun.
Like other adjectives in Spanish, they have to change for the feminine and
plural forms.

	Masculine	Feminine	Meaning
Singular	este	esta	this
	ese	esa	that (*close by*)
	aquel	aquella	that (*further away*)
Plural	estos	estas	these
	esos	esas	those (*close by*)
	aquellos	aquellas	those (*further away*)

➤ Use **este/esta/estos/estas** (meaning *this/these*) to talk about things and
people that are near <u>you</u>.

| Este bolígrafo no escribe. | This pen isn't working. |
| Me he comprado estos libros. | I've bought these books. |

➤ Use **ese/esa/esos/esas** and **aquel/aquella/aquellos/aquellas** (meaning
that/those) to talk about things that are further away.

Esa revista es muy mala.	That magazine is very bad.
¿Conoces a esos señores?	Do you know those gentlemen?
No le gusta aquella muñeca.	She doesn't like that doll.
Siga usted hasta aquellos árboles.	Carry on until you reach those trees (over there).

2 ese or aquel?

➤ In English we use *that* and *those* to talk about anything that is not close by, but
in Spanish you need to be a bit more precise.

➤ Use ese/esa/esos/esas:

- to talk about things and people that are nearer to the person you are talking to than to you

ese papel en el que escribes	that paper you're writing on
¿Por qué te has puesto **esas** medias?	Why are you wearing those tights?

- to talk about things and people that aren't very far away

No me gustan **esos** cuadros.	I don't like those pictures.

➤ Use aquel/aquella/aquellos/aquellas to talk about things that are further away

Me gusta más **aquella** mesa.	I prefer that table (over there).

Grammar Extra!

You should use ese/esa/esos/esas when you are talking about a definite date, month or year.

¿1999? No me acuerdo de dónde pasamos las vacaciones **ese** año.	1999? I can't remember where we went on holiday that year.

You should use aquel/aquella/aquellos/aquellas when you are talking about something in the past and not mentioning a definite date.

aquellas vacaciones que pasamos en Francia	those holidays we had in France

---

Key points

✔ <u>this</u> + noun = este/esta + noun

✔ <u>these</u> + noun = estos/estas + noun

✔ <u>that</u> + noun = ese/esa + noun (*when the object is not far away from you or the person you're talking to*)

✔ <u>that</u> + noun = aquel/aquella + noun (*when the object is more distant*)

✔ <u>those</u> + noun = esos/esas + noun (*when the objects are not far away from you or the person you're talking to*)

✔ <u>those</u> + noun = aquellos/aquellas + noun (*when the objects are more distant*)

Interrogative adjectives

> **What is an interrogative adjective?**
> An **interrogative adjective** is one of the question words and expressions used with a noun such as *which, what, how much* and *how many*; for example, *Which shirt are you going to wear?; How much time have we got?*

➤ In Spanish the interrogative adjectives are qué (meaning *which* or *what*) and cuánto/cuánta/cuántos/cuántas (meaning *how much/how many*). Note that like all other Spanish question words, qué and cuánto have accents on them.

➤ ¿qué? (meaning *which?* or *what?*) doesn't change for the feminine and plural forms.

¿Qué libro te gusta más?	Which book do you like best?
¿Qué clase de diccionario necesitas?	What kind of dictionary do you need?
¿Qué instrumentos tocas?	What instruments do you play?
¿Qué ofertas has recibido?	What offers have you received?

➤ ¿cuánto? means the same as *how much?* in English. It changes to ¿cuánta? in the feminine form.

¿Cuánto dinero te queda?	How much money have you got left?
¿Cuánta lluvia ha caído?	How much rain have we had?

[i] Note that with gente (meaning *people*), which is a feminine singular noun, cuánta must be used.

¿Cuánta gente ha venido?	How many people came?

➤ ¿cuántos? means the same as *how many?* in English. It changes to ¿cuántas? in the feminine plural.

¿Cuántos bolígrafos quieres?	How many pens would you like?
¿Cuántas personas van a venir?	How many people are coming?

> *Tip*
> Don't forget to add the opening upside-down question mark in Spanish questions.

For further explanation of grammatical terms, please see pages viii-xii.

Grammar Extra!

In English we can say, *Tell me what time it is, He asked me how much sugar there was* and *I don't know which dress to choose* to express doubt, report a question, or ask a question in a roundabout or indirect way. In Spanish you can use qué and cuánto/cuánta/cuántos/cuántas in the same way.

Dime <u>qué</u> hora es.	Tell me what time it is.
Me preguntó <u>cuánto</u> azúcar había.	He asked me how much sugar there was.
No sé <u>qué</u> vestido escoger.	I don't know which dress to choose.
No sé a <u>qué</u> hora llegó.	I don't know what time she arrived.
Dime <u>cuántas</u> postales quieres.	Tell me how many postcards you'd like.

Adjectives used in exclamations

➤ In Spanish ¡qué...! is often used where we might say *What a ...!* in English.

¡Qué lástima!	What a pity!
¡Qué sorpresa!	What a surprise!

Tip

Don't forget to add the opening upside-down exclamation mark in Spanish exclamations.

Grammar Extra!

¡qué...! combines with tan or más and an adjective in Spanish to mean *What (a) ...!* in English.

¡Qué día tan *or* más bonito!	What a lovely day!
¡Qué tiempo tan *or* más malo!	What awful weather!
¡Qué pasteles tan *or* más ricos!	What delicious cakes!

In Spanish cuánto/cuánta/cuántos/cuántas can be used to mean *What a lot of ...!* in English.

¡Cuánto dinero!	What a lot of money!
¡Cuánta gente!	What a lot of people!
¡Cuántos autobuses!	What a lot of buses!
¡Cuánto tiempo!	What a long time!

For further explanation of grammatical terms, please see pages viii-xii.

Possessive adjectives (1)

> **What is a possessive adjective?**
> In English a **possessive adjective** is one of the words *my, your, his, her, its, our* or *their* used with a noun to show that one person or thing belongs to another.

➤ Like other adjectives in Spanish, possessive adjectives have to change for the feminine and plural forms.

Singular		Plural		Meaning
masculine	feminine	masculine	feminine	
mi	mi	mis	mis	my
tu	tu	tus	tus	your (*belonging to someone you address as* tú)
su	su	sus	sus	his; her; its; your (*belonging to someone you address as* usted)
nuestro	nuestra	nuestros	nuestras	our
vuestro	vuestra	vuestros	vuestras	your (*belonging to people you address as* vosotros/vosotras)
su	su	sus	sus	their; your (*belonging to people you address as* ustedes)

⇨ *For more information on **Ways of saying 'you' in Spanish**, see page 44.*

¿Dónde está <u>tu</u> hermana?	Where's your sister?
José ha perdido <u>su</u> cartera.	José has lost his wallet.
¿Dónde están <u>nuestros</u> pasaportes?	Where are our passports?
¿Por qué no traéis a <u>vuestros</u> hijos?	Why don't you bring your children?
<u>Mis</u> tíos están vendiendo <u>su</u> casa.	My uncle and aunt are selling their house.

Tip

Possessive adjectives agree with what they describe <u>NOT</u> with the person who owns that thing.

Pablo ha perdido <u>su</u> bolígrafo.	Pablo has lost his pen.
Pablo ha perdido <u>sus</u> bolígrafos.	Pablo has lost his pens.

ℹ️ Note that possessive adjectives aren't normally used with parts of the body. You usually use the <u>definite article</u> instead.

Tiene <u>los</u> ojos verdes.	He's got green eyes.
No puedo mover <u>las</u> piernas.	I can't move my legs.

➡️ *For more information on* **Articles**, *see page 10.*

Tip

As **su** and **sus** can mean *his*, *her*, *its*, *your* or *their*, it can sometimes be a bit confusing. When you need to avoid confusion, you can say the Spanish equivalent of *of him* and so on.

<u>su</u> casa	→	la casa <u>de él</u>	his house (*literally: the house of him*)
<u>sus</u> amigos	→	los amigos <u>de usted</u>	your friends (*literally: the friends of you*)
<u>sus</u> coches	→	los coches <u>de ellos</u>	their cars (*literally: the cars of them*)
<u>su</u> abrigo	→	el abrigo <u>de ella</u>	her coat (*literally: the coat of her*)

➡️ *For more information on* **Personal pronouns**, *see page 42.*

Key points

✔ The Spanish possessive adjectives are:
- mi/tu/su/nuestro/vuestro/su with a masculine singular noun
- mi/tu/su/nuestra/vuestra/su with a feminine singular noun
- mis/tus/sus/nuestros/vuestros/sus with a masculine plural noun
- mis/tus/sus/nuestras/vuestras/sus with a feminine plural noun

✔ Possessive adjectives come before the noun they refer to. They agree with what they describe, rather than with the person who owns that thing.

✔ Possessive adjectives are not usually used with parts of the body. Use el/la/los or las as appropriate instead.

✔ To avoid confusion, it is sometimes clearer to use el coche de él/ella/ellas/ellos/usted and so on rather than su coche.

For further explanation of grammatical terms, please see pages viii-xii.

Possessive adjectives (2)

➤ In Spanish, there is a second set of possessive adjectives, which mean (of) mine, (of) yours and so on. Like other adjectives in Spanish, they change in the feminine and plural forms.

Singular		Plural		Meaning
masculine	feminine	masculine	feminine	
mío	mía	míos	mías	mine/of mine
tuyo	tuya	tuyos	tuyas	yours/of yours (belonging to tú)
suyo	suya	suyos	suyas	his/of his; hers/of hers; of its; yours/of yours (belonging to usted)
nuestro	nuestra	nuestros	nuestras	ours/of ours
vuestro	vuestra	vuestros	vuestras	yours/of yours (belonging to vosotros/as)
suyo	suya	suyos	suyas	theirs/of theirs; yours/of yours (belonging to ustedes)

⇨ For more information on **Ways of saying 'you' in Spanish**, see page 44.

un amigo <u>mío</u>	a (male) friend of mine, one of my (male) friends
una revista <u>tuya</u>	a magazine of yours, one of your magazines
una tía <u>suya</u>	an aunt of his/hers/theirs/yours, one of his/her/their/your aunts
una amiga <u>nuestra</u>	a (female) friend of ours, one of our friends
¿De quién es esta bufanda? – Es <u>mía</u>.	Whose scarf is this? – It's mine.

[i] Note that unlike the other possessive adjectives, these adjectives go <u>AFTER</u> the noun they describe.

un amigo <u>vuestro</u>	a (male) friend of yours, one of your friends

38 Adjectives

> ## Tip
>
> Possessive adjectives agree with what they describe <u>NOT</u> with the person who owns that thing.
>
> Estos apuntes son <u>míos</u>.   These notes are mine.

Grammar Extra!

mío/mía and so on are also used in exclamations and when addressing someone. In this case they mean the same as *my* in English.

¡Dios <u>mío</u>!	My God!
amor <u>mío</u>	my love
Muy señor <u>mío</u>	Dear Sir
hija <u>mía</u>	my dear daughter

For further explanation of grammatical terms, please see pages viii-xii.

Indefinite adjectives

> **What is an indefinite adjective?**
> An **indefinite adjective** is one of a small group of adjectives used to talk about people or things in a general way without saying exactly who or what they are, for example, *several*, *all*, *every*.

➤ In English indefinite adjectives do not change, but in Spanish most indefinite adjectives change for the feminine and plural forms.

Singular		Plural		Meaning
masculine	**feminine**	**masculine**	**feminine**	
algún	alguna	algunos	algunas	some; any
cada	cada			each; every
mismo	misma	mismos	mismas	same
mucho	mucha	muchos	muchas	a lot of
otro	otra	otros	otras	another; other
poco	poca	pocos	pocas	little; few
tanto	tanta	tantos	tantas	so much; so many
todo	toda	todos	todas	all; every
		varios	varias	several

algún día	some day
el mismo día	the same day
las mismas películas	the same films
otro coche	another car
mucha gente	a lot of people
otra manzana	another apple
pocos amigos	few friends

i Note that you can never use **otro** (meaning *other* or *another*) with **un** or **una**.

¿Me das otra manzana?	Will you give me another apple?
¿Tienes otro jersey?	Have you got another jumper?

Tip

Some and *any* are usually not translated before nouns that you can't count like bread, butter, water.

Hay pan en la mesa.	There's some bread on the table.
¿Quieres café?	Would you like some coffee?
¿Hay leche?	Is there any milk?
No hay mantequilla.	There isn't any butter.

➤ todo/toda/todos/todas (meaning *all* or *every*) can be followed by:
- a definite article (el, la, los, las)

Han estudiado durante toda la noche.	They've been studying all night.
Vienen todos los días.	They come every day.

- a demonstrative adjective (este, ese, aquel and so on)

Ha llovido toda esta semana.	It has rained all this week.

- a possessive adjective (mi, tu, su and so on)

Pondré en orden todos mis libros.	I'll sort out all my books.

- a place name

Lo sabe todo Madrid.	The whole of Madrid knows it.

⇨ *For more information on* **Articles**, **Demonstrative adjectives** *and* **Possessive adjectives**, *see pages* 10, 30 *and* 35.

➤ As in English, Spanish indefinite adjectives come <u>BEFORE</u> the noun they describe.

las mismas películas	the same films

Key points

✔ Like other adjectives, Spanish indefinite adjectives (such as otro and todo) must agree with what they describe.
✔ They go before the noun to which they relate.

Pronouns

What is a pronoun?
A **pronoun** is a word you use instead of a noun, when you do not need
or want to name someone or something directly, for example, *it, you, none*.

➤ There are several different types of pronoun:

- <u>Personal pronouns</u> such as *I, you, he, her* and *they*, which are used
  to refer to you, the person you are talking to, or other people and things.
  They can be either <u>subject pronouns</u> (*I, you, he* and so on) or <u>object
  pronouns</u> (*him, her, them*, and so on).

- <u>Possessive pronouns</u> like *mine* and *yours*, which show who someone or
  something belongs to.

- <u>Indefinite pronouns</u> like *someone* or *nothing*, which refer to people or things
  in a general way without saying exactly who or what they are.

- <u>Relative pronouns</u> like *who, which* or *that*, which link two parts of a
  sentence together.

- <u>Interrogative pronouns</u> like *who, what* or *which*, which are used in
  questions.

- <u>Demonstrative pronouns</u> like *this* or *those*, which point things or people
  out.

- <u>Reflexive pronouns</u>, a type of object pronoun that forms part of Spanish
  reflexive verbs like **lavarse** (meaning *to wash*) or **llamarse** (meaning
  to be called).

⇨   *For more information on **Reflexive verbs**, see page* 91.

➤ Pronouns often stand in for a noun to save repeating it.
>   I finished my homework and gave <u>it</u> to my teacher.
>   Do you remember Jack? I saw <u>him</u> at the weekend.

➤ Word order with personal pronouns is usually different in Spanish and English.

Personal pronouns: subject

> **What is a subject pronoun?**
> A **subject pronoun** is a word such as *I*, *he*, *she* and *they*, that carries out the action expressed by the verb. Pronouns stand in for nouns when it is clear who or what is being talked about, for example, *My brother isn't here at the moment. He'll be back in an hour.*

1 Using subject pronouns

➤ Here are the Spanish subject pronouns:

Singular	Meaning	Plural	Meaning
yo	I	nosotros (*masculine*)	we
tú	you	nosotras (*feminine*)	we
él	he	vosotros (*masculine*)	you
ella	she	vosotras (*feminine*)	you
usted (Vd.)	you	ellos (*masculine*)	they
		ellas (*feminine*)	they
		ustedes (Vds.)	you

[*i*] Note that there is an accent on **tú** (*you*) and **él** (*he*) so that they are not confused with **tu** (*your*) and **el** (*the*).

> *Tip*
> The abbreviations Vd. and Vds. are often used instead of **usted** and **ustedes**.

➤ In English we use subject pronouns all the time – *I walk*, *you eat*, *they are going*. In Spanish you don't need them if the verb endings and context make it clear who the subject is. For example **hablo español** can only mean *I speak Spanish* since the **-o** ending on the verb is only used with *I*. Similarly, **hablamos francés** can only mean *we speak French* since the **-amos** ending is only used with *we*. So the subject pronouns are not needed in these examples.

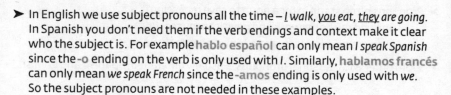

| Tengo un hermano. | *I*'ve got a brother. |
| Tenemos dos coches. | *We*'ve got two cars. |

ℹ️ Note that usted/Vd. and ustedes/Vds. are often used for politeness, even if they are not really needed.

¿Conoce <u>usted</u> al señor Martín?	Do you know Mr Martín?
Pasen <u>ustedes</u> por aquí.	Please come this way.

⇨ *For more information on **Ways of saying 'you' in Spanish**, see page 44.*

➤ Spanish subject pronouns are normally only used:
- for emphasis

¿Y <u>tú</u> qué piensas?	What do <u>you</u> think about it?
<u>Ellos</u> sí que llegaron tarde.	<u>They</u> really did arrive late.

- for contrast or clarity

<u>Yo</u> estudio español pero <u>él</u> estudia francés.	I study Spanish but <u>he</u> studies French.
<u>Él</u> lo hizo pero <u>ella</u> no.	<u>He</u> did it but <u>she</u> didn't.

- after ser (meaning *to be*)

Soy <u>yo</u>.	It's <u>me</u>.
¿Eres <u>tú</u>?	Is that <u>you</u>?

- in comparisons after que and como

Enrique es más alto que <u>yo</u>.	Enrique is taller than <u>I</u> am or than me.
Antonio no es tan alto como <u>tú</u>.	Antonio isn't as tall as <u>you</u> (are).

⇨ *For more information on **Making comparisons**, see page 26.*

- on their own without a verb

¿Quién dijo eso? – <u>Él</u>.	Who said that? – <u>He</u> did.
¿Quién quiere venir? – <u>Yo</u>.	Who wants to come? – <u>I</u> do.

- after certain prepositions

Es para <u>ella</u>.	It's for <u>her</u>.

⇨ *For more information on **Pronouns after prepositions**, see page 54.*

ℹ️ Note that *it* used as the subject, and *they* referring to things, are <u>NEVER</u> translated into Spanish.

¿Qué es? – Es una sorpresa.	What is it? – <u>It</u>'s a surprise.
¿Qué son? – Son abrelatas.	What are they? – <u>They</u> are tin openers.

2   Ways of saying 'you' in Spanish

➤ In English we have only <u>one</u> way of saying *you*. In Spanish, there are <u>several</u> words to choose from. The word you use depends on:
- whether you are talking to one person or more than one person
- whether you are talking to a friend or family member, or someone else.

➤ If you are talking to one person <u>you know well</u>, such as a friend, a young person or a relative, use **tú**.

➤ If you are talking to one person <u>you do not know so well</u>, such as your teacher, your boss or a stranger, use the polite form, **usted**.

➤ If you are talking to <u>more than one person</u> you know well, use **vosotros** (or **vosotras**, if you are talking to women only) in Spain. Use **ustedes** instead in Latin America.

➤ Use **ustedes** if you are talking to more than one person <u>you do not know so well</u>.

> *Tip*
>
> Remember that adjectives describing **tú** and **usted** should be feminine if you're talking to a woman or girl, while adjectives describing **ustedes** should be feminine plural if you're talking to women or girls only.

3   Using the plural subject pronouns

➤ When you are talking about males only, use **nosotros**, **vosotros** or **ellos**.

<u>Nosotros</u> no somos italianos.   <u>We</u> are not Italian.

➤ When you are talking about females only, use **nosotras**, **vosotras** or **ellas**.

Hablé con mis hermanas.   I spoke to my sisters.
<u>Ellas</u> estaban de acuerdo   <u>They</u> agreed with me.
conmigo.

➤ When you are talking about both males and females, use **nosotros**, **vosotros** or **ellos**.

<u>Ellos</u> sí que llegaron tarde.   <u>They</u> really did arrive late.

Key points

✔ The Spanish subject pronouns are: **yo, tú, él, ella, usted** in the singular, and **nosotros/nosotras, vosotros/vosotras, ellos/ellas, ustedes** in the plural.

✔ Don't use the subject pronouns (other than **usted** and **ustedes**) with verbs except for emphasis or clarity.

✔ Make sure you choose the correct form of the verb.

✔ Do use the subject pronouns:
  • after **ser** (meaning *to be*)
  • in comparisons after **que** and **como**
  • in one-word answers to questions.

✔ Choose the word for *you* carefully. Remember to think about how many people you are talking to and your relationship with them when deciding between **tú, vosotros, vosotras, usted** and **ustedes**.

✔ *It* as the subject of the verb, and *they* when it refers to things are <u>NOT</u> translated in Spanish.

✔ Use masculine plural forms (**nosotros, vosotros, ellos**) for groups made up of men and women.

✔ Remember to make any adjectives describing the subject agree.

Personal pronouns: direct object

> **What is a direct object pronoun?**
> A **direct object pronoun** is a word such as *me*, *him*, *us* and *them*, which is used instead of the noun to stand in for the person or thing most directly affected by the action expressed by the verb.

1 Using direct object pronouns

➤ Direct object pronouns stand in for nouns when it is clear who or what is being talked about, and save having to repeat the noun.

> I've lost my glasses. Have you seen <u>them</u>?
> 'Have you met Jo?' – 'Yes, I really like <u>her</u>!'

➤ Here are the Spanish direct object pronouns:

Singular	Meaning	Plural	Meaning
me	me	nos	us
te	you (*relating to* tú)	os	you (*relating to* vosotros/vosotras)
lo	him it (*masculine*) you (*relating to* usted – *masculine*)	los	them (*masculine*) you (*relating to* ustedes – *masculine*)
la	her it (*feminine*) you (*relating to* usted – *feminine*)	las	them (*feminine*) you (*relating to* ustedes – *feminine*)

<u>Te</u> quiero.   I love you.
No <u>los</u> toques.   Don't touch them.

i Note that you cannot use the Spanish direct object pronouns on their own without a verb or after a preposition such as **a** or **de**.

➡ *For more information on **Pronouns after prepositions**, see page 54.*

2 Word order with direct object pronouns

➤ The direct object pronoun usually comes <u>BEFORE</u> the verb.

¿<u>Las</u> ve usted?	Can you see them?
¿No <u>me</u> oís?	Can't you hear me?
Tu hija no <u>nos</u> conoce.	Your daughter doesn't know us.
¿<u>Lo</u> has visto?	Have you seen it?

➤ In orders and instructions telling someone <u>TO DO</u> something, the pronoun joins onto the end of the verb to form one word.

Ayúda<u>me</u>.	Help me.
Acompáña<u>nos</u>.	Come with us.

[i] Note that you will often need to add a written accent to preserve the spoken stress when adding pronouns to the end of verbs.

⇨ *For more information on **Stress**, see page 200.*

➤ In orders and instructions telling someone <u>NOT TO DO</u> something, the pronoun does <u>NOT</u> join onto the end of the verb.

No <u>los</u> toques.	Don't touch them.

➤ If the pronoun is the object of an infinitive (the *to* form of the verb) or a gerund (the *-ing* form of the verb), you always add the pronoun to the end of the verb to form one word, unless the infinitive or gerund follows another verb. Again, you may have to add a written accent to preserve the stress.

Se fue después de arreglar<u>lo</u>.	He left after fixing it.
Practicándo<u>lo</u>, aprenderás.	You'll learn by practising it.

⇨ *For more information on **Verbs** and **Gerunds**, see pages 69 and 125.*

➤ Where an infinitive or gerund follows another verb, you can put the pronoun either at the end of the infinitive or gerund, or before the other verb.

Vienen a ver<u>nos</u> *or*	
<u>Nos</u> vienen a ver.	They are coming to see us.
Está comiéndo<u>lo</u> *or*	
<u>Lo</u> está comiendo.	He's eating it.

⇨ *For further information on the **Order of object pronouns**, see page 52.*

48 Pronouns

3 | Special use of lo

➤ lo is sometimes used to refer back to an idea or information that has already been given. The word *it* is often missed out in English.

¿Va a venir María? – No lo sé.	Is María coming? – I don't know.
Habían comido ya pero no nos lo dijeron.	They had already eaten, but they didn't tell us.
Yo conduzco de prisa pero él lo hace despacio.	I drive fast but he drives slowly.

> **Key points**
> ✔ The Spanish direct object pronouns are: me, te, lo, la in the singular, and nos, os, los, las in the plural.
> ✔ The object pronoun usually comes before the verb.
> ✔ Object pronouns are joined to the end of infinitives, gerunds or verbs instructing someone to do something.
> ✔ If an infinitive or gerund follows another verb, you can choose whether to add the object pronoun to the end of the infinitive or gerund or to put it before the first verb.
> ✔ lo is sometimes used to refer back to an idea or information that has already been given.

Personal pronouns: indirect object

> **What is an indirect object pronoun?**
> An **indirect object pronoun** is used instead of a noun to show the person or thing an action is intended to benefit or harm, for example, *me* in *He gave me a book.; Can you get me a towel?; He wrote to me.*

1 Using indirect object pronouns

➤ It is important to understand the difference between direct and indirect object pronouns in English, as they can have different forms in Spanish.

➤ You can usually test whether an object is a direct object or an indirect one by asking questions about the action using *what* and *who*:

- an indirect object answers the question *who ... to?* or *who ... for?*, equally *what ... to?* or *what ... for?*

  He gave me a book. → *Who did he give the book to?* → me
  (*=indirect object pronoun*)

  Can you get me a towel? → *Who can you get a towel for?* → me
  (*=indirect object pronoun*)

  We got some varnish for it. → *What did you get the varnish for?* → it
  (*=indirect object pronoun*)

- if something answers the question *what* or *who*, then it is the direct object and <u>NOT</u> the indirect object.

  He gave me a book. → *What did he give me?* → a book
  (*=direct object*)

  I saw Mandy. → *Who did you see?* → Mandy
  (*=direct object*)

  We got some varnish for it. → *What did you get?* → some varnish
  (*=direct object*)

[*i*] Note that a verb won't necessarily have both a direct and an indirect object.

➤ Here are the Spanish indirect object pronouns:

Singular	Meaning	Plural	Meaning
me	me, to me, for me	nos	us, to us, for us
te	you, to you, for you (*relating to* tú)	os	you, to you, for you (*relating to* vosotros/vosotras)
le	him, to him, for him her, to her, for her it, to it, for it you, to you, for you (*relating to* usted)	les	them, to them, for them you, to you, for you (*relating to* ustedes)

➤ The pronouns shown in the table are used instead of using the preposition **a** with a noun.

> **Estoy escribiendo a Teresa.** I am writing to Teresa. →
> **Le estoy escribiendo.** I am writing to her.
> **Compra un regalo a los niños.** Buy the children a present. →
> **Cómprales un regalo.** Buy them a present.

➤ Some Spanish verbs like **mirar** (meaning *to look at*), **esperar** (meaning *to wait for*) and **buscar** (meaning *to look for*) take a direct object, because the Spanish construction is different from the English.

Grammar Extra!

You should usually use direct object pronouns rather than indirect object pronouns when replacing personal **a** + <u>noun</u>.

> **Vi a Teresa.** → **La vi.**   I saw Teresa. → I saw her.

⇨ *For more information on* **Personal** *a, see page 182.*

---

2 | Word order with indirect object pronouns

➤ The indirect object pronoun usually comes <u>BEFORE</u> the verb.

Sofía os ha escrito.	Sophie has written to you.
¿Os ha escrito Sofía?	Has Sofía written to you?
Carlos no nos habla.	Carlos doesn't speak to us.
¿Qué te pedían?	What were they asking you for?

➤ In orders and instructions telling someone <u>TO DO</u> something, the pronoun goes on the end of the verb to form one word.

> **Respóndeme.** Answer me.
> **Dime la respuesta.** Tell me the answer.

ℹ️ Note that you will often need to add a written accent to preserve the spoken stress.

⇨ *For more information on* **Stress**, *see page 200.*

➤ In orders and instructions telling someone <u>NOT TO DO</u> something, the pronoun does not join onto the end of the verb.

> **No me digas la respuesta.** Don't tell me the answer.

➤ If the pronoun is the object of an infinitive (the *to* form of the verb) or a gerund (the *-ing* form of the verb), you always add the pronoun to the end of the verb to form one word, unless the infinitive or gerund follows another verb. Again, you may have to add a written accent to preserve the stress.

Eso de dar**le** tu dirección no fue muy prudente.	It wasn't very wise to give him your address.
Gritándo**le** tanto lo vas a asustar.	You'll frighten him by shouting at him like that.

➤ Where an infinitive or gerund follows another verb, you can put the pronoun either at the end of the infinitive or gerund, or before the other verb.

Quiero decir**te** algo. *or* **Te** quiero decir algo.	I want to tell you something.
Estoy escribiéndo**le**. *or* **Le** estoy escribiendo.	I am writing to him/her.

⇨ *For further information on the **Order of object pronouns**, see page 52.*

> ### Key points
> ✔ The Spanish indirect object pronouns are: **me**, **te**, **le** in the singular, and **nos**, **os**, **les** in the plural.
> ✔ They can replace the preposition **a** (meaning *to*) + noun.
> ✔ Like the direct object pronoun, the indirect object pronoun usually comes before the verb.
> ✔ Object pronouns are joined to the end of infinitives, gerunds or verbs instructing someone to do something.
> ✔ If an infinitive or gerund follows another verb, you can choose whether to add the object pronoun to the end of the infinitive or gerund or to put it before the first verb.

Order of object pronouns

➤ Two object pronouns are often used together in the same sentence; for example: *he gave me them* or *he gave them to me*. In Spanish, you should always put the indirect object pronoun <u>BEFORE</u> the direct object pronoun.

Indirect		Direct
me	BEFORE	lo
te		la
nos		los
os		las

Ana <u>os lo</u> mandará mañana.	Ana will send it to you tomorrow.
¿<u>Te los</u> ha enseñado mi hermana?	Has my sister shown them to you?
No <u>me lo</u> digas.	Don't tell me (that).
Todos estaban pidiéndo<u>telo</u>.	They were all asking you for it.
No quiere prestár<u>nosla</u>.	He won't lend it to us.

➤ You have to use **se** instead of **le** (*to him, to her, to you*) and **les** (*to them, to you*), when you are using the object pronouns **lo**, **la**, **los**, or **las**.

<u>Se</u> lo di ayer.	I gave it to him/her/you/them yesterday.
<u>Se</u> las enviaré.	I'll send them to him/her/you/them.

> ### Key points
> ✔ When combining two object pronouns, put the indirect object pronoun before the direct object pronoun.
> ✔ Use **se** as the indirect object pronoun rather than **le** or **les** when there is more than one object pronoun.

For further explanation of grammatical terms, please see pages viii-xii.

Further information on object pronouns

➤ The object pronoun **le** can mean *(to) him, (to) her* and *(to) you*; **les** can mean *(to) them* and *(to) you*, and **se** can mean all of these things, which could lead to some confusion.

➤ To make it clear which one is meant, **a él** (meaning *to him*), **a ella** (meaning *to her*), **a usted** (meaning *to you*) and so on can be added to the phrase.

A ella le escriben mucho.	They write to her often.
A ellos se lo van a mandar pronto.	They will be sending it to them soon.

➤ When a noun object comes before the verb, the corresponding object pronoun must be used too.

A tu hermano lo conozco bien. I know your brother well.
(*literally: Your brother I know him well.*)
A María la vemos algunas veces. We sometimes see María.
(*literally: María we see her sometimes.*)

➤ Indirect object pronouns are often used in constructions with the definite article with parts of the body or items of clothing to show who they belong to. In English, we'd use a possessive adjective.

La chaqueta le estaba ancha.	His jacket was too loose.
Me duele el tobillo.	My ankle's sore.

⇨ *For more information on **The definite article** and **Possessive adjectives**, see pages 11, 35 and 37.*

➤ Indirect object pronouns can also be used in certain common phrases which use reflexive verbs.

Se me ha perdido el bolígrafo. I have lost my pen.

⇨ *For more information on **Reflexive verbs**, see page 91.*

ⓘ Note that in Spain, you will often hear **le** and **les** used instead of **lo** and **los** as direct object pronouns when referring to men and boys. It is probably better not to copy this practice since it is considered incorrect in some varieties of Spanish, particularly Latin American ones.

Pronouns after prepositions

➤ In English, we use *me, you, him* and so on after a preposition, for example, *he came towards me*; *it's for you*; *books by him*. In Spanish, there is a special set of pronouns which are used after prepositions.

➤ The pronouns used after a preposition in Spanish are the same as the subject pronouns, except for the forms mí (meaning *me*) ti (meaning *you*), and sí (meaning *himself, herself, yourself, themselves, yourselves*).

Singular	Meaning	Plural	Meaning
mí	me	nosotros	us (*masculine*)
ti	you	nosotras	us (*feminine*)
él	him	vosotros	you (*masculine*)
ella	her	vosotras	you (*feminine*)
usted (Vd.)	you	ellos	them (*masculine*)
sí	himself	ellas	them (*feminine*)
	herself	ustedes (Vds.)	you
	yourself	sí	themselves yourselves

Pienso <u>en ti</u>.	I think about you.
¿Son <u>para mí?</u>	Are they for me?
No he sabido nada <u>de él.</u>	I haven't heard from him.
Es <u>para ella</u>.	It's for her.
Iban <u>hacia ellos</u>.	They were going towards them.
Volveréis <u>sin nosotros</u>.	You'll come back without us.
Volaban <u>sobre vosotros</u>.	They were flying above you.

i Note that mí, sí and él each have an accent, to distinguish them from mi (meaning *my*), si (meaning *if*), and el (meaning *the*), but ti does not have an accent.

➤ These pronouns are often used for emphasis.

¿A <u>ti</u> no te escriben?	Don't they write to <u>you</u>?
Me lo manda a <u>mí</u>, no a <u>ti</u>.	She's sending it to <u>me</u>, not to you.

➤ con (meaning *with*) combines with mí, ti and sí to form:

- conmigo   with me
  Ven <u>conmigo</u>.   Come with me.
- contigo   with you
  Me gusta estar <u>contigo</u>.   I like being with you.

For further explanation of grammatical terms, please see pages viii-xii.

- **consigo**   with himself/herself/yourself/themselves/yourselves
  Lo trajeron <u>consigo</u>.   They brought it with them.

➤ **entre**, **hasta**, **salvo**, **menos** and **según** are always used with the <u>subject pronouns</u> (**yo** and **tú**), rather than with the object pronouns (**mí** and **ti**).

- **entre**   between, among
  <u>entre</u> tú y yo   between you and me
- **hasta**   even, including
  <u>Hasta</u> yo puedo hacerlo.   Even I can do it.
- **menos**   except
  todos <u>menos</u> yo   everybody except me
- **salvo**   except
  todos <u>salvo</u> yo   everyone except me
- **según**   according to
  <u>según</u> tú   according to you

⇨ *For more information on **Subject pronouns**, see page 42.*

Key points

✔ Most prepositions are followed by the forms: **mí**, **ti**, **sí** and so on.
✔ **con** combines with **mí**, **ti** and **sí** to form **conmigo**, **contigo** and **consigo**.
✔ **entre**, **hasta**, **menos**, **salvo** and **según** are followed by the subject pronouns **yo** and **tú**.

56 Pronouns

Possessive pronouns

What is a possessive pronoun?
A **possessive pronoun** is one of the words *mine, yours, hers, his, ours* or *theirs*, which are used instead of a noun to show that one person or thing belongs to another, for example, *Ask Carole if this pen is hers.; Mine's the blue one*.

➤ Here are the Spanish possessive pronouns:

Masculine singular	Feminine singular	Masculine plural	Feminine plural	Meaning
el mío	la mía	los míos	las mías	mine
el tuyo	la tuya	los tuyos	las tuyas	yours (*belonging to tú*)
el suyo	la suya	los suyos	las suyas	his; hers; its; yours (*belonging to usted*)
el nuestro	la nuestra	los nuestros	las nuestras	ours
el vuestro	la vuestra	los vuestros	las vuestras	yours (*belonging to vosotros/vosotras*)
el suyo	la suya	los suyos	las suyas	theirs; yours (*belonging to ustedes*)

For more information on **Ways of saying 'you' in Spanish**, see page 44.

Pregunta a Cristina si este bolígrafo es <u>el suyo</u>.	Ask Cristina if this pen is hers.
¿Qué equipo ha ganado, <u>el suyo</u> o <u>el nuestro</u>?	Which team won – theirs or ours?
Mi perro es más joven que <u>el tuyo</u>.	My dog is younger than yours.
Daniel pensó que esos libros eran <u>los suyos</u>.	Daniel thought those books were his.
Si no tienes lápices, te prestaré <u>los míos</u>.	If you haven't got any pencils, I'll lend you mine.
Las habitaciones son más pequeñas que <u>las vuestras</u>.	The rooms are smaller than yours.

For further explanation of grammatical terms, please see pages viii-xii.

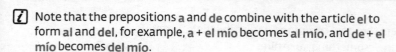

Tip

In Spanish, possessive pronouns agree with what they describe, NOT with the person who owns that thing. For example, el suyo can mean *his*, *hers*, *yours* or *theirs*, but can only be used to replace a masculine singular noun.

[i] Note that the prepositions a and de combine with the article el to form al and del, for example, a + el mío becomes al mío, and de + el mío becomes del mío.

Prefiero tu coche <u>al mío</u>.	I prefer your car to mine.
Su coche se parece <u>al vuestro</u>.	His/Her/Their car looks like yours.
Mi piso está encima <u>del tuyo</u>.	My flat is above yours.
Su colegio está cerca <u>del nuestro</u>.	His/Her/Your/Their school is near ours.

➤ Instead of el suyo/la suya/los suyos/las suyas, it is sometimes clearer to say el/la/los/las de usted, el/la/los/las de ustedes, el/la/los/las de ellos and so on. You choose between el/la/los/las to agree with the noun referred to.

mi libro y <u>el de</u> usted   my book and yours

➤ el/la/los/las de can also be used with a name or other noun referring to somebody.

Juan tiene un coche bonito pero yo prefiero <u>el de</u> Ana.	Juan's got a nice car, but I prefer Ana's.
Ellos tienen una casa bonita pero yo prefiero <u>la del</u> médico.	They've got a nice house but I prefer the doctor's.

Key points

✔ The Spanish possessive pronouns are el mío, el tuyo, el suyo, el nuestro, el vuestro and el suyo when they stand in for a masculine noun. If they stand in for a feminine or a plural noun, their forms change accordingly.

✔ In Spanish, the pronoun you choose has to agree with the noun it replaces, and <u>not</u> with the person who owns that thing.

✔ el/la/los/las de are used with a noun or pronoun to mean the *one(s) belonging to* ...

Indefinite pronouns

> **What is an indefinite pronoun?**
> An **indefinite pronoun** is one of a small group of pronouns such as *everything*, *nobody* and *something* which are used to refer to people or things in a general way without saying exactly who or what they are.

➤ Here are the most common Spanish indefinite pronouns:

- **algo**   something, anything

Tengo <u>algo</u> para ti.	I have something for you.
¿Viste <u>algo</u>?	Did you see anything?

- **alguien**   somebody, anybody

<u>Alguien</u> me lo ha dicho.	Somebody told me.
¿Has visto a <u>alguien</u>?	Have you seen anybody?

Típ

Don't forget to use personal a before indefinite pronouns referring to people when they are the object of a verb.

¿Viste <u>a</u> alguien?	Did you see anybody?
No vi <u>a</u> nadie.	I didn't see anybody.

➪ *For more information on **Personal** a, see page 182.*

- **alguno/alguna/algunos/algunas**   some, a few

<u>Algunos</u> de los niños ya saben leer.	Some of the children can already read.

- **cada uno/una**   each (one), everybody

Le dio una manzana a <u>cada uno</u>.	She gave each one an apple.
¡<u>Cada uno</u> a su casa!	Everybody home!

- **cualquiera**   anybody; any

<u>Cualquiera</u> puede hacerlo.	Anybody can do it.
<u>Cualquiera</u> de las explicaciones vale.	Any of the explanations is valid.

- **mucho/mucha/muchos/muchas**   much; many

<u>Muchas</u> de las casas no tenían jardín.	Many of the houses didn't have a garden.

For further explanation of grammatical terms, please see pages viii-xii.

- **nada**   nothing, anything

¿Qué tienes en la mano?	What have you got in your hand?
– <u>Nada</u>.	– Nothing.
No dijo <u>nada</u>.	He didn't say anything.

- **nadie**   nobody, anybody

¿A quién ves? – A <u>nadie</u>.	Who can you see? – Nobody.
No quiere ver a <u>nadie</u>.	He doesn't want to see anybody.

Tip

Don't forget to use personal <u>a</u> before indefinite pronouns referring to people when they are the object of a verb.

¿Viste <u>a</u> alguien?	Did you see anybody?
No vi <u>a</u> nadie.	I didn't see anybody.

⇨ *For more information on **Personal** a, see page 182.*

- **ninguno/ninguna**   none, any

¿Cuántas tienes? – <u>Ninguna</u>.	How many have you got? – None.
No me queda <u>ninguno</u>.	I haven't any left *or* I have none left.

- **otro/otra/otros/otras**   another one; others

No me gusta este modelo. ¿Tienes <u>otro</u>?	I don't like this model. Have you got another?

[*i*] Note that you can never put **un** or **una** before **otro** or **otra**.

- **poco/poca/pocos/pocas**   little; few

sólo unos <u>pocos</u>	only a few

- **tanto/tanta/tantos/tantas**   so much; so many

¿Se oía mucho ruido? – No <u>tanto</u>.	Was there a lot of noise? – Not so much.

- **todo/toda/todos/todas**   all; everything

Lo ha estropeado <u>todo</u>.	He has spoiled everything.
<u>Todo</u> va bien.	It's all going well.

- **uno … el otro/una … la otra**   (the) one … the other

<u>Uno</u> dijo que sí y <u>el otro</u> que no.	One said yes while the other said no.

- unos ... los otros/unas ... las otras   some ... the others

<u>Unos</u> cuestan 30 euros, <u>los otros</u> 40 euros.	Some cost 30 euros, the others 40 euros.

- varios/varias several

<u>Varios</u> de ellos me gustan mucho.	I like several of them very much.

Tip

Don't forget to make those pronouns that have feminine and plural forms agree with the noun they refer to.

He perdido mi goma pero tengo <u>otra</u>.	I've lost my rubber but I've got another one.

[*i*] Note that **algo**, **alguien** and **alguno** can <u>NEVER</u> be used after a negative such as **no**. Instead you must use the appropriate negative pronouns, **nada**, **nadie**, **ninguno**.

<u>No</u> veo a <u>nadie</u>.	I can't see anybody.
<u>No</u> tengo <u>nada</u> que hacer.	I haven't got anything to do.

➤ You use **nada**, **nadie** and **ninguno** on their own without **no** to answer questions.

¿Qué pasa? – <u>Nada</u>.	What's happening? – Nothing.
¿Quién habló? – <u>Nadie</u>.	Who spoke? – Nobody.
¿Cuántos quedan? – <u>Ninguno</u>.	How many are there left? – None.

➤ You also use **nada**, **nadie** and **ninguno** on their own without **no** when they come before a verb.

<u>Nada</u> lo asusta.	Nothing frightens him.
<u>Nadie</u> habló.	Nobody spoke.
<u>Ninguno</u> de mis amigos quiso venir.	None of my friends wanted to come.

⇨ *For more information on* **Negatives**, *see page 157.*

Key points

✔ Where indefinite pronouns have alternative endings, they must agree with the noun they refer to.

✔ *Anything* is usually translated by **algo** in questions and by **nada** in sentences containing **no**.

✔ *Anybody* is usually translated by **alguien** in questions and by **nadie** in sentences containing **no**.

✔ When **nada**, **nadie** or **ninguno** come <u>after</u> the verb, remember to put **no** before it. When they come <u>before</u> the verb, don't use **no**.

For further explanation of grammatical terms, please see pages viii-xii.

Relative pronouns

> **What is a relative pronoun?**
> In English, a **relative pronoun** is one of the words *who*, *which* and *that* (and the more formal *whom*) which can be used to introduce information that makes it clear which person or thing is being talked about, for example, *The man who has just come in is Ann's boyfriend.*; *The vase that you broke was quite valuable.*
> Relative pronouns can also introduce further information about someone or something, for example, *Peter, who is a brilliant painter, wants to study art.*; *Jane's house, which was built in 1890, needs a lot of repairs.*

1 Relative pronouns referring to people

➤ In English, we use the relative pronouns *who*, *whom* and *that* to talk about people. In Spanish, **que** is used.

el hombre <u>que</u> vino ayer	the man <u>who</u> came yesterday
Mi hermano, <u>que</u> tiene veinte años, es mecánico.	My brother, <u>who</u> is twenty, is a mechanic.
el hombre <u>que</u> vi en la calle	the man (<u>that</u>) I saw in the street

> *Tip*
>
> In English we often miss out the relative pronouns *who*, *whom* and *that*. For example, we can say both *the friends <u>that</u> I see most*, or *the friends I see most*.
>
> In Spanish, you can <u>NEVER</u> miss out **que** in this way.

➤ When the relative pronoun is used with a <u>preposition</u>, use **el/la/los/las que** or **quien/quienes** which must agree with the noun it replaces; **el que** changes for the feminine and plural forms, **quien** changes only in the plural.

➤ Here are the Spanish relative pronouns referring to people that are used after a preposition:

	Masculine	Feminine	Meaning
Singular	el que quien	la que quien	who, that, whom
Plural	los que quienes	las que quienes	who, that, whom

las mujeres con <u>las que</u> or con <u>quienes</u> estaba hablando	the women (that) she was talking to
La chica de <u>la que</u> or de <u>quien</u> te hablé llega mañana.	The girl (that) I told you about is coming tomorrow.
los niños de <u>los que</u> or de <u>quienes</u> se ocupa usted	the children (that) you look after

[*i*] Note that when de is used with el que, they combine to become del que. When a is used with el que, they combine to become al que.

el chico <u>del que</u> te hablé	the boy I told you about
Vive con un hombre <u>al que</u> adora.	She lives with a man she adores.

> *Tip*
>
> In English, we often put prepositions at the end of the sentence, for example, *the man she was talking to*. In Spanish, you can <u>never</u> put a preposition at the end of a sentence.
>
> | | |
> |---|---|
> | el hombre <u>con el que</u> or <u>con quien</u> estaba hablando | the man she was talking to |
>
> ⇨ *For more information on **Prepositions**, see page 178.*

2 **Relative pronouns referring to things**

➤ In English, we use the relative pronouns *which* and *that* to talk about things. In Spanish, que is used.

la novela <u>que</u> ganó el premio	the novel <u>that</u> or <u>which</u> won the prize
el coche <u>que</u> compré	the car (<u>that</u> or <u>which</u>) I bought

> *Tip*
>
> In English, we often miss out the relative pronouns *which* and *that*. For example, we can say both *the house <u>which</u> we want to buy*, or *the house we want to buy*.
>
> In Spanish, you can <u>NEVER</u> miss out que in this way.

➤ When the relative pronoun is used with a preposition, use **el/la/los/las que**, which must agree with the noun it replaces. Here are the Spanish relative pronouns referring to things that are used after a preposition:

	Masculine	Feminine	Meaning
Singular	el que	la que	which, that
Plural	los que	las que	which, that

la tienda a <u>la que</u> siempre va	the shop (that or which) she always goes to
los temas de <u>los que</u> habla	the subjects he talks about

i Note that when **de** is used with **el que**, they combine to become **del que**. When **a** is used with **el que**, they combine to become **al que**.

el programa <u>del que</u> te hablé	the programme I told you about
el banco <u>al que</u> fuiste	the bank you went to

➤ The neuter form **lo que** is used when referring to the whole of the previous part of the sentence.

Todo estaba en silencio, <u>lo que</u> me pareció raro.	All was silent, which I thought was odd.

⇨ *For more information on lo que, see page 17.*

> ## Tip
>
> In English, we often put prepositions at the end of the sentence, for example, *the shop she always goes to*. In Spanish, you can <u>never</u> put a preposition at the end of a sentence.
>
> | | |
> |---|---|
> | la tienda <u>a la que</u> siempre va | the shop she always goes <u>to</u> |
> | la película <u>de la que</u> te hablaba | the film I was telling you <u>about</u> |

Grammar Extra!

In English we can use *whose* to show possession, for example, *the woman whose son is ill*. In Spanish you use **cuyo/cuya/cuyos/cuyas**; **cuyo** is actually an adjective and must agree with the noun it describes **NOT** with the person who owns that thing.

La mujer, <u>cuyo</u> nombre era Antonia, estaba jubilada.	The woman, whose name was Antonia, was retired.
el señor en <u>cuya</u> casa me alojé	the gentleman whose house I stayed in

In your reading, you may come across the forms **el cual/la cual/los cuales/las cuales** which are a more formal alternative to **el que/la que/los que/las que** after a preposition.

las mujeres con <u>las cuales</u> estaba hablando	the women (that or who) she was talking to
la ventana desde <u>la cual</u> nos observaban	the window from which they were watching us

el cual/la cual/los cuales/las cuales are also useful to make it clear who you are talking about in other cases where the pronoun does not immediately follow the person or thing it refers to.

El padre de Elena, <u>el cual</u> tiene mucho dinero, es ...	Elena's father, who has a lot of money, is ...

---

3   **Other uses of** el que, la que, los que, las que

➤ You can use **el que, la que, los que, las que** to mean *the one(s) (who/which)* or *those who*.

Esa película es <u>la que</u> quiero ver.	That film is the one I want to see.
<u>los que</u> quieren irse	those who want to leave

Key points

- ✔ **que** can refer to both people and things in Spanish.
- ✔ In English we often miss out the relative pronouns *who*, *which* and *that*, but in Spanish you can never miss out **que**.
- ✔ After a preposition you use **el que/la que/los que/las que** or **quien/quienes** if you are referring to people; you use **el que/la que/los que/las que** if you are referring to things. **el que** and **quien** agree with the nouns they replace.
- ✔ **a + el que → al que**
  de + el que → del que
- ✔ <u>Never</u> put the preposition at the end of the sentence in Spanish.
- ✔ **el que/la que/los que** and **las que** are also used to mean *the one(s) who/which* or *those who*.

For further explanation of grammatical terms, please see pages viii-xii.

Interrogative pronouns

> **What is an interrogative pronoun?**
> In English, an **interrogative pronoun** is one of the words *who*, *which*, *whose*, *whom*, and *what* when they are used without a noun to ask questions.

➤ These are the interrogative pronouns in Spanish:

Singular	Plural	Meaning
¿qué?	¿qué?	what?
¿cuál?	¿cuáles?	which? which one(s)?; what?
¿quién?	¿quiénes?	who? (*as subject or after a preposition*)
¿cuánto?/¿cuánta?	¿cuántos?/¿cuántas?	how much? how many?

(i) Note that question words have an accent on them in Spanish.

1 ¿qué?

➤ ¿qué? is the equivalent of *what?* in English.

¿Qué están haciendo?	What are they doing?
¿Qué dices?	What are you saying?
¿Para qué lo quieres?	What do you want it for?

➤ You can use ¿por qué? in the same way as *why?* in English.

¿Por qué no vienes?	Why don't you come?

2 ¿cuál?, ¿cuáles?

➤ ¿cuál? and ¿cuáles? are usually the equivalent of *which?* in English and are used when there is a choice between two or more things.

¿Cuál de estos vestidos te gusta más?	Which of these dresses do you like best?
¿Cuáles quieres?	Which (ones) do you want?

(i) Note that you don't use **cuál** before a noun; use **qué** instead.

¿Qué libro es más interesante?	Which book is more interesting?

➩ *For more information on **Interrogative adjectives**, see page 32.*

3   qué es or cuál es?

➤ You should only use ¿qué es …? (meaning *what is…?*) and ¿qué son …? (meaning *what are…?*) when you are asking someone to define, explain or classify something.

¿Qué es esto?	What is this?
¿Qué son los genes?	What are genes?

➤ Use ¿cuál es …? and ¿cuáles son …? (also meaning *what is …?* and *what are …?*) when you want someone to specify a particular detail, number, name and so on.

¿Cuál es la capital de España?	What is the capital of Spain?
¿Cuál es tu consejo?	What's your advice?

4   ¿quién?

➤ ¿quién? and ¿quiénes? are the equivalent of *who?* in English when it is the subject of the verb or when used with a preposition.

¿Quién ganó la carrera?	Who won the race?
¿Con quiénes los viste?	Who did you see them with?
¿A quién se lo diste?	Who did you give it to?

➤ ¿a quién? and ¿a quiénes? are the equivalent of *who(m)?* when it is the object of the verb.

¿A quién viste?	Who did you see? *or* Whom did you see?
¿A quiénes ayudaste?	Who did you help? *or* Whom did you help?

➤ ¿de quién? and ¿de quiénes? are the equivalent of *whose?* in English.

¿De quién es este libro?	Whose is this book? *or* Whose book is this?
¿De quiénes son estos coches?	Whose are these cars? *or* Whose cars are these?

5   ¿cuánto?, ¿cuántos?

➤ ¿cuánto? (*masculine*) and ¿cuánta? (*feminine*) are the equivalent of *how much* in English. ¿cuántos? (*masculine plural*) and ¿cuántas? (*feminine plural*) are the equivalent of *how many?*

¿Cuánto es?	How much is it?
¿Cuántos tienes?	How many have you got?

Demonstrative pronouns

> **What is a demonstrative pronoun?**
> In English a **demonstrative pronoun** is one of the words *this, that, these*, and *those* used instead of a noun to point people or things out, for example, *That looks fun*.

1 **Using demonstrative pronouns**

➤ These are the demonstrative pronouns in Spanish:

	Masculine	Feminine	Neuter	Meaning
Singular	éste	ésta	esto	this, this one
	ése	ésa	eso	that, that one (*close by*)
	aquél	aquélla	aquello	that, that one (*further away*)
Plural	éstos	éstas		these, these ones
	ésos	ésas		those, those ones (*close by*)
	aquéllos	aquéllas		those, those ones (*further away*)

➤ The demonstrative pronouns in Spanish have to agree with the noun that they are replacing.

¿Qué abrigo te gusta más? – **Éste** de aquí. → Which coat do you like best? – This one here.

Aquella casa era más grande que **ésta**. → That house was bigger than this one.

estos libros y **aquéllos** → these books and those (over there)

Quiero estas sandalias y **ésas**. → I'd like these sandals and those ones.

2 **¿ése or aquél?**

➤ In English we use *that* and *those* to talk about anything that is not close by. In Spanish, you need to be a bit more precise.

➤ Use **ése/ésa** and so on to indicate things and people that are nearer to the person you're talking to than to you.

Me gusta más **ése** que tienes en la mano. → I prefer the one you've got in your hand.

➤ Use **ése/ésa** and so on to indicate things and people that aren't very far away.

Si quieres ver una película, podemos ir a **ésa** que dijiste. → If you want to see a film, we can go and see that one you mentioned.

68 Pronouns

➤ Use **aquél/aquélla** and so on to talk about things that are further away.

> **Aquélla** al fondo de la calle es
> mi casa.
>
> My house is that one at the end of
> the street.

[i] Note that the masculine and feminine forms of demonstrative <u>pronouns</u> usually have an accent, to distinguish them from demonstrative <u>adjectives</u>. Compare:

este bolígrafo	this pen	**éste**	this one
esa mesa	that table	**ésa**	that one

⇨ *For more information on **Demonstrative adjectives**, see page 30.*

➤ The neuter forms (**esto**, **eso**, **aquello**) are used to talk about an object you don't recognize or about an idea or statement.

> ¿Qué es <u>eso</u> que llevas en
> la mano?
>
> What's that you've got in your
> hand?

> No puedo creer que <u>esto</u> me
> esté pasando a mí.
>
> I can't believe this is really
> happening to me.

> <u>Aquello</u> sí que me gustó.
>
> I really did like that.

[i] Note that the neuter forms of demonstrative pronouns do <u>NOT</u> have an accent.

Key points

✔ Spanish demonstrative pronouns agree with the noun they are replacing.

✔ Masculine and feminine demonstrative pronouns usually have an accent on them in both the singular and the plural.

✔ In Spanish you have to choose the correct pronoun to emphasize the difference between something that is close to you and something that is further away:
- **éste/ésta/éstos** and **éstas** (meaning *this/these*) are used to indicate things and people that are very close.
- **ése/ésa/ésos** and **ésas** (meaning *that/those*) are used to indicate things and people that are near the person you are talking to or that aren't too far away.
- **aquél/aquélla/aquéllos/aquéllas** (meaning *that/those*) are used to indicate things and people that are further away.

✔ The neuter pronouns (**esto**, **eso** and **aquello**) are used to talk about things you don't recognize or to refer to statements or ideas. They don't have an accent.

Verbs

What is a verb?
A **verb** is a 'doing' word which describes what someone or something does, what someone or something is, or what happens to them, for example, *be*, *sing*, *live*.

Overview of verbs

➤ Verbs are frequently used with a noun, with somebody's name or, particularly in English, with a pronoun such as *I*, *you* or *she*. They can relate to the present, the past and the future; this is called their <u>tense</u>.

⇨   *For more information on **Nouns** and **Pronouns**, see pages 1 and 41.*

➤ Verbs are either:
  ● <u>**regular**</u>; their forms follow the normal rules
  ● <u>**irregular**</u>; their forms do not follow normal rules

➤ Almost all verbs have a form called the <u>infinitive</u>. This is a base form of the verb (for example, *walk*, *see*, *hear*) that hasn't had any endings added to it and doesn't relate to any particular tense. In English, the infinitive is usually shown with *to*, as in *to speak*, *to eat*, *to live*.

➤ In Spanish, the infinitive is always made up of just one word (never two as in *to speak* in English) and ends in **-ar**, **-er** or **-ir**: for example, hab<u>lar</u> (meaning *to speak*), com<u>er</u> (meaning *to eat*) and viv<u>ir</u> (meaning *to live*).
  All Spanish verbs belong to one of these three types, which are called <u>conjugations</u>. We will look at each of these three conjugations in turn on the next few pages.

➤ Regular English verbs have other forms apart from the infinitive: a form ending in -s (*walks*), a form ending in -*ing* (*walking*), and a form ending in -ed (*walked*).

➤ Spanish verbs have many more forms than this, which are made up of endings added to a <u>stem</u>. The stem of a verb can usually be worked out from the infinitive.

➤ Spanish verb endings change depending on who or what is doing the action and on when the action takes place. In fact, the ending is very often the only thing that shows you <u>who</u> is doing the action, as the Spanish equivalents of I, you, he and so on (yo, tú, él and so on) are not used very much. So, both hablo on its own and yo hablo mean I speak. Sometimes there is a name or a noun in the sentence to make it clear who is doing the action.

<u>José</u> habla español.	<u>José</u> speaks Spanish.
<u>El profesor</u> habla español.	<u>The teacher</u> speaks Spanish.

⇨ For more information on **Subject pronouns**, see page 42.

➤ Spanish verb forms also change depending on whether you are talking about the present, past or future, so (yo) habla<u>ré</u> means I will speak while (yo) hab<u>lé</u> means I spoke.

➤ Some verbs in Spanish do not follow the usual patterns. These <u>irregular verbs</u> include some very common and important verbs like ir (meaning to go), ser and estar (meaning to be) and hacer (meaning to do or to make). Other verbs are only slightly irregular, changing their stems in certain tenses.

⇨ For **Verb Tables**, see the middle section.

> ### Key points
> ✔ Spanish verbs have different forms depending on who or what is doing the action and on the tense.
> ✔ Spanish verb forms are made up of a stem and an ending. The stem is usually based on the infinitive of the verb. The ending depends on who or what is doing the action and on when the action takes place.
> ✔ Regular verbs follow the standard patterns for -ar, -er and -ir verbs. Irregular verbs do not.

The present tenses

> **What are the present tenses?**
> The **present tenses** are the verb forms that are used to talk about what is
> true at the moment, what happens regularly and what is happening now;
> for example, I'm a student; I travel to college by train; I'm studying languages.

➤ In English, there are two tenses you can use to talk about the present:

- the present simple tense

  I live here.
  They get up early.

- the present continuous tense

  He is eating an apple.
  You aren't working very hard.

➤ In Spanish, there is also a present simple and a present continuous tense.
As in English, the present simple in Spanish is used to talk about:

- things that are generally true

  En invierno hace frío.   It's cold in winter.

- things that are true at the moment

  Carlos no come carne.   Carlos doesn't eat meat.

- things that happen at intervals

  A menudo vamos al cine.   We often go to the cinema.

➤ The present continuous tense in Spanish is used to talk about things that are
happening right now or at the time of writing:

  Marta está viendo la televisión.   Marta is watching television.

➤ However, there are times where the use of the present tenses in the two
languages is not exactly the same.

⇨   For more information on the use of the **Present tenses**, see pages 79 and 84.

The present simple tense

1   Forming the present simple tense of regular -ar verbs

➤ If the infinitive of the Spanish verb ends in **-ar**, it means that the verb belongs to the <u>first conjugation</u>, for example, **hablar, lavar, llamar**.

➤ To know which form of the verb to use in Spanish, you need to work out what the stem of the verb is and then add the correct ending. The stem of regular **-ar** verbs in the present simple tense is formed by taking the <u>infinitive</u> and chopping off **-ar**.

Infinitive	Stem (without -ar)
hablar (to speak)	habl-
lavar (to wash)	lav-

➤ Now you know how to find the stem of a verb you can add the correct ending. The one you choose will depend on who or what is doing the action.

[i] Note that as the ending generally makes it clear who is doing the action, you usually don't need to add a subject pronoun such as **yo** (meaning *I*), **tú** (meaning *you*) as well.

⇨ For more information on **Subject pronouns**, see page 42.

➤ Here are the present simple endings for regular **-ar** verbs:

Present simple endings	Present simple of hablar	Meaning: to speak
-o	(yo) habl<u>o</u>	I speak
-as	(tú) habl<u>as</u>	you speak
-a	(él/ella) habl<u>a</u>	he/she/it speaks
	(usted) habl<u>a</u>	you speak
-amos	(nosotros/nosotras) habl<u>amos</u>	we speak
-áis	(vosotros/vosotras) habl<u>áis</u>	you speak
-an	(ellos/ellas) habl<u>an</u> (ustedes) habl<u>an</u>	they speak you speak

➤ You use the **él/ella** (*third person singular*) form of the verb with nouns and with people's names, when you are just talking about one person, animal or thing.

    Lydia estudia medicina.   Lydia studies or is studying medicine.

    Mi profesor me ayuda mucho.   My teacher helps me a lot.

For further explanation of grammatical terms, please see pages viii-xii.

➤ You use the **ellos/ellas** (*third person plural*) form of the verb with nouns and with people's names, when you are talking about more than one person, animal or thing.

Lydia y Carlos estudi<u>an</u> medicina.	Lydia and Carlos study *or* are studying medicine.
Mis profesores me ayud<u>an</u> mucho.	My teachers help me a lot.

i Note that even though you use the **él/ella** and **ellos/ellas** <u>forms</u> of the verb to talk about things in Spanish, you should <u>never</u> include the pronouns **él, ella, ellos** or **ellas** themselves in the sentence when referring to things.

Funciona bien.	It works well.
Funcionan bien.	They work well.

➾ For more information on **Ways of saying 'you' in Spanish**, see page 44.

Key points

✔ Verbs ending in **-ar** belong to the first conjugation. Regular **-ar** verbs form their present tense stem by losing the **-ar**.

✔ The present tense endings for regular **-ar** verbs are: **-o, -as, -a, -amos, -áis, -an**.

✔ You usually don't need to give a pronoun in Spanish as the ending of the verb makes it clear who or what is doing the action.

---

2 Forming the present simple tense of regular **-er** verbs

➤ If the infinitive of the Spanish verb ends in **-er**, it means that the verb belongs to the <u>second conjugation</u>, for example, **comer, depender**.

➤ The stem of regular **-er** verbs in the present simple tense is formed by taking the <u>infinitive</u> and chopping off **-er**.

Infinitive	Stem (without **-er**)
comer (*to eat*)	**com-**
depender (*to depend*)	**depend-**

➤ Now add the correct ending, depending on who or what is doing the action.

i Note that as the ending generally makes it clear who is doing the action, you usually don't need to add a subject pronoun such as **yo** (meaning *I*) or **tú** (meaning *you*) as well.

➾ For more information on **Subject pronouns**, see page 42.

➤ Here are the present simple endings for regular -er verbs:

Present simple endings	Present simple of comer	Meaning: to eat
-o	(yo) como	I eat
-es	(tú) comes	you eat
-e	(él/ella) come	he/she/it eats
	(usted) come	you eat
-emos	(nosotros/nosotras) comemos	we eat
-éis	(vosotros/vosotras) coméis	you eat
-en	(ellos/ellas) comen	they eat
	(ustedes) comen	you eat

➤ You use the **él/ella** (*third person singular*) form of the verb with nouns and with people's names, when you are just talking about one person, animal or thing.

> Juan come demasiado.   Juan eats too much.
> Mi padre me debe 15 euros.   My father owes me 15 euros.

➤ You use the **ellos/ellas** (*third person plural*) form of the verb with nouns and with people's names, when you talking about more than one person, animal or thing.

> Juan y Pedro comen demasiado.   Juan and Pedro eat too much.
> Mis padres me deben 15 euros.   My parents owe me 15 euros.

[i] Note that even though you use the **él/ella** and **ellos/ellas** forms of the verb to talk about things in Spanish, you should <u>never</u> include the pronouns **él**, **ella**, **ellos** or **ellas** themselves in the sentence when referring to things.

> Depende.   It depends.

⇨ *For more information on **Ways of saying 'you' in Spanish**, see page 44.*

Key points

✔ Verbs ending in **-er** belong to the second conjugation. Regular -er verbs form their present tense stem by losing the **-er**.

✔ The present tense endings for regular -er verbs are: **-o, -es, -e, -emos, -éis, -en**.

✔ You usually don't need to give a pronoun in Spanish as the ending of the verb makes it clear who or what is doing the action.

---

3 Forming the present simple tense of regular -ir verbs

➤ If the infinitive of the Spanish verb ends in -ir, it means that the verb belongs to the <u>third conjugation</u>, for example, vivir, recibir.

➤ The stem of regular -ir verbs in the present simple tense is formed by taking the <u>infinitive</u> and chopping off -ir.

Infinitive	Stem (without -ir)
vivir (to live)	viv-
recibir (to receive)	recib-

➤ Now add the correct ending depending on who or what is doing the action.

i Note that as the ending generally makes it clear who is doing the action, you usually don't need to add a subject pronoun such as yo (meaning *I*) or tú (meaning *you*) as well.

➪ For more information on **Subject pronouns**, see page 42.

➤ Here are the present simple endings for regular -ir verbs:

Present simple endings	Present simple of vivir	Meaning: to live
-o	(yo) vivo	I live
-es	(tú) vives	you live
-e	(él/ella) vive	he/she/it lives
	(usted) vive	you live
-imos	(nosotros/nosotras) vivimos	we live
-ís	(vosotros/vosotras) vivís	you live
-en	(ellos/ellas) viven	they live
	(ustedes) viven	you live

➤ You use the él/ella (*third person singular*) form of the verb with nouns and with people's names, when you are just talking about one person, animal or thing.

Javier vive aquí. Javier lives here.
Mi padre recibe muchas cartas. My father gets a lot of letters.

➤ You use the ellos/ellas (*third person plural*) form of the verb with nouns and with people's names, when you talking about more than one person, animal or thing.

Javier y Antonia viven aquí. Javier and Antonia live here.
Mis padres reciben muchas cartas. My parents get a lot of letters.

i Note that even though you use the él/ella and ellos/ellas forms of the verb to talk about things in Spanish, you should never include the pronouns él, ella, ellos or ellas themselves in the sentence when referring to things.

Ocurrió ayer.   It happened yesterday.

⇨ For more information on *Ways of saying 'you' in Spanish*, see page 44.

Key points

✔ Verbs ending in -ir belong to the third conjugation. Regular -ir verbs form their present tense stem by losing the -ir.

✔ The present tense endings for regular -ir verbs are: -o, -es, -e, -imos, -ís, -en.

✔ You usually don't need to give a pronoun in Spanish as the ending of the verb makes it clear who or what is doing the action.

---

4 Forming the present simple tense of less regular verbs

➤ Many Spanish verbs do not follow the regular patterns shown previously. There are lots of verbs that change their stem in the present tense when the stress is on the stem. This means that all forms are affected in the present simple APART FROM the nosotros and vosotros forms. Such verbs are often called radical-changing verbs, meaning root-changing verbs.

➤ For example, some verbs containing an -o in the stem change it to -ue in the present simple for all forms APART FROM the nosotros/nosotras and vosotros/vosotras forms.

	encontrar to find	recordar to remember	poder to be able	dormir to sleep
(yo)	encuentro	recuerdo	puedo	duermo
(tú)	encuentras	recuerdas	puedes	duermes
(él/ella/usted)	encuentra	recuerda	puede	duerme
(nosotros/as)	encontramos	recordamos	podemos	dormimos
(vosotros/as)	encontráis	recordáis	podéis	dormís
(ellos/ellas/ustedes)	encuentran	recuerdan	pueden	duermen

➤ Other verbs containing an -e in the stem change it to -ie for all forms <u>APART FROM</u> the **nosotros/nosotras** and **vosotros/vosotras** forms.

	cerrar to close	pensar to think	entender to understand	perder to lose	preferir to prefer
(yo)	cierro	pienso	entiendo	pierdo	prefiero
(tú)	cierras	piensas	entiendes	pierdes	prefieres
(él/ella/usted)	cierra	piensa	entiende	pierde	prefiere
(nosotros/as)	cerramos	pensamos	entendemos	perdemos	preferimos
(vosotros/as)	cerráis	pensáis	entendéis	perdéis	preferís
(ellos/ellas/ustedes)	cierran	piensan	entienden	pierden	prefieren

➤ A few -ir verbs containing -e in the stem change this to -i in the present simple for all forms <u>APART FROM</u> the **nosotros/nosotras** and **vosotros/vosotras** forms.

	pedir to ask (for)	servir to serve
(yo)	pido	sirvo
(tú)	pides	sirves
(él/ella/usted)	pide	sirve
(nosotros/as)	pedimos	servimos
(vosotros/as)	pedís	servís
(ellos/ellas/ustedes)	piden	sirven

➤ If you are not sure whether a Spanish verb belongs to this group of <u>radical-changing verbs</u>, you can look up the **Verb Tables** in the middle section.

⇨ *For more information on **Spelling**, see page 196.*

5   <u>Forming the present simple tense of common irregular verbs</u>

➤ There are many other verbs that do not follow the usual patterns in Spanish. These include some very common and important verbs such as **tener** (meaning *to have*), **hacer** (meaning *to do* or *to make*) and **ir** (meaning *to go*). These verbs are shown in full on the next page.

78 Verbs

➤ Here are the present simple tense endings for **tener**:

	tener	Meaning: *to have*
(yo)	tengo	I have
(tú)	tienes	you have
(él/ella/usted)	tiene	he/she/it has, you have
(nosotros/nosotras)	tenemos	we have
(vosotros/vosotras)	tenéis	you have
(ellos/ellas/ustedes)	tienen	they have, you have

Tengo dos hermanas.	I have two sisters.
No **tengo** dinero.	I haven't any money.
¿Cuántos sellos **tienes**?	How many stamps have you got?
Tiene el pelo rubio.	He has blond hair.

➤ Here are the present simple tense endings for **hacer**:

	hacer	Meaning: *to do, to make*
(yo)	hago	I do, I make
(tú)	haces	you do, you make
(él/ella/usted)	hace	he/she/it does, he/she/it makes, you do, you make
(nosotros/nosotras)	hacemos	we do, we make
(vosotros/vosotras)	hacéis	you do, you make
(ellos/ellas/ustedes)	hacen	they do, they make, you do, you make

Hago una tortilla.	I'm making an omelette.
No **hago** mucho deporte.	I don't do a lot of sport.
¿Qué **haces**?	What are you doing?
Hace calor.	It's hot.

➤ Here are the present simple tense endings for **ir**:

	ir	Meaning: *to go*
(yo)	voy	I go
(tú)	vas	you go
(él/ella/usted)	va	he/she/it goes, you go
(nosotros/nosotras)	vamos	we go
(vosotros/vosotras)	vais	you go
(ellos/ellas/ustedes)	van	they go, you go

For further explanation of grammatical terms, please see pages viii-xii.

Voy a Salamanca.	I'm going to Salamanca.
¿Adónde **vas**?	Where are you going?
No **va** al colegio.	He doesn't go to school.
No **van** a vender la casa.	They aren't going to sell the house.

⇨ *For other irregular verbs in the present simple tense, see* **Verb Tables** *in the middle section.*

6   How to use the present simple tense in Spanish

➤ The present simple tense is often used in Spanish in the same way as it is in English, although there are some differences.

➤ As in English, you use the Spanish **present** simple to talk about:

- things that are generally true

En verano **hace** calor.	It's hot in summer.

- things that are true now

Viven en Francia.	They live in France.

- things that happen all the time or at certain intervals or that you do as a habit

Marta **lleva** gafas.	Marta wears glasses.
Mi tío **vende** mariscos.	My uncle sells shellfish.

- things that you are planning to do

El domingo **jugamos** en León.	We're playing in León on Sunday.
Mañana **voy** a Madrid.	I am going to Madrid tomorrow.

➤ There are some instances when you would use the present simple in Spanish, but you wouldn't use it in English:

- to talk about current projects and activities that may not actually be going on right at this very minute

Construye una casa.	He's building a house.

- when you use certain time expressions in Spanish, especially **desde** (meaning *since*) and **desde hace** (meaning *for*), to talk about activities and states that started in the past and are still going on now

Jaime **vive** aquí **desde hace** dos años.	Jaime has been living here for two years.
Daniel **vive** aquí **desde** 1999.	Daniel has lived here since 1999.
Llevo horas esperando aquí.	I've been waiting here for hours.

⇨ *For more information on the use of tenses with* desde, *see page 189.*

permanent quality

ser and estar

➤ In Spanish there are two irregular verbs, **ser** and **estar**, that both mean *to be*, although they are used very differently. In the present simple tense, they follow the patterns shown below.

Pronoun	ser	estar	Meaning: *to be*
(yo)	soy	estoy	I am
(tú)	eres	estás	you are
(él/ella/usted)	es	está	he/she/it is, you are
(nosotros/nosotras)	somos	estamos	we are
(vosotros/vosotras)	sois	estáis	you are
(elllos/ellas/ustedes)	son	están	they/you are

➤ **ser** is used:

- with an adjective when talking about a characteristic or fairly permanent quality, for example, shape, size, height, colour, material, nationality.

Mi hermano **es** alto.	My brother is tall.
María **es** inteligente.	María is intelligent.
Es rubia.	She's blonde.
Es muy guapa.	She's very pretty.
Es rojo.	It's red.
Es de algodón.	It's made of cotton.
Sus padres **son** italianos.	His parents are Italian.
Es joven/viejo.	He's young/old.
Son muy ricos/pobres.	They're very rich/poor.

- with a following noun or pronoun that tells you what someone or something is

Miguel **es** camarero.	Miguel is a waiter.
Soy yo, Enrique.	It's me, Enrique.
Madrid **es** la capital de España.	Madrid is the capital of Spain.

- to say that something belongs to someone

La casa **es** de Javier.	The house belongs to Javier.
Es mío.	It's mine.

- to talk about where someone or something comes from

Yo **soy** de Escocia.	I'm from Scotland.
Mi mujer **es** de Granada.	My wife is from Granada.

For further explanation of grammatical terms, please see pages viii-xii.

- to say what time it is or what the date is

<u>Son</u> las tres y media.	It's half past three.
Mañana <u>es</u> sábado.	Tomorrow is Saturday.

- in calculations

Tres y dos <u>son</u> cinco.	Three and two are five.
¿Cuánto <u>es</u>? – <u>Son</u> dos euros.	How much is it? It's two euros.

- when followed by an infinitive

Lo importante <u>es</u> decir la verdad.	The important thing is to tell the truth.

⇨ *For more information on the Infinitive, see page 144.*

- to describe actions using the passive (for example *they are made, it is sold*)

<u>Son</u> fabricados en España.	They are made in Spain.

⇨ *For more information on the Passive, see page 122.*

➤ estar is used: Temporary

- to talk about where something or someone is

<u>Estoy</u> en Madrid.	I'm in Madrid.
¿Dónde <u>está</u> Burgos?	Where's Burgos?
<u>Está</u> cerca de aquí.	It's near here.

- with an adjective when there has been a change in the condition of someone or something or to suggest that there is something unexpected about them

El café <u>está</u> frío.	The coffee's cold.
¡Qué guapa <u>estás</u> con este vestido!	How pretty you look in that dress!
Hoy <u>estoy</u> de mal humor.	I'm in a bad mood today.

⇨ *For more information on Adjectives, see page 19.*

- with a past participle used as an adjective, to describe the state that something is in

Las tiendas <u>están</u> cerradas.	The shops are closed.
No <u>está</u> terminado.	It isn't finished.
El lavabo <u>está</u> ocupado.	The toilet is engaged.
<u>Está</u> roto.	It's broken.

⇨ *For more information on Past participles, see page 115.*

82 Verbs

- when talking about someone's health

| ¿Cómo están ustedes? | How are you? |
| Estamos todos bien. | We're all well. |

- to form continuous tenses such as the present continuous tense

| Está comiendo. | He's eating. |
| Estamos aprendiendo mucho. | We are learning a great deal. |

⇨ *For more information on the **Present continuous**, see page 84.*

➤ Both ser and estar can be used with certain adjectives, but the meaning changes depending on which is used.

➤ Use ser to talk about <u>permanent</u> qualities.

Marta es muy joven.	Marta is very young.
Es delgado.	He's slim.
Viajar es cansado.	Travelling is tiring.
La química es aburrida.	Chemistry is boring.

➤ Use estar to talk about <u>temporary</u> states or qualities.

Está muy joven con ese vestido.	She looks very young in that dress.
¡Estás muy delgada!	You're looking very slim!
Hoy estoy cansado.	I'm tired today.
Estoy aburrido.	I'm bored.

➤ ser is used with adjectives such as importante (meaning *important*) and imposible (meaning *impossible*) when the subject is *it* in English.

Es muy interesante.	It's very interesting.
Es imposible.	It's impossible.
Es fácil.	It's easy.

➤ ser is used in certain set phrases.

| Es igual *or* Es lo mismo. | It's all the same. |
| Es para ti. | It's for you. |

➤ estar is also used in some set phrases.

- estar de pie — to be standing
  Juan está de pie. — Juan is standing.
- estar de vacaciones — to be on holiday
  ¿Estás de vacaciones? — Are you on holiday?
- estar de viaje — to be on a trip
  Mi padre está de viaje. — My father's on a trip.
- estar de moda — to be in fashion

For further explanation of grammatical terms, please see pages viii-xii.

Las pantallas de plasma están de moda.	Plasma screens are in fashion.

- estar claro — to be obvious

Está claro que no entiendes.	It's obvious that you don't understand.

Grammar Extra!

Both **ser** and **estar** can be used with past participles.

Use **ser** and the past participle in passive constructions to describe an action.

Son fabricados en España.	They are made in Spain.

Use **estar** and the past participle to describe a state.

Está terminado.	It's finished.

⇨ *For more information on **Past participles**, see page 115.*

Key points

✔ **ser** and **estar** both mean *to be* in English, but are used very differently.

✔ **ser** and **estar** are irregular verbs. You have to learn them.

✔ Use **ser** with adjectives describing permanent qualities or characteristics; with nouns or pronouns telling you who or what somebody or something is; with time and dates; and to form the passive.

✔ Use **estar** to talk about location; health; with adjectives describing a change of state; and with past participles used as adjectives to describe states.

✔ **estar** is also used to form present continuous tenses.

✔ **ser** and **estar** can sometimes be used with the same adjectives, but the meaning changes depending on which verb is used.

✔ **ser** and **estar** are both used in a number of set phrases.

The present continuous tense

➤ In Spanish, the present continuous tense is used to talk about something that is happening at this very moment.

➤ The Spanish present continuous tense is formed from the <u>present tense</u> of estar and the <u>gerund</u> of the verb. The gerund is the form of the verb that ends in **-ando** (for **-ar** verbs) or **-iendo** (for **-er** and **-ir** verbs) and is the same as the *-ing* form of the verb in English (for example, *walking, swimming*).

<u>Estoy</u> trabaj<u>ando</u>	I'm working.
No <u>estamos</u> com<u>iendo</u>.	We aren't eating.
¿<u>Estás</u> escrib<u>iendo</u>?	Are you writing?

⇨ *For more information on estar and the **Gerund**, see pages 80 and 125.*

➤ To form the gerund of an **-ar** verb, take off the **-ar** ending of the infinitive and add **-ando**:

Infinitive	Meaning	Stem (without -ar)	Gerund	Meaning
hablar	to speak	habl-	habl<u>ando</u>	speaking
trabajar	to work	trabaj-	trabaj<u>ando</u>	working

➤ To form the gerund of an **-er** or **-ir** verb, take off the **-er** or **-ir** ending of the infinitive and add **-iendo**:

Infinitive	Meaning	Stem (without -er/-ir)	Gerund	Meaning
comer	to eat	com-	com<u>iendo</u>	eating
escribir	to write	escrib-	escrib<u>iendo</u>	writing

Tip

Only use the present continuous to talk about things that are in the middle of happening right now. Use the present simple tense instead to talk about activities which are current but which may not be happening at this minute.

Lydia <u>estudia</u> medicina.	Lydia's studying medicine.

⇨ *For more information on the **Present simple tense**, see page 72.*

Key points

✔ Only use the present continuous in Spanish for actions that are happening right now.

✔ To form the present continuous tense in Spanish, take the present tense of **estar** and add the gerund of the main verb.

For further explanation of grammatical terms, please see pages viii-xii.

The imperative

> **What is the imperative?**
> An **imperative** is a form of the verb used when giving orders and instructions, for example, *Sit down!; Don't go!; Let's start!*

1 Using the imperative

➤ In Spanish, the form of the imperative that you use for giving instructions depends on:

- whether you are telling someone to do something or not to do something
- whether you are talking to one person or to more than one person
- whether you are on familiar or more formal terms with the person or people

➤ These imperative forms correspond to the familiar **tú** and **vosotros/vosotras** and to the more formal **usted** and **ustedes**, although you don't actually say these pronouns when giving instructions.

➭ For more information on **Ways of saying 'you' in Spanish**, see page 44.

➤ There is also a form of the imperative that corresponds to *let's* in English.

2 Forming the imperative: instructions not to do something

➤ In orders that tell you <u>NOT</u> to do something and that have **no** in front of them in Spanish, the imperative forms for **tú**, **usted**, **nosotros/nosotras**, **vosotros/vosotras** and **ustedes** are all taken from a verb form called the <u>present subjunctive</u>. It's easy to remember because the endings for -ar and -er verbs are the opposite of what they are in the ordinary present tense.

➭ For more information on the **Present tense** and the **Subjunctive**, see pages 69 and 134.

➤ In regular -ar verbs, you take off the -as, -a, -amos, -áis and -an endings of the present tense and replace them with: -es, -e, -emos, -éis and -en.

-ar **verb**	trabajar	**to work**
tú form	¡no trabajes!	Don't work!
usted form	¡no trabaje!	Don't work!
nosotros/as form	¡no trabajemos!	Let's not work!
vosotros/as form	¡no trabajéis!	Don't work!
ustedes form	¡no trabajen!	Don't work!

➤ In regular -er verbs, you take off the **-es, -e, -emos, -éis** and **-en** endings of the present tense and replace them with **-as, -a, -amos, -áis** and **-an**.

-er **verb**	comer	**to eat**
tú form	¡no comas!	Don't eat!
usted form	¡no coma!	Don't eat!
nosotros/as form	¡no comamos!	Let's not eat!
vosotros/as form	¡no comáis!	Don't eat!
ustedes form	¡no coman!	Don't eat!

➤ In regular -ir verbs, you take off the **-es, -e, -imos, -ís** and **-en** endings of the present tense and replace them with **-as, -a, -amos, -áis** and **-an**.

-ir **verb**	decidir	**to decide**
tú form	¡no decidas!	Don't decide!
usted form	¡no decida!	Don't decide!
nosotros/as form	¡no decidamos!	Let's not decide!
vosotros/as form	¡no decidáis!	Don't decide!
ustedes form	¡no decidan!	Don't decide!

➤ A number of irregular verbs also have irregular imperative forms. These are shown in the table below.

	dar **to give**	decir **to say**	estar **to be**	hacer **to do/make**	ir **to go**
tú form	¡no des! don't give!	¡no digas! don't say!	¡no estés! don't be!	¡no hagas! don't do/make!	¡no vayas! don't go!
usted form	¡no dé! don't give!	¡no diga! don't say!	¡no esté! don't be!	¡no haga! don't do/make!	¡no vaya! don't go!
nosotros form	¡no demos! let's not give!	¡no digamos! let's not say!	¡no estemos! let's not be!	¡no hagamos! let's not do/make!	¡no vayamos! let's not go!
vosotros form	¡no deis! don't give!	¡no digáis! don't say!	¡no estéis! don't be!	¡no hagáis! don't do/make!	¡no vayáis! don't go!
ustedes form	¡no den! don't give!	¡no digan! don't say!	¡no estén! don't be!	¡no hagan! don't do/make!	¡no vayan! don't go!

	poner **to put**	salir **to leave**	ser **to be**	tener **to have**	venir **to come**
tú form	¡no pongas! don't put!	¡no salgas! don't leave!	¡no seas! don't be!	¡no tengas! don't have!	¡no vengas! don't come!
usted form	¡no ponga! don't put!	¡no salga! don't leave!	¡no sea! don't be!	¡no tenga! don't have!	¡no venga! don't come!
nosotros form	¡no pongamos! let's not put!	¡no salgamos! let's not leave!	¡no seamos! let's not be!	¡no tengamos! let's not have!	¡no vengamos! let's not come!
vosotros form	¡no pongáis! don't put!	¡no salgáis! don't leave!	¡no seáis! don't be!	¡no tengáis! don't have!	¡no vengáis! don't come!
ustedes form	¡no pongan! don't put!	¡no salgan! don't leave!	¡no sean! don't be!	¡no tengan! don't have!	¡no vengan! don't come!

[i] Note that if you take the **yo** form of the present tense, take off the -o and add the endings to this instead for instructions <u>NOT TO DO</u> something, some of these irregular forms will be more predictable.

digo	*I say*	→	negative imperative stem	→	**dig-**
hago	*I do*	→	negative imperative stem	→	**hag-**
pongo	*I put*	→	negative imperative stem	→	**pong-**
salgo	*I leave*	→	negative imperative stem	→	**salg-**
tengo	*I have*	→	negative imperative stem	→	**teng-**
vengo	*I come*	→	negative imperative stem	→	**veng-**

3   Forming the imperative: instructions to do something

➤ In instructions telling you <u>TO DO</u> something, the forms for **usted**, **nosotros** and **ustedes** are exactly the same as they are in negative instructions (instructions telling you not to do something) except that there isn't a **no**.

	trabajar to work	comer to eat	decidir to decide
usted form	¡Trabaje!	¡Coma!	¡Decida!
nosotros/as form	¡Trabajemos!	¡Comamos!	¡Decidamos!
ustedes form	¡Trabajen!	¡Coman!	¡Decidan!

➤ There are special forms of the imperative for **tú** and **vosotros/vosotras** in positive instructions (instructions telling you to do something).

➤ The **tú** form of the imperative is the same as the **tú** form of the ordinary present simple tense, but without the final -s.

trabajar	→	¡Trabaja!
to work		Work!
comer	→	¡Come!
to eat		Eat!
decidir	→	¡Decide!
to decide		Decide!

➪ *For more information on the **Present simple tense**, see page 72.*

➤ The **vosotros/vosotras** form of the imperative is the same as the infinitive, except that you take off the final -r and add -d instead.

trabajar	→	Trabajad!
to work		Work!
comer	→	Comed!
to eat		Eat!
decidir	→	Decidid!
to decide		Decide!

➤ There are a number of imperative forms that are irregular in Spanish. The irregular imperative forms for **usted**, **nosotros/nosotras** and **ustedes** are the same as the irregular negative imperative forms without the **no**. The **tú** and **vosotros/vosotras** forms are different again.

	dar to give	decir to say	estar to be	hacer to do/make	ir to go
tú form	¡da! give!	¡di! say!	¡está! be!	¡haz! do/make!	¡ve! go!
usted form	¡dé! give!	¡diga! say!	¡esté! be!	¡haga! do/make!	¡vaya! go!
nosotros/as form	¡demos! let's give!	¡digamos! let's say!	¡estemos! let's be!	¡hagamos! let's do/make!	¡vamos! let's go!
vosotros/as form	¡dad! give!	¡decid! say!	¡estad! be!	¡haced! do/make!	¡id! go!
ustedes form	¡den! give!	¡digan! say!	¡estén! be!	¡hagan! do/make!	¡vayan! go!

	poner to put	salir to leave	ser to be	tener to have	venir to come
tú form	¡pon! put!	¡sal! leave!	¡sé! be!	¡ten! have!	¡ven! come!
usted form	¡ponga! put!	¡salga! leave!	¡sea! be!	¡tenga! have!	¡venga! come!
nosotros/as form	¡pongamos! let's put!	¡salgamos! let's leave!	¡seamos! let's be!	¡tengamos! let's have!	¡vengamos! let's come!
vosotros/as form	¡poned! put!	¡salid! leave!	¡sed! be!	¡tened! have!	¡venid! come!
ustedes form	¡pongan! put!	¡salgan! leave!	¡sean! be!	¡tengan! have!	¡vengan! come!

i Note that the **nosotros/as** form for **ir** in instructions TO DO something is **vamos**; in instructions NOT TO DO something, it is **no vayamos**.

4 | Position of object pronouns

➤ An object pronoun is a word like *me* (meaning *me* or *to me*), *la* (meaning *her/it*) or *les* (meaning *to them/to you*) that is used instead of a noun as the object of a sentence. In orders and instructions, the position of these object pronouns in the sentence changes depending on whether you are telling someone TO DO something or NOT TO DO something.

*For more information on **Object pronouns**, see page 46.*

➤ If you are telling someone <u>NOT TO DO</u> something, the object pronouns go <u>BEFORE</u> the verb.

¡No **me lo** mandes!	Don't send it to me!
¡No **me** molestes!	Don't disturb me!
¡No **los** castigue!	Don't punish them!
¡No **se la** devolvamos!	Let's not give it back to him/her/them!
¡No **las** contestéis!	Don't answer them!

➤ If you are telling someone <u>TO DO</u> something, the object pronouns join on to the <u>END</u> of the verb. An accent is usually added to make sure that the stress in the imperative verb stays the same.

¡Explíca**melo**!	Explain it to me!
¡Perdóne**me**!	Excuse me!
¡Díga**me**!	Tell me!
¡Esperémos**la**!	Let's wait for her/it!

[i] Note that when there are two object pronouns, the indirect object pronoun always goes before the direct object pronoun.

⇨ *For more information on **Stress**, see page 200.*

5 **Other ways of giving instructions**

➤ For general instructions in instruction leaflets, recipes and so on, use the <u>infinitive</u> form instead of the imperative.

<u>Ver</u> página 9.	See page 9.

➤ **vamos a** with the infinitive is often used to mean *let's*.

<u>Vamos a</u> ver.	Let's see.
<u>Vamos a</u> empezar.	Let's start.

Key points

✔ In Spanish, in instructions <u>not to do</u> something, the endings are taken from the present subjunctive. They are the same as the corresponding endings for -ar and -er verbs in the ordinary present tense, except that the -e endings go on the -ar verbs and the -a endings go on the -er and -ir verbs.

✔ For -ar verbs the forms are: no hables (tú form); no hable (usted form); no hablemos (nosotros/as form); no habléis (vosotros/as form); no hablen (ustedes form)

✔ For -er verbs the forms are: no comas (tú form); no coma (usted form); no comamos (nosotros/as form); no comáis (vosotros/as form); no coman (ustedes form)

✔ For -ir verbs the forms are: no decidas (tú form); no decida (usted form); no decidamos (nosotros/as form); no decidáis (vosotros/as form); no decidan (ustedes form)

✔ In instructions <u>to do</u> something, the forms for usted, nosotros/as and ustedes are the same as they are in instructions not to do something.

✔ The forms for tú and vosotros/as are different:
- the tú form is the same as the corresponding form in the ordinary present tense, but without the final -s: trabaja; come; decide
- the vosotros/as form is the same as the infinitive but with a final -d instead of the -r: trabajad; comed; decidid

✔ A number of verbs have irregular imperative forms.

✔ The object pronouns in imperatives go before the verb when telling someone not to do something; they join onto the end of the verb when telling someone to do something.

For further explanation of grammatical terms, please see pages viii-xii.

Reflexive verbs

What is a reflexive verb?
A **reflexive verb** is one where the subject and object are the same, and where the action 'reflects back' on the subject. It is used with a reflexive pronoun such as *myself, yourself* and *herself* in English, for example, *I washed myself.; He shaved himself.*

1 Using reflexive verbs

➤ In Spanish, reflexive verbs are much more common than in English, and many are used in everyday language. The infinitive form of a reflexive verb has **se** attached to the end of it, for example, **secarse** (meaning *to dry oneself*). This is the way reflexive verbs are shown in dictionaries. **se** means *himself, herself, itself, yourself, themselves, yourselves* and *oneself*. **se** is called a <u>reflexive pronoun</u>.

➤ In Spanish, reflexive verbs are often used to describe things you do to yourself every day or that involve a change of some sort, for example, going to bed, sitting down, getting angry, and so on. Some of the most common reflexive verbs in Spanish are listed here.

acostarse	to go to bed
afeitarse	to shave
bañarse	to have a bath, to have a swim
dormirse	to go to sleep
ducharse	to have a shower
enfadarse	to get angry
lavarse	to wash
levantarse	to get up
llamarse	to be called
secarse	to get dried
sentarse	to sit down
vestirse	to get dressed

<u>Me baño</u> a las siete y media.	I have a bath at half past seven.
¡<u>Duérmete</u>!	Go to sleep!
Mi hermana <u>se ducha</u>.	My sister has a shower.
Mi madre <u>se enfada</u> mucho.	My mother often gets angry.
Mi hermano no <u>se lava</u>.	My brother doesn't wash.
<u>Me levanto</u> a las siete.	I get up at seven o'clock.
¿Cómo <u>te llamas</u>?	What's your name?
¿A qué hora <u>os acostáis</u>?	What time do you go to bed?
¡<u>Sentaos</u>!	Sit down!
<u>Nos vestimos</u>.	We're getting dressed.

i Note that **se**, **me** and so on are very rarely translated as *himself*, *myself* and so on in English. Instead of *he dresses himself* or *they bath themselves*, in English, we are more likely to say *he gets dressed* or *they have a bath*.

➤ Some Spanish verbs can be used both as reflexive verbs and as ordinary verbs (without the reflexive pronoun). When they are used as ordinary verbs, the person or thing doing the action is not the same as the person or thing receiving the action, so the meaning is different.

<u>Me lavo</u>.	I wash (myself).
<u>Lavo</u> la ropa a mano.	I wash the clothes by hand.
<u>Me llamo</u> Antonio.	I'm called Antonio.
¡<u>Llama</u> a la policía!	Call the police!
<u>Me acuesto</u> a las 11.	I go to bed at 11 o'clock.
<u>Acuesta</u> al niño.	He puts the child to bed.

Grammar Extra!

Some verbs mean <u>ALMOST</u> the same in the reflexive as when they are used on their own.

<u>Duermo</u>.	I sleep.
<u>Me duermo</u>.	I go to sleep.
¿Quieres <u>ir</u> al cine?	Do you want to go to the cinema?
Acaba de <u>irse.</u>	He has just left.

---

2 | Forming the present tense of reflexive verbs

➤ To use a reflexive verb in Spanish, you need to decide which reflexive pronoun to use. See how the reflexive pronouns in the table on the next page correspond to the subject pronouns.

Subject pronoun	Reflexive pronoun	Meaning
(yo)	me	myself
(tú)	te	yourself
(él) (ella) (uno) (usted)	se	himself herself oneself itself yourself
(nosotros/nosotras)	nos	ourselves
(vosotros/vosotras)	os	yourselves
(ellos) (ellas) (ustedes)	se	themselves yourselves

(Yo) <u>me</u> levanto temprano.	I get up early.
(Él) <u>se</u> acuesta a las once.	He goes to bed at eleven.
Ellos no <u>se</u> afeitan.	They don't shave.

➤ The present tense forms of a reflexive verb work in just the same way as an ordinary verb, except that the reflexive pronoun is used as well.

⇨ *For more information on the **Present tense**, see page 69.*

➤ The following table shows the reflexive verb **lavarse** in full.

Reflexive forms of lavarse	Meaning
(yo) me lavo	I wash (myself)
(tú) te lavas	you wash (yourself)
(él) se lava (ella) se lava (uno) se lava se lava (usted) se lava	he washes (himself) she washes (herself) one washes (oneself) it washes (itself) you wash (yourself)
(nosotros/nosotras) nos lavamos	we wash (ourselves)
(vosotros/vosotras) os laváis	you wash (yourselves)
(ellos) se lavan (ellas) se lavan (ustedes) se lavan	they wash (themselves) they wash (themselves) you wash (yourselves)

➤ Some reflexive verbs, such as **acostarse**, are irregular. Some of these irregular verbs are shown in the **Verb tables** in the middle section.

3   Position of reflexive pronouns

➤ In ordinary tenses such as the present simple, the reflexive pronoun goes <u>BEFORE</u> the verb.

<u>Me</u> acuesto temprano.	I go to bed early.
¿Cómo <u>se</u> llama usted?	What's your name?

⇨   *For more information on the **Present simple tense**, see page 72.*

➤ When telling someone <u>NOT TO DO</u> something, you also put the reflexive pronoun <u>BEFORE</u> the verb.

No <u>te</u> levantes.	Don't get up.
¡No <u>os</u> vayáis!	Don't go away!

➤ When telling someone <u>TO DO</u> something, you join the reflexive pronoun onto the end of the verb.

¡Siénten<u>se</u>!	Sit down!
¡Cálla<u>te</u>!	Be quiet!

⇨   *For more information on the **Imperative**, see page 85.*

> *Típ*
>
> When adding reflexive pronouns to the end of the imperative, you drop the final **-s** of the **nosotros** form and the final **-d** of the **vosotros** form, before the pronoun.
>
> | | |
> |---|---|
> | ¡Vámo<u>nos</u>! | Let's go! |
> | ¡Senta<u>os</u>! | Sit down! |

➤ You always join the reflexive pronoun onto the end of infinitives and gerunds (the **-ando** or **-iendo** forms of the verb) unless the infinitive or gerund follows another verb.

Hay que relajar<u>se</u> de vez en cuando.	You have to relax from time to time.
Acostándo<u>se</u> temprano, se descansa mejor.	You feel more rested by going to bed early.

➤ Where the infinitive or gerund follows another verb, you can put the reflexive pronoun either at the end of the infinitive or gerund or before the other verb.

Quiero bañar<u>me</u> *or* <u>Me</u> quiero bañar.	I want to have a bath.

Tienes que vestirte or **Te tienes que vestir.**	You must get dressed.
Está vistiéndose or **Se está vistiendo.**	She's getting dressed.
¿Estás duchándote? or **¿Te estás duchando?**	Are you having a shower?

⮕ *For more information on **Gerunds**, see page 125.*

ⓘ Note that, when adding pronouns to the ends of verb forms, you will often have to add a written accent to preserve the stress.

⮕ *For more information on **Stress**, see page 200.*

4 Using reflexive verbs with parts of the body and clothes

➤ In Spanish, you often talk about actions to do with your body or your clothing using a reflexive verb.

Se está secando el pelo.	She's drying her hair.
Nos lavamos los dientes.	We clean our teeth.
Se está poniendo el abrigo.	He's putting on his coat.

ⓘ Note that in Spanish you do not use a possessive adjective such as *my* and *her* when talking about parts of the body. You use **el**, **la**, **los** and **las** with a reflexive verb instead.

Me estoy lavando las manos.	I'm washing my hands.

⮕ *For more information on **Articles**, see page 10.*

5 Other uses of reflexive verbs

➤ In English we often use a passive construction, for example, *goods are transported all over the world, most of our tea is imported from India and China.* In Spanish, this construction is not used so much. Instead, very often a reflexive verb with **se** is used.

Aquí se vende café.	Coffee is sold here.
Aquí se venden muchos libros.	Lots of books are sold here.
Se habla inglés.	English is spoken here.
En Suiza se hablan tres idiomas.	Three languages are spoken in Switzerland.

ⓘ Note that the verb has to be singular or plural depending on whether the noun is singular or plural.

⮕ *For more information on the **Passive**, see page 122.*

➤ A reflexive verb with **se** is also used in some very common expressions.

¿Cómo <u>se dice</u> "siesta" en inglés?	How do you say "siesta" in English?
¿Cómo <u>se escribe</u> "Tarragona"?	How do you spell "Tarragona"?

➤ **se** is also used in impersonal expressions. In this case, it often corresponds to *one* (or *you*) in English.

No <u>se puede</u> entrar.	You can't go in.
No <u>se permite</u>.	You aren't *or* It isn't allowed.

⇨ *For more information on **Impersonal verbs**, see page 129.*

➤ **nos**, **os** and **se** are all also used to mean *each other* and *one another*.

<u>Nos</u> escribimos.	We write to one another.
<u>Nos</u> queremos.	We love each other.
Rachel y Julie <u>se</u> odian.	Rachel and Julie hate each other.
No <u>se</u> conocen.	They don't know each other.

> ### Key points
> ✔ A reflexive verb is made up of a reflexive pronoun and a verb.
> ✔ The reflexive pronouns are: **me**, **te**, **se**, **nos**, **os**, **se**.
> ✔ The reflexive pronoun goes before the verb, except when you are telling someone to do something and with infinitives and gerunds.

The future tense

> **What is the future tense?**
> The **future** tense is a verb tense used to talk about something that will happen or will be true in the future, for example, *He'll be here soon; I'll give you a call; What will you do?; It will be sunny tomorrow.*

1 Ways of talking about the future

➤ In Spanish, just as in English, you can often use the present tense to refer to something that is going to happen in the future.

Cogemos el tren de las once.	We're getting the eleven o'clock train.
Mañana **voy** a Madrid.	I am going to Madrid tomorrow.

➤ In English we often use *going to* with an infinitive to talk about the immediate future or our future plans. In Spanish, you can use the present tense of **ir** followed by **a** and an infinitive.

Va a perder el tren.	He's going to miss the train.
Va a llevar una media hora.	It's going to take about half an hour.
Voy a hacerlo mañana.	I'm going to do it tomorrow.

2 Forming the future tense

➤ In English we can form the future tense by putting *will* or its shortened form *'ll* before the verb. In Spanish you have to change the verb endings. So, just as **hablo** means *I speak*, **hablaré** means *I will speak* or *I shall speak*.

➤ To form the future tense of regular -ar, -er and -ir verbs, add the following endings to the <u>infinitive</u> of the verb: **-é, -ás, -á, -emos, -éis, -án**.

➤ The following table shows the future tense of three regular verbs: **hablar** (meaning *to speak*), **comer** (meaning *to eat*) and **vivir** (meaning *to live*).

(yo)	hablaré	comeré	viviré	I'll speak/eat/live
(tú)	hablarás	comerás	vivirás	you'll speak/eat/live
(él) (ella) (usted)	hablará	comerá	vivirá	he'll speak/eat/live she'll speak/eat/live it'll speak/eat/live you'll speak/eat/live
(nosotros/nosotras)	hablaremos	comeremos	viviremos	we'll speak/eat/live
(vosotros/vosotras)	hablaréis	comeréis	viviréis	you'll speak/eat/live
(ellos/ellas/ustedes)	hablarán	comerán	vivirán	they'll/you'll speak/eat/live

Habl<u>aré</u> con ella.		I'll speak to her.
Com<u>eremos</u> en casa de José.		We'll eat at José's.
No v<u>olverá</u>.		He won't come back.
¿Lo <u>entenderás</u>?		Will you understand it?

ⓘ Note that in the future tense only the **nosotros/nosotras** form doesn't have an accent.

> *Tip*
>
> Remember that Spanish has no direct equivalent of the word *will* in verb forms like *will rain* or *will look* and so on. You change the Spanish verb ending instead to form the future tense.

Grammar Extra!

In English, we sometimes use *will* with the meaning of *be willing to* rather than simply to express the future, for example, *Will you wait for me a moment?* In Spanish you don't use the future tense to say this; you use the verb **querer** (meaning *to want*) instead.

¿Me <u>quieres</u> esperar un momento, por favor?	Will you wait for me a moment, please?

3 | Verbs with irregular stems in the future tense

➤ There are a few verbs that <u>DO NOT</u> use their infinitives as the stem for the future tense. Here are some of the most common.

Verb	Stem	(yo)	(tú)	(él)(ella)(usted)	(nosotros)(nosotras)	(vosotros)(vosotras)	(ellos)(ellas)(ustedes)
decir to say	dir-	dir<u>é</u>	dir<u>ás</u>	dir<u>á</u>	dir<u>emos</u>	dir<u>éis</u>	dir<u>án</u>
haber to have	habr-	habr<u>é</u>	habr<u>ás</u>	habr<u>á</u>	habr<u>emos</u>	habr<u>éis</u>	habr<u>án</u>
hacer to do/make	har-	har<u>é</u>	har<u>ás</u>	har<u>á</u>	har<u>emos</u>	har<u>éis</u>	har<u>án</u>
poder to be able to	podr-	podr<u>é</u>	podr<u>ás</u>	podr<u>á</u>	podr<u>emos</u>	podr<u>éis</u>	podr<u>án</u>
poner to put	pondr-	pondr<u>é</u>	pondr<u>ás</u>	pondr<u>á</u>	pondr<u>emos</u>	pondr<u>éis</u>	pondr<u>án</u>
querer to want	querr-	querr<u>é</u>	querr<u>ás</u>	querr<u>á</u>	querr<u>emos</u>	querr<u>éis</u>	querr<u>án</u>
saber to know	sabr-	sabr<u>é</u>	sabr<u>ás</u>	sabr<u>á</u>	sabr<u>emos</u>	sabr<u>éis</u>	sabr<u>án</u>

For further explanation of grammatical terms, please see pages viii-xii.

Verb	Stem	(yo)	(tú)	(él) (ella) (usted)	(nosotros) (nosotras)	(vosotros) (vosotras)	(ellos) (ellas) (ustedes)
salir to leave	saldr-	saldré	saldrás	saldrá	saldremos	saldréis	saldrán
tener to have	tendr-	tendré	tendrás	tendrá	tendremos	tendréis	tendrán
venir to come	vendr-	vendré	vendrás	vendrá	vendremos	vendréis	vendrán

Lo haré mañana.	I'll do it tomorrow.
No podremos hacerlo.	We won't be able to do it.
Lo pondré aquí.	I'll put it here.
Saldrán por la mañana.	They'll leave in the morning.
¿A qué hora vendrás?	What time will you come?

[i] Note that the verb **haber** is only used when forming other tenses, such as the perfect tense, and in the expression **hay** (meaning *there is* or *there are*).

⇨ *For more information on the **Perfect tense** and on **hay**, see pages 115 and 130.*

4 Reflexive verbs in the future tense

➤ The future tense of reflexive verbs is formed in just the same way as for ordinary verbs, except that you have to remember to give the reflexive pronoun (**me**, **te**, **se**, **nos**, **os**, **se**).

    Me leventaré temprano.   I'll get up early.

Key points

✔ You can use a present tense in Spanish to talk about something that will happen or be true, just as in English.

✔ You can use **ir a** with an infinitive to talk about things that will happen in the immediate future.

✔ In Spanish there is no direct equivalent of the word *will* in verb forms like *will rain* and *will look*. You change the verb endings instead.

✔ To form the future tense, add the endings **-é**, **-ás**, **á**, **-emos**, **-éis**, **-án** to the infinitive.

✔ Some verbs have irregular stems in the future tense. It is worth learning these.

The conditional

> **What is the conditional?**
> The **conditional** is a verb form used to talk about things that would happen or that would be true under certain conditions, for example, I _would_ help you _if I could_.
> It is also used to say what you would like or need, for example, _Could_ you give me the bill?

1 Using the conditional

➤ You can often recognize a conditional in English by the word _would_ or its shortened form _'d_.

I _would_ be sad if you left.
If you asked him, he_'d_ help you.

➤ You use the conditional for:

- saying what you would like to do

  Me **gustaría** conocerlo.   I'd like to meet him.

- making suggestions

  Podrías alquilar una bici.   You could hire a bike.

- giving advice

  Deberías hacer más ejercicio.   You should take more exercise.

- saying what you would do

  Le dije que le **ayudaría**.   I said I would help him.

> _Tip_
> There is no direct Spanish translation of _would_ in verb forms like _would be_, _would like_, _would help_ and so on. You change the Spanish verb ending instead.

2 Forming the conditional

➤ To form the conditional of regular -ar, -er, and -ir verbs, add the following endings to the <u>infinitive</u> of the verb: -ía, -ías, -ía, -íamos, -íais, -ían.

➤ The following table shows the conditional tense of three regular verbs:
hablar (meaning *to speak*), **comer** (meaning *to eat*) and **vivir** (meaning *to live*).

(yo)	hablaría	comería	viviría	I would speak/eat/live
(tú)	hablarías	comerías	vivirías	you would speak/eat/live
(él) (ella) (usted)	hablaría	comería	viviría	he would speak/eat/live she would speak/eat/live it would speak/eat/live you would speak/eat/live
(nosotros/nosotras)	hablaríamos	comeríamos	viviríamos	we would speak/eat/live
(vosotros/vosotras)	hablaríais	comeríais	viviríais	you would speak/eat/live
(ellos/ellas) (ustedes)	hablarían	comerían	vivirían	they would speak/eat/live you would speak/eat/live

Me <u>gustaría</u> ir a China.	I'd like to go to China.
Dije que <u>hablaría</u> con ella.	I said that I would speak to her.
<u>Debería</u> llamar a mis padres.	I should ring my parents.

Tip

Don't forget to put an accent on the **í** in the conditional.

i Note that the endings in the conditional tense are identical to those of
the <u>imperfect tense</u> for -er and -ir verbs. The only difference is that they
are added to a different stem.

⇨ *For more information on the **Imperfect tense**, see page 110.*

3 Verbs with irregular stems in the conditional

➤ To form the conditional of irregular verbs, use the same stem as for the <u>future tense</u>, then add the usual endings for the conditional. The same verbs that are irregular in the future tense are irregular in the conditional.

Verb	Stem	(yo)	(tú)	(él) (ella) (usted)	(nosotros) (nosotras)	(vosotros) (vosotras)	(ellos) (ellas) (ustedes)
decir to say	dir-	diría	dirías	diría	diríamos	diríais	dirían
haber to have	habr-	habría	habrías	habría	habríamos	habríais	habrían
hacer to do/ make	har-	haría	harías	haría	haríamos	haríais	harían
poder to be able to	podr-	podría	podrías	podría	podríamos	podríais	podrían
poner to put	pondr-	pondría	pondrías	pondría	pondríamos	pondríais	pondrían
querer to want	querr-	querría	querrías	querría	querríamos	querríais	querrían
saber to know	sabr-	sabría	sabrías	sabría	sabríamos	sabríais	sabrían
salir to leave	saldr-	saldría	saldrías	saldría	saldríamos	saldríais	saldrían
tener to have	tendr-	tendría	tendrías	tendría	tendríamos	tendríais	tendrían
venir to come	vendr-	vendría	vendrías	<u>vendría</u>	vendríamos	vendríais	vendrían

⇨ *For more information on the **Future tense**, see page 97.*

¿Qué <u>harías</u> tú en mi lugar?	What would you do if you were me?
¿<u>Podrías</u> ayudarme?	Could you help me?
Yo lo <u>pondría</u> aquí.	I would put it here.

i Note that the verb **haber** is only used when forming other tenses, such as the perfect tense, and in the expression **hay** (meaning *there is/there are*).

⇨ *For more information on the **Perfect tense** and on **hay**, see pages 115 and 130.*

For further explanation of grammatical terms, please see pages viii-xii.

4 Reflexive verbs in the conditional

➤ The conditional of reflexive verbs is formed in just the same way as for ordinary verbs, except that you have to remember to give the reflexive pronoun (**me, te, se, nos, os, se**).

> **Le dije que <u>me levantaría</u> temprano.**   I said I would get up early.

> ### Key points
>
> ✔ In Spanish, there is no direct equivalent of the word *would* in verb forms like *would go* and *would look* and so on. You change the verb ending instead.
>
> ✔ To form the conditional tense, add the endings -ía, ías, -ía, -íamos, -íais, -ían to the infinitive. The conditional uses the same stem as for the future.
>
> ✔ Some verbs have irregular stems which are used for both the conditional and the future. It is worth learning these.

The preterite

> **What is the preterite?**
> The **preterite** is a form of the verb that is used to talk about actions that
> were completed in the past in Spanish. It often corresponds to the simple
> past in English, as in I _bought_ a new bike; Mary _went_ to the shops on Friday; I _typed_
> two reports yesterday.

1 Using the preterite

➤ In English, we use the <u>simple past tense</u> to talk about actions:
  - that were completed at a certain point in the past
    I <u>bought</u> a dress yesterday.
  - that were part of a series of events
    I <u>went</u> to the beach, <u>undressed</u> and <u>put on</u> my swimsuit.
  - that went on for a certain amount of time
    The war <u>lasted</u> three years.

➤ In English, we also use the <u>simple past tense</u> to describe actions which
  happened frequently (_Our parents <u>took</u> us swimming in the holidays_), and to
  describe settings (_It <u>was</u> a dark and stormy night_).

➤ In Spanish, the <u>preterite</u> is the most common tense for talking about the past.
  You use the preterite for actions:
  - that were completed at a certain point in the past

    Ayer <u>compré</u> un vestido.   I bought a dress yesterday.
  - that were part of a series of events

    <u>Fui</u> a la playa, me <u>quité</u> la ropa   I went to the beach, undressed and
    y me <u>puse</u> el bañador.   put on my swimsuit.
  - that went on for a certain amount of time

    La guerra <u>duró</u> tres años.   The war lasted for three years.

➤ However, you use the <u>imperfect tense</u> for actions that happened frequently
  (where you could use _used to_ in English) and for descriptions of settings.

⇨ _For more information on the **Imperfect tense**, see page 110._

2 Forming the preterite of regular verbs

➤ To form the preterite of any regular -**ar** verb, you take off the -**ar** ending to
  form the stem, and add the endings: -**é**, -**aste**, -**ó**, -**amos**, -**asteis**, -**aron**.

➤ To form the preterite of any regular -er or -ir verb, you also take off the -er or -ir ending to form the stem and add the endings: -í, -iste, -ió, -imos, -isteis, -ieron.

➤ The following table shows the preterite of three regular verbs: **hablar** (meaning *to speak*), **comer** (meaning *to eat*) and **vivir** (meaning *to live*).

(yo)	habl**é**	com**í**	viv**í**	I spoke/ate/lived
(tú)	habl**aste**	com**iste**	viv**iste**	you spoke/ate/lived
(él) (ella) (usted)	habl**ó**	com**ió**	viv**ió**	he spoke/ate/lived she spoke/ate/lived it spoke/ate/lived you spoke/ate/lived
(nosotros/nosotras)	habl**amos**	com**imos**	viv**imos**	we spoke/ate/lived
(vosotros/vosotras)	habl**asteis**	com**isteis**	viv**isteis**	you spoke/ate/lived
(ellos/ellas) (ustedes)	habl**aron**	com**ieron**	viv**ieron**	they spoke/ate/lived you spoke/ate/lived

Bail**é** con mi hermana.	I danced with my sister.
No habl**é** con ella.	I didn't speak to her.
Com**imos** en un restaurante.	We had lunch in a restaurant.
¿Cerr**aste** la ventana?	Did you close the window?

🛈 Note that Spanish has no direct translation of *did* or *didn't* in questions or negative sentences. You simply use a past tense and make it a question by making your voice go up at the end or changing the word order; you make it negative by adding **no**.

⇨ *For more information on **Questions** and **Negatives**, see pages 160 and 157.*

Tip

Remember the accents on the **yo** and **él/ella/usted** forms of regular verbs in the preterite. Only an accent shows the difference, for example, between **hablo** *I speak* and **habló** *he spoke*.

3 | Irregular verbs in the preterite

➤ A number of verbs have very irregular forms in the preterite. The table shows some of the most common.

Verb	(yo)	(tú)	(él) (ella) (usted)	(nosotros) (nosotras)	(vosotros) (vosotras)	(ellos) (ellas) (ustedes)
andar to walk	anduve	anduviste	anduvo	anduvimos	anduvisteis	anduvieron
conducir to drive	conduje	condujiste	condujo	condujimos	condujisteis	condujeron
dar to give	di	diste	dio	dimos	disteis	dieron
decir to say	dije	dijiste	dijo	dijimos	dijisteis	dijeron
estar to be	estuve	estuviste	estuvo	estuvimos	estuvisteis	estuvieron
hacer to do, to make	hice	hiciste	hizo	hicimos	hicisteis	hicieron
ir to go	fui	fuiste	fue	fuimos	fuisteis	fueron
poder to be able to	pude	pudiste	pudo	pudimos	pudisteis	pudieron
poner to put	puse	pusiste	puso	pusimos	pusisteis	pusieron
querer to want	quise	quisiste	quiso	quisimos	quisisteis	quisieron
saber to know	supe	supiste	supo	supimos	supisteis	supieron
ser to be	fui	fuiste	fue	fuimos	fuisteis	fueron
tener to have	tuve	tuviste	tuvo	tuvimos	tuvisteis	tuvieron
traer to bring	traje	trajiste	trajo	trajimos	trajisteis	trajeron
venir to come	vine	viniste	vino	vinimos	vinisteis	vinieron
ver to see	vi	viste	vio	vimos	visteis	vieron

i Note that **hizo** (the **él/ella/usted** form of **hacer**) is spelt with a **z**.

⇨ *For more information on **Spelling**, see page 196.*

For further explanation of grammatical terms, please see pages viii-xii.

<u>Fue</u> a Madrid.	He went to Madrid.
Te <u>vi</u> en el parque.	I saw you in the park.
No <u>vinieron</u>.	They didn't come.
¿Qué <u>hizo</u>?	What did she do?
Se lo <u>di</u> a Teresa.	I gave it to Teresa.
<u>Fue</u> en 1999.	It was in 1999.

Típ

The preterite forms of **ser** (meaning *to be*) are the same as the preterite forms of **ir** (meaning *to go*).

➤ Some other verbs are regular <u>EXCEPT FOR</u> the **él/ella/usted** and **ellos/ellas/ustedes** forms (*third persons singular and plural*). In these forms the stem vowel changes.

Verb	(yo)	(tú)	(él) (ella) (usted)	(nosotros) (nosotras)	(vosotros) (vosotras)	(ellos) (ellas) (ustedes)
dormir to sleep	dormí	dormiste	d<u>u</u>rmió	dormimos	dormisteis	d<u>u</u>rmieron
morir to die	morí	moriste	m<u>u</u>rió	morimos	moristeis	m<u>u</u>rieron
pedir to ask for	pedí	pediste	p<u>i</u>dió	pedimos	pedisteis	p<u>i</u>dieron
reír to laugh	reí	reíste	r<u>i</u>ó	reímos	reísteis	r<u>i</u>eron
seguir to follow	seguí	seguiste	s<u>i</u>guió	seguimos	seguisteis	s<u>i</u>guieron
sentir to feel	sentí	sentiste	s<u>i</u>ntió	sentimos	sentisteis	s<u>i</u>ntieron

i Note that **reír** also has an accent in all persons apart from the **ellos/ellas/ustedes** forms.

Antonio <u>durmió</u> diez horas.	Antonio slept for ten hours.
<u>Murió</u> en 1066.	He died in 1066.
<u>Pidió</u> paella.	He asked for paella.
¿Los <u>siguió</u>?	Did she follow them?
<u>Sintió</u> un dolor en la pierna.	He felt a pain in his leg.
Nos <u>reímos</u> mucho.	We laughed a lot.
Juan no se <u>rió</u>.	Juan didn't laugh.

➤ **caer** (meaning *to fall*) and **leer** (meaning *to read*) have an accent in all persons <u>apart from</u> the **ellos/ellas/ustedes** form (*third person plural*). In addition, the vowel changes to **y** in the **él/ella/usted** and **ellos/ellas/ustedes** forms (*third persons singular and plural*).

Verb	(yo)	(tú)	(él) (ella) (usted)	(nosotros) (nosotras)	(vosotros) (vosotras)	(ellos) (ellas) (ustedes)
caer to fall	caí	caíste	cayó	caímos	caísteis	cayeron
construir to build	construí	construiste	construyó	construimos	construisteis	construyeron
leer to read	leí	leíste	leyó	leímos	leísteis	leyeron

[i] Note that **construir** also changes to **y** in the **él/ella/usted** and **ellos/ellas/ustedes** forms (*third persons singular and plural*), but only has accents in the **yo** and **él/ella/usted** forms.

Se <u>cayó</u> por la ventana.	He fell out of the window.
Ayer <u>leí</u> un artículo muy interesante.	I read a very interesting article yesterday.
<u>Construyeron</u> una nueva autopista.	They built a new motorway.

4 Other spelling changes in the preterite

➤ Spanish verbs that end in **-zar**, **-gar** and **-car** in the infinitive change the **z** to **c**, the **g** to **gu** and the **c** to **qu** in the **yo** form (*first person singular*).

Verb	(yo)	(tú)	(él) (ella) (usted)	(nosotros) (nosotras)	(vosotros) (vosotras)	(ellos) (ellas) (ustedes)
cruzar to cross	cru<u>c</u>é	cruzaste	cruzó	cruzamos	cruzasteis	cruzaron
empezar to begin	empe<u>c</u>é	empezaste	empezó	empezamos	empezasteis	empezaron
pagar to pay for	pa<u>gu</u>é	pagaste	pagó	pagamos	pagasteis	pagaron
sacar to follow	sa<u>qu</u>é	sacaste	sacó	sacamos	sacasteis	sacaron

<u>Crucé</u> el río.	I crossed the river.
<u>Empecé</u> a hacer mis deberes.	I began doing my homework.
No <u>pagué</u> la cuenta.	I didn't pay the bill.
Me <u>saqué</u> las llaves del bolsillo.	I took my keys out of my pocket.

For further explanation of grammatical terms, please see pages viii-xii.

☐ Note that the change from **g** to **gu** and **c** to **qu** before **e** is to keep the sound hard.

⇨ *For more information on **Spelling**, see page 196.*

5   <u>Reflexive verbs in the preterite</u>

➤ The preterite of reflexive verbs is formed in just the same way as for ordinary verbs, except that you have to remember to give the reflexive pronoun (**me, te, se, nos, os, se**).

<u>Me levanté</u> a las siete.   I got up at seven.

Key points

✔ The preterite is the most common way to talk about the past in Spanish.

✔ To form the preterite of regular **-ar** verbs, take off the **-ar** ending and add the endings: **-é, -aste, -ó, -amos, -asteis, -aron**.

✔ To form the preterite of regular **-er** and **-ir** verbs, take off the **-er** and **-ir** endings and add the endings: **-í, -iste, -ió, -imos, -isteis, -ieron**.

✔ There are a number of verbs which are irregular in the preterite. These forms have to be learnt.

✔ With some verbs, the accents and spelling change in certain forms.

The imperfect tense

> **What is the imperfect tense?**
> The **imperfect tense** is one of the verb tenses used to talk about the past, especially in descriptions, and to say what was happening or used to happen, for example, *It was sunny at the weekend; We were living in Spain at the time; I used to walk to school.*

1 Using the imperfect tense

➤ In Spanish, the imperfect tense is used:

- to describe what things were like and how people felt in the past

Hacía calor.	It was hot.
No **teníamos** mucho dinero.	We didn't have much money.
Tenía hambre.	I was hungry.

- to say what used to happen or what you used to do regularly in the past

Cada día **llamaba** a su madre.	He used to ring his mother every day.

- to describe what was happening or what the situation was when something else took place

Tomábamos café.	We were having coffee.
Me **caí** cuando **cruzaba** la carretera.	I fell over when I was crossing the road.

Grammar Extra!

Sometimes, instead of the ordinary imperfect tense being used to describe what was happening at a given moment in the past when something else occurred interrupting it, the continuous form is used. This is made up of the imperfect tense of **estar** (**estaba, estabas** and so on), followed by the **-ando/-iendo** form of the main verb. The other verb – the one that relates the event that occurred – is in the preterite.

Montse **miraba** la televisión *or* Montse **estaba mirando** la televisión cuando sonó el teléfono.	Montse was watching television when the telephone rang.

⇨ *For further information on the Preterite, see page 104.*

---

2 Forming the imperfect tense

➤ To form the imperfect of any regular **-ar** verb, you take off the **-ar** ending of the infinitive to form the stem and add the endings: **-aba, -abas, -aba, -ábamos, -abais, -aban**.

For further explanation of grammatical terms, please see pages viii-xii.

➤ The following table shows the imperfect tense of one regular -ar verb: **hablar** (meaning *to speak*).

(yo)	hab<u>laba</u>	I spoke I was speaking I used to speak
(tú)	hab<u>labas</u>	you spoke you were speaking you used to speak
(él/ella/usted)	hab<u>laba</u>	he/she/it/you spoke he/she/it was speaking, you were speaking he/she/it/you used to speak
(nosotros/nosotras)	hab<u>lábamos</u>	we spoke we were speaking we used to speak
(vosotros/vosotras)	hab<u>labais</u>	you spoke you were speaking you used to speak
(ellos/ellas/ustedes)	hab<u>laban</u>	they/you spoke they/you were speaking they/you used to speak

i Note that in the imperfect tense of -ar verbs, the only accent is on the nosotros/nosotras form

Hablaba francés e italiano.	He spoke French and Italian.
Cuando era joven, mi tío trabajaba mucho.	My uncle worked hard when he was young.
Estudiábamos matemáticas e inglés.	We were studying maths and English.

➤ To form the imperfect of any regular -er or -ir verb, you take off the -er or -ir ending of the infinitive to form the stem and add the endings: -ía, -ías, -ía, -íamos, -íais, -ían.

➤ The following table shows the imperfect of two regular verbs: **comer** (meaning *to eat*) and **vivir** (meaning *to live*).

(yo)	comía	vivía	I ate/lived I was eating/living I used to eat/live
(tú)	comías	vivías	you ate/lived you were eating/living you used to eat/live
(él/ella/usted)	comía	vivía	he/she/it/you ate/lived he/she/it was eating/living, you were eating/living he/she/it was eating/living, you were eating/living
(nosotros/nosotras)	comíamos	vivíamos	we ate/lived we were eating/living we used to eat/live
(vosotros/vosotras)	comíais	vivíais	you ate/lived you were eating/living you used to eat/live
(ellos/ellas/ustedes)	comían	vivían	they/you ate/lived they/you were eating/living they/you used to eat/live

i Note that in the imperfect tense of **-er** and **-ir** verbs, there's an accent on all the endings.

A veces, <u>comíamos</u> en casa de Pepe.	We sometimes used to eat at Pepe's.
<u>Vivía</u> en un piso en la Avenida de Barcelona.	She lived in a flat in Avenida de Barcelona.
Cuando llegó el médico, ya se <u>sentían</u> mejor.	They were already feeling better when the doctor arrived.

> **Tip**
>
> The imperfect endings for **-er** and **-ir** verbs are the same as the endings used to form the conditional for all verbs. The only difference is that, in the conditional, the endings are added to the future stem.
>
> ➪ *For more information on the **Conditional**, see page 100.*

3   Irregular verbs in the imperfect tense

➤ ser, ir and ver are irregular in the imperfect tense.

	ser	Meaning: to be
(yo)	era	I was
(tú)	eras	you were
(él/ella/usted)	era	he/she/it was, you were
(nosotros/nosotras)	éramos	we were
(vosotros/vosotras)	erais	you were
(ellos/ellas/ustedes)	eran	they were/you were

Era un chico muy simpático.   He was a very nice boy.
Mi madre era profesora.   My mother was a teacher.

	ir	Meaning: to go
(yo)	iba	I went/used to go/was going
(tú)	ibas	you went/used to go/were going
(él/ella/usted)	iba	he/she/it went/used to go/was going, you went/used to go/were going
(nosotros/nosotras)	íbamos	we went/used to go/were going
(vosotros/vosotras)	ibais	you went/used to go/were going
(ellos/ellas/ustedes)	iban	they/you went/used to go/were going

Iba a la oficina cada día.   Every day he would go to the office.
¿Adónde iban?   Where were they going?

	ver	Meaning: to see/to watch
(yo)	veía	I saw/used to see I watched/used to watch/was watching
(tú)	veías	you saw/used to see you watched/used to watch/were watching
(él/ella/usted)	veía	he/she/it saw/used to see he/she/it watched/used to watch/was watching you saw/used to see you watched/used to watch/were watching
(nosotros/nosotras)	veíamos	we saw/used to see we watched/used to watch/were watching
(vosotros/vosotras)	veíais	you saw/used to see you watched/used to watch/were watching
(ellos/ellas/ustedes)	veían	they/you saw/used to see they/you watched/used to watch/were watching

| Los sábados, siempre lo veíamos. | We always used to see him on Saturdays. |
| Veía la televisión cuando llegó mi tío. | I was watching television when my uncle arrived. |

4 Reflexive verbs in the imperfect tense

➤ The imperfect of reflexive verbs is formed in just the same way as for ordinary verbs, except that you have to remember to give the reflexive pronoun (me, te, se, nos, os, se).

| Antes se levantaba temprano. | He used to get up early. |

Grammar Extra!

In Spanish, you also use the imperfect tense with certain time expressions, in particular with **desde** (meaning *since*), **desde hacía** (meaning *for*) and **hacía ... que** (meaning *for*) to talk about activities and states that had started previously and were still going on at a particular point in the past:

Estaba enfermo desde 2000.	He had been ill since 2000.
Conducía ese coche desde hacía tres meses.	He had been driving that car for three months.
Hacía mucho tiempo que salían juntos.	They had been going out together for a long time.
Hacía dos años que vivíamos en Madrid.	We had been living in Madrid for two years.

Compare the use of **desde**, **desde hacía** and **hacía ... que** with the imperfect with that of **desde**, **desde hace**, and **hace ... que** with the present.

⇨ *For more information on the use of tenses with* **desde**, *see page 189.*

Key points

✔ To form the imperfect tense of -ar verbs, take off the -ar ending and add the endings: -aba, -abas, -aba, -ábamos, -abais, -aban.

✔ To form the imperfect tense of -er and -ir verbs, take off the -er and -ir endings and add the endings: -ía, -ías, -ía, -íamos, -íais, -ían.

✔ ser, ir and ver are irregular in the imperfect.

The perfect tense

> **What is the perfect tense?**
> The **perfect** tense is a verb form used to talk about what has or hasn't happened; for example, *I've broken my glasses; We haven't spoken about it.*

1   Using the perfect tense

➤ In English, we use the perfect tense (*have*, *has* or their shortened forms '*ve* and '*s* followed by a past participle such as *spoken*, *eaten*, *lived*, *been*) to talk about what has or hasn't happened today, this week, this year or in our lives up to now.

➤ The Spanish perfect tense is used in a similar way.

He terminado el libro.	I've finished the book.
¿**Has fregado** el suelo?	Have you washed the floor?
Nunca **ha estado** en Bolivia.	He's never been to Bolivia.
Ha vendido su caballo.	She has sold her horse.
Todavía no **hemos comprado** un ordenador.	We still haven't bought a computer.
Ya se **han ido**.	They've already left.

Grammar Extra!

You may also come across uses of the perfect tense in Spanish to talk about actions completed in the very recent past. In English, we'd use the past simple tense in such cases.

¿Lo **has visto**?	Did you see that?

---

2   Forming the perfect tense

➤ As in English, the perfect tense in Spanish has two parts to it. These are:

- the <u>present</u> tense of the verb **haber** (meaning *to have*)
- a part of the main verb called the <u>past participle</u>.

3   Forming the past participle

➤ To form the past participle of regular **-ar** verbs, take off the **-ar** ending of the infinitive and add **-ado**.

    hablar (*to speak*)   →   **hablado** (*spoken*)

➤ To form the past participle of regular **-er** or **-ir** verbs, take off the **-er** or **-ir** ending of the infinitive and add **-ido**.

    comer (*to eat*)   →   **comido** (*eaten*)
    vivir (*to live*)   →   **vivido** (*lived*)

4 | The perfect tense of some regular verbs

➤ The following table shows how you can combine the present tense of haber with the past participle of any verb to form the perfect tense.

In this case, the past participles are taken from the following regular verbs: hablar (meaning to speak); trabajar (meaning to work); comer (meaning to eat); vender (meaning to sell); vivir (meaning to live); decidir (meaning to decide).

	Present of haber	Past participle	Meaning
(yo)	he	hablado	I have spoken
(tú)	has	trabajado	you have worked
(él/ella/usted)	ha	comido	he/she/it has eaten, you have eaten
(nosotros/nosotras)	hemos	vendido	we have sold
(vosotros/vosotras)	habéis	vivido	you have lived
(ellos/ellas/ustedes)	han	decidido	they/you have decided

Has trabajado mucho.	You've worked hard.
No he comido nada.	I haven't eaten anything.

i Note that you should not confuse haber with tener. Even though they both mean to have, haber is only used for forming tenses and in certain impersonal expressions such as hay and había meaning there is, there are, there was, there were, and so on.

⇨ *For further information on* **Impersonal verbs**, *see page 129.*

5 | Verbs with irregular past participles

➤ Some past participles are irregular. There aren't too many, so try to learn them.

abrir (to open)	→	abierto (opened)
cubrir (to cover)	→	cubierto (covered)
decir (to say)	→	dicho (said)
escribir (to write)	→	escrito (written)
freír (to fry)	→	frito (fried)
hacer (to do, to make)	→	hecho (done, made)
morir (to die)	→	muerto (died)
oír (to hear)	→	oído (heard)
poner (to put)	→	puesto (put)

For further explanation of grammatical terms, please see pages viii-xii.

romper (*to break*)	→	roto (*broken*)
ver (*to see*)	→	visto (*seen*)
volver (*to return*)	→	vuelto (*returned*)

<u>He abierto</u> una cuenta en el banco.	I've opened a bank account.
No <u>ha dicho</u> nada.	He hasn't said anything.
Hoy <u>he hecho</u> muchas cosas.	I've done a lot today.
Todavía no <u>he hecho</u> los deberes.	I haven't done my homework yet.
<u>Han muerto</u> tres personas.	Three people have died.
¿Dónde <u>has puesto</u> mis zapatos?	Where have you put my shoes?
Carlos <u>ha roto</u> el espejo.	Carlos has broken the mirror.
Jamás <u>he visto</u> una cosa parecida.	I've never seen anything like it.
¿<u>Ha vuelto</u> Ana?	Has Ana come back?

Tip

he/has/ha and so on must <u>NEVER</u> be separated from the past participle. Any object pronouns go before the form of haber being used, and <u>NOT</u> between the form of haber and the past participle.

No <u>lo</u> he visto.	I haven't seen it.
¿<u>Lo</u> has hecho ya?	Have you done it yet?

---

6   **Reflexive verbs in the perfect tense**

➤ The perfect tense of reflexive verbs is formed in the same way as for ordinary verbs. The reflexive pronouns (me, te, se, nos, os, se) come before he, has, ha, and so on. The table on the next page shows the perfect tense of lavarse in full.

Subject pronoun	Reflexive pronoun	Present tense of haber	Past Participle	Meaning
(yo)	me	he	lavado	I have washed
(tú)	te	has	lavado	you have washed
(él) (ella) (uno) (usted)	se	ha	lavado	he has washed she has washed one has washed it has washed you have washed
(nosotros) (nosotras)	nos	hemos	lavado	we have washed we have washed
(vosotros) (vosotras)	os	habéis	lavado	you have washed you have washed
(ellos) (ellas) (ustedes)	se	han	lavado	they have washed they have washed you have washed

Grammar Extra!

Don't use the perfect tense with **desde**, **desde hace** and **hace ... que** when talking about how long something has been going on for. Use the <u>present tense</u> instead.

<u>Está</u> enfermo desde julio.	He has been ill since July.
<u>Conduce</u> ese coche desde hace tres meses.	He has been driving that car for three months.
Hace mucho tiempo que <u>salen</u> juntos.	They have been going out together for a long time.

⇨ *For more information on the **Present tense**, see page 72.*

➤ In European Spanish you <u>CAN</u> use the perfect tense in the negative with **desde** and **desde hace**.

No lo <u>he visto</u> desde hace mucho tiempo.	I haven't seen him for a long time.

Key points

✔ The Spanish perfect tense is formed using the present tense of **haber** and a past participle.

✔ In Spanish, the perfect tense is used very much as it is in English.

✔ The past participle of regular **-ar** verbs ends in **-ado**, and the past participle of regular **-er** and **-ir** verbs ends in **-ido**.

✔ Make sure you know the following irregular past participle forms: abierto, cubierto, dicho, escrito, frito, hecho, muerto, puesto, roto, visto, vuelto.

For further explanation of grammatical terms, please see pages viii-xii.

The pluperfect or past perfect tense

> **What is the pluperfect tense?**
> The **pluperfect** is a verb tense that is used to talk about what had happened
> or had been true at a point in the past, for example, *I'd forgotten to finish my
> homework.*

1   Using the pluperfect tense

➤ When talking about the past, we sometimes refer to things that had
happened previously. In English, we often use *had* followed by a <u>past participle</u>
such as *spoken, eaten, lived* or *been* to do this. This tense is known as the
<u>pluperfect</u> or <u>past perfect</u> tense.

➤ The Spanish pluperfect tense is used and formed in a similar way.

Ya <u>habíamos comido</u> cuando llegó.	We'd already eaten when he arrived.
Nunca lo <u>había visto</u> antes de aquella noche.	I'd never seen it before that night.

2   Forming the pluperfect tense

➤ Like the perfect tense, the pluperfect tense in Spanish has <u>two</u> parts to it:

- the imperfect tense of the verb **haber** (meaning *to have*)
- the past participle.

⇨ *For more information on the **Imperfect tense** and **Past participles**, see pages 110
and 115.*

➤ The table below shows how you can combine the imperfect tense of **haber**
with the past participle of any verb to form the pluperfect tense. Here, the
past participles are taken from the following regular verbs: **hablar** (meaning
to speak); **trabajar** (meaning *to work*); **comer** (meaning *to eat*); **vender**
(meaning *to sell*); **vivir** (meaning *to live*); **decidir** (meaning *to decide*).

Subject pronoun	Imperfect of <u>haber</u>	Past Participle	Meaning
(yo)	había	hablado	I had spoken
(tú)	habías	trabajado	you had worked
(él/ella/usted)	había	comido	he/she/it/you had eaten
(nosotros/nosotras)	habíamos	vendido	we had sold
(vosotros/vosotras)	habíais	vivido	you had lived
(ellos/ellas/ustedes)	habían	decidido	they/you had decided

No <u>había trabajado</u> antes.	He hadn't worked before.
<u>Había vendido</u> su caballo.	She had sold her horse.

➤ Remember that some very common verbs have irregular past participles.

abrir (*to open*)	→	abierto (*opened*)
cubrir (*to cover*)	→	cubierto (*covered*)
decir (*to say*)	→	dicho (*said*)
escribir (*to write*)	→	escrito (*written*)
freír (*to fry*)	→	frito (*fried*)
hacer (*to do, to make*)	→	hecho (*done, made*)
morir (*to die*)	→	muerto (*died*)
oír (*to hear*)	→	oído (*heard*)
poner (*to put*)	→	puesto (*put*)
romper (*to break*)	→	roto (*broken*)
ver (*to see*)	→	visto (*seen*)
volver (*to return*)	→	vuelto (*returned*)

No <u>había dicho</u> nada.	He hadn't said anything.
Tres personas <u>habían muerto</u>.	Three people had died.

Tip

había/habías/habían and so on must <u>NEVER</u> be separated from the past participle. Any object pronouns go before the form of haber being used, and <u>NOT</u> between the form of haber and the past participle.

No lo había visto.	I hadn't seen it.

---

3 **Reflexive verbs in the pluperfect tense**

➤ The pluperfect tense of reflexive verbs is formed in the same way as for ordinary verbs. The reflexive pronouns (me, te, se, nos, os, se) come before había, habías, había, and so on. The table on the next page shows the pluperfect tense of lavarse in full.

Subject pronoun	Reflexive pronoun	Imperfect tense of haber	Past Participle	Meaning
(yo)	me	había	lavado	I had washed
(tú)	te	habías	lavado	you had washed
(él) (ella) (uno) (usted)	se	había	lavado	he had washed she had washed one had washed it had washed you had washed
(nosotros) (nosotras)	nos	habíamos	lavado	we had washed we had washed
(vosotros) (vosotras)	os	habíais	lavado	you had washed you had washed
(ellos) (ellas) (ustedes)	se	habían	lavado	they had washed they had washed you had washed

Grammar Extra!

Don't use the pluperfect with desde, desde hacía and hacía ... que when talking about how long something had been going on for. Use the imperfect instead.

<u>Estaba</u> enfermo desde 2000.	He had been ill since 2000.
<u>Conducía</u> ese coche desde hacía tres meses.	He had been driving that car for three months.
Hacía mucho tiempo que <u>salían</u> juntos.	They had been going out together for a long time.

⇨ *For more information on the Imperfect tense, see page 110.*

In European Spanish you <u>CAN</u> use the pluperfect tense in the negative with desde and desde hacía.

No lo <u>había visto</u> desde hacía mucho tiempo.	I hadn't seen him for a long time.

Key points

- ✔ The Spanish pluperfect tense is formed using the imperfect tense of haber and a past particple.
- ✔ In Spanish, the pluperfect tense is used very much as it is in English.
- ✔ The past participle of regular -ar verbs ends in -ado, while that of regular -er and -ir verbs ends in -ido.
- ✔ Make sure you know the irregular forms: abierto, cubierto, dicho, escrito, frito, hecho, muerto, puesto, roto, visto, vuelto.

The passive

> **What is the passive?**
> The **passive** is a verb form that is used when the subject of the verb is the person or thing that is affected by the action, for example, *Mary is liked by everyone; Two children were hurt in an accident; The house was sold.*

1   Using the passive

➤ Verbs can be either <u>active</u> or <u>passive</u>.

➤ In a normal or <u>active</u> sentence, the subject of the verb is the person or thing doing the action described by the verb. The object of the verb is the person or thing that the verb most directly affects.

> Peter (*subject*) wrote (*active verb*) a letter (*object*).
> Ryan (*subject*) hit (*active verb*) me (*object*).

➤ Provided the verb has an object, in English, as in Spanish, you can turn an <u>active</u> sentence round to make it a <u>passive</u> sentence by using *to be* followed by a past participle. In this case the person or thing directly affected by the action becomes the subject of the verb.

> A letter (*subject*) was written (*passive verb*).
> I (*subject*) was hit (*passive verb*).

➤ To show who or what is responsible for the action in a passive construction, in English you use *by*.

> I (*subject*) was hit (*passive verb*) <u>by</u> Ryan.

➤ You use the passive rather than the active when you want to focus attention on the person or thing <u>affected by</u> the action rather than the person or thing that carries it out.

> <u>John</u> was injured in an accident.

➤ You can also use the passive when you don't know who is responsible for the action.

> Several buses were vandalized.

2   Forming the passive

➤ In English we use the verb *to be* with a <u>past participle</u> (*was painted, were seen, are made*) to form the passive. In Spanish, the passive is formed in exactly the same way, using the verb **ser** (meaning *to be*) and a <u>past participle</u>. When you say who the action is or was done by, you use the preposition **por** (meaning *by*).

⇨ *For more information on the **Past participle**, see page 115.*

Son fabricados en España.	They're made in Spain.
Es hecho a mano.	It's made by hand.
Fue escrito por JK Rowling.	It was written by JK Rowling.
La casa fue construida en 1956.	The house was built in 1956.
El cuadro fue pintado por mi padre.	The picture was painted by my father.
El colegio va a ser modernizado.	The school is going to be modernized.

[*i*] Note that the ending of the past participle agrees with the subject of the verb ser in exactly the same way as an adjective would.

⇨ For more information on **Adjectives**, see page 19.

➤ Here is the preterite of the -ar verb enviar (meaning to send) in its passive form.

Subject pronoun	Preterite of ser	Past Participle	Meaning
(yo)	fui	enviado (masculine) enviada (feminine)	I was sent
(tú)	fuiste	enviado (masculine) enviada (feminine)	you were sent
(él) (ella) (usted)	fue	enviado enviada enviado (masculine) enviada (feminine)	he was sent she was sent you were sent
(nosotros) (nosotras)	fuimos fuimos	enviados enviadas	we were sent we were sent
(vosotros) (vosotras)	fuisteis	enviados enviadas	you were sent you were sent
(ellos) (ellas) (ustedes)	fueron	enviados enviadas enviados (masculine) enviadas (feminine)	they were sent they were sent you were sent you were sent

➤ You can form other tenses in the passive by changing the tense of the verb ser.

Future: **serán enviados**   they will be sent.

Perfect: **han sido enviados**   they have been sent.

➤ Irregular past participles are the same as they are in the perfect tense.

⇨ For more information on **Irregular past participles**, see page 116.

3 Avoiding the passive

➤ Passives are not as common in Spanish as they are in English. Spanish native speakers usually prefer to avoid using the passive by:

- using the active construction instead of the passive

La policía <u>interrogó</u> al sospechoso.	The suspect was interrogated by the police.
Su madre le <u>regaló</u> un libro.	He was given a book by his mother.

- using an active verb in the third person plural

<u>Ponen</u> demasiados anuncios en la televisión.	Too many adverts are shown on television.

- using a reflexive construction (as long as you don't need to say who the action is done by)

<u>Se fabrican</u> en España.	They're made in Spain.
<u>Se hace</u> a mano.	It's made by hand.
La casa <u>se construyó</u> en 1956.	The house was built in 1956.
Todos los libros <u>se han vendido</u>.	All the books have been sold.

⇨ *For more information on **Reflexive verbs**, see page 91.*

- using an impersonal **se** construction

<u>Se</u> cree que va a morir.	It is thought he will die.

⇨ *For more information on the impersonal **se** construction, see page 133.*

> ### Tip
> Active verbs often have both a direct object and an indirect object.
> He gave me (*indirect object*) a book (*direct object*).
> In English, both of these objects can be made the subject of a passive verb; *I was given a book.* or *A book was given to me.*
> In Spanish, an indirect object can <u>NEVER</u> become the subject of a passive verb.

Key points
- ✔ The passive is formed using **ser** + past participle, sometimes followed by **por** (meaning *by*).
- ✔ The past participle must agree with the subject of **ser**.
- ✔ Passive constructions are not as common as they are in English. You can often avoid the passive by using the third person plural of the active verb or by using a reflexive construction.

The gerund

> **What is a gerund?**
> The **gerund** is a verb form ending in -*ing* which is used to form verb tenses, and which in English may also be used as an adjective and a noun, for example, *What are you doing?*; the *setting* sun; *Swimming* is easy!

1   Using the gerund

➤ In Spanish, the gerund is a form of the verb that usually ends in -**ando** or -**iendo** and is used to form continuous tenses.

Estoy trabaj<u>ando</u>.	I'm work<u>ing</u>.
Estamos com<u>iendo</u>.	We are eat<u>ing</u>.

➤ It is used with **estar** to form continuous tenses such as:

- the present continuous

<u>**Está fregando**</u> los platos.	He's washing the dishes.
<u>**Estoy escribiendo**</u> una carta.	I'm writing a letter.

⇨ *For more information on the **Present continuous**, see page 84.*

- the imperfect continuous

<u>**Estaba reparando**</u> el coche.	She was fixing the car.
<u>**Estaban esperándo**</u>nos.	They were waiting for us.

[i] Note that continuous tenses should only be used in Spanish to describe action that is or was happening at the precise moment you are talking about.

Grammar Extra!

Sometimes another verb, such as **ir** or **venir** is used instead of **estar** with a gerund in continuous tenses. These verbs emphasize the gradualness or the slowness of the process.

<u>**Iba anocheciendo**</u>.	It was getting dark.
Eso lo <u>**vengo diciendo**</u> desde hace tiempo.	That's what I've been saying all along.

➤ The gerund is also used after certain other verbs:

- **seguir haciendo algo** and **continuar haciendo algo** are both used with the meaning of *to go on doing something* or *to continue doing something*.

Siguió cantando *or* **Continuó cantando.**	He went on singing *or* He continued singing.
Siguieron leyendo *or* **Continuaron leyendo.**	They went on reading *or* They continued reading.

- llevar with a time expression followed by the gerund is used to talk about how long someone has been doing something:

Lleva dos años estudiando inglés.	He's been studying English for two years.
Llevo una hora esperando aquí.	I've been waiting here for an hour.

i Note that the present tense of llevar followed by a gerund means the same as the English *have/has been + -ing*.

➤ pasar(se) with a time expression followed by the gerund is used to talk about how long you've spent doing something.

Pasé or Me pasé el fin de semana estudiando.	I spent the weekend studying.
Pasamos or Nos pasamos el día leyendo.	We spent the day reading.

➤ Verbs of movement, such as salir (meaning *to come out* or *to go out*), entrar (meaning *to come in* or *to go in*), and irse (meaning *to leave*) are sometimes followed by a gerund such as corriendo (meaning *running*) or cojeando (meaning *limping*). The English equivalent of salir corriendo, entrar corriendo or irse cojeando, would be *to run out*, *to run in* or *to limp off* in such cases.

Salió corriendo.	He ran out.
Se fue cojeando.	He limped off.

Tip

Use a past participle not a gerund to talk about physical position.

Estaba <u>tumbado</u> en el sofá.	He was lying on the sofa.
Estaba <u>sentada</u>.	She was sitting down.
Lo encontré <u>tendido</u> en el suelo.	I found him lying on the floor.
La escalera estaba <u>apoyada</u> contra la pared.	The ladder was leaning against the wall.

⇨ For more information on the **Past participles,** see page 115.

➤ You will also come across the gerund used in other ways. For example:

Los vimos jugando al fútbol.	We saw them playing football.
Estudiando, aprobarás.	By studying, *or* If you study, you'll pass.

2   Forming the gerund of regular verbs

➤ To form the gerund of regular -ar verbs, take off the -ar ending of the infinitive to form the stem, and add -ando.

Infinitive	Stem	Gerund
hablar	habl-	hablando
trabajar	trabaj-	trabajando

➤ To form the gerund of regular -er and -ir verbs, take off the -er and -ir ending of the infinitive to form the stem, and add -iendo.

Infinitive	Stem	Gerund
comer	com-	comiendo
vivir	viv-	viviendo

3   The gerund of irregular verbs

➤ Some verbs have an irregular gerund form. You have to learn these.

Infinitives	Meaning	Gerund	Meaning
decir	to say	diciendo	saying
dormir	to sleep	durmiendo	sleeping
freír	to fry	friendo	frying
morir	to die	muriendo	dying
pedir	to ask for	pidiendo	asking for
poder	to be able to	pudiendo	being able to
reír	to laugh	riendo	laughing
seguir	to follow	siguiendo	following
sentir	to feel	sintiendo	feeling
venir	to come	viniendo	coming
vestir	to dress	vistiendo	dressing

➤ In the next group of verbs there is a y rather than the normal i.

Infinitives	Meaning	Gerund	Meaning
caer	to fall	cayendo	falling
creer	to believe	creyendo	believing
leer	to read	leyendo	reading
oír	to hear	oyendo	hearing
traer	to bring	trayendo	bringing
ir	to go	yendo	going

> ### Tip
>
> In English, we often use *-ing* forms as adjectives, for example,
> *running water, shining eyes, the following day*. In Spanish, you cannot
> use the **-ando** and **-iendo** forms like this.
> Instead, there are sometimes corresponding forms ending in **-ante**
> and **-iente** that can be used as adjectives.
>
> | | |
> |---|---|
> | agua <u>corriente</u> | running water |
> | ojos <u>brillantes</u> | shining eyes |
> | Al día <u>siguiente</u>, visitamos Toledo. | The following day we visited Toledo. |
>
> Similarly, in English, we often use the *-ing* forms as nouns. In Spanish
> you have to use the <u>infinitive</u> instead.
>
> <u>Fumar</u> es malo para la salud.   <u>Smoking</u> is bad for you.

4   Position of pronouns with the gerund

➤ Object pronouns and reflexive pronouns are usually attached to the end of
the gerund, although you can also often put them before **estar** in continuous
tenses.

Estoy hablándo<u>te</u> *or* <u>Te</u> estoy hablando.	I'm talking to you.
Está vistiéndo<u>se</u> *or* <u>Se</u> está vistiendo.	He's getting dressed.
Estaban mostrándo<u>selo</u> *or* <u>Se lo</u> estaban mostrando.	They were showing it to him/her/them/you.

*Note that you will always have to add an accent to keep the stress in
the same place when adding pronouns to the end of a gerund.*

⇨ *For more information on **Stress**, see page 200.*

> ### Key points
> ✔ Use the gerund in continuous tenses with **estar** as well as after **seguir** and **continuar**.
> ✔ Gerunds for **-ar** verbs add **-ando** to the stem of the verb.
> ✔ Gerunds for **-er** and **-ir** verbs usually add **-iendo** to the stem of the verb.
> ✔ **-ando** and **-iendo** gerunds <u>cannot</u> be used as adjectives or nouns.
> ✔ You can attach pronouns to the end of the gerund, or sometimes put them before the previous verb.

Impersonal verbs

> **What is an impersonal verb?**
> An **impersonal verb** is a verb whose subject is *it*, but this 'it' does not refer to any specific thing; for example, *It's going to rain; It's nine o'clock*.

1 Verbs that are always used impersonally

➤ There are some verbs such as **llover** (meaning *to rain*) and **nevar** (meaning *to snow*), that are only used in the 'it' form, the infinitive, and as a gerund (the -*ing* form of the verb). These are called <u>impersonal verbs</u> because there is no person, animal or thing performing the action.

Llueve.	It's raining.
Está lloviendo.	It's raining.
Va a llover.	It's going to rain.
Nieva.	It's snowing.
Está nevando.	It's snowing.
Nevaba.	It was snowing.
Estaba nevando.	It was snowing.
Mañana nevará.	It will snow tomorrow.

2 Verbs that are sometimes used impersonally

➤ There are also some other very common verbs that are sometimes used as impersonal verbs, for example **hacer**, **haber** and **ser**.

➤ **hacer** is used in a number of impersonal expressions relating to the weather:

<u>Hace</u> frío/calor.	It's cold/hot.
Ayer <u>hacía</u> mucho frío/calor.	It was very cold/hot yesterday.
<u>Hace</u> sol/viento.	It's sunny/windy.
Va a <u>hacer</u> sol/viento.	It's going to be sunny/windy.
<u>Hace</u> un tiempo estupendo/horrible.	It's a lovely/horrible day.

➤ **hacer** is also used in combination with **que** and **desde** in impersonal time expressions, to talk about how long something has been going on for or how long it is since something happened.

<u>Hace</u> seis meses <u>que</u> vivo aquí. *or* Vivo aquí <u>desde hace</u> seis meses.	I've been living here for six months.

Hace tres años que estudio español or Estudio español desde hace tres años.	I've been studying Spanish for three years.
Hace mucho tiempo que no la veo or No la veo desde hace mucho tiempo.	I haven't seen her for ages or It is ages since I saw her.
Hace varias semanas que no voy por allí or No voy por allí desde hace varias semanas.	I haven't been there for several weeks or It is several weeks since I went there.

[i] Note the use of the present simple in Spanish in the above examples where in English we'd use the perfect tense or the past tense.

➤ hacer is also used impersonally in the expression (me/te/le) hace falta, which means it is necessary (for me/you/him).

Si hace falta, voy.	I'll go if necessary.
No hace falta llamar.	We/You/I needn't call.
Me hace falta otro vaso más.	I need another glass.
No hace falta ser un experto.	You don't need to be an expert.
No hacía falta.	It wasn't necessary.

[i] Note that not all impersonal expressions in Spanish are translated into English using impersonal expressions.

➤ haber too can be used impersonally with the meaning there is/there are, there was/there were, there will be, and so on. It has the special form hay in the present. For the other tenses, you take the third person singular (the 'it' form) of haber in the appropriate tense.

Hay un cine cerca de aquí.	There's a cinema near here.
Hay dos supermercados.	There are two supermarkets.
No hay bares.	There are no bars.
Había mucho ruido.	There was a lot of noise.
Había muchos coches.	There were a lot of cars.
Hubo un accidente.	There was an accident.
Hubo varios problemas.	There were several problems.
¿Habrá tiempo?	Will there be time?
¿Habrá suficientes sillas?	Will there be enough chairs?

[i] Note that you should ALWAYS use the singular form (never the plural), no matter how many things there are.

➤ **haber** is used in the construction **hay que** with an infinitive to talk about actions that need to be taken.

<u>Hay que</u> trabajar más.	We/You need to work harder.
<u>Hay que</u> ser respetuoso.	You/We/One must be respectful.
<u>Habrá</u> que decírselo.	We'll/You'll have to tell him.

➤ **ser** can be used in certain impersonal constructions with adjectives, for example:

- **es/era/fue** + adjective + infinitive

<u>Es</u> importante ahorrar dinero.	It's important to save money.
<u>Fue</u> torpe hacer eso.	It was silly to do that.
<u>Sería</u> mejor esperar.	It would be better to wait.

- **es/era/fue** + adjective + **que** + verb

<u>Es cierto que</u> tengo problemas.	It's true that I've got problems.
<u>Es verdad que</u> trabaja mucho.	It's true that he works hard.

📖 Note that when they are used in the negative (**no es cierto que…**; **no es verdad que…**), these expressions have to be followed by the subjunctive.

➪ *For more information on the **Subjunctive**, see page 134.*

Grammar Extra!

When impersonal expressions that don't state facts are followed by **que** (meaning *that*) and a verb, this verb must be in the <u>subjunctive</u>.

For this reason, the following non-factual impersonal expressions are all followed by the subjunctive:

- **Es posible que…** — It's possible that … / …might…
  Es posible que ganen. — They might win.
- **Es imposible que…** — It's impossible that… / …can't possibly…
  Es imposible que lo sepan. — They can't possibly know.
- **Es necesario que…** — It's necessary that…/ …need to…
  No es necesario que vengas. — You don't need to come.
- **Es mejor que…** — … be better to …
  Es mejor que lo pongas aquí. — You'd be better to put it here.

➪ *For more information on the **Subjunctive**, see page 134.*

➤ **ser** is also used impersonally with **de día** and **de noche** to say whether it's day or night.

Era de noche cuando llegamos.	It was night when we arrived.
Todavía **es de día** allí.	It's still day there.

⇨ *For other time expressions with* ser, *see page 80.*

➤ **basta con** is used impersonally:

- with a following <u>infinitive</u> to mean *it's enough to/all you need do is*

Basta con telefonear para reservar un asiento.	All you need do is to phone to reserve a seat.
Basta con dar una vuelta por la ciudad para...	You only need to take a walk round the city to ...

- with a <u>noun</u> or <u>pronoun</u> to mean *all you need is* or *all it takes is*

Basta con un error para que todo se estropee.	All it takes is one mistake to ruin everything.

➤ **(me) parece que** is used to give opinions.

Parece que va a llover.	It looks as if it's going to rain.
Me parece que estás equivocado.	I think that you are wrong.

ℹ Note that when **(me) parece que** is used in the negative, the following verb has to be in the <u>subjunctive</u>.

⇨ *For more information on the* **Subjunctive***, see page 134.*

➤ **vale la pena** is used to talk about what's worth doing.

Vale la pena.	It's worth it.
No vale la pena.	It's not worth it.
Vale la pena hacer el esfuerzo.	It's worth making the effort.
No vale la pena gastar tanto dinero.	It's not worth spending so much money.

Grammar Extra!

se is often used in impersonal expressions, especially with the verbs creer, decir, poder, and tratar. In such cases it often corresponds to it, one or you in English.

- Se cree que...

  It is thought or People think that...

  Se cree que es un mito.

  It is thought to be a myth.

- Se dice que...

  It is said or People say that...

  Se dice que es rico.

  He is said to be rich.

- Se puede...

  One can.../People can.../You can...

  Aquí se puede aparcar.

  One can park here.

- Se trata de...

  It's a question of .../It's about ...

  No se trata de dinero.

  It isn't a question of money.

  Se trata de resolverlo.

  We must solve it.

⇨ For more information on **Reflexive verbs**, see page 91.

Key points

✔ Impersonal verbs and expressions can only be used in the 'it' form, the infinitive and the gerund.

✔ Impersonal expressions relating to the weather are very common.

✔ Although in English we use there is or there are depending on the number of people or things that there are, in Spanish hay, había, hubo and so on are used in the singular form only.

✔ Some very common ordinary verbs are also used as impersonal verbs.

The subjunctive

What is the subjunctive?
The **subjunctive** is a verb form that is used in certain circumstances especially when expressing some sort of feeling or when there is doubt about whether something will happen or whether something is true. It is only used occasionally in modern English, for example, *If I were you, ...*; *So be it.*; *I wish you were here*.

---

1 Using the subjunctive

➤ Although you may not know it, you will already be familiar with many of the forms of the present subjunctive, as it is used when giving orders and instructions not to do something as well as in the **usted**, **ustedes** and **nosotros** forms of instructions to do something. For example, if you phone someone in Spain, they will probably answer with ¡diga! or ¡dígame!, an imperative form taken from the present subjunctive of **decir**.

⇨ For more information on **Imperatives**, see page 85.

➤ In Spanish the subjunctive is used after certain verbs and conjunctions when two parts of a sentence have different subjects.

Tengo miedo de que le ocurra algo.	I'm afraid <u>something</u> may (*subjunctive*) happen to him.

(The subject of the first part of the sentence is *I*; the subject of the second part of the sentence is *something*.).

➤ In English, in a sentence like *We want him/José to be happy*, we use an infinitive (*to be*) for the second verb even though *want* and *be happy* have different subjects (*we* and *him/José*).

➤ In Spanish you cannot do this. You have to use the <u>subjunctive</u> for the second verb.

Queremos que él sea feliz.	We want that he (*subjunctive*) be happy.
Queremos que José sea feliz.	We want that José (*subjunctive*) be happy.

➤ You <u>CAN</u> use an infinitive for the second verb in Spanish when the subject of both verbs is the same.

Queremos ser felices.	We want to be happy.

2 Coming across the subjunctive

➤ The subjunctive has several tenses, the main ones being the <u>present subjunctive</u> and the <u>imperfect subjunctive</u>. The tense used for the subjunctive verb depends on the tense of the previous verb.

For further explanation of grammatical terms, please see pages viii-xii.

⇨ *For more information on **Tenses with the subjunctive**, see page 139.*

➤ In sentences containing two verbs with different subjects, you will find that the second verb is in the subjunctive when the first verb:

- expresses a wish

Quiero que <u>vengan</u>.	I want them to come.
Quiero que se <u>vaya</u>.	I want him/her to go away.
Deseamos que <u>tengan</u> éxito.	We want them to be successful.

- expresses an emotion

Siento mucho que no <u>puedas</u> venir.	I'm very sorry that you can't come.
Espero que <u>venga</u>.	I hope he comes.
Me sorprende que no <u>esté</u> aquí.	I'm surprised that he isn't here.
Me alegro de que te <u>gusten</u>.	I'm pleased that you like them.

➤ If the subject of both verbs is the <u>same</u>, an infinitive is used as the second verb instead of a subjunctive.

➤ Compare the following examples. In the examples on the left, both the verb expressing the wish or emotion and the second verb have the same subject, so the second verb is an <u>infinitive</u>. In the examples on the right, each verb has a different subject, so the second verb is in the <u>subjunctive</u>.

Infinitive construction	Subjunctive construction
Quiero <u>estudiar</u>. I want to study.	Quiero que José <u>estudie</u>. I want José to study.
Maite quiere <u>irse</u>. Maite wants to leave.	Maite quiere que me <u>vaya</u>. Maite wants me to leave.
Siento no <u>poder</u> venir. I'm sorry I can't come.	Siento que no <u>puedas</u> venir. I'm sorry that you can't come.
Me alegro de <u>poder</u> ayudar. I'm pleased to be able to help.	Me alegro de que <u>puedas</u> ayudar. I'm pleased you can help.

➤ You will also come across the verb + **que** + subjunctive construction (often with a personal object such as **me**, **te** and so on) when the first verb is one you use to ask or advise somebody to do something.

Sólo te pido que <u>tengas</u> cuidado.	I'm only asking you to be careful.
Te aconsejo que no <u>llegues</u> tarde.	I'd advise you not to be late.

➤ You will also come across the subjunctive in the following cases:

- after verbs expressing doubt or uncertainty, and verbs saying what you think about something that are used with **no**

Dudo que <u>tenga</u> tiempo.	I doubt I'll have time.
No creo que <u>venga</u>.	I don't think she'll come.
No pienso que <u>esté</u> bien.	I don't think it's right.

- in impersonal constructions that show a need to do something

¿Hace falta que <u>vaya</u> Jaime?	Does Jaime need to go?
No es necesario que <u>vengas</u>.	You don't need to come.

- in impersonal constructions that do not express facts

Es posible que <u>tengan</u> razón.	They may be right.

⇨ *For more information on **Impersonal verbs**, see page 129.*

Grammar Extra!

Use the <u>indicative</u> (that is, any verb form that isn't subjunctive) after impersonal expressions that state facts provided they are <u>NOT</u> in the negative.

Es verdad que <u>es</u> interesante.	It's true that it's interesting.
Es cierto que me <u>gusta</u> el café.	It's true I like coffee.
Parece que se <u>va</u> a ir.	It seems that he's going to go.

➤ The subjunctive is used after **que** to express wishes.

¡Que lo <u>pases</u> bien!	Have a good time!
¡Que te <u>diviertas</u>!	Have fun!

➤ The subjunctive is also used after certain conjunctions linking two parts of a sentence which each have different subjects.

- antes de que — before

¿Quieres decirle algo antes de que se <u>vaya</u>?	Do you want to say anything to him before he goes?

- para que — so that

Es para que te <u>acuerdes</u> de mí.	It's so that you'll remember me.

- sin que — without

Salimos sin que nos <u>vieran</u>.	We left without them seeing us.

⇨ *For more information on **Conjunctions**, see page 192.*

For further explanation of grammatical terms, please see pages viii-xii.

> **Típ**
>
> Use para, sin and antes de with the <u>infinitive</u> when the subject of both verbs is the <u>same</u>.
>
> | | |
> |---|---|
> | Fue en taxi para no <u>llegar</u> tarde. | He went by taxi so that he wouldn't be late. |
> | Pedro se ha ido sin <u>esperar</u>nos. | Pedro's gone without waiting for us. |
> | Cenamos antes de <u>ir</u> al teatro. | We had dinner before we went to the theatre. |

3 Forming the present subjunctive

➤ To form the present subjunctive of most verbs, take off the -o ending of the yo form of the <u>present simple</u>, and add a fixed set of endings.

➤ For -ar verbs, the endings are: -e, -es, -e, -emos, -éis, -en.

➤ For both -er and -ir verbs, the endings are: -a, -as, -a, -amos, -áis, -an.

➤ The following table shows the present subjunctive of three regular verbs: hablar (meaning *to speak*), comer (meaning *to eat*) and vivir (meaning *to live*).

Infinitive	(yo)	(tú)	(él) (ella) (usted)	(nosotros) (nosotras)	(vosotros) (vosotras)	(ellos) (ellas) (ustedes)
hablar to speak	habl<u>e</u>	habl<u>es</u>	habl<u>e</u>	habl<u>emos</u>	habl<u>éis</u>	habl<u>en</u>
comer to eat	com<u>a</u>	com<u>as</u>	com<u>a</u>	com<u>amos</u>	com<u>áis</u>	com<u>an</u>
vivir to live	viv<u>a</u>	viv<u>as</u>	viv<u>a</u>	viv<u>amos</u>	viv<u>áis</u>	viv<u>an</u>

Quiero que <u>comas</u> algo.	I want you to eat something.
Me sorprende que no <u>hable</u> inglés.	I'm surprised he doesn't speak English.
No es verdad que <u>trabajen</u> aquí.	It isn't true that they work here.

➤ Some verbs have very irregular yo forms in the ordinary present tense and these irregular forms are reflected in the stem for the present subjunctive.

Infinitive	(yo)	(tú)	(él) (ella) (usted)	(nosotros) (nosotras)	(vosotros) (vosotras)	(ellos) (ellas) (ustedes)
decir to say	diga	digas	diga	digamos	digáis	digan
hacer to do/make	haga	hagas	haga	hagamos	hagáis	hagan
poner to put	ponga	pongas	ponga	pongamos	pongáis	pongan
salir to leave	salga	salgas	salga	salgamos	salgáis	salgan
tener to have	tenga	tengas	tenga	tengamos	tengáis	tengan
venir to come	venga	vengas	venga	vengamos	vengáis	vengan

Voy a limpiar la casa antes de que **vengan**.	I'm going to clean the house before they come.

[i] Note that only the **vosotros** form has an accent.

> ## Tip
>
> The present subjunctive endings are the opposite of what you'd expect, as **-ar** verbs have endings starting with **-e**, and **-er** and **-ir** verbs have endings starting with **-a**.

4 | Forming the present subjunctive of irregular verbs

➤ The following verbs have irregular subjunctive forms:

Infinitive	(yo)	(tú)	(él) (ella) (usted)	(nosotros) (nosotras)	(vosotros) (vosotras)	(ellos) (ellas) (ustedes)
dar to give	dé	des	dé	demos	deis	den
estar to be	esté	estés	esté	estemos	estéis	estén
haber to have	haya	hayas	haya	hayamos	hayáis	hayan
ir to go	vaya	vayas	vaya	vayamos	vayáis	vayan
saber to know	sepa	sepas	sepa	sepamos	sepáis	sepan
ser to be	sea	seas	sea	seamos	seáis	sean

No quiero que te **vayas**.	I don't want you to go.
Dudo que **esté** aquí.	I doubt if it's here.
No piensan que **sea** él.	They don't think it's him.
Es posible que **haya** problemas.	There may be problems.

For further explanation of grammatical terms, please see pages viii-xii.

➤ Verbs that change their stems (<u>radical-changing verbs</u>) in the ordinary present usually change them in the same way in the present subjunctive.

⇨ *For more information on **radical-changing verbs**, see page 76.*

Infinitive	(yo)	(tú)	(él) (ella) (usted)	(nosotros) (nosotras)	(vosotros) (vosotras)	(ellos) (ellas) (ustedes)
pensar to think	piense	pienses	piense	pensemos	penséis	piensen
entender to understand	entienda	entiendas	entienda	entendamos	entendáis	entiendan
poder to be able	pueda	puedas	pueda	podamos	podáis	puedan
querer to want	quiera	quieras	quiera	queramos	queráis	quieran
volver to return	vuelva	vuelvas	vuelva	volvamos	volváis	vuelvan

No hace falta que vuelvas.	There's no need for you to come back.
Es para que lo entiendas.	It's so that you understand.
Me alegro de que puedas venir.	I'm pleased you can come.

➤ Sometimes the stem of the **nosotros** and **vosotros** forms isn't the same as it is in the ordinary present tense.

Infinitive	(yo)	(tú)	(él) (ella) (usted)	(nosotros) (nosotras)	(vosotros) (vosotras)	(ellos) (ellas) (ustedes)
dormir to sleep	duerma	duermas	duerma	durmamos	durmáis	duerman
morir to die	muera	mueras	muera	muramos	muráis	mueran
pedir to ask for	pida	pidas	pida	pidamos	pidáis	pidan
seguir to follow	siga	sigas	siga	sigamos	sigáis	sigan
sentir to feel	sienta	sientas	sienta	sintamos	sintáis	sientan

Queremos hacerlo antes de que nos muramos.	We want to do it before we die.
Vendré a veros cuando os sintáis mejor.	I'll come and see you when you feel better.

5 Tenses with the subjunctive

➤ If the verb in the first part of the sentence is in the <u>present, future</u> or <u>imperative</u>, the second verb will usually be in the <u>present subjunctive</u>.

Quiero (*present*) **que lo hagas** (*present subjunctive*).
I want you to do it.

Iremos (*future*) **por aquí para que no nos vean** (*present subjunctive*). We'll go this way so that they won't see us.

➤ If the verb in the first part of the sentence is in the <u>conditional</u> or a <u>past tense</u>, the second verb will usually be in the <u>imperfect subjunctive</u>.

Me gustaría *(conditional)* que llegaras *(imperfect subjunctive)* temprano.
I'd like you to arrive early.
Les pedí *(preterite)* que me esperaran *(imperfect subjunctive)*.
I asked them to wait for me.

6 Indicative or subjunctive?

➤ Many expressions are followed by the <u>indicative</u> (the ordinary form of the verb) when they state facts, and by the <u>subjunctive</u> when they refer to possible or intended future events and outcomes.

➤ Certain conjunctions relating to time such as cuando (meaning *when*), hasta que (meaning *until*), en cuanto (meaning *as soon as*) and mientras (meaning *while*) are used with the <u>indicative</u> when the action has happened or when talking about what happens regularly.

¿Qué dijo cuando te <u>vio</u>?	What did he say when he saw you?
Siempre lo compro cuando <u>voy</u> a España.	I always buy it when I go to Spain.
Me quedé allí hasta que <u>volvió</u> Antonio.	I stayed there until Antonio came back.

➤ The same conjunctions are followed by the <u>subjunctive</u> when talking about a vague future time.

¿Qué quieres hacer cuando <u>seas</u> mayor?	What do you want to do when you grow up? *(but you're not grown up yet)*
¿Por qué no te quedas aquí hasta que <u>vuelva</u> Antonio?	Why don't you stay here until Antonio comes back? *(but Antonio hasn't come back yet)*
Lo haré en cuanto <u>pueda</u> *or* tan pronto como <u>pueda</u>.	I'll do it as soon as I can. *(but I'm not able to yet)*

Grammar Extra!

aunque is used with the <u>indicative</u> (the ordinary verb forms) when it means *although* or *even though*. In this case, the second part of the sentence is stating a fact.

Me gusta el francés aunque <u>prefiero</u> el alemán.	I like French although I prefer German.
Seguí andando aunque me <u>dolía</u> la pierna.	I went on walking even though my leg hurt.

aunque is used with the <u>subjunctive</u> when it means *even if*. Here, the second part of the sentence is not yet a fact.

Te llamaré cuando vuelva aunque <u>sea</u> tarde.	I'll ring you when I get back, even if it's late.

For further explanation of grammatical terms, please see pages viii-xii.

7 Forming the imperfect subjunctive

➤ For all verbs, there are <u>two</u> imperfect subjunctive forms that are exactly the same in meaning.

➤ The stem for both imperfect subjunctive forms is the same: you take off the -aron or -ieron ending of the **ellos** form of the preterite and add a fixed set of endings to what is left.

⇨ *For more information on the **Preterite**, see page 104.*

➤ For -ar verbs, the endings are: -ara, -aras, -ara, -áramos, -arais, -aran <u>or</u> -ase, -ases, -ase, -ásemos, -aseis, -asen. The first form is more common.

➤ For -er and -ir verbs, the endings are: -iera, -ieras, -iera, -iéramos, -ierais, -ieran <u>or</u> -iese, -ieses, -iese, -iésemos, -ieseis, -iesen. The first form is more common.

➤ The following table shows the imperfect subjunctive of three regular verbs: **hablar** (meaning *to speak*), **comer** (meaning *to eat*) and **vivir** (meaning *to live*).

Infinitive	(yo)	(tú)	(él) (ella) (usted)	(nosotros) (nosotras)	(vosotros) (vosotras)	(ellos) (ellas) (ustedes)
hablar to speak	hablara	hablaras	hablara	habláramos	hablarais	hablaran
	hablase	hablases	hablase	hablásemos	hablaseis	hablasen
comer to eat	comiera	comieras	comiera	comiéramos	comierais	comieran
	comiese	comieses	comiese	comiésemos	comieseis	comiesen
vivir to live	viviera	vivieras	viviera	viviéramos	vivierais	vivieran
	viviese	vivieses	viviese	viviésemos	vivieseis	viviesen

➤ Many verbs have irregular preterite forms which are reflected in the stem for the imperfect subjunctive. For example:

Infinitive	(yo)	(tú)	(él) (ella) (usted)	(nosotros) (nosotras)	(vosotros) (vosotras)	(ellos) (ellas) (ustedes)
dar to give	diera	dieras	diera	diéramos	dierais	dieran
	diese	dieses	diese	diésemos	dieseis	diesen
estar to be	estuviera	estuvieras	estuviera	estuviéramos	estuvierais	estuvieran
	estuviese	estuvieses	estuviese	estuviésemos	estuvieseis	estuviesen
hacer to do/ make	hiciera	hicieras	hiciera	hiciéramos	hicierais	hicieran
	hiciese	hicieses	hiciese	hiciésemos	hicieseis	hiciesen
poner to put	pusiera	pusieras	pusiera	pusiéramos	pusierais	pusieran
	pusiese	pusieses	pusiese	pusiésemos	pusieseis	pusiesen
tener to have	tuviera	tuvieras	tuviera	tuviéramos	tuvierais	tuvieran
	tuviese	tuvieses	tuviese	tuviésemos	tuvieseis	tuviesen
ser to be	fuera	fueras	fuera	fuéramos	fuerais	fueran
	fuese	fueses	fuese	fuésemos	fueseis	fuesen
venir to come	viniera	vinieras	viniera	viniéramos	vinierais	vinieran
	viniese	vinieses	viniese	viniésemos	vinieseis	viniesen

8 | Forming the imperfect subjunctive of some irregular -ir verbs

➤ In some irregular -ir verbs – the ones that don't have an i in the **ellos** form of the preterite – -era, -eras, -era, -éramos, -erais, -eran or -ese, -eses, -ese, -ésemos, -eseis, -esen are added to the preterite stem instead of -iera and -iese and so on.

⇨ *For more information on the **Preterite**, see page 104.*

Infinitive	(yo)	(tú)	(él) (ella) (usted)	(nosotros) (nosotras)	(vosotros) (vosotras)	(ellos) (ellas) (ustedes)
decir to say	dijera	dijeras	dijera	dijéramos	dijerais	dijeran
	dijese	dijeses	dijese	dijésemos	dijeseis	dijesen
ir to go	fuera	fueras	fuera	fuéramos	fuerais	fueran
	fuese	fueses	fuese	fuésemos	fueseis	fuesen

ⓘ Note that the imperfect subjunctive forms of **ir** and **ser** are identical.

> **Teníamos miedo de que se <u>fuera</u>.** We were afraid he might leave.
> **No era verdad que <u>fueran</u> ellos.** It wasn't true that it was them.

For further explanation of grammatical terms, please see pages viii-xii.

9   **Present indicative or imperfect subjunctive after si**

➤ Like some other conjunctions, si (meaning *if*) is sometimes followed by the ordinary present tense (the <u>present indicative</u>) and sometimes by the <u>imperfect subjunctive</u>.

➤ si is followed by the <u>present indicative</u> when talking about likely possibilities.

Si <u>quieres</u>, te dejo el coche.	If you like, I'll lend you the car. *(and you may well want to borrow the car)*
Compraré un bolígrafo si <u>tienen</u>.	I'll buy a pen if they have any. *(and there may well be some pens)*

➤ si is followed by the <u>imperfect subjunctive</u> when talking about unlikely or impossible conditions.

Si <u>tuviera</u> más dinero, me lo compraría.	If I had more money, I'd buy it. *(but I haven't got more money)*
Si yo <u>fuera</u> tú, lo compraría.	If I were you, I'd buy it. *(but I'm not you)*

Tip

You probably need the imperfect subjunctive in Spanish after si if the English sentence has *would* in it.

Key points

✔ After certain verbs you have to use a subjunctive in Spanish when there is a different subject in the two parts of the sentence.

✔ A subjunctive is also found after impersonal expressions, as well as after certain conjunctions.

✔ Structures with the subjunctive can often be avoided if the subject of both verbs is the same. An infinitive can often be used instead.

✔ The endings of the present subjunctive in regular -ar verbs are: -e, -es, -e, -emos, -éis, -en.

✔ The endings of the present subjunctive in regular -er and -ir verbs are: -a, -as, -a, -amos, -áis, -an.

✔ The endings of the imperfect subjunctive in regular -ar verbs are: -ara, -aras, -ara, -áramos, -arais, -aran or -ase, -ases, -ase, -ásemos, -aseis, -asen.

✔ The endings of the imperfect subjunctive in regular -er and -ir verbs are: -iera, -ieras, -iera, -iéramos, -ierais, -ieran or -iese, -ieses, -iese, -iésemos, -ieseis, -iesen.

✔ Some verbs have irregular subjunctive forms.

The infinitive

> **What is the infinitive?**
> The **infinitive** is a form of the verb that hasn't had any endings added to it and doesn't relate to any particular tense. In English, the infinitive is usually shown with *to*, as in *to speak, to eat, to live*.

1   Using the infinitive

➤ In English, the infinitive is usually thought of as being made up of two words, for example, *to speak*. In Spanish, the infinitive consists of one word and is the verb form that ends in **-ar**, **-er** or **-ir**, for example, **hablar**, **comer**, **vivir**.

➤ When you look up a verb in the dictionary, you will find that information is usually listed under the infinitive form.

➤ In Spanish, the infinitive is often used in the following ways:

- after a preposition such as **antes de** (meaning *before*), **después de** (meaning *after*)

Después de comer, fuimos a casa de Pepe.	<u>After eating</u>, we went round to Pepe's.
Salió <u>sin hacer</u> ruido.	She went out <u>without making</u> a noise.
Siempre veo la tele <u>antes de acostarme</u>.	I always watch TV <u>before going to bed</u>.

[*i*] Note that in English we always use the *-ing* form of the verb after a preposition, for example, *before going*. In Spanish you have to use the <u>infinitive</u> form after a preposition.

- in set phrases, particularly after adjectives or nouns

Estoy <u>encantada de poder ayudarte</u>.	I'm delighted to be able to help you.
Está <u>contento de vivir</u> aquí.	He's happy living here.
<u>Tengo ganas de salir</u>.	I feel like going out.
No <u>hace falta comprar</u> leche.	We/You don't need to buy any milk.
<u>Me dio</u> mucha <u>alegría verla</u>.	I was very pleased to see her.
<u>Me da miedo cruzar</u> la carretera.	I'm afraid of crossing the road.

- after another verb, sometimes as the object of it

Debo llamar a casa.	I must phone home.
Prefiero esquiar.	I prefer skiing.
Me gusta escuchar música.	I like listening to music.
Nos encanta nadar.	We love swimming.
¿**Te apetece ir** al cine?	Do you fancy going to the cinema?

i Note that, when it comes after another verb, the Spanish infinitive often corresponds to the *-ing* form in English.

- in instructions that are aimed at the general public – for example in cookery books or on signs

Cocer a fuego lento.	Cook on a low heat.
Prohibido **pisar** el césped.	Don't walk on the grass.

- as a noun, where in English we would use the *-ing* form of the verb

Lo importante es **intentar**lo.	Trying is the important thing.

i Note that, when the infinitive is the subject of another verb, it may have the article el before it, particularly if it starts the sentence.

El viajar tanto me resulta cansado.	I find so much travelling tiring.

> *Tip*
> Be especially careful when translating the English *-ing* form. It is often translated by the infinitive in Spanish.

2 Linking two verbs together

➤ There are three ways that verbs can be linked together when the second verb is an infinitive:

- with no linking word in between

¿Quieres venir?	Do you want to come?
Necesito hablar contigo.	I need to talk to you.

- with a preposition:

ir **a** hacer algo	to be going to do something
aprender **a** hacer algo	to learn to do something
dejar **de** hacer algo	to stop doing something

Voy **a** comprarme un móvil.	I'm going to buy a mobile.
Aprendimos **a** esquiar.	We learnt to ski.
Quiere dejar **de** fumar.	He wants to stop smoking.

i Note that you have to learn the preposition required for each verb.

- in set structures

tener que hacer algo	to have to do something
Tengo que salir.	I've got to go out.
Tendrías que comer más.	You should eat more.
Tuvo que devolver el dinero.	He had to pay back the money.

3 Verbs followed by the infinitive with no preposition

➤ Some Spanish verbs and groups of verbs can be followed by an infinitive with no preposition:

- **poder** (meaning *to be able to, can, may*), **saber** (meaning *to know how to, can*), **querer** (meaning *to want*) and **deber** (meaning *to have to, must*)

No <u>puede venir</u>.	He can't come.
¿<u>Sabes esquiar</u>?	Can you ski?
<u>Quiere estudiar</u> medicina.	He wants to study medicine.
<u>Debes hacerlo</u>.	You must do it.

- verbs like **gustar**, **encantar** and **apetecer**, where the infinitive is the subject of the verb

<u>Me gusta estudiar</u>.	I like studying.
<u>Nos encanta bailar</u>.	We love dancing.
¿<u>Te apetece ir</u> al cine?	Do you fancy going to the cinema?

- verbs that relate to seeing or hearing, such as **ver** (meaning *to see*) and **oír** (meaning *to hear*)

Nos <u>ha visto llegar</u>.	He saw us arrive.
Te <u>he oído cantar</u>.	I heard you singing.

- the verbs **hacer** (meaning *to make*) and **dejar** (meaning *to let*)

¡No me <u>hagas reír</u>!	Don't make me laugh!
Mis padres no me <u>dejan salir</u> por la noche.	My parents don't let me go out at night.

- the following common verbs

decidir	to decide
desear	to wish, want
esperar	to hope
evitar	to avoid
necesitar	to need
odiar	to hate
olvidar	to forget
pensar	to think
preferir	to prefer
recordar	to remember
sentir	to regret

Han **decidido comprarse** una casa.	They've decided to buy a house.
No **desea tener** más hijos.	She doesn't want to have any more children.
Espero poder ir.	I hope to be able to go.
Evita gastar demasiado dinero.	He avoids spending too much money.
Necesito salir un momento.	I need to go out for a moment.
Olvidó dejar su dirección.	She forgot to leave her address.
Pienso hacer una paella.	I'm thinking of making a paella.
Siento molestarte.	I'm sorry to bother you.

➤ Some of these verbs combine with infinitives to make set phrases with a special meaning:

- querer decir   to mean

  ¿Qué **quiere decir** eso?   What does that mean?

- dejar caer   to drop

  Dejó caer la bandeja.   She dropped the tray.

---

4   **Verbs followed by the preposition a and the infinitive**

➤ The following verbs are the most common ones that can be followed by **a** and the infinitive:

- verbs relating to movement such as **ir** (meaning *to go*) and **venir** (meaning *to come*)

Se va **a** comprar un caballo.	He's going to buy a horse.
Viene **a** vernos.	He's coming to see us.

- the following common verbs

aprender a hacer algo	to learn to do something
comenzar a hacer algo	to begin to do something
decidirse a hacer algo	to decide to do something
empezar a hacer algo	to begin to do something
llegar a hacer algo	to manage to do something
llegar a ser algo	to become something
probar a hacer algo	to try to do something
volver a hacer algo	to do something again

Me gustaría aprender a nadar.	I'd like to learn to swim.
No llegó a terminar la carrera.	He didn't manage to finish his degree course.
Llegó a ser primer ministro.	He became prime minister.
No vuelvas a hacerlo nunca más.	Don't ever do it again.

➤ The following verbs can be followed by a and a person's name or else by a and a noun or pronoun referring to a person, and then by another a and an infinitive.

ayudar a alguien a hacer algo	to help someone to do something
enseñar a alguien a hacer algo	to teach someone to do something
invitar a alguien a hacer algo	to invite someone to do something
¿Le podrías ayudar a Antonia a fregar los platos?	Could you help Antonia do the dishes?
Le enseñó a su hermano a nadar.	He taught his brother to swim.
Los he invitado a tomar unas copas en casa.	I've invited them over for drinks.

5 **Verbs followed by the preposition de and the infinitive**

➤ The following verbs are the most common ones that can be followed by de and the infinitive:

aburrirse de hacer algo	to get bored with doing something
acabar de hacer algo	to have just done something
acordarse de haber hecho/ de hacer algo	to remember having done/ doing something
alegrarse de hacer algo	to be glad to do something
dejar de hacer algo	to stop doing something
tener ganas de hacer algo	to want to do something
tratar de hacer algo	to try to do something

For further explanation of grammatical terms, please see pages viii-xii.

Me aburría <u>de</u> no poder salir de casa.	I was getting bored with not being able to leave the house.
Acabo <u>de</u> comprar un móvil.	I've just bought a mobile.
Acababan <u>de</u> llegar cuando...	They had just arrived when...
Me alegro <u>de</u> verte.	I'm glad to see you.
¿Quieres dejar <u>de</u> hablar?	Will you stop talking?
Tengo ganas <u>de</u> volver a España.	I want to go back to Spain.

6 Verbs followed by the preposition con and the infinitive

➤ The following verbs are the most common ones that can be followed by con and the infinitive:

amenazar <u>con</u> hacer algo	to threaten to do someting
soñar <u>con</u> hacer algo	to dream about doing something
Amenazó <u>con</u> denunciarlos.	He threatened to report them.
Sueño <u>con</u> vivir en España.	I dream about living in Spain.

7 Verbs followed by the preposition en and the infinitive

➤ The verb quedar is the most common one that can be followed by en and the infinitive:

quedar <u>en</u> hacer algo	to agree to do something
Habíamos quedado <u>en</u> encontrarnos a las ocho.	We had agreed to meet at eight.

Key points

✔ Infinitives are found after prepositions, set phrases and in instructions to the general public.

✔ They can also function as the subject or object of a verb, when the infinitive corresponds to the -ing form in English.

✔ Many Spanish verbs can be followed by another verb in the infinitive.

✔ The two verbs may be linked by nothing at all, or by a, de or another preposition.

✔ The construction in Spanish does not always match the English. It's best to learn these constructions when you learn a new verb.

Prepositions after verbs

➤ In English, there are some phrases which are made up of verbs and prepositions, for example, to _accuse_ somebody _of_ something, to _look forward to_ something and to _rely on_ something.

➤ In Spanish there are also lots of set phrases made up of verbs and prepositions. Often the prepositions in Spanish are not the same as they are in English, so you will need to learn them. Listed below are phrases using verbs and some common Spanish prepositions.

⇨ _For more information on verbs used with a preposition and the infinitive, see page 147._

1 Verbs followed by a

➤ **a** is often the equivalent of the English word _to_ when it is used with an indirect object after verbs like **enviar** (meaning _to send_), **dar** (meaning _to give_) and **decir** (meaning _to say_).

dar algo <u>a</u> alguien	to give something to someone
decir algo <u>a</u> alguien	to say something to someone
enviar algo <u>a</u> alguien	to send something to someone
escribir algo <u>a</u> alguien	to write something to someone
mostrar algo <u>a</u> alguien	to show something to someone

⇨ _For more information on **Indirect objects**, see page 49._

> ### Tip
> There is an important difference between Spanish and English with this type of verb. In English, you can say either to _give something to someone_ or to _give someone something_.
> You can <u>NEVER</u> miss out **a** in Spanish in the way that you can sometimes miss out _to_ in English.

➤ Here are some verbs taking **a** in Spanish that have a different construction in English.

asistir <u>a</u> algo	to attend something, to be at something
dirigirse <u>a</u> (un lugar)	to head for (a place)
dirigirse a alguien	to address somebody
jugar <u>a</u> algo	to play something (_sports/games_)
llegar <u>a</u> (un lugar)	to arrive at (a place)

oler a algo	to smell of something
parecerse a alguien/algo	to look like somebody/something
subir(se) a un autobús/un coche	to get on a bus/into a car
subir(se) a un árbol	to climb a tree
tener miedo a alguien	to be afraid of somebody

Este perfume huele a jazmín.	This perfume smells of jasmine.
¡De prisa, sube al coche!	Get into the car, quick!
Nunca tuvieron miedo a su padre.	They were never afraid of their father.

⇨ *For verbs such as* gustar, encantar *and* faltar, *see* **Verbal idioms** *on page 154.*

2 **Verbs followed by de**

➤ Here are some verbs taking **de** in Spanish that have a different construction in English:

acordarse de algo/alguien	to remember something/somebody
alegrarse de algo	to be glad about something
bajarse de un autobús/un coche	to get off a bus/out of a car
darse cuenta de algo	to realize something
depender de algo/alguien	to depend on something/somebody
despedirse de alguien	to say goodbye to somebody
preocuparse de algo/alguien	to worry about something/somebody
quejarse de algo	to complain about something
reírse de algo/alguien	to laugh at something/somebody
salir de (un cuarto/un edificio)	to leave (a room/a building)
tener ganas de algo	to want something
tener miedo de algo	to be afraid of something
trabajar de (camarero/secretario)	to work as (a waiter/secretary)
tratarse de algo/alguien	to be a question of something/to be about somebody

Nos acordamos muy bien de aquellas vacaciones.	We remember that holiday very well.
Se bajó del coche.	He got out of the car.
No depende de mí.	It doesn't depend on me.
Se preocupa mucho de su apariencia.	He worries a lot about his appearance.

3 **Verbs followed by con**

➤ Here are some verbs taking con in Spanish that have a different construction in English:

comparar algo/a alguien con algo/alguien	to compare something/somebody with something/somebody
contar con alguien/algo	to rely on somebody/something
encontrarse con alguien	to meet somebody (*by chance*)
enfadarse con alguien	to get annoyed with somebody
estar de acuerdo con alguien/algo	to agree with somebody/something
hablar con alguien	to talk to somebody
soñar con alguien/algo	to dream about somebody/something
Cuento contigo.	I'm relying on you.
Me encontré con ella al entrar en el banco.	I met her as I was going into the bank.
¿Puedo hablar con usted un momento?	May I talk to you for a moment?

4 **Verbs followed by en**

➤ Here are some verbs taking en in Spanish that have a different construction in English:

entrar en (un edificio/un cuarto)	to enter, go into (a building/a room)
pensar en algo/alguien	to think about something/somebody
trabajar en (una oficina/una fábrica)	to work in (an office/a factory)
No quiero pensar en eso.	I don't want to think about that.

5 **Verbs followed by por**

➤ Here are some verbs taking por in Spanish that have a different construction in English:

interesarse por algo/alguien	to ask about something/somebody
preguntar por alguien	to ask for/about somebody
preocuparse por algo/alguien	to worry about something/somebody

For further explanation of grammatical terms, please see pages viii-xii.

| Me interesaba mucho <u>por</u> la arqueología. | I was very interested in archaeology. |
| Se preocupa mucho <u>por</u> su apariencia. | He worries a lot about his appearance. |

6 Verbs taking a direct object in Spanish but not in English

➤ In English there are a few verbs that are followed by *at*, *for* or *to* which, in Spanish, are not followed by any preposition other than the personal a.

⇨ For more information on **Personal** a, see page 182.

mirar algo/a alguien	to look at something/somebody
escuchar algo/a alguien	to listen to something/somebody
buscar algo/a alguien	to look for something/somebody
pedir algo	to ask for something
esperar algo/a alguien	to wait for something/somebody
pagar algo	to pay for something

Mira esta foto.	Look at this photo.
Me gusta escuchar música.	I like listening to music.
Estoy buscando las gafas.	I'm looking for my glasses.
Pidió una taza de té.	He asked for a cup of tea.
Estamos esperando el tren.	We're waiting for the train.
Ya he pagado el billete.	I've already paid for my ticket.
Estoy buscando a mi hermano.	I'm looking for my brother.

Key points
✔ The prepositions used with Spanish verbs are often very different from those used in English, so make sure you learn common expressions involving prepositions in Spanish.
✔ The most common prepositions used with verbs in Spanish are a, de, con, en and por.
✔ Some Spanish verbs are not followed by a preposition, but are used with a preposition in English.

Verbal Idioms

1   Present tense of gustar

➤ You will probably already have come across the phrase **me gusta...** meaning *I like...* . Actually, **gustar** means literally *to please*, and if you remember this, you will be able to use **gustar** much more easily.

Me gusta el chocolate.	I like chocolate. (*literally: chocolate pleases me*)
Me gustan los animales.	I like animals. (*literally: animals please me*)
Nos gusta el español.	We like Spanish. (*literally: Spanish pleases us*)
Nos gustan los españoles.	We like Spanish people. (*literally: Spanish people please us*)

➤ Even though **chocolate**, **animales**, and so on, come after **gustar**, they are the subject of the verb (the person or thing performing the action) and therefore the endings of **gustar** change to agree with them.

➤ When the thing that you like is singular, you use **gusta** (*third person singular*), and when the thing that you like is plural, you use **gustan** (*third person plural*).

Le gusta Francia.	He/She likes France. (*literally: France pleases him/her*)
Le gustan los caramelos.	He/She likes sweets. (*literally: Sweets please him/her*)

📋 Note that **me**, **te**, **le**, **nos**, **os** and **les**, which are used with **gustar**, are indirect object pronouns.

➪ *For more information on **Indirect object pronouns**, see page 49.*

2   Other tenses of gustar

➤ You can use **gustar** in other tenses in Spanish.

Les gustó la fiesta.	They liked the party.
Les gustaron los fuegos artificiales.	They liked the fireworks.
Te va a gustar la película.	You'll like the film.
Te van a gustar las fotos.	You'll like the photos.
Les ha gustado mucho el museo.	They liked the museum a lot
Les han gustado mucho los cuadros.	They liked the paintings a lot.

➤ You can also use **más** with **gustar** to say what you prefer.

A mí me <u>gusta más</u> el rojo.	I prefer the red one. (*literally: the red one pleases me more*)
A mí me <u>gustan más</u> los rojos.	I prefer the red ones. (*literally: the red ones please me more*)

3 Other verbs like gustar

➤ There are several other verbs which behave in the same way as **gustar**:

- encantar

Me <u>encanta</u> el flamenco.	I love flamenco.
Me <u>encantan</u> los animales.	I love animals.

- faltar

Le <u>faltaba</u> un botón.	He had a button missing.
Le <u>faltaban</u> tres dientes.	He had three teeth missing.

- quedar

No les <u>queda</u> nada.	They have nothing left.
Sólo nos <u>quedan</u> dos kilómetros.	We've only got two kilometres left.

- doler

Le <u>dolía</u> la cabeza.	His head hurt.
Le <u>dolían</u> las muelas.	His teeth hurt.

- interesar

Te <u>interesará</u> el libro.	The book will interest you.
Te <u>interesarán</u> sus noticias.	His news will interest you.

- importar

No me <u>importa</u> la lluvia.	The rain doesn't matter to me. *or* I don't mind the rain.
Me <u>importan</u> mucho mis estudios.	My studies matter to me a lot.

- hacer falta

Nos <u>hace</u> falta un ordenador.	We need a computer.
Nos <u>hacen</u> falta libros.	We need books.

Grammar Extra!

All the examples given above are in the third persons singular and plural as these are by far the most common. However, it is also possible to use these verbs in other forms.

Creo que le <u>gustas</u>.	I think he likes you. (*literally: I think you please him*)

---

4 | **Verbal idioms used with another verb**

➤ In English you can say *I like playing football, we love swimming* and so on, and in Spanish you can also use another verb with most of the verbs like **gustar**. However, the verb form you use for the second verb in Spanish is the <u>infinitive</u>.

Le <u>gusta jugar</u> al fútbol.	He/She likes playing football.
No me <u>gusta bailar</u>.	I don't like dancing.
Nos <u>encanta estudiar</u>.	We love studying.
No me <u>importa tener</u> que esperar.	I don't mind having to wait.

➪ *For more information on the **Infinitive**, see page 144.*

> **Key points**
> ✔ There are a number of common verbs in Spanish which are used in the opposite way to English, for example, **gustar**, **encantar**, **hacer falta**, and so on. With all these verbs, the object of the English verb is the subject of the Spanish verb.
> ✔ The endings of these verbs change according to whether the thing liked or needed and so on is singular or plural.
> ✔ All these verbs can be followed by another verb in the infinitive.

Negatives

> **What is a negative?**
> A **negative** question or statement is one which contains a word such as *not*, *never* or *nothing* and is used to say that something is not happening, is not true or is absent.

1   no

➤ In English, we often make sentences negative by adding *don't*, *doesn't* or *didn't* before the verb. In Spanish you simply add **no** (meaning *not*) before the main verb.

Positive			Negative	
Trabaja.	He works.	→	**No** trabaja.	He doesn't work.
Comen.	They eat.	→	**No** comen.	They don't eat.
Salió.	She went out.	→	**No** salió.	She didn't go out.
Lo he visto.	I've seen it.	→	**No** lo he visto.	I haven't seen it.
Sabe nadar.	He can swim.	→	**No** sabe nadar.	He can't swim.

> *Típ*
> <u>NEVER</u> translate *don't*, *doesn't*, *didn't* using **hacer**.

➤ Where there is a subject (the person doing the action) in the sentence, put **no** between the subject and the verb.

Juan <u>no</u> vive aquí.	Juan doesn't live here.
Mi hermana <u>no</u> lee mucho.	My sister doesn't read much.
Mis padres <u>no</u> han llamado.	My parents haven't called.
Él <u>no</u> lo comprenderá.	He won't understand.

i Note that the Spanish word **no** also means *no* in answer to a question.

➤ Where the subject is only shown by the verb ending, **no** goes before the verb.

<u>No</u> tenemos tiempo.	We haven't got time.
Todavía <u>no</u> ha llegado.	He hasn't arrived yet.
<u>No</u> hemos comido.	We haven't eaten.
<u>No</u> llevará mucho tiempo.	It won't take long.

➤ If there are any object pronouns (for example, **me**, **te**, **lo**, **los**, **le** and so on) before the verb, **no** goes <u>BEFORE</u> them.

<u>No</u> lo he visto.	I didn't see it.
<u>No</u> me gusta el fútbol.	I don't like football.

➤ In phrases consisting only of *not* and another word, such as *not now* or *not me*, the Spanish **no** usually goes <u>AFTER</u> the other word.

Ahora <u>no</u>.	Not now.
Yo <u>no</u>.	Not me.
Todavía <u>no</u>.	Not yet.

➤ Some phrases have a special construction in Spanish.

Espero que sí.	I hope so.	→	Espero que no.	I hope not.
Creo que sí.	I think so.	→	Creo que no.	I don't think so.

2   Other negative words

➤ In Spanish, you can form negatives using pairs and groups of words, as you can in English.

- **no ... nunca**   never *or* not ... ever
  No la veo <u>nunca</u>.   I never see her *or*
  I don't ever see her.

- **no ... jamás**   never *or* not ... ever
  No la veo <u>jamás</u>.   I never see her *or*
  I don't ever see her.

- **no ... nada**   nothing *or* not ... anything
  No ha dicho <u>nada</u>.   He has said nothing *or*
  He hasn't said anything.

- **no ... nadie**   nobody *or* not ... anybody
  No hablaron con <u>nadie</u>.   They spoke to nobody *or*
  They didn't speak to anybody.

- **no ... tampoco**   not ... either
  Yo <u>no</u> la vi. – Yo <u>tampoco</u>.   I didn't see her. – Neither did I.
  or I didn't either. *or* Nor did I.

  A él <u>no</u> le gusta el café y a mí   He doesn't like coffee and neither
  <u>tampoco</u>.   do I.

- **no ... ni ... ni**   neither ... nor
  No vinieron <u>ni</u> Carlos <u>ni</u> Ana.   Neither Carlos nor Ana came.

- **no ... más**   no longer *or* not ... any more
  No te veré <u>más</u>.   I won't see you any more.

- **no ... ningún/ninguna** + *noun*   no *or* not ... any
  No tiene <u>ningún</u> interés en ir.   She has no interest in going.

For further explanation of grammatical terms, please see pages viii-xii.

➤ Most of these negative words can also be used without **no** provided they come before any verb.

<u>Nunca</u> or <u>Jamás</u> la veo.	I never see her.
<u>Nadie</u> vino.	No one came.
<u>Ni</u> Pedro <u>ni</u> Pablo fuman.	Neither Pedro nor Pablo smokes.
¿Quién te ha dicho eso? – <u>Nadie</u>.	Who told you that? - No one.
¿Qué has hecho? – <u>Nada</u>.	What have you done? – Nothing.

➤ Sometimes negative expressions combine with each other.

<u>Nunca</u> hacen <u>nada</u>.	They never do anything.
<u>Nunca</u> viene <u>nadie</u>.	No one ever comes.
<u>No</u> lo haré <u>nunca más</u>.	I'll never do it again.
<u>No</u> veo <u>nunca</u> a <u>nadie</u>.	I never see anyone.

3 **Word order with negatives**

➤ In English you can put words like *never* and *ever* between *have/has/had* and the past participle, for example, *We have never been to Argentina*. You should <u>NEVER</u> separate **he**, **has**, **ha**, **había** and so on from the past participle of the verb in Spanish.

<u>Nunca</u> hemos estado en Argentina.	We have never been to Argentina.
<u>Nunca</u> había visto <u>nada</u> así.	I had never seen anything like this.
<u>Ninguno</u> de nosotros había esquiado <u>nunca</u>.	None of us had ever skied.

⇨ *For more information on **Past participles**, see page 115.*

Key points

✔ The Spanish word **no** is equivalent to both *no* and *not* in English.

✔ You can make sentences negative by putting **no** before the verb (and before any object pronouns that are in front of the verb).

✔ Other negative words also exist, such as **nunca**, **nadie** and **nada**. Use them in combination with **no**, with the verb sandwiched in between. Most of them also work on their own provided they go <u>before</u> any verb.

✔ Never insert negative words, or anything else, between **he**, **has**, **ha**, **había** and so on and the past participle.

Questions

> **What is a question?**
> A **question** is a sentence which is used to ask someone about something and which often has the verb in front of the subject. Questions often include a question word such as *why*, *where*, *who*, *which* or *how*.

Asking questions in Spanish

There are three main ways of asking questions in Spanish:

- by making your voice go up at the end of the sentence
- by changing normal word order
- by using a question word

> *Tip*
>
> Don't forget the opening question mark in Spanish. It goes at the beginning of the question or of the question part of the sentence.
>
> | ¿No quieres tomar algo? | Wouldn't you like something to eat or drink? |
> | Eres inglés, ¿verdad? | You're English, aren't you? |

1 Asking a question by making your voice go up

➤ If you are expecting the answer *yes* or *no*, there is a very simple way of asking a question. You keep the word order exactly as it would be in a normal sentence but you turn it into a question by making your voice go up at the end.

¿Hablas español?	Do you speak Spanish?
¿Es profesor?	Is he a teacher?
¿Hay leche?	Is there any milk?
¿Te gusta la música?	Do you like music?

➤ When the subject (the person or thing doing the action) of the verb is a noun, pronoun or name it can be given before the verb, just as in an ordinary sentence. But you turn the statement into a question by making your voice go up at the end.

¿Tu hermana ha comprado pan?	Did your sister buy any bread?
¿Tú lo has hecho?	Did you do it?
¿Tu padre te ha visto?	Did your father see you?
¿El diccionario está aquí?	Is the dictionary here?

For further explanation of grammatical terms, please see pages viii-xii.

2 Asking a question by changing word order

➤ When the subject of the verb is specified, another even more common way of asking questions is to change the word order so that the verb comes <u>BEFORE</u> the subject instead of after it.

¿Lo has hecho tú?	Did you do it?
¿Te ha visto tu padre?	Did your father see you?
¿Está el diccionario aquí?	Is the dictionary here?

i Note that the position of object pronouns is not affected.

⇨ *For more information on **Word order with object pronouns**, see pages 47, 50 and 52.*

Grammar Extra!

If the verb has an object, such as *any bread* in *Did your sister buy any bread?*, the subject comes <u>AFTER</u> the object, provided the object is short.

¿Ha compado <u>pan</u> tu hermana?	Did your sister buy any bread?
¿Vio <u>la película</u> tu novio?	Did your boyfriend see the film?

If the object is made up of several words, the subject goes <u>BEFORE</u> it.

Se han comprado tus padres <u>aquella casa de que me hablaste</u>?	Have your parents bought that house you told me about?

When there is an adverbial phrase (*to the party*, *in Barcelona*) after the verb, the subject can go <u>BEFORE OR AFTER</u> the adverbial phrase.

¿Viene <u>a la fiesta</u> Andrés? *or* ¿Viene Andrés <u>a la fiesta</u>?	Is Andrés coming to the party?

---

3 Asking a question by using a question word

➤ Question words are words like *when*, *what*, *who*, *which*, *where* and *how* that are used to ask for information. In Spanish, <u>ALL</u> question words have an accent on them.

¿adónde?	where ... to?
¿cómo?	how?
¿cuál/cuáles?	which
¿cuándo?	when?
¿cuánto/cuánta?	how much?
¿cuántos/cuántas?	how many?
¿dónde?	where?
¿para qué?	what for?
¿por qué?	why?
¿qué?	what?, which?
¿quién?	who?

Tip

Be careful not to mix up **por qué** (meaning *why*) with **porque** (meaning *because*).

¿<u>Cuándo</u> se fue?	When did he go?
¿<u>Qué</u> te pasa?	What's the matter?
¿<u>Qué</u> chaqueta te vas a poner?	Which jacket are you going to wear?
¿<u>Cuál</u> de los dos quieres?	Which do you want?
¿<u>Cuánto</u> azúcar quieres?	How much sugar do you want?
¿<u>Cuánto</u> tiempo llevas esperando?	How long have you been waiting?

➪ For more information on question words, see **Interrogative adjectives** on page 32 and **Interrogative pronouns** on page 65.

➤ When the question starts with a question word that isn't the subject of the verb, the noun or pronoun (if given) that is the subject of the verb goes <u>AFTER</u> it.

¿De qué color es <u>la moqueta</u>?	What colour's the carpet?
¿A qué hora comienza <u>el concierto</u>?	What time does the concert start?
¿Dónde están <u>tus pantalones</u>?	Where are your trousers?
¿Adónde iba <u>tu padre</u>?	Where was your father going?
¿Cómo están <u>tus padres</u>?	How are your parents?
¿Cuándo volverán <u>ustedes</u>?	When will you come back?

4 **Which question word to use?**

➤ **qué** or **cuál** or **cuáles** can be used to mean *which*:

- always use **qué** before a noun

¿<u>Qué chaqueta</u> te vas a poner?	<u>Which jacket</u> are you going to wear?

- otherwise use **cuál** (*singular*) or **cuáles** (*plural*)

¿<u>Cuál</u> quieres?	<u>Which (one)</u> do you want?
¿<u>Cuáles</u> quieres?	<u>Which (ones)</u> do you want?

➤ **quién** or **quiénes** can be used to mean *who*:

- use **quién** when asking about one person

¿<u>Quién</u> ganó?	<u>Who</u> won?

- use **quiénes** when asking about more than one person

¿<u>Quiénes</u> estaban?	<u>Who</u> was there?

[i] Note that you need to put the personal **a** before **quién** and **quiénes** when it acts as an object.

¿A quién viste?	Who did you see?

⇨ *For more information on **Personal** a, see page 182.*

➤ **de quién** or **de quiénes** can be used to mean *whose*:

- use **de quién** when there is likely to be one owner

¿De quién es este abrigo?	Whose coat is this?

- use **de quiénes** when there is likely to be more than one owner

¿De quiénes son estos abrigos?	Whose coats are these?

[i] Note that the structure in Spanish is the equivalent of *Whose is this coat?/Whose are these coats?* Don't try putting ¿**de quién?** or ¿**de quiénes?** immediately before a noun.

➤ **qué**, **cómo**, **cuál** and **cuáles** can all be used to mean *what* although **qué** is the most common translation:

- use **cómo** not **qué** when asking someone to repeat something that you didn't hear properly

¿Cómo (has dicho)?	What (did you say)?

- use ¿**cuál es** ... ? and ¿**cuáles son** ... ? to mean *what is* ... ? and *what/are* ... ? when you aren't asking for a definition

¿Cuál es la capital de Francia?	What's the capital of France?
¿Cuál es su número de teléfono?	What's his telephone number?

- use ¿**qué es** ... ? and ¿**qué son** ... ? to mean *what is* ... ? and *what are* ... ? when you are asking for a definition

¿Qué son los genes?	What are genes?

- always use **qué** to mean *what* before another noun

¿Qué hora es?	What time is it?
¿Qué asignaturas estudias?	What subjects are you studying?

Típ

You can finish an English question (or sentence) with a preposition such as *about*, for example, *Who did you write to?*; *What are you talking about?* You can **NEVER** end a Spanish question or sentence with a preposition.

¿Con quién hablaste?	Who did you speak to?

Grammar Extra!

All the questions we have looked at so far have been straight questions, otherwise known as <u>direct questions</u>. However, sometimes instead of asking directly, for example, *Where is it?* or *Why did you do it?*, we ask the question in a more roundabout way, for example, *Can you tell me where it is?* or *Please tell me why you did it.* These are called <u>indirect questions.</u>

In indirect questions in English we say *where <u>it is</u>* instead of *where <u>is it</u>* and *why <u>you did it</u>* instead of *why <u>did you do it</u>*, but in Spanish you still put the subject <u>AFTER</u> the verb.

¿Sabes adónde <u>iba tu padre</u>?	Do you know where your father was going?
¿Puedes decirme para qué <u>sirven los diccionarios</u>?	Can you tell me what dictionaries are for?

The subject also goes <u>AFTER</u> the verb in Spanish when you report a question in indirect speech.

Quería saber adónde <u>iba mi padre</u>.	He wanted to know where my father was going.

[*i*] Note that you still put accents on question words in Spanish even when they are in indirect and reported questions or when they come after expressions of uncertainty:

No sé <u>qué</u> hacer.	I don't know what to do.
No sabemos <u>por qué</u> se fue.	We don't know why he left.

---

5   <u>Negative questions</u>

➤ When you want to make a negative question, put **no** before the verb in the same way that you do in statements (non-questions).

¿<u>No</u> vienes?	Aren't you coming?
¿<u>No</u> lo has visto?	Didn't you see it?

➤ You can also use **o no** at the end of a question in the same way that we can ask *or not* in English.

¿Vienes <u>o no</u>?	Are you coming <u>or not</u>?
¿Lo quieres <u>o no</u>?	Do you want it <u>or not</u>?

6   <u>Short questions</u>

➤ In English we sometimes check whether our facts and beliefs are correct by putting *isn't it?*, *don't they?*, *are they?* and so on at the end of a comment. In Spanish, you can add ¿verdad? in the same way.

Hace calor, <u>¿verdad</u>?	It's hot, <u>isn't it</u>?
Te gusta, <u>¿verdad</u>?	You like it, <u>don't you</u>?

For further explanation of grammatical terms, please see pages viii-xii.

No te olvidarás, <u>¿verdad?</u>	You won't forget, <u>will you</u>?
No vino, <u>¿verdad?</u>	He didn't come, <u>did he</u>?

➤ You can also use ¿no?, especially after positive comments.

Hace calor, <u>¿no?</u>	It's hot, <u>isn't it</u>?
Te gusta, <u>¿no?</u>	You like it, <u>don't you</u>?

7 Answering questions

➤ To answer a question which requires a *yes* or *no* answer, just use sí or no.

¿Te gusta? – Sí/No.	Do you like it? – Yes, I do/No, I don't.
¿Está aquí? – Sí/No.	Is he here? – Yes he is/No, he isn't.
¿Tienes prisa? – Sí/No.	Are you in a hurry? – Yes, I am/ No, I'm not.
No lo has hecho, ¿verdad? – Sí/No.	You haven't done it, have you? – Yes, I have/No, I haven't.

➤ You can also often answer sí or no followed by the verb in question. In negative answers this may mean that you say no twice.

Quieres acompañarme? – Sí, quiero.	Would you like to come with me? – Yes, I would.
¿Vas a ir a la fiesta? – No, no voy.	Are you going to the party? – No, I'm not.

Key points

✔ You ask a question in Spanish by making your voice go up at the end of the sentence, by changing normal word order, and by using question words.

✔ Question words always have an accent on them.

✔ To make a negative question, add no before the verb.

✔ You can add ¿verdad? to check whether your facts or beliefs are correct.

Adverbs

What is an adverb?
An **adverb** is a word usually used with verbs, adjectives or other adverbs that gives more information about when, how, where, or in what circumstances something happens, or to what degree something is true, for example, *quickly, happily, now, extremely, very*.

How adverbs are used

➤ In general, adverbs are used together with verbs, adjectives and other adverbs, for example, *act quickly*; *smile cheerfully*; *rather ill*; *a lot happier*; *really slowly*; *very well*.

➤ Adverbs can also relate to the whole sentence. In this case they often tell you what the speaker is thinking or feeling.

   Fortunately, Jan had already left.

How adverbs are formed

1 The basic rules

➤ In English, adverbs that tell you how something happened are often formed by adding -*ly* to an adjective, for example, *sweet → sweetly*. In Spanish, you form this kind of adverb by adding -**mente** to the feminine singular form of the adjective.

Masculine adjective	Feminine adjective	Adverb	Meaning
lento	lenta	lentamente	slowly
normal	normal	normalmente	normally

Habla muy lenta**mente**.	He speaks very slowly.
¡Hazlo inmediata**mente**!	Do it immediately!
Normal**mente** llego a las nueve.	I normally arrive at nine o'clock.

i Note that adverbs NEVER change their endings in Spanish to agree with anything.

> ### Tip
> You don't have to worry about adding or removing accents on the adjective when you add -**mente**; they stay as they are.
>
> fácil easy   →   fácilmente easily

For further explanation of grammatical terms, please see pages viii-xii.

Grammar Extra!

When there are two or more adverbs joined by a conjunction such as **y** (meaning *and*) or **pero** (meaning *but*), leave out the **-mente** ending on all but the last adverb.

> Lo hicieron <u>lenta</u> pero <u>eficazmente</u>. They did it slowly but efficiently.

Use the form **recién** rather than **recientemente** (meaning *recently*) before a past participle (the form of the verb ending in **-ado** and **-ido** in regular verbs).

> El comedor está <u>recién</u> pintado. The dining room has just been painted.

⇨ *For more information on **Past participles**, see page 115.*

In Spanish, adverbs ending in **-mente** are not as common as adverbs ending in *-ly* in English. For this reason, you will come across other ways of expressing an adverb in Spanish, for example, **con** used with a noun or **de manera** used with an adjective.

> Conduce <u>con cuidado</u>. Drive carefully.
> Todos estos cambios ocurren <u>de manera natural</u>. All these changes happen naturally.

---

2 Irregular adverbs

➤ The adverb that comes from **bueno** (meaning *good*) is **bien** (meaning *well*). The adverb that comes from **malo** (meaning *bad*) is **mal** (meaning *badly*).

> Habla <u>bien</u> el español. He speaks Spanish <u>well</u>.
> Está muy <u>mal</u> escrito. It's very <u>badly</u> written.

➤ Additionally, there are some other adverbs in Spanish which are exactly the same as the related masculine singular adjective:

- **alto** (adjective: *high, loud*; adverb: *high, loudly*)
  > El avión volaba <u>alto</u> sobre las montañas. The plane flew high over the mountains.
  > Pepe habla muy <u>alto</u>. Pepe talks very <u>loudly</u>.

- **bajo** (adjective: *low, quiet*; adverb: *low, quietly*)
  > El avión volaba muy <u>bajo</u>. The plane was flying very <u>low</u>.
  > ¡Habla <u>bajo</u>! Speak <u>quietly</u>.

- **barato** (adjective: *cheap*; adverb: *cheaply*)
  > Aquí se come muy <u>barato</u>. You can eat really <u>cheaply</u> here.

- **claro** (adjective: *clear*; adverb: *clearly*)
  > Lo oí muy <u>claro</u>. I heard it very <u>clearly</u>.

- **derecho** (adjective: *right, straight*; adverb: *straight*)
  > Vino <u>derecho</u> hacia mí. He came <u>straight</u> towards me.

- **fuerte** (adjective: *loud, hard*; adverb: *loudly, hard*)

  Habla muy <u>fuerte</u>. He talks very <u>loudly</u>.

  No lo golpees tan <u>fuerte</u>. Don't hit it so <u>hard</u>.

- **rápido** (adjective: *fast, quick*; adverb: *fast, quickly*)

  Conduces demasiado <u>rápido</u>. You drive too <u>fast</u>.

  Lo hice tan <u>rápido</u> como pude. I did it as <u>quickly</u> as I could.

i Note that, when used as adverbs, these words do <u>NOT</u> agree with anything.

⇨ *For more information on words which can be both adjectives and adverbs, see page 175.*

Grammar Extra!

Sometimes an <u>adjective</u> is used in Spanish where in English we would use an <u>adverb</u>.

  Esperaban <u>impacientes</u>. They were waiting <u>impatiently</u>.

  Vivieron muy <u>felices</u>. They lived very <u>happily</u>.

i Note that these Spanish <u>adjectives</u> describe the person or thing being talked about and therefore <u>MUST</u> agree with them.

Often you could equally well use an adverb or an adverbial expression in Spanish.

  Esperaban <u>impacientemente</u> *or* con impaciencia. They were waiting <u>impatiently</u>.

Key points

✔ To form adverbs that tell you how something happens, you can usually add **-mente** to the feminine singular adjective in Spanish.

✔ Adverbs don't agree with anything.

✔ Some Spanish adverbs are irregular, as in English.

✔ Some Spanish adverbs are identical in form to their corresponding adjectives; when used as adverbs, they never agree with anything.

Comparatives and superlatives of adverbs

1 Comparative adverbs

> **What is a comparative adverb?**
> A **comparative adverb** is one which, in English, has -er on the end of it or more or less in front of it, for example, *earlier*, *later*, *more/less often*.

➤ Adverbs can be used to make comparisons in Spanish, just as they can in English. The comparative of adverbs (*more often, more efficiently, faster*) is formed using the same phrases as for adjectives:

- más ... (que)   more ... (than)
  <u>más</u> rápido (<u>que</u>)   faster (than), more quickly (than)
  Corre <u>más</u> rápido que tú.   He runs faster than you do.

- menos ... (que)   less ... (than)
  <u>menos</u> rápido (<u>que</u>)   less fast (than), less quickly (than)
  Conduce <u>menos</u> rápido que tú.   He drives less fast than you do.

2 Superlative adverbs

> **What is a superlative adverb?**
> A **superlative adverb** is one which, in English, has -est on the end of it or most or least in front of it, for example, *soonest*, *most/least often*.

➤ The superlative of adverbs (*the most often, the most efficiently, the fastest*) is formed in the same way in Spanish as the comparative, using más and menos. In this case they mean *the most* and *the least*.

María es la que corre <u>más rápido</u>.	Maria is the one who runs (the) fastest.
la chica que sabe <u>más</u>	the girl who knows (the) most
la chica que sabe <u>menos</u>	the girl who knows (the) least
El que llegó <u>menos tarde</u> fue Miguel.	Miguel was the one who arrived least late.

Note that even though comparative and superlative adverbs are usually identical in Spanish, you can tell which one is meant by the rest of the sentence.

3 Irregular comparative and superlative adverbs

➤ Some common Spanish adverbs have irregular comparative and superlatives.

Adverb	Meaning	Comparative	Meaning	Superlative	Meaning
bien	well	mejor	better	mejor	(the) best
mal	badly	peor	worse	peor	(the) worst
mucho	a lot	más	more	más	(the) most
poco	little	menos	less	menos	(the) least

La conozco <u>mejor</u> que tú.	I know her <u>better</u> than you do.
¿Quién lo hace <u>mejor</u>?	Who does it (the) <u>best</u>?
Ahora salgo <u>más/menos</u>.	I go out <u>more/less</u> these days.

> ## Tip
>
> When saying *more than*, *less than* or *fewer than* followed by a number, use más and menos <u>de</u> rather than más and menos que.
>
> más/menos <u>de</u> veinte cajas   more/fewer than twenty boxes

i Note that in phrases like *it's the least one can expect* or *it's the least I can do*, where the adverb is qualified by further information, in Spanish you have to put lo before the adverb.

Es <u>lo menos que</u> se puede esperar.	It's the least one can expect.

4 Other ways of making comparisons

➤ There are other ways of making comparisons in Spanish:

- tanto como   as much as

No lee <u>tanto como</u> tú.	He doesn't read <u>as much as</u> you.

- tan ... como   as ... as

Vine <u>tan</u> pronto <u>como</u> pude.	I came <u>as</u> fast <u>as</u> I could.

Key points

✔ más + adverb (+ que) = *more* + adverb + (*than*)

✔ menos + adverb (+ que) = *less* + adverb + (*than*)

✔ más + adverb = (*the*) *most* + adverb

✔ menos + adverb = (*the*) *least* + adverb.

✔ There are a few irregular comparative and superlative adverbs.

✔ There are other ways of making comparisons in Spanish: tanto como, tan ... como.

Common adverbs

1 One-word adverbs not ending in -mente

➤ There are some common adverbs that do not end in **-mente**, most of which give more information about when or where something happens or to what degree something is true.

- **ahí** there

    ¡**Ahí** están!   There they are!

- **ahora** now

    ¿Dónde vamos **ahora**?   Where are we going now?

- **allá** there

    allá arriba   up there

- **allí** there

    Allí está.   There it is.

- **anoche** last night

    Anoche llovió.   It rained last night.

- **anteanoche** the night before last

    Anteanoche nevó.   It snowed the night before last.

- **anteayer** the day before yesterday

    Anteayer hubo tormenta.   There was a storm the day before yesterday.

- **antes** before

    Esta película ya la he visto **antes**.   I've seen this film before.

- **apenas** hardly

    Apenas podía levantarse.   He could hardly stand up.

- **aquí** here

    Aquí está el informe.   Here's the report.

- **arriba** above, upstairs

    Visto desde arriba parece más pequeño.   Seen from above it looks smaller.

    Arriba están los dormitorios.   The bedrooms are upstairs.

- **atrás**   behind
  Yo me quedé <u>atrás</u>.   I stayed <u>behind</u>.

- **aun**   even
  <u>Aun</u> sentado me duele la   <u>Even</u> when I'm sitting down, my
  pierna.   leg hurts.

- **aún**   still, yet
  ¿<u>Aún</u> te duele?   Does it <u>still</u> hurt?

Tip

The following mnemonic (memory jogger) should help you
remember when to use **aun** and when to use **aún**:
<u>Even</u> **aun** doesn't have an accent.
aún <u>still</u> has an accent.
aún hasn't lost its accent <u>yet</u>.

- **ayer**   yesterday
  <u>Ayer</u> me compré un bolso.   I bought a handbag <u>yesterday</u>.

- **casi**   almost
  Son <u>casi</u> las cinco.   It's <u>almost</u> five o'clock.

- **cerca**   near
  El colegio está muy <u>cerca</u>.   The school is very <u>near</u>.

- **claro**   clearly
  Lo oí muy <u>claro</u>.   I heard it very <u>clearly</u>.

- **debajo**   underneath
  Miré <u>debajo</u>.   I looked <u>underneath</u>.

- **dentro**   inside
  ¿Qué hay <u>dentro</u>?   What's <u>inside</u>?

- **despacio**   slowly
  Conduce <u>despacio</u>.   Drive <u>slowly</u>.

- **después**   afterwards
  <u>Después</u> estábamos muy   We were very tired <u>afterwards</u>.
  cansados.

- **detrás**   behind
  Vienen <u>detrás</u>.   They're coming along <u>behind</u>.

For further explanation of grammatical terms, please see pages viii-xii.

- enfrente opposite
  la casa de <u>enfrente</u>   the house <u>opposite</u>

- enseguida straightaway
  La ambulancia llegó <u>enseguida</u>. The ambulance arrived <u>straightaway</u>.

- entonces then
  ¿Qué hiciste <u>entonces</u>?   What did you do <u>then</u>?

- hasta even
  Estudia <u>hasta</u> cuando está de   He studies <u>even</u> when he's on
  vacaciones.   holiday.

- hoy today
  <u>Hoy</u> no tenemos clase.   We haven't any lessons <u>today</u>.

- jamás never
  <u>Jamás</u> he visto nada parecido.   I've <u>never</u> seen anything like it.

- lejos far
  ¿Está <u>lejos</u>?   Is it <u>far</u>?

- luego then, later
  <u>Luego</u> fuimos al cine.   <u>Then</u> we went to the cinema.

- muy very
  Estoy <u>muy</u> cansada.   I'm <u>very</u> tired.

- no no, not
  <u>No</u>, no me gusta.   <u>No</u>. I don't like it.

- nunca never
  No viene <u>nunca</u>.   He <u>never</u> comes.
  '¿Has estado alguna vez en   'Have you ever been to Argentina?'
  Argentina?' – 'No, <u>nunca</u>.'   – 'No, <u>never</u>.'

- pronto soon, early
  Llegarán <u>pronto</u>.   They'll be here <u>soon</u>.
  ¿Por qué has llegado tan   Why have you arrived so early?
  <u>pronto</u>?

- quizás perhaps
  <u>Quizás</u> está cansado.   <u>Perhaps</u> he's tired.

ℹ️ Note that you use the present subjunctive after **quizás** if referring to the future.

> **Quizás venga mañana.**　　Perhaps he'll come tomorrow.

⇨ *For more information on the **Subjunctive**, see page 134.*

- sí　yes

> ¿Te apetece un café? –　Do you fancy a coffee? – Yes,
> Sí, gracias.　please.

- siempre　always

> Siempre dicen lo mismo.　They always say the same thing.

- sólo　only

> Sólo cuesta tres euros.　It only costs three euros.

- también　also, too

> A mí también me gusta.　I like it too.

- tampoco　either, neither

> Yo tampoco lo compré.　I didn't buy it either.
> Yo no la vi. – Yo tampoco.　I didn't see her. – Neither did I.

- tan　as, so

> Vine tan pronto como pude.　I came as fast as I could.
> Habla tan deprisa que no　She speaks so fast that I can't
> la entiendo.　understand her.

- tarde　late

> Se está haciendo tarde.　It's getting late.

- temprano　early

> Tengo que levantarme　I've got to get up early.
> temprano.

- todavía　still, yet, even

> Todavía tengo dos.　I've still got two.
> Todavía no han llegado.　They haven't arrived yet.
> mejor todavía　even better

- ya　already

> Ya lo he hecho.　I've already done it.

2 | Words which are used both as adjectives and adverbs

➤ **bastante**, **demasiado**, **tanto**, **mucho** and **poco** can be used both as adjectives and as adverbs. When they are <u>adjectives</u>, their endings change in the feminine and plural to agree with what they describe. When they are <u>adverbs</u>, the endings don't change.

	Adjective use	Adverb use
bastante enough; quite a lot; quite	Hay <u>bastantes</u> libros. There are enough books.	Ya has comido <u>bastante</u>. You've had enough to eat. **Son** <u>bastante</u> **ricos.** They are quite rich.
demasiado too much (*plural*: too many); too	<u>demasiada</u> mantequilla too much butter <u>demasiados</u> libros too many books	He comido <u>demasiado</u>. I've eaten too much. **Llegamos** <u>demasiado</u> **tarde.** We arrived too late.
tanto as much (*plural*: as many); as often	Ahora no bebo <u>tanta</u> leche. I don't drink as much milk these days. Tengo <u>tantas</u> cosas que hacer. I've so many things to do.	Se preocupa <u>tanto</u> que no puede dormir. He worries so much that he can't sleep. Ahora no la veo <u>tanto.</u> I don't see her so often now.
mucho a lot (of), much (*plural*: many)	Había <u>mucha</u> gente. There were a lot of people. <u>muchas</u> cosas a lot of things	¿Lees <u>mucho</u>? Do you read a lot? ¿Está <u>mucho</u> más lejos? Is it much further?
poco little, not much, (*plural*: few, not many); not very	Hay <u>poca</u> leche. There isn't much milk. Tiene <u>pocos</u> amigos. He hasn't got many friends.	Habla muy <u>poco</u>. He speaks very little. **Es** <u>poco</u> **sociable.** He's not very sociable.

> *Tip*
>
> Don't confuse **poco**, which means *little, not much* or *not very*, with **un poco**, which means *a little* or *a bit*.
>
> Come <u>poco</u>. He eats <u>little</u>.
> ¿Me das un <u>poco</u>? Can I have <u>a bit</u>?

➤ **más** and **menos** can also be used both as adjectives and adverbs. However, they NEVER change their endings, even when used as adjectives.

	Adjective use	Adverb use
más more	No tengo <u>más</u> dinero. I haven't any more money. <u>más</u> libros more books	Es <u>más</u> inteligente que yo. He's more intelligent than I am. Mi hermano trabaja <u>más</u> ahora. My brother works more now.
menos less; fewer	<u>menos</u> mantequilla less butter Había <u>menos</u> gente que ayer. There were fewer people than yesterday.	Estoy <u>menos</u> sorprendida que tú. I'm less surprised than you are. Trabaja <u>menos</u> que yo. He doesn't work as hard as I do.

3   Adverbs made up of more than one word

➤ Just as in English, some Spanish adverbs are made up of two or more words instead of just one.

a veces	sometimes
a menudo	often
de vez en cuando	from time to time
todo el tiempo	all the time
hoy en día	nowadays
en seguida	immediately

Key points

✔ There are a number of common adverbs in Spanish which do not end in -mente.

✔ **bastante, demasiado, tanto, mucho** and **poco** can be used both as adjectives and as adverbs. Their endings change in the feminine and plural when they are adjectives, but when they are adverbs their endings <u>do not</u> change.

✔ **más** and **menos** can be both adjectives and adverbs – their endings <u>never</u> change.

✔ A number of Spanish adverbs are made up of more than one word.

Position of adverbs

1   Adverbs with verbs

➤ In English, adverbs can come in various places in a sentence, at the beginning, in the middle or at the end.

>I'm <u>never</u> coming back.
>See you <u>soon</u>!
><u>Suddenly</u>, the phone rang.
>I'd <u>really</u> like to come.

➤ In Spanish, the rules for the position of adverbs in a sentence are more fixed. The adverb can either go immediately <u>AFTER</u> the verb or <u>BEFORE</u> it for emphasis.

No conocemos <u>todavía</u> al nuevo médico.	We still haven't met the new doctor.
<u>Todavía</u> estoy esperando.	I'm still waiting.
<u>Siempre</u> le regalaban flores.	They always gave her flowers.

➤ When the adverb goes with a verb in the perfect tense or in the pluperfect, you can <u>NEVER</u> put the adverb between haber and the past participle.

Lo he hecho <u>ya</u>.	I've already done it.
No ha estado <u>nunca</u> en Italia.	She's never been to Italy.

⇨ *For more information on the **Perfect tense**, see page 115.*

2   Adverbs with adjectives and adverbs

➤ The adverb normally goes <u>BEFORE</u> any adjective or adverb it is used with.

un sombrero <u>muy</u> bonito	a very nice hat
hablar <u>demasiado</u> alto	to talk too loudly

Key points
- ✔ Adverbs follow the verb in most cases.
- ✔ Adverbs can go before verbs for emphasis.
- ✔ You can <u>never</u> separate haber, he, ha and so on from the following past participle (the -ado/-ido form of regular verbs).
- ✔ Adverbs generally come just before an adjective or another adverb.

Prepositions

What is a preposition?
A **preposition** is a word such as *at, for, with, into* or *from*, which is usually followed by a noun, pronoun or, in English, a word ending in *-ing*. Prepositions show how people and things relate to the rest of the sentence, for example, *She's at home.; a tool for cutting grass; It's from David.*

Using prepositions

➤ Prepositions are used in front of nouns and pronouns (such as *people, the man, me, him* and so on), and show the relationship between the noun or pronoun and the rest of the sentence. Although prepositions can be used before verb forms ending in *-ing* in English, in Spanish, they're followed by the <u>infinitive</u> – the form of the verb ending in **-ar, -er,** or **-ir.**

Le enseñé el billete <u>a</u> la revisora.	I showed my ticket <u>to</u> the ticket inspector.
Ven <u>con</u> nosotros.	Come <u>with</u> us.
Sirve <u>para</u> limpiar zapatos.	It's <u>for</u> cleaning shoes.

⇨ For more information on **Nouns**, **Pronouns** and **Infinitives**, see pages 1, 41 and 144.

➤ Prepositions are also used after certain adjectives and verbs and link them to the rest of the sentence.

Estoy muy contento <u>con</u> tu trabajo.	I'm very happy <u>with</u> your work.
Estamos hartos <u>de</u> repetirlo.	We're fed up <u>with</u> repeating it.
¿Te gusta jugar <u>al</u> fútbol?	Do you like playing football?

➤ As in English, Spanish prepositions can be made up of several words instead of just one.

delante de	in front of
antes de	before

For further explanation of grammatical terms, please see pages viii-xii.

➤ In English we can end a sentence with a preposition such as *for, with* or *into*, even though some people think this is not good grammar. You can <u>NEVER</u> end a Spanish sentence with a preposition.

¿<u>Para</u> qué es?	What's it <u>for</u>?
la chica <u>con</u> la que hablaste	the girl you spoke <u>to</u>

Tip

The choice of preposition in Spanish is not always what we might expect, coming from English. It is often difficult to give just one English equivalent for a particular Spanish preposition, since prepositions are used so differently in the two languages. This means that you need to learn how they are used and look up set phrases involving prepositions (such as *to be fond <u>of</u> somebody* or *dressed <u>in</u> white*) in a dictionary in order to find an equivalent expression in Spanish.

a, de, en, para and por

[handwritten: a = to / a + el = al = to the]

1 a

> **Tip**
> When a is followed by el, the two words merge to become al.

➤ a can mean *to* with places and destinations.

| Voy a Madrid. | I'm going to Madrid. |
| Voy al cine. | I'm going to the cinema. |

> **Tip**
> de is also used with a to mean *from ... to ...*
>
> | de la mañana a la noche | from morning to night |
> | de 10 a 12 | from 10 to 12 |

➤ a can mean *to* with indirect objects.

| Se lo dio a María. | He gave it to María. |

➤ a can mean *to* after ir when talking about what someone is *going to* do.

| Voy a verlo mañana. | I'm going to see him tomorrow. |

➤ a can mean *at* with times.

a las cinco	at five o'clock
a las dos y cuarto	at quarter past two
a medianoche	at midnight

➤ a can mean *at* with prices and rates.

| a dos euros el kilo | (at) two euros a kilo |
| a 100 km por hora | at 100 km per hour |

➤ a can mean *at* with ages.

| a los 18 años | at the age of 18 |

➤ a can mean *at* with places, but generally only after verbs suggesting movement.

| Te voy a buscar a la estación. | I'll meet you at the station. |
| cuando llegó al aeropuerto | when he arrived at the airport |

> **Típ**
>
> You can't use **a** to mean *at* when talking about a building, area, or village where someone is. Use **en** instead.
>
> Está **en** casa.   He's <u>at</u> home.

➤ **a** can mean *onto*.

    Se cayó **al** suelo.   He fell <u>onto</u> the floor.

➤ **a** can mean *into*.

    pegar una foto **al** álbum   to stick a photo <u>into</u> the album

➤ **a** is also used to talk about distance.

    a 8 km de aquí   (at a distance of) 8 km from here

➤ **a** is also used after certain adjectives and verbs.

    parecido **a** esto   similar to this

➤ **a** can mean *from* after certain verbs.

    Se lo compré **a** mi hermano.   I bought it <u>from</u> my brother.
    Les robaba dinero **a** sus   He was stealing money <u>from</u> his
    compañeros de clase.   classmates.

⇨ *For more information on **Prepositions after verbs**, see page 150.*

➤ **a** is used in set phrases.

    a final/finales/fines de mes   at the end of the month
    a veces   at times
    a menudo   often
    a la puerta   at the door
    a mano   by hand
    a caballo   on horseback
    a pie   on foot
    a tiempo   on time
    al sol   in the sun
    a la sombra   in the shade

***

Grammar Extra!

a is often used to talk about the manner in which something is done.

a la inglesa	in the English manner
a paso lento	slowly
poco a poco	little by little

The Spanish equivalent of the English construction *on* with a verb ending in *-ing* is al followed by the infinitive.

al levantarse	on getting up
al abrir la puerta	on opening the door

***

2 Personal a

➤ When the direct object of a verb is a specific person or pet animal, a is placed immediately before it.

Querían mucho a sus hijos.	They loved their children dearly.
Cuido a mi hermana pequeña.	I look after my little sister.

[i] Note that personal a is NOT used after the verb tener.

Tienen dos hijos.	They have two children.

⇨ *For more information on **Direct objects**, see page 46.*

3 de

> *Tip*
> When de is followed by el, the two words merge to become del.

➤ de can mean *from*.

Soy de Londres.	I'm from London.
un médico de Valencia	a doctor from Valencia

> *Tip*
> de is also used with a to mean *from ... to ...*
> | | |
> |---|---|
> | de la mañana a la noche | from morning to night |
> | de 10 a 12 | from 10 to 12 |

➤ **de** can mean *of*.

el presidente <u>de</u> Francia	the president <u>of</u> France
dos litros <u>de</u> leche	two litres <u>of</u> milk

➤ **de** shows who or what something belongs to.

el sombrero <u>de</u> mi padre	my father's hat
	(*literally: the hat <u>of</u> my father*)
la oficina <u>del</u> presidente	the president's office
	(*literally: the office <u>of</u> the president*)

➤ **de** can indicate what something is made of, what it contains or what it is used for.

un vestido <u>de</u> seda	a silk dress
una caja <u>de</u> cerillas	a box of matches
una taza <u>de</u> té	a cup of tea *or*
	a teacup
una silla <u>de</u> cocina	a kitchen chair
un traje <u>de</u> baño	a swimming costume

➤ **de** is used in comparisons when a number is mentioned.

Había más/menos <u>de</u> 100 personas.	There were more/fewer than 100 people.

[*i*] Note that you do <u>NOT</u> use **que** with **más** or **menos** when there is a number involved.

➤ **de** can mean *in* after superlatives (*the most…, the biggest, the least…*).

la ciudad más/menos contaminada <u>del</u> mundo	the most/least polluted city <u>in</u> the world

⇨ *For more information on **Superlative adjectives**, see page 26.*

➤ **de** is used after certain adjectives and verbs.

contento <u>de</u> ver	pleased to see
Es fácil/difícil <u>de</u> entender.	It's easy/difficult to understand.
Es capaz <u>de</u> olvidarlo.	He's quite capable of forgetting it.

⇨ *For more information on **Prepositions after verbs**, see page 150.*

Grammar Extra!

de is often used in descriptions.

la mujer <u>del</u> sombrero verde	the woman <u>in</u> the green hat
un chico <u>de</u> ojos azules	a boy <u>with</u> blue eyes

4 (en) *IN, at, on, by, into*

➤ **en** can mean *in* with places.

en el campo	**in** the country
en Londres	**in** London
en la cama	**in** bed
con un libro **en** la mano	with a book **in** his hand

➤ **en** can mean *at*.

en casa	**at** home
en el colegio	**at** school
en el aeropuerto	**at** the airport
en la parada de autobús	**at** the bus stop
en Navidad	**at** Christmas

➤ **en** can mean *in* with months, years and seasons and when saying how long something takes or took.

en marzo	**in** March
en 2005	**in** 2005
Nació **en** invierno.	He was born **in** winter.
Lo hice **en** dos días.	I did it **in** two days.

[*i*] Note the following time phrase which does not use *in* in English.

en este momento	**at** this moment

Tip

There are two ways of talking about a length of time in Spanish which translate the same in English, but have very different meanings.

Lo haré **dentro de** una semana. I'll do it **in** a week.

Lo haré **en** una semana. I'll do it **in** a week.

Though both can be translated in the same way, the first sentence means that you'll do it in a week's time; the second means that it will take you a week to do it.

➤ **en** can mean *in* with languages and in set phrases.

Está escrito **en** español.	It's written **in** Spanish.
en voz baja	**in** a low voice

For further explanation of grammatical terms, please see pages viii-xii.

➤ en can mean *on*.

sentado <u>en</u> una silla	sitting <u>on</u> a chair
<u>en</u> la planta baja	<u>on</u> the ground floor
Hay dos cuadros <u>en</u> la pared.	There are two pictures <u>on</u> the wall.

➤ en can mean *by* with most methods of transport.

<u>en</u> coche	<u>by</u> car
<u>en</u> avión	<u>by</u> plane
<u>en</u> tren	<u>by</u> train

➤ en can mean *into*.

No entremos <u>en</u> la casa.	Let's not go <u>into</u> the house.
Metió la mano <u>en</u> su bolso.	She put her hand <u>into</u> her handbag.

➤ en is also used after certain adjectives and verbs.

Es muy buena/mala <u>en</u> geografía.	She is very good/bad at geography.
Fueron los primeros/últimos/únicos <u>en</u> llegar.	They were the first/last/only ones to arrive.

⇨ *For more information on **Prepositions after verbs**, see page 150.*

5 **para** ~~for~~

➤ para can mean *for* with a person, destination or purpose.

Para mí un zumo de naranja.	An orange juice <u>for</u> me.
Salen <u>para</u> Cádiz.	They are leaving <u>for</u> Cádiz.
¿<u>Para</u> qué lo quieres?	What do you want it <u>for</u>?

[*i*] Note that you cannot end a sentence in Spanish with a preposition as you can in English.

➤ para can mean *for* with time.

Es <u>para</u> mañana.	It's <u>for</u> tomorrow.
una habitación <u>para</u> dos noches	a room <u>for</u> two nights

➤ para is also used with an infinitive with the meaning of *(in order) to*.

Lo hace <u>para</u> ganar dinero.	He does it <u>to</u> earn money.
Lo hice <u>para</u> ayudarte.	I did it <u>to</u> help you.

> *Tip*
> **para mí** can be used to mean *in my opinion*.
>   **Para mí, es estupendo.**   In my opinion, it's great.

6 por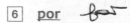

➤ **por** can mean *for* when it means *for the benefit of* or *because of*.

Lo hice por mis padres.	I did it for my parents.
Lo hago por ellos.	I'm doing it for them.
por la misma razón	for the same reason

➤ **por** can mean *for* when it means *in exchange for*.

¿Cuánto me darán por este libro?	How much will they give me for this book?
Te lo cambio por éste.	I'll swap you it for this one.

➤ **por** can mean *by* in passive constructions.

descubierto por unos niños	discovered by some children
odiado por sus enemigos	hated by his enemies

⇨ *For more information on the **Passive** see page 122.*

➤ **por** can mean *by* with means of transport when talking about freight.

por barco	by boat
por tren	by train
por avión	by airmail
por correo aéreo	by airmail

➤ **por** can mean *along*.

Vaya por ese camino.	Go along that path.

➤ **por** can mean *through*.

por el túnel	through the tunnel

➤ **por** can mean *around*.

pasear por el campo	to walk around the countryside

➤ **por** is used to talk vaguely about where something or someone is.

Tiene que estar por aquí.	It's got to be around here somewhere.
Lo busqué por todas partes.	I looked for him everywhere.

➤ **por** is used to talk about time.

<u>por</u> la mañana	<u>in</u> the morning
<u>por</u> la tarde	<u>in</u> the afternoon/evening
<u>por</u> la noche	<u>at</u> night

➤ **por** is used to talk about rates.

90 km <u>por</u> hora	90 km an hour
un cinco <u>por</u> ciento	five per cent
Ganaron <u>por</u> 3 a 0.	They won by 3 to 0.

➤ **por** is used in certain phrases which talk about the reason for something.

¿<u>por</u> qué?	why?, for what reason?
<u>por</u> todo eso	because of all that
<u>por</u> lo que he oído	judging by what I've heard

➤ **por** is used to talk about how something is done.

llamar <u>por</u> teléfono	to telephone
Lo oí <u>por</u> la radio.	I heard it on the radio.

Grammar Extra!

por is often combined with other Spanish prepositions and words, usually to show movement.

Saltó <u>por encima</u> de la mesa.	She jumped over the table.
Nadamos <u>por debajo del</u> puente.	We swam under the bridge.
Pasaron <u>por delante de</u> Correos.	They went past the post office.

Key points

✔ a, de, en, para and por are very frequently used prepositions which you will need to study carefully.

✔ Each of them has several possible meanings, which depend on the context they are used in.

Some other common prepositions

➤ The following prepositions are also frequently used in Spanish.

- **antes de** before

  <u>antes</u> de las 5　　　　　<u>before</u> 5 o'clock

[i] Note that, like many other prepositions, **antes de** is used before infinitives in Spanish where in English we'd usually use the -*ing* form of the verb.

<u>Antes de abrir</u> el paquete,　<u>Before opening</u> the packet, read
lea las instrucciones.　　　the instructions.

- **bajo** below, under

  un grado <u>bajo</u> cero　　　one degree <u>below</u> zero
  <u>bajo</u> la cama　　　　　<u>under</u> the bed

[i] Note that **debajo de** is more common than **bajo** when talking about the actual position of something.

<u>debajo de</u> la cama　　　<u>under</u> the bed

- **con** with

  Vino <u>con</u> su amigo.　　She came <u>with</u> her friend.

[i] Note that **con** can be used after certain adjectives as well as in a few very common phrases.

enfadado <u>con</u> ellos　　　angry <u>with</u> them
un café <u>con</u> leche　　　a white coffee
un té <u>con</u> limón　　　　a (cup of) tea <u>with</u> a slice of lemon

- **contra** against

  Estaba apoyado <u>contra</u>　　He was leaning <u>against</u> the wall.
  la pared.
  El domingo jugamos <u>contra</u>　We play <u>against</u> Malaga on Sunday.
  el Málaga.

- **debajo de** under

  <u>debajo de</u> la cama　　　<u>under</u> the bed

- **delante de** in front of

  Iba <u>delante de</u> mí.　　　He was walking <u>in front of</u> me.

- **desde**   from, since

<u>Desde</u> aquí se puede ver.	You can see it <u>from</u> here.
Llamaron <u>desde</u> España.	They phoned <u>from</u> Spain.
<u>desde</u> otro punto de vista	<u>from</u> a different point of view
<u>desde</u> entonces	<u>from</u> then onwards
<u>desde</u> la una <u>hasta</u> las siete	<u>from</u> one o'clock <u>to</u> seven
<u>desde</u> la boda	<u>since</u> the wedding

Tip

Spanish uses the <u>present tense</u> with **desde** (meaning *since*) and the expressions **desde hace** and **hace … que** (meaning *for*) to talk about actions that started in the past and are still going on.

<u>Estoy</u> aquí desde las diez.	I've been here since ten o'clock.
<u>Estoy</u> aquí desde hace dos horas. *or* Hace dos horas que <u>estoy</u> aquí.	I've been here for two hours.

If you are saying how long something has NOT happened for, in European Spanish you can use the <u>perfect tense</u> with **desde** and **desde hace**.

No <u>ha trabajado</u> desde el accidente.	He hasn't worked since the accident.
No <u>ha trabajado</u> desde hace dos meses.	He hasn't worked for two months.

⇨ *For more information on the **Present tense** and the **Perfect tense**, see pages 69 and 115.*

- **después de**   after

<u>después del</u> partido	<u>after</u> the match

[i] Note that, like many other prepositions, **después de** is used before infinitives in Spanish where in English we'd usually use the *-ing* form of the verb.

<u>Después de ver</u> la televisión me fui a la cama.	<u>After watching</u> television I went to bed.

- **detrás de**   behind

Están <u>detrás de</u> la puerta.	They are <u>behind</u> the door.

- **durante**   during, for

<u>durante</u> la guerra	<u>during</u> the war
Anduvieron <u>durante</u> 3 días.	They walked <u>for</u> 3 days.

- entre   between, among
    entre 8 y 10 | between 8 and 10
    Hablaban entre sí. | They were talking among themselves.

- hacia   towards, around
    Van hacia ese edificio. | They're going towards that building.
    hacia las tres | at around three (o'clock)
    hacia finales de enero | around the end of January

Grammar Extra!

hacia can also combine with some adverbs to show movement in a particular direction.

hacia arriba	upwards
hacia abajo	downwards
hacia adelante	forwards
hacia atrás	backwards

- hasta   until, as far as, to, up to
    hasta la noche | until night
    Fueron en coche hasta Sevilla. | They drove as far as Seville.
    desde la una hasta las tres | from one o'clock to three
    Hasta ahora no ha llamado nadie. | No one has called up to now.

i Note that there are some very common ways of saying goodbye using hasta.

    ¡Hasta luego! | See you!
    ¡Hasta mañana! | See you tomorrow!

- sin   without
    sin agua/dinero | without any water/money
    sin mi marido | without my husband

Tip

Whereas in English we say *without a doubt*, *without a hat* and so on, in Spanish the indefinite article isn't given after sin.

    sin duda | without a doubt
    sin sombrero | without a hat

➪ For more information on **Articles**, see page 10.

For further explanation of grammatical terms, please see pages viii-xii.

[i] Note that **sin** is used before infinitives in Spanish where in English we would use the *-ing* form of the verb.

Se fue <u>sin decir</u> nada.	He left <u>without saying</u> anything.

- **sobre**   on, about

<u>sobre</u> la cama	<u>on</u> the bed
Ponlo <u>sobre</u> la mesa.	Put it <u>on</u> the table.
un libro <u>sobre</u> Shakespeare	a book <u>on</u> *or* <u>about</u> Shakespeare
Madrid tiene <u>sobre</u> 4 millones de habitantes.	Madrid has <u>about</u> 4 million inhabitants.
Vendré <u>sobre</u> las cuatro.	I'll come <u>about</u> four o'clock.

➤ Spanish prepositions can be made up of more than one word, for example, **antes de**, **detrás de**. Here are some more common prepositions made up of two or more words:

- **a causa de**   because of

No salimos <u>a causa de</u> la lluvia.	We didn't go out <u>because of</u> the rain.

- **al lado de**   beside, next to

<u>al lado de</u> la tele	<u>beside</u> the TV

- **cerca de**   near, close to

Está <u>cerca de</u> la iglesia.	It's <u>near</u> the church.

- **encima de**   on, on top of

Ponlo <u>encima de</u> la mesa.	Put it <u>on</u> the table.

- **por encima de**   above, over

Saltó <u>por encima de</u> la mesa.	He jumped <u>over</u> the table.

- **en medio de**   in the middle of

Está <u>en medio de</u> la plaza.	It's <u>in the middle of</u> the square.

- **junto a**   by

Está <u>junto al</u> cine.	It's <u>by</u> the cinema.

- **junto con**   together with

Fue detenido <u>junto con</u> su hijo.	He was arrested <u>together with</u> his son.

- **lejos de**   far from

No está <u>lejos de</u> aquí.	It isn't <u>far from</u> here.

Conjunctions

> **What is a conjunction?**
> A **conjunction** is a word such as *and*, *but*, *or*, *so*, *if* and *because*, that links two words or phrases of a similar type, or two parts of a sentence, for example, *Diane <u>and</u> I have been friends for years.; I left <u>because</u> I was bored.*

y, o, pero, porque and si

➤ y, o, pero, porque and si are the most common conjunctions that you need to know in Spanish:

- **y** and

  el coche y la casa   the car <u>and</u> the house

[i] Note that you use e instead of y before words beginning with i or hi (but not hie).

     Diana e Isabel   Diana <u>and</u> Isabel
     madre e hija   mother <u>and</u> daughter
     BUT
     árboles y hierba   trees <u>and</u> grass

- **o** or

  patatas fritas o arroz   chips <u>or</u> rice

[i] Note that you use u instead of o before words beginning with o or ho.

     diez u once   ten <u>or</u> eleven
     minutos u horas   minutes <u>or</u> hours

[i] Note that you use ó instead of o between numerals to avoid confusion with zero.

     37 ó 38   37 or 38

⇨ *For more information on **Numbers**, see page 206.*

- **pero** but

  Me gustaría ir, <u>pero</u> estoy muy   I'd like to go, <u>but</u> I am very tired.
  cansado.

[i] Note that you use sino in direct contrasts after a negative.

     No es escocesa, <u>sino</u> irlandesa.   She's not Scottish <u>but</u> Irish.

For further explanation of grammatical terms, please see pages viii–xii.

Split conjunctions

In English we have conjunctions which are made up of two parts (*both ... and*, *neither ... nor*). Spanish also has conjunctions which have more than one part, the commonest of which are probably ni ... ni (meaning *neither ... nor*) and o ... o (meaning *either ... or*):

- ni ... ni   neither ... nor

    Ni Carlos **ni** Sofía vinieron. *or*   <u>Neither</u> Carlos <u>nor</u> Sofía came.
    No vinieron <u>ni</u> Carlos <u>ni</u> Sofía.

ℹ Note that if you're putting ni ... ni after the verb you must put no before the verb.

    No tengo <u>ni</u> hermanos <u>ni</u>   I have <u>neither</u> brothers <u>nor</u>
    hermanas.   sisters.

- o ... o   either ... or

    Puedes tomar <u>o</u> helado <u>o</u> yogur.   You can have <u>either</u> ice cream <u>or</u> yoghurt.

> **Key points**
> ✔ y, o, pero, porque and si are the most common conjunctions that you need to know in Spanish.
> ✔ Use e rather than y before words beginning with i or hi (but not with hie).
> ✔ Use u rather than o before words beginning with o or ho.
> ✔ que very often means *that*. *That* is often missed out in English, but que can never be left out in Spanish.
> ✔ Some conjunctions such as ni ... ni and o ... o consist of two parts.

Spelling

1 | Sounds that are spelled differently depending on the letter that follows

➤ Certain sounds are spelled differently in Spanish depending on what letter follows them. For example, the hard [k] sound heard in the English word *car* is usually spelled:
- c before a, o and u
- qu before e and i

➤ This means that the Spanish word for *singer* is spelled cantante (pronounced [*kan-tan-tay*]); the word for *coast* is spelled costa (pronounced [*ko-sta*]); and the word for *cure* is spelled cura (pronounced [*koo-ra*]).

➤ However, the Spanish word for cheese is spelled queso (pronounced [*kay-so*]) and the word for *chemistry* is spelled química (pronounced [*kee-mee-ka*]).

[*i*] Note that although the letter k is not much used in Spanish, it is found in words relating to *kilos*, *kilometres* and *kilograms*; for example un kilo (meaning *a kilo*); un kilogramo (meaning *a kilogram*); un kilómetro (meaning *a kilometre*).

➤ Similarly, the [g] sound heard in the English word *gone* is spelled:
- g before a, o and u
- gu before e and i

➤ This means that the Spanish word for *cat* is spelled gato (pronounced [*ga-toe*]); the word for *goal* is spelled gol (pronounced [*gol*]); and the word for *worm* is spelled gusano (pronounced [*goo-sa-no*]).

➤ However, the Spanish word for *war* is spelled guerra (pronounced [*gair-ra*]) and the word for *guitar* is spelled guitarra (pronounced [*ghee-tar-ra*]).

Letters that are pronounced differently depending on what follows

➤ Certain letters are pronounced differently depending on what follows them. As we have seen, when c comes before a, o or u, it is pronounced like a [k]. When it comes before e or i, in European Spanish it is pronounced like the [th] in the English word *pith* and in Latin American Spanish it is pronounced like the [s] in *sing*.

➤ This means that casa (meaning *house*) is pronounced [ka-sa], but centro (meaning *centre*) is pronounced [then-tro] in European Spanish and [sen-tro] in Latin American Spanish. Similarly, cita (meaning *date*) is pronounced [the-ta] in European Spanish and [see-ta] in Latin American Spanish.

➤ In the same way, when g comes before a, o or u, it is pronounced like the [g] in *gone*. When it comes before e or i, however, it is pronounced like the [ch] in *loch*, as it is pronounced in Scotland.

➤ This means that gas (meaning *gas*) is pronounced [gas] but gente (meaning *people*) is pronounced [chen-tay]. Similarly, gimnasio (meaning *gym*) is pronounced [cheem-na-see-o].

3 **Spelling changes that are needed in verbs to reflect the pronunciation**

➤ Because c sounds like [k] before a, o and u, and like [th] or [s] before e and i, you sometimes have to alter the spelling of a verb when adding a particular ending to ensure the word reads as it is pronounced:

● In verbs ending in -car (which is pronounced [kar]), you have to change the c to qu before endings starting with an e to keep the hard [k] pronunciation. So the yo form of the preterite tense of sacar (meaning *to take out*) is spelled saqué. This spelling change affects the preterite and the present subjunctive of verbs ending in -car.

● In verbs ending in -cer and -cir (which are pronounced [ther] and [thir] or [ser] and [sir]), you have to change the c to z before endings starting with a or o to keep the soft [th/s] pronunciation. So while the yo form of the preterite tense of hacer is spelled hice, the él/ella/usted form is spelled hizo. This spelling change affects the ordinary present tense as well as the present subjunctive of verbs ending in -cer or -cir.

➤ Because g sounds like the [g] of *gone* before a, o and u, and like the [ch] of *loch* before e and i, you also sometimes have to alter the spelling of a verb when adding a particular ending to ensure the verb still reads as it is pronounced:

- In verbs ending in **-gar** (which is pronounced [*gar*]), you have to change the g to **gu** before endings starting with an e or an i to keep the hard [g] pronunciation. So the **yo** form of the preterite tense of **pagar** (meaning *to pay*) is spelled **pagué**. This spelling change affects the preterite and the present subjunctive of verbs ending in **-gar**.

- In verbs ending in **-ger** and **-gir** (which are pronounced [*cher*] and [*chir*]), you have to change the g to j before endings starting with a or o to keep the soft [ch] pronunciation. So while the **él/ella/usted** form of the present tense of **coger** (meaning *to take* or *to catch*) is spelled **coge**, the **yo** form is spelled **cojo**. This spelling change affects the ordinary present tense as well as the present subjunctive of verbs ending in **-ger** or **-gir**.

➤ Because **gui** sounds like [*ghee*] in verbs ending in **-guir**, but **gua** and **guo** sound like [*gwa*] and [*gwo*], you have to drop the u before a and o in verbs ending in **-guir**. So while the **él/ella/usted** form of the present tense of **seguir** (meaning *to follow*) is spelled **sigue**, the **yo** form is spelled **sigo**. This spelling change affects the ordinary present tense as well as the present subjunctive of verbs ending in **-guir**.

➤ Finally, although z is always pronounced [*th*] in European Spanish and [*s*] in Latin American Spanish, in verbs ending in **-zar** the z spelling is changed to c before e. So, while the **él/ella/usted** form of the preterite tense of **cruzar** is spelled **cruzó**, the **yo** form is spelled **crucé**. This spelling change affects the preterite and the present subjunctive of verbs ending in **-zar**.

---

4 **Spelling changes that are needed when making nouns and adjectives plural**

➤ In the same way that you have to make some spelling changes when modifying the endings of certain verbs, you sometimes have to change the spelling of nouns and adjectives when making them plural.

➤ This affects nouns and adjectives ending in **-z**. When adding the **-es** ending of the plural, you have to change the z to c.

una vez	once, one time	→	dos veces	twice, two times
una luz	a light	→	unas luces	some lights
capaz	capable (*singular*)	→	capaces	capable (*plural*)

For further explanation of grammatical terms, please see pages viii-xii.

➤ The following table shows the usual spelling of the various sounds discussed above:

	Usual spelling				
	before a	before o	before u	before e	before i
[k] sound (as in *cap*)	ca: casa house	co: cosa thing	cu: cubo bucket	que: queso cheese	qui: química chemistry
[g] sound (as in *gap*)	ga: gato cat	go: gordo fat	gu: gusto taste	gue: guerra war	gui: guitarra guitar
[th] sound (as in *pith*) (pronounced [s] in Latin America)	za: zapato shoe	zo: zorro fox	zu: zumo juice	ce: cero zero	ci: cinta ribbon
[ch] sound (as in *loch*)	ja: jardín garden	jo: joven young	ju: jugar to play	ge: gente people	gi: gigante giant

[i] Note that because j is still pronounced [ch] even when it comes before e or i, there are quite a number of words that contain je or ji; for example,

el jefe/la jefa	the boss
el jerez	sherry
el jersey	jersey
el jinete	jockey
la jirafa	giraffe
el ejemplo	the example
dije/dijiste	I said/you said
dejé	I left

Similarly, because z is also pronounced [th] or [s] even when it comes before i or e, there are one or two exceptions to the spelling rules described above; for example, **el zigzag** (meaning *zigzag*) and **la zeta** (the name of the letter z in Spanish).

Which syllable to stress

➤ Most words can be broken up into <u>syllables</u>. These are the different sounds that words are broken up into. They are shown in this section by | and the stressed syllable is underlined.

➤ There are some very simple rules to help you remember which part of the word to stress in Spanish, and when to write an accent.

➤ Words <u>DON'T</u> have a written acute accent if they follow the normal stress rules for Spanish. If they do not follow the normal stress rules, they <u>DO</u> need an accent.

> *Tip*
>
> The accent that shows stress is always an <u>acute</u> accent in Spanish (´). To remember which way an acute accents slopes try thinking of this saying:
> *It's low on the left, with the height on the right.*

1 <u>Words ending in a vowel or -n or -s</u>

➤ Words ending in a vowel (*a*, *e*, *i*, *o* or *u*) or **-n** or **-s** are normally stressed on the <u>last syllable but one</u>. If this is the case, they do <u>NOT</u> have any written accents.

<u>ca</u>|sa	house	<u>ca</u>|sas	houses
pa|<u>la</u>|bra	word	pa|<u>la</u>|bras	words
<u>tar</u>|de	afternoon	<u>tar</u>|des	afternoons
<u>ha</u>|bla	he/she speaks	<u>ha</u>|blan	they speak
<u>co</u>|rre	he/she runs	<u>co</u>|rren	they run

➤ Whenever words ending in a vowel or **-n** or **-s** are <u>NOT</u> stressed on the last syllable but one, they have a written accent on the vowel that is stressed.

<u>úl</u>|ti|mo	last
<u>jó</u>|ve|nes	young people
<u>crí</u>|me|nes	crimes

2   Words ending in a consonant other than -n or -s

➤ Words ending in a consonant (a letter that isn't a vowel) other than -n or -s are normally stressed on the <u>last syllable</u>. If this is the case, they do <u>NOT</u> have an accent.

re|<u>loj</u>	clock, watch
ver|<u>dad</u>	truth
trac|<u>tor</u>	tractor

➤ Whenever words ending in a consonant other than -n or -s are <u>NOT</u> stressed on the last syllable, they have an accent.

ca|<u>rác</u>|ter	character
di|<u>fí</u>|cil	difficult
<u>fá</u>|cil	easy

3   Accents on feminine and plural forms

➤ The same syllable is stressed in the plural form of adjectives and nouns as in the singular. To show this, you need to:

- add an accent in the plural in the case of unaccented nouns and adjectives of more than one syllable ending in -n

<u>or</u>|den	order	<u>ór</u>|de|nes	orders
e|<u>xa</u>|men	exam	e|<u>xá</u>|me|nes	exams
BUT: tren	train	<u>tre</u>|nes	trains

ⓘ Note that in the case of one-syllable words ending in -n or -s, such as tren above, no accent is needed in the plural, since the stress falls naturally on the last syllable but one thanks to the plural -es ending.

- drop the accent in the plural form of nouns and adjectives ending in -n or -s which have an accent on the last syllable in the singular

| au\|to\|<u>bús</u> | bus | au\|to\|<u>bu</u>\|ses | buses |
| re\|vo\|lu\|<u>ción</u> | revolution | re\|vo\|lu\|<u>cio</u>\|nes | revolutions |

➤ The feminine forms of nouns or adjectives whose masculine form ends in an accented vowel followed by -n or -s do <u>NOT</u> have an accent.

| un franc<u>és</u> | a Frenchman |
| una franc<u>e</u>sa | a French woman |

> **Tip**
>
> Just because a word has a written accent in the singular does not necessarily mean it has one in the plural, and vice versa.
>
> **jo|ven**
> *Ends in **n**, so rule is to stress last syllable but one; follows rule, so <u>no</u> accent needed in singular*
>
> **jó|ve|nes**
> *Ends in **s**, so rule is to stress last syllable but one; breaks rule, so accent <u>is</u> needed in plural to keep stress on jo-*
>
> **lec|ción**
> *Ends in **n**, so rule is to stress last syllable but one; breaks rule, so accent <u>is</u> needed in singular*
>
> **lec|cio|nes**
> *Ends in **s**, so rule is to stress last syllable but one; follows rule, so <u>no</u> accent needed in plural to keep stress on -cio-*

4   <u>Which vowel to stress in vowel combinations</u>

➤ The vowels **i** and **u** are considered to be <u>weak</u>. The vowels **a**, **e** and **o** are considered to be <u>strong</u>.

➤ When a weak vowel (**i** or **u**) combines with a strong one (**a**, **e** or **o**), they form <u>ONE</u> sound that is part of the <u>SAME</u> syllable. Technically speaking, this is called a <u>diphthong</u>. The strong vowel is emphasized more.

b<u>ai</u>|le	dance
c<u>ie</u>|rra	he/she/it closes
b<u>oi</u>|na	beret
p<u>ei</u>|ne	comb
c<u>au</u>|sa	cause

> **Tip**
>
> To remember which are the weak vowels, try thinking of this saying:
> *U and I are weaklings and always lose out to other vowels!*

➤ When **i** is combined with **u** or **u** with **i** (the two weak vowels), they also form <u>ONE</u> sound within the <u>SAME</u> syllable; there is more emphasis on the second vowel.

ci<u>u</u>dad	city, town
fu<u>i</u>	I went

➤ When you combine two strong vowels (**a**, **e** or **o**), they form <u>TWO</u> separate sounds and are part of <u>DIFFERENT</u> syllables.

ca|er	to fall
ca|os	chaos
fe|o	ugly

For further explanation of grammatical terms, please see pages viii–xii.

5   Adding accents to some verb forms

➤ When object pronouns are added to the end of certain verb forms, an accent is often required to show that the syllable stressed in the verb form does not change. These verb forms are:

- the gerund whenever one or more pronouns are added

| comprando | buying |
| comprándo(se)lo | buying it (for him/her/them) |

- the infinitive, when followed by two pronouns

| vender | to sell |
| vendérselas | to sell them to him/her/them |

- imperative forms

compra	buy
cómpralo	buy it
hagan	do
háganselo	do it for him/her/them
BUT:	
comprad	buy
compradlo	buy it

➪ For more information on **Gerunds**, **Infinitives** and the **Imperative**, see pages 125, 144 and 85.

6   Accents on adjectives and adverbs

➤ Adjectives ending in -ísimo always have an accent on -ísimo. This means that any other accents are dropped.

caro	→	carísimo
expensive		very expensive
difícil	→	dificilísimo
difficult		very difficult

➤ Accents on adjectives are NOT affected when you add -mente to turn them into adverbs.

| fácil | → | fácilmente |
| easy | | easily |

The acute accent used to show meaning

➤ The acute accent is often used to distinguish between the written forms of some words which are pronounced the same but have a different meaning or function.

Without an accent		With an accent	
mi	my	mí	me
tu	your	tú	you
te	you	té	tea
si	if	sí	yes; himself
el	the	él	he
de	of	dé	give
solo	alone; by oneself	sólo	only
mas	but	más	more

Han robado <u>mi</u> coche.	They've stolen my car.
A <u>mí</u> no me vio.	He didn't see me.
¿Te gusta <u>tu</u> trabajo?	Do you like your job?
<u>Tú</u>, ¿qué opinas?	What do you think?
...<u>si</u> no viene	...if he doesn't come
<u>Sí</u> que lo sabe.	Yes, he does know.
<u>El</u> puerto está cerca.	The harbour's nearby.
<u>Él</u> lo hará.	He'll do it.
Vino <u>solo</u>.	He came alone or by himself.
<u>Sólo</u> lo sabe él.	Only he knows.

➤ The acute accent is often used on the <u>demonstrative pronouns</u> (éste/ésta, aquél/aquélla, ése/ésa and so on) to distinguish them from the <u>demonstrative adjectives</u> (este/esta, aquel/aquella, ese/esa and so on).

Me gusta <u>esta</u> casa. (= adjective)	I like this house.
Me quedo con <u>ésta</u>. (= pronoun)	I'll take this one.
¿Ves <u>aquellos</u> edificios? (= adjective)	Can you see those buildings?
<u>Aquéllos</u> son más bonitos. (= pronoun)	Those are prettier.

[i] Note that no accent is given on the neuter pronouns esto, eso and aquello since there is no adjective form with which they might be confused.

⇨ *For more information on **Demonstrative adjectives** and **Demonstrative pronouns**, see pages 30 and 67.*

➤ An accent is needed on question words in direct and indirect questions as well as after expressions of uncertainty.

¿<u>Cómo</u> estás?	How are you?
Dime <u>cómo</u> estás.	Tell me how you are.
Me preguntó <u>cómo</u> estaba.	He asked me how I was.
¿Con <u>quién</u> viajaste?	Who did you travel with?
¿<u>Dónde</u> encontraste eso?	Where did you find that?
No sé <u>dónde</u> está.	I don't know where it is.

⇨ *For more information on* **Questions**, *see page 160.*

➤ An accent is also needed on exclamation words.

¡<u>Qué</u> asco!	How revolting!
¡<u>Qué</u> horror!	How awful!
¡<u>Qué</u> raro!	How strange!
¡<u>Cuánta</u> gente!	What a lot of people!

Key points

✔ When deciding whether or not to write an accent on a word, think about how it sounds and what letter it ends in, as there are certain rules to say when an accent should be used.

✔ The vowels i and u are considered to be weak. The vowels a, e and o are considered to be strong. They can combine in a number of ways.

✔ Accents are added to written forms of words which are pronounced the same but have a different meaning, for example, mi/mí, tu/tú and so on.

✔ Accents are also added to most demonstrative pronouns so that they are not confused with demonstrative adjectives.

✔ Adjectives ending in -ísimo always have an accent on -ísimo, but no accent is added when adverbs are formed by adding -mente to adjectives.

✔ Question words used in direct and indirect questions as well as exclamation words always have an acute accent.

Numbers

1	uno (un, una)	31	treinta y uno (un, una)
2	dos	40	cuarenta
3	tres	41	cuarenta y uno (un, una)
4	cuatro	50	cincuenta
5	cinco	52	cincuenta y dos
6	seis	60	sesenta
7	siete	65	sesenta y cinco
8	ocho	70	setenta
9	nueve	76	setenta y seis
10	diez	80	ochenta
11	once	87	ochenta y siete
12	doce	90	noventa
13	trece	99	noventa y nueve
14	catorce	100	cien (ciento)
15	quince	101	ciento uno (un, una)
16	dieciséis	200	doscientos/doscientas
17	diecisiete	212	doscientos/doscientas doce
18	dieciocho	300	trescientos/trescientas
19	diecinueve	400	cuatrocientos/cuatrocientas
20	veinte	500	quinientos/quinientas
21	veintiuno (veintiún, veintiuna)	600	seiscientos/seiscientas
22	veintidós	700	setecientos/setecientas
23	veintitrés	800	ochocientos/ochocientas
24	veinticuatro	900	novecientos/novecientas
25	veinticinco	1000	mil
26	veintiséis	1001	mil (y) uno (un, una)
27	veintisiete	2000	dos mil
28	veintiocho	2500	dos mil quinientos/quinientas
29	veintinueve	1.000.000	un millón
30	treinta		(in English: 1,000,000)

EJEMPLOS	EXAMPLES
Vive en el número diez.	He lives at number ten.
en la página diecinueve	on page nineteen
un diez por ciento	10%
un cien por cien(to)	100%

For further explanation of grammatical terms, please see pages viii-xii.

1 uno, un or una?

➤ Use uno when counting, unless referring to something or someone feminine.

➤ Use un before a masculine noun and una before a feminine noun even when the nouns are plural.

un hombre	one man
una mujer	one woman
treinta y un días	thirty-one days
treinta y una noches	thirty-one nights
veintiún años	twenty-one years
veintiuna chicas	twenty-one girls

2 cien or ciento?

➤ Use cien before both masculine and feminine nouns as well as before mil (meaning *thousand*) and millones (meaning *million* in the plural):

cien libros	one hundred books
cien mil hombres	one hundred thousand men
cien millones	one hundred million

➤ Use ciento before other numbers.

ciento un perros	one hundred and one dogs
ciento una ovejas	one hundred and one sheep
ciento cincuenta	one hundred and fifty

[i] Note that you don't translate the *and* in 101, 220 and so on.

➤ Make doscientos/doscientas, trescientos/trescientas, quinientos/quinientas and so on agree with the noun in question.

doscientas veinte libras	two hundred and twenty pounds
quinientos alumnos	five hundred students

[i] Note that setecientos and setecientas have no i after the first s. Similarly, novecientos and novecientas have an o rather than the ue you might expect.

3 Full stop or comma?

➤ Use a full stop, not a comma, to separate thousands and millions in figures.

700.000 (setecientos mil)	700,000 (seven hundred thousand)
5.000.000 (cinco millones)	5,000,000 (five million)

➤ Use a comma instead of a decimal point to show decimals in Spanish.

0,5 (cero coma cinco)	0.5 (nought point five)
3,4 (tres coma cuatro)	3.4 (three point four)

1st	primero (1º), primer (1er), primera (1ª)
2nd	segundo (2º), segunda (2ª)
3rd	tercero (3º), tercer (3er), tercera (3ª)
4th	cuarto (4º), cuarta (4ª)
5th	quinto (5º), quinta (5ª)
6th	sexto (6º), sexta (6ª)
7th	séptimo (7º), séptima (7ª)
8th	octavo (8º), octava (8ª)
9th	noveno (9º), novena (9ª)
10th	décimo (10º), décima (10ª)
100th	centésimo (100º), centésima (100ª)
101st	centésimo primero (101º), centésima primera (101ª)
1000th	milésimo (1000º), milésima (1000ª)

EJEMPLOS	EXAMPLES
Vive en el quinto (piso).	He lives on the fifth floor.
Llegó tercero.	He came in third.

> *Tip*
>
> Shorten **primero** (meaning *first*) to **primer**, and **tercero** (meaning *third*) to **tercer** before a <u>masculine singular noun</u>.
>
> su <u>primer</u> cumpleaños — his first birthday
> el <u>tercer</u> premio — the third prize

[i] Note that when you are writing these numbers in figures, don't write *1st*, *2nd*, *3rd* as in English. Use 1º, 1ª, 1er, 2º, 2ª and 3º, 3ª, 3er as required by the noun.

la 2ª lección — the 2nd lesson
el 3er premio — the 3rd prize

4 primero, segundo, tercero or uno, dos, tres?

➤ Apart from **primero** (meaning *first*) up to **décimo** (meaning *tenth*), as well as **centésimo** (meaning *one hundredth*) and **milésimo** (meaning *one thousandth*), the ordinal numbers tend not to be used very much in Spanish. Cardinal numbers (ordinary numbers) are used instead.

Carlos <u>tercero</u> — Carlos the third
Alfonso <u>trece</u> — Alfonso the thirteenth

⇨ *For numbers used in dates, see page 211.*

LA HORA | THE TIME

¿Qué hora es? | **What time is it?**

Es la una menos veinte.	It's twenty to one.
Es la una menos cuarto.	It's (a) quarter to one.
Es la una.	It's one o'clock.
Es la una y diez.	It's ten past one.
Es la una y cuarto.	It's (a) quarter past one.
Es la una y media.	It's half past one.
Son las dos menos veinticinco.	It's twenty-five to two.
Son las dos menos cuarto.	It's (a) quarter to two.
Son las dos.	It's two o'clock.
Son las dos y diez.	It's ten past two.
Son las dos y cuarto.	It's (a) quarter past two.
Son las dos y media.	It's half past two.
Son las tres.	It's three o'clock.

> *Tip*
> Use **son las** for all times not involving **una** (meaning *one*).

¿A qué hora? | **At what time?**

a medianoche	at midnight
a mediodía	at midday
a la una (del mediodía)	at one o'clock (in the afternoon)
a las ocho (de la tarde)	at eight o'clock (in the evening)
a las 9:25 *or* a las nueve (y) veinticinco	at nine twenty-five
a las 16:50 *or* a las dieciséis (y) cincuenta	at 16:50 *or* sixteen fifty

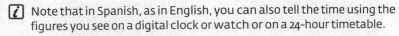 Note that in Spanish, as in English, you can also tell the time using the figures you see on a digital clock or watch or on a 24-hour timetable.

LA FECHA | THE DATE

Los días de la semana | **The days of the week**

lunes	Monday
martes	Tuesday
miércoles	Wednesday
jueves	Thursday
viernes	Friday
sábado	Saturday
domingo	Sunday

¿Cuándo?	When?
el lunes	on Monday
los lunes	on Mondays
todos los lunes	every Monday
el martes pasado	last Tuesday
el viernes que viene	next Friday
el sábado que viene no, el otro	a week on Saturday
dentro de tres sábados	two weeks on Saturday

i Note that days of the week <u>DON'T</u> have a capital letter in Spanish.

Los meses	Months of the year
enero	January
febrero	February
marzo	March
abril	April
mayo	May
junio	June
julio	July
agosto	August
septiembre	September
octubre	October
noviembre	November
diciembre	December

¿Cuándo?	When?
en febrero	in February
el 1 or uno de diciembre	on December 1st or first December
en 1998 (mil novecientos noventa y ocho)	in 1998 (nineteen ninety-eight)
el 15 de diciembre de 2008	on 15th December, 2008
el año dos mil	(the year) two thousand
dos mil cinco	two thousand and five

¿Qué día es hoy?	What day is it today?
Es...	It's...
lunes 26 de febrero	Monday, 26th February
domingo 1 de octubre	Sunday, 1st October
lunes veintiséis de febrero	Monday, the twenty-sixth of February
domingo uno de octubre	Sunday, the first of October

i Note that months of the year are <u>DON'T</u> have a capital letter in Spanish.

For further explanation of grammatical terms, please see pages viii-xii.

> ### Tip
> Although in English we use *first*, *second*, *third* and so on in dates, in Spanish you use the equivalent of *one*, *two*, *three* and so on.
>
> el dos de mayo   the second of May

FRASES ÚTILES / USEFUL PHRASES

¿Cuándo? — **When?**

hoy	today
esta mañana	this morning
esta tarde	this afternoon
esta noche	this evening

¿Con qué frecuencia? — **How often?**

todos los días	every day
cada dos días	every other day
una vez por semana	once a week
dos veces por semana	twice a week
una vez al mes	once a month

¿Cuándo pasó? — **When did it happen?**

por la mañana	in the morning
por la noche	in the evening
ayer	yesterday
ayer por la mañana	yesterday morning
ayer por la tarde	yesterday afternoon/evening
ayer por la noche	yesterday evening/last night
anoche	last night
anteayer	the day before yesterday
hace una semana	a week ago
hace quince días	two weeks ago
la semana pasada	last week
el año pasado	last year

¿Cuándo va a pasar? — **When is it going to happen?**

mañana	tomorrow
mañana por la mañana	tomorrow morning
mañana por la tarde	tomorrow afternoon/evening
mañana por la noche	tomorrow evening/night
pasado mañana	the day after tomorrow
dentro de dos días	in two days' time
dentro de una semana	in a week's time
dentro de quince días	in two weeks' time
el mes que viene	next month
el año que viene	next year

Main Index

Index **215**

Verb Tables

VERB TABLES

Introduction

The **Verb Tables** in the following section contain 120 tables of Spanish verbs (some regular and some irregular) in alphabetical order. Each table shows you the following forms: **Present, Present Perfect, Preterite, Imperfect, Future, Conditional, Present Subjunctive, Imperfect Subjunctive, Imperative** and the **Past Participle** and **Gerund**. For more information on these tenses and how they are formed you should look at the section on Verbs on pages 69–156.

In order to help you use the verbs shown in Verb Tables correctly, there are also a number of example phrases at the bottom of each page to show the verb as it is used in context.

In Spanish there are both **regular** verbs (their forms follow the normal rules) and **irregular** verbs (their forms do not follow the normal rules). The regular verbs in these tables that you can use as models for other regular verbs are:

hablar (regular -ar verb, Verb Table 336–337)
comer (regular -er verb, Verb Table 270–271)
vivir (regular -ir verb, Verb Table 452–453)

The irregular verbs are shown in full.

The **Verb Index** at the end of this section contains over 1200 verbs, each of which is cross-referred to one of the verbs given in the Verb Tables. The table shows the patterns that the verb listed in the index follows.

abolir (to abolish)

	PRESENT		PRESENT PERFECT
(yo)			he abolido
(tú)			has abolido
(él/ella/usted)			ha abolido
(nosotros/as)	abolimos		hemos abolido
(vosotros/as)	abolís		habéis abolido
(ellos/ellas/ ustedes)			han abolido

Present tense only used in persons shown

	PRETERITE	IMPERFECT
(yo)	abolí	abolía
(tú)	aboliste	abolías
(él/ella/usted)	abolió	abolía
(nosotros/as)	abolimos	abolíamos
(vosotros/as)	abolisteis	abolíais
(ellos/ellas/ ustedes)	abolieron	abolían

GERUND

aboliendo

PAST PARTICIPLE

abolido

EXAMPLE PHRASES

Hay que **abolirlo**. It ought to be abolished.

¿Por qué no **abolimos** esta ley? Why don't we abolish this law?

Han abolido la pena de muerte. They have abolished the death penalty.

Abolieron la esclavitud. They abolished slavery.

Remember that subject pronouns are not used very often in Spanish.

abolir

	FUTURE	CONDITIONAL
(yo)	aboliré	aboliría
(tú)	abolirás	abolirías
(él/ella/usted)	abolirá	aboliría
(nosotros/as)	aboliremos	aboliríamos
(vosotros/as)	aboliréis	aboliríais
(ellos/ellas/ ustedes)	abolirán	abolirían

	PRESENT SUBJUNCTIVE	IMPERFECT SUBJUNCTIVE
(yo)	*not used*	aboliera or aboliese
(tú)		abolieras or abolieses
(él/ella/usted)		aboliera or aboliese
(nosotros/as)		aboliéramos or aboliésemos
(vosotros/as)		abolierais or abolieseis
(ellos/ellas/ ustedes)		abolieran or aboliesen

IMPERATIVE

abolid

EXAMPLE PHRASES

Sólo unidos **aboliremos** la injusticia. Only if we are united, will we abolish injustice.

Prometieron que **abolirían** la censura. They promised they'd abolish censorship.

Si lo **abolieran**, se producirían disturbios. There would be riots if it were abolished.

Remember that subject pronouns are not used very often in Spanish.

abrir (to open)

	PRESENT		PRESENT PERFECT
(yo)	abro		he abierto
(tú)	abres		has abierto
(él/ella/usted)	abre		ha abierto
(nosotros/as)	abrimos		hemos abierto
(vosotros/as)	abrís		habéis abierto
(ellos/ellas/ustedes)	abren		han abierto

	PRETERITE		IMPERFECT
(yo)	abrí		abría
(tú)	abriste		abrías
(él/ella/usted)	abrió		abría
(nosotros/as)	abrimos		abríamos
(vosotros/as)	abristeis		abríais
(ellos/ellas/ustedes)	abrieron		abrían

GERUND

abriendo

PAST PARTICIPLE

abierto

EXAMPLE PHRASES

Hoy **se abre** el plazo de matrícula. Registration begins today.

Han abierto un restaurante cerca de aquí. They've opened a new restaurant near here.

¿Quién **abrió** la ventana? Who opened the window?

La llave **abría** el armario. The key opened the cupboard.

Remember that subject pronouns are not used very often in Spanish.

abrir

	FUTURE	CONDITIONAL
(yo)	abriré	abriría
(tú)	abrirás	abrirías
(él/ella/usted)	abrirá	abriría
(nosotros/as)	abriremos	abriríamos
(vosotros/as)	abriréis	abriríais
(ellos/ellas/ ustedes)	abrirán	abrirían

	PRESENT SUBJUNCTIVE	IMPERFECT SUBJUNCTIVE
(yo)	abra	abriera or abriese
(tú)	abras	abrieras or abrieses
(él/ella/usted)	abra	abriera or abriese
(nosotros/as)	abramos	abriéramos or abriésemos
(vosotros/as)	abráis	abrierais or abrieseis
(ellos/ellas/ ustedes)	abran	abrieran or abriesen

IMPERATIVE

abre / abrid

Use the present subjunctive in all cases other than these tú and vosotros affirmative forms.

EXAMPLE PHRASES

Abrirán todas las puertas de la catedral. They'll open all the doors of the cathedral.

Me dijo que hoy **abrirían** sólo por la tarde. He told me that today they'd be open only in the evening.

No creo que **abran** un nuevo supermercado por aquí. I don't think they'll open a new supermarket here.

No **abras** ese grifo. Don't turn on that tap.

Remember that subject pronouns are not used very often in Spanish.

actuar (to act)

	PRESENT		PRESENT PERFECT
(yo)	actúo		he actuado
(tú)	actúas		has actuado
(él/ella/usted)	actúa		ha actuado
(nosotros/as)	actuamos		hemos actuado
(vosotros/as)	actuáis		habéis actuado
(ellos/ellas/ ustedes)	actúan		han actuado

	PRETERITE		IMPERFECT
(yo)	actué		actuaba
(tú)	actuaste		actuabas
(él/ella/usted)	actuó		actuaba
(nosotros/as)	actuamos		actuábamos
(vosotros/as)	actuasteis		actuabais
(ellos/ellas/ ustedes)	actuaron		actuaban

GERUND	PAST PARTICIPLE
actuando	actuado

EXAMPLE PHRASES

Actúa de una forma muy rara. He's acting very strangely.

Ha actuado siguiendo un impulso. He acted on impulse.

Actuó en varias películas. He was in several films.

Actuaba como si no supiera nada. She was behaving as if she didn't know anything about it.

Remember that subject pronouns are not used very often in Spanish.

actuar

	FUTURE	CONDITIONAL
(yo)	actuaré	actuaría
(tú)	actuarás	actuarías
(él/ella/usted)	actuará	actuaría
(nosotros/as)	actuaremos	actuaríamos
(vosotros/as)	actuaréis	actuaríais
(ellos/ellas/ ustedes)	actuarán	actuarían

	PRESENT SUBJUNCTIVE	IMPERFECT SUBJUNCTIVE
(yo)	actúe	actuara or actuase
(tú)	actúes	actuaras or actuases
(él/ella/usted)	actúe	actuara or actuase
(nosotros/as)	actuemos	actuáramos or actuásemos
(vosotros/as)	actuéis	actuarais or actuaseis
(ellos/ellas/ ustedes)	actúen	actuaran or actuasen

IMPERATIVE

actúa / actuad

Use the present subjunctive in all cases other than these tú and vosotros affirmative forms.

EXAMPLE PHRASES

¿Quién **actuará** en su próxima película? Who will be in his next film?

Yo nunca **actuaría** así. I'd never behave like that.

Si **actuara** de forma más lógica, sería más fácil atraparle. It would be easier to catch him if he behaved in a more logical way.

Actuad como mejor os parezca. Do as you think best.

Remember that subject pronouns are not used very often in Spanish.

adquirir (to acquire)

	PRESENT		PRESENT PERFECT
(yo)	adquiero		he adquirido
(tú)	adquieres		has adquirido
(él/ella/usted)	adquiere		ha adquirido
(nosotros/as)	adquirimos		hemos adquirido
(vosotros/as)	adquirís		habéis adquirido
(ellos/ellas/ ustedes)	adquieren		han adquirido

	PRETERITE		IMPERFECT
(yo)	adquirí		adquiría
(tú)	adquiriste		adquirías
(él/ella/usted)	adquirió		adquiría
(nosotros/as)	adquirimos		adquiríamos
(vosotros/as)	adquiristeis		adquiríais
(ellos/ellas/ ustedes)	adquirieron		adquirían

GERUND

adquiriendo

PAST PARTICIPLE

adquirido

EXAMPLE PHRASES

Adquiere cada vez mayor importancia. It's becoming more and more important.

Está adquiriendo una reputación que no merece. It's getting a reputation it doesn't deserve.

Hemos adquirido una colección de sellos. We've bought a stamp collection.

Con el tiempo **adquirió** cierta madurez. Over the years he gained a certain maturity.

Remember that subject pronouns are not used very often in Spanish.

adquirir

	FUTURE	CONDITIONAL
(yo)	adquiriré	adquiriría
(tú)	adquirirás	adquirirías
(él/ella/usted)	adquirirá	adquiriría
(nosotros/as)	adquiriremos	adquiriríamos
(vosotros/as)	adquiriréis	adquiriríais
(ellos/ellas/ ustedes)	adquirirán	adquirirían

	PRESENT SUBJUNCTIVE	IMPERFECT SUBJUNCTIVE
(yo)	adquiera	adquiriera or adquiriese
(tú)	adquieras	adquirieras or adquirieses
(él/ella/usted)	adquiera	adquiriera or adquiriese
(nosotros/as)	adquiramos	adquiriéramos or adquiriésemos
(vosotros/as)	adquiráis	adquirierais or adquirieseis
(ellos/ellas/ ustedes)	adquieran	adquirieran or adquiriesen

IMPERATIVE
adquiere / adquirid

Use the present subjunctive in all cases other than these tú and vosotros affirmative forms.

EXAMPLE PHRASES

Al final **adquirirán** los derechos de publicación. They will get the publishing rights in the end.

¿Lo **adquirirías** por ese precio? Would you buy it for that price?

Adquiera o no la nacionalidad, podrá permanecer en el país. She'll be able to stay in the country whether she becomes naturalized or not.

Tenía gran interés en que **adquiriera** el cuadro. He was very keen that she should buy the picture.

Remember that subject pronouns are not used very often in Spanish.

advertir (to warn, to notice)

	PRESENT		PRESENT PERFECT
(yo)	advierto		he advertido
(tú)	adviertes		has advertido
(él/ella/usted)	advierte		ha advertido
(nosotros/as)	advertimos		hemos advertido
(vosotros/as)	advertís		habéis advertido
(ellos/ellas/ustedes)	advierten		han advertido

	PRETERITE		IMPERFECT
(yo)	advertí		advertía
(tú)	advertiste		advertías
(él/ella/usted)	advirtió		advertía
(nosotros/as)	advertimos		advertíamos
(vosotros/as)	advertisteis		advertíais
(ellos/ellas/ustedes)	advirtieron		advertían

GERUND

advirtiendo

PAST PARTICIPLE

advertido

EXAMPLE PHRASES

Te **advierto** que no va a ser nada fácil. **I must warn you that it won't be at all easy.**

No **he advertido** nada extraño en su comportamiento. **I haven't noticed anything strange about his behaviour.**

Ya te **advertí** que no intervinieras. **I warned you not to get involved.**

Las señales **advertían** del peligro. **The signs warned of danger.**

Remember that subject pronouns are not used very often in Spanish.

advertir

	FUTURE	CONDITIONAL
(yo)	advertiré	advertiría
(tú)	advertirás	advertirías
(él/ella/usted)	advertirá	advertiría
(nosotros/as)	advertiremos	advertiríamos
(vosotros/as)	advertiréis	advertiríais
(ellos/ellas/ustedes)	advertirán	advertirían

	PRESENT SUBJUNCTIVE	IMPERFECT SUBJUNCTIVE
(yo)	advierta	advirtiera or advirtiese
(tú)	adviertas	advirtieras or advirtieses
(él/ella/usted)	advierta	advirtiera or advirtiese
(nosotros/as)	advirtamos	advirtiéramos or advirtiésemos
(vosotros/as)	advirtáis	advirtierais or advirtieseis
(ellos/ellas/ustedes)	adviertan	advirtieran or advirtiesen

IMPERATIVE

advierte / advertid

Use the present subjunctive in all cases other than these tú and vosotros affirmative forms.

EXAMPLE PHRASES

Si **advirtiera** algún cambio, llámenos. If you should notice any change, give us a call.

Adviértele del riesgo que entraña. Warn him about the risk involved.

Remember that subject pronouns are not used very often in Spanish.

almorzar (to have lunch)

	PRESENT		PRESENT PERFECT
(yo)	almuerzo		he almorzado
(tú)	almuerzas		has almorzado
(él/ella/usted)	almuerza		ha almorzado
(nosotros/as)	almorzamos		hemos almorzado
(vosotros/as)	almorzáis		habéis almorzado
(ellos/ellas/ ustedes)	almuerzan		han almorzado

	PRETERITE		IMPERFECT
(yo)	almorcé		almorzaba
(tú)	almorzaste		almorzabas
(él/ella/usted)	almorzó		almorzaba
(nosotros/as)	almorzamos		almorzábamos
(vosotros/as)	almorzasteis		almorzabais
(ellos/ellas/ ustedes)	almorzaron		almorzaban

GERUND

almorzando

PAST PARTICIPLE

almorzado

EXAMPLE PHRASES

¿Dónde vais a **almorzar**? Where are you going to have lunch?

¿A qué hora **almuerzas**? What time do you have lunch?

Ya **hemos almorzado**. We've already had lunch.

Almorcé en un bar. I had lunch in a bar.

Siempre **almorzaba** un bocadillo. He always had a sandwich for lunch.

Remember that subject pronouns are not used very often in Spanish.

almorzar

	FUTURE	CONDITIONAL
(yo)	almorzaré	almorzaría
(tú)	almorzarás	almorzarías
(él/ella/usted)	almorzará	almorzaría
(nosotros/as)	almorzaremos	almorzaríamos
(vosotros/as)	almorzaréis	almorzaríais
(ellos/ellas/ ustedes)	almorzarán	almorzarían

	PRESENT SUBJUNCTIVE	IMPERFECT SUBJUNCTIVE
(yo)	almuerce	almorzara or almorzase
(tú)	almuerces	almorzaras or almorzases
(él/ella/usted)	almuerce	almorzara or almorzase
(nosotros/as)	almorcemos	almorzáramos or almorzásemos
(vosotros/as)	almorcéis	almorzarais or almorzaseis
(ellos/ellas/ ustedes)	almuercen	almorzaran or almorzasen

IMPERATIVE

almuerza / almorzad

Use the present subjunctive in all cases other than these tú and vosotros affirmative forms.

EXAMPLE PHRASES

Mañana **almorzaremos** todos juntos. We'll all have lunch together tomorrow.

Almuerce o no siempre me entra sueño a esta hora. I always feel sleepy at this time of the day, regardless of whether I've had lunch or not.

Si **almorzara** así todos los días, estaría mucho más gordo. I'd be much fatter if I had this sort of lunch every day.

Remember that subject pronouns are not used very often in Spanish.

amanecer (to get light, to wake up)

	PRESENT		PRESENT PERFECT
(yo)	amanezco		he amanecido
(tú)	amaneces		has amanecido
(él/ella/usted)	amanece		ha amanecido
(nosotros/as)	amanecemos		hemos amanecido
(vosotros/as)	amanecéis		habéis amanecido
(ellos/ellas/ ustedes)	amanecen		han amanecido

	PRETERITE		IMPERFECT
(yo)	amanecí		amanecía
(tú)	amaneciste		amanecías
(él/ella/usted)	amaneció		amanecía
(nosotros/as)	amanecimos		amanecíamos
(vosotros/as)	amanecisteis		amanecíais
(ellos/ellas/ ustedes)	amanecieron		amanecían

GERUND

amaneciendo

PAST PARTICIPLE

amanecido

EXAMPLE PHRASES

Siempre **amanece** nublado. The day always starts off cloudy.

Justo en ese momento **estaba amaneciendo**. Just then dawn was breaking.

Hoy **ha amanecido** a las ocho. Today it got light at eight o'clock.

La ciudad **amaneció** desierta. In the morning the town was deserted.

Amanecía de un humor de perros. She would wake up in a really bad mood.

Remember that subject pronouns are not used very often in Spanish.

amanecer

	FUTURE	CONDITIONAL
(yo)	amaneceré	amanecería
(tú)	amanecerás	amanecerías
(él/ella/usted)	amanecerá	amanecería
(nosotros/as)	amaneceremos	amaneceríamos
(vosotros/as)	amaneceréis	amaneceríais
(ellos/ellas/ ustedes)	amanecerán	amanecerían

	PRESENT SUBJUNCTIVE	IMPERFECT SUBJUNCTIVE
(yo)	amanezca	amaneciera or amaneciese
(tú)	amanezcas	amanecieras or amanecieses
(él/ella/usted)	amanezca	amaneciera or amaneciese
(nosotros/as)	amanezcamos	amaneciéramos or amaneciésemos
(vosotros/as)	amanezcáis	amanecierais or amanecieseis
(ellos/ellas/ ustedes)	amanezcan	amanecieran or amaneciesen

IMPERATIVE
amanece / amaneced

Use the present subjunctive in all cases other than these tú and vosotros affirmative forms.

EXAMPLE PHRASES
Pronto **amanecerá**. It will soon be daylight.

Saldremos en cuanto **amanezca**. We'll set off as soon as it gets light.

Si **amanecieras** con fiebre, toma una de estas pastillas. If you should wake up with a temperature, take one of these pills.

Remember that subject pronouns are not used very often in Spanish.

andar (to walk)

	PRESENT		PRESENT PERFECT
(yo)	ando		he andado
(tú)	andas		has andado
(él/ella/usted)	anda		ha andado
(nosotros/as)	andamos		hemos andado
(vosotros/as)	andáis		habéis andado
(ellos/ellas/ustedes)	andan		han andado

	PRETERITE		IMPERFECT
(yo)	anduve		andaba
(tú)	anduviste		andabas
(él/ella/usted)	anduvo		andaba
(nosotros/as)	anduvimos		andábamos
(vosotros/as)	anduvisteis		andabais
(ellos/ellas/ustedes)	anduvieron		andaban

GERUND

andando

PAST PARTICIPLE

andado

EXAMPLE PHRASES

Andar es un ejercicio muy sano. Walking is very good exercise.

Hemos andado todo el camino hasta aquí. We walked all the way here.

Anduvimos al menos 10 km. We walked at least 10 km.

Por aquel entonces **andaban** mal de dinero. Back then they were short of money.

Voy **andando** al trabajo todos los días. I walk to work every day.

Remember that subject pronouns are not used very often in Spanish.

andar

	FUTURE	CONDITIONAL
(yo)	andaré	andaría
(tú)	andarás	andarías
(él/ella/usted)	andará	andaría
(nosotros/as)	andaremos	andaríamos
(vosotros/as)	andaréis	andaríais
(ellos/ellas/ ustedes)	andarán	andarían

	PRESENT SUBJUNCTIVE	IMPERFECT SUBJUNCTIVE
(yo)	ande	anduviera or anduviese
(tú)	andes	anduvieras or anduvieses
(él/ella/usted)	ande	anduviera or anduviese
(nosotros/as)	andemos	anduviéramos or anduviésemos
(vosotros/as)	andéis	anduvierais or anduvieseis
(ellos/ellas/ ustedes)	anden	anduvieran or anduviesen

IMPERATIVE

anda / andad

Use the present subjunctive in all cases other than these tú and vosotros affirmative forms.

EXAMPLE PHRASES

Andará por los cuarenta. He must be about forty.

Yo **me andaría** con pies de plomo. I'd tread very carefully.

El médico le ha aconsejado que **ande** varios kilómetros al día. The doctor has advised him to walk several kilometres a day.

Si **anduvieras** con más cuidado, no te pasarían esas cosas. If you were more careful, this sort of thing wouldn't happen to you.

Remember that subject pronouns are not used very often in Spanish.

apoderarse (to take possession)

	PRESENT	PRESENT PERFECT
(yo)	me apodero	me he apoderado
(tú)	te apoderas	te has apoderado
(él/ella/usted)	se apodera	se ha apoderado
(nosotros/as)	nos apoderamos	nos hemos apoderado
(vosotros/as)	os apoderáis	os habéis apoderado
(ellos/ellas/ ustedes)	se apoderan	se han apoderado

	PRETERITE	IMPERFECT
(yo)	me apoderé	me apoderaba
(tú)	te apoderaste	te apoderabas
(él/ella/usted)	se apoderó	se apoderaba
(nosotros/as)	nos apoderamos	nos apoderábamos
(vosotros/as)	os apoderasteis	os apoderabais
(ellos/ellas/ ustedes)	se apoderaron	se apoderaban

GERUND	PAST PARTICIPLE
apoderando	apoderado

EXAMPLE PHRASES

En esas situaciones, el miedo **se apodera** de mí. In situations like that,
I find myself gripped by fear.

Poco a poco **se han ido apoderando** de las riquezas del país. Little by little,
they've taken possession of the country's riches.

Se apoderaron de las joyas y huyeron. They ran off with the jewels.

El desánimo **se apoderaba** de nosotros por momentos. We were feeling more
and more discouraged by the minute.

Remember that subject pronouns are not used very often in Spanish.

apoderarse

	FUTURE	CONDITIONAL
(yo)	me apoderaré	me apoderaría
(tú)	te apoderarás	te apoderarías
(él/ella/usted)	se apoderará	se apoderaría
(nosotros/as)	nos apoderaremos	nos apoderaríamos
(vosotros/as)	os apoderaréis	os apoderaríais
(ellos/ellas/ustedes)	se apoderarán	se apoderarían

	PRESENT SUBJUNCTIVE	IMPERFECT SUBJUNCTIVE
(yo)	me apodere	me apoderara or apoderase
(tú)	te apoderes	te apoderaras or apoderases
(él/ella/usted)	se apodere	se apoderara or apoderase
(nosotros/as)	nos apoderemos	nos apoderáramos or apoderásemos
(vosotros/as)	os apoderéis	os apoderarais or apoderaseis
(ellos/ellas/ustedes)	se apoderen	se apoderaran or apoderasen

IMPERATIVE

apodérate / apoderaos

Use the present subjunctive in all cases other than these tú and vosotros affirmative forms.

EXAMPLE PHRASES

No dejes que la curiosidad **se apodere** de ti. Don't let curiosity get the better of you.

aprobar (to pass, to approve of)

	PRESENT	PRESENT PERFECT
(yo)	apruebo	he aprobado
(tú)	apruebas	has aprobado
(él/ella/usted)	aprueba	ha aprobado
(nosotros/as)	aprobamos	hemos aprobado
(vosotros/as)	aprobáis	habéis aprobado
(ellos/ellas/ ustedes)	aprueban	han aprobado

	PRETERITE	IMPERFECT
(yo)	aprobé	aprobaba
(tú)	aprobaste	aprobabas
(él/ella/usted)	aprobó	aprobaba
(nosotros/as)	aprobamos	aprobábamos
(vosotros/as)	aprobasteis	aprobabais
(ellos/ellas/ ustedes)	aprobaron	aprobaban

GERUND

aprobando

PAST PARTICIPLE

aprobado

EXAMPLE PHRASES

No **apruebo** esa conducta. I don't approve of that sort of behaviour.

Este año lo **estoy aprobando** todo. So far this year I've passed everything.

Han aprobado una ley antitabaco. They've passed an anti-smoking law.

¿**Aprobaste** el examen? Did you pass the exam?

La decisión **fue aprobada** por mayoría. The decision was approved by a majority.

Remember that subject pronouns are not used very often in Spanish.

aprobar

	FUTURE	CONDITIONAL
(yo)	aprobaré	aprobaría
(tú)	aprobarás	aprobarías
(él/ella/usted)	aprobará	aprobaría
(nosotros/as)	aprobaremos	aprobaríamos
(vosotros/as)	aprobaréis	aprobaríais
(ellos/ellas/ustedes)	aprobarán	aprobarían

	PRESENT SUBJUNCTIVE	IMPERFECT SUBJUNCTIVE
(yo)	apruebe	aprobara or aprobase
(tú)	apruebes	aprobaras or aprobases
(él/ella/usted)	apruebe	aprobara or aprobase
(nosotros/as)	aprobemos	aprobáramos or aprobásemos
(vosotros/as)	aprobéis	aprobarais or aprobaseis
(ellos/ellas/ustedes)	aprueben	aprobaran or aprobasen

IMPERATIVE

aprueba / aprobad

Use the present subjunctive in all cases other than these tú and vosotros affirmative forms.

arrancar (to pull up)

	PRESENT	PRESENT PERFECT
(yo)	arranco	he arrancado
(tú)	arrancas	has arrancado
(él/ella/usted)	arranca	ha arrancado
(nosotros/as)	arrancamos	hemos arrancado
(vosotros/as)	arrancáis	habéis arrancado
(ellos/ellas/ ustedes)	arrancan	han arrancado

	PRETERITE	IMPERFECT
(yo)	arranqué	arrancaba
(tú)	arrancaste	arrancabas
(él/ella/usted)	arrancó	arrancaba
(nosotros/as)	arrancamos	arrancábamos
(vosotros/as)	arrancasteis	arrancabais
(ellos/ellas/ ustedes)	arrancaron	arrancaban

GERUND	PAST PARTICIPLE
arrancando	arrancado

EXAMPLE PHRASES

Lo tienes que **arrancar** de raíz. You must pull it up by its roots.

Estaba **arrancando** malas hierbas. I was pulling up weeds.

Me has **arrancado** un botón. You've pulled off one of my buttons.

El viento **arrancó** varios árboles. Several trees were uprooted in the wind.

Remember that subject pronouns are not used very often in Spanish.

arrancar

	FUTURE	CONDITIONAL
(yo)	arrancaré	arrancaría
(tú)	arrancarás	arrancarías
(él/ella/usted)	arrancará	arrancaría
(nosotros/as)	arrancaremos	arrancaríamos
(vosotros/as)	arrancaréis	arrancaríais
(ellos/ellas/ ustedes)	arrancarán	arrancarían

	PRESENT SUBJUNCTIVE	IMPERFECT SUBJUNCTIVE
(yo)	arranque	arrancara *or* arrancase
(tú)	arranques	arrancaras *or* arrancases
(él/ella/usted)	arranque	arrancara *or* arrancase
(nosotros/as)	arranquemos	arrancáramos *or* arrancásemos
(vosotros/as)	arranquéis	arrancarais *or* arrancaseis
(ellos/ellas/ ustedes)	arranquen	arrancaran *or* arrancasen

IMPERATIVE

arranca / arrancad

Use the present subjunctive in all cases other than these tú *and* vosotros *affirmative forms.*

EXAMPLE PHRASES

No **arranques** hojas del cuaderno. **Don't go tearing pages out of the exercise book.**

Arranca y vámonos. **Start the engine and let's get going.**

Remember that subject pronouns are not used very often in Spanish.

arrepentirse (to be sorry)

	PRESENT		PRESENT PERFECT
(yo)	me arrepiento		me he arrepentido
(tú)	te arrepientes		te has arrepentido
(él/ella/usted)	se arrepiente		se ha arrepentido
(nosotros/as)	nos arrepentimos		nos hemos arrepentido
(vosotros/as)	os arrepentís		os habéis arrepentido
(ellos/ellas/ ustedes)	se arrepienten		se han arrepentido

	PRETERITE		IMPERFECT
(yo)	me arrepentí		me arrepentía
(tú)	te arrepentiste		te arrepentías
(él/ella/usted)	se arrepintió		se arrepentía
(nosotros/as)	nos arrepentimos		nos arrepentíamos
(vosotros/as)	os arrepentisteis		os arrepentíais
(ellos/ellas/ ustedes)	se arrepintieron		se arrepentían

GERUND

arrepintiéndose, etc

PAST PARTICIPLE

arrepentido

EXAMPLE PHRASES

¡Te vas a **arrepentir** de esto! You'll be sorry you did that!

No **me arrepiento** de nada. I don't regret anything.

¿Nunca **te has arrepentido** de haberte ido de casa? Haven't you ever regretted leaving home?

Se arrepintieron y decidieron no vender la casa. They changed their minds and decided not to sell the house.

Remember that subject pronouns are not used very often in Spanish.

arrepentirse

	FUTURE	CONDITIONAL
(yo)	me arrepentiré	me arrepentiría
(tú)	te arrepentirás	te arrepentirías
(él/ella/usted)	se arrepentirá	se arrepentiría
(nosotros/as)	nos arrepentiremos	nos arrepentiríamos
(vosotros/as)	os arrepentiréis	os arrepentiríais
(ellos/ellas/ ustedes)	se arrepentirán	se arrepentirían

	PRESENT SUBJUNCTIVE	IMPERFECT SUBJUNCTIVE
(yo)	me arrepienta	me arrepintiera or arrepintiese
(tú)	te arrepientas	te arrepintieras or arrepintieses
(él/ella/usted)	se arrepienta	se arrepintiera or arrepintiese
(nosotros/as)	nos arrepintamos	nos arrepintiéramos or arrepintiésemos
(vosotros/as)	os arrepintáis	os arrepintierais or arrepintieseis
(ellos/ellas/ ustedes)	se arrepientan	se arrepintieran or arrepintiesen

IMPERATIVE

arrepiéntete / arrepentíos

Use the present subjunctive in all cases other than these tú and vosotros affirmative forms.

EXAMPLE PHRASES

Algún día **se arrepentirá** de no haber estudiado una carrera. One day he'll be sorry he didn't go to university.

No **te arrepientas** nunca de haber dicho la verdad. Don't ever regret having told the truth.

Remember that subject pronouns are not used very often in Spanish.

atravesar (to cross, to go through)

	PRESENT		PRESENT PERFECT
(yo)	atravieso		he atravesado
(tú)	atraviesas		has atravesado
(él/ella/usted)	atraviesa		ha atravesado
(nosotros/as)	atravesamos		hemos atravesado
(vosotros/as)	atravesáis		habéis atravesado
(ellos/ellas/ustedes)	atraviesan		han atravesado

	PRETERITE		IMPERFECT
(yo)	atravesé		atravesaba
(tú)	atravesaste		atravesabas
(él/ella/usted)	atravesó		atravesaba
(nosotros/as)	atravesamos		atravesábamos
(vosotros/as)	atravesasteis		atravesabais
(ellos/ellas/ustedes)	atravesaron		atravesaban

GERUND

atravesando

PAST PARTICIPLE

atravesado

EXAMPLE PHRASES

Atravesamos un mal momento. **We're going through a bad patch.**

En este momento **está atravesando** la ciudad en un coche descubierto. **Right know he's being driven through the city in an open-topped vehicle.**

Hemos atravesado el río a nado. **We swam across the river.**

La bala le **atravesó** el cráneo. **The bullet went through his skull.**

Un camión **se** nos **atravesó** en la carretera. **A lorry came out into the road in front of us.**

Remember that subject pronouns are not used very often in Spanish.

atravesar

	FUTURE	CONDITIONAL
(yo)	atravesaré	atravesaría
(tú)	atravesarás	atravesarías
(él/ella/usted)	atravesará	atravesaría
(nosotros/as)	atravesaremos	atravesaríamos
(vosotros/as)	atravesaréis	atravesaríais
(ellos/ellas/ ustedes)	atravesarán	atravesarían

	PRESENT SUBJUNCTIVE	IMPERFECT SUBJUNCTIVE
(yo)	atraviese	atravesara or atravesase
(tú)	atravieses	atravesaras or atravesases
(él/ella/usted)	atraviese	atravesara or atravesase
(nosotros/as)	atravesemos	atravesáramos or atravesásemos
(vosotros/as)	atraveséis	atravesarais or atravesaseis
(ellos/ellas/ ustedes)	atraviesen	atravesaran or atravesasen

IMPERATIVE

atraviesa / atravesad

Use the present subjunctive in all cases other than these tú and vosotros affirmative forms.

EXAMPLE PHRASES

El túnel **atravesará** la montaña. The tunnel will go under the mountain.

aunar (to join together)

	PRESENT		PRESENT PERFECT
(yo)	aúno		he aunado
(tú)	aúnas		has aunado
(él/ella/usted)	aúna		ha aunado
(nosotros/as)	aunamos		hemos aunado
(vosotros/as)	aunáis		habéis aunado
(ellos/ellas/ustedes)	aúnan		han aunado

	PRETERITE		IMPERFECT
(yo)	auné		aunaba
(tú)	aunaste		aunabas
(él/ella/usted)	aunó		aunaba
(nosotros/as)	aunamos		aunábamos
(vosotros/as)	aunasteis		aunabais
(ellos/ellas/ustedes)	aunaron		aunaban

GERUND
aunando

PAST PARTICIPLE
aunado

EXAMPLE PHRASES

En esta obra **se han aunado** imaginación y técnica. This play combines imagination and technique.

Aunaron esfuerzos. They joined forces.

La pintura barroca **aunaba** conocimientos de geometría y anatomía. Baroque painting brought knowledge of geometry and anatomy together.

Remember that subject pronouns are not used very often in Spanish.

aunar

	FUTURE	CONDITIONAL
(yo)	aunaré	aunaría
(tú)	aunarás	aunarías
(él/ella/usted)	aunará	aunaría
(nosotros/as)	aunaremos	aunaríamos
(vosotros/as)	aunaréis	aunaríais
(ellos/ellas/ ustedes)	aunarán	aunarían

	PRESENT SUBJUNCTIVE	IMPERFECT SUBJUNCTIVE
(yo)	aúne	aunara or aunase
(tú)	aúnes	aunaras or aunases
(él/ella/usted)	aúne	aunara or aunase
(nosotros/as)	aunemos	aunáramos or aunásemos
(vosotros/as)	aunéis	aunarais or aunaseis
(ellos/ellas/ ustedes)	aúnen	aunaran or aunasen

IMPERATIVE

aúna / aunad

Use the present subjunctive in all cases other than these tú *and* vosotros *affirmative forms.*

Remember that subject pronouns are not used very often in Spanish.

avergonzar (to shame)

	PRESENT		PRESENT PERFECT
(yo)	avergüenzo		he avergonzado
(tú)	avergüenzas		has avergonzado
(él/ella/usted)	avergüenza		ha avergonzado
(nosotros/as)	avergonzamos		hemos avergonzado
(vosotros/as)	avergonzáis		habéis avergonzado
(ellos/ellas/ ustedes)	avergüenzan		han avergonzado

	PRETERITE		IMPERFECT
(yo)	avergoncé		avergonzaba
(tú)	avergonzaste		avergonzabas
(él/ella/usted)	avergonzó		avergonzaba
(nosotros/as)	avergonzamos		avergonzábamos
(vosotros/as)	avergonzasteis		avergonzabais
(ellos/ellas/ ustedes)	avergonzaron		avergonzaban

GERUND	PAST PARTICIPLE
avergonzando	avergonzado

EXAMPLE PHRASES

Tendrías que **avergonzarte**. You should be ashamed of yourself.

Le **avergüenza** no tener dinero. He's ashamed of having no money.

Cuando me lo dijo **me avergoncé**. I was embarrassed when he told me.

Se avergonzaba de su familia. He was ashamed of his family.

Avergonzándote no arreglas nada. Being ashamed doesn't solve anything.

Remember that subject pronouns are not used very often in Spanish.

avergonzar

	FUTURE	CONDITIONAL
(yo)	avergonzaré	avergonzaría
(tú)	avergonzarás	avergonzarías
(él/ella/usted)	avergonzará	avergonzaría
(nosotros/as)	avergonzaremos	avergonzaríamos
(vosotros/as)	avegónzaréis	avergonzaríais
(ellos/ellas/ ustedes)	avergonzarán	avergonzarían

	PRESENT SUBJUNCTIVE	IMPERFECT SUBJUNCTIVE
(yo)	avergüence	avergonzara or avergonzase
(tú)	avergüences	avergonzaras or avergonzases
(él/ella/usted)	avergüence	avergonzara or avergonzase
(nosotros/as)	avergoncemos	avergonzáramos or avergonzásemos
(vosotros/as)	avergoncéis	avergonzarais or avergonzaseis
(ellos/ellas/ ustedes)	avergüencen	avergonzaran or avergonzasen

IMPERATIVE
avergüenza / avergonzad

Use the present subjunctive in all cases other than these tú and vosotros affirmative forms.

EXAMPLE PHRASES

Si hubiera sabido que **te avergonzarías** tanto, no te lo habría dicho.
I wouldn't have told you if I'd known you'd be so embarrassed.

Si de verdad **se avergonzaran**, no se comportarían así. They wouldn't behave
like that if they were really ashamed.

Remember that subject pronouns are not used very often in Spanish.

averiguar (to find out)

	PRESENT		PRESENT PERFECT
(yo)	averiguo		he averiguado
(tú)	averiguas		has averiguado
(él/ella/usted)	averigua		ha averiguado
(nosotros/as)	averiguamos		hemos averiguado
(vosotros/as)	averiguáis		habéis averiguado
(ellos/ellas/ ustedes)	averiguan		han averiguado

	PRETERITE	IMPERFECT
(yo)	averigüé	averiguaba
(tú)	averiguaste	averiguabas
(él/ella/usted)	averiguó	averiguaba
(nosotros/as)	averiguamos	averiguábamos
(vosotros/as)	averiguasteis	averiguabais
(ellos/ellas/ ustedes)	averiguaron	averiguaban

GERUND

averiguando

PAST PARTICIPLE

averiguado

EXAMPLE PHRASES

Trataron de **averiguar** su paradero. They tried to find out his whereabouts.

Poco a poco van **averiguando** más cosas sobre su vida. They're gradually finding out more about his life.

¿Cómo **has averiguado** dónde vivo? How did you find out where I lived?

¿Cuándo lo **averiguaron**? When did they find out?

Remember that subject pronouns are not used very often in Spanish.

averiguar

	FUTURE	CONDITIONAL
(yo)	averiguaré	averiguaría
(tú)	averiguarás	averiguarías
(él/ella/usted)	averiguará	averiguaría
(nosotros/as)	averiguaremos	averiguaríamos
(vosotros/as)	averiguaréis	averiguaríais
(ellos/ellas/ ustedes)	averiguarán	averiguarían

	PRESENT SUBJUNCTIVE	IMPERFECT SUBJUNCTIVE
(yo)	averigüe	averiguara or averiguase
(tú)	averigües	averiguaras or averiguases
(él/ella/usted)	averigüe	averiguara or averiguase
(nosotros/as)	averigüemos	averiguáramos or averiguásemos
(vosotros/as)	averigüéis	averiguarais or averiguaseis
(ellos/ellas/ ustedes)	averigüen	averiguaran or averiguasen

IMPERATIVE

averigua / averiguad

Use the present subjunctive in all cases other than these tú and vosotros affirmative forms.

EXAMPLE PHRASES

Lo **averiguaré** pronto. I'll find out soon.

Dijo que si le dábamos tiempo lo **averiguaría**. She said that she'd find out if we gave her time.

En cuanto lo **averigüe** te lo digo. I'll tell you as soon as I find out.

¡**Averígualo** inmediatamente! Check it out immediately!

Remember that subject pronouns are not used very often in Spanish.

bendecir (to bless)

	PRESENT		PRESENT PERFECT
(yo)	bendigo		he bendecido
(tú)	bendices		has bendecido
(él/ella/usted)	bendice		ha bendecido
(nosotros/as)	bendecimos		hemos bendecido
(vosotros/as)	bendecís		habéis bendecido
(ellos/ellas/ ustedes)	bendicen		han bendecido

	PRETERITE		IMPERFECT
(yo)	bendije		bendecía
(tú)	bendijiste		bendecías
(él/ella/usted)	bendijo		bendecía
(nosotros/as)	bendijimos		bendecíamos
(vosotros/as)	bendijisteis		bendecíais
(ellos/ellas/ ustedes)	bendijeron		bendecían

GERUND

bendiciendo

PAST PARTICIPLE

bendecido

EXAMPLE PHRASES

Su padre **bendice** siempre la mesa. His father always says grace.

La vida me **ha bendecido** con unos hijos maravillosos. I've been blessed with wonderful children.

Jesús **bendijo** los panes y los peces. Jesus blessed the fish and the bread.

Bendecía el día en que lo conoció. She blessed the day she met him.

Remember that subject pronouns are not used very often in Spanish.

bendecir

	FUTURE	CONDITIONAL
(yo)	bendeciré	bendeciría
(tú)	bendecirás	bendecirías
(él/ella/usted)	bendecirá	bendeciría
(nosotros/as)	bendeciremos	bendeciríamos
(vosotros/as)	bendeciréis	bendeciríais
(ellos/ellas/ ustedes)	bendecirán	bendecirían

	PRESENT SUBJUNCTIVE	IMPERFECT SUBJUNCTIVE
(yo)	bendiga	bendijera or bendijese
(tú)	bendigas	bendijeras or bendijeses
(él/ella/usted)	bendiga	bendijera or bendijese
(nosotros/as)	bendigamos	bendijéramos or bendijésemos
(vosotros/as)	bendigáis	bendijerais or bendijeseis
(ellos/ellas/ ustedes)	bendigan	bendijeran or bendijesen

IMPERATIVE
bendice / bendecid

Use the present subjunctive in all cases other than these tú and vosotros affirmative forms.

EXAMPLE PHRASES

El Papa **bendecirá** a los fieles desde el balcón. The Pope will bless the faithful from the balcony.

Quieren que sea él quien **bendiga** su unión. They want him to marry them.

Pidieron a un sacerdote que **bendijera** su nueva casa. They asked a priest to bless their new house.

Remember that subject pronouns are not used very often in Spanish.

caber (to fit)

	PRESENT		PRESENT PERFECT
(yo)	quepo		he cabido
(tú)	cabes		has cabido
(él/ella/usted)	cabe		ha cabido
(nosotros/as)	cabemos		hemos cabido
(vosotros/as)	cabéis		habéis cabido
(ellos/ellas/ ustedes)	caben		han cabido

	PRETERITE		IMPERFECT
(yo)	cupe		cabía
(tú)	cupiste		cabías
(él/ella/usted)	cupo		cabía
(nosotros/as)	cupimos		cabíamos
(vosotros/as)	cupisteis		cabíais
(ellos/ellas/ ustedes)	cupieron		cabían

GERUND

cabiendo

PAST PARTICIPLE

cabido

EXAMPLE PHRASES

No te preocupes, que va a **caber**. Don't worry, it will fit.
Aquí no **cabe**. There isn't enough room for it here.
Al final **ha cabido** todo. In the end everything went in.
No le **cupo** la menor duda. She wasn't in any doubt.
No **cabía** en sí de gozo. She was beside herself with joy.

Remember that subject pronouns are not used very often in Spanish.

caber

	FUTURE	CONDITIONAL
(yo)	cabré	cabría
(tú)	cabrás	cabrías
(él/ella/usted)	cabrá	cabría
(nosotros/as)	cabremos	cabríamos
(vosotros/as)	cabréis	cabríais
(ellos/ellas/ustedes)	cabrán	cabrían

	PRESENT SUBJUNCTIVE	IMPERFECT SUBJUNCTIVE
(yo)	quepa	cupiera or cupiese
(tú)	quepas	cupieras or cupieses
(él/ella/usted)	quepa	cupiera or cupiese
(nosotros/as)	quepamos	cupiéramos or cupiésemos
(vosotros/as)	quepáis	cupierais or cupieseis
(ellos/ellas/ustedes)	quepan	cupieran or cupiesen

IMPERATIVE

cabe / cabed

Use the present subjunctive in all cases other than these tú and vosotros affirmative forms.

EXAMPLE PHRASES

¿Crees que **cabrá**? Do you think there will be enough room for it?

Cabría cuestionarse si es la mejor solución. We should ask ourselves whether it's the best solution.

Hizo lo imposible para que le **cupiera** la redacción en una página.
He did everything he could to fit the composition onto one page.

Remember that subject pronouns are not used very often in Spanish.

caer (to fall)

	PRESENT	PRESENT PERFECT
(yo)	caigo	he caído
(tú)	caes	has caído
(él/ella/usted)	cae	ha caído
(nosotros/as)	caemos	hemos caído
(vosotros/as)	caéis	habéis caído
(ellos/ellas/ ustedes)	caen	han caído

	PRETERITE	IMPERFECT
(yo)	caí	caía
(tú)	caíste	caías
(él/ella/usted)	cayó	caía
(nosotros/as)	caímos	caíamos
(vosotros/as)	caísteis	caíais
(ellos/ellas/ ustedes)	cayeron	caían

GERUND

cayendo

PAST PARTICIPLE

caído

EXAMPLE PHRASES

Su cumpleaños **cae** en viernes. Her birthday falls on a Friday.

Ese edificio se **está cayendo**. That building's falling down.

Se me **ha caído** un guante. I've dropped one of my gloves.

Me **caí** por las escaleras. I fell down the stairs.

Me **caía** muy bien. I really liked him.

Remember that subject pronouns are not used very often in Spanish.

caer

	FUTURE	CONDITIONAL
(yo)	caeré	caería
(tú)	caerás	caerías
(él/ella/usted)	caerá	caería
(nosotros/as)	caeremos	caeríamos
(vosotros/as)	caeréis	caeríais
(ellos/ellas/ustedes)	caerán	caerían

	PRESENT SUBJUNCTIVE	IMPERFECT SUBJUNCTIVE
(yo)	caiga	cayera or cayese
(tú)	caigas	cayeras or cayeses
(él/ella/usted)	caiga	cayera or cayese
(nosotros/as)	caigamos	cayéramos or cayésemos
(vosotros/as)	caigáis	cayerais or cayeseis
(ellos/ellas/ustedes)	caigan	cayeran or cayesen

IMPERATIVE

cae / caed

Use the present subjunctive in all cases other than these tú and vosotros affirmative forms.

EXAMPLE PHRASES

Tarde o temprano, **caerá** en manos del enemigo. Sooner or later, it will fall into enemy hands.

Yo me **caería** con esos tacones. I'd fall over if I wore heels like those.

Seguirá adelante **caiga** quien **caiga**. She'll go ahead no matter how many heads have to roll.

No **caigas** tan bajo. Don't stoop so low.

Remember that subject pronouns are not used very often in Spanish.

cambiar (to change)

	PRESENT		PRESENT PERFECT
(yo)	cambio		he cambiado
(tú)	cambias		has cambiado
(él/ella/usted)	cambia		ha cambiado
(nosotros/as)	cambiamos		hemos cambiado
(vosotros/as)	cambiáis		habéis cambiado
(ellos/ellas/ ustedes)	cambian		han cambiado

	PRETERITE		IMPERFECT
(yo)	cambié		cambiaba
(tú)	cambiaste		cambiabas
(él/ella/usted)	cambió		cambiaba
(nosotros/as)	cambiamos		cambiábamos
(vosotros/as)	cambiasteis		cambiabais
(ellos/ellas/ ustedes)	cambiaron		cambiaban

GERUND

cambiando

PAST PARTICIPLE

cambiado

EXAMPLE PHRASES

Necesito **cambiar** de ambiente. I need a change of scene.

Te **cambio** mi bolígrafo por tu goma. I'll swap my ballpoint for your rubber.

He cambiado de idea. I've changed my mind.

Cambié varias veces de trabajo. I changed jobs several times.

Cambiaban de coche cada año. They changed their car every year.

Remember that subject pronouns are not used very often in Spanish.

cambiar

	FUTURE	CONDITIONAL
(yo)	cambiaré	cambiaría
(tú)	cambiarás	cambiarías
(él/ella/usted)	cambiará	cambiaría
(nosotros/as)	cambiaremos	cambiaríamos
(vosotros/as)	cambiaréis	cambiaríais
(ellos/ellas/ ustedes)	cambiarán	cambiarían

	PRESENT SUBJUNCTIVE	IMPERFECT SUBJUNCTIVE
(yo)	cambie	cambiara or cambiase
(tú)	cambies	cambiaras or cambiases
(él/ella/usted)	cambie	cambiara or cambiase
(nosotros/as)	cambiemos	cambiáramos or cambiásemos
(vosotros/as)	cambiéis	cambiarais or cambiaseis
(ellos/ellas/ ustedes)	cambien	cambiaran or cambiasen

IMPERATIVE

cambia / cambiad

Use the present subjunctive in all cases other than these tú and vosotros affirmative forms.

EXAMPLE PHRASES

Cuando la conozcas, **cambiarás** de idea. You'll change your mind when you meet her.

Si pudiéramos, **nos cambiaríamos** de casa. If we could, we'd move houses.

No quiero que **cambies**. I don't want you to change.

Cámbiate, que se nos hace tarde. Get changed, it's getting late.

Remember that subject pronouns are not used very often in Spanish.

cazar (to hunt, to shoot)

	PRESENT		PRESENT PERFECT
(yo)	cazo		he cazado
(tú)	cazas		has cazado
(él/ella/usted)	caza		ha cazado
(nosotros/as)	cazamos		hemos cazado
(vosotros/as)	cazáis		habéis cazado
(ellos/ellas/ ustedes)	cazan		han cazado

	PRETERITE		IMPERFECT
(yo)	cacé		cazaba
(tú)	cazaste		cazabas
(él/ella/usted)	cazó		cazaba
(nosotros/as)	cazamos		cazábamos
(vosotros/as)	cazasteis		cazabais
(ellos/ellas/ ustedes)	cazaron		cazaban

GERUND

cazando

PAST PARTICIPLE

cazado

EXAMPLE PHRASES

Salieron a **cazar** ciervos. They went deer-hunting.

Caza las cosas al vuelo. She's very quick on the uptake.

No **he cazado** nada de lo que ha dicho. I didn't understand a word he said.

Los **cacé** robando. I caught them stealing.

Cazaban con lanza. They hunted with spears.

Remember that subject pronouns are not used very often in Spanish.

cazar

	FUTURE	CONDITIONAL
(yo)	cazaré	cazaría
(tú)	cazarás	cazarías
(él/ella/usted)	cazará	cazaría
(nosotros/as)	cazaremos	cazaríamos
(vosotros/as)	cazaréis	cazaríais
(ellos/ellas/ ustedes)	cazarán	cazarían

	PRESENT SUBJUNCTIVE	IMPERFECT SUBJUNCTIVE
(yo)	cace	cazara or cazase
(tú)	caces	cazaras or cazases
(él/ella/usted)	cace	cazara or cazase
(nosotros/as)	cacemos	cazáramos or cazásemos
(vosotros/as)	cacéis	cazarais or cazaseis
(ellos/ellas/ ustedes)	cacen	cazaran or cazasen

IMPERATIVE

caza / cazad

Use the present subjunctive in all cases other than these tú *and* vosotros *affirmative forms.*

EXAMPLE PHRASES

¡Quién **cazara** a un millonario! I wish I could land myself a millionaire!

Remember that subject pronouns are not used very often in Spanish.

cerrar (to close)

	PRESENT		PRESENT PERFECT
(yo)	cierro		he cerrado
(tú)	cierras		has cerrado
(él/ella/usted)	cierra		ha cerrado
(nosotros/as)	cerramos		hemos cerrado
(vosotros/as)	cerráis		habéis cerrado
(ellos/ellas/ ustedes)	cierran		han cerrado

	PRETERITE		IMPERFECT
(yo)	cerré		cerraba
(tú)	cerraste		cerrabas
(él/ella/usted)	cerró		cerraba
(nosotros/as)	cerramos		cerrábamos
(vosotros/as)	cerrasteis		cerrabais
(ellos/ellas/ ustedes)	cerraron		cerraban

GERUND
cerrando

PAST PARTICIPLE
cerrado

EXAMPLE PHRASES

No puedo **cerrar** la maleta. I can't shut this suitcase.
No **cierran** al mediodía. They don't close at midday.
Ha cerrado la puerta con llave. She's locked the door.
Cerró el libro. He closed the book.
Se le cerraban los ojos. She couldn't keep her eyes open.

Remember that subject pronouns are not used very often in Spanish.

cerrar

	FUTURE	CONDITIONAL
(yo)	cerraré	cerraría
(tú)	cerrarás	cerrarías
(él/ella/usted)	cerrará	cerraría
(nosotros/as)	cerraremos	cerraríamos
(vosotros/as)	cerraréis	cerraríais
(ellos/ellas/ ustedes)	cerrrarán	cerrarían

	PRESENT SUBJUNCTIVE	IMPERFECT SUBJUNCTIVE
(yo)	cierre	cerrara or cerrase
(tú)	cierres	cerraras or cerrases
(él/ella/usted)	cierre	cerraras or cerrases
(nosotros/as)	cerremos	cerráramos or cerrásemos
(vosotros/as)	cerréis	cerrarais or cerraseis
(ellos/ellas/ ustedes)	cierren	cerraran or cerrasen

IMPERATIVE

cierra / cerrad

Use the present subjunctive in all cases other than these tú and vosotros affirmative forms.

EXAMPLE PHRASES

No dejes que **se cierre** la puerta de golpe. Don't let the door slam shut.

No **cierres** la ventana. Don't close the window.

Cierra el grifo. Turn off the tap.

Remember that subject pronouns are not used very often in Spanish.

cocer (to boil, to cook)

	PRESENT		PRESENT PERFECT
(yo)	cuezo		he cocido
(tú)	cueces		has cocido
(él/ella/usted)	cuece		ha cocido
(nosotros/as)	cocemos		hemos cocido
(vosotros/as)	cocéis		habéis cocido
(ellos/ellas/ ustedes)	cuecen		han cocido

	PRETERITE		IMPERFECT
(yo)	cocí		cocía
(tú)	cociste		cocías
(él/ella/usted)	coció		cocía
(nosotros/as)	cocimos		cocíamos
(vosotros/as)	cocisteis		cocíais
(ellos/ellas/ ustedes)	cocieron		cocían

GERUND

cociendo

PAST PARTICIPLE

cocido

EXAMPLE PHRASES

Las gambas **se cuecen** en un momento. Prawns take no time to cook.

Aquí nos **estamos cociendo**. It's boiling in here.

He cocido todo junto. I've cooked everything together.

Coció el pan en el horno. He baked the bread in the oven.

Remember that subject pronouns are not used very often in Spanish.

cocer

	FUTURE	CONDITIONAL
(yo)	coceré	cocería
(tú)	cocerás	cocerías
(él/ella/usted)	cocerá	cocería
(nosotros/as)	coceremos	coceríamos
(vosotros/as)	coceréis	coceríais
(ellos/ellas/ustedes)	cocerán	cocerían

	PRESENT SUBJUNCTIVE	IMPERFECT SUBJUNCTIVE
(yo)	cueza	cociera or cociese
(tú)	cuezas	cocieras or cocieses
(él/ella/usted)	cueza	cociera or cociese
(nosotros/as)	cozamos	cociéramos or cociésemos
(vosotros/as)	cozáis	cocierais or cocieseis
(ellos/ellas/ustedes)	cuezan	cocieran or cociesen

IMPERATIVE

cuece / coced

Use the present subjunctive in all cases other than these tú and vosotros affirmative forms.

EXAMPLE PHRASES

Así se **cocerá** antes. This way it will be ready sooner.

Te dije que lo **cocieras** tapado. I told you to cook it with the lid on.

No lo **cuezas** demasiado. Don't overcook it.

Cuécelo a fuego lento. Cook it over a gentle heat.

Remember that subject pronouns are not used very often in Spanish.

coger (to catch, to take)

	PRESENT		PRESENT PERFECT
(yo)	cojo		he cogido
(tú)	coges		has cogido
(él/ella/usted)	coge		ha cogido
(nosotros/as)	cogemos		hemos cogido
(vosotros/as)	cogéis		habéis cogido
(ellos/ellas/ ustedes)	cogen		han cogido

	PRETERITE		IMPERFECT
(yo)	cogí		cogía
(tú)	cogiste		cogías
(él/ella/usted)	cogió		cogía
(nosotros/as)	cogimos		cogíamos
(vosotros/as)	cogisteis		cogíais
(ellos/ellas/ ustedes)	cogieron		cogían

GERUND

cogiendo

PAST PARTICIPLE

cogido

EXAMPLE PHRASES

¿Por qué no **coges** el tren de las seis? Why don't you get the six o'clock train?

Estuvimos **cogiendo** setas. We were picking mushrooms.

Le **he cogido** cariño al gato. I've grown fond of the cat.

La **cogí** entre mis brazos. I took her in my arms.

Cogía el metro todos los días. I used to take the tube every day.

Remember that subject pronouns are not used very often in Spanish.

coger

	FUTURE	CONDITIONAL
(yo)	cogeré	cogería
(tú)	cogerás	cogerías
(él/ella/usted)	cogerá	cogería
(nosotros/as)	cogeremos	cogeríamos
(vosotros/as)	cogeréis	cogeríais
(ellos/ellas/ ustedes)	cogerán	cogerían

	PRESENT SUBJUNCTIVE	IMPERFECT SUBJUNCTIVE
(yo)	coja	cogiera or cogiese
(tú)	cojas	cogieras or cogieses
(él/ella/usted)	coja	cogiera or cogiese
(nosotros/as)	cojamos	cogiéramos or cogiésemos
(vosotros/as)	cojáis	cogierais or cogieseis
(ellos/ellas/ ustedes)	cojan	cogieran or cogiesen

IMPERATIVE

coge / coged

Use the present subjunctive in all cases other than these tú *and* vosotros *affirmative forms.*

EXAMPLE PHRASES

Se **cogerá** un resfriado. **He'll catch a cold.**

Yo **cogería** el azul. **I'd take the blue one.**

No le **cojas** los juguetes a tu hermana. **Don't take your sister's toys.**

Coja la primera calle a la derecha. **Take the first street on the right.**

Remember that subject pronouns are not used very often in Spanish.

colgar (to hang)

	PRESENT		PRESENT PERFECT
(yo)	cuelgo		he colgado
(tú)	cuelgas		has colgado
(él/ella/usted)	cuelga		ha colgado
(nosotros/as)	colgamos		hemos colgado
(vosotros/as)	colgáis		habéis colgado
(ellos/ellas/ ustedes)	cuelgan		han colgado

	PRETERITE		IMPERFECT
(yo)	colgué		colgaba
(tú)	colgaste		colgabas
(él/ella/usted)	colgó		colgaba
(nosotros/as)	colgamos		colgábamos
(vosotros/as)	colgasteis		colgabais
(ellos/ellas/ ustedes)	colgaron		colgaban

GERUND

colgando

PAST PARTICIPLE

colgado

EXAMPLE PHRASES

Cada día **cuelgan** el cartel de "no hay billetes". Every day the "sold out" sign goes up.

Hay telarañas **colgando** del techo. There are cobwebs hanging from the ceiling.

Te **he colgado** la chaqueta en la percha. I've hung your jacket on the hanger.

Me **colgó** el teléfono. He hung up on me.

De la pared **colgaba** un espejo. There was a mirror hanging on the wall.

Remember that subject pronouns are not used very often in Spanish.

colgar

	FUTURE	CONDITIONAL
(yo)	colgaré	colgaría
(tú)	colgarás	colgarías
(él/ella/usted)	colgará	colgaría
(nosotros/as)	colgaremos	colgaríamos
(vosotros/as)	colgaréis	colgaríais
(ellos/ellas/ ustedes)	colgarán	colgarían

	PRESENT SUBJUNCTIVE	IMPERFECT SUBJUNCTIVE
(yo)	cuelgue	colgara or colgase
(tú)	cuelgues	colgaras or colgases
(él/ella/usted)	cuelgue	colgara or colgase
(nosotros/as)	colguemos	colgáramos or colgásemos
(vosotros/as)	colguéis	colgarais or colgaseis
(ellos/ellas/ ustedes)	cuelguen	colgaran or colgasen

IMPERATIVE

cuelga / colgad

Use the present subjunctive in all cases other than these tú and vosotros affirmative forms.

EXAMPLE PHRASES

Colgaremos el cuadro en esa pared. We'll hang the picture on that wall.

¡Que lo **cuelguen**! Hang him!

No **cuelgue**, por favor. Please don't hang up.

¡**Cuelga**, por favor, que quiero hacer una llamada! Please hang up. I want to use the phone!

Remember that subject pronouns are not used very often in Spanish.

comer (to eat)

	PRESENT		PRESENT PERFECT
(yo)	como		he comido
(tú)	comes		has comido
(él/ella/usted)	come		ha comido
(nosotros/as)	comemos		hemos comido
(vosotros/as)	coméis		habéis comido
(ellos/ellas/ustedes)	comen		han comido

	PRETERITE		IMPERFECT
(yo)	comí		comía
(tú)	comiste		comías
(él/ella/usted)	comió		comía
(nosotros/as)	comimos		comíamos
(vosotros/as)	comisteis		comíais
(ellos/ellas/ustedes)	comieron		comían

GERUND

comiendo

PAST PARTICIPLE

comido

EXAMPLE PHRASES

No **come** carne. He doesn't eat meat.

Se lo **ha comido** todo. He's eaten it all.

Comimos en un restaurante. We had lunch in a restaurant.

Siempre **comían** demasiado. They always ate too much.

Remember that subject pronouns are not used very often in Spanish.

comer

	FUTURE		CONDITIONAL
(yo)	comeré		comería
(tú)	comerás		comerías
(él/ella/usted)	comerá		comería
(nosotros/as)	comeremos		comeríamos
(vosotros/as)	comeréis		comeríais
(ellos/ellas/ ustedes)	comerán		comerían

	PRESENT SUBJUNCTIVE		IMPERFECT SUBJUNCTIVE
(yo)	coma		comiera or comiese
(tú)	comas		comieras or comieses
(él/ella/usted)	coma		comiera or comiese
(nosotros/as)	comamos		comiéramos or comiésemos
(vosotros/as)	comáis		comierais or comieseis
(ellos/ellas/ ustedes)	coman		comieran or comiesen

IMPERATIVE

come / comed

Use the present subjunctive in all cases other than these tú and vosotros affirmative forms.

EXAMPLE PHRASES

Me lo **comeré** yo. I'll eat it.

Si no fuera por mí, no **comeríamos**. We wouldn't eat if it weren't for me.

Si **comieras** más, no estarías tan delgado. You wouldn't be so thin if you ate more.

No **comas** tan deprisa. Don't eat so fast.

Remember that subject pronouns are not used very often in Spanish.

conducir (to drive, to lead)

	PRESENT		PRESENT PERFECT
(yo)	conduzco		he conducido
(tú)	conduces		has conducido
(él/ella/usted)	conduce		ha conducido
(nosotros/as)	conducimos		hemos conducido
(vosotros/as)	conducís		habéis conducido
(ellos/ellas/ustedes)	conducen		han conducido

	PRETERITE		IMPERFECT
(yo)	conduje		conducía
(tú)	condujiste		conducías
(él/ella/usted)	condujo		conducía
(nosotros/as)	condujimos		conducíamos
(vosotros/as)	condujisteis		conducíais
(ellos/ellas/ustedes)	condujeron		conducían

GERUND

conduciendo

PAST PARTICIPLE

conducido

EXAMPLE PHRASES

No sé **conducir**. I can't drive.

Conduces muy bien. You're a very good driver.

Enfadarte no te **ha conducido** a nada. Getting angry hasn't got you anywhere.

La pista nos **condujo** hasta él. The clue led us to him.

¿**Conducías** tú? Was it you driving?

Remember that subject pronouns are not used very often in Spanish.

conducir

	FUTURE	CONDITIONAL
(yo)	conduciré	conduciría
(tú)	conducirás	conducirías
(él/ella/usted)	conducirá	conduciría
(nosotros/as)	conduciremos	conduciríamos
(vosotros/as)	conduciréis	conduciríais
(ellos/ellas/ ustedes)	conducirán	conducirían

	PRESENT SUBJUNCTIVE	IMPERFECT SUBJUNCTIVE
(yo)	conduzca	condujera or condujese
(tú)	conduzcas	condujeras or condujeses
(él/ella/usted)	conduzca	condujera or condujese
(nosotros/as)	conduzcamos	condujéramos or condujésemos
(vosotros/as)	conduzcáis	condujerais or condujeseis
(ellos/ellas/ ustedes)	conduzcan	condujeran or condujesen

IMPERATIVE

conduce / conducid

Use the present subjunctive in all cases other than these tú *and* vosotros *affirmative forms.*

EXAMPLE PHRASES

El camarero les **conducirá** a su mesa. The waiter will show you to your table.

Si bebes, no **conduzcas**. Don't drink and drive.

Le pedí que **condujera** más despacio. I asked him to drive more slowly.

Conduzca con cuidado. Drive carefully.

Remember that subject pronouns are not used very often in Spanish.

conocer (to know)

	PRESENT		PRESENT PERFECT
(yo)	conozco		he conocido
(tú)	conoces		has conocido
(él/ella/usted)	conoce		ha conocido
(nosotros/as)	conocemos		hemos conocido
(vosotros/as)	conocéis		habéis conocido
(ellos/ellas/ ustedes)	conocen		han conocido

	PRETERITE		IMPERFECT
(yo)	conocí		conocía
(tú)	conociste		conocías
(él/ella/usted)	conoció		conocía
(nosotros/as)	conocimos		conocíamos
(vosotros/as)	conocisteis		conocíais
(ellos/ellas/ ustedes)	conocieron		conocían

GERUND

conociendo

PAST PARTICIPLE

conocido

EXAMPLE PHRASES

Conozco un restaurante donde se come bien. I know a restaurant where the food is very good.

Nunca **he conocido** a nadie así. I've never met anybody like that.

La **conocí** en una fiesta. I met her at a party.

Nos conocíamos desde hacía años. We'd known each other for years.

Remember that subject pronouns are not used very often in Spanish.

conocer

	FUTURE	CONDITIONAL
(yo)	conoceré	conocería
(tú)	conocerás	conocerías
(él/ella/usted)	conocerá	conocería
(nosotros/as)	conoceremos	conoceríamos
(vosotros/as)	conoceréis	conoceríais
(ellos/ellas/ustedes)	conocerán	conocerían

	PRESENT SUBJUNCTIVE	IMPERFECT SUBJUNCTIVE
(yo)	conozca	conociera or conociese
(tú)	conozcas	conocieras or conocieses
(él/ella/usted)	conozca	conociera or conociese
(nosotros/as)	conozcamos	conociéramos or conociésemos
(vosotros/as)	conozcáis	conocierais or conocieseis
(ellos/ellas/ustedes)	conozcan	conocieran or conociesen

IMPERATIVE
conoce / conoced

Use the present subjunctive in all cases other than these tú and vosotros affirmative forms.

EXAMPLE PHRASES
No sé si la **conocerás** cuando la veas. I don't know if you'll recognize her when you see her.

No quiero que mis padres le **conozcan**. I don't want my parents to meet him.

Si no la **conociera**, pensaría que lo hizo queriendo. If I didn't know her better, I'd think she had done it on purpose.

Remember that subject pronouns are not used very often in Spanish.

construir (to build)

	PRESENT	**PRESENT PERFECT**
(yo)	construyo	he construido
(tú)	construyes	has construido
(él/ella/usted)	construye	ha construido
(nosotros/as)	construimos	hemos construido
(vosotros/as)	construís	habéis construido
(ellos/ellas/ustedes)	construyen	han construido

	PRETERITE	**IMPERFECT**
(yo)	construí	construía
(tú)	construiste	construías
(él/ella/usted)	construyó	construía
(nosotros/as)	construimos	construíamos
(vosotros/as)	construisteis	construíais
(ellos/ellas/ustedes)	construyeron	construían

GERUND

construyendo

PAST PARTICIPLE

construido

EXAMPLE PHRASES

Construyen casas de madera. They build wooden houses.

Están construyendo una escuela. They're building a new school.

Ha construido la casa él solo. He built the house on his own.

Lo **construyó** sin planos. He built it without any plans.

Su empresa **construía** puentes. His company built bridges.

Remember that subject pronouns are not used very often in Spanish.

construir

	FUTURE	CONDITIONAL
(yo)	construiré	construiría
(tú)	construirás	construirías
(él/ella/usted)	construirá	construiría
(nosotros/as)	construiremos	construiríamos
(vosotros/as)	construiréis	construiríais
(ellos/ellas/ustedes)	construirán	construirían

	PRESENT SUBJUNCTIVE	IMPERFECT SUBJUNCTIVE
(yo)	construya	construyera or construyese
(tú)	construyas	construyeras or construyeses
(él/ella/usted)	construya	construyera or construyese
(nosotros/as)	construyamos	construyéramos or construyésemos
(vosotros/as)	construyáis	construyerais or construyeseis
(ellos/ellas/ustedes)	construyan	construyeran or construyesen

IMPERATIVE
construye / construid
Use the present subjunctive in all cases other than these tú and vosotros affirmative forms.

EXAMPLE PHRASES
Aquí **construirán** una autopista. They're going to build a new motorway here.
Yo **construiría** la oración de otra forma. I'd construct the sentence differently.
Le pedí que lo **construyera** así. I asked him to build it like this.

Remember that subject pronouns are not used very often in Spanish.

contar (to tell, to count)

	PRESENT		PRESENT PERFECT
(yo)	cuento		he contado
(tú)	cuentas		has contado
(él/ella/usted)	cuenta		ha contado
(nosotros/as)	contamos		hemos contado
(vosotros/as)	contáis		habéis contado
(ellos/ellas/ustedes)	cuentan		han contado

	PRETERITE		IMPERFECT
(yo)	conté		contaba
(tú)	contaste		contabas
(él/ella/usted)	contó		contaba
(nosotros/as)	contamos		contábamos
(vosotros/as)	contasteis		contabais
(ellos/ellas/ustedes)	contaron		contaban

GERUND
contando

PAST PARTICIPLE
contado

EXAMPLE PHRASES

Sabe **contar** hasta diez. She can count up to ten.

Estoy contando los días. I'm counting the days.

¿**Has contado** el dinero? Have you counted the money?

Nos **contó** un secreto. He told us a secret.

Para él sólo **contaba** su carrera. The only thing that mattered to him was his career.

Remember that subject pronouns are not used very often in Spanish.

contar

	FUTURE	CONDITIONAL
(yo)	contaré	contaría
(tú)	contarás	contarías
(él/ella/usted)	contará	contaría
(nosotros/as)	contaremos	contaríamos
(vosotros/as)	contaréis	contaríais
(ellos/ellas/ ustedes)	contarán	contarían

	PRESENT SUBJUNCTIVE	IMPERFECT SUBJUNCTIVE
(yo)	cuente	contara or contase
(tú)	cuentes	contaras or contases
(él/ella/usted)	cuente	contara or contase
(nosotros/as)	contemos	contáramos or contásemos
(vosotros/as)	contéis	contarais or contaseis
(ellos/ellas/ ustedes)	cuenten	contaran or contasen

IMPERATIVE

cuenta / contad

Use the present subjunctive in all cases other than these tú and vosotros affirmative forms.

EXAMPLE PHRASES

Prométeme que no se lo **contarás** a nadie. Promise you won't tell anyone.

Quiero que me **cuente** exactamente qué pasó. I want you to tell me exactly what happened.

Quería que le **contara** un cuento. She wanted me to tell her a story.

No **cuentes** conmigo. Don't count on me.

Venga, **cuéntamelo**. Come on, tell me.

Remember that subject pronouns are not used very often in Spanish.

crecer (to grow)

	PRESENT		PRESENT PERFECT
(yo)	crezco		he crecido
(tú)	creces		has crecido
(él/ella/usted)	crece		ha crecido
(nosotros/as)	crecemos		hemos crecido
(vosotros/as)	crecéis		habéis crecido
(ellos/ellas/ ustedes)	crecen		han crecido

	PRETERITE		IMPERFECT
(yo)	crecí		crecía
(tú)	creciste		crecías
(él/ella/usted)	creció		crecía
(nosotros/as)	crecimos		crecíamos
(vosotros/as)	crecisteis		crecíais
(ellos/ellas/ ustedes)	crecieron		crecían

GERUND
creciendo

PAST PARTICIPLE
crecido

EXAMPLE PHRASES

Esas plantas **crecen** en Chile. Those plants grow in Chile.

¡Cómo **has crecido**! Haven't you grown!

Crecimos juntos. We grew up together.

La ciudad **crecía** a pasos agigantados. The city was growing by leaps and bounds.

Sigue **creciendo** la inflación. Inflation is still going up.

Remember that subject pronouns are not used very often in Spanish.

crecer

	FUTURE	CONDITIONAL
(yo)	creceré	crecería
(tú)	crecerás	crecerías
(él/ella/usted)	crecerá	crecería
(nosotros/as)	creceremos	creceríamos
(vosotros/as)	creceréis	creceríais
(ellos/ellas/ustedes)	crecerán	crecerían

	PRESENT SUBJUNCTIVE	IMPERFECT SUBJUNCTIVE
(yo)	crezca	creciera or creciese
(tú)	crezcas	crecieras or crecieses
(él/ella/usted)	crezca	creciera or creciese
(nosotros/as)	crezcamos	creciéramos or creciésemos
(vosotros/as)	crezcáis	crecierais or crecieseis
(ellos/ellas/ustedes)	crezcan	crecieran or creciesen

IMPERATIVE

crece / creced

Use the present subjunctive in all cases other than these tú and vosotros affirmative forms.

EXAMPLE PHRASES

Este año la economía **crecerá** un 2%. The economy will grow by 2% this year.

Crecería mejor en un ambiente húmedo. It would grow better in a humid environment.

Cuando **crezca**, ya verás. When he grows up, you'll see.

Quería que sus hijos **crecieran** en otro ambiente. She wanted her children to grow up in a different environment.

Remember that subject pronouns are not used very often in Spanish.

cruzar (to cross)

	PRESENT		PRESENT PERFECT
(yo)	cruzo		he cruzado
(tú)	cruzas		has cruzado
(él/ella/usted)	cruza		ha cruzado
(nosotros/as)	cruzamos		hemos cruzado
(vosotros/as)	cruzáis		habéis cruzado
(ellos/ellas/ ustedes)	cruzan		han cruzado

	PRETERITE		IMPERFECT
(yo)	crucé		cruzaba
(tú)	cruzaste		cruzabas
(él/ella/usted)	cruzó		cruzaba
(nosotros/as)	cruzamos		cruzábamos
(vosotros/as)	cruzasteis		cruzabais
(ellos/ellas/ ustedes)	cruzaron		cruzaban

GERUND	PAST PARTICIPLE
cruzando	cruzado

EXAMPLE PHRASES

Hace tiempo que no **me cruzo** con él. I haven't seen him for a long time.

La caravana **está cruzando** el desierto. The caravan is crossing the dessert.

Se me **han cruzado** los cables. I got mixed up.

Cruzaron el puente. They crossed the bridge.

La carretera **cruzaba** la urbanización. The road went through the housing estate.

Remember that subject pronouns are not used very often in Spanish.

cruzar

	FUTURE	CONDITIONAL
(yo)	cruzaré	cruzaría
(tú)	cruzarás	cruzarías
(él/ella/usted)	cruzará	cruzaría
(nosotros/as)	cruzaremos	cruzaríamos
(vosotros/as)	cruzaréis	cruzaríais
(ellos/ellas/ ustedes)	cruzarán	cruzarían

	PRESENT SUBJUNCTIVE	IMPERFECT SUBJUNCTIVE
(yo)	cruce	cruzara or cruzase
(tú)	cruces	cruzaras or cruzases
(él/ella/usted)	cruce	cruzara or cruzase
(nosotros/as)	crucemos	cruzáramos or cruzásemos
(vosotros/as)	crucéis	cruzarais or cruzaseis
(ellos/ellas/ ustedes)	crucen	cruzaran or cruzasen

IMPERATIVE

cruza / cruzad

Use the present subjunctive in all cases other than these tú and vosotros affirmative forms.

EXAMPLE PHRASES

Cruzarán varias especies distintas. They'll cross several different species.

Crucemos los dedos. Let's keep our fingers crossed.

Le dije que **cruzara** por el paso de cebra. I told her to cross at the pedestrian crossing.

No **cruces** la calle con el semáforo en rojo. Don't cross the road when the signal's at red.

Remember that subject pronouns are not used very often in Spanish.

cubrir (to cover)

	PRESENT		PRESENT PERFECT
(yo)	cubro		he cubierto
(tú)	cubres		has cubierto
(él/ella/usted)	cubre		ha cubierto
(nosotros/as)	cubrimos		hemos cubierto
(vosotros/as)	cubrís		habéis cubierto
(ellos/ellas/ ustedes)	cubren		han cubierto

	PRETERITE		IMPERFECT
(yo)	cubrí		cubría
(tú)	cubriste		cubrías
(él/ella/usted)	cubrió		cubría
(nosotros/as)	cubrimos		cubríamos
(vosotros/as)	cubristeis		cubríais
(ellos/ellas/ ustedes)	cubrieron		cubrían

GERUND
cubriendo

PAST PARTICIPLE
cubierto

EXAMPLE PHRASES

Esto no **cubre** los gastos. This isn't enough to cover expenses.

Le **han cubierto** con una manta. They've covered him with a blanket.

Se **cubrió** la cara con las manos. She covered her face with her hands.

La nieve **cubría** la montaña. The mountain was covered in snow.

cubrir

	FUTURE	CONDITIONAL
(yo)	cubriré	cubriría
(tú)	cubrirás	cubrirías
(él/ella/usted)	cubrirá	cubriría
(nosotros/as)	cubriremos	cubriríamos
(vosotros/as)	cubriréis	cubriríais
(ellos/ellas/ ustedes)	cubrirán	cubrirían

	PRESENT SUBJUNCTIVE	IMPERFECT SUBJUNCTIVE
(yo)	cubra	cubriera or cubriese
(tú)	cubras	cubrieras or cubrieses
(él/ella/usted)	cubra	cubriera or cubriese
(nosotros/as)	cubramos	cubriéramos or cubriésemos
(vosotros/as)	cubráis	cubrierais or cubrieseis
(ellos/ellas/ ustedes)	cubran	cubrieran or cubriesen

IMPERATIVE
cubre / cubrid

Use the present subjunctive in all cases other than these tú and vosotros affirmative forms.

EXAMPLE PHRASES
Los corredores **cubrirán** una distancia de 2 km. The runners will cover a distance of 2 km.

¿Quién **cubriría** la vacante? Who'd fill the vacancy?

Quiero que **cubras** la noticia. I want you to cover that news story.

Remember that subject pronouns are not used very often in Spanish.

dar (to give)

	PRESENT	PRESENT PERFECT
(yo)	doy	he dado
(tú)	das	has dado
(él/ella/usted)	da	ha dado
(nosotros/as)	damos	hemos dado
(vosotros/as)	dais	habéis dado
(ellos/ellas/ustedes)	dan	han dado

	PRETERITE	IMPERFECT
(yo)	di	daba
(tú)	diste	dabas
(él/ella/usted)	dio	daba
(nosotros/as)	dimos	dábamos
(vosotros/as)	disteis	dabais
(ellos/ellas/ustedes)	dieron	daban

GERUND	PAST PARTICIPLE
dando	dado

EXAMPLE PHRASES

Me **da** miedo la oscuridad. **I'm afraid of the dark.**

Le **han dado** varios premios a su película. **His film has been awarded several prizes.**

Nos **dieron** un par de entradas gratis. **They gave us a couple of free tickets.**

Mi ventana **daba** al jardín. **My window looked out on the garden.**

Remember that subject pronouns are not used very often in Spanish.

dar

	FUTURE	CONDITIONAL
(yo)	daré	daría
(tú)	darás	darías
(él/ella/usted)	dará	daría
(nosotros/as)	daremos	daríamos
(vosotros/as)	daréis	daríais
(ellos/ellas/ ustedes)	darán	darían

	PRESENT SUBJUNCTIVE	IMPERFECT SUBJUNCTIVE
(yo)	dé	diera or diese
(tú)	des	dieras or dieses
(él/ella/usted)	dé	diera or diese
(nosotros/as)	demos	diéramos or diésemos
(vosotros/as)	deis	dierais or dieseis
(ellos/ellas/ ustedes)	den	dieran or diesen

IMPERATIVE
da / dad

Use the present subjunctive in all cases other than these tú and vosotros affirmative forms.

EXAMPLE PHRASES

Te **daré** el número de mi móvil. I'll give you my mobile phone number.

Me **daría** mucha alegría volver a verla. It would be really good to see her again.

Quiero que me lo **des** ahora mismo. I want you to give it to me right now.

Déme 2 kilos. 2 kilos please.

Remember that subject pronouns are not used very often in Spanish.

decir (to say, to tell)

	PRESENT		PRESENT PERFECT
(yo)	digo		he dicho
(tú)	dices		has dicho
(él/ella/usted)	dice		ha dicho
(nosotros/as)	decimos		hemos dicho
(vosotros/as)	decís		habéis dicho
(ellos/ellas/ ustedes)	dicen		han dicho

	PRETERITE		IMPERFECT
(yo)	dije		decía
(tú)	dijiste		decías
(él/ella/usted)	dijo		decía
(nosotros/as)	dijimos		decíamos
(vosotros/as)	dijisteis		decíais
(ellos/ellas/ ustedes)	dijeron		decían

GERUND

diciendo

PAST PARTICIPLE

dicho

EXAMPLE PHRASES

Pero ¿qué **dices**? What are you saying?

¿Te **ha dicho** lo de la boda? Has he told you about the wedding?

Me lo **dijo** ayer. He told me yesterday.

Siempre nos **decía** que tuviéramos cuidado. She always used to tell us to be careful.

Remember that subject pronouns are not used very often in Spanish.

decir

	FUTURE	CONDITIONAL
(yo)	diré	diría
(tú)	dirás	dirías
(él/ella/usted)	dirá	diría
(nosotros/as)	diremos	diríamos
(vosotros/as)	diréis	diríais
(ellos/ellas/ ustedes)	dirán	dirían

	PRESENT SUBJUNCTIVE	IMPERFECT SUBJUNCTIVE
(yo)	diga	dijera or dijese
(tú)	digas	dijeras or dijeses
(él/ella/usted)	diga	dijera or dijese
(nosotros/as)	digamos	dijéramos or dijésemos
(vosotros/as)	digáis	dijerais or dijeseis
(ellos/ellas/ ustedes)	digan	dijeran or dijesen

IMPERATIVE

di / decid

Use the present subjunctive in all cases other than these tú and vosotros affirmative forms.

EXAMPLE PHRASES

Yo **diría** que miente. I'd say he's lying.

Diga lo que **diga** no le voy a creer. Whatever he says I won't believe him.

Si me **dijeras** lo que pasa, a lo mejor podría ayudar. If you told me what was going on, I could maybe help.

No le **digas** que me has visto. Don't tell him you've seen me.

Remember that subject pronouns are not used very often in Spanish.

despreocuparse (to stop worrying)

	PRESENT	PRESENT PERFECT
(yo)	me despreocupo	me he despreocupado
(tú)	te despreocupas	te has despreocupado
(él/ella/usted)	se despreocupa	se ha despreocupado
(nosotros/as)	nos despreocupamos	nos hemos despreocupado
(vosotros/as)	os despreocupáis	os habéis despreocupado
(ellos/ellas/ ustedes)	se despreocupan	se han despreocupado

	PRETERITE	IMPERFECT
(yo)	me despreocupé	me despreocupaba
(tú)	te despreocupaste	te despreocupabas
(él/ella/usted)	se despreocupó	se despreocupaba
(nosotros/as)	nos despreocupamos	nos despreocupábamos
(vosotros/as)	os despreocupasteis	os despreocupabais
(ellos/ellas/ ustedes)	se despreocuparon	se despreocupaban

GERUND
despreocupándose, etc

PAST PARTICIPLE
despreocupado

EXAMPLE PHRASES

Deberías **despreocuparte** un poco más de las cosas. You shouldn't worry so much about things.

Se **despreocupa** de todo. He shows no concern for anything.

Se **despreocupó** del asunto. He forgot about the matter.

Remember that subject pronouns are not used very often in Spanish.

despreocuparse

	FUTURE	CONDITIONAL
(yo)	me despreocuparé	me despreocuparía
(tú)	te despreocuparás	te despreocuparías
(él/ella/usted)	se despreocupará	se despreocuparía
(nosotros/as)	nos despreocuparemos	nos despreocuparíamos
(vosotros/as)	os despreocuparéis	os despreocuparíais
(ellos/ellas/ ustedes)	se despreocuparán	se despreocuparían

	PRESENT SUBJUNCTIVE	IMPERFECT SUBJUNCTIVE
(yo)	me despreocupe	me despreocupara or despreocupase
(tú)	te despreocupes	te despreocuparas or despreocupases
(él/ella/usted)	se despreocupe	se despreocupara or despreocupase
(nosotros/as)	nos despreocupemos	nos despreocupáramos or despreocupásemos
(vosotros/as)	os despreocupéis	os despreocuparais or despreocupaseis
(ellos/ellas/ ustedes)	se despreocupen	se despreocuparan or despreocupasen

IMPERATIVE
despreocúpate / despreocupaos
Use the present subjunctive in all cases other than these tú and vosotros affirmative forms.

EXAMPLE PHRASES
Yo **me despreocuparía** de él. I wouldn't worry about him.
Despreocúpate porque ya no tiene remedio. Stop worrying because there's nothing we can do about it now.

Remember that subject pronouns are not used very often in Spanish.

detener (to stop, to arrest)

	PRESENT		PRESENT PERFECT
(yo)	detengo		he detenido
(tú)	detienes		has detenido
(él/ella/usted)	detiene		ha detenido
(nosotros/as)	detenemos		hemos detenido
(vosotros/as)	detenéis		habéis detenido
(ellos/ellas/ ustedes)	detienen		han detenido

	PRETERITE		IMPERFECT
(yo)	detuve		detenía
(tú)	detuviste		detenías
(él/ella/usted)	detuvo		detenía
(nosotros/as)	detuvimos		deteníamos
(vosotros/as)	detuvisteis		deteníais
(ellos/ellas/ ustedes)	detuvieron		detenían

GERUND

deteniendo

PAST PARTICIPLE

detenido

EXAMPLE PHRASES

Han detenido a los ladrones. They've arrested the thieves.

Nos detuvimos en el semáforo. We stopped at the lights.

¡Queda **detenido**! You are under arrest!

Remember that subject pronouns are not used very often in Spanish.

detener

	FUTURE	**CONDITIONAL**
(yo)	detendré	detendría
(tú)	detendrás	detendrías
(él/ella/usted)	detendrá	detendría
(nosotros/as)	detendremos	detendríamos
(vosotros/as)	detendréis	detendríais
(ellos/ellas/ ustedes)	detendrán	detendrían

	PRESENT SUBJUNCTIVE	**IMPERFECT SUBJUNCTIVE**
(yo)	detenga	detuviera or detuviese
(tú)	detengas	detuvieras or detuvieses
(él/ella/usted)	detenga	detuviera or detuviese
(nosotros/as)	detengamos	detuviéramos or detuviésemos
(vosotros/as)	detengáis	detuvierais or detuvieseis
(ellos/ellas/ ustedes)	detengan	detuvieran or detuviesen

IMPERATIVE

detén / detened

Use the present subjunctive in all cases other than these tú and vosotros affirmative forms.

EXAMPLE PHRASES

Nada la **detendrá**. Nothing will stop her.

Si **te detuvieras** a pensar, nunca harías nada. If you stopped to think, you'd never do anything.

¡**Deténgase**! Stop!

¡No **te detengas**! Don't stop!

Remember that subject pronouns are not used very often in Spanish.

dirigir (to direct, to run)

	PRESENT		PRESENT PERFECT
(yo)	dirijo		he dirigido
(tú)	diriges		has dirigido
(él/ella/usted)	dirige		ha dirigido
(nosotros/as)	dirigimos		hemos dirigido
(vosotros/as)	dirigís		habéis dirigido
(ellos/ellas/ ustedes)	dirigen		han dirigido

	PRETERITE		IMPERFECT
(yo)	dirigí		dirigía
(tú)	dirigiste		dirigías
(él/ella/usted)	dirigió		dirigía
(nosotros/as)	dirigimos		dirigíamos
(vosotros/as)	dirigisteis		dirigíais
(ellos/ellas/ ustedes)	dirigieron		dirigían

GERUND
dirigiendo

PAST PARTICIPLE
dirigido

EXAMPLE PHRASES

Dirijo esta empresa desde hace dos años. I've been running this company for two years.

Ha dirigido varias películas. She has directed several films.

No le **dirigió** la palabra. She didn't say a word to him.

Se dirigía a la parada de autobús. He was making his way to the bus stop.

Remember that subject pronouns are not used very often in Spanish.

dirigir

	FUTURE	CONDITIONAL
(yo)	dirigiré	dirigiría
(tú)	dirigirás	dirigirías
(él/ella/usted)	dirigirá	dirigiría
(nosotros/as)	dirigiremos	dirigiríamos
(vosotros/as)	dirigiréis	dirigiríais
(ellos/ellas/ ustedes)	dirigirán	dirigirían

	PRESENT SUBJUNCTIVE	IMPERFECT SUBJUNCTIVE
(yo)	dirija	dirigiera or dirigiese
(tú)	dirijas	dirigieras or dirigieses
(él/ella/usted)	dirija	dirigiera or dirigiese
(nosotros/as)	dirijamos	dirigiéramos or dirigiésemos
(vosotros/as)	dirijáis	dirigierais or dirigieseis
(ellos/ellas/ ustedes)	dirijan	dirigieran or dirigiesen

IMPERATIVE
dirige / dirigid

Use the present subjunctive in all cases other than these tú and vosotros affirmative forms.

EXAMPLE PHRASES
Dirigirá la expedición. He'll be leading the expedition.

Para más información **diríjase** al apartado de correos número 1002.
For further information write to PO Box 1002.

Remember that subject pronouns are not used very often in Spanish.

distinguir (to distinguish)

	PRESENT	PRESENT PERFECT
(yo)	distingo	he distinguido
(tú)	distingues	has distinguido
(él/ella/usted)	distingue	ha distinguido
(nosotros/as)	distinguimos	hemos distinguido
(vosotros/as)	distinguís	habéis distinguido
(ellos/ellas/ ustedes)	distinguen	han distinguido

	PRETERITE	IMPERFECT
(yo)	distinguí	distinguía
(tú)	distinguiste	distinguías
(él/ella/usted)	distinguió	distinguía
(nosotros/as)	distinguimos	distinguíamos
(vosotros/as)	distinguisteis	distinguíais
(ellos/ellas/ ustedes)	distinguieron	distinguían

GERUND
distinguiendo

PAST PARTICIPLE
distinguido

EXAMPLE PHRASES

No lo **distingo** del azul. I can't tell the difference between it and the blue one.

Nos **ha distinguido** con su presencia. He has honoured us with his presence.

Se **distinguió** por su gran valentía. He distinguished himself by his bravery.

Se **distinguía** desde lejos. You could see it from the distance.

Remember that subject pronouns are not used very often in Spanish.

distinguir

	FUTURE	CONDITIONAL
(yo)	distinguiré	distinguiría
(tú)	distinguirás	distinguirías
(él/ella/usted)	distinguirá	distinguiría
(nosotros/as)	distinguiremos	distinguiríamos
(vosotros/as)	distinguiréis	distinguiríais
(ellos/ellas/ ustedes)	distinguirán	distinguirían

	PRESENT SUBJUNCTIVE	IMPERFECT SUBJUNCTIVE
(yo)	distinga	distinguiera or distinguiese
(tú)	distingas	distinguieras or distinguieses
(él/ella/usted)	distinga	distinguiera or distinguiese
(nosotros/as)	distingamos	distinguiéramos or distinguiésemos
(vosotros/as)	distingáis	distinguierais or distinguieseis
(ellos/ellas/ ustedes)	distingan	distinguieran or distinguiesen

IMPERATIVE
distingue / distinguid

Use the present subjunctive in all cases other than these tú and vosotros affirmative forms.

EXAMPLE PHRASES
Al final **distinguirás** unas notas de otras. Eventually you'll be able to tell one note from another.

No los **distinguiría**. I wouldn't be able to tell them apart.

divertir (to entertain)

	PRESENT		PRESENT PERFECT
(yo)	divierto		he divertido
(tú)	diviertes		has divertido
(él/ella/usted)	divierte		ha divertido
(nosotros/as)	divertimos		hemos divertido
(vosotros/as)	divertís		habéis divertido
(ellos/ellas/ ustedes)	divierten		han divertido

	PRETERITE		IMPERFECT
(yo)	divertí		divertía
(tú)	divertiste		divertías
(él/ella/usted)	divirtió		divertía
(nosotros/as)	divertimos		divertíamos
(vosotros/as)	divertisteis		divertíais
(ellos/ellas/ ustedes)	divirtieron		divertían

GERUND
divirtiendo

PAST PARTICIPLE
divertido

EXAMPLE PHRASES

Cantamos sólo para **divertirnos**. We sing just for fun.

Me **divierte** verlos tan serios. It's amusing to see them looking so serious.

¿**Os habéis divertido** en la fiesta? Did you enjoy the party?

Nos **divirtió** con sus anécdotas. He entertained us with his stories.

Nos divertíamos mucho jugando en la playa. We had a great time playing on the beach.

Remember that subject pronouns are not used very often in Spanish.

divertir

	FUTURE	CONDITIONAL
(yo)	divertiré	divertiría
(tú)	divertirás	divertirías
(él/ella/usted)	divertirá	divertiría
(nosotros/as)	divertiremos	divertiríamos
(vosotros/as)	divertiréis	divertiríais
(ellos/ellas/ustedes)	divertirán	divertirían

	PRESENT SUBJUNCTIVE	IMPERFECT SUBJUNCTIVE
(yo)	divierta	divirtiera or divirtiese
(tú)	diviertas	divirtieras or divirtieses
(él/ella/usted)	divierta	divirtiera or divirtiese
(nosotros/as)	divirtamos	divirtiéramos or divirtiésemos
(vosotros/as)	divirtáis	divirtierais or divirtieseis
(ellos/ellas/ustedes)	diviertan	divirtieran or divirtiesen

IMPERATIVE
divierte / divertid

Use the present subjunctive in all cases other than these tú and vosotros affirmative forms.

EXAMPLE PHRASES

Si fueras, **te divertirías** mucho. If you went you'd have a great time.

Hizo lo posible por que **se divirtieran**. He did everything he could to make it fun for them.

¡Que **te diviertas**! Have a good time!

dormir (to sleep)

	PRESENT	**PRESENT PERFECT**
(yo)	duermo	he dormido
(tú)	duermes	has dormido
(él/ella/usted)	duerme	ha dormido
(nosotros/as)	dormimos	hemos dormido
(vosotros/as)	dormís	habéis dormido
(ellos/ellas/ ustedes)	duermen	han dormido

	PRETERITE	**IMPERFECT**
(yo)	dormí	dormía
(tú)	dormiste	dormías
(él/ella/usted)	durmió	dormía
(nosotros/as)	dormimos	dormíamos
(vosotros/as)	dormisteis	dormíais
(ellos/ellas/ ustedes)	durmieron	dormían

GERUND
durmiendo

PAST PARTICIPLE
dormido

EXAMPLE PHRASES

No **duermo** muy bien. I don't sleep very well.

Está **durmiendo**. She's asleep.

He **dormido** de un tirón. I slept like a log.

Se me **durmió** la pierna. My leg went to sleep.

Se **dormía** en clase. She would fall asleep in class.

Remember that subject pronouns are not used very often in Spanish.

dormir

	FUTURE	CONDITIONAL
(yo)	dormiré	dormiría
(tú)	dormirás	dormirías
(él/ella/usted)	dormirá	dormiría
(nosotros/as)	dormiremos	dormiríamos
(vosotros/as)	dormiréis	dormiríais
(ellos/ellas/ustedes)	dormirán	dormirían

	PRESENT SUBJUNCTIVE	IMPERFECT SUBJUNCTIVE
(yo)	duerma	durmiera or durmiese
(tú)	duermas	durmieras or durmieses
(él/ella/usted)	duerma	durmiera or durmiese
(nosotros/as)	durmamos	durmiéramos or durmiésemos
(vosotros/as)	durmáis	durmierais or durmieseis
(ellos/ellas/ustedes)	duerman	durmieran or durmiesen

IMPERATIVE
duerme / dormid

Use the present subjunctive in all cases other than these tú and vosotros affirmative forms.

EXAMPLE PHRASES

Si no tomo café, **me dormiré**. I'll fall asleep if I don't have some coffee.

Yo no **dormiría** en esa casa. I wouldn't sleep in that house.

Quiero que **duermas** la siesta. I want you to have a nap.

Si **durmieras** más horas, no estarías tan cansada. You wouldn't be so tired if you slept for longer.

Remember that subject pronouns are not used very often in Spanish.

elegir (to choose)

	PRESENT	PRESENT PERFECT
(yo)	elijo	he elegido
(tú)	eliges	has elegido
(él/ella/usted)	elige	ha elegido
(nosotros/as)	elegimos	hemos elegido
(vosotros/as)	elegís	habéis elegido
(ellos/ellas/ ustedes)	eligen	han elegido

	PRETERITE	IMPERFECT
(yo)	elegí	elegía
(tú)	elegiste	elegías
(él/ella/usted)	eligió	elegía
(nosotros/as)	elegimos	elegíamos
(vosotros/as)	elegisteis	elegíais
(ellos/ellas/ ustedes)	eligieron	elegían

GERUND
eligiendo

PAST PARTICIPLE
elegido

EXAMPLE PHRASES

Te dan a **elegir** entre dos modelos. You get a choice of two models.

Nosotros no **elegimos** a nuestros padres, ni ellos nos **eligen** a nosotros.
    We don't choose our parents and they don't choose us either.

Creo que **ha elegido** bien. I think he's made a good choice.

No lo **eligieron** ellos. It wasn't they who chose it.

Remember that subject pronouns are not used very often in Spanish.

elegir

	FUTURE	CONDITIONAL
(yo)	elegiré	elegiría
(tú)	elegirás	elegirías
(él/ella/usted)	elegirá	elegiría
(nosotros/as)	elegiremos	elegiríamos
(vosotros/as)	elegiréis	elegiríais
(ellos/ellas/ ustedes)	elegirán	elegirían

	PRESENT SUBJUNCTIVE	IMPERFECT SUBJUNCTIVE
(yo)	elija	eligiera or eligiese
(tú)	elijas	eligieras or eligieses
(él/ella/usted)	elija	eligiera or eligiese
(nosotros/as)	elijamos	eligiéramos or eligiésemos
(vosotros/as)	elijáis	eligierais or eligieseis
(ellos/ellas/ ustedes)	elijan	eligieran or eligiesen

IMPERATIVE
elige / elegid

Use the present subjunctive in all cases other than these tú and vosotros affirmative forms.

EXAMPLE PHRASES
Yo **elegiría** el más caro. I'd choose the most expensive one.

Elija una carta. Choose a card.

empezar (to begin)

	PRESENT		PRESENT PERFECT
(yo)	empiezo		he empezado
(tú)	empiezas		has empezado
(él/ella/usted)	empieza		ha empezado
(nosotros/as)	empezamos		hemos empezado
(vosotros/as)	empezáis		habéis empezado
(ellos/ellas/ ustedes)	empiezan		han empezado

	PRETERITE		IMPERFECT
(yo)	empecé		empezaba
(tú)	empezaste		empezabas
(él/ella/usted)	empezó		empezaba
(nosotros/as)	empezamos		empezábamos
(vosotros/as)	empezasteis		empezabais
(ellos/ellas/ ustedes)	empezaron		empezaban

GERUND

empezando

PAST PARTICIPLE

empezado

EXAMPLE PHRASES

Está a punto de **empezar**. It's about to start.

¿Cuándo **empiezas** a trabajar en el sitio nuevo? When do you start work at the new place?

Ha empezado a nevar. It's begun to snow.

Las vacaciones **empezaron** el quince. The holidays started on the fifteenth.

Empezaba por p. It began with p.

Remember that subject pronouns are not used very often in Spanish.

empezar

	FUTURE	CONDITIONAL
(yo)	empezaré	empezaría
(tú)	empezarás	empezarías
(él/ella/usted)	empezará	empezaría
(nosotros/as)	empezaremos	empezaríamos
(vosotros/as)	empezaréis	empezaríais
(ellos/ellas/ ustedes)	empezarán	empezarían

	PRESENT SUBJUNCTIVE	IMPERFECT SUBJUNCTIVE
(yo)	empiece	empezara *or* empezase
(tú)	empieces	empezaras *or* empezases
(él/ella/usted)	empiece	empezara *or* empezase
(nosotros/as)	empecemos	empezáramos *or* empezásemos
(vosotros/as)	empecéis	empezarais *or* empezaseis
(ellos/ellas/ ustedes)	empiecen	empezaran *or* empezasen

IMPERATIVE

empieza / empezad

Use the present subjunctive in all cases other than these tú and vosotros affirmative forms.

EXAMPLE PHRASES

La semana que viene **empezaremos** un curso nuevo. We'll start a new course next week.

Yo **empezaría** desde cero. I'd start from scratch.

Quiero que **empieces** ya. I want you to start now.

Si **empezáramos** ahora, acabaríamos a las diez. If we started now, we'd be finished by ten.

Empieza por aquí. Start here.

Remember that subject pronouns are not used very often in Spanish.

enfrentarse (a to face)

	PRESENT	PRESENT PERFECT
(yo)	me enfrento	me he enfrentado
(tú)	te enfrentas	te has enfrentado
(él/ella/usted)	se enfrenta	se ha enfrentado
(nosotros/as)	nos enfrentamos	nos hemos enfrentado
(vosotros/as)	os enfrentáis	os habéis enfrentado
(ellos/ellas/ustedes)	se enfrentan	se han enfrentado

	PRETERITE	IMPERFECT
(yo)	me enfrenté	me enfrentaba
(tú)	te enfrentaste	te enfrentabas
(él/ella/usted)	se enfrentó	se enfrentaba
(nosotros/as)	nos enfrentamos	nos enfrentábamos
(vosotros/as)	os enfrentasteis	os enfrentabais
(ellos/ellas/ustedes)	se enfrentaron	se enfrentaban

GERUND

enfrentándose, etc

PAST PARTICIPLE

enfrentado

EXAMPLE PHRASES

Tienes que **enfrentarte** al problema. You have to face up to the problem.

Hoy **se enfrentan** los dos semifinalistas. The two semifinalists meet today.

Padre e hijo **se han enfrentado** varias veces. Father and son have had several confrontations.

Se enfrentaban a un futuro incierto. They faced an uncertain future.

Remember that subject pronouns are not used very often in Spanish.

enfrentarse

	FUTURE	CONDITIONAL
(yo)	me enfrentaré	me enfrentaría
(tú)	te enfrentarás	te enfrentarías
(él/ella/usted)	se enfrentará	se enfrentaría
(nosotros/as)	nos enfrentaremos	nos enfrentaríamos
(vosotros/as)	os enfrentaréis	os enfrentaríais
(ellos/ellas/ ustedes)	se enfrentarán	se enfrentarían

	PRESENT SUBJUNCTIVE	IMPERFECT SUBJUNCTIVE
(yo)	me enfrente	me enfrentara or enfrentase
(tú)	te enfrentes	te enfrentaras or enfrentases
(él/ella/usted)	se enfrente	se enfrentara or enfrentase
(nosotros/as)	nos enfrentemos	nos enfrentáramos or enfrentásemos
(vosotros/as)	os enfrentéis	os enfrentarais or enfrentaseis
(ellos/ellas/ ustedes)	se enfrenten	se enfrentaran or enfrentasen

IMPERATIVE

enfréntate / enfrentaos

Use the present subjunctive in all cases other than these tú and vosotros affirmative forms.

EXAMPLE PHRASES

El héroe **se enfrentará** a todo tipo de peligros. The hero will have to face all kinds of dangers.

No **te enfrentes** con él. Don't confront him.

Remember that subject pronouns are not used very often in Spanish.

entender (to understand)

	PRESENT		PRESENT PERFECT
(yo)	entiendo		he entendido
(tú)	entiendes		has entendido
(él/ella/usted)	entiende		ha entendido
(nosotros/as)	entendemos		hemos entendido
(vosotros/as)	entendéis		habéis entendido
(ellos/ellas/ ustedes)	entienden		han entendido

	PRETERITE		IMPERFECT
(yo)	entendí		entendía
(tú)	entendiste		entendías
(él/ella/usted)	entendió		entendía
(nosotros/as)	entendimos		entendíamos
(vosotros/as)	entendisteis		entendíais
(ellos/ellas/ ustedes)	entendieron		entendían

GERUND

entendiendo

PAST PARTICIPLE

entendido

EXAMPLE PHRASES

No lo vas a **entender**. You won't understand.

No lo **entiendo**. I don't understand.

Estás entendiéndolo todo al revés. You're getting the wrong end of the stick.

Creo que lo **he entendido** mal. I think I've misunderstood.

¿**Entendiste** lo que dijo? Did you understand what she said?

Mi padre **entendía** mucho de caballos. My father knew a lot about horses.

Remember that subject pronouns are not used very often in Spanish.

entender

	FUTURE	CONDITIONAL
(yo)	entenderé	entendería
(tú)	entenderás	entenderías
(él/ella/usted)	entenderá	entendería
(nosotros/as)	entenderemos	entenderíamos
(vosotros/as)	entenderéis	entenderíais
(ellos/ellas/ustedes)	entenderán	entenderían

	PRESENT SUBJUNCTIVE	IMPERFECT SUBJUNCTIVE
(yo)	entienda	entendiera or entendiese
(tú)	entiendas	entendieras or entendieses
(él/ella/usted)	entienda	entendiera or entendiese
(nosotros/as)	entendamos	entendiéramos or entendiésemos
(vosotros/as)	entendáis	entendierais or entendieseis
(ellos/ellas/ustedes)	entiendan	entendieran or entendiesen

IMPERATIVE

entiende / entended

Use the present subjunctive in all cases other than these tú and vosotros affirmative forms.

EXAMPLE PHRASES

Con el tiempo lo **entenderás**. You'll understand one day.

Yo no lo **entendería** así. I wouldn't interpret it like that.

Si de verdad me **entendieras**, no habrías dicho eso. If you really understood me, you would never have said that.

No me **entiendas** mal. Don't misunderstand me.

Remember that subject pronouns are not used very often in Spanish.

enviar (to send)

	PRESENT		PRESENT PERFECT
(yo)	envío		he enviado
(tú)	envías		has enviado
(él/ella/usted)	envía		ha enviado
(nosotros/as)	enviamos		hemos enviado
(vosotros/as)	enviáis		habéis enviado
(ellos/ellas/ ustedes)	envían		han enviado

	PRETERITE		IMPERFECT
(yo)	envié		enviaba
(tú)	enviaste		enviabas
(él/ella/usted)	envió		enviaba
(nosotros/as)	enviamos		enviábamos
(vosotros/as)	enviasteis		enviabais
(ellos/ellas/ ustedes)	enviaron		enviaban

GERUND

enviando

PAST PARTICIPLE

enviado

EXAMPLE PHRASES

¿Cómo lo vas a **enviar**? How are you going to send it?

Les **envío** el trabajo por correo electrónico. I send them my work by email.

Ya **está enviando** las invitaciones. She has already started sending out the invitations.

La **han enviado** a Guatemala. They've sent her to Guatemala.

Le **envió** el regalo por correo. He posted her the present.

Me **enviaba** siempre a mí a hacer los recados. She always sent me to do the errands.

Remember that subject pronouns are not used very often in Spanish.

enviar

	FUTURE	CONDITIONAL
(yo)	enviaré	enviaría
(tú)	enviarás	enviarías
(él/ella/usted)	enviará	enviaría
(nosotros/as)	enviaremos	enviaríamos
(vosotros/as)	enviaréis	enviaríais
(ellos/ellas/ustedes)	enviarán	enviarían

	PRESENT SUBJUNCTIVE	IMPERFECT SUBJUNCTIVE
(yo)	envíe	enviara or enviase
(tú)	envíes	enviaras or enviases
(él/ella/usted)	envíe	enviara or enviase
(nosotros/as)	enviemos	enviáramos or enviásemos
(vosotros/as)	enviéis	enviarais or enviaseis
(ellos/ellas/ustedes)	envíen	enviaran or enviasen

IMPERATIVE

envía / enviad

Use the present subjunctive in all cases other than these tú and vosotros affirmative forms.

EXAMPLE PHRASES

Nos **enviarán** más información. They'll send us further information.

Yo lo **enviaría** por mensajero. I'd send it by courier.

Necesitamos que lo **envíes** inmediatamente. We need you to send it immediately.

Si lo **enviaras** ahora, llegaría el lunes. If you sent it now it would get there on Monday.

No lo **envíes** sin repasarlo antes. Don't send it in without checking it first.

Envíe sus datos personales. Send in your details.

Remember that subject pronouns are not used very often in Spanish.

equivocarse (to make a mistake, to be wrong)

	PRESENT		PRESENT PERFECT
(yo)	me equivoco		me he equivocado
(tú)	te equivocas		te has equivocado
(él/ella/usted)	se equivoca		se ha equivocado
(nosotros/as)	nos equivocamos		nos hemos equivocado
(vosotros/as)	os equivocáis		os habéis equivocado
(ellos/ellas/ ustedes)	se equivocan		se han equivocado

	PRETERITE		IMPERFECT
(yo)	me equivoqué		me equivocaba
(tú)	te equivocaste		te equivocabas
(él/ella/usted)	se equivocó		se equivocaba
(nosotros/as)	nos equivocamos		nos equivocábamos
(vosotros/as)	os equivocasteis		os equivocabais
(ellos/ellas/ ustedes)	se equivocaron		se equivocaban

GERUND

equivocándose, etc

PAST PARTICIPLE

equivocado

EXAMPLE PHRASES

Si crees que voy a dejarte ir, **te equivocas**. If you think I'm going to let you go,
  you're wrong.

Perdone, **me he equivocado** de número. Sorry, I've got the wrong number.

Se equivocaron de tren. They got the wrong train.

Siempre **se equivocaba** de calle. He always went down the wrong street.

Remember that subject pronouns are not used very often in Spanish.

equivocarse

	FUTURE	CONDITIONAL
(yo)	me equivocaré	me equivocaría
(tú)	te equivocarás	te equivocarías
(él/ella/usted)	se equivocará	se equivocaría
(nosotros/as)	nos equivocaremos	nos equivocaríamos
(vosotros/as)	os equivocaréis	os equivocaríais
(ellos/ellas/ ustedes)	se equivocarán	se equivocarían

	PRESENT SUBJUNCTIVE	IMPERFECT SUBJUNCTIVE
(yo)	me equivoque	me equivocara or equivocase
(tú)	te equivoques	te equivocaras or equivocases
(él/ella/usted)	se equivoque	se equivocara or equivocase
(nosotros/as)	nos equivoquemos	nos equivocáramos or equivocásemos
(vosotros/as)	os equivoquéis	os equivocarais or equivocaseis
(ellos/ellas/ ustedes)	se equivoquen	se equivocaran or equivocasen

IMPERATIVE

equivócate / equivocaos

Use the present subjunctive in all cases other than these tú and vosotros affirmative forms.

EXAMPLE PHRASES

Sobre todo, no **te equivoques** de hora. **Above all, don't get the time wrong.**

Si **te equivocaras**, quedarías eliminado del juego. **If you made a mistake, you'd be out of the game.**

Remember that subject pronouns are not used very often in Spanish.

erguir (to erect)

	PRESENT		PRESENT PERFECT
(yo)	yergo		he erguido
(tú)	yergues		has erguido
(él/ella/usted)	yergue		ha erguido
(nosotros/as)	erguimos		hemos erguido
(vosotros/as)	erguís		habéis erguido
(ellos/ellas/ ustedes)	yerguen		han erguido

	PRETERITE		IMPERFECT
(yo)	erguí		erguía
(tú)	erguiste		erguías
(él/ella/usted)	irguió		erguía
(nosotros/as)	erguimos		erguíamos
(vosotros/as)	erguisteis		erguías
(ellos/ellas/ ustedes)	irguieron		erguían

GERUND

irguiendo

PAST PARTICIPLE

erguido

EXAMPLE PHRASES

El perro **irguió** las orejas. The dog pricked up its ears.

La montaña **se erguía** majestuosa sobre el valle. The mountain rose majestically above the valley.

Tú mantén siempre la cabeza bien **erguida**. You must always hold your head high.

Remember that subject pronouns are not used very often in Spanish.

erguir

	FUTURE	**CONDITIONAL**
(yo)	erguiré	erguiría
(tú)	erguirás	erguirías
(él/ella/usted)	erguirá	erguiría
(nosotros/as)	erguiremos	erguiríamos
(vosotros/as)	erguiréis	erguiríais
(ellos/ellas/ ustedes)	erguirán	erguirían

	PRESENT SUBJUNCTIVE	**IMPERFECT SUBJUNCTIVE**
(yo)	yerga	irguiera or irguiese
(tú)	yergas	irguieras or irguieses
(él/ella/usted)	yerga	irguiera or irguiese
(nosotros/as)	irgamos	irguiéramos or irguiésemos
(vosotros/as)	irgáis	irguierais or irguieseis
(ellos/ellas/ ustedes)	yergan	irguieran or irguiesen

IMPERATIVE

yergue / erguid

Use the present subjunctive in all cases other than these tú and vosotros affirmative forms.

Remember that subject pronouns are not used very often in Spanish.

errar (to err)

	PRESENT		PRESENT PERFECT
(yo)	yerro		he errado
(tú)	yerras		has errado
(él/ella/usted)	yerra		ha errado
(nosotros/as)	erramos		hemos errado
(vosotros/as)	erráis		habéis errado
(ellos/ellas/ ustedes)	yerran		han errado

	PRETERITE		IMPERFECT
(yo)	erré		erraba
(tú)	erraste		errabas
(él/ella/usted)	erró		erraba
(nosotros/as)	erramos		errábamos
(vosotros/as)	errasteis		errabais
(ellos/ellas/ ustedes)	erraron		erraban

GERUND

errando

PAST PARTICIPLE

errado

EXAMPLE PHRASES

Errar es humano. To err is human.

Ha errado en su decisión. She has made the wrong decision.

Erró el tiro. He missed.

Remember that subject pronouns are not used very often in Spanish.

errar

	FUTURE	CONDITIONAL
(yo)	erraré	erraría
(tú)	errarás	errarías
(él/ella/usted)	errará	erraría
(nosotros/as)	erraremos	erraríamos
(vosotros/as)	erraréis	erraríais
(ellos/ellas/ ustedes)	errarán	errarían

	PRESENT SUBJUNCTIVE	IMPERFECT SUBJUNCTIVE
(yo)	yerre	errara or errase
(tú)	yerres	erraras or errases
(él/ella/usted)	yerre	errara or errase
(nosotros/as)	erremos	erráramos or errásemos
(vosotros/as)	erréis	errarais or erraseis
(ellos/ellas/ ustedes)	yerren	erraran or errasen

IMPERATIVE

yerra / errad

Use the present subjunctive in all cases other than these tú *and* vosotros *affirmative forms.*

Remember that subject pronouns are not used very often in Spanish.

escribir (to write)

	PRESENT		PRESENT PERFECT
(yo)	escribo		he escrito
(tú)	escribes		has escrito
(él/ella/usted)	escribe		ha escrito
(nosotros/as)	escribimos		hemos escrito
(vosotros/as)	escribís		habéis escrito
(ellos/ellas/ ustedes)	escriben		han escrito

	PRETERITE		IMPERFECT
(yo)	escribí		escribía
(tú)	escribiste		escribías
(él/ella/usted)	escribió		escribía
(nosotros/as)	escribimos		escribíamos
(vosotros/as)	escribisteis		escribíais
(ellos/ellas/ ustedes)	escribieron		escribían

GERUND

escribiendo

PAST PARTICIPLE

escrito

EXAMPLE PHRASES

¿Cómo **se escribe** su nombre? How do you spell your name?

¿**Estás escribiendo** la carta? Are you writing the letter?

Eso lo **he escrito** yo. I wrote that.

Nos escribimos durante un tiempo. We wrote to each other for a while.

Escribía canciones. She wrote songs.

Remember that subject pronouns are not used very often in Spanish.

escribir

	FUTURE	CONDITIONAL
(yo)	escribiré	escribiría
(tú)	escribirás	escribirías
(él/ella/usted)	escribirá	escribiría
(nosotros/as)	escribiremos	escribiríamos
(vosotros/as)	escribiréis	escribiríais
(ellos/ellas/ustedes)	escribirán	escribirían

	PRESENT SUBJUNCTIVE	IMPERFECT SUBJUNCTIVE
(yo)	escriba	escribiera or escribiese
(tú)	escribas	escribieras or escribieses
(él/ella/usted)	escriba	escribiera or escribiese
(nosotros/as)	escribamos	escribiéramos or escribiésemos
(vosotros/as)	escribáis	escribierais or escribieseis
(ellos/ellas/ustedes)	escriban	escribieran or escribiesen

IMPERATIVE

escribe / escribid

Use the present subjunctive in all cases other than these tú *and* vosotros *affirmative forms.*

EXAMPLE PHRASES

¿Me **escribirás**? Will you write to me?

Yo lo **escribiría** con mayúscula. I'd write it with a capital letter.

Te he dicho que no **escribas** en la mesa. I've told you not to write on the table.

Si de verdad **escribiera** bien, ya le habrían publicado algún libro. If he really wrote well, he'd have had a book published by now.

Escríbelo en la pizarra. Write it on the blackboard.

Remember that subject pronouns are not used very often in Spanish.

esforzarse (to make an effort)

	PRESENT		PRESENT PERFECT
(yo)	me esfuerzo		me he esforzado
(tú)	te esfuerzas		te has esforzado
(él/ella/usted)	se esfuerza		se ha esforzado
(nosotros/as)	nos esforzamos		nos hemos esforzado
(vosotros/as)	os esforzáis		os habéis esforzado
(ellos/ellas/ ustedes)	se esfuerzan		se han esforzado

	PRETERITE		IMPERFECT
(yo)	me esforcé		me esforzaba
(tú)	te esforzaste		te esforzabas
(él/ella/usted)	se esforzó		se esforzaba
(nosotros/as)	nos esforzamos		nos esforzábamos
(vosotros/as)	os esforzasteis		os esforzabais
(ellos/ellas/ ustedes)	se esforzaron		se esforzaban

GERUND

esforzándose, etc

PAST PARTICIPLE

esforzado

EXAMPLE PHRASES

Tienes que **esforzarte** si quieres ganar. You have to make an effort if you
   want to win.

No **te esfuerzas** lo suficiente. You don't make enough effort.

Me he esforzado, pero nada. I've tried my best but haven't got anywhere.

Se esforzó todo lo que pudo por aprobar el examen. He did everything he
   could to get through the exam.

Me esforzaba por entenderla. I tried hard to understand her.

Remember that subject pronouns are not used very often in Spanish.

esforzarse

	FUTURE	CONDITIONAL
(yo)	me esforzaré	me esforzaría
(tú)	te esforzarás	te esforzarías
(él/ella/usted)	se esforzará	se esforzaría
(nosotros/as)	nos esforzaremos	nos esforzaríamos
(vosotros/as)	os esforzaréis	os esforzaríais
(ellos/ellas/ustedes)	se esforzarán	se esforzarían

	PRESENT SUBJUNCTIVE	IMPERFECT SUBJUNCTIVE
(yo)	me esfuerce	me esforzara or esforzase
(tú)	te esfuerces	te esforzaras or esforzases
(él/ella/usted)	se esfuerce	se esforzara or esforzase
(nosotros/as)	nos esforcemos	nos esforzáramos or esforzásemos
(vosotros/as)	os esforcéis	os esforzarais or esforzaseis
(ellos/ellas/ustedes)	se esfuercen	se esforzaran or esforzasen

IMPERATIVE

esfuérzate / esforzaos

Use the present subjunctive in all cases other than these tú and vosotros affirmative forms.

EXAMPLE PHRASES

No **te esfuerces**, no me vas a convencer. **Stop struggling, you're not going to convince me.**

Si **te esforzaras** un poco más, lo conseguirías. **You'd manage it if you made a bit more of an effort.**

Remember that subject pronouns are not used very often in Spanish.

establecer (to establish)

	PRESENT	PRESENT PERFECT
(yo)	establezco	he establecido
(tú)	estableces	has establecido
(él/ella/usted)	establece	ha establecido
(nosotros/as)	establecemos	hemos establecido
(vosotros/as)	establecéis	habéis establecido
(ellos/ellas/ ustedes)	establecen	han establecido

	PRETERITE	IMPERFECT
(yo)	establecí	establecía
(tú)	estableciste	establecías
(él/ella/usted)	estableció	establecía
(nosotros/as)	establecimos	establecíamos
(vosotros/as)	establecisteis	establecíais
(ellos/ellas/ ustedes)	establecieron	establecían

GERUND

estableciendo

PAST PARTICIPLE

establecido

EXAMPLE PHRASES

Han logrado **establecer** contacto con el barco. They've managed to make contact with the boat.

La ley **establece** que... The law states that...

Se ha establecido una buena relación entre los dos países. A good relationship has been established between the two countries.

En 1945, la familia **se estableció** en Madrid. In 1945, the family settled in Madrid.

Remember that subject pronouns are not used very often in Spanish.

establecer

	FUTURE	CONDITIONAL
(yo)	estableceré	establecería
(tú)	establecerás	establecerías
(él/ella/usted)	establecerá	establecería
(nosotros/as)	estableceremos	estableceríamos
(vosotros/as)	estableceréis	estableceríais
(ellos/ellas/ustedes)	establecerán	establecerían

	PRESENT SUBJUNCTIVE	IMPERFECT SUBJUNCTIVE
(yo)	establezca	estableciera or estableciese
(tú)	establezcas	establecieras or establecieses
(él/ella/usted)	establezca	estableciera or estableciese
(nosotros/as)	establezcamos	estableciéramos or estableciésemos
(vosotros/as)	establezcáis	establecierais or establecieseis
(ellos/ellas/ustedes)	establezcan	establecieran or estableciesen

IMPERATIVE

establece / estableced

Use the present subjunctive in all cases other than these tú and vosotros affirmative forms.

EXAMPLE PHRASES

El año que viene **se establecerá** por su cuenta. Next year she'll set up on her own.

estar (to be)

	PRESENT		PRESENT PERFECT
(yo)	estoy		he estado
(tú)	estás		has estado
(él/ella/usted)	está		ha estado
(nosotros/as)	estamos		hemos estado
(vosotros/as)	estáis		habéis estado
(ellos/ellas/ ustedes)	están		han estado

	PRETERITE	IMPERFECT
(yo)	estuve	estaba
(tú)	estuviste	estabas
(él/ella/usted)	estuvo	estaba
(nosotros/as)	estuvimos	estábamos
(vosotros/as)	estuvisteis	estabais
(ellos/ellas/ ustedes)	estuvieron	estaban

GERUND

estando

PAST PARTICIPLE

estado

EXAMPLE PHRASES

Estoy cansado. I'm tired.

¿Cómo **estás**? How are you?

¿**Has estado** alguna vez en París? Have you ever been to Paris?

Estuvimos en casa de mis padres. We were at my parents'.

¿Dónde **estabas**? Where were you?

Remember that subject pronouns are not used very often in Spanish.

estar

	FUTURE	CONDITIONAL
(yo)	estaré	estaría
(tú)	estarás	estarías
(él/ella/usted)	estará	estaría
(nosotros/as)	estaremos	estaríamos
(vosotros/as)	estaréis	estaríais
(ellos/ellas/ustedes)	estarán	estarían

	PRESENT SUBJUNCTIVE	IMPERFECT SUBJUNCTIVE
(yo)	esté	estuviera or estuviese
(tú)	estés	estuvieras or estuvieses
(él/ella/usted)	esté	estuviera or estuviese
(nosotros/as)	estemos	estuviéramos or estuviésemos
(vosotros/as)	estéis	estuvierais or estuvieseis
(ellos/ellas/ustedes)	estén	estuvieran or estuviesen

IMPERATIVE

está / estad

Use the present subjunctive in all cases other than these tú and vosotros affirmative forms.

EXAMPLE PHRASES

¿A qué hora **estarás** en casa? What time will you be home?

Dijo que **estaría** aquí a las ocho. She said she'd be here at eight o'clock.

Avísame cuando **estés** lista. Let me know when you're ready.

No sabía que **estuviera** tan lejos. I didn't know it was so far.

¡**Estáte** quieto! Stay still!

Remember that subject pronouns are not used very often in Spanish.

evacuar (to evacuate)

	PRESENT	PRESENT PERFECT
(yo)	evacuo	he evacuado
(tú)	evacuas	has evacuado
(él/ella/usted)	evacua	ha evacuado
(nosotros/as)	evacuamos	hemos evacuado
(vosotros/as)	evacuáis	habéis evacuado
(ellos/ellas/ ustedes)	evacuan	han evacuado

	PRETERITE	IMPERFECT
(yo)	evacué	evacuaba
(tú)	evacuaste	evacuabas
(él/ella/usted)	evacuó	evacuaba
(nosotros/as)	evacuamos	evacuábamos
(vosotros/as)	evacuasteis	evacuabais
(ellos/ellas/ ustedes)	evacuaron	evacuaban

GERUND
evacuando

PAST PARTICIPLE
evacuado

EXAMPLE PHRASES

Van a **evacuar** a los heridos. They're going to evacuate the injured.

Han evacuado la zona. The area has been evacuated.

Remember that subject pronouns are not used very often in Spanish.

evacuar

	FUTURE	CONDITIONAL
(yo)	evacuaré	evacuaría
(tú)	evacuarás	evacuarías
(él/ella/usted)	evacuará	evacuaría
(nosotros/as)	evacuaremos	evacuaríamos
(vosotros/as)	evacuaréis	evacuaríais
(ellos/ellas/ ustedes)	evacuarán	evacuarían

	PRESENT SUBJUNCTIVE	IMPERFECT SUBJUNCTIVE
(yo)	evacue	evacuara or evacuase
(tú)	evacues	evacuaras or evacuases
(él/ella/usted)	evacue	evacuara or evacuase
(nosotros/as)	evacuemos	evacuáramos or evacuásemos
(vosotros/as)	evacuéis	evacuarais or evacuaseis
(ellos/ellas/ ustedes)	evacuen	evacuaran or evacuasen

IMPERATIVE

evacua / evacuad

Use the present subjunctive in all cases other than these tú and vosotros affirmative forms.

EXAMPLE PHRASES

Seguirá existiendo peligro mientras no **evacuen** el edificio. The danger won't be over while there are still people inside the building.

freír (to fry)

	PRESENT	PRESENT PERFECT
(yo)	frío	he frito
(tú)	fríes	has frito
(él/ella/usted)	fríe	ha frito
(nosotros/as)	freímos	hemos frito
(vosotros/as)	freís	habéis frito
(ellos/ellas/ ustedes)	fríen	han frito

	PRETERITE	IMPERFECT
(yo)	freí	freía
(tú)	freíste	freías
(él/ella/usted)	frió	freía
(nosotros/as)	freímos	freíamos
(vosotros/as)	freísteis	freíais
(ellos/ellas/ ustedes)	frieron	freían

GERUND	PAST PARTICIPLE
friendo	frito

EXAMPLE PHRASES

No sabe ni **freír** un huevo. **He can't even fry an egg.**

He **frito** el pescado. **I've fried the fish.**

Se está **friendo** demasiado por ese lado. **It's getting overdone on that side.**

Lo **frió** en manteca. **She fried it in lard.**

Nos **freíamos** de calor. **We were roasting in the heat.**

Remember that subject pronouns are not used very often in Spanish.

freír

	FUTURE	CONDITIONAL
(yo)	freiré	freiría
(tú)	freirás	freirías
(él/ella/usted)	freirá	freiría
(nosotros/as)	freiremos	freiríamos
(vosotros/as)	freiréis	freiríais
(ellos/ellas/ ustedes)	freirán	freirían

	PRESENT SUBJUNCTIVE	IMPERFECT SUBJUNCTIVE
(yo)	fría	friera or friese
(tú)	frías	frieras or frieses
(él/ella/usted)	fría	friera or friese
(nosotros/as)	friamos	friéramos or friésemos
(vosotros/as)	friáis	frierais or frieseis
(ellos/ellas/ ustedes)	frían	frieran or friesen

IMPERATIVE
fríe / freíd

Use the present subjunctive in all cases other than these tú and vosotros affirmative forms.

EXAMPLE PHRASES
Yo lo **freiría** con menos aceite. **I'd fry it using less oil.**
Fríelo en esa sartén. **Fry it in that pan.**

gruñir (to grumble, to growl)

	PRESENT		PRESENT PERFECT
(yo)	gruño		he gruñido
(tú)	gruñes		has gruñido
(él/ella/usted)	gruñe		ha gruñido
(nosotros/as)	gruñimos		hemos gruñido
(vosotros/as)	gruñís		habéis gruñido
(ellos/ellas/ ustedes)	gruñen		han gruñido

	PRETERITE		IMPERFECT
(yo)	gruñí		gruñía
(tú)	gruñiste		gruñías
(él/ella/usted)	gruñó		gruñía
(nosotros/as)	gruñimos		gruñíamos
(vosotros/as)	gruñisteis		gruñíais
(ellos/ellas/ ustedes)	gruñeron		gruñían

GERUND

gruñendo

PAST PARTICIPLE

gruñido

EXAMPLE PHRASES

¿A quién **gruñe** el perro? Who's the dog growling at?

Siempre **está gruñendo**. He's always grumbling.

El oso nos **gruñía** sin parar. The bear kept growling at us.

Remember that subject pronouns are not used very often in Spanish.

gruñir

	FUTURE	CONDITIONAL
(yo)	gruñiré	gruñiría
(tú)	gruñirás	gruñirías
(él/ella/usted)	gruñirá	gruñiría
(nosotros/as)	gruñiremos	gruñiríamos
(vosotros/as)	gruñiréis	gruñiríais
(ellos/ellas/ ustedes)	gruñirán	gruñirían

	PRESENT SUBJUNCTIVE	IMPERFECT SUBJUNCTIVE
(yo)	gruña	gruñera or gruñese
(tú)	gruñas	gruñeras or gruñeses
(él/ella/usted)	gruña	gruñera or gruñese
(nosotros/as)	gruñamos	gruñéramos or gruñésemos
(vosotros/as)	gruñáis	gruñerais or gruñeseis
(ellos/ellas/ ustedes)	gruñan	gruñeran or gruñesen

IMPERATIVE

gruñe / gruñid

Use the present subjunctive in all cases other than these tú and vosotros affirmative forms.

EXAMPLE PHRASES

¡No **gruñas** tanto! Don't grumble so much.

Remember that subject pronouns are not used very often in Spanish.

guiar (to guide)

	PRESENT	PRESENT PERFECT
(yo)	guío	he guiado
(tú)	guías	has guiado
(él/ella/usted)	guía	ha guiado
(nosotros/as)	guiamos	hemos guiado
(vosotros/as)	guiais	habéis guiado
(ellos/ellas/ustedes)	guían	han guiado

	PRETERITE	IMPERFECT
(yo)	guie	guiaba
(tú)	guiaste	guiabas
(él/ella/usted)	guio	guiaba
(nosotros/as)	guiamos	guiábamos
(vosotros/as)	guiasteis	guiabais
(ellos/ellas/ustedes)	guiaron	guiaban

GERUND
guiando

PAST PARTICIPLE
guiado

EXAMPLE PHRASES

Los perros **se guían** por su olfato. Dogs follow their sense of smell.

Me **he guiado** por el instinto. I followed my instinct.

Nos **guiamos** por un mapa que teníamos. We found our way using a map we had.

Siempre me protegía y me **guiaba**. He always protected me and guided me.

Remember that subject pronouns are not used very often in Spanish.

guiar

	FUTURE	CONDITIONAL
(yo)	guiaré	guiaría
(tú)	guiarás	guiarías
(él/ella/usted)	guiará	guiaría
(nosotros/as)	guiaremos	guiaríamos
(vosotros/as)	guiaréis	guiaríais
(ellos/ellas/ustedes)	guiarán	guiarían

	PRESENT SUBJUNCTIVE	IMPERFECT SUBJUNCTIVE
(yo)	guíe	guiara or guiase
(tú)	guíes	guiaras or guiases
(él/ella/usted)	guíe	guiara or guiase
(nosotros/as)	guiemos	guiáramos or guiásemos
(vosotros/as)	guieis	guiarais or guiaseis
(ellos/ellas/ustedes)	guíen	guiaran or guiasen

IMPERATIVE

guía / guiad

Use the present subjunctive in all cases other than these tú and vosotros affirmative forms.

EXAMPLE PHRASES

Les **guiaré** hasta allí. I'll take you there.

Guíate por la razón. Use reason as your guide.

haber (to have – *auxiliary*)

	PRESENT	PRESENT PERFECT
(yo)	he	*not used except impersonally*
(tú)	has	*See* hay
(él/ella/usted)	ha	
(nosotros/as)	hemos	
(vosotros/as)	habéis	
(ellos/ellas/ ustedes)	han	

	PRETERITE	IMPERFECT
(yo)	hube	había
(tú)	hubiste	habías
(él/ella/usted)	hubo	había
(nosotros/as)	hubimos	habíamos
(vosotros/as)	hubisteis	habíais
(ellos/ellas/ ustedes)	hubieron	habían

GERUND

habiendo

PAST PARTICIPLE

habido

EXAMPLE PHRASES

De **haberlo** sabido, **habría** ido. If I'd known, I would have gone.

¿**Has** visto eso? Did you see that?

Eso nunca **había** pasado antes. That had never happened before.

Remember that subject pronouns are not used very often in Spanish.

haber

	FUTURE	CONDITIONAL
(yo)	habré	habría
(tú)	habrás	habrías
(él/ella/usted)	habrá	habría
(nosotros/as)	habremos	habríamos
(vosotros/as)	habréis	habríais
(ellos/ellas/ ustedes)	habrán	habrían

	PRESENT SUBJUNCTIVE	IMPERFECT SUBJUNCTIVE
(yo)	haya	hubiera or hubiese
(tú)	hayas	hubieras or hubieses
(él/ella/usted)	haya	hubiera or hubiese
(nosotros/as)	hayamos	hubiéramos or hubiésemos
(vosotros/as)	hayáis	hubierais or hubieseis
(ellos/ellas/ ustedes)	hayan	hubieran or hubiesen

IMPERATIVE

not used

EXAMPLE PHRASES

Habrá que repasarlo. We'll have to check it.
Habría que limpiarlo. We should clean it.
Como se **hayan** olvidado los mato. I'll kill them if they've forgotten.
Si me lo **hubieras** dicho, te lo **habría** traído. I'd have brought it, if you'd said.

Remember that subject pronouns are not used very often in Spanish.

hablar (to speak, to talk)

	PRESENT	PRESENT PERFECT
(yo)	hablo	he hablado
(tú)	hablas	has hablado
(él/ella/usted)	habla	ha hablado
(nosotros/as)	hablamos	hemos hablado
(vosotros/as)	habláis	habéis hablado
(ellos/ellas/ustedes)	hablan	han hablado

	PRETERITE	IMPERFECT
(yo)	hablé	hablaba
(tú)	hablaste	hablabas
(él/ella/usted)	habló	hablaba
(nosotros/as)	hablamos	hablábamos
(vosotros/as)	hablasteis	hablabais
(ellos/ellas/ustedes)	hablaron	hablaban

GERUND

hablando

PAST PARTICIPLE

hablado

EXAMPLE PHRASES

María no **habla** inglés. María doesn't speak English.

No **nos hablamos** desde hace tiempo. We haven't spoken to each other for a long time.

Está **hablando** por teléfono. He's on the phone.

Hoy **he hablado** con mi hermana. I've spoken to my sister today.

¿**Has hablado** ya con el profesor? Have you spoken to the teacher yet?

Remember that subject pronouns are not used very often in Spanish.

hablar

	FUTURE	CONDITIONAL
(yo)	hablaré	hablaría
(tú)	hablarás	hablarías
(él/ella/usted)	hablará	hablaría
(nosotros/as)	hablaremos	hablaríamos
(vosotros/as)	hablaréis	hablaríais
(ellos/ellas/ ustedes)	hablarán	hablarían

	PRESENT SUBJUNCTIVE	IMPERFECT SUBJUNCTIVE
(yo)	hable	hablara or hablase
(tú)	hables	hablaras or hablases
(él/ella/usted)	hable	hablara or hablase
(nosotros/as)	hablemos	habláramos or hablásemos
(vosotros/as)	habléis	hablarais or hablaseis
(ellos/ellas/ ustedes)	hablen	hablaran or hablasen

IMPERATIVE

habla / hablad

Use the present subjunctive in all cases other than these tú and vosotros affirmative forms.

EXAMPLE PHRASES

Luego **hablaremos** de ese tema. We'll talk about that later.

Recuérdame que **hable** con Daniel. Remind me to speak to Daniel.

¿Quieres que **hablemos**? Shall we talk?

Hay que darles una oportunidad para que **hablen**. We need to give them an opportunity to speak.

Remember that subject pronouns are not used very often in Spanish.

hacer (to do, to make)

	PRESENT		PRESENT PERFECT
(yo)	hago		he hecho
(tú)	haces		has hecho
(él/ella/usted)	hace		ha hecho
(nosotros/as)	hacemos		hemos hecho
(vosotros/as)	hacéis		habéis hecho
(ellos/ellas/ustedes)	hacen		han hecho

Past Tense

	PRETERITE		IMPERFECT
(yo)	hice		hacía
(tú)	hiciste		hacías
(él/ella/usted)	hizo		hacía
(nosotros/as)	hicimos		hacíamos
(vosotros/as)	hicisteis		hacíais
(ellos/ellas/ustedes)	hicieron		hacían

Past, talk about describ "g was doing M.TR. et te time"

GERUND *making*
haciendo *doing*

PAST PARTICIPLE
hecho

EXAMPLE PHRASES

¿Qué **hace** tu padre? What does your father do?

Están haciendo mucho ruido. They're making a lot of noise.

¿Quién **hizo** eso? Who did that?

Hicieron pintar la fachada del colegio. They had the front of the school painted.

Lo **hacía** para fastidiarme. He did it to annoy me.

Remember that subject pronouns are not used very often in Spanish.

hacer

	FUTURE	CONDITIONAL
(yo)	haré	haría
(tú)	harás	harías
(él/ella/usted)	hará	haría
(nosotros/as)	haremos	haríamos
(vosotros/as)	haréis	haríais
(ellos/ellas/ustedes)	harán	harían

	PRESENT SUBJUNCTIVE	IMPERFECT SUBJUNCTIVE
(yo)	haga	hiciera or hiciese
(tú)	hagas	hicieras or hicieses
(él/ella/usted)	haga	hiciera or hiciese
(nosotros/as)	hagamos	hiciéramos or hiciésemos
(vosotros/as)	hagáis	hicierais or hicieseis
(ellos/ellas/ustedes)	hagan	hicieran or hiciesen

IMPERATIVE

haz / haced

Use the present subjunctive in all cases other than these tú and vosotros affirmative forms.

EXAMPLE PHRASES

Lo **haré** yo mismo. I'll do it myself.

Dijiste que lo **harías**. You said you'd do it.

¿Quieres que **haga** las camas? Do you want me to make the beds?

Preferiría que **hiciera** menos calor. I'd rather it weren't so hot.

Hazlo como te he dicho. Do it the way I told you.

Remember that subject pronouns are not used very often in Spanish.

hay (there is, there are)

PRESENT

hay

PRESENT PERFECT

ha habido

PRETERITE

hubo

IMPERFECT

había

GERUND

habiendo

PAST PARTICIPLE

habido

EXAMPLE PHRASES

Esta tarde va a **haber** una manifestación. **There's going to be a demonstration** this evening.

Hay una iglesia en la esquina. **There's a church on the corner.**

Ha habido una tormenta. **There's been a storm.**

Hubo una guerra. **There was a war.**

Había mucha gente. **There were a lot of people.**

Remember that subject pronouns are not used very often in Spanish.

hay

FUTURE
habrá

CONDITIONAL
habría

PRESENT SUBJUNCTIVE
haya

IMPERFECT SUBJUNCTIVE
hubiera *or* hubiese

IMPERATIVE
not used

EXAMPLE PHRASES

¿**Habrá** suficiente? **Will there be enough?**

De este modo **habría** menos accidentes. **That way there would be fewer accidents.**

No creo que **haya** mucha gente en el recital. **I don't think there'll be many people at the concert.**

Si **hubiera** más espacio, pondría un sofá. **I'd have a sofa if there were more room.**

Remember that subject pronouns are not used very often in Spanish.

herir (to injure)

	PRESENT		PRESENT PERFECT
(yo)	hiero		he herido
(tú)	hieres		has herido
(él/ella/usted)	hiere		ha herido
(nosotros/as)	herimos		hemos herido
(vosotros/as)	herís		habéis herido
(ellos/ellas/ ustedes)	hieren		han herido

	PRETERITE		IMPERFECT
(yo)	herí		hería
(tú)	heriste		herías
(él/ella/usted)	hirió		hería
(nosotros/as)	herimos		heríamos
(vosotros/as)	heristeis		heríais
(ellos/ellas/ ustedes)	hirieron		herían

GERUND
hiriendo

PAST PARTICIPLE
herido

EXAMPLE PHRASES

Vas a **herir** sus sentimientos. You're going to hurt her feelings.

Me **hiere** que me digas eso. I'm hurt that you should say such a thing.

La **han herido** en el brazo. Her arm's been injured.

Lo **hirieron** en el pecho. He was wounded in the chest.

La **hería** en lo más hondo. She was deeply hurt.

Remember that subject pronouns are not used very often in Spanish.

herir

	FUTURE	CONDITIONAL
(yo)	heriré	heriría
(tú)	herirás	herirías
(él/ella/usted)	herirá	heriría
(nosotros/as)	heriremos	heriríamos
(vosotros/as)	heriréis	heriríais
(ellos/ellas/ ustedes)	herirán	herirían

	PRESENT SUBJUNCTIVE	IMPERFECT SUBJUNCTIVE
(yo)	hiera	hiriera or hiriese
(tú)	hieras	hirieras or hirieses
(él/ella/usted)	hiera	hiriera or hiriese
(nosotros/as)	hiramos	hiriéramos or hiriésemos
(vosotros/as)	hiráis	hirierais or hirieseis
(ellos/ellas/ ustedes)	hieran	hirieran or hiriesen

IMPERATIVE

hiere / herid

Use the present subjunctive in all cases other than these tú and vosotros affirmative forms.

Remember that subject pronouns are not used very often in Spanish.

huir (to escape)

	PRESENT		PRESENT PERFECT
(yo)	huyo		he huido
(tú)	huyes		has huido
(él/ella/usted)	huye		ha huido
(nosotros/as)	huimos		hemos huido
(vosotros/as)	huis		habéis huido
(ellos/ellas/ustedes)	huyen		han huido

	PRETERITE		IMPERFECT
(yo)	hui		huía
(tú)	huiste		huías
(él/ella/usted)	huyó		huía
(nosotros/as)	huimos		huíamos
(vosotros/as)	huisteis		huíais
(ellos/ellas/ustedes)	huyeron		huían

GERUND

huyendo

PAST PARTICIPLE

huido

EXAMPLE PHRASES

No sé por qué me **huye**. I don't know why he's avoiding me.

Salió **huyendo**. He ran away.

Ha huido de la cárcel. He has escaped from prison.

Huyeron del país. They fled the country.

Remember that subject pronouns are not used very often in Spanish.

huir

	FUTURE	CONDITIONAL
(yo)	huiré	huiría
(tú)	huirás	huirías
(él/ella/usted)	huirá	huiría
(nosotros/as)	huiremos	huiríamos
(vosotros/as)	huiréis	huiríais
(ellos/ellas/ ustedes)	huirán	huirían

	PRESENT SUBJUNCTIVE	IMPERFECT SUBJUNCTIVE
(yo)	huya	huyera *or* huyese
(tú)	huyas	huyeras *or* huyeses
(él/ella/usted)	huya	huyera *or* huyese
(nosotros/as)	huyamos	huyéramos *or* huyésemos
(vosotros/as)	huyáis	huyerais *or* huyeseis
(ellos/ellas/ ustedes)	huyan	huyeran *or* huyesen

IMPERATIVE

huye / huid

Use the present subjunctive in all cases other than these tú and vosotros affirmative forms.

EXAMPLE PHRASES

No quiero que **huyas** como un cobarde. I dont wont you to run away like a coward.

¡**Huye**! Si te atrapan, te matarán. Run! If they catch you, they'll kill you.

Remember that subject pronouns are not used very often in Spanish.

imponer (to impose)

	PRESENT		PRESENT PERFECT
(yo)	impongo		he impuesto
(tú)	impones		has impuesto
(él/ella/usted)	impone		ha impuesto
(nosotros/as)	imponemos		hemos impuesto
(vosotros/as)	imponéis		habéis impuesto
(ellos/ellas/ ustedes)	imponen		han impuesto

	PRETERITE	IMPERFECT
(yo)	impuse	imponía
(tú)	impusiste	imponías
(él/ella/usted)	impuso	imponía
(nosotros/as)	impusimos	imponíamos
(vosotros/as)	impusisteis	imponíais
(ellos/ellas/ ustedes)	impusieron	imponían

GERUND

imponiendo

PAST PARTICIPLE

impuesto

EXAMPLE PHRASES

La vista desde el acantilado **impone** un poco. The view from the cliff top is quite impressive.

La minifalda **se está imponiendo** de nuevo. The miniskirt is in fashion again.

Han impuesto la enseñanza religiosa. They have made religious education compulsory.

El corredor nigeriano **se impuso** en la segunda carrera. The Nigerian runner triumphed in the second race.

Mi abuelo **imponía** mucho respeto. My grandfather commanded a lot of respect.

Remember that subject pronouns are not used very often in Spanish.

imponer

	FUTURE	CONDITIONAL
(yo)	impondré	impondría
(tú)	impondrás	impondrías
(él/ella/usted)	impondrá	impondría
(nosotros/as)	impondremos	impondríamos
(vosotros/as)	impondréis	impondríais
(ellos/ellas/ ustedes)	impondrán	impondrían

	PRESENT SUBJUNCTIVE	IMPERFECT SUBJUNCTIVE
(yo)	imponga	impusiera or impusiese
(tú)	impongas	impusieras or impusieses
(él/ella/usted)	imponga	impusiera or impusiese
(nosotros/as)	impongamos	impusiéramos or impusiésemos
(vosotros/as)	impongáis	impusierais or impusieseis
(ellos/ellas/ ustedes)	impongan	impusieran or impusiesen

IMPERATIVE

impón / imponed

Use the present subjunctive in all cases other than these tú and vosotros affirmative forms.

EXAMPLE PHRASES

Impondrán multas de hasta 50 euros. **They'll impose fines of up to 50 euros.**

Remember that subject pronouns are not used very often in Spanish.

imprimir (to print)

	PRESENT	PRESENT PERFECT
(yo)	imprimo	he imprimido
(tú)	imprimes	has imprimido
(él/ella/usted)	imprime	ha imprimido
(nosotros/as)	imprimimos	hemos imprimido
(vosotros/as)	imprimís	habéis imprimido
(ellos/ellas/ ustedes)	imprimen	han imprimido

	PRETERITE	IMPERFECT
(yo)	imprimí	imprimía
(tú)	imprimiste	imprimías
(él/ella/usted)	imprimió	imprimía
(nosotros/as)	imprimimos	imprimíamos
(vosotros/as)	imprimisteis	imprimíais
(ellos/ellas/ ustedes)	imprimieron	imprimían

GERUND

imprimiendo

PAST PARTICIPLE

imprimido, impreso

EXAMPLE PHRASES

Una experiencia así **imprime** carácter. **An experience like that is character-building.**

¿**Has imprimido** el documento? **Have you printed out the file?**

Se imprimieron sólo doce copias del libro. **Only twelve copies of the book were printed.**

El sillón **imprimía** un cierto aire de distinción al salón. **The chair gave the living-room a certain air of distinction.**

Remember that subject pronouns are not used very often in Spanish.

imprimir

	FUTURE	CONDITIONAL
(yo)	imprimiré	imprimiría
(tú)	imprimirás	imprimirías
(él/ella/usted)	imprimirá	imprimiría
(nosotros/as)	imprimiremos	imprimiríamos
(vosotros/as)	imprimiréis	imprimiríais
(ellos/ellas/ ustedes)	imprimirán	imprimirían

	PRESENT SUBJUNCTIVE	IMPERFECT SUBJUNCTIVE
(yo)	imprima	imprimiera or imprimiese
(tú)	imprimas	imprimieras or imprimieses
(él/ella/usted)	imprima	imprimiera or imprimiese
(nosotros/as)	imprimamos	imprimiéramos or imprimiésemos
(vosotros/as)	imprimáis	imprimierais or imprimieseis
(ellos/ellas/ ustedes)	impriman	imprimieran or imprimiesen

IMPERATIVE

imprime / imprimid

Use the present subjunctive in all cases other than these tú and vosotros affirmative forms.

Remember that subject pronouns are not used very often in Spanish.

ir (to go)

	PRESENT		PRESENT PERFECT
(yo)	voy		he ido
(tú)	vas		has ido
(él/ella/usted)	va		ha ido
(nosotros/as)	vamos		hemos ido
(vosotros/as)	vais		habéis ido
(ellos/ellas/ustedes)	van		han ido

	PRETERITE		IMPERFECT
(yo)	fui		iba
(tú)	fuiste		ibas
(él/ella/usted)	fue		iba
(nosotros/as)	fuimos		íbamos
(vosotros/as)	fuisteis		ibais
(ellos/ellas/ustedes)	fueron		iban

GERUND

yendo

PAST PARTICIPLE

ido

EXAMPLE PHRASES

¿Puedo **ir** contigo? Can I come with you?

¿**Vamos** a comer al campo? Shall we have a picnic in the country?

Estoy **yendo** a clases de natación. I'm taking swimming lessons.

Ha ido a comprar el pan. She's gone to buy some bread.

Anoche **fuimos** al cine. We went to the cinema last night.

Remember that subject pronouns are not used very often in Spanish.

ir

	FUTURE	CONDITIONAL
(yo)	iré	iría
(tú)	irás	irías
(él/ella/usted)	irá	iría
(nosotros/as)	iremos	iríamos
(vosotros/as)	iréis	iríais
(ellos/ellas/ ustedes)	irán	irían

	PRESENT SUBJUNCTIVE	IMPERFECT SUBJUNCTIVE
(yo)	vaya	fuera or fuese
(tú)	vayas	fueras or fueses
(él/ella/usted)	vaya	fuera or fuese
(nosotros/as)	vayamos	fuéramos or fuésemos
(vosotros/as)	vayáis	fuerais or fueseis
(ellos/ellas/ ustedes)	vayan	fueran or fuesen

IMPERATIVE

ve / id

Use the present subjunctive in most cases other than these tú and vosotros affirmative forms.
However, in the 'let's' affirmative form, vamos is more common than vayamos.

EXAMPLE PHRASES

El domingo **iré** a Edimburgo. **I'll go to Edinburgh on Sunday.**

Dijeron que **irían** andando. **They said they'd walk.**

¡Que te **vaya** bien! **Take care of yourself!**

Quería pedirte que **fueras** en mi lugar. **I wanted to ask you if you'd take my place.**

No **te vayas** sin despedirte. **Don't go without saying goodbye.**

Vete a hacer los deberes. **Go and do your homework.**

Remember that subject pronouns are not used very often in Spanish.

jugar (to play)

	PRESENT		PRESENT PERFECT
(yo)	juego		he jugado
(tú)	juegas		has jugado
(él/ella/usted)	juega		ha jugado
(nosotros/as)	jugamos		hemos jugado
(vosotros/as)	jugáis		habéis jugado
(ellos/ellas/ ustedes)	juegan		han jugado

	PRETERITE		IMPERFECT
(yo)	jugué		jugaba
(tú)	jugaste		jugabas
(él/ella/usted)	jugó		jugaba
(nosotros/as)	jugamos		jugábamos
(vosotros/as)	jugasteis		jugabais
(ellos/ellas/ ustedes)	jugaron		jugaban

GERUND

jugando

PAST PARTICIPLE

jugado

EXAMPLE PHRASES

Juego al fútbol todos los domingos. **I play football every Sunday.**

Están jugando en el jardín. **They're playing in the garden.**

Le **han jugado** una mala pasada. **They played a dirty trick on him.**

Después de cenar **jugamos** a las cartas. **After dinner we played cards.**

Se jugaba la vida continuamente. **She was constantly risking her life.**

Remember that subject pronouns are not used very often in Spanish.

jugar

	FUTURE	**CONDITIONAL**
(yo)	jugaré	jugaría
(tú)	jugarás	jugarías
(él/ella/usted)	jugará	jugaría
(nosotros/as)	jugaremos	jugaríamos
(vosotros/as)	jugaréis	jugaríais
(ellos/ellas/ ustedes)	jugarán	jugarían

	PRESENT SUBJUNCTIVE	**IMPERFECT SUBJUNCTIVE**
(yo)	juegue	jugara or jugase
(tú)	juegues	jugaras or jugases
(él/ella/usted)	juegue	jugara or jugase
(nosotros/as)	juguemos	jugáramos or jugásemos
(vosotros/as)	juguéis	jugarais or jugaseis
(ellos/ellas/ ustedes)	jueguen	jugaran or jugasen

IMPERATIVE

juega / jugad

Use the present subjunctive in all cases other than these tú and vosotros affirmative forms.

EXAMPLE PHRASES

Jugarán contra el Real Madrid. **They'll play Real Madrid.**

Jugarías mejor si estuvieras más relajado. **You'd play better if you were more relaxed.**

No **juegues** con tu salud. **Don't take risks with your health.**

El médico le aconsejó que **jugara** más y leyera menos. **The doctor advised him to play more and read less.**

Remember that subject pronouns are not used very often in Spanish.

leer (to read)

	PRESENT		PRESENT PERFECT
(yo)	leo		he leído
(tú)	lees		has leído
(él/ella/usted)	lee		ha leído
(nosotros/as)	leemos		hemos leído
(vosotros/as)	leéis		habéis leído
(ellos/ellas/ustedes)	leen		han leído

	PRETERITE		IMPERFECT
(yo)	leí		leía
(tú)	leíste		leías
(él/ella/usted)	leyó		leía
(nosotros/as)	leímos		leíamos
(vosotros/as)	leísteis		leíais
(ellos/ellas/ustedes)	leyeron		leían

GERUND
leyendo

PAST PARTICIPLE
leído

EXAMPLE PHRASES

Hace mucho tiempo que no **leo** nada. I haven't read anything for ages.
Estoy leyendo un libro muy interesante. I'm reading a very interesting book.
¿**Has leído** esta novela? Have you read this novel?
Lo **leí** hace tiempo. I read it a while ago.
Antes **leía** mucho más. I used to read much more than now.

Remember that subject pronouns are not used very often in Spanish.

leer

	FUTURE	CONDITIONAL
(yo)	leeré	leería
(tú)	leerás	leerías
(él/ella/usted)	leerá	leería
(nosotros/as)	leeremos	leeríamos
(vosotros/as)	leeréis	leeríais
(ellos/ellas/ustedes)	leerán	leerían

	PRESENT SUBJUNCTIVE	IMPERFECT SUBJUNCTIVE
(yo)	lea	leyera or leyese
(tú)	leas	leyeras or leyeses
(él/ella/usted)	lea	leyera or leyese
(nosotros/as)	leamos	leyéramos or leyésemos
(vosotros/as)	leáis	leyerais or leyeseis
(ellos/ellas/ustedes)	lean	leyeran or leyesen

IMPERATIVE

lee / leed

Use the present subjunctive in all cases other than these tú and vosotros affirmative forms.

EXAMPLE PHRASES

Si os portáis bien, os **leeré** un cuento. If you behave yourselves, I'll read you a story.

Yo **leería** también la letra pequeña. I'd read the small print as well.

Quiero que lo **leas** y me digas qué piensas. I want you to read it and tell me what you think.

No **leas** tan deprisa. Don't read so fast.

Remember that subject pronouns are not used very often in Spanish.

levantar (to lift)

	PRESENT		PRESENT PERFECT
(yo)	levanto		he levantado
(tú)	levantas		has levantado
(él/ella/usted)	levanta		ha levantado
(nosotros/as)	levantamos		hemos levantado
(vosotros/as)	levantáis		habéis levantado
(ellos/ellas/ ustedes)	levantan		han levantado

	PRETERITE		IMPERFECT
(yo)	levanté		levantaba
(tú)	levantaste		levantabas
(él/ella/usted)	levantó		levantaba
(nosotros/as)	levantamos		levantábamos
(vosotros/as)	levantasteis		levantabais
(ellos/ellas/ ustedes)	levantaron		levantaban

GERUND

levantando

PAST PARTICIPLE

levantado

EXAMPLE PHRASES

No me importa **levantarme** temprano. I don't mind getting up early.

Siempre **se levanta** de mal humor. He's always in a bad mood when he gets up.

Hoy **me he levantado** temprano. I got up early this morning.

Levantó la maleta como si no pesara nada. He lifted up the suitcase as if it weighed nothing.

Me **levanté** y seguí caminando. I got up and carried on walking.

Remember that subject pronouns are not used very often in Spanish.

levantar

	FUTURE	CONDITIONAL
(yo)	levantaré	levantaría
(tú)	levantarás	levantarías
(él/ella/usted)	levantará	levantaría
(nosotros/as)	levantaremos	levantaríamos
(vosotros/as)	levantaréis	levantaríais
(ellos/ellas/ ustedes)	levantarán	levantarían

	PRESENT SUBJUNCTIVE	IMPERFECT SUBJUNCTIVE
(yo)	levante	levantara or levantase
(tú)	levantes	levantaras or levantases
(él/ella/usted)	levante	levantara or levantase
(nosotros/as)	levantemos	levantáramos or levantásemos
(vosotros/as)	levantéis	levantarais or levantaseis
(ellos/ellas/ ustedes)	levanten	levantaran or levantasen

IMPERATIVE

levanta / levantad

Use the present subjunctive in all cases other than these tú and vosotros affirmative forms.

EXAMPLE PHRASES

La noticia le **levantará** el ánimo. This news will raise her spirits

Sí pudiera **me levantaría** siempre tarde. I'd sleep in every day, if I could.

No me **levantes** la voz. Don't raise your voice to me.

Levanta la tapa. Lift the lid.

Levantad la mano si tenéis alguna duda. Put up your hands if you are unclear about anything.

Remember that subject pronouns are not used very often in Spanish.

llover (to rain)

PRESENT
llueve

PRESENT PERFECT
ha llovido

PRETERITE
llovió

IMPERFECT
llovía

GERUND
lloviendo

PAST PARTICIPLE
llovido

EXAMPLE PHRASES

Hace semanas que no **llueve**. It hasn't rained for weeks.

Está lloviendo. It's raining.

Le **han llovido** las ofertas. He's received lots of offers.

Llovió sin parar. It rained non-stop.

Llovía a cántaros. It was pouring down.

Remember that subject pronouns are not used very often in Spanish.

llover

FUTURE
lloverá

CONDITIONAL
llovería

PRESENT SUBJUNCTIVE
llueva

IMPERFECT SUBJUNCTIVE
lloviera *or* lloviese

IMPERATIVE
not used

EXAMPLE PHRASES

Sabía que le **lloverían** las críticas. She knew she would be much criticized.

Espero que no **llueva** este fin de semana. I hope it won't rain this weekend.

Si no **lloviera** podríamos salir a dar una vuelta. We could go for a walk if it weren't raining.

Remember that subject pronouns are not used very often in Spanish.

lucir (to shine)

	PRESENT		PRESENT PERFECT
(yo)	luzco		he lucido
(tú)	luces		has lucido
(él/ella/usted)	luce		ha lucido
(nosotros/as)	lucimos		hemos lucido
(vosotros/as)	lucís		habéis lucido
(ellos/ellas/ustedes)	lucen		han lucido

	PRETERITE		IMPERFECT
(yo)	lucí		lucía
(tú)	luciste		lucías
(él/ella/usted)	lució		lucía
(nosotros/as)	lucimos		lucíamos
(vosotros/as)	lucisteis		lucíais
(ellos/ellas/ustedes)	lucieron		lucían

GERUND

luciendo

PAST PARTICIPLE

lucido

EXAMPLE PHRASES

Ahí no **luce** nada. It doesn't look very good there.

¡Anda, que **te has lucido**! Well, you've excelled yourself!

Lucían las estrellas. The stars were shining.

Remember that subject pronouns are not used very often in Spanish.

lucir

	FUTURE	CONDITIONAL
(yo)	luciré	luciría
(tú)	lucirás	lucirías
(él/ella/usted)	lucirá	luciría
(nosotros/as)	luciremos	luciríamos
(vosotros/as)	luciréis	luciríais
(ellos/ellas/ ustedes)	lucirán	lucirían

	PRESENT SUBJUNCTIVE	IMPERFECT SUBJUNCTIVE
(yo)	luzca	luciera *or* luciese
(tú)	luzcas	lucieras *or* lucieses
(él/ella/usted)	luzca	luciera *or* luciese
(nosotros/as)	luzcamos	luciéramos *or* luciésemos
(vosotros/as)	luzcáis	lucierais *or* lucieseis
(ellos/ellas/ ustedes)	luzcan	lucieran *or* luciesen

IMPERATIVE

luce / lucid

Use the present subjunctive in all cases other than these tú *and* vosotros *affirmative forms.*

EXAMPLE PHRASES

Lucirá un traje muy elegante. **She will be wearing a very smart dress.**
Luciría más con otros zapatos. **It would look much better with another pair of shoes.**
Quiero que esta noche **luzcas** tú el collar. **I want you to wear the necklace tonight.**

Remember that subject pronouns are not used very often in Spanish.

morir (to die)

	PRESENT		PRESENT PERFECT
(yo)	muero		he muerto
(tú)	mueres		has muerto
(él/ella/usted)	muere		ha muerto
(nosotros/as)	morimos		hemos muerto
(vosotros/as)	morís		habéis muerto
(ellos/ellas/ ustedes)	mueren		han muerto

	PRETERITE		IMPERFECT
(yo)	morí		moría
(tú)	moriste		morías
(él/ella/usted)	murió		moría
(nosotros/as)	morimos		moríamos
(vosotros/as)	moristeis		moríais
(ellos/ellas/ ustedes)	murieron		morían

GERUND	PAST PARTICIPLE
muriendo	muerto

EXAMPLE PHRASES

¡Me muero de hambre! I'm starving!

Se está muriendo. She's dying.

Se le ha muerto el gato. His cat has died.

Se murió el mes pasado. He died last month.

Me moría de ganas de contárselo. I was dying to tell her.

Remember that subject pronouns are not used very often in Spanish.

morir

	FUTURE	CONDITIONAL
(yo)	moriré	moriría
(tú)	morirás	morirías
(él/ella/usted)	morirá	moriría
(nosotros/as)	moriremos	moriríamos
(vosotros/as)	moriréis	moriríais
(ellos/ellas/ ustedes)	morirán	morirían

	PRESENT SUBJUNCTIVE	IMPERFECT SUBJUNCTIVE
(yo)	muera	muriera or muriese
(tú)	mueras	murieras or murieses
(él/ella/usted)	muera	muriera or muriese
(nosotros/as)	muramos	muriéramos or muriésemos
(vosotros/as)	muráis	murierais or murieseis
(ellos/ellas/ ustedes)	mueran	murieran or muriesen

IMPERATIVE
muere / morid

Use the present subjunctive in all cases other than these tú and vosotros affirmative forms.

EXAMPLE PHRASES

Cuando te lo cuente **te morirás** de risa. You'll kill yourself laughing when
   I tell you.

Yo **me moriría** de vergüenza. I'd die of shame.

Cuando **me muera**... When I die...

¡Por favor, no **te mueras**! Please don't die!

Estoy muerto de miedo. I'm scared stiff.

Remember that subject pronouns are not used very often in Spanish.

mover (to move)

	PRESENT		PRESENT PERFECT
(yo)	muevo		he movido
(tú)	mueves		has movido
(él/ella/usted)	mueve		ha movido
(nosotros/as)	movemos		hemos movido
(vosotros/as)	movéis		habéis movido
(ellos/ellas/ustedes)	mueven		han movido

	PRETERITE		IMPERFECT
(yo)	moví		movía
(tú)	moviste		movías
(él/ella/usted)	movió		movía
(nosotros/as)	movimos		movíamos
(vosotros/as)	movisteis		movíais
(ellos/ellas/ustedes)	movieron		movían

GERUND
moviendo

PAST PARTICIPLE
movido

EXAMPLE PHRASES

El perro no dejaba de **mover** la cola. **The dog kept wagging its tail.**

Se está **moviendo**. **It's moving.**

¿**Has movido** ese mueble de sitio? **Have you moved that piece of furniture?**

No **se movieron** de casa. **They didn't leave the house.**

Antes **se movía** en esos ambientes. **He used to move in those circles.**

Remember that subject pronouns are not used very often in Spanish.

mover

	FUTURE	CONDITIONAL
(yo)	moveré	movería
(tú)	moverás	moverías
(él/ella/usted)	moverá	movería
(nosotros/as)	moveremos	moveríamos
(vosotros/as)	moveréis	moveríais
(ellos/ellas/ ustedes)	moverán	moverían

	PRESENT SUBJUNCTIVE	IMPERFECT SUBJUNCTIVE
(yo)	mueva	moviera or moviese
(tú)	muevas	movieras or movieses
(él/ella/usted)	mueva	moviera or moviese
(nosotros/as)	movamos	moviéramos or moviésemos
(vosotros/as)	mováis	movierais or movieseis
(ellos/ellas/ ustedes)	muevan	movieran or moviesen

IMPERATIVE

mueve / moved

Use the present subjunctive in all cases other than these tú *and* vosotros *affirmative forms.*

EXAMPLE PHRASES

Prométeme que no **te moverás** de aquí. Promise me you won't move from here.

No **te muevas**. Don't move.

Mueve un poco las cajas para que podamos pasar. Move the boxes a bit so that we can get past.

Remember that subject pronouns are not used very often in Spanish.

nacer (to be born)

	PRESENT	PRESENT PERFECT
(yo)	nazco	he nacido
(tú)	naces	has nacido
(él/ella/usted)	nace	ha nacido
(nosotros/as)	nacemos	hemos nacido
(vosotros/as)	nacéis	habéis nacido
(ellos/ellas/ ustedes)	nacen	han nacido

	PRETERITE	IMPERFECT
(yo)	nací	nacía
(tú)	naciste	nacías
(él/ella/usted)	nació	nacía
(nosotros/as)	nacimos	nacíamos
(vosotros/as)	nacisteis	nacíais
(ellos/ellas/ ustedes)	nacieron	nacían

GERUND

naciendo

PAST PARTICIPLE

nacido

EXAMPLE PHRASES

Nacen cuatro niños por minuto. Four children are born every minute.

Ha nacido antes de tiempo. It was premature.

Nació en 1980. He was born in 1980.

¿Cuándo **naciste**? When were you born?

En aquella época había muchos más niños que **nacían** en casa. Many more babies were born at home in those days.

Remember that subject pronouns are not used very often in Spanish.

nacer

	FUTURE	CONDITIONAL
(yo)	naceré	nacería
(tú)	nacerás	nacerías
(él/ella/usted)	nacerá	nacería
(nosotros/as)	naceremos	naceríamos
(vosotros/as)	naceréis	naceríais
(ellos/ellas/ustedes)	nacerán	nacerían

	PRESENT SUBJUNCTIVE	IMPERFECT SUBJUNCTIVE
(yo)	nazca	naciera or naciese
(tú)	nazcas	nacieras or nacieses
(él/ella/usted)	nazca	naciera or naciese
(nosotros/as)	nazcamos	naciéramos or naciésemos
(vosotros/as)	nazcáis	nacierais or nacieseis
(ellos/ellas/ustedes)	nazcan	nacieran or naciesen

IMPERATIVE

nace / naced

Use the present subjunctive in all cases other than these tú and vosotros affirmative forms.

EXAMPLE PHRASES

Nacerá el año que viene. It will be born next year.

Queremos que **nazca** en España. We want it to be born in Spain.

Si **naciera** hoy, sería tauro. He'd be a Taurus if he were born today.

Remember that subject pronouns are not used very often in Spanish.

negar (to deny, to refuse)

	PRESENT		PRESENT PERFECT
(yo)	niego		he negado
(tú)	niegas		has negado
(él/ella/usted)	niega		ha negado
(nosotros/as)	negamos		hemos negado
(vosotros/as)	negáis		habéis negado
(ellos/ellas/ ustedes)	niegan		han negado

	PRETERITE		IMPERFECT
(yo)	negué		negaba
(tú)	negaste		negabas
(él/ella/usted)	negó		negaba
(nosotros/as)	negamos		negábamos
(vosotros/as)	negasteis		negabais
(ellos/ellas/ ustedes)	negaron		negaban

GERUND

negando

PAST PARTICIPLE

negado

EXAMPLE PHRASES

No lo puedes **negar**. You can't deny it.

Me **niego** a creerlo. I refuse to believe it.

Me **ha negado** el favor. He wouldn't do me this favour.

Se **negó** a venir con nosotros. She refused to come with us.

Decían que era el ladrón, pero él lo **negaba**. They said that he was the thief, but he denied it.

Remember that subject pronouns are not used very often in Spanish.

negar

	FUTURE	CONDITIONAL
(yo)	negaré	negaría
(tú)	negarás	negarías
(él/ella/usted)	negará	negaría
(nosotros/as)	negaremos	negaríamos
(vosotros/as)	negaréis	negaríais
(ellos/ellas/ ustedes)	negarán	negarían

	PRESENT SUBJUNCTIVE	IMPERFECT SUBJUNCTIVE
(yo)	niegue	negara or negase
(tú)	niegues	negaras or negases
(él/ella/usted)	niegue	negara or negase
(nosotros/as)	neguemos	negáramos or negásemos
(vosotros/as)	neguéis	negarais or negaseis
(ellos/ellas/ ustedes)	nieguen	negaran or negasen

IMPERATIVE
niega / negad

Use the present subjunctive in all cases other than these tú and vosotros affirmative forms.

EXAMPLE PHRASES
No me **negarás** que es barato. **You can't say it's not cheap.**

Si lo **negaras**, nadie te creería. **If you denied it, nobody would believe you.**

No lo **niegues**. **Don't deny it.**

Remember that subject pronouns are not used very often in Spanish.

oír (to hear)

	PRESENT	PRESENT PERFECT
(yo)	oigo	he oído
(tú)	oyes	has oído
(él/ella/usted)	oye	ha oído
(nosotros/as)	oímos	hemos oído
(vosotros/as)	oís	habéis oído
(ellos/ellas/ustedes)	oyen	han oído

	PRETERITE	IMPERFECT
(yo)	oí	oía
(tú)	oíste	oías
(él/ella/usted)	oyó	oía
(nosotros/as)	oímos	oíamos
(vosotros/as)	oísteis	oíais
(ellos/ellas/ustedes)	oyeron	oían

GERUND	PAST PARTICIPLE
oyendo	oído

EXAMPLE PHRASES

No **oigo** nada. I can't hear anything.

Hemos estado oyendo las noticias. We've been listening to the news.

¿**Has oído** eso? Did you hear that?

Lo **oí** por casualidad. I heard it by chance.

No **oía** muy bien. He couldn't hear very well.

Remember that subject pronouns are not used very often in Spanish.

oír

	FUTURE	CONDITIONAL
(yo)	oiré	oiría
(tú)	oirás	oirías
(él/ella/usted)	oirá	oiría
(nosotros/as)	oiremos	oiríamos
(vosotros/as)	oiréis	oiríais
(ellos/ellas/ ustedes)	oirán	oirían

	PRESENT SUBJUNCTIVE	IMPERFECT SUBJUNCTIVE
(yo)	oiga	oyera or oyese
(tú)	oigas	oyeras or oyeses
(él/ella/usted)	oiga	oyera or oyese
(nosotros/as)	oigamos	oyéramos or oyésemos
(vosotros/as)	oigáis	oyerais or oyeseis
(ellos/ellas/ ustedes)	oigan	oyeran or oyesen

IMPERATIVE

oye / oíd

Use the present subjunctive in all cases other than these tú and vosotros affirmative forms.

EXAMPLE PHRASES

Oirías mal. You must have misunderstood.

¡Oiga! ¡A ver si mira por dónde va! Excuse me! Why don't you look where you're going?

Óyeme bien, no vuelvas a hacer eso. Now listen carefully; don't do that again.

Remember that subject pronouns are not used very often in Spanish.

oler (to smell)

	PRESENT	PRESENT PERFECT
(yo)	huelo	he olido
(tú)	hueles	has olido
(él/ella/usted)	huele	ha olido
(nosotros/as)	olemos	hemos olido
(vosotros/as)	oléis	habéis olido
(ellos/ellas/ustedes)	huelen	han olido

	PRETERITE	IMPERFECT
(yo)	olí	olía
(tú)	oliste	olías
(él/ella/usted)	olió	olía
(nosotros/as)	olimos	olíamos
(vosotros/as)	olisteis	olíais
(ellos/ellas/ustedes)	olieron	olían

GERUND
oliendo

PAST PARTICIPLE
olido

EXAMPLE PHRASES

Huele a pescado. It smells of fish.

El perro **estaba oliendo** la basura. The dog was sniffing the rubbish.

Se ha olido algo. He's started to suspect.

A mí el asunto me **olió** mal. I thought there was something fishy about it.

Olía muy bien. It smelled really nice.

Remember that subject pronouns are not used very often in Spanish.

oler

	FUTURE	CONDITIONAL
(yo)	oleré	olería
(tú)	olerás	olerías
(él/ella/usted)	olerá	olería
(nosotros/as)	oleremos	oleríamos
(vosotros/as)	oleréis	oleríais
(ellos/ellas/ustedes)	olerán	olerían

	PRESENT SUBJUNCTIVE	IMPERFECT SUBJUNCTIVE
(yo)	huela	oliera or oliese
(tú)	huelas	olieras or olieses
(él/ella/usted)	huela	oliera or oliese
(nosotros/as)	olamos	oliéramos or oliésemos
(vosotros/as)	oláis	olierais or olieseis
(ellos/ellas/ustedes)	huelan	olieran or oliesen

IMPERATIVE
huele / oled

Use the present subjunctive in all cases other than these tú and vosotros affirmative forms.

EXAMPLE PHRASES
Con esto ya no **olerá**. This will take the smell away.
Si te **oliera** a quemado, apágalo. If it should smell hot, turn it off.

Remember that subject pronouns are not used very often in Spanish.

pagar (to pay, to pay for)

	PRESENT	PRESENT PERFECT
(yo)	pago	he pagado
(tú)	pagas	has pagado
(él/ella/usted)	paga	ha pagado
(nosotros/as)	pagamos	hemos pagado
(vosotros/as)	pagáis	habéis pagado
(ellos/ellas/ustedes)	pagan	han pagado

	PRETERITE	IMPERFECT
(yo)	pagué	pagaba
(tú)	pagaste	pagabas
(él/ella/usted)	pagó	pagaba
(nosotros/as)	pagamos	pagábamos
(vosotros/as)	pagasteis	pagabais
(ellos/ellas/ustedes)	pagaron	pagaban

GERUND	PAST PARTICIPLE
pagando	pagado

EXAMPLE PHRASES

Se puede **pagar** con tarjeta de crédito. You can pay by credit card.

¿Cuánto te **pagan** al mes? How much do they pay you a month?

No **han pagado** el alquiler. They haven't paid the rent.

Lo **pagué** en efectivo. I paid for it in cash.

Me **pagaban** muy poco. I got paid very little.

Remember that subject pronouns are not used very often in Spanish.

pagar

	FUTURE	CONDITIONAL
(yo)	pagaré	pagaría
(tú)	pagarás	pagarías
(él/ella/usted)	pagará	pagaría
(nosotros/as)	pagaremos	pagaríamos
(vosotros/as)	pagaréis	pagaríais
(ellos/ellas/ustedes)	pagarán	pagarían

	PRESENT SUBJUNCTIVE	IMPERFECT SUBJUNCTIVE
(yo)	pague	pagara or pagase
(tú)	pagues	pagaras or pagases
(él/ella/usted)	pague	pagara or pagase
(nosotros/as)	paguemos	pagáramos or pagásemos
(vosotros/as)	paguéis	pagarais or pagaseis
(ellos/ellas/ustedes)	paguen	pagaran or pagasen

IMPERATIVE

paga / pagad

Use the present subjunctive in all cases other than these tú and vosotros affirmative forms.

EXAMPLE PHRASES

Yo te **pagaré** la entrada. I'll pay for your ticket.

¡Quiero que **pague** por lo que me ha hecho! I want him to pay for what he's done to me!

Si **pagase** sus deudas, se quedaría sin nada. He'd be left with nothing if he paid his debts.

No les **pagues** hasta que lo hayan hecho. Don't pay them until they've done it.

Págame lo que me debes. Pay me what you owe me.

Remember that subject pronouns are not used very often in Spanish.

partir (to leave)

	PRESENT	PRESENT PERFECT
(yo)	parto	he partido
(tú)	partes	has partido
(él/ella/usted)	parte	ha partido
(nosotros/as)	partimos	hemos partido
(vosotros/as)	partís	habéis partido
(ellos/ellas/ustedes)	parten	han partido

	PRETERITE	IMPERFECT
(yo)	partí	partía
(tú)	partiste	partías
(él/ella/usted)	partió	partía
(nosotros/as)	partimos	partíamos
(vosotros/as)	partisteis	partíais
(ellos/ellas/ustedes)	partieron	partían

GERUND
partiendo

PAST PARTICIPLE
partido

EXAMPLE PHRASES

¿Te **parto** un trozo de queso? Shall I cut you a piece of cheese?

Partiendo de la base de que... Assuming that...

El remo **se partió** en dos. The oar broke in two.

Se partían de risa. They were splitting their sides laughing.

Remember that subject pronouns are not used very often in Spanish.

partir

	FUTURE	CONDITIONAL
(yo)	partiré	partiría
(tú)	partirás	partirías
(él/ella/usted)	partirá	partiría
(nosotros/as)	partiremos	partiríamos
(vosotros/as)	partiréis	partiríais
(ellos/ellas/ ustedes)	partirán	partirían

	PRESENT SUBJUNCTIVE	IMPERFECT SUBJUNCTIVE
(yo)	parta	partiera or partiese
(tú)	partas	partieras or partieses
(él/ella/usted)	parta	partiera or partiese
(nosotros/as)	partamos	partiéramos or partiésemos
(vosotros/as)	partáis	partierais or partieseis
(ellos/ellas/ ustedes)	partan	partieran or partiesen

IMPERATIVE

parte / partid

Use the present subjunctive in all cases other than these tú and vosotros affirmative forms.

EXAMPLE PHRASES

La expedición **partirá** mañana de París. **The expedition is to leave from Paris tomorrow.**

Eso le **partiría** el corazón. **That would break his heart.**

No **partas** todavía el pan. **Don't slice the bread yet.**

Pártelo por la mitad. **Cut it in half.**

Remember that subject pronouns are not used very often in Spanish.

pedir (to ask for, to ask)

	PRESENT		PRESENT PERFECT
(yo)	pido		he pedido
(tú)	pides		has pedido
(él/ella/usted)	pide		ha pedido
(nosotros/as)	pedimos		hemos pedido
(vosotros/as)	pedís		habéis pedido
(ellos/ellas/ ustedes)	piden		han pedido

	PRETERITE		IMPERFECT
(yo)	pedí		pedía
(tú)	pediste		pedías
(él/ella/usted)	pidió		pedía
(nosotros/as)	pedimos		pedíamos
(vosotros/as)	pedisteis		pedíais
(ellos/ellas/ ustedes)	pidieron		pedían

GERUND

pidiendo

PAST PARTICIPLE

pedido

EXAMPLE PHRASES

¿Cuánto **pide** por el coche? How much is he asking for the car?

La casa **está pidiendo** a gritos una mano de pintura. The house is crying out to be painted.

Hemos pedido dos cervezas. We've ordered two beers.

No nos **pidieron** el pasaporte. They didn't ask us for our passports.

Pedían dos millones de rescate. They were demanding a two-million ransom.

Remember that subject pronouns are not used very often in Spanish.

pedir

	FUTURE	CONDITIONAL
(yo)	pediré	pediría
(tú)	pedirás	pedirías
(él/ella/usted)	pedirá	pediría
(nosotros/as)	pediremos	pediríamos
(vosotros/as)	pediréis	pediríais
(ellos/ellas/ ustedes)	pedirán	pedirían

	PRESENT SUBJUNCTIVE	IMPERFECT SUBJUNCTIVE
(yo)	pida	pidiera or pidiese
(tú)	pidas	pidieras or pidieses
(él/ella/usted)	pida	pidiera or pidiese
(nosotros/as)	pidamos	pidiéramos or pidiésemos
(vosotros/as)	pidáis	pidierais or pidieseis
(ellos/ellas/ ustedes)	pidan	pidieran or pidiesen

IMPERATIVE

pide / pedid

Use the present subjunctive in all cases other than these tú and vosotros affirmative forms.

EXAMPLE PHRASES

Si se entera, te **pedirá** explicaciones. If he finds out, he'll ask you for an explanation.

Nunca te **pediría** que hicieras una cosa así. I'd never ask you to do anything like that.

Y que sea lo último que me **pidas**. And don't ask me for anything else.

Pídele el teléfono. Ask her for her telephone number.

Remember that subject pronouns are not used very often in Spanish.

pensar (to think)

	PRESENT		PRESENT PERFECT
(yo)	pienso		he pensado
(tú)	piensas		has pensado
(él/ella/usted)	piensa		ha pensado
(nosotros/as)	pensamos		hemos pensado
(vosotros/as)	pensáis		habéis pensado
(ellos/ellas/ustedes)	piensan		han pensado

	PRETERITE		IMPERFECT
(yo)	pensé		pensaba
(tú)	pensaste		pensabas
(él/ella/usted)	pensó		pensaba
(nosotros/as)	pensamos		pensábamos
(vosotros/as)	pensasteis		pensabais
(ellos/ellas/ustedes)	pensaron		pensaban

GERUND

pensando

PAST PARTICIPLE

pensado

EXAMPLE PHRASES

¿**Piensas** que vale la pena? Do you think it's worth it?

¿Qué **piensas** del aborto? What do you think about abortion?

Está **pensando** en comprarse un piso. He's thinking about buying a flat.

¿Lo **has pensado** bien? Have you thought about it carefully?

Pensaba que vendrías. I thought you'd come.

Remember that subject pronouns are not used very often in Spanish.

pensar

	FUTURE	CONDITIONAL
(yo)	pensaré	pensaría
(tú)	pensarás	pensarías
(él/ella/usted)	pensará	pensaría
(nosotros/as)	pensaremos	pensaríamos
(vosotros/as)	pensaréis	pensaríais
(ellos/ellas/ ustedes)	pensarán	pensarían

	PRESENT SUBJUNCTIVE	IMPERFECT SUBJUNCTIVE
(yo)	piense	pensara *or* pensase
(tú)	pienses	pensaras *or* pensases
(él/ella/usted)	piense	pensara *or* pensase
(nosotros/as)	pensemos	pensáramos *or* pensásemos
(vosotros/as)	penséis	pensarais *or* pensaseis
(ellos/ellas/ ustedes)	piensen	pensaran *or* pensasen

IMPERATIVE

piensa / pensad

Use the present subjunctive in all cases other than these tú *and* vosotros *affirmative forms.*

EXAMPLE PHRASES

Yo no me lo **pensaría** dos veces. I wouldn't think about it twice.

Me da igual lo que **piensen**. I don't care what they think.

Si **pensara** eso, te lo diría. If I thought that, I'd tell you.

No **pienses** que no quiero ir. Don't think that I don't want to go.

No lo **pienses** más. Don't think any more about it.

Remember that subject pronouns are not used very often in Spanish.

perder (to lose)

	PRESENT		PRESENT PERFECT
(yo)	pierdo		he perdido
(tú)	pierdes		has perdido
(él/ella/usted)	pierde		ha perdido
(nosotros/as)	perdemos		hemos perdido
(vosotros/as)	perdéis		habéis perdido
(ellos/ellas/ ustedes)	pierden		han perdido

	PRETERITE		IMPERFECT
(yo)	perdí		perdía
(tú)	perdiste		perdías
(él/ella/usted)	perdió		perdía
(nosotros/as)	perdimos		perdíamos
(vosotros/as)	perdisteis		perdíais
(ellos/ellas/ ustedes)	perdieron		perdían

GERUND

perdiendo

PAST PARTICIPLE

perdido

EXAMPLE PHRASES

Siempre **pierde** las llaves. He's always losing his keys.

Ana es la que saldrá **perdiendo**. Ana is the one who will lose out.

He perdido dos kilos. I've lost two kilos.

Perdimos dos a cero. We lost two nil.

Perdían siempre. They always used to lose.

Remember that subject pronouns are not used very often in Spanish.

perder

	FUTURE	CONDITIONAL
(yo)	perderé	perdería
(tú)	perderás	perderías
(él/ella/usted)	perderá	perdería
(nosotros/as)	perderemos	perderíamos
(vosotros/as)	perderéis	perderíais
(ellos/ellas/ ustedes)	perderán	perderían

	PRESENT SUBJUNCTIVE	IMPERFECT SUBJUNCTIVE
(yo)	pierda	perdiera or perdiese
(tú)	pierdas	perdieras or perdieses
(él/ella/usted)	pierda	perdiera or perdiese
(nosotros/as)	perdamos	perdiéramos or perdiésemos
(vosotros/as)	perdáis	perdierais or perdieseis
(ellos/ellas/ ustedes)	pierdan	perdieran or perdiesen

IMPERATIVE
pierde / perded

Use the present subjunctive in all cases other than these tú and vosotros affirmative forms.

EXAMPLE PHRASES
Date prisa o **perderás** el tren. Hurry up or you'll miss the train.

¡No **te** lo **pierdas**! Don't miss it!

No **pierdas** esta oportunidad. Don't miss this opportunity.

Remember that subject pronouns are not used very often in Spanish.

poder (to be able to)

	PRESENT	PRESENT PERFECT
(yo)	puedo	he podido
(tú)	puedes	has podido
(él/ella/usted)	puede	ha podido
(nosotros/as)	podemos	hemos podido
(vosotros/as)	podéis	habéis podido
(ellos/ellas/ustedes)	pueden	han podido

	PRETERITE	IMPERFECT
(yo)	pude	podía
(tú)	pudiste	podías
(él/ella/usted)	pudo	podía
(nosotros/as)	pudimos	podíamos
(vosotros/as)	pudisteis	podíais
(ellos/ellas/ustedes)	pudieron	podían

GERUND

pudiendo

PAST PARTICIPLE

podido

EXAMPLE PHRASES

¿**Puedo** entrar? **Can I come in?**

Puede que llegue mañana. **He may arrive tomorrow.**

No **he podido** venir antes. **I couldn't come before.**

Pudiste haberte hecho daño. **You could have hurt yourself.**

¡Me lo **podías** haber dicho! **You could have told me!**

Remember that subject pronouns are not used very often in Spanish.

poder

	FUTURE		CONDITIONAL
(yo)	podré		podría
(tú)	podrás		podrías
(él/ella/usted)	podrá		podría
(nosotros/as)	podremos		podríamos
(vosotros/as)	podréis		podríais
(ellos/ellas/ ustedes)	podrán		podrían

	PRESENT SUBJUNCTIVE		IMPERFECT SUBJUNCTIVE
(yo)	pueda		pudiera *or* pudiese
(tú)	puedas		pudieras *or* pudieses
(él/ella/usted)	pueda		pudiera *or* pudiese
(nosotros/as)	podamos		pudiéramos *or* pudiésemos
(vosotros/as)	podáis		pudierais *or* pudieseis
(ellos/ellas/ ustedes)	puedan		pudieran *or* pudiesen

IMPERATIVE

puede / poded

Use the present subjunctive in all cases other than these tú and vosotros affirmative forms.

EXAMPLE PHRASES

Estoy segura de que **podrá** conseguirlo. I'm sure he'll succeed.

¿**Podrías** ayudarme? Could you help me?

Ven en cuanto **puedas**. Come as soon as you can.

Si no **pudiera** encontrar la casa, te llamaría al móvil. If I weren't able to find
the house, I'd call you on your mobile.

Remember that subject pronouns are not used very often in Spanish.

poner (to put)

	PRESENT		PRESENT PERFECT
(yo)	pongo		he puesto
(tú)	pones		has puesto
(él/ella/usted)	pone		ha puesto
(nosotros/as)	ponemos		hemos puesto
(vosotros/as)	ponéis		habéis puesto
(ellos/ellas/ustedes)	ponen		han puesto

	PRETERITE		IMPERFECT
(yo)	puse		ponía
(tú)	pusiste		ponías
(él/ella/usted)	puso		ponía
(nosotros/as)	pusimos		poníamos
(vosotros/as)	pusisteis		poníais
(ellos/ellas/ustedes)	pusieron		ponían

GERUND

poniendo

PAST PARTICIPLE

puesto

EXAMPLE PHRASES

¿Dónde **pongo** mis cosas? Where shall I put my things?

¿Qué **pone** en la carta? What does the letter say?

¿Le **has puesto** azúcar a mi café? Have you put any sugar in my coffee?

Todos **nos pusimos** de acuerdo. We all agreed.

Remember that subject pronouns are not used very often in Spanish.

poner

	FUTURE	CONDITIONAL
(yo)	pondré	pondría
(tú)	pondrás	pondrías
(él/ella/usted)	pondrá	pondría
(nosotros/as)	pondremos	pondríamos
(vosotros/as)	pondréis	pondríais
(ellos/ellas/ ustedes)	pondrán	pondrían

	PRESENT SUBJUNCTIVE	IMPERFECT SUBJUNCTIVE
(yo)	ponga	pusiera or pusiese
(tú)	pongas	pusieras or pusieses
(él/ella/usted)	ponga	pusiera or pusiese
(nosotros/as)	pongamos	pusiéramos or pusiésemos
(vosotros/as)	pongáis	pusierais or pusieseis
(ellos/ellas/ ustedes)	pongan	pusieran or pusiesen

IMPERATIVE
pon / poned

Use the present subjunctive in all cases other than these tú and vosotros affirmative forms.

EXAMPLE PHRASES
Lo **pondré** aquí. I'll put it here.

¿Le **pondrías** más sal? Would you add more salt?

Ponlo ahí encima. Put it on there.

Remember that subject pronouns are not used very often in Spanish.

prohibir (to ban, to prohibit)

	PRESENT		PRESENT PERFECT
(yo)	prohíbo		he prohibido
(tú)	prohíbes		has prohibido
(él/ella/usted)	prohíbe		ha prohibido
(nosotros/as)	prohibimos		hemos prohibido
(vosotros/as)	prohibís		habéis prohibido
(ellos/ellas/ustedes)	prohíben		han prohibido

	PRETERITE		IMPERFECT
(yo)	prohibí		prohibía
(tú)	prohibiste		prohibías
(él/ella/usted)	prohibió		prohibía
(nosotros/as)	prohibimos		prohibíamos
(vosotros/as)	prohibisteis		prohibíais
(ellos/ellas/ustedes)	prohibieron		prohibían

GERUND

prohibiendo

PAST PARTICIPLE

prohibido

EXAMPLE PHRASES

Deberían **prohibirlo**. It should be banned.

Te **prohíbo** que me hables así. I won't have you talking to me like that!

Han prohibido el acceso a la prensa. The press have been banned.

Le **prohibieron** la entrada en el bingo. She was not allowed into the bingo hall.

El tratado **prohibía** el uso de armas químicas. The treaty prohibited the use of chemical weapons.

Remember that subject pronouns are not used very often in Spanish.

prohibir

	FUTURE	CONDITIONAL
(yo)	prohibiré	prohibiría
(tú)	prohibirás	prohibirías
(él/ella/usted)	prohibirá	prohibiría
(nosotros/as)	prohibiremos	prohibiríamos
(vosotros/as)	prohibiréis	prohibiríais
(ellos/ellas/ustedes)	prohibirán	prohibirían

	PRESENT SUBJUNCTIVE	IMPERFECT SUBJUNCTIVE
(yo)	prohíba	prohibiera or prohibiese
(tú)	prohíbas	prohibieras or prohibieses
(él/ella/usted)	prohíba	prohibiera or prohibiese
(nosotros/as)	prohibamos	prohibiéramos or prohibiésemos
(vosotros/as)	prohibáis	prohibierais or prohibieseis
(ellos/ellas/ustedes)	prohíban	prohibieran or prohibiesen

IMPERATIVE

prohíbe / prohibid

Use the present subjunctive in all cases other than these tú and vosotros affirmative forms.

EXAMPLE PHRASES

Lo **prohibirán** más tarde o más temprano. **Sooner or later they'll ban it.**

Yo esa música la **prohibiría**. If it were up to me, that music would be banned.

"**prohibido** fumar" "no smoking"

Remember that subject pronouns are not used very often in Spanish.

querer (to want, to love)

	PRESENT	PRESENT PERFECT
(yo)	quiero	he querido
(tú)	quieres	has querido
(él/ella/usted)	quiere	ha querido
(nosotros/as)	queremos	hemos querido
(vosotros/as)	queréis	habéis querido
(ellos/ellas/ustedes)	quieren	han querido

	PRETERITE	IMPERFECT
(yo)	quise	quería
(tú)	quisiste	querías
(él/ella/usted)	quiso	quería
(nosotros/as)	quisimos	queríamos
(vosotros/as)	quisisteis	queríais
(ellos/ellas/ustedes)	quisieron	querían

GERUND
queriendo

PAST PARTICIPLE
querido

EXAMPLE PHRASES

Lo hice sin **querer**. I didn't mean to do it.

Te **quiero**. I love you.

Quiero que vayas. I want you to go.

Tú lo **has querido**. You were asking for it.

No **quería** decírmelo. She didn't want to tell me.

Remember that subject pronouns are not used very often in Spanish.

querer

	FUTURE	CONDITIONAL
(yo)	querré	querría
(tú)	querrás	querrías
(él/ella/usted)	querrá	querría
(nosotros/as)	querremos	querríamos
(vosotros/as)	querréis	querríais
(ellos/ellas/ ustedes)	querrán	querrían

	PRESENT SUBJUNCTIVE	IMPERFECT SUBJUNCTIVE
(yo)	quiera	quisiera or quisiese
(tú)	quieras	quisieras or quisieses
(él/ella/usted)	quiera	quisiera or quisiese
(nosotros/as)	queramos	quisiéramos or quisiésemos
(vosotros/as)	queráis	quisierais or quisieseis
(ellos/ellas/ ustedes)	quieran	quisieran or quisiesen

IMPERATIVE

quiere / quered

Use the present subjunctive in all cases other than these tú and vosotros affirmative forms.

EXAMPLE PHRASES

¿**Querrá** firmarme un autógrafo? Will you give me your autograph?

Querría que no hubiera pasado nunca. I wish it had never happened.

¡Por lo que más **quieras**! ¡Cállate! For goodness' sake, shut up!

Quisiera preguntar una cosa. I'd like to ask something.

Remember that subject pronouns are not used very often in Spanish.

reducir (to reduce)

	PRESENT		PRESENT PERFECT
(yo)	reduzco		he reducido
(tú)	reduces		has reducido
(él/ella/usted)	reduce		ha reducido
(nosotros/as)	reducimos		hemos reducido
(vosotros/as)	reducís		habéis reducido
(ellos/ellas/ ustedes)	reducen		han reducido

	PRETERITE		IMPERFECT
(yo)	reduje		reducía
(tú)	redujiste		reducías
(él/ella/usted)	redujo		reducía
(nosotros/as)	redujimos		reducíamos
(vosotros/as)	redujisteis		reducíais
(ellos/ellas/ ustedes)	redujeron		reducían

GERUND

reduciendo

PAST PARTICIPLE

reducido

EXAMPLE PHRASES

Al final todo **se reduce** a eso. In the end it all comes down to that.

Le **han reducido** la pena a dos meses. His sentence has been reduced to two months.

Se ha reducido la tasa de natalidad. The birth rate has fallen.

Sus gastos **se redujeron** a la mitad. Their expenses were cut by half.

Remember that subject pronouns are not used very often in Spanish.

reducir

	FUTURE	CONDITIONAL
(yo)	reduciré	reduciría
(tú)	reducirás	reducirías
(él/ella/usted)	reducirá	reduciría
(nosotros/as)	reduciremos	reduciríamos
(vosotros/as)	reduciréis	reduciríais
(ellos/ellas/ ustedes)	reducirán	reducirían

	PRESENT SUBJUNCTIVE	IMPERFECT SUBJUNCTIVE
(yo)	reduzca	redujera *or* redujese
(tú)	reduzcas	redujeras *or* redujeses
(él/ella/usted)	reduzca	redujera *or* redujese
(nosotros/as)	reduzcamos	redujéramos *or* redujésemos
(vosotros/as)	reduzcáis	redujerais *or* redujeseis
(ellos/ellas/ ustedes)	reduzcan	redujeran *or* redujesen

IMPERATIVE
reduce / reducid

Use the present subjunctive in all cases other than these tú *and* vosotros *affirmative forms.*

EXAMPLE PHRASES
Reducirán la producción en un 20%. **They'll cut production by 20%.**
Reduzca la velocidad. **Reduce speed.**

Remember that subject pronouns are not used very often in Spanish.

rehusar (to refuse)

	PRESENT		PRESENT PERFECT
(yo)	rehúso		he rehusado
(tú)	rehúsas		has rehusado
(él/ella/usted)	rehúsa		ha rehusado
(nosotros/as)	rehusamos		hemos rehusado
(vosotros/as)	rehusáis		habéis rehusado
(ellos/ellas/ ustedes)	rehúsan		han rehusado

	PRETERITE		IMPERFECT
(yo)	rehusé		rehusaba
(tú)	rehusaste		rehusabas
(él/ella/usted)	rehusó		rehusaba
(nosotros/as)	rehusamos		rehusábamos
(vosotros/as)	rehusasteis		rehusabais
(ellos/ellas/ ustedes)	rehusaron		rehusaban

GERUND

rehusando

PAST PARTICIPLE

rehusado

EXAMPLE PHRASES

Rehúso tomar parte en esto. I refuse to take part in this.

Ha rehusado la oferta de trabajo. He declined the job offer.

Su familia **rehusó** hacer declaraciones. His family refused to comment.

Remember that subject pronouns are not used very often in Spanish.

rehusar

	FUTURE	CONDITIONAL
(yo)	rehusaré	rehusaría
(tú)	rehusarás	rehusarías
(él/ella/usted)	rehusará	rehusaría
(nosotros/as)	rehusaremos	rehusaríamos
(vosotros/as)	rehusaréis	rehusaríais
(ellos/ellas/ ustedes)	rehusarán	rehusarían

	PRESENT SUBJUNCTIVE	IMPERFECT SUBJUNCTIVE
(yo)	rehúse	rehusara or rehusase
(tú)	rehúses	rehusaras or rehusases
(él/ella/usted)	rehúse	rehusara or rehusase
(nosotros/as)	rehusemos	rehusáramos or rehusásemos
(vosotros/as)	rehuséis	rehusarais or rehusaseis
(ellos/ellas/ ustedes)	rehúsen	rehusaran or rehusasen

IMPERATIVE

rehúsa / rehusad

Use the present subjunctive in all cases other than these tú and vosotros affirmative forms.

Remember that subject pronouns are not used very often in Spanish.

reír (to laugh)

	PRESENT		PRESENT PERFECT
(yo)	río		he reído
(tú)	ríes		has reído
(él/ella/usted)	ríe		ha reído
(nosotros/as)	reímos		hemos reído
(vosotros/as)	reís		habéis reído
(ellos/ellas/ ustedes)	ríen		han reído

	PRETERITE		IMPERFECT
(yo)	reí		reía
(tú)	reíste		reías
(él/ella/usted)	rió		reía
(nosotros/as)	reímos		reíamos
(vosotros/as)	reísteis		reíais
(ellos/ellas/ ustedes)	rieron		reían

GERUND
riendo

PAST PARTICIPLE
reído

EXAMPLE PHRASES

Se echó a reír. She burst out laughing.

Se ríe de todo. She doesn't take anything seriously.

¿De qué te ríes? What are you laughing at?

Siempre están riéndose en clase. They're always laughing in class.

Me reía mucho con él. I always had a good laugh with him.

Remember that subject pronouns are not used very often in Spanish.

reír

	FUTURE	CONDITIONAL
(yo)	reiré	reiría
(tú)	reirás	reirías
(él/ella/usted)	reirá	reiría
(nosotros/as)	reiremos	reiríamos
(vosotros/as)	reiréis	reiríais
(ellos/ellas/ ustedes)	reirán	reirían

	PRESENT SUBJUNCTIVE	IMPERFECT SUBJUNCTIVE
(yo)	ría	riera or riese
(tú)	rías	rieras or rieses
(él/ella/usted)	ría	riera or riese
(nosotros/as)	riamos	riéramos or riésemos
(vosotros/as)	riáis	rierais or rieseis
(ellos/ellas/ ustedes)	rían	rieran or riesen

IMPERATIVE

ríe / reíd

Use the present subjunctive in all cases other than these tú *and* vosotros *affirmative forms.*

EXAMPLE PHRASES

Te **reirás** cuando te lo cuente. You'll have a laugh when I tell you about it.

Que **se rían** lo que quieran. Let them laugh as much as they want.

No **te rías** de mí. Don't laugh at me.

¡Tú **ríete**, pero he pasado muchísimo miedo! You may laugh, but I was really frightened.

Remember that subject pronouns are not used very often in Spanish.

reñir (to scold, to quarrel)

	PRESENT	PRESENT PERFECT
(yo)	riño	he reñido
(tú)	riñes	has reñido
(él/ella/usted)	riñe	ha reñido
(nosotros/as)	reñimos	hemos reñido
(vosotros/as)	reñís	habéis reñido
(ellos/ellas/ustedes)	riñen	han reñido

	PRETERITE	IMPERFECT
(yo)	reñí	reñía
(tú)	reñiste	reñías
(él/ella/usted)	riñó	reñía
(nosotros/as)	reñimos	reñíamos
(vosotros/as)	reñisteis	reñíais
(ellos/ellas/ustedes)	riñeron	reñían

GERUND
riñendo

PAST PARTICIPLE
reñido

EXAMPLE PHRASES

Se pasan el día entero **riñendo**. They spend the whole day quarrelling.

Ha reñido con su novio. She has fallen out with her boyfriend.

Les **riñó** por llegar tarde a casa. She told them off for getting home late.

Nos **reñía** sin motivo. She used to tell us off for no reason.

reñir

	FUTURE	CONDITIONAL
(yo)	reñiré	reñiría
(tú)	reñirás	reñirías
(él/ella/usted)	reñirá	reñiría
(nosotros/as)	reñiremos	reñiríamos
(vosotros/as)	reñiréis	reñiríais
(ellos/ellas/ustedes)	reñirán	reñirían

	PRESENT SUBJUNCTIVE	IMPERFECT SUBJUNCTIVE
(yo)	riña	riñera or riñese
(tú)	riñas	riñeras or riñeses
(él/ella/usted)	riña	riñera or riñese
(nosotros/as)	riñamos	riñéramos or riñésemos
(vosotros/as)	riñáis	riñerais or riñeseis
(ellos/ellas/ustedes)	riñan	riñeran or riñesen

IMPERATIVE

riñe / reñid

Use the present subjunctive in all cases other than these tú and vosotros affirmative forms.

EXAMPLE PHRASES

Si se entera, te **reñirá**. He'll tell you off if he finds out.

No la **riñas**, no es culpa suya. Don't tell her off, it's not her fault.

¡Niños, no **riñáis**! Children, don't quarrel!

Remember that subject pronouns are not used very often in Spanish.

repetir (to repeat)

	PRESENT		PRESENT PERFECT
(yo)	repito		he repetido
(tú)	repites		has repetido
(él/ella/usted)	repite		ha repetido
(nosotros/as)	repetimos		hemos repetido
(vosotros/as)	repetís		habéis repetido
(ellos/ellas/ ustedes)	repiten		han repetido

	PRETERITE		IMPERFECT
(yo)	repetí		repetía
(tú)	repetiste		repetías
(él/ella/usted)	repitió		repetía
(nosotros/as)	repetimos		repetíamos
(vosotros/as)	repetisteis		repetíais
(ellos/ellas/ ustedes)	repitieron		repetían

GERUND

repitiendo

PAST PARTICIPLE

repetido

EXAMPLE PHRASES

¿Podría **repetirlo**, por favor? **Could you repeat that, please?**

Le **repito** que es imposible. **I repeat that it is impossible.**

Se lo **he repetido** mil veces, pero no escucha. **I've told him hundreds of times but he won't listen.**

Repetía una y otra vez que era inocente. **He kept repeating that he was innocent.**

Remember that subject pronouns are not used very often in Spanish.

repetir

	FUTURE	**CONDITIONAL**
(yo)	repetiré	repetiría
(tú)	repetirás	repetirías
(él/ella/usted)	repetirá	repetiría
(nosotros/as)	repetiremos	repetiríamos
(vosotros/as)	repetiréis	repetiríais
(ellos/ellas/ ustedes)	repetirán	repetirían

	PRESENT SUBJUNCTIVE	**IMPERFECT SUBJUNCTIVE**
(yo)	repita	repitiera or repitiese
(tú)	repitas	repitieras or repitieses
(él/ella/usted)	repita	repitiera or repitiese
(nosotros/as)	repitamos	repitiéramos or repitiésemos
(vosotros/as)	repitáis	repitierais or repitieseis
(ellos/ellas/ ustedes)	repitan	repitieran or repitiesen

IMPERATIVE

repite / repetid

Use the present subjunctive in all cases other than these tú and vosotros affirmative forms.

EXAMPLE PHRASES

Si sigue así, **repetirá** curso. If she goes on like this, she'll end up having to repeat the year.

Espero que no **se repita**. I hope this won't happen again.

Repetid detrás de mí... Repeat after me...

Remember that subject pronouns are not used very often in Spanish.

resolver (to solve)

	PRESENT		PRESENT PERFECT
(yo)	resuelvo		he resuelto
(tú)	resuelves		has resuelto
(él/ella/usted)	resuelve		ha resuelto
(nosotros/as)	resolvemos		hemos resuelto
(vosotros/as)	resolvéis		habéis resuelto
(ellos/ellas/ ustedes)	resuelven		han resuelto

	PRETERITE		IMPERFECT
(yo)	resolví		resolvía
(tú)	resolviste		resolvías
(él/ella/usted)	resolvió		resolvía
(nosotros/as)	resolvimos		resolvíamos
(vosotros/as)	resolvisteis		resolvíais
(ellos/ellas/ ustedes)	resolvieron		resolvían

GERUND

resolviendo

PAST PARTICIPLE

resuelto

EXAMPLE PHRASES

Trataré de **resolver** tus dudas. I'll try to answer your questions.

Enfadarse no **resuelve** nada. Getting angry doesn't help at all.

No **hemos resuelto** los problemas. We haven't solved the problems.

Resolvimos el problema entre todos. We solved the problem together.

Remember that subject pronouns are not used very often in Spanish.

resolver

	FUTURE	CONDITIONAL
(yo)	resolveré	resolvería
(tú)	resolverás	resolverías
(él/ella/usted)	resolverá	resolvería
(nosotros/as)	resolveremos	resolveríamos
(vosotros/as)	resolveréis	resolveríais
(ellos/ellas/ ustedes)	resolverán	resolverían

	PRESENT SUBJUNCTIVE	IMPERFECT SUBJUNCTIVE
(yo)	resuelva	resolviera or resolviese
(tú)	resuelvas	resolvieras or resolvieses
(él/ella/usted)	resuelva	resolviera or resolviese
(nosotros/as)	resolvamos	resolviéramos or resolviésemos
(vosotros/as)	resolváis	resolvierais or resolvieseis
(ellos/ellas/ ustedes)	resuelvan	resolvieran or resolviesen

IMPERATIVE
resuelve / resolved

Use the present subjunctive in all cases other than these tú and vosotros affirmative forms.

EXAMPLE PHRASES

No te preocupes, ya lo **resolveremos**. Don't worry, we'll get it sorted.

Yo lo **resolvería** de otra forma. I'd sort it out another way.

Hasta que no lo **resuelva** no descansaré. I won't rest until I've sorted it out.

Remember that subject pronouns are not used very often in Spanish.

reunir (to put together, to gather)

	PRESENT	PRESENT PERFECT
(yo)	reúno	he reunido
(tú)	reúnes	has reunido
(él/ella/usted)	reúne	ha reunido
(nosotros/as)	reunimos	hemos reunido
(vosotros/as)	reunís	habéis reunido
(ellos/ellas/ ustedes)	reúnen	han reunido

	PRETERITE	IMPERFECT
(yo)	reuní	reunía
(tú)	reuniste	reunías
(él/ella/usted)	reunió	reunía
(nosotros/as)	reunimos	reuníamos
(vosotros/as)	reunisteis	reuníais
(ellos/ellas/ ustedes)	reunieron	reunían

GERUND	PAST PARTICIPLE
reuniendo	reunido

EXAMPLE PHRASES

Hemos conseguido **reunir** suficiente dinero. We've managed to raise enough money.

Hace tiempo que no **me reúno** con ellos. I haven't seen them for ages.

Reunió a todos para comunicarles la noticia. He called them all together to tell them the news.

No **reunía** los requisitos. She didn't satisfy the requirements.

Remember that subject pronouns are not used very often in Spanish.

reunir

	FUTURE	CONDITIONAL
(yo)	reuniré	reuniría
(tú)	reunirás	reunirías
(él/ella/usted)	reunirá	reuniría
(nosotros/as)	reuniremos	reuniríamos
(vosotros/as)	reuniréis	reuniríais
(ellos/ellas/ ustedes)	reunirán	reunirían

	PRESENT SUBJUNCTIVE	IMPERFECT SUBJUNCTIVE
(yo)	reúna	reuniera or reuniese
(tú)	reúnas	reunieras or reunieses
(él/ella/usted)	reúna	reuniera or reuniese
(nosotros/as)	reunamos	reuniéramos or reuniésemos
(vosotros/as)	reunáis	reunierais or reunieseis
(ellos/ellas/ ustedes)	reúnan	reunieran or reuniesen

IMPERATIVE

reúne / reunid

Use the present subjunctive in all cases other than these tú and vosotros affirmative forms.

EXAMPLE PHRASES

Se **reunirán** el viernes. They'll meet on Friday.

Necesito encontrar un local que **reúna** las condiciones. I need to find premises that will meet the requirements.

Consiguió que su familia se **reuniera** tras una larga separación. She managed to get her family back together again after a long separation.

Antes de acusarle, **reúne** las pruebas suficientes. Get enough evidence together before accusing him.

Remember that subject pronouns are not used very often in Spanish.

rogar (to beg, to pray)

	PRESENT	PRESENT PERFECT
(yo)	ruego	he rogado
(tú)	ruegas	has rogado
(él/ella/usted)	ruega	ha rogado
(nosotros/as)	rogamos	hemos rogado
(vosotros/as)	rogáis	habéis rogado
(ellos/ellas/ ustedes)	ruegan	han rogado

	PRETERITE	IMPERFECT
(yo)	rogué	rogaba
(tú)	rogaste	rogabas
(él/ella/usted)	rogó	rogaba
(nosotros/as)	rogamos	rogábamos
(vosotros/as)	rogasteis	rogabais
(ellos/ellas/ ustedes)	rogaron	rogaban

GERUND
rogando

PAST PARTICIPLE
rogado

EXAMPLE PHRASES

Les **rogamos** acepten nuestras disculpas. Please accept our apologies.

Te **ruego** que me lo devuelvas. Please give it back to me.

"**Se ruega** no fumar" "Please do not smoke"

Me **rogó** que le perdonara. He begged me to forgive him.

Le **rogaba** a Dios que se curara. I prayed to God to make him better.

Remember that subject pronouns are not used very often in Spanish.

rogar

	FUTURE	CONDITIONAL
(yo)	rogaré	rogaría
(tú)	rogarás	rogarías
(él/ella/usted)	rogará	rogaría
(nosotros/as)	rogaremos	rogaríamos
(vosotros/as)	rogaréis	rogaríais
(ellos/ellas/ ustedes)	rogarán	rogarían

	PRESENT SUBJUNCTIVE	IMPERFECT SUBJUNCTIVE
(yo)	ruegue	rogara or rogase
(tú)	ruegues	rogaras or rogases
(él/ella/usted)	ruegue	rogara or rogase
(nosotros/as)	roguemos	rogáramos or rogásemos
(vosotros/as)	roguéis	rogarais or rogaseis
(ellos/ellas/ ustedes)	rueguen	rogaran or rogasen

IMPERATIVE

ruega / rogad

Use the present subjunctive in all cases other than these tú and vosotros affirmative forms.

EXAMPLE PHRASES

Ruega por mí. Pray for me.

Remember that subject pronouns are not used very often in Spanish.

romper (to break)

	PRESENT	PRESENT PERFECT
(yo)	rompo	he roto
(tú)	rompes	has roto
(él/ella/usted)	rompe	ha roto
(nosotros/as)	rompemos	hemos roto
(vosotros/as)	rompéis	habéis roto
(ellos/ellas/ ustedes)	rompen	han roto

	PRETERITE	IMPERFECT
(yo)	rompí	rompía
(tú)	rompiste	rompías
(él/ella/usted)	rompió	rompía
(nosotros/as)	rompimos	rompíamos
(vosotros/as)	rompisteis	rompíais
(ellos/ellas/ ustedes)	rompieron	rompían

GERUND

rompiendo

PAST PARTICIPLE

roto

EXAMPLE PHRASES

La cuerda **se** va a **romper**. The rope is going to snap.

Siempre **están rompiendo** cosas. They're always breaking things.

Se ha roto una taza. A cup has got broken.

Se rompió el jarrón. The vase broke.

Remember that subject pronouns are not used very often in Spanish.

romper

	FUTURE	CONDITIONAL
(yo)	romperé	rompería
(tú)	romperás	romperías
(él/ella/usted)	romperá	rompería
(nosotros/as)	romperemos	romperíamos
(vosotros/as)	romperéis	romperíais
(ellos/ellas/ustedes)	romperán	romperían

	PRESENT SUBJUNCTIVE	IMPERFECT SUBJUNCTIVE
(yo)	rompa	rompiera or rompiese
(tú)	rompas	rompieras or rompieses
(él/ella/usted)	rompa	rompiera or rompiese
(nosotros/as)	rompamos	rompiéramos or rompiésemos
(vosotros/as)	rompáis	rompierais or rompieseis
(ellos/ellas/ustedes)	rompan	rompieran or rompiesen

IMPERATIVE

rompe / romped

Use the present subjunctive in all cases other than these tú and vosotros affirmative forms.

EXAMPLE PHRASES

Yo nunca **rompería** una promesa. **I'd never break a promise.**

Si lo **rompiera**, tendría que pagarlo. **If you broke it, you'd have to pay for it.**

Rompe con él, si ya no le quieres. **If you don't love him any more, finish with him.**

Cuidado, no lo **rompas**. **Careful you don't break it.**

Remember that subject pronouns are not used very often in Spanish.

saber (to know)

	PRESENT	PRESENT PERFECT
(yo)	sé	he sabido
(tú)	sabes	has sabido
(él/ella/usted)	sabe	ha sabido
(nosotros/as)	sabemos	hemos sabido
(vosotros/as)	sabéis	habéis sabido
(ellos/ellas/ustedes)	saben	han sabido

	PRETERITE	IMPERFECT
(yo)	supe	sabía
(tú)	supiste	sabías
(él/ella/usted)	supo	sabía
(nosotros/as)	supimos	sabíamos
(vosotros/as)	supisteis	sabíais
(ellos/ellas/ustedes)	supieron	sabían

GERUND	PAST PARTICIPLE
sabiendo	sabido

EXAMPLE PHRASES

No lo **sé**. I don't know.

¿**Sabes** una cosa? Do you know what?

¿Cuándo lo **has sabido**? When did you find out?

No **supe** qué responder. I didn't know what to answer.

Pensaba que lo **sabías**. I thought you knew.

Remember that subject pronouns are not used very often in Spanish.

saber

	FUTURE	CONDITIONAL
(yo)	sabré	sabría
(tú)	sabrás	sabrías
(él/ella/usted)	sabrá	sabría
(nosotros/as)	sabremos	sabríamos
(vosotros/as)	sabréis	sabríais
(ellos/ellas/ ustedes)	sabrán	sabrían

	PRESENT SUBJUNCTIVE	IMPERFECT SUBJUNCTIVE
(yo)	sepa	supiera or supiese
(tú)	sepas	supieras or supieses
(él/ella/usted)	sepa	supiera or supiese
(nosotros/as)	sepamos	supiéramos or suplésemos
(vosotros/as)	sepáis	supierais or supieseis
(ellos/ellas/ ustedes)	sepan	supieran or supiesen

IMPERATIVE

sabe / sabed

Use the present subjunctive in all cases other than these tú and vosotros affirmative forms.

EXAMPLE PHRASES

Nunca se **sabrá** quién la mató. We'll never know who killed her.

Si no le tuvieras tanto miedo al agua, ya **sabrías** nadar. If you weren't so afraid of water, you'd already be able to swim.

Que yo **sepa**, vive en París. As far as I know, she lives in Paris.

¡Si **supiéramos** al menos dónde está! If only we knew where he was!

Remember that subject pronouns are not used very often in Spanish.

sacar (to take out)

	PRESENT	PRESENT PERFECT
(yo)	saco	he sacado
(tú)	sacas	has sacado
(él/ella/usted)	saca	ha sacado
(nosotros/as)	sacamos	hemos sacado
(vosotros/as)	sacáis	habéis sacado
(ellos/ellas/ ustedes)	sacan	han sacado

	PRETERITE	IMPERFECT
(yo)	saqué	sacaba
(tú)	sacaste	sacabas
(él/ella/usted)	sacó	sacaba
(nosotros/as)	sacamos	sacábamos
(vosotros/as)	sacasteis	sacabais
(ellos/ellas/ ustedes)	sacaron	sacaban

GERUND
sacando

PAST PARTICIPLE
sacado

EXAMPLE PHRASES

¿**Me sacas** una foto? Will you take a photo of me?

Estás sacando las cosas de quicio. You're blowing things out of all proportion.

Ya **he sacado** las entradas. I've already bought the tickets.

Saqué un 7 en el examen. I got 7 marks in the exam.

¿De dónde **sacaba** tanto dinero? Where did he get so much money from?

Remember that subject pronouns are not used very often in Spanish.

sacar

	FUTURE	CONDITIONAL
(yo)	sacaré	sacaría
(tú)	sacarás	sacarías
(él/ella/usted)	sacará	sacaría
(nosotros/as)	sacaremos	sacaríamos
(vosotros/as)	sacaréis	sacaríais
(ellos/ellas/ ustedes)	sacarán	sacarían

	PRESENT SUBJUNCTIVE	IMPERFECT SUBJUNCTIVE
(yo)	saque	sacara or sacase
(tú)	saques	sacaras or sacases
(él/ella/usted)	saque	sacara or sacase
(nosotros/as)	saquemos	sacáramos or sacásemos
(vosotros/as)	saquéis	sacarais or sacaseis
(ellos/ellas/ ustedes)	saquen	sacaran or sacasen

IMPERATIVE

saca / sacad

Use the present subjunctive in all cases other than these tú and vosotros affirmative forms.

EXAMPLE PHRASES

Yo no **sacaría** todavía ninguna conclusión. I wouldn't draw any conclusions yet.

Quiero que **saques** inmediatamente esa bicicleta de casa. I want you to get that bike out of the house immediately.

Si te **sacaras** el carnet de conducir, serías mucho más independiente. You'd be much more independent if you got your driving licence.

No **saques** la cabeza por la ventanilla. Don't lean out of the window.

Remember that subject pronouns are not used very often in Spanish.

salir (to go out)

	PRESENT		PRESENT PERFECT
(yo)	salgo		he salido
(tú)	sales		has salido
(él/ella/usted)	sale		ha salido
(nosotros/as)	salimos		hemos salido
(vosotros/as)	salís		habéis salido
(ellos/ellas/ ustedes)	salen		han salido

	PRETERITE		IMPERFECT
(yo)	salí		salía
(tú)	saliste		salías
(él/ella/usted)	salió		salía
(nosotros/as)	salimos		salíamos
(vosotros/as)	salisteis		salíais
(ellos/ellas/ ustedes)	salieron		salían

GERUND

saliendo

PAST PARTICIPLE

salido

EXAMPLE PHRASES

Hace tiempo que no **salimos**. We haven't been out for a while.

Está saliendo con un compañero de trabajo. She's going out with a colleague from work.

Ha salido. She's gone out.

Su foto **salió** en todos los periódicos. Her picture appeared in all the newspapers.

Salía muy tarde de trabajar. He used to finish work very late.

Remember that subject pronouns are not used very often in Spanish.

salir

	FUTURE	CONDITIONAL
(yo)	saldré	saldría
(tú)	saldrás	saldrías
(él/ella/usted)	saldrá	saldría
(nosotros/as)	saldremos	saldríamos
(vosotros/as)	saldréis	saldríais
(ellos/ellas/ ustedes)	saldrán	saldrían

	PRESENT SUBJUNCTIVE	IMPERFECT SUBJUNCTIVE
(yo)	salga	saliera or saliese
(tú)	salgas	salieras or salieses
(él/ella/usted)	salga	saliera or saliese
(nosotros/as)	salgamos	saliéramos or saliésemos
(vosotros/as)	salgáis	salierais or salieseis
(ellos/ellas/ ustedes)	salgan	salieran or saliesen

IMPERATIVE

sal / salid

Use the present subjunctive in all cases other than these tú and vosotros affirmative forms.

EXAMPLE PHRASES

Te dije que **saldría** muy caro. I told you it would work out very expensive.

Espero que todo **salga** bien. I hope everything works out all right.

Si **saliera** elegido... If I were elected...

Por favor, **salgan** por la puerta de atrás. Please leave via the back door.

Remember that subject pronouns are not used very often in Spanish.

satisfacer (to satisfy)

	PRESENT	PRESENT PERFECT
(yo)	satisfago	hè satisfecho
(tú)	satisfaces	has satisfecho
(él/ella/usted)	satisface	ha satisfecho
(nosotros/as)	satisfacemos	hemos satisfecho
(vosotros/as)	satisfacéis	habéis satisfecho
(ellos/ellas/ustedes)	satisfacen	han satisfecho

	PRETERITE	IMPERFECT
(yo)	satisfice	satisfacía
(tú)	satisficiste	satisfacías
(él/ella/usted)	satisfizo	satisfacía
(nosotros/as)	satisficimos	satisfacíamos
(vosotros/as)	satisficisteis	satisfacíais
(ellos/ellas/ustedes)	satisficieron	satisfacían

GERUND

satisfaciendo

PAST PARTICIPLE

satisfecho

EXAMPLE PHRASES

No me **satisface** nada el resultado. I'm not at all satisfied with the result.

Ha **satisfecho** mis expectativas. It came up to my expectations.

Eso **satisfizo** mi curiosidad. That satisfied my curiosity.

Aquella vida **satisfacía** todas mis necesidades. That lifestyle satisfied all my needs.

Remember that subject pronouns are not used very often in Spanish.

satisfacer

	FUTURE	**CONDITIONAL**
(yo)	satisfaré	satisfaría
(tú)	satisfarás	satisfarías
(él/ella/usted)	satisfará	satisfaría
(nosotros/as)	satisfaremos	satisfaríamos
(vosotros/as)	satisfaréis	satisfaríais
(ellos/ellas/ ustedes)	satisfarán	satisfarían

	PRESENT SUBJUNCTIVE	**IMPERFECT SUBJUNCTIVE**
(yo)	satisfaga	satisficiera *or* satisficiese
(tú)	satisfagas	satisficieras *or* satisficieses
(él/ella/usted)	satisfaga	satisficiera *or* satisficiese
(nosotros/as)	satisfagamos	satisficiéramos *or* satisficiésemos
(vosotros/as)	satisfagáis	satisficierais *or* satisficieseis
(ellos/ellas/ ustedes)	satisfagan	satisficieran *or* satisficiesen

IMPERATIVE

satisfaz *or* satisface / satisfaced

Use the present subjunctive in all cases other than these tú and vosotros affirmative forms.

EXAMPLE PHRASES

Le **satisfará** saber que hemos cumplido nuestros objetivos. **You'll be happy to know that we have achieved our objectives.**

Me **satisfaría** mucho más que estudiaras una carrera. **I'd be far happier if you went to university.**

Remember that subject pronouns are not used very often in Spanish.

seguir (to follow)

	PRESENT	PRESENT PERFECT
(yo)	sigo	he seguido
(tú)	sigues	has seguido
(él/ella/usted)	sigue	ha seguido
(nosotros/as)	seguimos	hemos seguido
(vosotros/as)	seguís	habéis seguido
(ellos/ellas/ustedes)	siguen	han seguido

	PRETERITE	IMPERFECT
(yo)	seguí	seguía
(tú)	seguiste	seguías
(él/ella/usted)	siguió	seguía
(nosotros/as)	seguimos	seguíamos
(vosotros/as)	seguisteis	seguíais
(ellos/ellas/ustedes)	siguieron	seguían

GERUND	PAST PARTICIPLE
siguiendo	seguido

EXAMPLE PHRASES

Si **sigues** así, acabarás mal. If you go on like this you'll end up badly.

¿Te **han seguido**? Have you been followed?

Siguió cantando como si nada. He went on singing as if nothing was the matter.

El ordenador **seguía** funcionando a pesar del apagón. The computer went on working in spite of the power cut.

Les **estuvimos siguiendo** mucho rato. We followed them for a long time.

Remember that subject pronouns are not used very often in Spanish.

seguir

	FUTURE	**CONDITIONAL**
(yo)	seguiré	seguiría
(tú)	seguirás	seguirías
(él/ella/usted)	seguirá	seguiría
(nosotros/as)	seguiremos	seguiríamos
(vosotros/as)	seguiréis	seguiríais
(ellos/ellas/ ustedes)	seguirán	seguirían

	PRESENT SUBJUNCTIVE	**IMPERFECT SUBJUNCTIVE**
(yo)	siga	siguiera or siguiese
(tú)	sigas	siguieras or siguieses
(él/ella/usted)	siga	siguiera or siguiese
(nosotros/as)	sigamos	siguiéramos or siguiésemos
(vosotros/as)	sigáis	siguierais or siguieseis
(ellos/ellas/ ustedes)	sigan	siguieran or siguiesen

IMPERATIVE

sigue / seguid

Use the present subjunctive in all cases other than these tú and vosotros affirmative forms.

EXAMPLE PHRASES

Nos seguiremos viendo. We will go on seeing each other.

Quiero que **sigas** estudiando. I want you to go on with your studies.

Si **siguieras** mis consejos, te iría muchísimo mejor. You'd be much better off if you followed my advice.

Siga por esta calle hasta el final. Go on till you get to the end of the street.

Remember that subject pronouns are not used very often in Spanish.

sentir (to feel, to be sorry)

	PRESENT		PRESENT PERFECT
(yo)	siento		he sentido
(tú)	sientes		has sentido
(él/ella/usted)	siente		ha sentido
(nosotros/as)	sentimos		hemos sentido
(vosotros/as)	sentís		habéis sentido
(ellos/ellas/ ustedes)	sienten		han sentido

	PRETERITE		IMPERFECT
(yo)	sentí		sentía
(tú)	sentiste		sentías
(él/ella/usted)	sintió		sentía
(nosotros/as)	sentimos		sentíamos
(vosotros/as)	senteisteis		sentíais
(ellos/ellas/ ustedes)	sintieron		sentían

GERUND

sintiendo

PAST PARTICIPLE

sentido

EXAMPLE PHRASES

Te vas a **sentir** sola. You'll feel lonely.

Siento mucho lo que pasó. I'm really sorry about what happened.

Ha sentido mucho la muerte de su padre. He has been greatly affected by
his father's death.

Sentí un pinchazo en la pierna. I felt a sharp pain in my leg.

Me **sentía** muy mal. I didn't feel well at all.

Remember that subject pronouns are not used very often in Spanish.

sentir

	FUTURE	CONDITIONAL
(yo)	sentiré	sentiría
(tú)	sentirás	sentirías
(él/ella/usted)	sentirá	sentiría
(nosotros/as)	sentiremos	sentiríamos
(vosotros/as)	sentiréis	sentiríais
(ellos/ellas/ ustedes)	sentirán	sentirían

	PRESENT SUBJUNCTIVE	IMPERFECT SUBJUNCTIVE
(yo)	sienta	sintiera or sintiese
(tú)	sientas	sintieras or sintieses
(él/ella/usted)	sienta	sintiera or sintiese
(nosotros/as)	sintamos	sintiéramos or sintiésemos
(vosotros/as)	sintáis	sintierais or sintieseis
(ellos/ellas/ ustedes)	sientan	sintieran or sintiesen

IMPERATIVE

siente / sentid

Use the present subjunctive in all cases other than these tú and vosotros affirmative forms.

EXAMPLE PHRASES

Al principio **te sentirás** un poco raro. You'll feel a bit strange at first.

Yo **sentiría** mucho que se fuera de la empresa. I'd be really sorry if you left the firm.

No creo que lo **sienta**. I don't think she's sorry.

Sería mucho más preocupante si no **sintiera** la pierna. It would be much more worrying if he couldn't feel his leg.

Remember that subject pronouns are not used very often in Spanish.

ser (to be)

	PRESENT	PRESENT PERFECT
(yo)	soy	he sido
(tú)	eres	has sido
(él/ella/usted)	es	ha sido
(nosotros/as)	somos	hemos sido
(vosotros/as)	sois	habéis sido
(ellos/ellas/ ustedes)	son	han sido

	PRETERITE	IMPERFECT
(yo)	fui	era
(tú)	fuiste	eras
(él/ella/usted)	fue	era
(nosotros/as)	fuimos	éramos
(vosotros/as)	fuisteis	erais
(ellos/ellas/ ustedes)	fueron	eran

GERUND
siendo

PAST PARTICIPLE
sido

EXAMPLE PHRASES

Soy español. I'm Spanish.

Estás siendo muy paciente con él. You're being very patient with him.

Ha sido un duro golpe. It was a major blow.

¿Fuiste tú el que llamó? Was it you who phoned?

Era de noche. It was dark.

Remember that subject pronouns are not used very often in Spanish.

ser

	FUTURE	CONDITIONAL
(yo)	seré	sería
(tú)	serás	serías
(él/ella/usted)	será	sería
(nosotros/as)	seremos	seríamos
(vosotros/as)	seréis	seríais
(ellos/ellas/ ustedes)	serán	serían

	PRESENT SUBJUNCTIVE	IMPERFECT SUBJUNCTIVE
(yo)	sea	fuera or fuese
(tú)	seas	fueras or fueses
(él/ella/usted)	sea	fuera or fuese
(nosotros/as)	seamos	fuéramos or fuésemos
(vosotros/as)	seáis	fuerais or fueseis
(ellos/ellas/ ustedes)	sean	fueran or fuesen

IMPERATIVE

sé / sed

Use the present subjunctive in all cases other than these tú and vosotros affirmative forms.

EXAMPLE PHRASES

Será de Joaquín. It must be Joaquin's.

Eso **sería** estupendo. That would be great.

O **sea**, que no vienes. So you're not coming.

No **seas** tan perfeccionista. Don't be such a perfectionist.

¡**Sed** buenos! Behave yourselves!

Remember that subject pronouns are not used very often in Spanish.

soler (to be wont to)

	PRESENT		PRESENT PERFECT
(yo)	suelo		*not used*
(tú)	sueles		
(él/ella/usted)	suele		
(nosotros/as)	solemos		
(vosotros/as)	soléis		
(ellos/ellas/ ustedes)	suelen		

	PRETERITE		IMPERFECT
(yo)	*not used*		solía
(tú)			solías
(él/ella/usted)			solía
(nosotros/as)			solíamos
(vosotros/as)			solíais
(ellos/ellas/ ustedes)			solían

GERUND

soliendo

PAST PARTICIPLE

not used

EXAMPLE PHRASES

Suele salir a las ocho. **He usually leaves at eight.**

Solíamos ir todos los años a la playa. **We used to go to the beach every year.**

Remember that subject pronouns are not used very often in Spanish.

soler

	FUTURE	**CONDITIONAL**
(yo)	*not used*	*not used*
(tú)		
(él/ella/usted)		
(nosotros/as)		
(vosotros/as)		
(ellos/ellas/ ustedes)		

	PRESENT SUBJUNCTIVE	**IMPERFECT SUBJUNCTIVE**
(yo)	suela	soliera *or* soliese
(tú)	suelas	solieras *or* solieses
(él/ella/usted)	suela	soliera *or* soliese
(nosotros/as)	solamos	soliéramos *or* soliésemos
(vosotros/as)	soláis	solierais *or* solieseis
(ellos/ellas/ ustedes)	suelan	solieran *or* soliesen

IMPERATIVE

not used

Remember that subject pronouns are not used very often in Spanish.

soltar (to let go of, to release)

	PRESENT		PRESENT PERFECT
(yo)	suelto		he soltado
(tú)	sueltas		has soltado
(él/ella/usted)	suelta		ha soltado
(nosotros/as)	soltamos		hemos soltado
(vosotros/as)	soltáis		habéis soltado
(ellos/ellas/ ustedes)	sueltan		han soltado

	PRETERITE		IMPERFECT
(yo)	solté		soltaba
(tú)	soltaste		soltabas
(él/ella/usted)	soltó		soltaba
(nosotros/as)	soltamos		soltábamos
(vosotros/as)	soltasteis		soltabais
(ellos/ellas/ ustedes)	soltaron		soltaban

GERUND	**PAST PARTICIPLE**
soltando	soltado

EXAMPLE PHRASES

Al final logró **soltarse**. Eventually she managed to break free.

No para de **soltar** tacos. He swears all the time.

¿Por qué no **te sueltas** el pelo? Why don't you have your hair loose?

Han soltado a los rehenes. They've released the hostages.

Soltó una carcajada. He burst out laughing.

Remember that subject pronouns are not used very often in Spanish.

soltar

	FUTURE	CONDITIONAL
(yo)	soltaré	soltaría
(tú)	soltarás	soltarías
(él/ella/usted)	soltará	soltaría
(nosotros/as)	soltaremos	soltaríamos
(vosotros/as)	soltaréis	soltaríais
(ellos/ellas/ustedes)	soltarán	soltarían

	PRESENT SUBJUNCTIVE	IMPERFECT SUBJUNCTIVE
(yo)	suelte	soltara or soltase
(tú)	sueltes	soltaras or soltases
(él/ella/usted)	suelte	soltara or soltase
(nosotros/as)	soltemos	soltáramos or soltásemos
(vosotros/as)	soltéis	soltarais or soltaseis
(ellos/ellas/ustedes)	suelten	soltaran or soltasen

IMPERATIVE

suelta / soltad

Use the present subjunctive in all cases other than these tú and vosotros affirmative forms.

EXAMPLE PHRASES

Te **soltaré** el brazo si me dices dónde está. I'll let go of your arm if you tell me where he is.

Te dije que lo **soltaras**. I told you to let it go.

No **sueltes** la cuerda. Don't let go of the rope.

¡Suéltame! Let me go!

Remember that subject pronouns are not used very often in Spanish.

sonar (to sound, to ring)

	PRESENT	PRESENT PERFECT
(yo)	sueno	he sonado
(tú)	suenas	has sonado
(él/ella/usted)	suena	ha sonado
(nosotros/as)	sonamos	hemos sonado
(vosotros/as)	sonáis	habéis sonado
(ellos/ellas/ ustedes)	suenan	han sonado

	PRETERITE	IMPERFECT
(yo)	soné	sonaba
(tú)	sonaste	sonabas
(él/ella/usted)	sonó	sonaba
(nosotros/as)	sonamos	sonábamos
(vosotros/as)	sonasteis	sonabais
(ellos/ellas/ ustedes)	sonaron	sonaban

GERUND

sonando

PAST PARTICIPLE

sonado

EXAMPLE PHRASES

¿Te suena su nombre? Does her name sound familiar?

Ha sonado tu móvil. Your mobile rang.

Justo en ese momento sonó el timbre. Just then the bell rang.

Sonabas un poco triste por teléfono. You sounded a bit sad on the phone.

Estaba sonando el teléfono. The phone was ringing.

Remember that subject pronouns are not used very often in Spanish.

sonar

	FUTURE	CONDITIONAL
(yo)	sonaré	sonaría
(tú)	sonarás	sonarías
(él/ella/usted)	sonará	sonaría
(nosotros/as)	sonaremos	sonaríamos
(vosotros/as)	sonaréis	sonaríais
(ellos/ellas/ ustedes)	sonarán	sonarían

	PRESENT SUBJUNCTIVE	IMPERFECT SUBJUNCTIVE
(yo)	suene	sonara or sonase
(tú)	suenes	sonaras or sonases
(él/ella/usted)	suene	sonara or sonase
(nosotros/as)	sonemos	sonáramos or sonásemos
(vosotros/as)	sonéis	sonarais or sonaseis
(ellos/ellas/ ustedes)	suenen	sonaran or sonasen

IMPERATIVE

suena / sonad

Use the present subjunctive in all cases other than these tú and vosotros affirmative forms.

EXAMPLE PHRASES

Hay que esperar a que **suene** un pitido. We have to wait until we hear a beep.

¡**Suénate** la nariz! Blow your nose!

temer (to be afraid)

	PRESENT	PRESENT PERFECT
(yo)	temo	he temido
(tú)	temes	has temido
(él/ella/usted)	teme	ha temido
(nosotros/as)	tememos	hemos temido
(vosotros/as)	teméis	habéis temido
(ellos/ellas/ ustedes)	temen	han temido

	PRETERITE	IMPERFECT
(yo)	temí	temía
(tú)	temiste	temías
(él/ella/usted)	temío	temía
(nosotros/as)	temimos	temíamos
(vosotros/as)	temisteis	temíais
(ellos/ellas/ ustedes)	temieron	temían

GERUND

temiendo

PAST PARTICIPLE

temido

EXAMPLE PHRASES

Me temo que no. I'm afraid not.

Se temen lo peor. They fear the worst.

–Ha empezado a llover. –**Me** lo **temía**. "It's started raining." – "I was afraid it would."

Temí ofenderles. I was afraid of offending them.

Temían por su seguridad. They feared for their security.

Remember that subject pronouns are not used very often in Spanish.

temer

	FUTURE	CONDITIONAL
(yo)	temeré	temería
(tú)	temerás	temerías
(él/ella/usted)	temerá	temería
(nosotros/as)	temeremos	temeríamos
(vosotros/as)	temeréis	temeríais
(ellos/ellas/ ustedes)	temerán	temerían

	PRESENT SUBJUNCTIVE	IMPERFECT SUBJUNCTIVE
(yo)	tema	temiera or temiese
(tú)	temas	temieras or temieses
(él/ella/usted)	tema	temiera or temiese
(nosotros/as)	temamos	temiéramos or temiésemos
(vosotros/as)	temáis	temierais or temieseis
(ellos/ellas/ ustedes)	teman	temieran or temiesen

IMPERATIVE

teme / temed

Use the present subjunctive in all cases other than these tú and vosotros affirmative forms.

EXAMPLE PHRASES

No **temas**. Don't be afraid.

tener (to have)

	PRESENT		PRESENT PERFECT
(yo)	tengo		he tenido
(tú)	tienes		has tenido
(él/ella/usted)	tiene		ha tenido *has had*
(nosotros/as)	tenemos		hemos tenido
(vosotros/as)	tenéis		habéis tenido
(ellos/ellas/ ustedes)	tienen		ha tenido

	PRETERITE		IMPERFECT
(yo)	tuve		tenía
(tú)	tuviste		tenías
(él/ella/usted)	tuvo		tenía *didn't have*
(nosotros/as)	tuvimos *We had to*		teníamos
(vosotros/as)	tuvisteis		teníais
(ellos/ellas/ ustedes)	tuvieron		tenían

GERUND

teniendo *are having*

PAST PARTICIPLE

tenido

EXAMPLE PHRASES

Tengo sed. I'm thirsty.

Están teniendo muchos problemas con el coche. They're having a lot of trouble with the car.

Ha tenido una gripe muy fuerte. She's had very bad flu.

Tuvimos que irnos. We had to leave.

No **tenía** suficiente dinero. She didn't have enough money.

Remember that subject pronouns are not used very often in Spanish.

tener

	FUTURE	CONDITIONAL
(yo)	tendré	tendría
(tú)	tendrás	tendrías
(él/ella/usted)	tendrá	tendría
(nosotros/as)	tendremos	tendríamos
(vosotros/as)	tendréis	tendríais
(ellos/ellas/ ustedes)	tendrán	tendrían

	PRESENT SUBJUNCTIVE	IMPERFECT SUBJUNCTIVE
(yo)	tenga	tuviera or tuviese
(tú)	tengas	tuvieras or tuvieses
(él/ella/usted)	tenga	tuviera or tuviese
(nosotros/as)	tengamos	tuviéramos or tuviésemos
(vosotros/as)	tengáis	tuvierais or tuvieseis
(ellos/ellas/ ustedes)	tengan	tuvieran or tuviesen

IMPERATIVE

ten / tened

Use the present subjunctive in all cases other than these tú and vosotros affirmative forms.

EXAMPLE PHRASES

Tendrás que pagarlo tú. **You'll have to pay for it yourself.**

Tendrías que comer más. **You should eat more.**

No creo que **tenga** suficiente dinero. **I don't think I've got enough money.**

Si **tuviera** tiempo, haría un curso de catalán. **If I had time, I'd do a Catalan course.**

Ten cuidado. **Be careful.**

No **tengas** miedo. **Don't be afraid.**

Remember that subject pronouns are not used very often in Spanish.

tocar (to touch, to play)

	PRESENT		PRESENT PERFECT
(yo)	toco		he tocado
(tú)	tocas		has tocado
(él/ella/usted)	toca		ha tocado
(nosotros/as)	tocamos		hemos tocado
(vosotros/as)	tocáis		habéis tocado
(ellos/ellas/ ustedes)	tocan		han tocado

	PRETERITE		IMPERFECT
(yo)	toqué		tocaba
(tú)	tocaste		tocabas
(él/ella/usted)	tocó		tocaba
(nosotros/as)	tocamos		tocábamos
(vosotros/as)	tocasteis		tocabais
(ellos/ellas/ ustedes)	tocaron		tocaban

GERUND
tocando

PAST PARTICIPLE
tocado

EXAMPLE PHRASES

Toca el violín. He plays the violin.

Te **toca** fregar los platos. It's your turn to do the dishes.

Me **ha tocado** el peor asiento. I've ended up with the worst seat.

Le **tocó** la lotería. He won the lottery.

Me **tocaba** tirar a mí. It was my turn.

Remember that subject pronouns are not used very often in Spanish.

tocar

	FUTURE	CONDITIONAL
(yo)	tocaré	tocaría
(tú)	tocarás	tocarías
(él/ella/usted)	tocará	tocaría
(nosotros/as)	tocaremos	tocaríamos
(vosotros/as)	tocaréis	tocaríais
(ellos/ellas/ ustedes)	tocarán	tocarían

	PRESENT SUBJUNCTIVE	IMPERFECT SUBJUNCTIVE
(yo)	toque	tocara *or* tocase
(tú)	toques	tocaras *or* tocases
(él/ella/usted)	toque	tocara *or* tocase
(nosotros/as)	toquemos	tocáramos *or* tocásemos
(vosotros/as)	toquéis	tocarais *or* tocaseis
(ellos/ellas/ ustedes)	toquen	tocaran *or* tocasen

IMPERATIVE

toca / tocad

Use the present subjunctive in all cases other than these tú *and* vosotros *affirmative forms.*

EXAMPLE PHRASES

Sabía que me **tocaría** ir a mí. I knew I'd be the one to have to go.

No lo **toques**. Don't touch it.

Tócalo, verás que suave. Touch it and see how soft it is.

torcer (to twist)

	PRESENT	PRESENT PERFECT
(yo)	tuerzo	he torcido
(tú)	tuerces	has torcido
(él/ella/usted)	tuerce	ha torcido
(nosotros/as)	torcemos	hemos torcido
(vosotros/as)	torcéis	habéis torcido
(ellos/ellas/ustedes)	tuercen	han torcido

	PRETERITE	IMPERFECT
(yo)	torcí	torcía
(tú)	torciste	torcías
(él/ella/usted)	torció	torcía
(nosotros/as)	torcimos	torcíamos
(vosotros/as)	torcisteis	torcíais
(ellos/ellas/ustedes)	torcieron	torcían

GERUND

torciendo

PAST PARTICIPLE

torcido

EXAMPLE PHRASES

Acaba de **torcer** la esquina. **She has just turned the corner.**

El sendero **tuerce** luego a la derecha. **Later on the path bends round to the right.**

Se le **ha torcido** la muñeca. **She's sprained her wrist.**

Se me **torció** el tobillo. **I twisted my ankle.**

Remember that subject pronouns are not used very often in Spanish.

torcer

	FUTURE	CONDITIONAL
(yo)	torceré	torcería
(tú)	torcerás	torcerías
(él/ella/usted)	torcerá	torcería
(nosotros/as)	torceremos	torceríamos
(vosotros/as)	torceréis	torceríais
(ellos/ellas/ ustedes)	torcerán	torcerían

	PRESENT SUBJUNCTIVE	IMPERFECT SUBJUNCTIVE
(yo)	tuerza	torciera or torciese
(tú)	tuerzas	torcieras or torcieses
(él/ella/usted)	tuerza	torciera or torciese
(nosotros/as)	torzamos	torciéramos or torciésemos
(vosotros/as)	torzáis	torcierais or torcieseis
(ellos/ellas/ ustedes)	tuerzan	torcieran or torciesen

IMPERATIVE

tuerce / torced

Use the present subjunctive in all cases other than these tú and vosotros affirmative forms.

EXAMPLE PHRASES

Tuerza a la izquierda. Turn left.
Tuércelo un poco más. Twist it a little more.

traer (to bring)

	PRESENT		PRESENT PERFECT
(yo)	traigo		he traído
(tú)	traes		has traído
(él/ella/usted)	trae		ha traído
(nosotros/as)	traemos		hemos traído
(vosotros/as)	traéis		habéis traído
(ellos/ellas/ustedes)	traen		han traído

	PRETERITE		IMPERFECT
(yo)	traje		traía
(tú)	trajiste		traías
(él/ella/usted)	trajo		traía
(nosotros/as)	trajimos		traíamos
(vosotros/as)	trajisteis		traíais
(ellos/ellas/ustedes)	trajeron		traían

GERUND

trayendo

PAST PARTICIPLE

traído

EXAMPLE PHRASES

¿Me puedes **traer** una toalla? Can you bring me a towel?

Nos **está trayendo** muchos problemas. It's causing us a lot of trouble.

¿**Has traído** lo que te pedí? Have you brought what I asked for?

Traía un vestido nuevo. She was wearing a new dress.

No **trajo** el dinero. He didn't bring the money.

Remember that subject pronouns are not used very often in Spanish.

traer

	FUTURE	CONDITIONAL
(yo)	traeré	traería
(tú)	traerás	traerías
(él/ella/usted)	traerá	traería
(nosotros/as)	traeremos	traeríamos
(vosotros/as)	traeréis	traeríais
(ellos/ellas/ ustedes)	traerán	traerían

	PRESENT SUBJUNCTIVE	IMPERFECT SUBJUNCTIVE
(yo)	traiga	trajera *or* trajese
(tú)	traigas	trajeras *or* trajeses
(él/ella/usted)	traiga	trajera *or* trajese
(nosotros/as)	traigamos	trajéramos *or* trajésemos
(vosotros/as)	traigáis	trajerais *or* trajeseis
(ellos/ellas/ ustedes)	traigan	trajeran *or* trajesen

IMPERATIVE

trae / traed

Use the present subjunctive in all cases other than these tú and vosotros affirmative forms.

EXAMPLE PHRASES

Me pregunto qué **se traerán** entre manos. I wonder what they're up to.

Se lo **traería** de África. He must have brought it over from Africa.

Dile que **traiga** a algún amigo. Tell him to bring a friend with him.

Trae eso. Give that here.

Remember that subject pronouns are not used very often in Spanish.

valer (to be worth)

	PRESENT		PRESENT PERFECT
(yo)	valgo		he valido
(tú)	vales		has valido
(él/ella/usted)	vale		ha valido
(nosotros/as)	valemos		hemos valido
(vosotros/as)	valéis		habéis valido
(ellos/ellas/ ustedes)	valen		han valido

	PRETERITE		IMPERFECT
(yo)	valí		valía
(tú)	valiste		valías
(él/ella/usted)	valió		valía
(nosotros/as)	valimos		valíamos
(vosotros/as)	valisteis		valíais
(ellos/ellas/ ustedes)	valieron		valían

GERUND

valiendo

PAST PARTICIPLE

valido

EXAMPLE PHRASES

No puede **valerse** por sí mismo. He can't look after himself.

¿Cuánto **vale** eso? How much is that?

¿**Vale**? OK?

No le **valió** de nada suplicar. Begging got her nowhere.

No **valía** la pena. It wasn't worth it.

Remember that subject pronouns are not used very often in Spanish.

valer

	FUTURE	CONDITIONAL
(yo)	valdré	valdría
(tú)	valdrás	valdrías
(él/ella/usted)	valdrá	valdría
(nosotros/as)	valdremos	valdríamos
(vosotros/as)	valdréis	valdríais
(ellos/ellas/ustedes)	valdrán	valdrían

	PRESENT SUBJUNCTIVE	IMPERFECT SUBJUNCTIVE
(yo)	valga	valiera or valiese
(tú)	valgas	valieras or valieses
(él/ella/usted)	valga	valiera or valiese
(nosotros/as)	valgamos	valiéramos or valiésemos
(vosotros/as)	valgáis	valierais or valieseis
(ellos/ellas/ustedes)	valgan	valieran or valiesen

IMPERATIVE

vale / valed

Use the present subjunctive in all cases other than these tú and vosotros affirmative forms.

EXAMPLE PHRASES

Valdrá unos 500 euros. It must cost around 500 euros.

Yo no **valdría** para enfermera. I'd make a hopeless nurse.

Valga lo que **valga**, lo compro. I'll buy it, no matter how much it costs.

Remember that subject pronouns are not used very often in Spanish.

vencer (to win, to beat)

	PRESENT	PRESENT PERFECT
(yo)	venzo	he vencido
(tú)	vences	has vencido
(él/ella/usted)	vence	ha vencido
(nosotros/as)	vencemos	hemos vencido
(vosotros/as)	vencéis	habéis vencido
(ellos/ellas/ ustedes)	vencen	han vencido

	PRETERITE	IMPERFECT
(yo)	vencí	vencía
(tú)	venciste	vencías
(él/ella/usted)	venció	vencía
(nosotros/as)	vencimos	vencíamos
(vosotros/as)	vencisteis	vencíais
(ellos/ellas/ ustedes)	vencieron	vencían

GERUND

venciendo

PAST PARTICIPLE

vencido

EXAMPLE PHRASES

Tienes que **vencer** el miedo. You must overcome your fear.

El plazo de matrícula **vence** mañana. Tomorrow is the last day for registration.

Finalmente le **ha vencido** el sueño. At last, he was overcome by sleep.

Vencimos por dos a uno. We won two-one.

Le **vencía** la curiosidad. His curiosity got the better of him.

Remember that subject pronouns are not used very often in Spanish.

vencer

	FUTURE	CONDITIONAL
(yo)	venceré	vencería
(tú)	vencerás	vencerías
(él/ella/usted)	vencerá	vencería
(nosotros/as)	venceremos	venceríamos
(vosotros/as)	venceréis	venceríais
(ellos/ellas/ ustedes)	vencerán	vencerían

	PRESENT SUBJUNCTIVE	IMPERFECT SUBJUNCTIVE
(yo)	venza	venciera or venciese
(tú)	venzas	vencieras or vencieses
(él/ella/usted)	venza	venciera or venciese
(nosotros/as)	venzamos	venciéramos or venciésemos
(vosotros/as)	venzáis	vencierais or vencieseis
(ellos/ellas/ ustedes)	venzan	vencieran or venciesen

IMPERATIVE

vence / venced

Use the present subjunctive in all cases other than these tú and vosotros affirmative forms.

EXAMPLE PHRASES

Nuestro ejército **vencerá**. Our army will be victorious.

No dejes que te **venza** la impaciencia. Don't let your impatience get the better of you.

Remember that subject pronouns are not used very often in Spanish.

venir (to come)

	PRESENT	PRESENT PERFECT
(yo)	vengo	he venido
(tú)	vienes	has venido
(él/ella/usted)	viene	ha venido
(nosotros/as)	venimos	hemos venido
(vosotros/as)	venís	habéis venido
(ellos/ellas/ustedes)	vienen	han venido

	PRETERITE	IMPERFECT
(yo)	vine	venía
(tú)	viniste	venías
(él/ella/usted)	vino	venía
(nosotros/as)	vinimos	veníamos
(vosotros/as)	vinisteis	veníais
(ellos/ellas/ustedes)	vinieron	venían

GERUND
viniendo

PAST PARTICIPLE
venido

EXAMPLE PHRASES

Vengo andando desde la playa. I've walked all the way from the beach.

La casa **se está viniendo** abajo. The house is falling apart.

Ha venido en taxi. He came by taxi.

Vinieron a verme al hospital. They came to see me in hospital.

La noticia **venía** en el periódico. The news was in the paper.

Remember that subject pronouns are not used very often in Spanish.

venir

	FUTURE	CONDITIONAL
(yo)	vendré	vendría
(tú)	vendrás	vendrías
(él/ella/usted)	vendrá	vendría
(nosotros/as)	vendremos	vendríamos
(vosotros/as)	vendréis	vendríais
(ellos/ellas/ ustedes)	vendrán	vendrían

	PRESENT SUBJUNCTIVE	IMPERFECT SUBJUNCTIVE
(yo)	venga	viniera or viniese
(tú)	vengas	vinieras or vinieses
(él/ella/usted)	venga	viniera or viniese
(nosotros/as)	vengamos	viniéramos or viniésemos
(vosotros/as)	vengáis	vinierais or vinieseis
(ellos/ellas/ ustedes)	vengan	vinieran or viniesen

IMPERATIVE

ven / venid

Use the present subjunctive in all cases other than these tú and vosotros affirmative forms.

EXAMPLE PHRASES

¿**Vendrás** conmigo al cine? Will you come to the cinema with me?

A mí me **vendría** mejor el sábado. Saturday would be better for me.

¡**Venga**, vámonos! Come on, let's go!

No **vengas** si no quieres. Don't come if you don't want to.

¡**Ven** aquí! Come here!

Remember that subject pronouns are not used very often in Spanish.

ver (to see)

	PRESENT		PRESENT PERFECT
(yo)	veo		he visto
(tú)	ves		has visto
(él/ella/usted)	ve		ha visto
(nosotros/as)	vemos		hemos visto
(vosotros/as)	veis		habéis visto
(ellos/ellas/ustedes)	ven		han visto

	PRETERITE		IMPERFECT
(yo)	vi		veía
(tú)	viste		veías
(él/ella/usted)	vio		veía
(nosotros/as)	vimos		veíamos
(vosotros/as)	visteis		veíais
(ellos/ellas/ustedes)	vieron		veían

GERUND	PAST PARTICIPLE
viendo	visto

EXAMPLE PHRASES

No **veo** muy bien. I can't see very well.

Están **viendo** la televisión. They're watching television.

No **he visto** esa película. I haven't seen that film.

¿**Viste** lo que pasó? Did you see what happened?

Los **veía** a todos desde la ventana. I could see them all from the window.

Remember that subject pronouns are not used very often in Spanish.

ver

	FUTURE	CONDITIONAL
(yo)	veré	vería
(tú)	verás	verías
(él/ella/usted)	verá	vería
(nosotros/as)	veremos	veríamos
(vosotros/as)	veréis	veríais
(ellos/ellas/ ustedes)	verán	verían

	PRESENT SUBJUNCTIVE	IMPERFECT SUBJUNCTIVE
(yo)	vea	viera or viese
(tú)	veas	vieras or vieses
(él/ella/usted)	vea	viera or viese
(nosotros/as)	veamos	viéramos or viésemos
(vosotros/as)	veáis	vierais or vieseis
(ellos/ellas/ ustedes)	vean	vieran or viesen

IMPERATIVE

ve / ved

Use the present subjunctive in all cases other than these tú and vosotros affirmative forms.

EXAMPLE PHRASES

Eso ya se **verá**. We'll see.

No **veas** cómo se puso. He got incredibly worked up.

¡Si **vieras** cómo ha cambiado todo aquello! If you could see how everything has changed.

Veamos, ¿qué le pasa? Let's see now, what's the matter?

Remember that subject pronouns are not used very often in Spanish.

verter (to pour)

	PRESENT		PRESENT PERFECT
(yo)	vierto		he vertido
(tú)	viertes		has vertido
(él/ella/usted)	vierte		ha vertido
(nosotros/as)	vertemos		hemos vertido
(vosotros/as)	vertéis		habéis vertido
(ellos/ellas/ ustedes)	vierten		han vertido

	PRETERITE		IMPERFECT
(yo)	vertí		vertía
(tú)	vertiste		vertías
(él/ella/usted)	vertió		vertía
(nosotros/as)	vertimos		vertíamos
(vosotros/as)	vertisteis		vertíais
(ellos/ellas/ ustedes)	vertieron		vertían

GERUND

vertiendo

PAST PARTICIPLE

vertido

EXAMPLE PHRASES

Primero **viertes** el contenido del sobre en un recipiente. **First you empty out the contents of the packet into a container.**

Me **has vertido** agua encima. **You've spilt water on me.**

Vertió un poco de leche en el cazo. **He poured some milk into the saucepan.**

Se vertían muchos residuos radioactivos en el mar. **A lot of nuclear waste was dumped in the sea.**

Remember that subject pronouns are not used very often in Spanish.

verter

	FUTURE	CONDITIONAL
(yo)	verteré	vertería
(tú)	verterás	verterías
(él/ella/usted)	verterá	vertería
(nosotros/as)	verteremos	verteríamos
(vosotros/as)	verteréis	verteríais
(ellos/ellas/ ustedes)	verterán	verterían

	PRESENT SUBJUNCTIVE	IMPERFECT SUBJUNCTIVE
(yo)	vierta	vertiera or vertiese
(tú)	viertas	vertieras or vertieses
(él/ella/usted)	vierta	vertiera or vertiese
(nosotros/as)	vertamos	vertiéramos or vertiésemos
(vosotros/as)	vertáis	vertierais or vertieseis
(ellos/ellas/ ustedes)	viertan	vertieran or vertiesen

IMPERATIVE

vierte / verted

Use the present subjunctive in all cases other than these tú *and* vosotros *affirmative forms.*

EXAMPLE PHRASES

Se vertirán muchas lágrimas por esto. A lot of tears will be shed over this.

Ten cuidado no **viertas** el café. Be careful you don't knock over the coffee.

Por favor, **vierta** el contenido del bolso sobre la mesa. Please empty out your bag on the table.

Remember that subject pronouns are not used very often in Spanish.

vestir (to dress)

	PRESENT		PRESENT PERFECT
(yo)	visto		he vestido
(tú)	vistes		has vestido
(él/ella/usted)	viste		ha vestido
(nosotros/as)	vestimos		hemos vestido
(vosotros/as)	vestís		habéis vestido
(ellos/ellas/ustedes)	visten		han vestido

	PRETERITE		IMPERFECT
(yo)	vestí		vestía
(tú)	vestiste		vestías
(él/ella/usted)	vistió		vestía
(nosotros/as)	vestimos		vestíamos
(vosotros/as)	vestisteis		vestíais
(ellos/ellas/ustedes)	vistieron		vestían

GERUND

vistiendo

PAST PARTICIPLE

vestido

EXAMPLE PHRASES

Tengo una familia que **vestir** y que alimentar. I have a family to feed and clothe.

Viste bien. She's a smart dresser.

Estaba **vistiendo** a los niños. I was dressing the children

Me he vestido en cinco minutos. It took me five minutes to get dressed.

Remember that subject pronouns are not used very often in Spanish.

vestir

	FUTURE	CONDITIONAL
(yo)	vestiré	vestiría
(tú)	vestirás	vestirías
(él/ella/usted)	vestirá	vestiría
(nosotros/as)	vestiremos	vestiríamos
(vosotros/as)	vestiréis	vestiríais
(ellos/ellas/ ustedes)	vestirán	vestirían

	PRESENT SUBJUNCTIVE	IMPERFECT SUBJUNCTIVE
(yo)	vista	vistiera or vistiese
(tú)	vistas	vistieras or vistieses
(él/ella/usted)	vista	vistiera or vistiese
(nosotros/as)	vistamos	vistiéramos or vistiésemos
(vosotros/as)	vistáis	vistierais or vistieseis
(ellos/ellas/ ustedes)	vistan	vistieran or vistiesen

IMPERATIVE

viste / vestid

Use the present subjunctive in all cases other than these tú *and* vosotros *affirmative forms.*

EXAMPLE PHRASES

Se **vistió** de princesa. She dressed up as a princess

Vestía pantalones vaqueros y una camiseta. He was wearing jeans and a T-shirt.

Su padre **vestirá** de uniforme. Her father will wear a uniform.

¡**Vístete** de una vez! For the last time, go and get dressed!

Remember that subject pronouns are not used very often in Spanish.

vivir (to live)

	PRESENT	PRESENT PERFECT
(yo)	vivo	he vivido
(tú)	vives	has vivido
(él/ella/usted)	vive	ha vivido
(nosotros/as)	vivimos	hemos vivido
(vosotros/as)	vivís	habéis vivido
(ellos/ellas/ustedes)	viven	han vivido

	PRETERITE	IMPERFECT
(yo)	viví	vivía
(tú)	viviste	vivías
(él/ella/usted)	vivió	vivía
(nosotros/as)	vivimos	vivíamos
(vosotros/as)	vivisteis	vivíais
(ellos/ellas/ustedes)	vivieron	vivían

GERUND

viviendo

PAST PARTICIPLE

vivido

EXAMPLE PHRASES

Me gusta **vivir** sola. I like living on my own.

¿Dónde **vives**? Where do you live?

Siempre **han vivido** muy bien. They've always had a very comfortable life.

Vivían de su pensión. They lived on his pension.

Remember that subject pronouns are not used very often in Spanish.

vivir

	FUTURE	CONDITIONAL
(yo)	viviré	viviría
(tú)	vivirás	vivirías
(él/ella/usted)	vivirá	viviría
(nosotros/as)	viviremos	viviríamos
(vosotros/as)	viviréis	viviríais
(ellos/ellas/ ustedes)	vivirán	vivirían

	PRESENT SUBJUNCTIVE	IMPERFECT SUBJUNCTIVE
(yo)	viva	viviera or viviese
(tú)	vivas	vivieras or vivieses
(él/ella/usted)	viva	viviera or viviese
(nosotros/as)	vivamos	viviéramos or viviésemos
(vosotros/as)	viváis	vivierais or vivieseis
(ellos/ellas/ ustedes)	vivan	vivieran or viviesen

IMPERATIVE

vive / vivid

Use the present subjunctive in all cases other than these tú and vosotros affirmative forms.

EXAMPLE PHRASES

Viviremos en el centro de la ciudad. We'll live in the city centre.

Si pudiéramos, **viviríamos** en el campo. We'd live in the country if we could.

Si **vivierais** más cerca, nos veríamos más a menudo. We'd all see one another more often if you lived nearer.

!Viva! Hurray!

Remember that subject pronouns are not used very often in Spanish.

volcar (to overturn)

	PRESENT		PRESENT PERFECT
(yo)	vuelco		he volcado
(tú)	vuelcas		has volcado
(él/ella/usted)	vuelca		ha volcado
(nosotros/as)	volcamos		hemos volcado
(vosotros/as)	volcáis		habéis volcado
(ellos/ellas/ustedes)	vuelcan		han volcado

	PRETERITE		IMPERFECT
(yo)	volqué		volcaba
(tú)	volcaste		volcabas
(él/ella/usted)	volcó		volcaba
(nosotros/as)	volcamos		volcábamos
(vosotros/as)	volcasteis		volcabais
(ellos/ellas/ustedes)	volcaron		volcaban

GERUND
volcando

PAST PARTICIPLE
volcado

EXAMPLE PHRASES

Se **vuelca** en su trabajo. She throws herself into her work.
Se **han volcado** con nosotros. They've been very kind to us.
El camión **volcó**. The lorry overturned.

Remember that subject pronouns are not used very often in Spanish.

volcar

	FUTURE	CONDITIONAL
(yo)	volcaré	volcaría
(tú)	volcarás	volcarías
(él/ella/usted)	volcará	volcaría
(nosotros/as)	volcaremos	volcaríamos
(vosotros/as)	volcaréis	volcaríais
(ellos/ellas/ ustedes)	volcarán	volcarían

	PRESENT SUBJUNCTIVE	IMPERFECT SUBJUNCTIVE
(yo)	vuelque	volcara or volcase
(tú)	vuelques	volcaras or volcases
(él/ella/usted)	vuelque	volcara or volcase
(nosotros/as)	volquemos	volcáramos or volcásemos
(vosotros/as)	volquéis	volcarais or volcaseis
(ellos/ellas/ ustedes)	vuelquen	volcaran or volcasen

IMPERATIVE

vuelca / volcad

Use the present subjunctive in all cases other than these tú *and* vosotros *affirmative forms.*

EXAMPLE PHRASES

Si sigues moviéndote, harás que **vuelque** el bote. If you keep on moving like that, you'll make the boat capsize.

Ten cuidado, no **vuelques** el vaso. Be careful not to knock over the glass.

Vuelca el contenido sobre la cama. Empty the contents onto the bed.

Remember that subject pronouns are not used very often in Spanish.

volver (to return)

	PRESENT		PRESENT PERFECT
(yo)	vuelvo		he vuelto
(tú)	vuelves		has vuelto
(él/ella/usted)	vuelve		ha vuelto
(nosotros/as)	volvemos		hemos vuelto
(vosotros/as)	volvéis		habéis vuelto
(ellos/ellas/ ustedes)	vuelven		han vuelto

	PRETERITE	IMPERFECT
(yo)	volví	volvía
(tú)	volviste	volvías
(él/ella/usted)	volvió	volvía
(nosotros/as)	volvimos	volvíamos
(vosotros/as)	volvisteis	volvíais
(ellos/ellas/ ustedes)	volvieron	volvían

GERUND

volviendo

PAST PARTICIPLE

vuelto

EXAMPLE PHRASES

Mi padre **vuelve** mañana. My father's coming back tomorrow.

Se **está volviendo** muy pesado. He's becoming a real pain in the neck.

Ha vuelto a casa. He's gone back home.

Me **volví** para ver quién era. I turned round to see who it was.

Volvía agotado de trabajar. I used to come back exhausted from work.

Remember that subject pronouns are not used very often in Spanish.

volver

	FUTURE	CONDITIONAL
(yo)	volveré	volvería
(tú)	volverás	volverías
(él/ella/usted)	volverá	volvería
(nosotros/as)	volveremos	volveríamos
(vosotros/as)	volveréis	volveríais
(ellos/ellas/ ustedes)	volverán	volverían

	PRESENT SUBJUNCTIVE	IMPERFECT SUBJUNCTIVE
(yo)	vuelva	volviera *or* volviese
(tú)	vuelvas	volvieras *or* volvieses
(él/ella/usted)	vuelva	volviera *or* volviese
(nosotros/as)	volvamos	volviéramos *or* volviésemos
(vosotros/as)	volváis	volvierais *or* volvieseis
(ellos/ellas/ ustedes)	vuelvan	volvieran *or* volviesen

IMPERATIVE

vuelve / volved

Use the present subjunctive in all cases other than these tú and vosotros affirmative forms.

EXAMPLE PHRASES

Todo **volverá** a la normalidad. **Everything will go back to normal.**

Yo **volvería** a intentarlo. **I'd try again.**

No quiero que **vuelvas** a las andadas. **I don't want you to go back to your old ways.**

No **vuelvas** por aquí. **Don't come back here.**

¡**Vuelve** a la cama! **Go back to bed!**

Remember that subject pronouns are not used very often in Spanish.

zurcir (to darn)

	PRESENT		PRESENT PERFECT
(yo)	zurzo		he zurcido
(tú)	zurces		has zurcido
(él/ella/usted)	zurce		ha zurcido
(nosotros/as)	zurcimos		hemos zurcido
(vosotros/as)	zurcís		habéis zurcido
(ellos/ellas/ ustedes)	zurcen		han zurcido

	PRETERITE		IMPERFECT
(yo)	zurcí		zurcía
(tú)	zurciste		zurcías
(él/ella/usted)	zurció		zurcía
(nosotros/as)	zurcimos		zurcíamos
(vosotros/as)	zurcisteis		zurcíais
(ellos/ellas/ ustedes)	zurcieron		zurcían

GERUND
zurciendo

PAST PARTICIPLE
zurcido

EXAMPLE PHRASES

¿Quién le **zurce** las camisas? Who darns his shirts?

Se pasa el día **zurciéndole** la ropa. She spends the whole day darning his clothes.

Remember that subject pronouns are not used very often in Spanish.

zurcir

	FUTURE	CONDITIONAL
(yo)	zurciré	zurciría
(tú)	zurcirás	zurcirías
(él/ella/usted)	zurcirá	zurciría
(nosotros/as)	zurciremos	zurciríamos
(vosotros/as)	zurciréis	zurciríais
(ellos/ellas/ ustedes)	zurcirán	zurcirían

	PRESENT SUBJUNCTIVE	IMPERFECT SUBJUNCTIVE
(yo)	zurza	zurciera or zurciese
(tú)	zurzas	zurcieras or zurcieses
(él/ella/usted)	zurza	zurciera or zurciese
(nosotros/as)	zurzamos	zurciéramos or zurciésemos
(vosotros/as)	zurzáis	zurcierais or zurcieseis
(ellos/ellas/ ustedes)	zurzan	zurcieran or zurciesen

IMPERATIVE

zurce / zurcid

Use the present subjunctive in all cases other than these tú *and* vosotros *affirmative forms.*

EXAMPLE PHRASES

¡Que te **zurzan**! Get lost!

How to use the Verb Index

The verbs in bold are the model verbs which you will find in the verb tables. All the other verbs follow one of these patterns, so the number next to each verb indicates which pattern fits this particular verb. For example, acampar (*to camp*) follows the same pattern as hablar (number 336 in the verb tables).

All the verbs are in alphabetical order. Superior numbers (¹ etc) refer you to notes on page 464. These notes explain any differences between verbs and their model.

Notes

[1] The verbs **anochecer, atardecer, granizar, helar, llover, nevar, nublarse** and **tronar** are used almost exclusively in the infinitive and third person singular forms.

[2] The **past participle** of the verb pudrir is podrido.

Vocabulary

contents 467

This vocabulary section is divided into 50 topics, arranged in alphabetical order. This thematic approach enables you to learn related words and phrases together, so that you can become confident in using particular vocabulary in context.

Vocabulary within each topic is divided into nouns and useful phrases which are aimed at helping you to express yourself in idiomatic Spanish. Vocabulary within each topic is graded to help you prioritize your learning. Essential words include the basic words you will need to be able to communicate effectively, important words help expand your knowledge, and useful words provide additional vocabulary which will enable you to express yourself more fully.

Nouns are grouped by gender: masculine ("el") nouns are given on the left-hand page, and feminine ("la") nouns on the right-hand page, enabling you to memorize words according to their gender. In addition, all feminine forms of adjectives are shown, as are irregular plurals.

At the end of the section you will find a list of supplementary vocabulary, grouped according to part of speech – adjective, verb, noun and so on. This is vocabulary which you will come across in many everyday situations.

ABBREVIATIONS

adj	adjective
adv	adverb
algn	alguien
conj	conjunction
f	feminine
inv	invariable
LAm	word used in Latin America
m	masculine
m+f	masculine and feminine form
Mex	word used in Mexico
n	noun
pl	plural
prep	preposition
sb	somebody
sing	singular
Sp	word used in Spain
sth	something

The swung dash ~ is used to indicate the basic elements of the compound and appropriate endings are then added.

PLURALS AND GENDER

In Spanish, if a noun ends in a vowel it generally takes –s in the plural (casa > casas). If it ends in a consonant (including y) it generally takes –es in the plural (reloj > relojes). If it doesn't follow these rules, then the plural will be given in the text.

Although most masculine nouns take "el" and most feminine nouns take "la", you will find a few nouns grouped under feminine words which take "el" (el agua water; el arca chest; el aula classroom) because they are actually feminine.

ESSENTIAL WORDS (*masculine*)

el	**aeropuerto**	airport
el	**agente de viajes**	travel agent
el	**alquiler de coches**	car hire
el	**avión** (*pl* aviones)	plane
el	**billete** (*Sp*), el **boleto** (*LAm*)	ticket
el	**bolso**	bag
el	**carnet** (*or* carné) **de identidad**	ID card
	(*pl* carnets *or* carnés ~ ~)	
el	**enlace**	connection
el	**equipaje**	luggage
el	**equipaje de mano**	hand luggage
el	**horario**	timetable
el	**número**	number
el	**oficial de aduanas**	customs officer
el	**pasajero**	passenger
el	**pasaporte**	passport
el	**(precio del) billete** (*Sp*) *or* boleto (*LAm*)	fare
el	**retraso**	delay
los	**servicios**	toilets
el	**taxi**	taxi
el	**turista**	tourist
el	**viaje**	trip
el	**viajero**	traveller

USEFUL PHRASES

viajar en avión **to travel by plane**
un billete (*Sp*) *or* boleto (*LAm*) de ida **a single ticket**
un billete (*Sp*) *or* boleto (*LAm*) de ida y vuelta, un boleto redondo (*Mex*)
  a return ticket
reservar un billete (*Sp*) *or* boleto (*LAm*) de avión **to book a plane ticket**
"por avión" **"by airmail"**
facturar el equipaje **to check in one's luggage**
perdí el enlace **I missed my connection**
el avión ha despegado/ha aterrizado **the plane has taken off/has landed**
el panel de llegadas/salidas **the arrivals/departures board**
el vuelo número 776 procedente de Madrid/con destino Madrid **flight
  number 776 from Madrid/to Madrid**

ESSENTIAL WORDS (*feminine*)

la **aduana**	customs
la **agente de viajes**	travel agent
la **cancelación** (*pl* cancelaciones)	cancellation
la **duty free**	duty-free (shop)
la **entrada**	entrance
la **información** (*pl* informaciones)	information desk; information
la **llegada**	arrival
la **maleta**	bag; suitcase
la **oficial de aduanas**	customs officer
la **pasajera**	passenger
la **puerta de embarque**	departure gate
la **reserva**	reservation
la **salida**	departure; exit
la **salida de emergencia**	emergency exit
la **tarifa**	fare
la **tarjeta de embarque**	boarding card
la **turista**	tourist
la **viajera**	traveller

USEFUL PHRASES

recoger el equipaje to collect one's luggage
"recogida de equipajes" "baggage reclaim"
pasar por la aduana to go through customs
tengo algo que declarar I have something to declare
no tengo nada que declarar I have nothing to declare
registrar el equipaje to search the luggage

IMPORTANT WORDS (*masculine*)

el	**accidente de avión**	plane crash
el	**billete electrónico**	e-ticket
el	**carrito**	trolley
el	**cinturón de seguridad**	seat belt
	(*pl* cinturones ~~)	
el	**helicóptero**	helicopter
el	**mapa**	map
el	**mareo** (en avión)	airsickness
el	**piloto**	pilot
el	**reloj**	clock
el	**vuelo**	flight

USEFUL WORDS (*masculine*)

el	**asiento**	seat
el	**aterrizaje**	landing
el	**auxiliar de vuelo**	steward; flight attendant
el	**cambiador para bebés**	mother and baby room
el	**control de seguridad**	security check
el	**controlador aéreo**	air-traffic controller
los	**derechos de aduana**	customs duty
el	**despegue**	take-off
el	**detector de metales**	metal detector
el	**embarque**	boarding
el	**horario**	timetable
el	**jumbo**	jumbo jet
los	**mandos**	controls
el	**paracaídas** (*pl inv*)	parachute
el	**radar**	radar
el	**reactor**	jet plane/engine
el	**satélite**	satellite terminal
el	**veraneante**	holiday-maker

USEFUL PHRASES

a bordo on board; "prohibido fumar" "no smoking"
"abróchense el cinturón de seguridad" "fasten your seat belts"
estamos sobrevolando Londres we are flying over London
me estoy mareando I am feeling sick; secuestrar un avión to hijack a plane

IMPORTANT WORDS *(feminine)*

la	**duración** *(pl* duraciones)	length; duration
la	**escalera mecánica**	escalator
la	**piloto**	pilot
la	**sala de embarque**	departure lounge
la	**velocidad**	speed

USEFUL WORDS *(feminine)*

el	**ala** *(pl f* las alas)	wing
la	**altitud**	altitude
la	**altura**	height
la	**auxiliar de vuelo**	air hostess; flight attendant
la	**barrera del sonido**	sound barrier
la	**bolsa de aire**	air pocket
la	**caja negra**	black box
la	**cinta transportadora**	carousel
la	**controladora aérea**	air-traffic controller
la	**escala**	stopover
la	**etiqueta**	label
la	**hélice**	propeller
la	**línea aérea**	airline
la	**pista (de aterrizaje)**	runway
la	**terminal**	terminal
la	**tienda libre de impuestos**	duty-free shop
la	**torre de control**	control tower
la	**tripulación** *(pl* tripulaciones)	crew
la	**turbulencia**	turbulence
la	**ventanilla**	window
la	**veraneante**	holiday-maker

USEFUL PHRASES

"pasajeros del vuelo AB251 con destino Madrid embarquen por la puerta 51"
  "flight AB251 to Madrid now boarding at gate 51"
hicimos escala en Nueva York we stopped over in New York
un aterrizaje forzoso *or* de emergencia an emergency landing
un aterrizaje violento a crash landing
cigarrillos libres de impuestos duty-free cigarettes

ESSENTIAL WORDS *(masculine)*

el	**animal**	animal
el	**buey** *(pl ~es)*	ox
el	**caballo**	horse
el	**cachorro**	puppy
el	**cerdo**	pig
el	**conejo**	rabbit
el	**cordero**	lamb
el	**elefante**	elephant
el	**gato**	cat
el	**gatito**	kitten
el	**hámster** *(pl ~s)*	hamster
el	**león** *(pl* leones)	lion
el	**pájaro**	bird
el	**perro**	dog
el	**perrito**	puppy
el	**pelaje**	fur, coat
el	**pelo**	coat, hair
el	**pescado**	fish
el	**pez** *(pl* peces)	fish
el	**potro**	foal
el	**ratón** *(pl* ratones)	mouse
el	**ternero**	calf
el	**tigre**	tiger
el	**zoo** *(pl ~s)*	zoo
el	**zoológico**	zoo

USEFUL PHRASES

me gustan los gatos, odio las serpientes, prefiero los ratones I like cats,
 I hate snakes, I prefer mice

tenemos 12 animales en casa we have 12 pets in our house

no tenemos animales en casa we have no pets in our house

los animales salvajes wild animals

los animales domésticos *or* las mascotas pets

el ganado livestock

meter un animal en una jaula to put an animal in a cage

liberar un animal to set an animal free

ESSENTIAL WORDS *(feminine)*

el **ave** (*pl f* las aves)	bird
la **gata**	cat *(female)*
la **oveja**	ewe
la **perra**	dog *(female)*
la **tortuga**	tortoise
la **vaca**	cow

IMPORTANT WORDS *(feminine)*

la **cola**	tail
la **jaula**	cage

USEFUL PHRASES

el perro ladra the dog barks; gruñe it growls
el gato maulla the cat miaows; ronronea it purrs
me gusta la equitación *or* montar a caballo I like horse-riding
a caballo on horseback
"cuidado con el perro" "beware of the dog"
"no se admiten perros" "no dogs allowed"
"¡quieto!" (*to dog*) "down!"
los derechos de los animales animal rights

USEFUL WORDS (masculine)

el	asno	donkey
el	burro	donkey
el	camello	camel
el	canguro	kangaroo
el	caparazón (pl caparazones)	shell (of tortoise)
el	casco	hoof
el	cerdo	pig
el	ciervo	stag
el	cocodrilo	crocodile
el	colmillo	tusk
el	conejillo de Indias	guinea pig
el	cuerno	horn
el	erizo	hedgehog
el	hipopótamo	hippopotamus
el	hocico	snout
el	lobo	wolf
el	macho cabrío	billy goat
el	mono	monkey
el	mulo	mule
el	murciélago	bat
el	oso	bear
el	oso polar	polar bear
el	pavo	turkey
el	pony (pl ~s)	pony
el	rinoceronte	rhinoceros
el	sapo	toad
el	tiburón (pl tiburones)	shark
el	topo	mole
el	toro	bull
el	zorro	fox

USEFUL WORDS *(feminine)*

la	ardilla	squirrel
el	asta *(pl f* las astas)	antler
la	ballena	whale
la	boca	mouth
la	bolsa	pouch *(of kangaroo)*
la	cabra	(nanny) goat
la	crin	mane
la	culebra	(grass) snake
la	foca	seal
la	garra	claw
la	jirafa	giraffe
la	joroba	hump *(of camel)*
la	leona	lioness
la	liebre	hare
la	melena	mane
la	mula	mule
la	pajarería	pet shop
la	pata	paw
la	pezuña	hoof
la	piel	fur; hide *(of cow, elephant etc)*
la	rana	frog
las	rayas	stripes *(of zebra)*
la	serpiente	snake
la	tienda de animales	pet shop
la	tigresa	tigress
la	trampa	trap
la	trompa	trunk *(of elephant)*
la	yegua	mare
la	zebra	zebra

ESSENTIAL WORDS (*masculine*)

el	casco	helmet
el	ciclismo	cycling
el	ciclista	cyclist
el	faro	lamp
el	freno	brake
el	neumático	tyre

IMPORTANT WORDS (*masculine*)

el	pinchazo	puncture

USEFUL WORDS (*masculine*)

el	ascenso	climb
el	candado	padlock
el	carril bici	cycle lane
el	descarrilamiento	derailleur
el	descenso	descent
el	eje	hub
el	guardabarros (*pl inv*) (*Sp*)	mudguard
el	kit de reparación de pinchazos (*pl* ~s ~~~~)	puncture repair kit
el	manillar	handlebars
el	pedal	pedal
el	portaequipajes (*pl inv*)	carrier
el	radio	spoke
el	reflector	reflector
el	sillín (*pl* sillines)	saddle
el	timbre	bell

USEFUL PHRASES

ir en bici(cleta) to go by bike, to cycle
vine en bici(cleta) I came by bike
viajar to travel
a toda velocidad at full speed
cambiar de marchas to change gears
pararse to stop
frenar bruscamente to brake suddenly

ESSENTIAL WORDS (feminine)

la	**bici**	bike
la	**bicicleta**	bicycle
la	**bicicleta de montaña**	mountain bike
la	**vuelta ciclista a España**	Tour of Spain

IMPORTANT WORDS (feminine)

la	**rueda**	wheel
la	**velocidad**	speed; gear

USEFUL WORDS (feminine)

la	**alforja**	pannier
la	**barra**	crossbar
la	**bomba**	pump
la	**cadena**	chain
la	**cuesta**	slope
la	**cumbre**	top (of hill)
la	**dínamo**	dynamo
la	**luz delantera** (pl luces ~s)	front light
la	**pendiente**	slope
la	**salpicadera** (Mex)	mudguard
la	**subida**	climb
la	**válvula**	valve

USEFUL PHRASES

dar una vuelta *or* pasear en bici(cleta) **to go for a bike ride**
tener un pinchazo *or* una rueda pinchada **to have a puncture**
arreglar un pinchazo **to mend a puncture**
la rueda delantera/trasera **the front/back wheel**
inflar las ruedas **to blow up the tyres**
brillante, reluciente **shiny**
oxidado(a) **rusty**
fluorescente **fluorescent**

ESSENTIAL WORDS (*masculine*)

el	**cielo**	sky
el	**gallo**	cock
el	**ganso**	goose
el	**loro**	parrot
el	**pájaro**	bird
el	**pato**	duck
el	**pavo**	turkey
el	**periquito**	budgie

USEFUL WORDS (*masculine*)

el	**avestruz** (*pl* avestruces)	ostrich
el	**búho**	owl
el	**buitre**	vulture
el	**canario**	canary
el	**chochín** (*pl* chochines)	wren
el	**cisne**	swan
el	**cuervo**	raven; crow
el	**cuco**	cuckoo
el	**estornino**	starling
el	**faisán** (*pl* faisanes)	pheasant
el	**gorrión** (*pl* gorriones)	sparrow
el	**halcón** (*pl* halcones)	falcon
el	**herrerillo**	bluetit
el	**huevo**	egg
el	**martín pescador** (*pl* martines ~es)	kingfisher
el	**mirlo**	blackbird
el	**nido**	nest
el	**pájaro carpintero**	woodpecker
el	**pavo real**	peacock
el	**petirrojo**	robin
el	**pico**	beak
el	**pingüino**	penguin
el	**ruiseñor**	nightingale
el	**tordo**	thrush
el	**urogallo**	grouse

ESSENTIAL WORDS *(feminine)*

la	**gallina**	hen

USEFUL WORDS *(feminine)*

el	**águila** *(pl f* las águilas)	eagle
el	**ala** *(pl f* las alas)	wing
la	**alondra**	lark
el	**ave** *(pl f* las aves)	bird
el	**ave de rapiña** *(pl f* las ~s ~~)	bird of prey
el	**ave rapaz** *(pl f* las ~s rapaces)	bird of prey
la	**cigüeña**	stork
la	**codorniz** *(pl* codornices)	quail
la	**gaviota**	seagull
la	**golondrina**	swallow
la	**grajilla**	jackdaw
la	**jaula**	cage
la	**paloma**	pigeon; dove
la	**perdiz** *(pl* perdices)	partridge
la	**pluma**	feather
la	**urraca**	magpie

USEFUL PHRASES

volar **to fly**
emprender vuelo **to fly away**
construir un nido **to build a nest**
silbar **to whistle**
cantar **to sing**
la gente los mete en jaulas **people put them in cages**
hibernar **to hibernate**
poner un huevo **to lay an egg**
un ave migratoria **a migratory bird**

ESSENTIAL WORDS *(masculine)*

el	**brazo**	arm
el	**cabello**	hair
el	**corazón** (*pl* corazones)	heart
el	**cuerpo**	body
el	**dedo**	finger
el	**diente**	tooth
el	**estómago**	stomach
el	**ojo**	eye
el	**pelo**	hair
el	**pie**	foot
el	**rostro**	face

IMPORTANT WORDS *(masculine)*

el	**cuello**	neck
el	**hombro**	shoulder
el	**pecho**	chest; bust
el	**pulgar**	thumb
el	**tobillo**	ankle

USEFUL PHRASES

de pie standing
sentado(a) sitting
tumbado(a) lying

ESSENTIAL WORDS *(feminine)*

la	**boca**	mouth
la	**cabeza**	head
la	**espalda**	back
la	**garganta**	throat
la	**mano**	hand
la	**nariz** *(pl narices)*	nose
la	**oreja**	ear
la	**pierna**	leg
la	**rodilla**	knee

IMPORTANT WORDS *(feminine)*

la	**barbilla**	chin
la	**cara**	face
la	**ceja**	eyebrow
la	**frente**	forehead
la	**lengua**	tongue
la	**mejilla**	cheek
la	**piel**	skin
la	**sangre**	blood
la	**voz** *(pl voces)*	voice

USEFUL PHRASES

grande big
alto(a) tall
pequeño(a) small
bajo(a) short
gordo(a) fat
flaco(a) skinny
delgado(a) slim
bonito(a) pretty
feo(a) ugly

USEFUL WORDS (*masculine*)

el	cerebro	brain
el	codo	elbow
el	cutis (*pl inv*)	skin, complexion
el	dedo del pie	toe
el	dedo índice	forefinger
el	dedo gordo	the big toe
los	dedos del pie	toes
el	esqueleto	skeleton
el	gesto	gesture
el	hígado	liver
el	hueso	bone
el	labio	lip
el	músculo	muscle
el	muslo	thigh
el	párpado	eyelid
el	pulmón (*pl* pulmones)	lung
el	puño	fist
el	rasgo	feature
el	riñón (*pl* riñones)	kidney
el	seno	breast
el	talle	waist
el	talón (*pl* talones)	heel
el	trasero	bottom

USEFUL PHRASES

sonarse (la nariz) to blow one's nose
cortarse las uñas to cut one's nails
cortarse el pelo to have one's hair cut
encogerse de hombros to shrug one's shoulders
asentir/decir que sí con la cabeza to nod one's head
negar/decir que no con la cabeza to shake one's head
ver to see; oír to hear; sentir to feel
oler to smell; tocar to touch; probar to taste
estrechar la mano a alguien to shake hands with somebody
saludar a alguien con la mano to wave at somebody
señalar algo to point at something

USEFUL WORDS (feminine)

la	**arteria**	artery
la	**cadera**	hip
la	**carne**	flesh
la	**columna (vertebral)**	spine
la	**costilla**	rib
la	**facción** (pl facciones)	feature
la	**mandíbula**	jaw
la	**muñeca**	wrist
la	**nuca**	nape of the neck
la	**pantorrilla**	calf (of leg)
la	**pestaña**	eyelash
la	**planta del pie**	sole of the foot
la	**pupila**	pupil (of the eye)
la	**sien**	temple (of head)
la	**talla**	size
la	**tez** (pl teces)	complexion
la	**uña**	nail
la	**vena**	vein

USEFUL PHRASES

contorno de caderas hip measurement
cintura waist measurement
contorno de pecho chest measurement
sordo(a) deaf
ciego(a) blind
mudo(a) mute
discapacitado(a) disabled
disminuido(a) psíquico(a) person with learning difficulties
él es más alto que tú he is taller than you
ella ha crecido mucho she has grown a lot
estoy demasiado gordo(a) or tengo sobrepeso I am overweight
ella ha engordado/adelgazado she has put on/lost weight
ella mide 1,47 metros she is 1.47 metres tall
él pesa 40 kilos he weighs 40 kilos

488 calendar

SEASONS

la	primavera	spring
el	verano	summer
el	otoño	autumn
el	invierno	winter

MONTHS

enero	January	julio	July
febrero	February	agosto	August
marzo	March	septiembre	September
abril	April	octubre	October
mayo	May	noviembre	November
junio	June	diciembre	December

DAYS OF THE WEEK

lunes	Monday
martes	Tuesday
miércoles	Wednesday
jueves	Thursday
viernes	Friday
sábado	Saturday
domingo	Sunday

USEFUL PHRASES

en primavera/verano/otoño/invierno in spring/summer/autumn/winter
en mayo in May
el 10 de julio de 2006 on 10 July 2006
es 3 de diciembre it's 3rd December
los sábados voy a la piscina on Saturdays I go to the swimming pool
el sábado fui a la piscina on Saturday I went to the swimming pool
el próximo sábado/el sábado pasado next/last Saturday
el sábado anterior/siguiente the previous/following Saturday

CALENDAR

el **calendario**	calendar
el **día**	day
los **días de la semana**	days of the week
el **día festivo**	public holiday
la **estación** (*pl* estaciones)	season
el **mes**	month
la **semana**	week

USEFUL PHRASES

el día de los (Santos) Inocentes April Fools' Day (*celebrated on 28 December in Spain*)

la broma del día de los (Santos) Inocentes April fool's trick

el primero de mayo May Day

el día de la Hispanidad Columbus Day (*Spain's national day, celebrated on 12 October*)

el himno nacional de España Spain's national anthem

el día D D-Day

el día de San Valentín St Valentine's Day

el día de Todos los Santos All Saints' Day

la Semana Santa Easter

el Domingo de Resurrección *or* Pascua Easter Sunday

el Lunes de Pascua Easter Monday

el Miércoles de Ceniza Ash Wednesday

el Viernes Santo Good Friday

la Cuaresma Lent

la Pascua judía Passover

el Ramadán Ramadan

el Hanukkah Hanukkah *or* Hanukah

el Divali *or* el Festival de la Luz Divali *or* Diwali

el Adviento Advent

la Nochebuena Christmas Eve

la Navidad Christmas

en Navidad at Christmas

el día de Navidad Christmas Day

la Nochevieja New Year's Eve

el día de Año Nuevo New Year's Day

la cena *or* fiesta de Fin de Año New Year's Eve dinner *or* party

ESSENTIAL WORDS (*masculine*)

el	**aniversario de boda**	wedding anniversary
el	**cumpleaños** (*pl inv*)	birthday
el	**(día del) santo**	saint's day
el	**divorcio**	divorce
el	**matrimonio**	marriage
el	**regalo**	present

IMPORTANT WORDS (*masculine*)

el	**compromiso**	engagement
el	**festival**	festival
los	**fuegos artificiales**	fireworks; firework display
el	**nacimiento**	birth
el	**parque de atracciones**	fun fair

USEFUL WORDS (*masculine*)

el	**bautismo**	christening
el	**cementerio**	cemetery
el	**entierro**	funeral
el	**festival folclórico**	folk festival
el	**testigo**	witness
el	**regalo de Navidad**	Christmas present

USEFUL PHRASES

celebrar el cumpleaños to celebrate one's birthday
mi hermana nació en 1995 my sister was born in 1995
ella acaba de cumplir 17 años she's just turned 17
él me dio este regalo he gave me this present
¡te lo regalo! I'm giving it to you!
gracias thank you
divorciarse to get divorced
casarse to get married
comprometerse (con algn) to get engaged (to sb)
mi padre murió hace dos años my father died two years ago
enterrar to bury

ESSENTIAL WORDS (feminine)

la	boda	wedding
la	cita	appointment, date
la	fecha	date
la	fiesta	festival; fair; party

IMPORTANT WORDS (feminine)

las	fiestas	festivities
la	feria	fair
la	muerte	death
la	hoguera	bonfire

USEFUL WORDS (feminine)

la	ceremonia	ceremony
la	dama de honor	bridesmaid
la	invitación de boda (pl invitaciones ~~)	wedding invitation
la	jubilación (pl jubilaciones)	retirement
la	luna de miel	honeymoon
la	procesión (pl procesiones)	procession; march
la	tarjeta de felicitación	greetings card
la	testigo	witness

USEFUL PHRASES

bodas de plata/oro/diamante silver/golden/diamond wedding anniversary
desear a algn (un) Feliz Año to wish sb a happy New Year
dar or hacer una fiesta to have a party
invitar a los amigos to invite one's friends
elegir un regalo to choose a gift
¡Feliz navidad! or ¡Felices Pascuas! Happy Christmas!
¡Feliz cumpleaños! happy birthday!
(con) nuestros mejores deseos best wishes

ESSENTIAL WORDS *(masculine)*

los	**aseos**	toilets
los	**baños** *(LAm)*	washrooms; toilets
el	**bote**	tin, can
el	**camping** *(pl ~s)*	camping; campsite
el	**campista**	camper
el	**cerillo** *(LAm)*	match
el	**cubo de la basura**	dustbin
el	**cuchillo**	knife
el	**depósito de butano**	butane store
el	**emplazamiento**	pitch, site
el	**espejo**	mirror
el	**gas**	gas
el	**guarda**	warden
el	**lavabo**	washbasin
el	**plato**	plate
los	**servicios** *(Sp)*	washrooms; toilets
el	**suplemento**	extra charge
el	**tenedor**	fork
el	**trailer** *(pl ~s) (LAm)*	trailer
el	**vehículo**	vehicle

IMPORTANT WORDS *(masculine)*

el	**abrelatas** *(pl inv)*	tin-opener
el	**colchón inflable** *(pl colchones ~s)*	airbed
el	**detergente**	washing powder
el	**enchufe**	socket
el	**hornillo**	stove
el	**sacacorchos** *(pl inv)*	corkscrew
el	**saco de dormir**	sleeping bag

USEFUL PHRASES

ir de *or* hacer camping to go camping
acampar to camp
bien equipado(a) well equipped
hacer una hoguera to make a fire

ESSENTIAL WORDS *(feminine)*

el	**agua (no) potable** *(f)*	(non-)drinking water
la	**alberca** *(Mex)*	swimming pool
la	**caja**	box
la	**cama plegable**	camp bed
la	**campista**	camper
la	**caravana**	caravan; motorhome
la	**carpa** *(LAm)*	tent
la	**cerilla**	match
la	**comida enlatada**	tinned food
la	**cuchara**	spoon
la	**ducha**	shower
la	**hoguera de campamento**	campfire
la	**lata**	tin, can
la	**lavadora**	washing machine
la	**linterna**	torch
la	**mesa**	table
la	**navaja**	penknife
la	**noche**	night
la	**piscina** *(Sp)*	swimming pool
la	**sala**	room; hall
la	**tienda (de campaña)** *(Sp)*	tent
la	**tumbona**	deckchair

IMPORTANT WORDS *(feminine)*

la	**barbacoa**	barbecue
la	**colada**	washing
las	**instalaciones sanitarias**	washing facilities
la	**lavandería**	launderette
la	**mochila**	rucksack
las	**normas**	rules
la	**sala de juegos**	games room
la	**sombra**	shade; shadow
la	**toma de corriente**	socket

USEFUL PHRASES

montar una tienda **to pitch a tent**
asar unas salchichas (a la parrilla) **to grill some sausages**

ESSENTIAL WORDS *(masculine)*

el	aeromozo *(LAm)*	steward; flight attendant
el	agricultor	farmer
el	auxiliar de vuelo *(Sp)*	steward; flight attendant
el	banco	bank
el	bombero	fireman
el	cajero	check-out assistant
el	cartero	postman
el	diseñador de páginas web	web designer
el	electricista	electrician
el	empleado	employee
el	empresario	employer
el	enfermero	nurse
el	farmacéutico	chemist
el	informático	computer programmer
el	jefe	boss
el	maquinista	engineer; train driver
el	mecánico	mechanic
el	médico	doctor
el	minero	miner
el	oficio	trade
el	orientador profesional	careers adviser
el	policía	policeman
el	profesor	teacher
el	propietario de un taller (mecánico *or* de reparaciones)	garage owner
el	redactor	editor
el	soldado	soldier
el	sueldo	wages
el	taxista	taxi driver
el	trabajo	job; work
el	vendedor	sales assistant, shop assistant

USEFUL PHRASES

interesante/poco interesante interesting/not very interesting
él es cartero he is a postman; él/ella es médico he/she is a doctor
trabajar to work
hacerse, volverse to become

ESSENTIAL WORDS (feminine)

la	aeromoza (LAm)	stewardess; flight attendant
la	agricultora	farmer
la	ambición (pl ambiciones)	ambition
la	auxiliar de vuelo	stewardess; flight attendant
la	cajera	check-out assistant
la	cartera	postwoman
la	consejera profesional	careers adviser
la	empleada	employee
la	enfermera	nurse
la	estrella (m+f)	star
la	fábrica	factory
la	informática	computer programmer
la	jefa	boss
la	jubilación (pl jubilaciones)	retirement
la	mecanógrafa	typist
la	médico	doctor
la	oficina	office
la	profesión (pl profesiones)	profession
la	profesora	teacher
la	recepcionista	receptionist
la	redactora	editor
la	secretaria	secretary
la	vendedora	sales assistant, shop assistant
la	vida	life
la	vida laboral	working life

USEFUL PHRASES

trabajar para ganarse la vida to work for one's living
mi ambición es ser juez(a) it is my ambition to be a judge
¿en qué trabajas? what do you do (for a living)?
solicitar un trabajo to apply for a job

IMPORTANT WORDS (*masculine*)

el	**aprendizaje**	apprenticeship
el	**asalariado**	wage-earner
el	**aumento**	rise
el	**autor**	author
el	**bombero**	fireman
el	**colega**	colleague
el	**comerciante**	shopkeeper
el	**contrato**	contract
el	**conserje**	caretaker
el	**decorador**	decorator
el	**desempleado**	unemployed person
el	**desempleo**	unemployment
el	**empleo**	job; situation
el	**fontanero** (*Sp*)	plumber
el	**futuro**	future
el	**gerente**	manager
el	**hombre de negocios**	businessman
el	**INEM**	employment organization; institute of employment
el	**interino**	temp
el	**jefe**	boss
el	**mercado laboral**	job market
el	**negocio** *or* los **negocios**	business
el	**óptico**	optician
el	**peluquero**	hairdresser
el	**piloto**	pilot
el	**pintor**	painter
el	**plomero** (*Mex*)	plumber
el	**presidente**	president; chairperson
el	**sindicato**	trade union
el	**trabajador**	worker
el	**trabajo**	job

USEFUL PHRASES

estar desempleado(a) *or* en paro **to be unemployed**
despedir a algn **to make sb redundant**
contrato indefinido/temporal/a término fijo **permanent/temporary/ fixed term contract**

IMPORTANT WORDS *(feminine)*

la	acomodadora	usher
la	agencia de trabajo temporal	temping agency
la	asalariada	wage-earner
la	biblioteca	library
la	carrera	career
la	carta adjunta	covering letter
la	cocinera	cook
la	colega	colleague
la	conserje	caretaker
la	entrevista (de trabajo)	(job) interview
la	gerente	manager
la	huelga	strike
la	interina	temp
la	limpiadora	cleaner
la	mujer de negocios	businesswoman
la	oficina de empleo	job centre
la	peluquera	hairdresser
la	pintora	painter
la	política	politics
la	presidenta	president; chairperson
la	solicitud	application
la	trabajadora	worker

USEFUL PHRASES

"demandas de empleo" **"situations wanted"**
"ofertas de empleo" **"situations vacant"**
estar en/pertenercer a un sindicato **to be in a union**
ganar 150 libras a la semana **to earn £150 a week**
una subida *or* un aumento de sueldo **a pay rise**
ponerse *or* declararse en huelga **to go on strike**
estar en huelga **to be on strike**
trabajar jornada completa/media jornada **to work full-time/part-time**
trabajar horas extra(s) **to work overtime**
reducción de la jornada laboral **reduction in working hours**

USEFUL WORDS (*masculine*)

el	**abogado**	lawyer
el	**agente comercial**	sales rep
el	**albañil**	mason
el	**arquitecto**	architect
el	**artista**	artist
el	**carpintero**	joiner
el	**cirujano**	surgeon
el	**contable** (*Sp*), el **contador** (*LAm*)	accountant
el	**cosmonauta**	cosmonaut
el	**cura**	priest
el	**curso de formación**	training course
el	**diputado**	MP
el	**diseñador**	fashion designer
el	**ejecutivo**	executive
el	**escritor**	writer
el	**fotógrafo**	photographer
el	**funcionario**	civil servant
el	**horario**	schedule
el	**ingeniero**	engineer
el	**intérprete**	interpreter
el	**investigador**	researcher
el	**juez** (*pl* jueces)	judge
el	**marinero**	sailor
el	**modelo**	model (*person*)
el	**monitor de actividades**	activity leader
el	**negocio**	business
el	**notario**	notary
el	**paro**	unemployment benefit
el	**periodista**	journalist
el	**(período de) trabajo en prácticas**	work placement
el	**personal**	staff
el	**político**	politician
el	**director ejecutivo**	managing director
el	**procurador**	solicitor
el	**representante**	rep; sales rep
el	**sacerdote**	priest
el	**traductor**	translator
el	**veterinario**	vet
el	**viticultor**	wine grower

USEFUL WORDS *(feminine)*

la	**abogada**	lawyer
la	**administración** (*pl* administraciones)	administration
el	**ama de casa** (*pl f* amas ~~)	housewife
la	**monitora de actividades**	activity leader
la	**artista**	artist
la	**compañía**	company
la	**contable** (*Sp*), la **contadora** (*LAm*)	accountant
la	**empresa**	company
la	**formación**	training
la	**funcionaria**	civil servant
la	**huelga de celo**	work-to-rule; go-slow
la	**indemnización por desempleo**	redundancy payment
la	**intérprete**	interpreter
la	**jueza**	judge
la	**locutora**	announcer
la	**modelo**	model (*person*)
la	**modista**	dressmaker
la	**monja**	nun
la	**orientación profesional**	careers guidance
la	**periodista**	journalist
la	**policía**	policewoman
la	**religiosa**	nun
la	**representante**	rep; sales rep
la	**taquimecanógrafa**	shorthand typist
la	**traductora**	translator

USEFUL PHRASES

el trabajo temporal **seasonal work**
un empleo temporal/permanente **a temporary/permanent job**
un trabajo a tiempo parcial (*Sp*) *or* a medio tiempo (*LAm*) **a part-time job**
ser contratado(a) **to be taken on**; ser despedido(a) **to be dismissed**
despedir *or* echar a algn **to give sb the sack**
buscar trabajo **to look for work**
hacer un curso de formación profesional **to go on a training course**
fichar al entrar a/al salir de trabajar **to clock in/out**
trabajar en horario flexible **to work flexitime**

ESSENTIAL WORDS (*masculine*)

el	**aceite**	oil
el	**agente de policía**	policeman
el	**aparcamiento** (*Sp*)	car park
el	**atasco**	traffic jam
el	**autoestop**	hitch-hiking
el	**autoestopista**	hitch-hiker
el	**automóvil**	car
el	**aventón** (*Mex*)	hitch-hiking
el	**callejero**	street map
el	**camión** (*pl* camiones)	lorry, truck
el	**carnet** or **carné de conducir** (*Sp*) (*pl* ~s or ~s ~~)	driving licence
el	**carro** (*LAm*)	car
el	**chófer**	driver; chauffeur
el	**ciclista**	cyclist
el	**coche** (*Sp*)	car
el	**conductor**	driver
el	**cruce**	crossroads
el	**diesel**	diesel
el	**estacionamiento** (*LAm*)	car park
los	**faros**	headlights
el	**freno**	brake
el	**garaje**	garage
el	**gasoil**	diesel (*oil*)
el	**kilómetro**	kilometre
el	**litro**	litre
el	**mapa de carreteras**	road map
el	**mecánico**	mechanic
el	**neumático**	tyre
el	**número**	number
el	**parking** (*pl* ~s)	car park
el	**peaje**	toll
el	**peatón** (*pl* peatones)	pedestrian
el	**radar**	speed camera
el	**semáforo**	traffic lights
el	**trailer** (*pl* ~s) (*LAm*)	caravan
el	**viaje**	journey

ESSENTIAL WORDS *(feminine)*

el	**agua** *(f)*	water
la	**autoestopista**	hitch-hiker
la	**autopista**	motorway
la	**autopista de peaje**	toll motorway
la	**caravana** *(Sp)*	caravan
la	**carretera**	road
la	**carretera nacional**	main road
la	**chófer**	driver; chauffeur
la	**ciclista**	cyclist
la	**cochera**	garage
la	**conductora**	driver
la	**desviación** *(pl* desviaciones)	diversion
la	**dirección** *(pl* direcciones)	direction
la	**dirección asistida** *(pl* direcciones ~s)	power steering
la	**distancia**	distance
la	**estación de servicio** *(pl* estaciones ~ ~)	petrol station
la	**gasolina**	petrol
la	**gasolina sin plomo**	unleaded petrol
la	**libreta de manejar** *(Mex)*	driving licence
la	**matrícula** *(Sp)*, la **placa** *(LAm)*	(car) registration document
la	**policía**	police
la	**póliza de seguros**	insurance certificate

USEFUL PHRASES

frenar bruscamente **to brake suddenly**
100 kilómetros por hora **100 kilometres an hour**
¿tienes carné *(or* carnet) de conducir? **do you have a driving licence?**
vamos a dar una vuelta (en coche) **we're going for a drive (in the car)**
¡lleno, por favor!, ¡llénelo, por favor! **fill her up please!**
tomar la carretera a/hacia Córdoba **take the road to Córdoba**
es un viaje de tres horas **it's a 3-hour journey**
¡buen viaje! **have a good journey!**
¡vámonos!, ¡en marcha! **let's go!**
de camino vimos ... **on the way we saw ...**
adelantar a un coche **to overtake a car**

IMPORTANT WORDS (*masculine*)

el	accidente (de carretera)	(road) accident
el	aparcamiento	parking
el	atasco	traffic jam
el	camionero	lorry driver
el	choque	collision
el	cinturón de seguridad	seat belt
	(*pl* cinturones ~~)	
el	claxon (*pl* cláxones *or* ~s)	horn
el	código de la circulación	highway code
el	daño	damage
el	embrague	clutch
el	encargado de una gasolinera	petrol pump attendant
el	faro	headlight
el	maletero (*Sp*)	boot
el	motociclista	motorcyclist
el	motor	engine
el	motorista	motorist
los	papeles (del coche)	official papers
el	pinchazo	puncture
el	pito	horn
el	salpicadero	dashboard
el	seguro	insurance
el	surtidor (de gasolina)	petrol pump
el	tráfico	traffic
el	túnel de lavado de coches	car wash

USEFUL PHRASES

primero enciendes *or* pones el motor en marcha **first you switch on the engine**

el motor arranca *or* se pone en marcha **the engine starts up**

el coche se pone en marcha **the car moves off**

estamos circulando **we're driving along**

acelerar **to accelerate**; continuar **to continue**

reducir *or* aminorar la velocidad *or* la marcha **to slow down**

detenerse **to stop**; aparcar (el coche) **to park (the car)**

apagar el motor **to switch off the engine**

parar con el semáforo en rojo **to stop at the red light**

IMPORTANT WORDS (feminine)

la	autoescuela (Sp)	driving school
la	avería	breakdown
la	batería	battery
la	cajuela (Mex)	boot
la	calle de sentido único	one-way street
la	carrocería	body work
la	colisión (pl colisiones)	collision
la	documentación (del coche)	official papers
la	esculela de conductores (LAm) or de manejo (Mex)	driving school
la	frontera	border
la	glorieta	roundabout
la	grúa	breakdown van
la	ITV (inspección técnica de vehículos) (Sp)	MOT test
la	marca	make (of car)
la	motociclista	motorcyclist
la	motorista	motorist
la	pieza de repuesto	spare part
la	póliza de seguros	insurance policy
la	prioridad	right of way
la	prueba del alcohol	Breathalyser® test
la	puerta	(car) door
la	rotonda	roundabout
la	rueda	tyre
la	rueda de repuesto	spare tyre
la	velocidad	speed; gear
la	zona azul	restricted parking zone

USEFUL PHRASES

ha habido un accidente **there's been an accident**

hubo seis heridos en el accidente **six people were injured in the accident**

¿puedo ver la documentación *or* los papeles del coche, por favor? **may I see your papers please?**

pinchar, tener un pinchazo **to have a puncture**; arreglar **to fix**

averiarse *or* tener una avería **to break down**

me he quedado sin gasolina **I've run out of petrol**

USEFUL WORDS (*masculine*)

el acelerador	accelerator
el arcén (*pl* arcenes)	hard shoulder
el autolavado	car-wash
el botón de arranque (*pl* botones ~~)	starter
el capó	bonnet
el carburador	carburettor
el carril	lane
el catalizador	catalytic converter
el conductor novel	learner driver
el consumo de gasolina	petrol consumption
el cuentakilómetros (*pl inv*)	speedometer
el desvío	detour
el guardia de tráfico	traffic warden
el herido	casualty
el intermitente	indicator
el lavacoches (*pl inv*)	car-wash
el límite de velocidad	speed limit
el limpiaparabrisas (*pl inv*)	windscreen wiper
el parabrisas (*pl inv*)	windscreen
el parachoques (*pl inv*)	bumper
el parquímetro	parking meter
el pedal	pedal
el policía motorizado	motorcycle policeman
el profesor de autoescuela	driving instructor
el remolque	trailer
el retrovisor	rear-view mirror
el (sistema de navegación) GPS	satellite navigation system
el volante	steering wheel

USEFUL PHRASES

en la hora punta **at rush hour**
le pusieron una multa de 100 euros **he got a 100-euro fine**
¿está asegurado? **are you insured?**
no olviden ponerse los cinturones de seguridad **don't forget to put on your
   seat belts**
en la frontera **at the border**
hacer autoestop **to hitch-hike**

USEFUL WORDS *(feminine)*

el **área de descanso** *(pl f* las áreas ~~)	lay-by
el **área de servicio** *(pl f* las áreas ~~)	service area
la **baca**	roof rack
la **caja de cambios**	gearbox
la **carretera de circunvalación**	ring road
la **clase de conducir**	driving lesson
la **curva**	bend
la **estación de servicio** *(pl* estaciones ~~)	filling station
la **gasolinera**	filling station
la **guardia de tráfico**	traffic warden
la **infracción de tráfico** *(pl* infracciones ~~)	traffic offence
la **matrícula**	number plate
la **mediana**	central reservation
la **multa**	fine
la **parada de emergencia**	emergency stop
la **presión**	pressure
la **señal de tráfico**	road sign
la **vía**	way, road; lane *(on road)*
la **vía de acceso**	slip road
la **víctima** *(m+f)*	casualty
la **zona urbanizada**	built-up area

USEFUL PHRASES

la rueda delantera/trasera **the front/back wheel**
tenemos que desviarnos **we have to make a detour**
una multa por exceso de velocidad **a fine for speeding**
contratar a un conductor **to book a driver**

"ceda el paso a la derecha" **"give way to the right"**
"circule por la derecha" **"keep to the right"**
"prohibido el paso" **"no entry"**
"prohibido aparcar" **"no parking"**
"obras" **"roadworks"**

ESSENTIAL WORDS (masculine)

el	abrigo	overcoat; coat
el	anorak (pl inv or ~s)	anorak
el	bañador	swimming trunks; swimsuit
el	bolso	bag
el	botón (pl botones)	button
el	calcetín (pl calcetines)	sock
los	calzoncillos	pants; boxer shorts
los	calzones (LAm)	knickers
el	camisón (pl camisones)	nightdress
el	chubasquero	raincoat
el	cuello	collar
el	jersey (pl ~s)	jumper
el	número (de pie)	(shoe) size
el	pantalón (pl pantalones)	trousers
los	(pantalones) vaqueros	jeans
el	pañuelo	handkerchief
el	paraguas (pl inv)	umbrella
el	pijama	pyjamas
el	sombrero	hat
el	talle	waist
el	traje	suit (for man); costume
el	traje de chaqueta	suit
el	vestido	dress
el	zapato	shoe

IMPORTANT WORDS (masculine)

el	bolsillo	pocket
el	bolso	handbag
el	cinturón (pl cinturones)	belt
el	guante	glove
el	impermeable	raincoat
los	pantalones cortos	shorts
el	uniforme	uniform

ESSENTIAL WORDS *(feminine)*

la	braga (del bikini)	bikini bottoms
las	bragas *(Sp)*	pants; knickers
la	camisa	shirt
la	camiseta	T-shirt
la	capucha	hood
la	chaqueta	jacket
la	corbata	tie
la	falda	skirt
las	medias	tights
la	moda	fashion
la	parka	parka
la	ropa	clothes
la	ropa interior	underwear
la	sandalia	sandal
la	talla	size

IMPORTANT WORDS *(feminine)*

la	americana	jacket *(for man)*
la	blusa	blouse
la	bota	boot
las	prendas de vestir	clothes
la	zapatilla	slipper

USEFUL PHRASES

por la mañana me visto **in the morning I get dressed**
por la tarde me desvisto **in the evening I get undressed**
cuando llego a casa del colegio me cambio **when I get home from school
I get changed**
llevar, llevar puesto **to wear**
ponerse **to put on**
eso es muy elegante **that's very smart**
(eso) te queda bien **that suits you**
¿qué talla tienes (*or* tiene)? **what size do you take?**
¿qué número de pie tienes (*or* tiene)? **what shoe size do you take?**
tengo un 38 (de pie), calzo un 38 **I take size 38 in shoes**

USEFUL WORDS (*masculine*)

los	**accesorios**	accessories
el	**bastón** (*pl* bastones)	walking stick
el	**bolso bandolera** (*pl* ~s ~)	shoulder bag
el	**cárdigan** (*pl* ~s)	cardigan
el	**chaleco**	vest; waistcoat
el	**chándal** (*pl* ~s)	tracksuit
los	**cordones**	(shoe)laces
el	**delantal**	apron
el	**desfile de moda**	fashion show
el	**foulard** (*pl* ~s)	scarf
el	**lazo**	ribbon
el	**mono**	overalls
el	**ojal**	buttonhole
los	**pantis**	tights
el	**pañuelo**	scarf
el	**peto**	overalls; dungarees
el	**polar**	fleece
el	**polo**	polo shirt
el	**probador**	fitting room
el	**sujetador**	bra
el	**traje de chaqueta**	suit (*for woman*)
el	**traje de etiqueta**	evening dress (*for man*)
el	**traje de noche**	evening dress (*for woman*)
el	**traje pantalón** (*pl* ~s ~)	trouser suit
los	**tirantes**	braces
el	**vestido de novia**	wedding dress
los	**zapatos de tacón**	high heels
los	**zapatos de tacón de aguja**	stiletto heels

USEFUL WORDS (feminine)

la	alpargata	espadrille
la	alta costura	haute couture
la	bandolera	shoulder bag
la	bata	dressing gown
las	bermudas	Bermuda shorts
la	boina	beret
la	bufanda	scarf
la	camiseta con capucha	hooded top
la	camiseta sin mangas	tank top
las	chanclas	flip flops
la	cinta	ribbon
la	colada	washing
la	combinación (pl combinaciones)	underskirt
la	cremallera	zip
la(s)	enagua(s)	underskirt
la	falda pantalón (pl ~s ~)	culottes
la	gorra	cap
la	limpieza en seco	dry-cleaning
la	manga	sleeve
las	medias	stockings
la	pajarita	bow tie
la	rebeca	cardigan
la	ropa blanca	washing
la	sudadera	sweatshirt
las	zapatillas de deporte	trainers

USEFUL PHRASES

largo(a) long; corto(a) short
un vestido de manga corta/larga a short-sleeved/long-sleeved dress
estrecho(a), ajustado(a) tight
amplio(a), suelto(a) loose
una falda ajustada or ceñida a tight skirt
a rayas, de rayas striped; a cuadros, de cuadros checked; de lunares spotted
ropa de sport, ropa informal casual clothes
con vestido de noche in evening dress
a la moda, de moda fashionable; moderno(a) trendy
pasado(a) de moda, anticuado(a) old-fashioned

amarillo(a)	yellow
azul	blue
azul celeste	sky blue
azul claro	pale blue
azul marino	navy blue
azul oscuro	dark blue
azul real	royal blue
beige, beis	beige
blanco(a)	white
burdeos (*pl inv*)	maroon
crudo(a)	natural
dorado(a)	golden
granate	maroon
gris	grey
malva	mauve
marrón (*pl* marrones)	brown
morado(a)	purple
naranja	orange
negro(a)	black
rojo(a)	red
rojo fuerte *or* intenso	bright red
rosa	pink
turquesa	turquoise
verde	green
violeta	violet

USEFUL PHRASES

el color colour

¿de qué color tienes (or tiene) los ojos/el pelo? what colour are your eyes/
 is your hair?

el azul te sienta bien blue suits you; the blue one suits you

pintar algo de azul to paint sth blue

los zapatos azules blue shoes

los zapatos azul claro light blue shoes

(ella) tiene los ojos verdes she has green eyes

cambiar de color to change colour

la Casa Blanca the White House

un (hombre) blanco a white man

una (mujer) blanca a white woman

un (hombre) negro a black man

una (mujer) negra a black woman

blanco como la nieve as white as snow

Blancanieves Snow White

Caperucita Roja Little Red Riding Hood

ponerse colorado(a) or rojo(a) to turn red

sonrojarse de vergüenza to blush with shame

blanco(a) como el papel as white as a sheet

muy moreno(a), muy bronceado(a) as brown as a berry

(él) estaba cubierto de cardenales he was black and blue

un ojo morado a black eye

un filete muy poco hecho a very rare steak, an underdone steak

ESSENTIAL WORDS (*masculine*)

el	ordenador (personal)	(personal) computer
el	programa	program
el	programador	programmer
el	ratón (*pl* ratones)	mouse

USEFUL WORDS (*masculine*)

el	cartucho de tinta	ink cartridge
el	CD-ROM (*pl inv*)	CD-ROM
el	corrector ortográfico	spellchecker
el	correo electrónico	email
el	cursor	cursor
los	datos	data
el	disco duro	hard disk
el	disquete	floppy disk
el	documento	document
el	fichero	file
el	icono	icon
el	internauta	internet user
el	Internet	internet
el	juego de ordenador	computer game
el	mail (*pl* ~s)	email
el	menú	menu
el	módem (*pl* ~s)	modem
el	monitor	monitor
el	navegador	browser
el	ordenador portátil	laptop
el	paquete de programas	software package
el	pirata informático	hacker
el	procesador de textos	wordprocessor
el	servidor	server
el	sitio web	website
el	software (*pl inv*)	software
el	soporte (físico)	hardware
el	teclado	keyboard
el	virus (*pl inv*)	virus
el	Web (*pl* ~s)	Web
el	wifi	wifi

ESSENTIAL WORDS (feminine)

la	impresora	printer
la	informática	computer science; computer studies

USEFUL WORDS (feminine)

la	aplicación (pl aplicaciones)	program
la	banda ancha	broadband
la	base de datos	database
la	computadora (personal) (LAm)	(personal) computer
la	copia de seguridad	back-up
la	copia impresa	print-out
la	dirección de correo (electrónico) (pl direcciones ~~ (~))	e-mail address
la	función (pl funciones)	function
la	grabadora de DVD	DVD writer
la	hoja de cálculo	spreadsheet
la	interfaz (pl interfaces)	interface
la	internauta	internet user
la	Internet	Internet
la	llave USB	USB key
la	memoria	memory
la	memoria RAM	RAM, random-access memory
la	memoria ROM	ROM, read-only Memory
la	página de inicio	home page
la	pantalla	screen
la	papelera de reciclaje	recycle bin
la	red	network
la	unidad de disco	disk drive
la	ventana	window
la	Web (pl ~s)	Web
la	webcam (pl ~s)	webcam

USEFUL PHRASES

copiar to copy; eliminar, suprimir to delete; formatear to format
descargar un archivo to download a file
guardar to save; imprimir to print; teclear to key
navegar por Internet to surf the internet

COUNTRIES

ESSENTIAL WORDS (*masculine*)

Canadá	Canada
EE.UU.	USA
Estados Unidos	United States
país	country
Países Bajos	Netherlands
Reino Unido	United Kingdom

USEFUL WORDS (*masculine*)

Brasil	Brazil
Ecuador	Ecuador
El Salvador	El Salvador
Japón	Japan
Marruecos	Morocco
México	Mexico
Pakistán	Pakistan
Panamá	Panama
Paraguay	Paraguay
Perú	Peru
Tercer Mundo	Third World
Túnez	Tunisia
Uruguay	Uruguay

USEFUL PHRASES

mi país de origen **my native country**
la capital de España **the capital of Spain**
¿de qué país eres (*or* es)? **what country do you come from?**
soy de (los) Estados Unidos/de Canadá **I come from the United States/ from Canada**
nací en Escocia **I was born in Scotland**
me voy a los Países Bajos **I'm going to the Netherlands**
acabo de regresar de (los) Estados Unidos **I have just come back from the United States**
los países en (vías de) desarrollo **the developing countries**
países de habla hispana **Spanish-speaking countries**

ESSENTIAL WORDS (feminine)

América	America
América del Sur	South America
Alemania	Germany
Bélgica	Belgium
Escocia	Scotland
España	Spain
Europa	Europe
Francia	France
Gran Bretaña	Great Britain
Holanda	Holland
Inglaterra	England
Irlanda (del Norte)	(Northern) Ireland
Italia	Italy
(el País de) Gales	Wales
Sudamérica	South America
Suiza	Switzerland
USA	USA

USEFUL WORDS (feminine)

África	Africa
Argelia	Algeria
Asia	Asia
Bolivia	Bolivia
Colombia	Colombia
Costa Rica	Costa Rica
Cuba	Cuba
Francia	France
Grecia	Greece
Guatemala	Guatemala
la India	India
Nicaragua	Nicaragua
la República Dominicana	the Dominican Republic
la Unión Europea, UE	the European Union, the EU
Venezuela	Venezuela

NATIONALITIES

ESSENTIAL WORDS *(masculine)*

un	**alemán** (*pl* alemanes)	a German
un	**americano**	an American
un	**belga**	a Belgian
un	**británico**	a Briton
un	**canadiense**	a Canadian
un	**escocés** (*pl* escoceses)	a Scot
un	**español**	a Spaniard
un	**europeo**	a European
un	**francés** (*pl* franceses)	a Frenchman
un	**galés** (*pl* galeses)	a Welshman
un	**holandés** (*pl* holandeses)	a Dutchman
un	**inglés** (*pl* ingleses)	an Englishman
un	**irlandés** (*pl* irlandeses)	an Irishman
un	**italiano**	an Italian
un	**pakistaní** (*pl* ~es *or* ~s)	a Pakistani
un	**suizo**	a Swiss (man *or* boy)

USEFUL PHRASES
(él) es irlandés he is Irish
(ella) es irlandesa she is Irish
la campiña irlandesa the Irish countryside
una ciudad irlandesa an Irish town

ESSENTIAL WORDS *(feminine)*

una	**alemana**	a German
una	**americana**	an American
una	**belga**	a Belgian
una	**británica**	a Briton, a British woman *or* girl
una	**canadiense**	a Canadian
una	**escocesa**	a Scot
una	**española**	a Spaniard
una	**europea**	a European
una	**francesa**	a Frenchwoman, a French girl
una	**galesa**	a Welshwoman, a Welsh girl
una	**holandesa**	a Dutchwoman, a Dutch girl
una	**inglesa**	an Englishwoman, an English girl
una	**irlandesa**	an Irishwoman, an Irish girl
una	**italiana**	an Italian
una	**pakistaní** (*pl* ~es *or* ~s)	a Pakistani
una	**suiza**	a Swiss girl *or* woman

USEFUL PHRASES

soy escocés – hablo inglés **I am Scottish – I speak English**
soy escocesa **I am Scottish**
un(a) extranjero(a) **a foreigner**
en el extranjero **abroad**
la nacionalidad **nationality**

USEFUL WORDS (*masculine*)

un	africano	an African
un	antillano	a West Indian
un	árabe	an Arab
un	argelino	an Algerian
un	argentino	an Argentinian
un	boliviano	a Bolivian
un	brasileño	a Brazilian
un	chileno	a Chilean
un	chino	a Chinese
un	colombiano	a Colombian
un	costarricense	a Costa Rican
un	cubano	a Cuban
un	dominicano	a Dominican
un	ecuatoriano	an Ecuadorean
un	griego	a Greek
un	guatemalteco	a Guatemalan
un	indio	an Indian
un	japonés (*pl* japoneses)	a Japanese
un	marroquí (*pl* ~es *or* ~s)	a Moroccan
un	mexicano	a Mexican
un	nicaragüense	a Nicaraguan
un	panameño	a Panamanian
un	paraguayo	a Paraguayan
un	peruano	a Peruvian
un	ruso	a Russian
un	salvadoreño	a Salvadorian
un	tunecino	a Tunisian
un	turco	a Turk
un	uruguayo	a Uruguayan
un	venezolano	a Venezuelan

USEFUL WORDS *(feminine)*

una	africana	an African
una	antillana	a West Indian
una	árabe	an Arab
una	argelina	an Algerian
una	argentina	an Argentinian
una	boliviana	a Bolivian
una	brasileña	a Brazilian
una	chilena	a Chilean
una	china	a Chinese
una	colombiana	a Colombian
una	costarricense	a Costa Rican
una	cubana	a Cuban
una	dominicana	a Dominican
una	ecuatoriana	an Ecuadorean
una	griega	a Greek
una	guatemalteca	a Guatemalan
una	india	an Indian
una	japonesa	a Japanese
una	marroquí *(pl ~es or ~s)*	a Moroccan
una	mexicana	a Mexican
una	nicaragüense	a Nicaraguan
una	panameña	a Panamanian
una	paraguaya	a Paraguayan
una	peruana	a Peruvian
una	rusa	a Russian
una	salvadoreña	a Salvadorian
una	tunecina	a Tunisian
una	turca	a Turk
una	uruguaya	a Uruguayan
una	venezolana	a Venezuelan

ESSENTIAL WORDS *(masculine)*

el	aire	air
el	albergue juvenil	youth hostel
el	árbol	tree
el	arroyo	stream
el	bastón *(pl* bastones)	walking stick
el	bosque	wood; forest
el	camino	way
el	campesino	countryman; farmer
el	campo	country; countryside
el	castillo	castle
el	cazador	hunter
el	granjero	farmer
el	mercado	market
el	paisaje	scenery
el	paseo	walk
el	picnic *(pl inv or ~*s)	picnic
el	prado	field
el	pueblo	village
el	puente	bridge
el	río	river
el	ruido	noise
el	sendero	path; track
el	terreno	soil; ground
el	turista	tourist
el	valle	valley

USEFUL PHRASES

al aire libre **in the open air**
sé el camino al pueblo **I know the way to the village**
salir en bicicleta **to go cycling**
los vecinos *or* los habitantes de la zona **the locals**
fuimos de picnic **we went for a picnic**

ESSENTIAL WORDS *(feminine)*

la	**barrera**	gate; fence
la	**camioneta** (*Sp*)	van
la	**campesina**	countrywoman; farmer
la	**carretera**	road
la	**cazadora**	hunter
la	**excursión** (*pl* excursiones)	hike
la	**granja**	farm, farmhouse
la	**granjera**	farmer
la	**montaña**	mountain
la	**piedra**	stone; rock
la	**región** (*pl* regiones)	district
la	**tierra**	land; earth; soil; ground
la	**torre**	tower
la	**turista**	tourist
la	**vagoneta** (*Mex*)	van
la	**valla**	fence

USEFUL PHRASES

en el campo **in the country**
ir (de excursión) al campo **to go into the country**
vivir en el campo/en la ciudad **to live in the country/in town**
cultivar la tierra **to cultivate the land**

IMPORTANT WORDS (masculine)

el	agricultor (Sp)	farmer
el	guardia civil	civil guard (person)
el	lago	lake
el	mesón (pl mesones)	inn
el	polvo	dust
el	ranchero (Mex)	farmer

USEFUL WORDS (masculine)

los	anteojos de larga vista (LAm)	binoculars
el	arbusto	bush
el	barro	mud
el	brezo	heather
el	charco	puddle
el	estanque	pond
el	guijarro	pebble
el	heno	hay
el	matorral	bush
el	molino (de viento)	(wind)mill
el	palo	stick
el	pantano	marsh
el	páramo	moor
el	poste telegráfico	telegraph pole
el	prado	meadow
los	prismáticos (Sp)	binoculars
el	seto	hedge
el	trigo	corn; wheat

USEFUL PHRASES

agrícola agricultural
apacible, tranquilo(a) peaceful
en la cima de la colina at the top of the hill
caer en una trampa to fall into a trap

IMPORTANT WORDS *(feminine)*

la	**agricultora** *(Sp)*	farmer
la	**agricultura**	agriculture
la	**calzada**	road surface
la	**catiusca, katiuska**	(wellington) boot
la	**cima**	top *(of hill)*
la	**colina**	hill
la	**gente del campo**	country people
la	**guardia civil**	civil guard *(person)*
la	**Guardia Civil**	Civil Guard
la	**hoja**	leaf
la	**posada**	inn
la	**propiedad**	property; estate
la	**ranchera** *(Mex)*	farmer
la	**tranquilidad**	peace

USEFUL WORDS *(feminine)*

la	**aldea**	hamlet
la	**bota de goma**	(wellington) boot
la	**cantera**	quarry
la	**cascada**	waterfall
la	**caverna**	cave
la	**caza**	hunting; shooting
la	**cosecha**	crop; harvest
la	**fuente**	spring; source
la	**furgoneta**	van
la	**llanura**	plain
la	**orilla**	bank *(of river)*
las	**ruinas**	ruins
la	**señal**	signpost
la	**trampa**	trap
la	**vendimia**	grape harvest
la	**zanja**	ditch

USEFUL PHRASES

perderse **to lose one's way**
recoger la cosecha **to bring in the harvest**
vendimiar, hacer la vendimia **to harvest the grapes**

ESSENTIAL WORDS (*masculine*)

el	**aspecto**	appearance
el	**bigote**	moustache
el	**cabello**	hair
el	**color**	colour
los	**ojos**	eyes
el	**talle**	waist

USEFUL PHRASES

alegre **cheerful**
alto(a) **tall**
amable **nice**
antiguo(a) **old**
asqueroso(a) **disgusting**
bajo(a) **short**
barbudo(a), con barba **bearded, with a beard**
bonito(a) **pretty**
bueno(a) **kind**
calvo(a) **bald**
delgado(a) **skinny**
desagradable **unpleasant**
dinámico(a) **dynamic**
divertido(a), entretenido(a) **amusing, entertaining**
educado(a) **polite**
esbelto(a) **slim**
estupendo(a) **great**
feliz (*pl* felices) **happy**
feo(a) **ugly**
gordo(a) **fat**
gracioso(a) **funny**
grosero(a) **rude**
guapo **handsome**; guapa **beautiful**
horrible **hideous**
infeliz (*pl* infelices), desgraciado(a) **unhappy, unfortunate**
inquieto(a) **agitated**
inteligente **intelligent**

ESSENTIAL WORDS *(feminine)*

la	barba	beard
la	edad	age
la	estatura	height; size
las	gafas	glasses
la	identidad	ID
la	lágrima	tear
la	persona	person
la	talla	size; height

USEFUL PHRASES

joven *(pl* jóvenes) **young**

largo(a) **long**

malo(a) **naughty**

mono(a) **cute**

nervioso(a), tenso(a) **nervous, tense**

optimista/pesimista **optimistic/pessimistic**

pequeño(a) **small, little**

que se porta bien **well-behaved**

serio(a) **serious**

tímido(a) **shy**

tonto(a) **stupid**

tranquilo(a) **calm**

viejo(a) **old**

(ella) parece triste **she looks sad**

(él) estaba llorando **he was crying**

(él) sonreía **he was smiling**

(él) tenía lágrimas en los ojos **he had tears in his eyes**

un hombre de estatura mediana **a man of average height**

mido 1 metro 70 *or* uno setenta *or* 1,70 **I am 1 metre 70 tall**

¿de qué color son tus (*or* sus) ojos/es tu (*or* su) pelo? **what colour are your eyes/is your hair?**

tengo el pelo rubio **I have fair hair**

tengo los ojos azules/verdes **I have blue/green eyes**

pelo moreno *or* castaño **dark *or* brown hair**

pelo castaño **light brown hair**; pelo rizado **curly hair**; pelirrojo(a) **red-haired**

pelo negro/canoso **black/grey hair**

pelo teñido **dyed hair**

IMPORTANT WORDS (*masculine*)

el **carácter** (*pl* caracteres)	character; nature
el **grano**	spot
el **humor**	mood

USEFUL WORDS (*masculine*)

el **cerquillo** (*LAm*)	fringe
el **defecto**	fault
el **fleco** (*Mex*), el **flequillo** (*Sp*)	fringe
el **gesto**	gesture
el **gigante**	giant
los **hoyuelos**	dimples
el **lunar**	mole, beauty spot
el **parecido**	resemblance
el **peso**	weight
el **rizo**	curl

USEFUL PHRASES

(él) tiene buen carácter **he is good-tempered**
(él) tiene mal genio *or* carácter **he is bad-tempered**
tener la tez pálida *or* muy blanca **to have a pale complexion**
llevar gafas/lentes de contacto *or* lentillas **to wear glasses/contact lenses**

IMPORTANT WORDS (feminine)

la	belleza	beauty
la	calidad	(good) quality
la	costumbre	habit
la	curiosidad	curiosity
la	expresión (pl expresiones)	expression
la	fealdad	ugliness
las	lentillas	contact lenses
la	mirada	look
la	sonrisa	smile
la	tez (pl teces)	complexion
la	voz (pl voces)	voice

USEFUL WORDS (feminine)

las	arrugas	wrinkles
la	cicatriz (pl cicatrices)	scar
la	dentadura (postiza)	false teeth
las	pecas	freckles
la	permanente	perm
la	timidez	shyness

USEFUL PHRASES

siempre estoy de buen humor **I am always in a good mood**
(él) está de mal humor **he is in a bad mood**
(él) se enfadó **he got angry**
(ella) se parece a su madre **she looks like her mother**
(él) se muerde las uñas **he bites his nails**

ESSENTIAL WORDS *(masculine)*

el	alemán	German
el	alfabeto	alphabet
el	alumno	pupil; schoolboy
el	amigo	pal
el	aprendizaje	apprenticeship
el	club *(pl* ~s *or* ~es)	club
el	colegio	school
el	colegio de secundaria	secondary school
el	comedor	dining hall
el	comienzo del curso	beginning of term
el	compañero de clase	school friend
el	concierto	concert
el	cuaderno	notebook; exercise book
los	deberes	homework
el	día	day
el	dibujo	drawing
el	director	headmaster
el	dormitorio	dormitory
el	error	mistake
el	escolar	schoolboy
el	español	Spanish
el	estudiante	student
el	estudio (de)	study (of)
los	estudios	studies
el	examen *(pl* exámenes)	exam
el	examen de prueba	mock exam
	(pl exámenes ~~)	
el	experimento	experiment
el	fallo	mistake
el	francés	French
el	gimnasio	gym
el	grupo	group
el	horario	timetable
el	IES (Instituto de	comprehensive school
	Enseñanza Secundaria)	
el	inglés	English
el	instituto	secondary school
el	intercambio	exchange
el	italiano	Italian

ESSENTIAL WORDS *(feminine)*

la	alberca *(Mex)*	swimming pool
la	alumna	pupil; schoolgirl
la	amiga	pal
el	aula *(pl f* las aulas)	classroom
la	biología	biology
la	cafetería	canteen
las	ciencias	science
la	clase	class; year; classroom
las	clases	lessons
las	clases prácticas	practical class
la	compañera de clase	school friend
la	directora	headmistress
la	educación física	PE
la	electrónica	electronics
la	enseñanza	education; teaching
la	escolar	schoolgirl
la	escuela	school
la	escuela de primaria	primary school
la	escuela infantil	nursery school
la	estudiante	student
la	excursión *(pl* excursiones)	trip; outing
la	exposición *(pl* exposiciones)	presentation
la	física	physics
la	frase	sentence
la	geografía	geography
la	gimnasia	gym
la	goma (de borrar)	rubber
la	grabadora	tape recorder
la	guardería	nursery school
la	historia	history; story
la	informática	computer studies
la	lección *(pl* lecciones)	lesson
la	lectura	reading
las	lenguas (modernas)	(modern) languages
la	maestra de primaria *or* de infantil	primary schoolteacher
las	matemáticas	mathematics
la	materia (escolar)	(school) subject

ESSENTIAL WORDS *(masculine continued)*

el	laboratorio	laboratory
el	lápiz (*pl* lápices)	pencil
el	libro	book
el	maestro de primaria	primary schoolteacher
	or de infantil	
el	mapa	map
el	ordenador	computer
el	premio	prize
el	profesor	teacher
el	progreso	progress
el	recreo	break; playtime
el	resultado	result
el	semestre	semester
el	trabajo	work
los	trabajos manuales	handicrafts

USEFUL PHRASES

trabajar **to work**
aprender **to learn**
estudiar **to study**
¿cuánto tiempo llevas (*or* lleva) aprendiendo español? **how long have you been learning Spanish?**
aprenderse algo de memoria **to learn sth off by heart**
tengo deberes/tareas todos los días *or* a diario **I have homework every day**
mi hermana pequeña va a primaria/al colegio – yo voy a secundaria *or* al instituto **my little sister goes to primary school – I go to secondary school**
enseñar español **to teach Spanish**
el/la profesor(a) de alemán **the German teacher**
he mejorado en matemáticas **I have made progress in maths**
hacer un examen **to sit an exam**
aprobar un examen **to pass an exam**
suspender un examen **to fail an exam**
sacar un aprobado **to get a pass mark**

ESSENTIAL WORDS *(feminine continued)*

las	mates	maths
la	música	music
la	natación	swimming
la	nota	mark
la	palabra	word
la	piscina	swimming pool
la	pizarra	blackboard
la	pregunta	question
la	profesora	teacher
la	química	chemistry
la	respuesta	answer
la	sala de profesores	staffroom
la	tarea	homework; task
la	universidad	university
las	vacaciones	holidays
las	vacaciones de verano	summer holidays

USEFUL PHRASES

fácil **easy**; difícil **difficult**

interesante **interesting**

aburrido(a) **boring**

leer **to read**; escribir **to write**

escuchar **to listen (to)**

mirar **to look at, watch**

repetir **to repeat**

responder **to reply**

hablar **to speak**

es la primera *or* mejor de la clase **she is top of the class**

es la última *or* peor de la clase **she is bottom of the class**

entrar en clase **to go into the classroom**

cometer un error *or* fallo **to make a mistake**

corregir **to correct**

cometí un error gramatical **I made a grammatical error**

he sacado buena nota **I got a good mark**

¡responde a la pregunta! **answer the question!**

¡levantad la mano! **put your hand up!**

IMPORTANT WORDS *(masculine)*

el **bachillerato**, el **bachiller**	higher school-leaving course/certificate
el **certificado**	certificate
el **colegio concertado**	grant-aided school
el **colegio privado**	private school
el **colegio público**	state school
el **despacho**	office
el **día libre**	day off
el **diploma**	diploma
el **estuche**	pencil case
el **examen escrito** (*pl* exámenes ~s)	written exam
el **examen oral** (*pl* exámenes ~es)	oral exam
el **expediente**	file
el **papel**	paper
el **pasillo**	corridor
el **patio (de recreo)**	playground

USEFUL PHRASES

mi amigo se está preparando la selectividad **my friend is sitting his university entrance exam**

repasar (la lección) **to revise**

repasaré otra vez la lección mañana **I'll go over the lesson again tomorrow**

IMPORTANT WORDS (feminine)

la	**ausencia**	absence
la	**carpeta**	folder; file
la	**conferencia**	lecture
las	**normas**	rules
las	**notas**	report
la	**oposición** (pl oposiciones)	competitive exam
la	**regla**	rule; ruler
la	**selectividad** (Sp)	entrance examination
la	**traducción** (pl traducciones)	translation
la	**versión** (pl versiones)	translation (from foreign language to English)

USEFUL PHRASES

en segundo de primaria **in year two**
en primero de ESO **in year seven**
en segundo de ESO **in year eight**
en tercero de ESO **in year nine**
en cuarto de ESO **in year ten**
en primero de bachillerato **in year eleven**

presente **present**
ausente **absent**
castigar a un(a) alumno(a) **to punish a pupil**
el/la profesor(a) los castigó sin recreo **the teacher kept them in at break time**
¡silencio!, ¡callaos! **be quiet!**

USEFUL WORDS (*masculine*)

el	bedel	janitor
el	bloc (*pl* ~s)	jotter
el	boli, bolígrafo	Biro®
el	borrador	rough copy
el	cálculo	sum
el	castigo	detention; punishment
el	comportamiento	behaviour
el	corrector (líquido)	correction fluid
el	diccionario	dictionary
el	ejercicio	exercise
el	examinador	examiner
el	griego	Greek
el	jefe de estudios	director of studies
el	inspector	school inspector
el	internado	boarding school
el	interno	boarder
el	latín	Latin
el	libro de texto	textbook
el	maletín (*pl* maletines)	briefcase
el	parte (de faltas *or* ausencias)	absence sheet
el	parvulario	nursery school
el	profesor consejero	form tutor
el	pupitre	desk
el	rotulador	felt-tip pen
el	sacapuntas (*pl inv*)	pencil sharpener
el	test (*pl* ~s)	test
el	trabajo	essay; class exam
el	trimestre	term
el	vestuario	cloakroom
el	vocabulario	vocabulary

USEFUL WORDS (*feminine*)

el	álgebra (*f*)	algebra
la	aritmética	arithmetic
la	bedel	janitor
la	calculadora	calculator
la	caligrafía	handwriting
la	carpintería	woodwork
la	cartera	satchel; schoolbag; briefcase
las	ciencias del medio ambiente	natural science
las	ciencias naturales	natural history
la	enseñanza religiosa	religious instruction
la	entrega de premios	prize-giving
la	ESO (Educación Secundaria Obligatoria) (*Sp*)	compulsory secondary education
la	facultad	faculty
la	fila	row (*of seats etc*)
la	FP (formación profesional) (*Sp*)	technical college
la	geometría	geometry
la	gramática	grammar
la	inspectora	school inspector
la	interna	boarder
la	mancha	blot
la	nota media	pass mark; average mark
la	ortografía	spelling
la	pizarra (electrónica) interactiva	interactive whiteboard
la	poesía	poetry; poem
la	prueba	test
las	TIC (tecnologías de la información y la comunicación)	ICT
la	tinta	ink
la	tiza	chalk
la	traducción inversa (*pl* traducciones ~s)	prose translation

ESSENTIAL WORDS (*masculine*)

el	aerogenerador	wind turbine
el	agujero	hole
el	aire	air
los	animales	animals
los	árboles	trees
el	bosque	wood
el	coche	car
el	diesel	diesel
el	ecologista	environmentalist
el	gas	gas
los	gases de escape	exhaust fumes
el	gasoil	diesel
los	habitantes	inhabitants
el	mapa	map
el	mar	sea
el	medio ambiente	environment
el	mundo	world
el	país	country
el	pescado	fish
el	tiempo	weather; time
los	Verdes	the Greens
el	vidrio	glass

IMPORTANT WORDS (*masculine*)

el	acontecimiento	event
el	aluminio	aluminium
el	calor	heat
el	clima	climate
el	contaminante	pollutant
el	daño	damage
el	detergente	detergent; washing powder
el	futuro	future
el	gobierno	government
el	impuesto	tax
el	lago	lake
el	parque eólico	windfarm
el	planeta	planet
el	río	river

ESSENTIAL WORDS (feminine)

el	**agua** (f)	water
las	**botellas**	bottles
la	**contaminación**	pollution
la	**costa**	coast
la	**cuestión** (pl cuestiones)	question
la	**ecología**	ecology
la	**especie**	species
la	**fábrica**	factory
la	**flor**	flower
la	**fruta**	fruit
la	**gasolina**	petrol
la	**isla**	island
la	**lluvia**	rain
la	**montaña**	mountain
la	**planta**	plant
la	**playa**	beach
la	**región** (pl regiones)	region; area
la	**temperatura**	temperature
la	**tierra**	earth
la(s)	**verdura(s)**	vegetables

IMPORTANT WORDS (feminine)

la	**central nuclear**	nuclear plant
la	**crisis** (pl inv)	crisis
la	**legumbre**	vegetable
la	**selva**	forest; jungle
la	**solución** (pl soluciones)	solution
la	**zona**	zone

USEFUL WORDS (*masculine*)

el	aerosol	aerosol
los	alimentos orgánicos	organic food
el	calentamiento global	global warming
el	canal	canal
el	catalizador	catalytic converter
el	CFC (clorofluorocarbono)	CFC
los	científicos	scientists
el	combustible	fuel
el	continente	continent
el	desarrollo sostenible	sustainable development
el	desierto	desert
el	ecosistema	ecosystem
el	fertilizante	(artificial) fertilizer
el	investigador	researcher
el	océano	ocean
el	OGM (organismo genéticamente modificado)	GMO
el	producto	product
los	productos químicos	chemicals
el	reciclado, el reciclaje	recycling
los	residuos nucleares/ industriales	nuclear/industrial waste
el	universo	universe
el	vertedero	dumping ground

USEFUL PHRASES

(él) es muy respetuoso con el medio ambiente **he's very environmentally-minded**

un producto ecológico **an eco-friendly product**

en el futuro **in the future**

destruir **to destroy**

contaminar **to contaminate; to pollute**

prohibir **to ban**

salvar **to save**

reciclar **to recycle**

verde **green**

USEFUL WORDS *(feminine)*

las	**aguas residuales**	sewage
la	**capa de ozono**	ozone layer
la	**catástrofe**	disaster
la	**contaminación acústica**	noise pollution
la	**energía eólica**	wind power
la	**energía nuclear**	nuclear power
la	**energía renovable**	renewable energy
la	**lluvia ácida**	acid rain
la	**luna**	moon
la	**marea negra**	oil slick
la	**población** *(pl* poblaciones)	population
la	**selva tropical**	tropical rainforest

USEFUL PHRASES

biodegradable **biodegradable**

nocivo(a) *or* dañino(a) para el medio ambiente **harmful to the environment**

orgánico(a), biológico(a), ecológico(a) **organic**

gasolina sin plomo **unleaded petrol**

(las) especies en peligro de extinción **endangered species**

ESSENTIAL WORDS *(masculine)*

el	**abuelo**	grandfather
los	**abuelos**	grandparents
los	**adultos**	adults
el	**apellido**	surname
el	**apellido de soltera**	maiden name
el	**bebé**	baby
la	**edad**	age
el	**hermano**	brother
el	**hijo**	son
el	**hombre**	man
el	**joven** (*pl* jóvenes)	youth, young man
los	**jóvenes**	young people
el	**marido**	husband
el	**niño**	child, boy
el	**nombre**	name
el	**nombre (de pila)**	first *or* Christian name
el	**novio**	fiancé
el	**padre**	father
los	**padres**	parents
el	**papá**	daddy
el	**pariente**	relative
el	**primo**	cousin
el	**prometido**	fiancé
el	**tío**	uncle

USEFUL PHRASES

¿qué edad tiene (*or* tienes)?, ¿cuántos años tiene (*or* tienes)? how old are you?
tengo 15 años – él tiene 40 años I'm 15 – he is 40
¿cómo se llama (*or* te llamas)? what is your name?
me llamo Daniela my name is Daniela
él se llama Paco his name is Paco
prometido(a) engaged
casado(a) married
divorciado(a) divorced
separado(a) separated
casarse con algn to marry sb
casarse to get married; divorciarse to get divorced

ESSENTIAL WORDS *(feminine)*

la	**abuela**	grandmother
la	**familia**	family
la	**gente**	people
la	**hermana**	sister
la	**hija**	daughter; girl
la	**joven** *(pl* jóvenes)	youth
la	**madre**	mother
la	**mamá**	mummy
los	**mayores**	grown-ups
la	**mujer**	woman; wife
la	**niña**	child, girl
la	**novia**	fiancée
la	**persona**	person
la	**prima**	cousin
la	**prometida**	fiancée
la	**señora**	lady
la	**tía**	aunt

USEFUL PHRASES

más joven/mayor que yo **younger/older than me**
¿tiene (*or* tienes) hermanos? **do you have any brothers or sisters?**
tengo un hermano y una hermana **I have one brother and one sister**
no tengo hermanos **I don't have any brothers or sisters**
soy hijo(a) único(a) **I am an only child**
toda la familia **the whole family**
crecer **to grow**
envejecer, hacerse viejo(a) **to get old**
me llevo bien con mis padres **I get on well with my parents**
mi madre trabaja **my mother works**

IMPORTANT WORDS (*masculine*)

el	adolescente	teenager
el	esposo	husband
el	nieto	grandson
los	nietos	grandchildren
el	padrastro	stepfather
el	sobrino	nephew
el	soltero	bachelor
el	subsidio familiar (por hijos)	child benefit
el	suegro	father-in-law
el	vecino	neighbour
el	viudo	widower

USEFUL WORDS (*masculine*)

el	ahijado	godson
el	anciano	old man
el	apodo	nickname
el	chaval, el chico	kid
el	cuñado	brother-in-law
los	gemelos	identical twins
el	hermanastro	stepbrother
el	hijastro	stepson
el	huérfano	orphan
el	jubilado	pensioner
el	marido	bridegroom
los	mellizos	twins
el	mote	nickname
el	padrino	godfather
los	recién casados	newlyweds
los	trillizos	triplets
el	viejo	old man
el	yerno	son-in-law

USEFUL PHRASES

nacer to be born; vivir to live; morir to die
nací en 1990 I was born in 1990
mi abuela murió *or* está muerta my grandmother is dead
ella murió en 1995 she died in 1995

IMPORTANT WORDS *(feminine)*

la **adolescente**	teenager
la **au pair** (*pl inv*)	au pair girl
la **esposa**	wife
la **madrastra**	stepmother
la **nieta**	granddaughter
la **sobrina**	niece
la **soltera**	single woman
la **suegra**	mother-in-law
la **vecina**	neighbour
la **viuda**	widow

USEFUL WORDS *(feminine)*

la **ahijada**	goddaughter
el **ama de casa** (*pl f* las amas ~ ~)	housewife
la **anciana**	old woman
la **chavala**, la **chica**	kid
la **cuñada**	sister-in-law
las **gemelas**	identical twins
la **hermanastra**	stepsister
la **hijastra**	stepdaughter
la **huérfana**	orphan
la **jubilada**	pensioner
la **madrina**	godmother
las **mellizas**	twins, twin sisters
la **niñera**	nanny
la **novia**	bride
la **nuera**	daughter-in-law
la **pareja**	couple
la **vejez**	old age
la **vieja**	old woman

USEFUL PHRASES

él/ella es soltero(a) he/she is single
él es viudo he is a widower; ella es viuda she is a widow
soy el/la más joven I am the youngest; soy el/la mayor I am the eldest
mi hermana mayor my older sister

ESSENTIAL WORDS (*masculine*)

el	**agricultor** (*Sp*)	farmer
el	**animal**	animal
el	**bosque**	forest
el	**buey**	ox
el	**caballo**	horse
el	**cabrito**	kid
el	**campo**	field; country
el	**cerdo**	pig
el	**chivo**	kid
el	**gato**	cat
el	**granjero**	farmer
el	**invernadero**	greenhouse
el	**pato**	duck
el	**pavo**	turkey
el	**perro**	dog
el	**perro pastor** (*pl* ~s ~)	sheepdog
el	**pollo**	chicken
el	**pueblo**	village
el	**ranchero** (*Mex*)	farmer
el	**ternero**	calf

IMPORTANT WORDS (*masculine*)

el	**campesino**	countryman
el	**cordero**	lamb
el	**gallo**	cock
el	**tractor**	tractor

USEFUL PHRASES

un trigal, un maizal **a cornfield**
la agricultura ecológica **organic farming**
los pollos de granja **free range chickens**
los huevos de corral **free range eggs**
cuidar los animales **to look after the animals**
recolectar **to harvest**
recoger la cosecha **to bring in the harvest/crops**

ESSENTIAL WORDS *(feminine)*

la	**agricultora** *(Sp)*	farmer
la	**camioneta** *(Sp)*	van
la	**cerda**	sow
la	**finca**	farm
la	**gallina**	hen
la	**granja**	farm; farmhouse
la	**granjera**	farmer; farmer's wife
la	**oveja**	sheep; ewe
la	**puerta**	gate
la	**ranchera** *(Mex)*	farmer
la	**tierra**	earth; ground
la	**vaca**	cow
la	**vagoneta** *(Mex)*	van
la	**valla**	fence
la	**verja**	gate
la	**yegua**	mare

IMPORTANT WORDS *(feminine)*

la	**campesina**	countrywoman
la	**colina**	hill

USEFUL PHRASES

vivir en el campo **to live in the country**
trabajar en una granja **to work on a farm**
recolectar el heno **to make hay**

USEFUL WORDS (*masculine*)

el	abono	manure; fertilizer
el	almiar	haystack
el	arado	plough
el	barro	mud
el	burro	donkey
el	carnero	ram
el	centeno	rye
el	cerdo	pig
el	cereal	cereal, crop
el	cobertizo	shed
el	corral	farmyard
el	espantapájaros (*pl inv*)	scarecrow
el	establo	cow shed, byre
el	estanque	pond
el	estiércol	manure
el	gallinero	henhouse
el	ganado	cattle
el	ganso	goose
el	granero	barn
el	grano	grain, seed
el	heno	hay
el	maíz (*pl* maices)	maize
el	molino (de viento)	(wind)mill
el	paisaje	landscape
el	pajar	loft
el	páramo	moor, heath
el	pastor	shepherd
el	pollito	chick
el	potro	foal
el	pozo	well
el	prado	meadow
el	rebaño	(*sheep*) flock; (*cattle*) herd
el	suelo	ground, earth
el	surco	furrow
el	toro	bull
el	trigo	corn; wheat

USEFUL WORDS (*feminine*)

la	avena	oats
la	cabra	goat
la	cabritilla	kid
la	carretilla	cart
la	casita (con el tejado de paja)	(thatched) cottage
la	cebada	barley
la	cosecha	crop
la	cosechadora	combine harvester
la	cuadra	stable
la	escalera	ladder
la	ganadería	cattle farm
la	lana	wool
la	lonja	market
la	paja	straw
la	pocilga	pigsty
la	recolección (*pl* recolecciones)	harvest
la	uva	grapes
la	vendimia	grape harvest, grape picking
la	viña	vine
la	zanja	ditch

ESSENTIAL WORDS (*masculine*)

el **marisco**	seafood
el **pez** (*pl* peces)	fish
el **pez de colores** (*pl* peces ~~)	goldfish

IMPORTANT WORDS (*masculine*)

el **cangrejo**	crab
el **insecto**	insect

USEFUL WORDS (*masculine*)

el **acuario**	aquarium
el **arenque**	herring
el **atún** (*pl* atunes)	tuna
el **avispón** (*pl* avispones)	hornet
el **bacalao**	cod
el **calamar**	squid
el **camarón** (*pl* camarones)	shrimp
el **cangrejo de río**	crayfish
el **chinche**	bug
el **eglefino**	haddock
el **grillo**	cricket
el **gusano**	worm
el **gusano de seda**	silkworm
los **langostinos**	scampi
el **lenguado**	sole
el **lucio**	pike
el **mejillón** (*pl* mejillones)	mussel
el **mosquito**	mosquito
el **pulpo**	octopus
el **renacuajo**	tadpole
el **salmón** (*pl* salmones)	salmon
el **saltamontes** (*pl inv*)	grasshopper
el **tiburón** (*pl* tiburones)	shark

USEFUL PHRASES

nadar **to swim**
volar **to fly**
vamos a ir a pescar **we're going fishing**

ESSENTIAL WORDS (feminine)

el **agua** (f)	water

IMPORTANT WORDS (feminine)

la **mosca**	fly
la **sardina**	sardine
la **trucha**	trout

USEFUL WORDS (feminine)

la **abeja**	bee
el **ala** (pl f las alas)	wing
la **anguila**	eel
la **araña**	spider
la **avispa**	wasp
la **cigala**	crayfish
la **cigarra**	cicada
la **cucaracha**	cockroach
la **hormiga**	ant
la **langosta**	lobster
la **libélula**	dragonfly
la **mariposa**	butterfly
la **mariquita**	ladybird
la **medusa**	jellyfish
la **mosquilla**	midge
la **mosquita**	midge
la **oruga**	caterpillar
la **ostra**	oyster
la **pescadilla**	whiting
la **polilla**	moth
la **pulga**	flea
la **rana**	frog

USEFUL PHRASES
una picadura de avispa a wasp sting
una tela de araña a spider's web

ESSENTIAL WORDS *(masculine)*

el	aceite	oil
el	agua mineral	(mineral) water
el	alcohol	alcohol
el	almuerzo	lunch
el	aperitivo	aperitif
el	arroz	rice
el	asado	roast
el	autoservicio	self-service restaurant
el	azúcar	sugar
el	bar	bar
el	bistec *(pl inv or ~s)*	steak
el	bol	bowl
el	bote	tin, can
el	café	coffee; café
el	café con leche	coffee with milk
el	café con más leche	milky coffee
el	camarero *(Sp)*	waiter
los	caramelos	sweets
el	cerdo	pork
los	cereales	cereal
el	chocolate (caliente)	(hot) chocolate
el	cocinero	cook
el	consomé	soup
el	croissant *or* el cruasán *(pl* cruasanes)	croissant
el	cuarto	quarter *(bottle/litre etc)*
el	cuenco	bowl
el	cuchillo	knife
el	desayuno	breakfast
el	dueño	owner
los	entrantes	hors d'œuvres, starters
el	entrecot *(pl inv or ~s)*	(entrecôte) steak
el	filete	steak
el	helado	ice cream
el	huevo	egg
el	huevo duro *or* cocido	hard-boiled egg
el	huevo pasado por agua	soft-boiled egg
el	jamón *(pl* jamones)	ham

ESSENTIAL WORDS *(feminine)*

la	aceituna	olive
la	baguette *(pl inv or ~s)*	French loaf
la	bandeja	tray
la	bebida	drink
la	botella	bottle
la	caja	box
la	carne	meat
la	carne de vaca	beef
la	carta	menu
la	cena	dinner
la	cerveza	beer
la	Coca-Cola® *(pl ~s)*	Coke®
la	comida	lunch; meal
la	comida precocinada *or* preparada	ready-made meal
las	conservas	canned food
la	cuchara	spoon
la	cuenta	bill
la	ensalada	salad
la	ensalada mixta	mixed salad
la	fruta	fruit
el	hambre *(f)*	hunger
la	hamburguesa	hamburger
la	lata	tin, can
la	leche	milk
la	limonada	lemonade
la	loncha (de)	slice (of)
la	mantequilla	butter
la	mermelada	jam
la	mermelada (de cítricos)	marmalade
la	mesa	table
la	pastelería	pastry; cake shop
las	patatas fritas	chips; crisps
la	pescadería	fish shop
la	pieza de fruta	piece of fruit
la	repostería	pastry; cake shop
la	sal	salt
la	salchicha	sausage

ESSENTIAL WORDS *(masculine continued)*

el **marisco**	seafood
el **menú del día**	fixed-price menu
el **mesero** *(LAm)*	waiter
el **pan**	bread
el **paté**	pâté
el **pescado**	fish
el **picnic** *(pl inv or ~s)*	picnic
el **platillo**	saucer
el **plato**	plate; dish; course
el **plato del día**	today's special
el **pollo (asado)**	(roast) chicken
el **postre**	dessert
el **primero**, el **primer plato**	first course, starter
el **queso**	cheese
el **quiche** *(pl inv)*	quiche
el **restaurante**	restaurant
el **salami**, el **salchichón**	salami
(pl salchichones*)*	
el **sándwich** *(pl ~s or ~es)*	sandwich
el **self-service** *(pl inv)*	self-service restaurant
el **servicio**	service
el **té**	tea
el **tenedor**	fork
el **vaso**	glass
el **vinagre**	vinegar
el **vino**	wine
el **yogur(t)**	yoghurt
el **zumo de fruta**	fruit juice

USEFUL PHRASES

cocinar **to cook**; comer **to eat**
beber **to drink**; tragar **to swallow**
mi plato favorito **my favourite dish**
¿qué vas (*or* va) a beber? **what are you having to drink?**
está bueno *or* rico **it's nice**
estar hambriento, tener hambre **to be hungry**
estar sediendo, tener sed **to be thirsty**

ESSENTIAL WORDS *(feminine continued)*

la	sed *(pl inv)*	thirst
la	sidra	cider
la	sopa	soup
la	tarta	cake
la	taza	cup
la	ternera	veal
la	tortilla francesa	omelette
la	tortita	pancake
la	tostada	toast
la	vajilla	dishes
las	verduras	vegetables

IMPORTANT WORDS *(feminine)*

la	cafetería	cafeteria
la	camarera	waitress
la	carne asada *or* a la parrilla	grilled meat
la	cerveza de barril	draught beer
la	chef *(pl inv or* ~s)	chef
la	chuleta de cerdo	pork chop
la	cucharilla	teaspoon
la	cucharita (de postre)	dessertspoon
la	cuchara de servir	tablespoon
la	garrafa	carafe
la	harina	flour
la	jarra	jug
la	mayonesa	mayonnaise
la	mostaza	mustard
la	nata	cream
las	patatas fritas (de bolsa)	crisps
la	pimienta	pepper
la	pizza	pizza
la	propina	tip
la	receta	recipe
la	selección *(pl* selecciones)	choice
la	tarta	tart
la	tetera	teapot
la	vainilla	vanilla

IMPORTANT WORDS (masculine)

el	ajo	garlic
el	almíbar	syrup
el	aperitivo	snack
el	camarero	waiter
los	caracoles	snails
el	carrito	trolley
el	chef (pl inv or ~s)	chef
el	cocinero jefe	chef
el	conejo	rabbit
el	cordero	lamb; mutton
el	cubierto	cover charge; place setting
el	gusto	taste
el	olor	smell
el	precio con todo incluido	inclusive price
el	precio fijo	set price
el	refresco concentrado	cordial
el	restaurante	restaurant
el	sabor	flavour
el	suplemento	extra charge
el	tentempié	snack

USEFUL WORDS (masculine)

el	abrelatas (pl inv)	tin opener
el	aperitivo	snack
el	beicon	bacon
el	biscote	Melba toast
el	bollito	roll
el	bollo	bun
el	cacao	cocoa
el	champán (pl champanes)	champagne
el	coñac (pl inv)	brandy
el	corcho	cork
el	cubito (de hielo)	ice cube
el	estofado	stew
el	foie gras (pl inv)	liver pâté
el	hígado	liver
el	ketchup (pl inv)	ketchup
el	mantel	tablecloth

USEFUL WORDS *(feminine)*

las	aves	poultry
la	carta de vinos	wine list
la	caza	game
la	chuleta	chop
la	clara	shandy
la	comida	food
la	gelatina	jelly
la	infusión *(pl infusiones)*	herbal tea
la	jarra	jug
la	margarina	margarine
la	miel	honey
la	miga	crumb
la	nata montada	whipped cream
las	natillas	custard
la	pajita	straw
la	pasta	pasta
la	rebanada	piece of bread and butter
la	salsa	sauce
la	salsa de jugo de carne	gravy
la	servilleta	napkin
la	tisana	herbal tea
las	tripas	tripe
la	tostada	slice of toast
la	vinagreta	vinaigrette dressing

USEFUL PHRASES

fregar los platos to do the dishes

cuando volvemos del colegio merendamos we have a snack when we come back from school

desayunar, tomar el desayuno to have breakfast

delicioso(a) delicious; repugnante disgusting

¡que aproveche! enjoy your meal!; ¡salud! cheers!

¡la cuenta, por favor! the bill please!

"servicio (no) incluido" "service (not) included"

comer fuera to eat out

invitar a algn a comer to invite sb to lunch

tomar algo de beber, beber algo to have drinks

USEFUL WORDS (*masculine continued*)

los	**mejillones**	mussels
el	**panecillo**	roll
el	**paté de carne**	potted meat
el	**paté de hígado**	liver pâté
el	**paté de oca**	goose pâté
el	**puré de patatas**	mashed potatoes
los	**riñones**	kidneys
el	**rosbif** (*pl inv or* ~s)	roast beef
el	**sacacorchos** (*pl inv*)	corkscrew
el	**tapón** (*pl* tapones)	cork
el	**termo**	flask
el	**torrezno**	diced bacon
el	**whisky, whiskey** (*pl* ~s)	whisky
el	**zumo natural de limón**	freshly-squeezed lemon juice

USEFUL PHRASES

poner la mesa **to set the table**; quitar la mesa **to clear the table**
comer, almorzar **to have lunch**
cenar **to have dinner**
probar algo **to taste sth**
¡eso huele bien! **that smells good!**
vino blanco/rosado/tinto **white/rosé/red wine**
un filete poco hecho/en su punto/bien hecho **a rare/medium/**
  well-done steak
un sándwich (tostado) de jamón y queso **a ham and cheese toastie**

SMOKING

el	cenicero	ashtray
la	cerilla	match
el	cigarrillo	cigarette
el	cigarro	cigar
el	estanco	tobacconist's
el	mechero	lighter
la	pipa	pipe
el	tabaco	tobacco

USEFUL PHRASES

una caja de cerillas a box of matches

¿tienes (or tiene) fuego? do you have a light?

encender un cigarrillo to light up

"prohibido fumar" "no smoking"

no fumo I don't smoke

he dejado de fumar, he dejado el tabaco I've stopped smoking

fumar es perjudicial para tí or la salud smoking is very bad for you

ESSENTIAL WORDS (*masculine*)

el	ajedrez	chess
el	amigo por correspondencia	pen friend
el	baile	dance
el	billete (*Sp*)	ticket
el	boleto (*LAm*)	ticket
el	cantante	singer
el	canto	singing
el	CD (*pl inv or* ~s)	CD
el	cine	cinema
el	club (*pl* ~s *or* ~es)	club
el	concierto	concert
los	deportes	sports
el	dinero de bolsillo	pocket money
el	disco	record
el	DVD (*pl inv or* ~s)	DVD
el	espectáculo	show
el	fin de semana	weekend
el	folleto	leaflet
el	futbolín (*pl* futbolines)	table football
el	hobby (*pl* hobbies)	hobby
el	Internet	internet
el	juego	game
el	lector de CD/DVD/MP3	CD/DVD/MP3 player
el	miembro	member
el	museo	museum; art gallery
el	paseo	walk
el	periódico	newspaper
el	programa	programme
el	teatro	theatre
el	(teléfono) móvil (*Sp*) *or* celular (*LAm*)	mobile (phone)
el	tiempo libre	free time
el	videojuego	video game
el	walkman® (*pl* ~s)	personal stereo

ESSENTIAL WORDS *(feminine)*

la	**afición** *(pl* aficiones)	hobby
la	**amiga por correspondencia**	pen friend
la	**cadena de televisión**	TV channel
la	**cámara (de fotos)**	camera
la	**canción** *(pl* canciones)	song
la	**cantante**	singer
las	**cartas**	cards
la	**disco(teca)**	disco
la	**diversión** *(pl* diversiones)	entertainment
la	**estrella (de cine)** *(m+f)*	(film) star
la	**excursión** *(pl* excursiones)	trip; outing; hike
la	**fiesta**	party
la	**foto**	photo
la	**historieta**	comic strip
la	**lectura**	reading
la	**música (pop/clásica)**	(pop/classical) music
las	**noticias**	news
la	**novela**	novel
la	**novela policíaca** *or* **policiaca**	detective novel
la	**película**	film
la	**pista de patinaje**	skating rink
la	**prensa**	the press
la	**publicidad**	publicity
la	**radio**	radio
la	**revista**	magazine
la	**tele(visión)** *(pl* teles, televisiones)	television, TV
la	**videoconsola**	games console

USEFUL PHRASES

salgo con mis amigos I go out with my friends
leo el periódico I read the newspaper
veo la televisión I watch television
juego al fútbol/al tenis/a las cartas I play football/tennis/cards
hacer bricolaje to do DIY
hacer de canguro to baby-sit
hacer zapping to channel-hop
ir de discoteca *or* marcha *(Sp)* to go clubbing

IMPORTANT WORDS *(masculine)*

el	**anuncio**	notice; poster
los	**anuncios por palabras**	adverts; small ads
el	**carrete**	film *(for camera)*
el	**compact disc** *(pl ~ ~s)*	compact disc, CD
el	**concurso**	competition
los	**dibujos animados**	cartoon
el	**juguete**	toy
el	**mensaje de texto**	text message
el	**noticiero** *(LAm)*	news
el	**novio**	boyfriend
el	**ordenador (personal)** *(Sp)*	personal computer
los	**pasatiempos**	leisure activities
el	**PC** *(pl inv)*	PC
el	**programa**	programme
el	**punto**	knitting
el	**SMS** *(pl inv)*	text message
el	**telediario** *(Sp)*	news
el	**vídeo** *(Sp)*, el **video** *(LAm)*	video recorder
el	**website**	website

USEFUL WORDS *(masculine)*

el	**aficionado**	fan
el	**blog**	blog
el	**campamento de verano**	holiday camp
el	**chat**	chat; chatroom
el	**club nocturno** *(pl ~s or ~es ~s)*	night club
el	**coro**	choir
el	**crucigrama**	crossword puzzle(s)
el	**explorador**	scout
el	**juego de mesa**	board game
el	**monopatín** *(pl monopatines)*	skateboard
el	**videoclub** *(pl ~s or ~es)*	video shop

USEFUL PHRASES

emocionante exciting
aburrido(a) boring
divertido(a) funny

IMPORTANT WORDS *(feminine)*

la	**cámara digital**	digital camera
la	**casa de la juventud**	youth club
la	**cinta**	tape
la	**cinta de vídeo**	video cassette
la	**colección** *(pl* colecciones)	collection
la	**computadora (personal)** *(LAm)*	personal computer
la	**exposición** *(pl* exposiciones)	exhibition
la	**filmadora** *(LAm)*	camcorder
la	**grabadora de CD/DVD**	CD/DVD writer
la	**noche**	evening
la	**novia**	girlfriend
la	**pintura**	painting
la	**reunión** *(pl* reuniones)	meeting
la	**serie**	serial
la	**tarde**	evening
la	**telenovela**	soap (opera)
la	**videocámara** *(Sp)*	camcorder

USEFUL WORDS *(feminine)*

la	**aficionada**	fan
la	**diapositiva**	slide
la	**exploradora**	(girl) guide, girl scout
la	**fotografía**	photograph; photography
la	**lista de éxitos**	charts

USEFUL PHRASES

no está mal **it's not bad**
bastante bien **quite good**
bailar **to dance**
hacer fotos **to take photos**
estoy aburrido(a) **I'm bored**
quedamos los viernes **we meet on Fridays**
estoy ahorrando para comprarme un DVD **I'm saving up to buy a DVD**
me gustaría dar la vuelta al mundo **I'd like to go round the world**

ESSENTIAL WORDS (*masculine*)

el **albaricoque**	apricot
el **limón** (*pl* limones)	lemon
el **melocotón** (*pl* melocotones)	peach
el **plátano**	banana
el **pomelo**	grapefruit
el **tomate**	tomato

IMPORTANT WORDS (*masculine*)

el **árbol frutal**	fruit tree
el **melón** (*pl* melones)	melon

USEFUL WORDS (*masculine*)

el **aguacate**	avocado
el **anacardo**	cashew nut
el **arándano**	blueberry
el **cacahuete**	peanut
el **coco**	coconut
el **dátil**	date
el **higo**	fig
el **hueso**	stone (*in fruit*)
el **kiwi**	kiwi fruit
el **ruibarbo**	rhubarb

ESSENTIAL WORDS *(feminine)*

la	**castaña (asada)**	(roasted) chestnut
la	**cereza**	cherry
la	**frambuesa**	raspberry
la	**fresa**	strawberry
la	**fruta**	fruit
la	**manzana**	apple
la	**naranja**	orange
la	**pasa**	raisin
la	**pera**	pear
la	**piel**	skin
la	**(pieza de) fruta**	(piece of) fruit
la	**piña**	pineapple
la	**uva**	grape(s)

USEFUL WORDS *(feminine)*

la	**avellana**	hazelnut
la	**baya**	berry
la	**ciruela**	plum
la	**ciruela pasa**	prune
la	**granada**	pomegranate
la	**grosella espinosa**	gooseberry
la	**grosella negra**	blackcurrant
la	**grosella (roja)**	redcurrant
la	**mandarina**	tangerine
la	**mora**	blackberry
la	**nuez** (*pl* nueces)	nut; walnut
la	**pepita**	pip (*in fruit*)
la	**vid**	vine

USEFUL PHRASES

un zumo de naranja/piña **an orange/a pineapple juice**
un racimo de uvas **a bunch of grapes**
maduro(a) **ripe**
verde **unripe**
pelar una fruta **to peel a fruit**
resbalar al pisar una cáscara de plátano **to slip on a banana skin**

ESSENTIAL WORDS *(masculine)*

el	armario *(Sp)*	cupboard; wardrobe
el	calefactor	heater
el	congelador	freezer
el	equipo (de música)	stereo system
el	espejo	mirror
el	frigo	fridge
el	frigorífico *(Sp)*	fridge
el	mueble	piece of furniture
los	muebles	furniture
el	radiodespertador	radio alarm
el	refrigerador *(LAm)*	fridge
el	reloj	clock
el	ropero *(LAm)*	cupboard; wardrobe
el	sillón *(pl* sillones)	armchair
el	teléfono	telephone
el	transistor	transistor

IMPORTANT WORDS *(masculine)*

el	aparador	sideboard
el	aparato	appliance
el	casete	tape recorder
el	cuadro	picture
el	escritorio	(writing) desk
el	hervidor	kettle
el	horno microondas	microwave oven
el	inalámbrico	cordless phone
el	lavavajillas *(pl inv)*	dishwasher
el	lector de CD/DVD	CD/DVD player
el	piano	piano
el	portátil	laptop
el	sofá	sofa
el	(teléfono) móvil *(Sp)* or celular *(LAm)*	mobile phone
el	vídeo *(Sp),* el video *(LAm)*	video recorder

ESSENTIAL WORDS *(feminine)*

la	**balda**	shelf
la	**cama**	bed
la	**cocina (eléctrica/de gas)**	(electric/gas) cooker
la	**estufa**	heater
la	**habitación** (*pl* habitaciones)	room
la	**lámpara**	lamp
la	**lavadora**	washing machine
la	**mesa**	table
la	**pantalla (de lámpara)**	lampshade
la	**radio**	radio
la	**silla**	chair
la	**televisión** (*pl* televisiones)	television

IMPORTANT WORDS *(feminine)*

el	**arca** (*f pl* las arcas)	chest
la	**aspiradora**	vacuum cleaner
la	**librería**	bookcase
la	**mesa de centro**	coffee table
la	**pintura**	painting
la	**plancha**	iron
la	**radio digital**	digital radio
la	**secadora**	tumble-dryer

USEFUL WORDS *(masculine)*

la **altavoz** *(pl* altavoces)	loudspeaker
el **asiento**	seat
el **cajón** *(pl* cajones)	drawer
el **camión de mudanzas** *(pl* camiones ~ ~)	removal van
el **carrito**	trolley
el **colchón** *(pl* colchones)	mattress
el **contestador**	answering machine
el **horno**	oven
el **mando a distancia**	remote control
el **marco**	frame
el **mobiliario**	furniture
el **operario de mudanzas**	removal man
el **paragüero**	umbrella stand
el **peso**	scales
los **postigos**	shutters
el **robot de cocina** *(pl* ~ s ~ ~)	food processor
el **secador (de pelo)**	hairdryer
el **taburete**	stool
el **teléfono inalámbrico**	cordless telephone
el **tocador**	dressing table

USEFUL PHRASES
un apartamento *or* piso amueblado a furnished flat
encender/apagar el calefactor *or* la estufa to switch the heater on/off
he hecho la cama I've made my bed
sentarse to sit down
poner *or* meter algo en el horno to put sth in the oven
correr las cortinas to draw the curtains
cerrar los postigos *or* las contraventanas to close the shutters

USEFUL WORDS *(feminine)*

la	alfombra	rug
la	antena	aerial
la	antena parabólica	satellite dish
la	cadena de música	music centre
la	cámara cinematográfica	cine camera
la	cómoda	chest of drawers
las	contraventanas	shutters
la	cuna	cradle; cot
la	estantería	shelves
la	lámpara de pie	standard lamp
la	lámpara halógena	halogen lamp
las	literas	bunk beds
la	máquina de coser	sewing machine
la	máquina de escribir	typewriter
la	mesilla de noche	bedside table
la	moqueta	fitted carpet
la	mudanza	move
la	persiana	blind
la	tabla de planchar	ironing board
la	videocámara	video camera, camcorder

USEFUL PHRASES

es un piso de 4 habitaciones it's a 4-roomed flat

¡ya está el desayuno/la comida/la cena! breakfast/lunch/dinner is ready!

ESSENTIAL WORDS

los	Alpes	the Alps
	Andalucía	Andalusia
el	Atlántico	the Atlantic
	Barcelona	Barcelona
	Bruselas	Brussels
	Castilla	Castile
	Cataluña	Catalonia
la	Costa del Sol	the Costa del Sol
el	este	the east
las	Islas Baleares	the Balearic Islands
las	Islas Canarias	the Canary Islands
la	Coruña	Corunna
	Londres	London
	Málaga	Malaga
	Mallorca	Majorca
el	Mar Cantábrico	the Bay of Biscay
el	Mediterráneo	the Mediterranean
	Menorca	Minorca
el	norte	the north
el	oeste	the west
el	País Vasco	the Basque Country
el	Peñón (de Gibraltar)	the Rock (of Gibraltar)
los	Pirineos	the Pyrenees
	Sevilla	Seville
la	sierra	mountain range
el	sur	the south
	Vizcaya	Biscay
	Zaragoza	Saragossa

IMPORTANT WORDS

	Edimburgo	Edinburgh
el	Támesis	the Thames

USEFUL WORDS

	Atenas	Athens
	Berlín	Berlin
la	capital	capital
la	comunidad autónoma	autonomous region (*of Spain*)
el	Extremo Oriente	the Far East
	Ginebra	Geneva
las	Islas Británicas	the British Isles
la	Haya	The Hague
	Lisboa	Lisbon
	Marruecos	Morocco
	Moscú	Moscow
el	Oriente Medio	the Middle East
el	Oriente Próximo	the Near East
el	Pacífico	the Pacific
	París	Paris
	Pekín	Beijing
el	Polo Norte/Sur	the North/South Pole
la	provincia	province
	Roma	Rome
	Varsovia	Warsaw
	Venecia	Venice
	Viena	Vienna

USEFUL PHRASES

ir a Londres/Sevilla **to go to London/Seville**

ir a Andalucía **to go to Andalusia**

vengo de Barcelona/del País Vasco **I come from Barcelona/the Basque Country**

en el *or* al norte **in** *or* **to the north**

en el *or* al sur **in** *or* **to the south**

en el *or* al este **in** *or* **to the east**

en el *or* al oeste **in** *or* **to the west**

GREETINGS

hola hello
¿cómo está usted (or estás)? how are you?
¿qué tal? how are you?
bien fine (*in reply*)
encantado(a) pleased to meet you
¿dígame? hello (*on telephone*)
buenas tardes good afternoon; good evening
buenas noches good evening; good night
adiós goodbye; hello (*when passing one another*)
hasta mañana see you tomorrow
hasta luego see you later

BEST WISHES

feliz cumpleaños happy birthday
feliz Navidad merry Christmas
feliz Año Nuevo happy New Year
felices Pascuas happy Easter
recuerdos best wishes
saludos best wishes
bienvenido(a) welcome
enhorabuena congratulations
que aproveche enjoy your meal
que le vaya (or te vaya) bien all the best
que te diviertas (or se divierta) enjoy yourself
buena suerte good luck
buen viaje safe journey
jesús bless you (*after a sneeze*)
salud cheers
a tu (or vuestra, etc) salud good health

SURPRISE

Dios mío my goodness
¿qué?, ¿cómo? what?
entiendo oh, I see
vaya well, well
pues… well…
(¿)de verdad(?), (¿)sí(?) really(?)
(¿)estás (or está) de broma(?) you're kidding; are you kidding?
¡qué suerte! how lucky!

POLITENESS

perdone I'm sorry; excuse me
por favor please
gracias thank you
no, gracias no thank you
sí, gracias yes please
de nada not at all, don't mention it, you're welcome
con mucho gusto gladly

AGREEMENT

sí yes
por supuesto of course
de acuerdo, vale (Sp) OK
bueno fine

DISAGREEMENT

no no
que no no (*contradicting a positive statement*)
que sí yes (*contradicting a negative statement*)
claro que no of course not
ni hablar no way
en absoluto not at all
al contrario on the contrary
no me digas well I never
qué cara what a cheek
no te metas en lo que no te importa mind your own business

DIFFICULTIES

socorro help
fuego fire
ay ouch
perdón (I'm) sorry, excuse me, I beg your pardon
lo siento I'm sorry
qué pena what a pity
qué pesadez, qué rollo what a nuisance; how boring
estoy harto(a) I'm fed up
no aguanto más I can't stand it any more
vaya (por Dios) oh dear
qué horror how awful

ORDERS

cuidado be careful
para (*or* **pare**) stop
oiga, usted hey, you there
fuera de aquí clear off
silencio shh
basta ya that's enough
prohibido fumar no smoking
vamos, venga come on, let's go
sigue go ahead, go on
vámonos let's go

OTHERS

no tengo (ni) idea no idea
quizá, quizás perhaps, maybe
no (lo) sé I don't know
¿qué desea? can I help you?
aquí tienes there, there you are
ya voy just coming
no te preocupes don't worry
no merece la pena it's not worth it
a propósito by the way
cariño, querido(a) darling
el (*or* **la**) **pobre** poor thing
tanto mejor so much the better
no me importa I don't mind
a mí me da igual it's all the same to me
mala suerte too bad
depende it depends
¿qué voy a hacer? what shall I do?
¿para qué? what's the point?
me molesta it annoys me
me saca de quicio it gets on my nerves

ESSENTIAL WORDS *(masculine)*

el	**accidente**	accident
el	**dentista**	dentist
el	**doctor**	doctor
el	**enfermero**	(male) nurse
el	**enfermo**	patient
el	**estómago**	stomach
el	**hospital**	hospital
el	**médico**	doctor

IMPORTANT WORDS *(masculine)*

el	**algodón (hidrófilo)**	cotton wool
el	**antiséptico**	antiseptic
el	**comprimido**	tablet
el	**dolor**	pain
el	**esparadrapo**	(sticking) plaster
el	**farmacéutico**	chemist
el	**jarabe**	syrup
el	**medicamento**	medicine, drug
el	**paciente**	patient
el	**resfriado**	cold
el	**seguro**	insurance

USEFUL PHRASES

ha habido un accidente there's been an accident

ingresar en el hospital to be admitted to hospital

debe permanecer en cama you must stay in bed

estar enfermo(a) to be ill; sentirse mejor to feel better

cuidar to look after

me he hecho daño I have hurt myself

me he hecho un corte en el dedo I have cut my finger

me he torcido el tobillo I have sprained my ankle

se ha roto el brazo he has broken his arm

me he quemado I have burnt myself

me duele la garganta/la cabeza/ el estómago I've got a sore throat/ a headache/a stomach ache

tener fiebre to have a temperature

ESSENTIAL WORDS (feminine)

la	aspirina	aspirin
la	cama	bed
la	cita	appointment
la	dentista	dentist
la	doctora	doctor
la	enferma	patient
la	enfermera	nurse
la	farmacia	chemist's (shop)
la	médico	doctor
la	pastilla	tablet, pill
la	salud	health
la	temperatura	temperature

IMPORTANT WORDS (feminine)

la	ambulancia	ambulance
la	camilla	stretcher
la	clínica	clinic, private hospital
la	consulta	surgery
la	crema	cream, ointment
la	cucharada	spoonful
la	diarrea	diarrhoea
la	enfermedad	illness
la	escayola	plaster cast
la	farmacéutica	chemist
la	gripe	flu
la	herida	wound, injury
la	insolación (pl insolaciones)	sunstroke
la	inyección (pl inyecciones)	injection
la	medicina	medicine
la	operación (pl operaciones)	operation
la	paciente	patient
la	píldora	pill; the Pill
las	quemaduras del sol	sunburn
la	receta	prescription
la	sangre	blood
la	tableta	tablet
las	urgencias	Accident and Emergency
la	venda	bandage

USEFUL WORDS *(masculine)*

el	absceso	abscess
el	acné	acne
el	arañazo	scratch
el	ataque	fit
el	ataque al corazón	heart attack
el	cáncer	cancer
el	cardenal	bruise
el	embarazo	pregnancy
el	estrés	stress
el	mareo	dizzy spell; sickness
el	microbio	germ
el	nervio	nerve
el	preservativo	condom
los	primeros auxilios	first aid
el	pulso	pulse
el	régimen	diet
el	reposo	rest
el	SAMU	emergency medical service
el	sarampión	measles
el	shock	shock
el	sida	AIDS
el	tónico	tonic
el	vendaje	dressing
el	veneno	poison

USEFUL PHRASES

tengo sueño I'm sleepy
tengo naúseas I feel sick
adelgazar to lose weight
engordar to put on weight
tragar to swallow
sangrar to bleed
vomitar to vomit
estar en forma to be in good shape
reposar, descansar to rest

USEFUL WORDS (*feminine*)

la	amigdalitis	tonsillitis
las	anginas	sore throat; tonsillitis
la	apendicitis	appendicitis
la	astilla	splinter
la	cicatriz (*pl* cicatrices)	scar
la	dentadura postiza	false teeth
la	dieta	diet
la	epidemia	epidemic
la	fiebre del heno	hay fever
la	migraña	migraine
la	muleta	crutch
la	náusea	nausea
las	paperas	mumps
la	pomada	ointment
la	radiografía	X-ray
la	recuperación	recovery
la	rubeola	German measles
la	silla de ruedas	wheelchair
la	tos	cough
la	tos ferina	whooping cough
la	transfusión (de sangre) (*pl* transfusiones (~ ~))	blood transfusion
la	varicela	chickenpox
la	viruela	smallpox

USEFUL PHRASES

curar to cure; curarse to get better
gravemente herido(a) seriously injured
¿tiene seguro? are you insured?
estoy resfriado(a) I have a cold
¡eso duele! that hurts!; me duele it hurts!
respirar to breathe
desmayarse to faint
toser to cough
morir to die
perder el conocimiento to lose consciousness
llevar el brazo en cabestrillo to have one's arm in a sling

ESSENTIAL WORDS *(masculine)*

el	**almuerzo**	lunch
el	**ascensor**	lift
el	**balcón** (*pl* balcones)	balcony
los	**baños públicos** (*LAm*)	toilets
el	**bar**	bar
el	**camarero**	waiter
el	**cambio**	change
el	**cheque**	cheque
el	**cuarto de baño**	bathroom
el	**depósito**	deposit
el	**desayuno**	breakfast
el	**director**	manager
el	**equipaje**	luggage
el	**hotel**	hotel
el	**huésped**	guest
el	**impreso**	form
el	**maletero**	porter
el	**número**	number
el	**pasaporte**	passport
el	**piso**	floor; storey
el	**precio**	price
el	**recepcionista**	receptionist
el	**restaurante**	restaurant
el	**ruido**	noise
los	**servicios**	toilets
el	**teléfono**	telephone

USEFUL PHRASES

quisiera reservar una habitación I would like to book a room
una habitación con ducha/con baño a room with a shower/
   with a bathroom
una habitación individual a single room
una habitación doble a double room

ESSENTIAL WORDS *(feminine)*

la	cama de matrimonio	double bed
la	camarera	waitress
las	camas separadas	twin beds
la	comida	lunch; meal
la	comodidad	comfort
la	cuenta	bill
la	directora	manager
la	ducha	shower
la	entrada	entrance
la	escalera	stairs
la	estancia	stay
la	fecha	date
la	ficha	form
la	habitación (*pl* habitaciones)	room
la	huésped	guest
la	llave	key
la	maleta	suitcase
la	media pensión	half board
la	noche	night
la	pensión (*pl* pensiones)	guest house
la	pensión completa	full board
la	piscina	swimming pool
la	planta	floor; storey
la	planta baja	ground floor
la	recepción	reception
la	recepcionista	receptionist
la	salida de incendios	fire escape
la	tarifa	rate, rates
la	televisión (*pl* televisiones)	television
la	vista	view

USEFUL PHRASES

¿lleva algún documento de identidad? do you have any ID?
¿a qué hora se sirve el desayuno? what time is breakfast served?
limpiar la habitación to clean the room
"se ruega no molestar" "do not disturb"

IMPORTANT WORDS (*masculine*)

el	albergue	inn
el	baño	bathroom
el	interruptor	switch
el	lavabo	washbasin; bathroom
el	precio total	inclusive price
el	recibo	receipt

USEFUL WORDS (*masculine*)

el	cocinero	cook
el	maître	head waiter
el	sumiller	wine waiter
el	vestíbulo	foyer

USEFUL PHRASES

ocupado(a) **occupied**
libre **vacant**
limpio(a) **clean**
sucio(a) **dirty**
dormir **to sleep**
despertar **to wake**
"con todas las comodidades" **"with all facilities"**
¿podrían despertarme (*or* llamarme) mañana por la mañana a las siete?
   I'd like a 7 o'clock alarm call tomorrow morning, please
una habitación con vistas al mar **a room overlooking the sea**

IMPORTANT WORDS *(feminine)*

la	**bañera**	bathtub
la	**bienvenida**	welcome
la	**camarera (de habitaciones)**	chambermaid
la	**casa de huéspedes**	guest house
la	**factura**	bill
la	**guía turística**	guidebook
la	**propina**	tip
la	**reclamación** (*pl* reclamaciones)	complaint

USEFUL WORDS *(feminine)*

la	**cocinera**	cook

USEFUL PHRASES

una habitación con media pensión **room with half board**
¿nos sentamos fuera *or* en la terraza? **shall we sit outside?**
nos sirvieron la cena fuera *or* en la terraza **we were served dinner outside**
un hotel de tres estrellas **a three-star hotel**
IVA incluido **inclusive of VAT**

ESSENTIAL WORDS (masculine)

el	aparcamiento (Sp)	car park; parking space
el	apartamento	flat, apartment
el	ascensor	lift
el	balcón (pl balcones)	balcony
el	bloque de departamentos (LAm)	block of flats
el	bloque de pisos (Sp)	block of flats
el	comedor	dining room
el	cuarto de baño	bathroom
el	departamento (LAm)	flat, apartment
el	dormitorio	bedroom
el	edificio	building
el	estacionamiento (LAm)	car park; parking space
el	exterior	exterior
el	garaje	garage
el	interior	interior
el	jardín (pl jardines)	garden
el	mueble	piece of furniture
los	muebles	furniture
el	numéro de teléfono	phone number
el	patio	yard
el	piso	floor, storey; (Sp) flat, apartment
el	pueblo	village
el	salón (pl salones)	living room
el	sótano	basement
el	terreno	plot of land

USEFUL PHRASES

cuando vaya a casa when I go home
mirar por la ventana to look out of the window
en mi/tu/nuestra casa at my/your/our house
mudarse de casa to move house
alquilar un apartamento or un piso to rent a flat

ESSENTIAL WORDS (feminine)

la	**avenida**	avenue
la	**bodega**	cellar
la	**calefacción (central)**	(central) heating
	(pl calefacciones (~es))	
la	**calle**	street
la	**casa**	house
la	**ciudad**	town; city
la	**cocina**	kitchen
la	**comodidad**	comfort
la	**dirección** (pl direcciones)	address
la	**ducha**	shower
la	**entrada**	entrance
la	**entrada para coches** (Sp)	drive
	or **para carros** (LAm)	
la	**escalera**	stairs
la	**habitación** (pl habitaciones)	room
la	**llave**	key
la	**parcela**	plot of land
la	**pared**	wall
la	**planta**	floor, storey
la	**planta baja**	ground floor
la	**plaza de parking** or **de garaje**	parking space (in car park)
la	**puerta**	door
la	**puerta principal**	front door
la	**sala de estar**	living room
la	**urbanización** (pl urbanizaciones)	housing estate
la	**ventana**	window
la	**vista**	view

USEFUL PHRASES

vivo en una casa/en un apartamento or un piso I live in a house /a flat
(en el piso de) arriba upstairs
(en el piso de) abajo downstairs
en el primer piso on the first floor
en la planta baja on the ground floor
en casa at home

IMPORTANT WORDS (*masculine*)

el	alojamiento	accommodation
el	alquiler	rent
el	baño	toilet
el	césped	lawn
el	dueño	landlord; owner
el	humo	smoke
el	lavabo	toilet; washbasin
el	mantenimiento	upkeep
el	mobiliario	furniture
el	pasillo	corridor
el	piso amueblado	furnished flat
el	portero	caretaker
el	propietario	owner; landlord
el	rellano	landing
el	tejado	roof
el	trastero	lumber room; (*Mex*) cupboard
el	vecino	neighbour

USEFUL WORDS (*masculine*)

el	ático	penthouse; attic
el	chalet (*pl* ~s)	bungalow; detached house
el	cristal	window pane
el	despacho	study
el	escalón (*pl* escalones)	step
el	estudio	studio flat
el	inquilino	tenant; lodger
el	muro	wall
el	parquet (*pl* ~s)	parquet floor
el	piso piloto	show flat
el	seto	hedge
el	suelo	floor
el	techo	ceiling
el	timbre	door bell
el	tragaluz (*pl* tragaluces)	skylight
el	umbral	doorstep
el	vestíbulo	hall
el	vidrio	window pane

IMPORTANT WORDS (feminine)

la	casa de campo	cottage
la	chimenea	chimney; fireplace
la	dueña	landlady; owner
la	mudanza	move
la	portera	caretaker
la	propietaria	owner; landlady
la	señora de la limpieza	cleaner
la	vecina	neighbour
la	vivienda	housing

USEFUL WORDS (feminine)

el	ama de casa (*f pl* amas ~ ~)	housewife
la	antena	aerial
la	baldosa	tile
la	buhardilla	attic
la	caldera	boiler
la	contraventana	shutter
la	cristalera (*Sp*)	French window
la	decoración (*pl* decoraciones)	decoration
la	fachada	front (*of house*)
la	habitación de los invitados	spare room
la	inquilina	tenant; lodger
la	persiana	blind
la	portería	caretaker's room
la	puerta ventana	French window
la	teja	roof tile; slate
la	tubería	pipe
la	vivienda de protección oficial	council flat *or* house

USEFUL PHRASES

llamar a la puerta to knock at the door
acaba de sonar el timbre the doorbell's just gone
desde fuera from the outside
dentro on the inside
hasta el techo up to the ceiling

ESSENTIAL WORDS *(masculine)*

el	**armario**	cupboard; wardrobe
el	**bote de la basura** (*Mex*)	dustbin
el	**buzón** (*pl* buzones)	letterbox
el	**cazo**	saucepan
el	**cenicero**	ashtray
el	**cepillo**	brush
el	**cuadro**	picture
el	**cubo de la basura**	dustbin
el	**despertador**	alarm clock
el	**espejo**	mirror
el	**fregadero**	sink
el	**frigorífico** (*Sp*)	fridge
el	**gas**	gas
el	**grifo**	tap
el	**interruptor**	switch
el	**jabón** (*pl* jabones)	soap
el	**lavabo**	washbasin; toilet
la	**pasta de dientes**	toothpaste
el	**póster** (*pl* ~es *or* ~s)	poster
el	**radiador**	radiator
el	**refrigerador** (*LAm*)	fridge
el	**televisor**	television set
el	**vídeo** (*Sp*) *or* video (*LAm*)	video recorder

USEFUL PHRASES

darse un baño, bañarse to have a bath
darse una ducha, ducharse to have a shower
hacer la limpieza de la casa to do the housework
me gusta cocinar I like cooking

ESSENTIAL WORDS *(feminine)*

el	**agua** (*f*)	water
la	**alfombra**	carpet, rug
la	**almohada**	pillow
la	**balanza**	scales
la	**bandeja**	tray
la	**bañera**	bath
la	**cacerola**	saucepan
la	**cafetera**	coffee pot; coffee maker
la	**cazuela**	saucepan
la	**cocina**	cooker
las	**cortinas**	curtains
la	**ducha**	shower
la	**electricidad**	electricity
la	**foto**	photo
la	**lámpara**	lamp
la	**lavadora**	washing machine
la	**luz** (*pl* luces)	light
la	**manta**	blanket
la	**radio**	radio
la	**refrigeradora** (*LAm*)	fridge
la	**sábana**	sheet
la	**servilleta**	napkin
las	**tareas domésticas**	housework
la	**televisión** (*pl* televisiones)	television
la	**toalla**	towel
la	**vajilla**	dishes

USEFUL PHRASES

ver la televisión to watch television
en televisión on television
encender/apagar la tele to switch on/off the TV
tirar algo al cubo de la basura to throw sth in the dustbin
lavar *or* fregar los platos to do the dishes

IMPORTANT WORDS *(masculine)*

el **bidé**	bidet
el **detergente (en polvo)**	washing powder
el **enchufe**	plug; socket
el **horno**	oven
el **lavavajillas** *(pl inv)*	dishwasher; washing-up liquid
el **mueble de cocina**	cooker
el **polvo**	dust

USEFUL WORDS *(masculine)*

el **adorno**	ornament
el **almohadón** *(pl* almohadones)	bolster
el **cojín** *(pl* cojines)	cushion
el **cubo**	bucket
el **edredón nórdico** *(pl* edredones ~s)	duvet
el **horno microondas**	microwave oven
el **jarrón** *(pl* jarrones)	vase
el **molinillo de café**	coffee grinder
el **paño de cocina**	dishcloth
el **papel pintado**	wallpaper
el **picaporte**	door handle
el **trapo (del polvo)**	duster

USEFUL PHRASES

enchufar/desenchufar **to plug in/to unplug**
pasar la aspiradora **to hoover**
hacer la colada **to do the washing**

IMPORTANT WORDS *(feminine)*

la	aspiradora	vacuum cleaner
la	bombilla	light bulb
la	cerradura	lock
la	colada	(clean) washing
la	estufa	heater
la	pintura	paint; painting
la	receta	recipe
la	ropa de cama	bedclothes
la	ropa sucia	(dirty) washing, laundry
la	sartén (*pl* sartenes)	frying pan
la	señora de la limpieza	cleaner

USEFUL WORDS *(feminine)*

la	basura	rubbish
la	batidora	blender
la	bayeta	duster
la	escalera (de mano)	ladder
la	escoba	broom
la	esponja	sponge
la	manta eléctrica	electric blanket
la	moqueta	fitted carpet
la	olla a presión	pressure cooker
la	papelera	waste paper basket
la	percha	coat hanger
la	plancha	iron
la	tabla de planchar	ironing board
la	tapa	lid
la	tapicería	upholstery
la	tostadora	toaster

USEFUL PHRASES

barrer to sweep (up)
limpiar to clean
recoger uno sus cosas to tidy away one's things
dejar uno sus cosas por ahí tiradas to leave one's things lying about

ESSENTIAL WORDS (*masculine*)

el	**banco**	bank
el	**billete (de banco)**	banknote
el	**bolígrafo**	Biro®
el	**buzón** (*pl* buzones)	postbox
el	**cambio**	change
el	**carnet** *or* **carné de identidad** (*Sp*)	ID card
	(*pl* ~s ~~)	
el	**cartero**	postman
el	**céntimo de euro**	euro cent
el	**cheque**	cheque
el	**código postal**	postcode
el	**contrato telefónico**	phone contract
el	**correo electrónico**	email
el	**documento de identidad**	ID card
el	**empleado**	counter clerk
el	**error**	mistake
el	**euro**	euro
el	**fax**	fax; fax machine
el	**impreso**	form
el	**ingreso**	deposit
el	**justificante**	written proof
el	**mensaje de texto**	text message
el	**mostrador**	counter
el	**prefijo**	dialling code
el	**número**	number
el	**paquete**	parcel
el	**pasaporte**	passport
el	**precio**	price
el	**sello**	stamp
el	**sobre**	envelope
el	**teléfono**	telephone
el	**tono de marcado**	dialling tone

USEFUL PHRASES

el banco más cercano **the nearest bank**
quisiera cobrar un cheque/cambiar dinero **I would like to cash a cheque/change some money**

ESSENTIAL WORDS (feminine)

la	caja	check-out
la	carta	letter
la	cartera	postwoman; wallet; (LAm) handbag
la	cédula de identidad (LAm)	ID card
la	compañía de teléfonos	phone company
la	dirección (pl direcciones)	address
la	empleada	counter clerk
la	firma	signature
la	información	information; directory enquiries
la	libra (esterlina)	pound (sterling)
la	llamada	call
la	oficina de correos	post office
la	oficina de información y turismo	tourist information office
la	pluma	pen
la	respuesta	reply
la	tarjeta de crédito	credit card
la	tarjeta de débito	debit card
la	(tarjeta) postal	postcard

USEFUL PHRASES

una llamada telefónica a phone call
llamar a algn por teléfono, telefonear a algn to phone sb
descolgar el teléfono to lift the receiver
marcar (el número) to dial (the number)
hola – soy el Dr Pérez or el Dr Pérez al habla hello, this is Dr. Pérez
la línea está ocupada the line is engaged
no cuelgue hold the line
me he equivocado de número I got the wrong number
colgar to hang up
quisiera hacer una llamada internacional I'd like to make an international
  phone call

IMPORTANT WORDS *(masculine)*

el **archivo adjunto**	attachment
el **buzón de voz** *(pl* buzones ~~ *)*	voicemail
el **cheque de viaje**	traveller's cheque
el **cibercafé**	internet café
el **contestador (automático)**	answerphone
el **correo**	mail
el **crédito**	credit
el **domicilio**	home address
el **gasto**	expense
el **impuesto**	tax
el **mail** *(pl* ~s *)*	email
el **monedero**	purse
el **pago**	payment
el **papel de carta**	writing paper
el **recargo**	extra charge
el **SMS** *(pl inv)*	text message
el **talonario de cheques**	cheque book
el **telefonista**	operator
el **(teléfono) fijo**	landline
el **(teléfono) móvil**	mobile (phone)
el **telegrama**	telegram
el **tipo de cambio**	exchange rate

USEFUL WORDS *(masculine)*

el **apartado de correos**	PO box
el **auricular**	receiver
el **destinatario**	addressee
el **documento adjunto**	attachment
el **giro postal**	postal order
el **nombre de acceso** *(or* entrada*)* al sistema	login
el **papel de envolver**	wrapping paper
el **remitente**	sender
el **tono de llamada**	ringtone

IMPORTANT WORDS (feminine)

la	banda ancha	broadband
la	cabina telefónica	callbox
la	contraseña	password
la	cuenta (bancaria)	(bank) account
la	estampilla	stamp
la	guía telefónica	telephone directory
la	llamada telefónica	phone call
la	oficina de objetos perdidos	lost property office
la	peseta	peseta
la	ranura	slot
la	recogida	collection
la	recompensa	reward
la	tarjeta telefónica	(*prepaid*) phonecard
la	tarjeta de recarga (del móvil)	top-up (card)
la	telefonista	operator

USEFUL WORDS (feminine)

la	carta certificada	registered letter
la	destinataria	addressee
la	llamada internacional	international call
la	llamada local	local call
la	llamada nacional	inter-city call
la	oficina de cambio	bureau de change
la	remitente	sender
la	tarjeta SIM (*pl* ~s ~)	SIM card

USEFUL PHRASES

he perdido la cartera **I've lost my wallet**
rellenar un impreso **to fill in a form**
en mayúsculas **in block letters**
hacer una llamada a cobro revertido **to make a reverse charge call**

GENERAL SITUATIONS

¿cuál es su dirección? what is your address?
¿cómo se escribe? how do you spell that?
¿tiene cambio de 100 euros? do you have change of 100 euros?
escribir to write
responder to reply
firmar to sign
¿me puede ayudar por favor? can you help me please?
¿cómo se va a la estación? how do I get to the station?
todo recto straight on
a la derecha to or on the right; **a la izquierda** to or on the left

LETTERS

Querido Carlos Dear Carlos
Querida Ana Dear Ana
Estimado señor Dear Sir
Estimada señora Dear Madam
recuerdos, saludos best wishes
un abrazo de, un beso de, besos de love from
le saluda atentamente or **cordialmente** kind regards
besos y abrazos love and kisses
atentamente yours faithfully
reciba un atento saludo, le saluda atentamente yours sincerely
sigue PTO

E-MAILS

mandarle un correo electrónico a algn to mail or email sb

MOBILES

mandarle un mensaje de texto a algn to text sb

PRONUNCIATION GUIDE

Pronounced approximately as:

A	ah
B	bay
C	thay, say
D	day
E	ay
F	efay
G	khay
H	atchay
I	ee
J	khota
K	kah
L	elay
LL	elyay
M	emay
N	enay
Ñ	enyay
O	oh
P	pay
Q	koo
R	eray
S	essay
T	tay
U	oo
V	oobay (*Sp*), bay korta (*LAm*)
W	oobay doblay (*Sp*), doblay bay (*LAm*)
X	ekees
Y	ee griayga
Z	theta, seta

ESSENTIAL WORDS (*masculine*)

el	**abogado**	lawyer
el	**accidente**	accident
el	**carnet de identidad** (*Sp*) (*pl* ~s ~~)	ID card
el	**documento de identidad**	ID card
el	**incendio**	fire
el	**policía**	policeman
el	**problema**	problem
el	**robo**	burglary; theft

IMPORTANT WORDS (*masculine*)

el	**atracador**	armed robber; mugger
el	**atraco**	hold-up; mugging
el	**consulado**	consulate
el	**control policial**	checkpoint; roadblock
el	**culpable**	culprit
el	**daño** *or* los **daños**	damage
el	**ejército**	army
el	**espía**	spy
el	**gobierno**	government
el	**guardia civil**	civil guard (*person*)
los	**impuestos**	income tax
el	**ladrón** (*pl* ladrones)	burglar; thief; robber
el	**monedero**	purse
el	**muerto**	dead man
el	**permiso**	permission
el	**propietario**	owner
el	**testigo**	witness

USEFUL PHRASES

robar **to burgle; to steal; to rob**
¡me han robado la cartera! **someone has stolen my wallet!**
ilegal **illegal**; inocente **innocent**
no es culpa mía **it's not my fault**
¡socorro! **help!**; ¡al ladrón! **stop thief!**
¡fuego! **fire!**; ¡arriba las manos! **hands up!**
robar un banco **to rob a bank**
encarcelar **to imprison**; fugarse, escapar **to escape**

ESSENTIAL WORDS *(feminine)*

la	**abogada**	lawyer
la	**cédula de identidad** *(LAm)*	identity card
la	**culpa**	fault
la	**documentación**	papers
la	**identidad**	identity
la	**policía**	police; policewoman
la	**verdad**	truth

IMPORTANT WORDS *(feminine)*

la	**atracadora**	armed robber; mugger
la	**banda**	gang
la	**cartera**	wallet; *(LAm)* handbag
la	**comisaría**	police station
la	**culpable**	culprit
la	**denuncia**	report
la	**espía**	spy
la	**Guardia Civil**	Civil Guard
la	**guardia civil**	civil guard *(person)*
la	**ladrona**	burglar; thief; robber
la	**manifestación** *(pl* manifestaciones)	demonstration
la	**muerta**	dead woman
la	**muerte**	death
la	**multa**	fine
la	**pena de muerte**	death penalty
la	**póliza de seguros**	insurance policy
la	**propietaria**	owner
la	**recompensa**	reward
la	**testigo**	witness

USEFUL PHRASES

un atraco a mano armada **a hold-up**
raptar *or* secuestrar a un niño **to abduct a child**
un grupo de gamberros **a bunch of hooligans**
en la cárcel **in prison**
pelearse **to fight;** arrestar **to arrest;** acusar **to charge**
estar detenido(a) **to be remanded in custody**
acusar a algn de algo **to accuse sb of sth; to charge sb with sth**

USEFUL WORDS *(masculine)*

el	arresto	arrest
el	asesinato	murder
el	asesino	murderer
el	botín *(pl* botines)	loot
el	cadáver	corpse
el	crimen *(pl* crímenes)	murder; crime
el	criminal	criminal
el	detective privado	private detective
el	disparo (de arma)	(gun) shot
el	drogadicto	drug addict
el	encarcelamiento	imprisonment
el	estafador	crook
el	gamberro	hooligan
el	gángster *(pl* ~s)	gangster
el	guarda	guard; warden
el	guardia	guard; policeman
el	inmigrante ilegal	illegal immigrant
el	intento	attempt
el	juez *(pl* jueces)	judge
el	juicio	trial
el	jurado	jury
el	levantamiento	uprising
el	pirómano	arsonist
el	poli	cop
el	preso	prisoner
el	rehén *(pl* rehenes)	hostage
el	rescate	ransom; rescue
el	revólver	revolver
el	secuestrador	kidnapper; hijacker
el	secuestro	kidnapping
el	secuestro aéreo	hijacking
el	terrorismo	terrorism
el	terrorista	terrorist
el	traficante de drogas	drug dealer
el	tribunal	court
los	tribunales	law courts
el	valor	bravery

law 599

USEFUL WORDS *(feminine)*

la	**acusación** *(pl* acusaciones)	the prosecution; charge
el	**arma** *(pl f* las **armas)**	weapon
la	**asesina**	murderer
la	**bomba**	bomb
la	**cárcel**	prison
la	**celda**	cell
la	**criminal**	criminal
la	**declaración** *(pl* declaraciones)	statement
la	**defensa**	defence
la	**detective privada**	private detective
la	**detención** *(pl* detenciones)	arrest
la	**droga**	drug
la	**drogadicta**	drug addict
la	**estafadora**	crook
la	**fuga**	escape
la	**gamberra**	hooligan
la	**guarda**	guard; warden
la	**guardia**	guard; policewoman
la	**inmigrante ilegal**	illegal immigrant
la	**investigación** *(pl* investigaciones)	inquiry
la	**ley**	law
la	**multa**	fine
la	**pelea**	fight
la	**pirómana**	arsonist
la	**pistola**	gun
la	**poli**	the cops; cop
la	**prisión** *(pl* prisiones)	prison
la	**presa**	prisoner
la	**prueba**	proof
las	**pruebas**	evidence
la	**redada**	raid
la	**rehén** *(pl* rehenes)	hostage
la	**riña**	argument
la	**secuestradora**	kidnapper; hijacker
la	**suplantación de personalidad** *(pl* suplantaciones ~~)	identity theft
la	**terrorista**	terrorist
la	**traficante de drogas**	drug dealer

ESSENTIAL WORDS (*masculine*)

el	**acero**	steel
el	**algodón**	cotton
el	**caucho**	rubber
el	**cristal**	glass
el	**cuero**	leather
el	**gas**	gas
el	**gasoil**	diesel
el	**hierro**	iron
el	**metal**	metal
el	**oro**	gold
el	**plástico**	plastic
el	**vidrio**	glass

IMPORTANT WORDS (*masculine*)

el	**acero inoxidable**	stainless steel
el	**aluminio**	aluminium
el	**cartón**	cardboard
el	**estado**	condition
el	**hierro forjado**	wrought iron
el	**ladrillo**	brick
el	**papel**	paper
el	**tejido**	fabric

USEFUL PHRASES

una silla de madera **a wooden chair**
una caja de plástico **a plastic box**
un anillo de oro **a gold ring**
en buen estado, en buenas condiciones **in good condition**
en mal estado, en malas condiciones **in bad condition**

ESSENTIAL WORDS *(feminine)*

la	**lana**	wool
la	**madera**	wood
la	**piedra**	stone
la	**piel**	fur; leather
la	**plata**	silver
la	**tela**	fabric

IMPORTANT WORDS *(feminine)*

la	**fibra sintética**	synthetic fibre
la	**seda**	silk

USEFUL PHRASES

un abrigo de piel a fur coat
un jersey de lana a woollen jumper
oxidado(a) rusty

USEFUL WORDS (*masculine*)

el	acrílico	acrylic
el	alambre	wire
el	ante	suede
el	bronce	bronze
el	carbón	coal
el	cemento	concrete
el	cobre	copper
el	encaje	lace
el	estaño	tin
el	hilo	thread
el	latón	brass
el	lino	linen
el	líquido	liquid
el	mármol	marble
el	material	material
el	mimbre	wickerwork
el	pegamento	glue
el	plomo	lead
el	raso	satin
el	terciopelo	velvet
el	tweed	tweed

USEFUL WORDS *(feminine)*

la	**arcilla**	clay
la	**cera**	wax
la	**cerámica**	ceramics
la	**cola**	glue
la	**cuerda**	string
la	**escayola**	plaster
la	**gomaespuma**	foam rubber
la	**hojalata**	tin, tinplate
la	**lona**	canvas
la	**loza**	pottery
la	**paja**	straw
la	**pana**	corduroy
la	**porcelana**	china

ESSENTIAL WORDS *(masculine)*

el	director de orquesta	conductor
el	grupo	band
el	instrumento musical	musical instrument
el	músico	musician
el	piano	piano
el	violín *(pl* violines)	violin

USEFUL WORDS *(masculine)*

el	acorde	chord
el	acordeón *(pl* acordeones)	accordion
el	arco	bow
el	atril	music stand
el	bombo	bass drum
el	clarinete	clarinet
el	contrabajo	double bass
el	estuche	case
el	estudio de grabación	recording studio
el	fagot	bassoon
los	instrumentos de cuerda	string instruments
los	instrumentos de percusión	percussion instruments
los	instrumentos de viento	wind instruments
el	jazz	jazz
los	metales	brass
el	micrófono	microphone
el	minidisco	minidisc
el	oboe	oboe
el	órgano	organ
los	platillos	cymbals
el	saxofón *(pl* saxofones)	saxophone
el	solfeo	music theory
el	solista	soloist
el	tambor	drum
el	triángulo	triangle
el	trombón *(pl* trombones)	trombone
el	violonchelo	cello

ESSENTIAL WORDS (feminine)

la	**batería**	drums, drum kit
la	**directora de orquesta**	conductor
la	**flauta**	flute
la	**flauta dulce**	recorder
la	**guitarra**	guitar
la	**música**	music; musician
la	**orquesta**	orchestra

USEFUL WORDS (feminine)

la	**armónica**	harmonica
el	**arpa**	harpe
la	**batuta**	conductor's baton
la	**composición** (pl composiciones)	composition
la	**corneta**	bugle
la	**cuerda**	string
la	**gaita**	bagpipes
la	**grabación digital**	digital recording
	(pl grabaciones ~es)	
la	**megafonía**	PA system
la	**mesa de mezclas**	mixing deck
la	**nota**	note
la	**pandereta**	tambourine
la	**solista**	soloist
la	**tecla (de piano)**	(piano) key
la	**trompeta**	trumpet
la	**viola**	viola

USEFUL PHRASES

tocar or interpretar una pieza to play a piece
tocar alto/bajo to play loudly/softly
tocar afinado/desafinado to play in tune/out of tune
tocar el piano/la guitarra to play the piano/the guitar
tocar la batería to play drums
Pedro a la batería Pedro on drums
practicar el piano to practise the piano
¿tocas en un grupo? do you play in a band?
una nota falsa a wrong note

CARDINAL NUMBERS

cero	0	zero
uno (m), una (f)	1	one
dos	2	two
tres	3	three
cuatro	4	four
cinco	5	five
seis	6	six
siete	7	seven
ocho	8	eight
nueve	9	nine
diez	10	ten
once	11	eleven
doce	12	twelve
trece	13	thirteen
catorce	14	fourteen
quince	15	fifteen
dieciséis	16	sixteen
diecisiete	17	seventeen
dieciocho	18	eighteen
diecinueve	19	nineteen
veinte	20	twenty
veintiuno(a)	21	twenty-one
veintidós	22	twenty-two
veintitrés	23	twenty-three
treinta	30	thirty
treinta y uno(a)	31	thirty-one
treinta y dos	32	thirty-two
cuarenta	40	forty
cincuenta	50	fifty
sesenta	60	sixty
setenta	70	seventy
ochenta	80	eighty
noventa	90	ninety
cien	100	one hundred

CARDINAL NUMBERS (continued)

ciento uno(a)	101	a hundred and one
ciento dos	102	a hundred and two
ciento diez	110	a hundred and ten
ciento ochenta y dos	182	a hundred and eighty-two
doscientos(as)	200	two hundred
doscientos(as) uno(a)	201	two hundred and one
doscientos(as) dos	202	two hundred and two
trescientos(as)	300	three hundred
cuatrocientos(as)	400	four hundred
quinientos(as)	500	five hundred
seiscientos(as)	600	six hundred
setecientos(as)	700	seven hundred
ochocientos(as)	800	eight hundred
novecientos(as)	900	nine hundred
mil	1000	one thousand
mil uno(a)	1001	a thousand and one
mil dos	1002	a thousand and two
dos mil	2000	two thousand
dos mil seis	2006	two thousand and six
diez mil	10000	ten thousand
cien mil	100000	one hundred thousand
un millón	1000000	one million
dos millones	2000000	two million

USEFUL PHRASES

mil euros **a thousand euros**
un millón de dólares **one million dollars**
tres coma dos (3,2) **three point two (3.2)**

ORDINAL NUMBERS

primero(a)	1º, 1ª	first
segundo(a)	2º, 2ª	second
tercero(a)	3º, 3ª	third
cuarto(a)	4º, 4ª	fourth
quinto(a)	5º, 5ª	fifth
sexto(a)	6º, 6ª	sixth
séptimo(a)	7º, 7ª	seventh
octavo(a)	8º, 8ª	eighth
noveno(a)	9º, 9ª	ninth
décimo(a)	10º, 10ª	tenth
undécimo(a)	11º, 11ª	eleventh
duodécimo(a)	12º, 12ª	twelfth
decimotercero(a)	13º, 13ª	thirteenth
decimocuarto(a)	14º, 14ª	fourteenth
decimoquinto(a)	15º, 15ª	fifteenth
decimosexto(a)	16º, 16ª	sixteenth
decimoséptimo(a)	17º, 17ª	seventeenth
decimoctavo(a)	18º, 18ª	eighteenth
decimonoveno(a), decimonono(a)	19º, 19ª	nineteenth
vigésimo(a)	20º, 20ª	twentieth

Note:
Ordinal numbers are hardly ever used above 10th in spoken Spanish, and rarely at all above 20th. It's normal to use the cardinal numbers instead, except for **milésimo(a)**.

milésimo(a)	1000º, 1000ª	thousandth
dos milésimo(a)	2000º, 2000ª	two thousandth
millonésimo(a)	1000000º, 1000000ª	millionth
dos millonésimo(a)	2000000º, 2000000ª	two millionth

FRACTIONS

un medio	$\frac{1}{2}$	a half
uno(a) y medio(a)	$1\frac{1}{2}$	one and a half
dos y medio(a)	$2\frac{1}{2}$	two and a half
un tercio, la tercera parte	$\frac{1}{3}$	a third
dos tercios, las dos terceras partes	$\frac{2}{3}$	two thirds
un cuarto, la cuarta parte	$\frac{1}{4}$	a quarter
tres cuartos, las tres cuartas partes	$\frac{3}{4}$	three quarters
un sexto, la sexta parte	$\frac{1}{6}$	a sixth
tres y cinco sextos	$3\frac{5}{6}$	three and five sixths
un séptimo, la séptima parte	$\frac{1}{7}$	a seventh
un octavo, la octava parte	$\frac{1}{8}$	an eighth
un noveno, la novena parte	$\frac{1}{9}$	a ninth
un décimo, la décima parte	$\frac{1}{10}$	a tenth
un onceavo, la onceava parte	$\frac{1}{11}$	an eleventh
un doceavo, la doceava parte	$\frac{1}{12}$	a twelfth
siete doceavos, las siete doceavas partes	$\frac{7}{12}$	seven twelfths
un centésimo, la centésima parte	$\frac{1}{100}$	a hundredth
un milésimo, la milésima parte	$\frac{1}{1000}$	a thousandth

USEFUL PHRASES

ambos (ƒambas), los dos (ƒlas dos) both of them
un bocado de a mouthful of
un bote de a jar of; a tin or can of
una botella de a bottle of
un botellín (de cerveza) a small bottle (of beer)
una caja de a box of
(gran) cantidad de lots of
una caña (de cerveza) a small glass of beer
cien gramos de a hundred grammes of
un centenar de (about) a hundred
un cuarto de a quarter of
tres cuartos de three quarters of
una cucharada de a spoonful of
una docena de (about) a dozen
un grupo de a group of
una jarra de a jug of; a mug of (beer)
un kilo de a kilo of
un litro de a litre of
la mayoría (de), la mayor parte (de) most (of)
media docena de half a dozen
medio litro de half a litre of
una loncha de jamón a slice of ham
un metro de a metre of
miles de thousands of

USEFUL PHRASES

la mitad de **half of**
un montón de **a pile of**
mucho(a) **a lot of, much**
muchos (*f* muchas) **a lot of, many**
multitud de, montones de **loads of**
un paquete de **a packet of**
un par de **a pair of**
un plato de **a plate of**
un poco de **a little; some**
una porción de **a portion of**
un puñado de **a handful of**
una rebanada de pan **a slice of bread**
un rebaño de **a herd of** (*cattle*); **a flock of** (*sheep*)
una rodaja de merluza **a slice of hake**
un sobre de sopa **a packet of soup**
una taza de **a cup of**
un tazón de **a bowl of**
un terrón de azúcar **a lump of sugar**
un tonel de **a barrel of**
un trozo de papel/pastel **a piece of paper/cake**
a unos metros de **a few metres from**
un vaso de **a glass of**
varios **several**
a varios kilómetros de **a few kilometres from**

ESSENTIAL WORDS *(masculine)*

el	anillo	ring
el	cepillo	brush
el	cepillo de dientes	toothbrush
el	champú	shampoo
el	desodorante	deodorant
el	espejo	mirror
el	maquillaje	make-up
el	peine	comb
el	perfume	perfume
el	reloj	watch

USEFUL WORDS *(masculine)*

el	aftershave	aftershave
el	broche	brooch
el	colgante	pendant
el	collar	necklace
el	dentífrico	toothpaste
el	diamante	diamond
los	efectos personales	personal effects
el	esmalte (de uñas)	nail varnish
el	gemelo	cufflink
el	kleenex® (pl inv)	tissue
el	lápiz de labios (pl lápices ~ ~)	lipstick
el	llavero	key-ring
el	maquillaje	make-up
el	neceser	toilet bag
el	papel higiénico	toilet paper
el	peinado	hairstyle
el	pendiente	earring
los	polvos compactos	face powder
los	polvos para la cara	face powder
el	quitaesmalte	nail varnish remover
el	rímel	mascara
el	rulo	roller
el	secador	hairdryer

ESSENTIAL WORDS (feminine)

el	agua de colonia (f)	eau de toilette
la	cadena	chain
la	crema para la cara	face cream
la	cuchilla de afeitar	razor
la	joya	jewel
la	maquinilla de afeitar	(safety) razor
la	pasta de dientes	toothpaste
la	pulsera	bracelet

USEFUL WORDS (feminine)

la	alianza	wedding ring
la	base de maquillaje	foundation
la	brocha de afeitar	shaving brush
la	crema de afeitar	shaving cream
la	esponja	sponge
la	espuma de afeitar	shaving foam
la	manicura	manicure
la	perla	pearl
la	polvera	(powder) compact
la	sombra de ojos	eye shadow

USEFUL PHRASES

maquillarse to put on one's make-up
desmaquillarse to take off one's make-up
hacerse un peinado to do one's hair
peinarse to comb one's hair
cepillarse el pelo to brush one's hair
afeitarse to shave
lavarse los dientes, limpiarse los dientes to clean or brush one's teeth

ESSENTIAL WORDS *(masculine)*

el	**árbol**	tree
el	**césped**	lawn
el	**jardín** (*pl* jardines)	garden
el	**jardinero**	gardener
el	**sol**	sun

IMPORTANT WORDS *(masculine)*

el	**arbusto**	bush
el	**banco**	bench
el	**camino**	path
el	**cultivo**	cultivation; crop
el	**ramo de flores**	bunch of flowers

USEFUL PHRASES

plantar **to plant**
quitar las malas hierbas, desherbar **to weed**
regalar a algn un ramo de flores **to give sb a bunch of flowers**
cortar el césped **to mow the lawn**
"no pisar el césped" **"keep off the grass"**
a mi padre le gusta la jardinería **my father likes gardening**

ESSENTIAL WORDS *(feminine)*

la	flor	flower
la	hierba	grass
la	hoja	leaf
la	jardinera	gardener; flower bed
la	jardinería	gardening
la	lluvia	rain
la	planta	plant
la	rama	branch
la	rosa	rose
la	tierra	land; soil; ground
las	verduras	vegetables

IMPORTANT WORDS *(feminine)*

la	abeja	bee
la	avispa	wasp
las	malas hierbas	weeds
la	raíz (*pl* raíces)	root
la	sombra	shade; shadow
la	valla	fence
la	verja	gate

USEFUL PHRASES

las flores están creciendo **the flowers are growing**
en el suelo **on the ground**
regar las plantas **to water the flowers**
coger flores **to pick flowers**
irse a la sombra **to go into the shade**
quedarse en la sombra **to remain in the shade**
a la sombra de un árbol **in the shade of a tree**

USEFUL WORDS (*masculine*)

el	**arriate**	flowerbed
el	**azafrán** (*pl* azafranes)	crocus
el	**brote**	bud
el	**clavel**	carnation
el	**cortacésped**	lawnmower
el	**crisantemo**	chrysanthemum
el	**diente de león**	dandelion
el	**estanque**	(ornamental) pool
el	**follaje**	leaves
el	**girasol**	sunflower
el	**gusano**	worm
el	**huerto**	vegetable garden
el	**invernadero**	greenhouse
el	**invierno**	winter
el	**jacinto**	hyacinth
el	**lirio**	lily
el	**lirio del valle**	lily of the valley
el	**narciso**	daffodil
el	**otoño**	autumn, fall
el	**parterre**	flowerbed
el	**pensamiento**	pansy
el	**ranúnculo**	buttercup
el	**rocío**	dew
el	**rosal**	rose bush
el	**sendero**	path
el	**seto**	hedge
el	**suelo**	ground; soil
el	**tallo**	stalk
el	**tronco**	trunk (*of tree*)
el	**tulipán** (*pl* tulipanes)	tulip
el	**verano**	summer

USEFUL WORDS (feminine)

la	amapola	poppy
la	baya	berry
la	campanilla	campanula, bellflower
la	campanilla de invierno	snowdrop
la	carretilla	wheelbarrow
la	cerca	fence
la	cosecha	crop
la	espina	thorn
la	herramienta	tool
la	hiedra	ivy
la	hortensia	hydrangea
las	lilas	lilac
la	madreselva	honeysuckle
la	manguera	hose
la	margarita	daisy
la	mariposa	butterfly
la	orquídea	orchid
la	peonía	peony
la	primavera	spring; primrose
la	regadera	watering can
la	semilla	seed
la	violeta	violet

ESSENTIAL WORDS (*masculine*)

los	anteojos de sol (*LAm*)	sunglasses
el	bañador	swimming trunks; swimsuit
el	bañista	swimmer
el	barco	boat; ship
el	barco de pesca	fishing boat
el	bikini	bikini
el	bote	boat
el	mar	sea
el	muelle	quay
el	paseo	walk
el	pescador	fisherman
el	pesquero	fishing boat
el	picnic (*pl* ~s)	picnic
el	puerto	port, harbour
el	puerto deportivo	marina
el	remo	rowing; oar
el	traje de baño	swimming trunks; swimsuit

IMPORTANT WORDS (*masculine*)

el	cangrejo	crab
el	castillo de arena	sandcastle
el	fondo	bottom
el	horizonte	horizon
el	mareo	seasickness
el	veraneante	holiday-maker

USEFUL PHRASES

en la playa **at the seaside; at** *or* **on the beach**
en el horizonte **on the horizon**
está mareado **he is seasick**
nadar **to swim**
ahogarse **to drown**
me voy a dar un baño **I'm going for a swim**
tirarse al agua, zambullirse **to dive into the water**
flotar **to float**

ESSENTIAL WORDS *(feminine)*

el	**agua** (*f*)	water
la	**arena**	sand
la	**bañista**	swimmer
la	**barca**	boat
la	**costa**	coast
las	**gafas de sol** (*Sp*)	sunglasses
la	**isla**	island
la	**natación**	swimming
la	**pescadora**	fisherwoman
la	**piedra**	stone
la	**playa**	beach; seaside
las	**quemaduras de sol**	sunburn
la	**toalla**	towel

IMPORTANT WORDS *(feminine)*

la	**colchoneta inflable**	airbed, lilo
la	**crema (de protección) solar**	suncream
la	**tabla de windsurf**	windsurfing board
la	**travesía**	crossing
la	**tumbona**	deckchair
la	**veraneante**	holiday-maker

USEFUL PHRASES

en el fondo del mar **at the bottom of the sea**
hacer la travesía en barco **to go across by boat**
broncearse, ponerse moreno(a) **to get a tan**
estar moreno(a) **to be tanned**
sabe nadar **he can swim**

USEFUL WORDS (*masculine*)

el	acantilado	cliff
el	aire de mar	sea air
el	balde	bucket
el	(barco de) vapor	steamer
los	binoculares	binoculars
el	bote de pedales	pedalo
el	cabo	headland
el	crucero	cruise
el	cubo	bucket
el	embarcadero	pier
el	estuario	estuary
el	faro	lighthouse
el	guijarro	pebble
el	marinero	sailor
el	marino	sailor; naval officer
el	mástil	mast
el	naufragio	shipwreck
los	náufragos	shipwrecked people, castaways
el	océano	ocean
el	oleaje	swell
el	pedal (*Sp*)	pedalo
los	prismáticos	binoculars
el	puente (de mando)	bridge (*of ship*)
los	restos de un naufragio	wreckage
el	salvavidas (*pl inv*)	lifeguard; lifebelt
el	socorrista	lifeguard
el	timón (*pl* timones)	rudder
el	transbordador	ferry

USEFUL WORDS *(feminine)*

las	**algas**	seaweed
el	**ancla** *(pl f* las **anclas)**	anchor
la	**bahía**	bay
la	**balsa**	raft
la	**bandera**	flag
la	**barca**	small boat
la	**boya**	buoy
la	**brisa marina**	sea breeze
la	**carga**	cargo
la	**concha**	shell
la	**corriente**	current
la	**desembocadura**	mouth *(of river)*
la	**espuma**	foam
la	**gaviota**	seagull
la	**insolación** *(pl* insolaciones)	sunstroke
la	**marea**	tide
la	**marina**	navy
la	**marinera**	sailor
la	**marina**	sailor; naval officer
la	**nave**	vessel
la	**ola**	wave
la	**orilla**	shore
la	**pala**	spade
la	**pasarela**	gangway
la	**ría**	estuary
la	**roca**	rock
la	**salvavidas** *(pl inv) or* **socorrista**	lifeguard
la	**sombrilla**	parasol
la	**tripulación** *(pl* tripulaciones)	crew
la	**vela**	sail; sailing

USEFUL PHRASES

tuve una insolación I had sunstroke
con la marea baja/alta at low/high tide
hacer vela to go sailing

ESSENTIAL WORDS (*masculine*)

el	banco	bank
el	billete (de banco)	banknote
el	cambio	change
el	céntimo	cent
el	centro comercial	shopping centre
el	cheque	cheque
el	cliente	customer
el	departamento	department
el	dependiente	shop assistant, sales assistant
el	descuento	discount
el	dinero	money
el	estanco	tobacconist's
el	euro	euro
los	grandes almacenes	department store
el	hipermercado	hypermarket
el	mercado	market
el	número (de zapato)	(shoe) size
el	precio	price
el	regalo	present
el	souvenir (*pl* ~s)	souvenir
el	supermercado	supermarket
el	talonario de cheques	cheque book
el	vendedor	salesman

USEFUL PHRASES

comprar/vender to buy/sell

¿cuánto cuesta? how much does it cost?

¿cuánto es? how much does it come to?

pagué veinte euros por esto, esto me costó veinte euros I paid 20 euros for that

en la carnicería/la panadería at the butcher's/bakery

ESSENTIAL WORDS (feminine)

la	agencia de viajes	travel agent's
la	alimentación	food
la	caja	checkout; cash desk
la	carnicería	butcher's
la	charcutería	pork butcher's
la	clienta	customer
la	compra	purchase
la	dependienta	shop assistant, sales assistant
la	farmacia	chemist's
la	floristería	flower shop
la	frutería	fruiterer's
la	lista	list
la	oficina de correos	post office
la	panadería	bakery
la	pastelería	cake shop
la	perfumería	perfume shop/department
la	pescadería	fishmonger's
la	rebaja	reduction
las	rebajas	sales
la	sección (pl secciones)	department
la	talla	size
la	tarjeta de crédito	credit card
la	tarjeta de débito	debit card
la	tienda	shop
la	tienda de alimentación or de comestibles	grocer's
la	vendedora	saleswoman
la	verdulería	greengrocer's
la	zapatería	shoe shop

IMPORTANT WORDS *(masculine)*

el	artículo	article
el	carnicero	butcher
el	charcutero	pork butcher
el	comerciante	shopkeeper
el	comercio	trade; shop
el	comercio justo	fair trade
el	encargado	manager
el	frutero	fruiterer
el	mercadillo	street market
el	monedero	purse
el	mostrador	counter
el	panadero	baker
el	pastelero	confectioner
el	peluquero	hairdresser
el	pescadero	fishmonger
el	rastro (*Sp*)	flea market
el	recibo	receipt
el	tícket (*pl* ~s)	receipt; ticket
el	vendedor de periódicos	newsagent
el	verdulero	greengrocer
el	zapatero	cobbler

USEFUL PHRASES

sólo estoy mirando I'm just looking
es demasiado caro it's too expensive
algo más barato something cheaper
es barato it's cheap
"pague en caja" "pay at the checkout"
¿lo quiere para regalo? would you like it gift-wrapped?
debe de haber un error there must be some mistake

IMPORTANT WORDS *(feminine)*

la **biblioteca**	library
la **boutique**	boutique
la **calculadora**	calculator
la **carnicera**	butcher
la **cartera**	wallet; purse; *(LAm)* handbag
la **charcutera**	pork butcher
la **comerciante**	shopkeeper
la **encargada**	manager
la **escalera mecánica**	escalator
la **frutera**	fruiterer
la **librería**	bookshop
la **marca**	brand
la **panadera**	baker
la **pastelera**	confectioner
la **peluquera**	hairdresser
la **pescadera**	fishmonger
la **promoción** *(pl* promociones)	special offer
la **reclamación** *(pl* reclamaciones)	complaint
la **tintorería**	dry-cleaner's
la **vendedora de periódicos**	newsagent
la **verdulera**	greengrocer
la **vitrina**	display case; *(LAm)* shop window

USEFUL PHRASES

¿algo más? **anything else?**
S.A. (= *Sociedad Anónima*) Ltd
S.L. (= *Sociedad Limitada*) limited liability company
y Cía & Co
"de venta aquí" "on sale here"
un coche de ocasión a used car
en oferta, de oferta on special offer
el café de comercio justo fair-trade coffee

USEFUL WORDS *(masculine)*

el	agente inmobiliario	estate agent
el	color	colour
el	escaparate	shop window
el	ferretero	ironmonger
el	gerente	manager
el	joyero	jeweller; jewellery box
el	librero	bookseller
el	óptico	optician
el	producto	product
los	productos	produce
el	recado	errand
el	relojero	watchmaker; clockmaker
el	tendero	grocer
el	trato	deal
el	videoclub *(pl ~s)*	video shop

USEFUL PHRASES

ir a ver escaparates, ir de escaparates **to go window shopping**
horario **opening hours**
pagar en metálico **to pay cash**
pagar con un cheque **to pay by cheque**
pagar con tarjeta de crédito **to pay by credit card**

USEFUL WORDS *(feminine)*

la	**agencia de viajes**	travel agent's
la	**agencia inmobiliaria**	estate agent's
la	**agente inmobiliario**	estate agent
la	**caja de ahorros**	savings bank
la	**cola**	queue
la	**compra**	purchase; shopping
las	**compras**	shopping
la	**confitería**	sweetshop
la	**droguería**	hardware shop
la	**ferretera**	ironmonger
la	**ferretería**	ironmonger's
la	**gerente**	manager
la	**joyera**	jeweller
la	**joyería**	jeweller's
la	**lavandería**	laundry
la	**librería**	bookseller
la	**mercancía**	goods
la	**óptica**	optician; optician's
la	**papelería**	stationer's
la	**rebaja**	discount
la	**relojera**	watchmaker; clockmaker
la	**relojería**	watchmaker's; clockmaker's
la	**sucursal**	branch
la	**talla de cuello**	collar size
la	**tendera**	grocer
la	**venta**	sale

USEFUL PHRASES

en el escaparate in the window
ir de compras to go shopping
hacer la compra to do the shopping
gastar to spend

ESSENTIAL WORDS *(masculine)*

el	**aerobic**	aerobics
el	**ajedrez**	chess
el	**arco** *(LAm)*	goal
el	**balón** *(pl* balones)	ball *(large)*
el	**baloncesto**	basketball
el	**balonvolea**	volleyball
el	**billar**	billiards
el	**campeón** *(pl* campeones)	champion
el	**campeonato**	championship
el	**campo**	field, *(football)* pitch; *(golf)* course; *(basketball)* court
el	**ciclismo**	cycling
el	**críket**	cricket
el	**deporte**	sport
el	**equipo**	team
el	**esquí**	skiing; ski
el	**esquí acuático**	water skiing
el	**estadio**	stadium
el	**fútbol**	football
el	**gimnasta**	gymnast
el	**golf**	golf
el	**hockey**	hockey
el	**juego**	game; play
el	**jugador**	player
el	**partido**	match, game
el	**paseo**	walk
el	**resultado**	result
el	**rugby**	rugby
el	**tenis**	tennis

USEFUL PHRASES

jugar al fútbol/tenis **to play football/tennis**
marcar un gol/un punto **to score a goal/a point**
llevar la cuenta de los tantos **to keep the score**
el campeón/la campeona del mundo **the world champion**
ganar/perder un partido **to win/lose a match**
mi deporte preferido **my favourite sport**

ESSENTIAL WORDS (feminine)

la	campeona	champion
la	cancha	(basketball/tennis) court; (LAm) field, (football) pitch
la	cancha de tenis (LAm)	tennis court
la	equitación	horse-riding
la	gimnasia	gymnastics
la	gimnasta	gymnast
la	jugadora	player
la	natación	swimming
la	partida	game (chess etc)
la	pelota	ball
la	pesca	fishing
la	piscina	swimming pool
la	pista	track
la	pista de tenis (Sp)	tennis court
la	portería	goal
la	tabla de windsurf	windsurfing board
la	vela	sailing; sail

USEFUL PHRASES

empatar to equalize; to draw
correr to run; saltar to jump; lanzar to throw
ganar or derrotar or vencer a algn to beat sb
entrenarse to train
el Liverpool gana por 2 a 1 Liverpool is leading by 2 goals to 1
un partido de tenis a game of tennis
es socio de un club he belongs to a club
ir de pesca to go fishing
ir a la piscina to go to the swimming pool
¿sabes nadar? can you swim?
hacer deporte to do sport
montar en bicicleta or hacer ciclismo to go cycling
hacer vela to go sailing
hacer footing/alpinismo to go jogging/climbing
patín de cuchilla/de ruedas/en línea (ice) skate/roller skate/Rollerblade®
tiro al arco/al blanco archery/target practice

IMPORTANT WORDS (*masculine*)

los	**bolos**	skittles
el	**encuentro**	match

USEFUL WORDS (*masculine*)

el	**adversario**	opponent
el	**alpinismo**	mountaineering
el	**árbitro**	referee; umpire (*tennis*)
el	**atletismo**	athletics
el	**bádminton**	badminton
el	**boxeo**	boxing
el	**buceo**	diving
el	**chándal**	tracksuit
el	**cronómetro**	stopwatch
el	**descanso**	half-time
el	**entrenador**	trainer; coach
el	**espectador**	spectator
el	**footing**	jogging
el	**ganador**	winner
el	**gol**	goal
el	**hipódromo**	race course
los	**Juegos Olímpicos**	Olympic Games
el	**Mundial (de Fútbol)**	World Cup
el	**parapente**	paragliding
el	**patín**	skate
el	**patinaje sobre hielo**	(ice) skating
el	**perdedor**	loser
el	**portero**	goalkeeper
el	**principiante**	beginner
el	**remo**	rowing; oar
el	**resultado**	score
el	**salto de altura**	high jump
el	**salto de longitud**	long jump
el	**squash**	squash
el	**tanto**	goal; point
el	**tiro**	shooting
el	**torneo**	tournament
el	**trineo**	sledge

IMPORTANT WORDS (feminine)

la	bola	ball (small)
la	carrera	race
las	carreras (de caballos)	horse-racing
la	defensa	defence
la	petanca	pétanque
la	pista de esquí	ski slope

USEFUL WORDS (feminine)

la	adversaria	opponent
la	árbitra	referee; umpire (tennis)
la	camiseta (de deporte)	jersey, shirt
la	caña de pescar	fishing rod
la	caza	hunting
la	copa	cup
la	Copa del Mundo	World Cup
la	eliminatoria	heat
la	entrenadora	trainer, coach
la	esgrima	fencing
la	espectadora	spectator
la	estación de esquí (pl estaciones de ~)	ski resort
la	etapa	stage
la	final	final
la	ganadora	winner
la	jabalina	javelin
la	lucha libre	wrestling
la	perdedora	loser
la	pesca	fishing
la	pista de hielo	ice rink
la	pista de patinaje	skating rink
la	portera	goalkeeper
la	principiante	beginner
la	prórroga	extra time
la	raqueta	racket
la	red	net
la	tribuna	stand
las	zapatillas de deporte	sports shoes; trainers
las	zapatillas de tenis	tennis shoes

ESSENTIAL WORDS (*masculine*)

el	**actor**	actor
el	**ambiente**	atmosphere
el	**anfiteatro**	dress circle
el	**asiento**	seat
el	**auditorio**	auditorium; audience
el	**boleto** (*LAm*)	ticket
el	**cine**	cinema
el	**circo**	circus
el	**cómico**	comedian
el	**espectáculo**	show
el	**patio de butacas**	stalls
el	**payaso**	clown
el	**programa**	programme
el	**público**	audience
el	**teatro**	theatre
el	**vestuario**	costume
el	**videoclip** (*pl* ~s)	music video
el	**western** (*pl* ~s)	western

IMPORTANT WORDS (*masculine*)

el	**acomodador**	usher
el	**actor principal**	leading man
el	**ballet** (*pl* ~s)	ballet
el	**cartel**	notice; poster
el	**director**	director
el	**entreacto**	interval
el	**intermedio**	interval
el	**maquillaje**	make-up

USEFUL PHRASES

ir al teatro/al cine **to go to the theatre/to the cinema**
reservar un asiento **to book a seat**
un asiento en el patio de butacas **a seat in the stalls**
mi actor preferido/actriz preferida **my favourite actor/actress**
durante el intermedio **during the interval**
salir a escena **to come on stage**
interpretar el papel de **to play the part of**

ESSENTIAL WORDS (feminine)

la	actriz (pl actrices)	actress
la	banda sonora	soundtrack
la	boletería (LAm)	box office
la	cómica	comedian
la	cortina	curtain
la	entrada	ticket
la	estrella de cine	film star
la	música	music
la	obra (de teatro)	play
la	ópera	opera
la	orquesta	orchestra
la	payasa	clown
la	película	film
la	sala	auditorium; cinema
la	salida	exit
la	sesión (pl sesiones)	performance; showing
la	taquilla	box office

USEFUL PHRASES

interpretar to play
bailar to dance
cantar to sing
filmar una película to shoot a film
"próxima sesión: 21 horas" "next showing: 9 p.m."
"versión original" "original version"
"subtitulada" "subtitled"
"localidades agotadas" "full house"
aplaudir to clap
¡bis! encore!
¡bravo! bravo!
una película de ciencia ficción/de amor a science fiction film/a romance
una película de aventuras/de terror an adventure/horror film

IMPORTANT WORDS (*masculine continued*)

el **primer actor**	leading man
el **protagonista**	star
el **subtítulo**	subtitle
el **título**	title

USEFUL WORDS (*masculine*)

el **anfiteatro**	circle
los **aplausos**	applause
el **apuntador**	prompter
el **argumento**	plot
los **bastidores**	wings
el **crítico**	critic
el **culebrón** (*pl* culebrones)	soap (opera)
el **decorado**	scenery
el **director de escena**	producer; stage manager
el **dramaturgo**	playwright
el **ensayo (general)**	(dress) rehearsal
el **escenario**	stage; scene
el **espectador**	member of the audience
el **estrado**	platform
el **estreno**	first night, premiere
el **foco**	spotlight
el **foso de la orquesta**	orchestra pit
el **gallinero**	the "gods"
el **guardarropa**	cloakroom
el **guión** (*pl* guiones)	script
el **guionista**	scriptwriter
el **musical**	musical
el **palco**	box
el **papel**	part
el **personaje**	character
el **productor**	producer
el **realizador**	director (*cinema*); producer (*TV*)
el **regidor**	stage manager
el **reparto**	cast
el **serial**	serial
el **vestíbulo**	foyer

IMPORTANT WORDS *(feminine)*

la	**acomodadora**	usherette
la	**actriz principal** (*pl* actrices ~es)	leading lady
la	**butaca**	seat
la	**cartelera**	hoarding, billboard; listings section
la	**comedia**	comedy
la	**directora**	director
la	**platea**	stalls
la	**primera actriz** (*pl* ~s actrices)	leading lady
la	**propina**	tip
la	**protagonista**	star
la	**reserva**	booking

USEFUL WORDS *(feminine)*

la	**actuación** (*pl* actuaciones)	acting, performance
la	**apuntadora**	prompter
las	**candilejas**	footlights
la	**crítica**	review; critics; critic
la	**directora de escena**	producer; stage manager
la	**dramaturga**	playwright
la	**escena**	scene
la	**escenografía**	scenery
la	**espectadora**	member of the audience
la	**farsa**	farce
la	**función** (*pl* funciones)	performance
la	**guionista**	scriptwriter
la	**pantalla**	screen
la	**platea**	stalls
la	**productora**	producer
la	**puesta en escena**	production
la	**realizadora**	director (*cinema*); producer (*TV*)
la	**regidora**	stage manager
la	**representación** (*pl* representaciones)	performance
la	**serie**	series
la	**tragedia**	tragedy

ESSENTIAL WORDS *(masculine)*

el	**año**	year
el	**cuarto de hora**	quarter of an hour
el	**despertador**	alarm clock
el	**día**	day
el	**fin de semana**	weekend
el	**instante**	moment
el	**mes**	month
el	**minuto**	minute
el	**momento**	moment
el	**reloj**	watch; clock
el	**segundo**	second
el	**siglo**	century
el	**tiempo**	time

USEFUL PHRASES

a mediodía at midday
a medianoche at midnight
pasado mañana the day after tomorrow
hoy today
hoy en día nowadays
anteayer, antes de ayer the day before yesterday
mañana tomorrow
ayer yesterday
hace dos días 2 days ago
dentro de dos días in 2 days
una semana a week
una quincena a fortnight
todos los días every day
¿a qué día estamos?, ¿qué día es hoy? what day is it?
¿cuál es la fecha de hoy? what's the date?
de momento at the moment
las tres menos cuarto a quarter to 3
las tres y cuarto a quarter past 3
en el siglo XXI in the 21st century
ayer por la noche last night, yesterday evening

ESSENTIAL WORDS *(feminine)*

la	**hora**	hour; time (*in general*)
la	**jornada**	day
la	**mañana**	morning
la	**media hora**	half an hour
la	**noche**	night; evening
la	**quincena**	fortnight
la	**semana**	week
la	**tarde**	afternoon; evening

USEFUL PHRASES

el año pasado/próximo last/next year
la semana/el año que viene next week/year
dentro de media hora in half an hour
una vez once
dos/tres veces two/three times
varias veces several times
tres veces al año three times a year
nueve de cada diez veces nine times out of ten
érase una vez once upon a time there was
diez a la vez ten at a time
¿qué hora es? what time is it?
¿tiene hora? have you got the time?
son las seis/las seis menos diez/las seis y media it is 6 o'clock/10 to 6/
  half past 6
son las dos en punto it is 2 o'clock exactly
hace un rato a while ago
dentro de un rato in a while
temprano early
tarde late
esta noche (*past*) last night; (*to come*) tonight

IMPORTANT WORDS (*masculine*)

el	**día siguiente**	next day
el	**futuro**	future; future tense
el	**pasado**	past; past tense
el	**presente**	present (*time*); present tense
el	**retraso**	delay

USEFUL WORDS (*masculine*)

el	**año bisiesto**	leap year
el	**calendario**	calendar
el	**cronómetro**	stopwatch
el	**reloj de pie**	grandfather clock
el	**reloj de pulsera**	wristwatch

USEFUL PHRASES

pasado mañana **the day after tomorrow**
dos días después **two days later**
el día antes *or* el día anterior **the day before**
un día sí y otro no **every other day**
en el futuro **in the future**
un día libre **a day off**
un día de fiesta **a public holiday**
un día laborable **a weekday**
en un día de lluvia, en un día lluvioso **on a rainy day**
al amanecer, al alba **at dawn**
la mañana/tarde siguiente **the following morning/evening**
ahora **now**

USEFUL WORDS (*feminine*)

las	**agujas**	hands (*of clock*)
la	**década**	decade
la	**Edad Media**	Middle Ages
la	**época**	time; era
la	**esfera**	face (*of clock*)
las	**manecillas**	hands (*of clock*)

USEFUL PHRASES

llegas tarde **you are late**
llegas temprano **you are early**
este reloj adelanta/atrasa **this watch is fast/slow**
llegar a tiempo, llegar a la hora **to arrive on time**
¿cuánto tiempo? **how long?**
el tercer milenio **the third millennium**
no levantarse hasta tarde **to have a lie-in**
de un momento a otro **any minute now**
dentro de una semana **in a week's time**
el lunes que viene no el otro **a week on Monday**
la noche antes, la noche anterior **the night before**
en esa época **at that time**

ESSENTIAL WORDS *(masculine)*

el	**bricolaje**	DIY
el	**manitas** *(pl inv)*	handyman
el	**taller**	workshop

USEFUL WORDS *(masculine)*

el	**alambre (de espino)**	(barbed) wire
los	**alicates**	pliers
el	**andamio**	scaffolding
el	**candado**	padlock
el	**celo** *(Sp)*	Sellotape®
el	**chinche** *(LAm)*	drawing pin
el	**cincel**	chisel
el	**clavo**	nail
el	**destornillador**	screwdriver
el	**durex®** *(LAm)*	Sellotape®
el	**martillo**	hammer
el	**muelle**	spring
el	**pico**	pickaxe
el	**pincel**	paintbrush
el	**taladro**	drill
el	**tornillo**	screw

USEFUL PHRASES

hacer bricolaje, hacer chapuzas **to do odd jobs**
clavar un clavo con el martillo **to hammer in a nail**
"recién pintado(a)" **"wet paint"**
pintar **to paint**
empapelar **to wallpaper**

ESSENTIAL WORDS (feminine)

la	**cuerda**	rope
la	**herramienta**	tool
la	**llave**	key; (LAm) tap
la	**llave inglesa**	spanner
la	**manitas** (pl inv)	handywoman
la	**máquina**	machine

USEFUL WORDS (feminine)

la	**aguja**	needle
la	**batería**	battery (in car)
la	**caja de herramientas**	toolbox
la	**cerradura**	lock
la	**chinche** (LAm)	drawing pin
la	**chincheta** (Sp)	drawing pin
la	**cola**	glue
la	**escalera (de mano)**	ladder
la	**goma (elástica)**	rubber band
la	**horca**	(garden) fork
la	**lima**	file
la	**obra**	construction site
la	**pala**	spade
la	**pila**	battery (in radio etc)
la	**sierra**	saw
la	**tabla**	plank
la	**taladradora**	pneumatic drill
las	**tijeras**	scissors

USEFUL PHRASES

"prohibido el paso a la obra" "construction site: keep out"
práctico(a) handy
cortar to cut
reparar to mend
atornillar to screw (in)
desatornillar to unscrew

ESSENTIAL WORDS *(masculine)*

los	**alrededores**	surroundings
el	**aparcamiento** (*Sp*)	car park; parking space
el	**autobús** (*pl* autobuses)	bus
el	**ayuntamiento**	town hall; town council
el	**banco**	bank; bench
el	**barrio**	district
el	**bloque de departamentos** (*LAm*)	block of flats
el	**bloque de pisos** (*Sp*)	block of flats
el	**café**	café; coffee
el	**carro** (*LAm*)	car
el	**centro de la ciudad**	town centre
el	**cine**	cinema
el	**coche** (*Sp*)	car
el	**edificio**	building
el	**estacionamiento** (*LAm*)	car park; parking space
el	**habitante**	inhabitant
el	**hotel**	hotel
el	**mercado**	market
el	**metro**	underground, subway
el	**museo**	museum; art gallery
el	**parking** (*pl* ~s)	car park
el	**parque**	park
el	**peatón** (*pl* peatones)	pedestrian
el	**policía**	policeman
el	**puente**	bridge
el	**restaurante**	restaurant
el	**suburbio**	suburb; slum area
el	**taxi**	taxi
el	**teatro**	theatre
el	**tour** (*pl* ~s)	tour
el	**turista**	tourist

ESSENTIAL WORDS *(feminine)*

la **boutique**	boutique
la **calle**	street
la **carretera**	road
la **catedral**	cathedral
la **ciudad**	town, city
la **comisaría**	police station
la **contaminación**	air pollution
la **esquina**	corner
la **estación (de trenes)**	(train) station
(*pl* estaciones (~~))	
la **estación de autobuses**	bus station
(*pl* estaciones ~~)	
la **fábrica**	factory
la **gasolinera**	petrol station
la **habitante**	inhabitant
la **lavandería automática**	launderette
la **oficina**	office
la **oficina de correos**	post office
la **parada de autobús**	bus stop
la **parada de taxis**	taxi rank
la **piscina**	swimming pool
la **plaza**	square
la **policía**	policewoman; police
la **tienda**	shop
la **torre**	tower
la **turista**	tourist
la **vista**	view
la **vivienda de protección oficial**	council flat

USEFUL PHRASES

voy a la ciudad *or* al centro I'm going into town
en el centro (de la ciudad) in the town centre
en la plaza in the square
una calle de sentido único a one-way street
una zona muy urbanizada a built-up area
"dirección prohibida" "no entry"
cruzar la calle to cross the road

IMPORTANT WORDS *(masculine)*

el	**abono**	season ticket
el	**agente (de policía)**	police officer
el	**alcalde**	mayor
el	**atasco**	traffic jam
el	**cartel**	notice; poster
el	**castillo**	castle
el	**cibercafé**	internet café
el	**cruce**	crossroads
los	**jardines públicos**	park
el	**lugar**	place
el	**monumento**	monument
el	**parquímetro**	parking meter
el	**quiosco de periódicos**	news stand
el	**semáforo**	traffic lights
el	**sitio**	place
el	**tráfico**	traffic
el	**transeúnte**	passer-by
el	**zoológico**	zoo

USEFUL PHRASES

en la esquina de la calle at the corner of the street
vivir en las afueras to live in the outskirts
andar, caminar to walk
tomar el autobús/el metro, coger el autobús/el metro *(Sp)* to take the
   bus/the underground
comprar una tarjeta multiviajes to buy a multiple-journey ticket
picar to punch *(ticket)*

IMPORTANT WORDS *(feminine)*

la	**acera**	pavement
la	**agente (de policía)**	police officer
la	**alcaldesa**	mayor
la	**biblioteca**	library
la	**calle principal**	main street
la	**calzada**	road
la	**circulación**	traffic
la	**desviación** (*pl* desviaciones)	diversion
la	**estación de servicio** (*pl* estaciones ~~)	petrol station
la	**iglesia**	church
la	**máquina expendedora de billetes** (*Sp*) *or* **de boletos** (*LAm*)	ticket machine
la	**mezquita**	mosque
la	**parte antigua**	old town
la	**polución**	air pollution
la	**sinagoga**	synagogue
la	**tarjeta multiviajes**	multiple-journey ticket
la	**transeúnte**	passer-by
la	**zona azul**	restricted parking zone
la	**zona industrial**	industrial estate
la	**zona peatonal**	pedestrian precinct

USEFUL PHRASES

industrial **industrial**
histórico(a) **historic**
bonito(a) **pretty**
feo(a) **ugly**
limpio(a) **clean**
sucio(a) **dirty**

USEFUL WORDS *(masculine)*

el	**adoquín** (*pl* adoquines)	cobblestone
el	**barrio residencial**	residential area
el	**callejón sin salida** (*pl* callejones ~~)	cul-de-sac, dead end
el	**camino de bicicletas**	cycle path
el	**carril bici**	cycle lane
el	**cementerio**	cemetery
el	**ciudadano**	citizen
el	**cochecito (de niño)**	pram, buggy
el	**concejo municipal**	town council
el	**desfile**	parade
el	**distrito**	district
el	**edificio**	building
el	**embotellamiento**	traffic jam
el	**folleto**	leaflet
los	**lugares de interés**	sights, places of interest
el	**paradero de autobús** (*LAm*)	bus stop
el	**parque de bomberos** (*Sp*)	fire station
el	**paso de cebra**	zebra crossing
el	**paso de peatones**	pedestrian crossing
el	**pavimento**	road surface
el	**rascacielos** (*pl inv*)	skyscraper
el	**sondeo de opinión**	opinion poll

USEFUL WORDS (feminine)

las	afueras	outskirts
la	alcantarilla	sewer
la	cafetería	coffee shop, café; canteen
la	calle sin salida	cul-de-sac, dead end
la	camioneta de reparto	delivery van
la	cárcel	prison
la	ciudadana	citizen
la	cola	queue
la	ciudad universitaria	university campus
la	curva	bend
la	estación de bomberos (pl estaciones ~ ~) (LAm)	fire station
la	estatua	statue
la	farola	street lamp
la	flecha	arrow
la	galería de arte	art gallery
la	isla peatonal	traffic island
la	muchedumbre	crowd
la	multitud	crowd
la	muralla	rampart
la	parada de autobús	bus stop
la	población (pl poblaciones)	population
la	señal de tráfico	road sign

ESSENTIAL WORDS *(masculine)*

el	**andén** *(pl* andenes)	platform
el	**asiento**	seat
el	**AVE**	high-speed train
el	**billete** *(Sp)*	ticket
el	**billete de ida** *(Sp)*	single ticket
el	**billete de ida y vuelta** *(Sp)*	return ticket
el	**billete sencillo** *(Sp)*	single ticket
el	**boleto** *(LAm)*	ticket
el	**boleto de ida** *(LAm)*	single ticket
el	**boleto de ida y vuelta** *(LAm)*	return ticket
el	**bolso** *(Sp)*	handbag
el	**compartimento**	compartment
el	**descuento**	reduction
el	**enlace**	connection
el	**equipaje**	luggage
el	**expreso**	fast train
el	**freno**	brake
el	**horario**	timetable
el	**maletero**	porter
el	**metro**	underground, subway
el	**número**	number
el	**oficial de aduanas**	customs officer
el	**pasaporte**	passport
el	**plano**	map
el	**precio del billete** *(Sp)* or del boleto *(LAm)*	fare
el	**puente**	bridge
el	**recargo**	extra charge
el	**retraso**	delay
el	**taxi**	taxi
el	**tícket** *(pl ~s)*	ticket; receipt
el	**tren**	train
el	**vagón** *(pl* vagones)	carriage
el	**viaje**	journey
el	**viajero**	traveller

ESSENTIAL WORDS *(feminine)*

la	**aduana**	customs
la	**bici**	bike
la	**bicicleta**	bicycle
la	**boletería** (*LAm*)	ticket office
la	**bolsa**	bag
la	**cafetería (de la estación)**	station buffet
la	**cantina (de la estación)**	station buffet
la	**cartera**	wallet; (*LAm*) handbag
la	**clase**	class
la	**conexión** (*pl* conexiones)	connection
la	**consigna**	left-luggage office
la	**consigna automática**	left-luggage locker
la	**dirección** (*pl* direcciones)	direction
la	**entrada**	entrance
la	**estación** (*pl* estaciones)	station
la	**estación de metro** (*pl* estaciones ~ ~)	underground station
la	**información**	information
la	**línea**	line
la	**llegada**	arrival
la	**maleta**	suitcase
la	**oficial de aduanas**	customs officer
la	**oficina de objetos perdidos**	lost property office
la	**parada de taxis**	taxi rank
la	**petaca** (*Mex*)	suitcase
la	**reserva**	reservation
la	**sala de espera**	waiting room
la	**salida**	departure; exit
la	**taquilla**	ticket office; locker
la	**vía**	track, line
la	**viajera**	traveller

USEFUL PHRASES

reservar un asiento **to book a seat**

pagar un recargo, pagar un suplemento **to pay an extra charge, to pay a surcharge**

hacer/deshacer el equipaje **to pack/unpack**

IMPORTANT WORDS (*masculine*)

el **coche-cama** (*pl* ~s~)	sleeping car
el **coche-comedor** (*pl* ~s~)	dining car
el **conductor**	driver
el **destino**	destination
el **ferrocarril**	railway
el **revisor**	ticket collector

USEFUL WORDS (*masculine*)

el **abono**	season ticket
el **baúl**	trunk
el **carnet joven** (*pl* ~s ~)	young persons' discount card
el **coche**	carriage
el **descarrilamiento**	derailment
el **jefe de estación**	stationmaster
el **maquinista**	engine-driver
el **panel informativo**	noticeboard
el **paso a nivel**	level crossing
el **silbato**	whistle
el **suplemento**	extra charge, supplement
el **trayecto**	journey
el **(tren de) mercancías** (*pl* (~es ~) ~)	goods train

USEFUL PHRASES

tomar el tren, coger el tren (*Sp*) to take the train
perder el tren to miss the train
montarse en el tren to get on the train
bajar del tren to get off the train
¿está libre este asiento? is this seat free?
el tren lleva retraso the train is late
un vagón de fumadores/no fumadores a smoking/ non-smoking
  compartment
"prohibido asomarse por la ventanilla" "do not lean out of the window"

IMPORTANT WORDS *(feminine)*

la **barrera**	barrier
la **conductora**	driver
la **duración** (*pl* duraciones)	length (of time)
la **escalera mecánica**	escalator
la **frontera**	border
la **litera**	couchette
la **propina**	tip
la **RENFE**	Spanish Railway
la **revisora**	ticket collector
la **tarifa**	fare

USEFUL WORDS *(feminine)*

la **alarma**	alarm
la **etiqueta**	label
la **jefa de estación**	stationmaster
la **locomotora**	locomotive
la **maquinista**	engine-driver
la **vía férrea**	(railway) line or track
las **vías**	rails

USEFUL PHRASES

te acompañaré a la estación **I'll go to the station with you**
iré a buscarte a la estación **I'll come and pick you up at the station**
el tren de las diez con destino a/procedente de Madrid **the 10 o'clock train to/from Madrid**

ESSENTIAL WORDS (*masculine*)

el	**árbol**	tree
el	**bosque**	wood

USEFUL WORDS (*masculine*)

el	**abedul**	birch
el	**abeto**	fir tree
el	**acebo**	holly
el	**albaricoque**	apricot tree
el	**árbol frutal**	fruit tree
el	**arbusto**	bush
el	**arce**	maple
el	**boj**	box tree
el	**brote**	bud
el	**castaño**	chestnut tree
el	**cerezo**	cherry tree
el	**chabacano** (*Mex*)	apricot tree
el	**chopo**	poplar
el	**duraznero** (*LAm*)	peach tree
el	**espino**	hawthorn
el	**follaje**	foliage
el	**fresno**	ash
el	**huerto**	orchard
el	**limonero**	lemon tree
el	**manzano**	apple tree
el	**melocotonero** (*Sp*)	peach tree
el	**naranjo**	orange tree
el	**nogal**	walnut tree
el	**olmo**	elm
el	**peral**	pear tree
el	**pino**	pine
el	**platanero**	banana tree
el	**plátano**	plane tree
el	**roble**	oak
el	**sauce llorón** (*pl* ~s llorones)	weeping willow
el	**tejo**	yew
el	**tilo**	lime tree
el	**tronco**	trunk
el	**viñedo**	vineyard

ESSENTIAL WORDS *(feminine)*

la	**hoja**	leaf
la	**rama**	branch
la	**selva** (tropical)	rain forest

USEFUL WORDS *(feminine)*

la	**baya**	berry
la	**corteza**	bark
la	**encina**	ilex, holm oak
el	**haya** (*pl f* las hayas)	beech
la	**higuera**	fig tree
la	**raíz** (*pl* raíces)	root
la	**viña**	vineyard

ESSENTIAL WORDS *(masculine)*

el	**ajo**	garlic
los	**champiñones**	mushrooms
los	**chícharos** *(Mex)*	peas
los	**ejotes** *(Mex)*	French beans
los	**guisantes** *(Sp)*	peas
el	**pimiento**	pepper
el	**tomate**	tomato

USEFUL WORDS *(masculine)*

el	**apio**	celery
el	**berro**	watercress
el	**brécol**	broccoli
el	**calabacín** *(pl* calabacines)	courgette
el	**elote** *(Mex)*	sweetcorn
los	**espárragos**	asparagus
los	**frijoles** *(LAm)*	beans
los	**garbanzos**	chickpeas
el	**maíz (dulce** *or* **tierno)**	sweetcorn
el	**nabo**	turnip
el	**pepino**	cucumber
el	**perejil**	parsley
el	**pimiento morrón** *(pl* ~s morrones)	(sweet) pepper
el	**puerro**	leek
el	**rábano**	radish
el	**repollo**	cabbage

USEFUL PHRASES

cultivar verduras to grow vegetables

una mazorca de maíz *(Sp)*, una mazorca de choclo *(Mex)* corn on the cob

ESSENTIAL WORDS *(feminine)*

las	arvejas *(LAm)*	peas
la	cebolla	onion
la	coliflor	cauliflower
la	ensalada	salad
las	habichuelas *(LAm)*	French beans
las	judías verdes *(Sp)*	French beans
la	papa *(LAm, Southern Sp)*,	potato
la	patata *(Sp)*	
las	verduras	vegetables
la	zanahoria	carrot

USESFUL WORDS *(feminine)*

la	alcachofa	artichoke
las	alubias *(Sp)*	beans
la	berenjena	aubergine
la	calabacita *(Mex)*	courgette
la	calabaza	pumpkin
la	cebolleta	spring onion
la	col	cabbage
las	coles de Bruselas	Brussels sprouts
la	endibia	endive, chicory
la	escarola	curly endive
las	espinacas	spinach
las	judías	beans
las	judías blancas	haricot beans
la	lechuga	lettuce
las	legumbres	pulses
las	lentejas	lentils
la	remolacha	beetroot

USEFUL PHRASES

zanahoria rallada grated carrot
biológico(a) organic
vegetariano(a) vegetarian

ESSENTIAL WORDS (*masculine*)

el	**autobús** (*pl* autobuses)	bus
el	**autocar**	coach
el	**avión** (*pl* aviones)	plane
el	**barco de vela**	sailing ship; sailing boat
el	**bote**	boat
el	**bote de remos**	rowing boat
el	**camión** (*pl* camiones)	lorry
el	**carro**	cart; (*LAm*) car
el	**casco**	helmet
el	**ciclomotor**	moped
el	**coche** (*Sp*)	car
el	**coche de línea**	coach
el	**helicóptero**	helicopter
el	**medio de transporte**	means of transport
el	**metro**	underground, subway
el	**precio del billete** (*Sp*) *or* del boleto (*LAm*)	fare
el	**taxi**	taxi
el	**transbordador**	ferry
el	**transporte público**	public transport
el	**tren**	train
el	**vehículo**	vehicle
el	**vehículo pesado**	heavy goods vehicle

IMPORTANT WORDS (*masculine*)

el	**coche de bomberos**	fire engine

USEFUL PHRASES
viajar **to travel**
ha ido a Barcelona en avión **he flew to Barcelona**
tomar el autobús/el metro/el tren, coger (*Sp*) el autobús/el metro/el tren **to take the bus/the subway/the train**
montar en bicicleta **to go cycling**
se puede ir en coche **you can go there by car**

ESSENTIAL WORDS (feminine)

la	**bici**	bike
la	**bicicleta**	bicycle
la	**camioneta**	van
la	**caravana**	caravan
la	**distancia**	distance
la	**moto**	motorbike
la	**motocicleta**	motorcycle, motorbike
la	**parte de atrás**	back
la	**parte de delante**	front
la	**parte delantera**	front
la	**parte trasera**	back
la	**vespa®**	scooter

IMPORTANT WORDS (feminine)

la	**ambulancia**	ambulance
la	**grúa**	breakdown van

USEFUL PHRASES

reparar el coche de algn to repair sb's car
un coche de alquiler a hire car
un coche deportivo a sports car
un coche de carreras a racing car
un coche de empresa a company car
"coches de ocasión" "used cars"
arrancar to start, to move off

USEFUL WORDS *(masculine)*

el	**aerodeslizador**	hovercraft
el	**(barco de) vapor**	steamer
el	**bulldozer** (*pl* ~s)	bulldozer
el	**buque**	ship
el	**camión articulado** (*pl* camiones ~s)	articulated lorry
el	**camión cisterna** (*pl* camiones ~)	tanker
el	**cochecito (de niño)**	pram, buggy
el	**cohete**	rocket
el	**hidroavión** (*pl* hidroaviones)	seaplane
el	**jeep** (*pl* ~s)	jeep
el	**navío**	ship
el	**ovni (objeto volante no identificado)**	UFO (*unidentified flying object*)
el	**petrolero**	oil tanker (*ship*)
el	**planeador**	glider
el	**platillo volante**	flying saucer
el	**portaaviones** (*pl inv*)	aircraft carrier
el	**remolcador**	tug
el	**remolque**	trailer
el	**riesgo**	risk
el	**submarino**	submarine
el	**tanque**	tank
el	**teleférico**	cable car
el	**telesilla**	chairlift
el	**tranvía**	tram
el	**velero**	sailing ship; sailing boat
el	**velomotor**	moped
el	**yate**	yacht; pleasure cruiser

USEFUL WORDS *(feminine)*

la	barcaza	barge
la	camioneta de reparto	delivery van
la	canoa	canoe
la	carreta	waggon; cart
la	golondrina	pleasure boat
la	lancha	boat *(small)*; launch
la	lancha de salvamento	lifeboat
la	lancha de socorro	lifeboat
la	lancha neumática	rubber dinghy
la	lancha rápida	speedboat
la	locomotora	locomotive
la	ranchera	estate car

ESSENTIAL WORDS (*masculine*)

el	**aire**	air
el	**boletín meteorológico**	weather report
	(*pl* boletines ~s)	
el	**calor**	heat
el	**cielo**	sky
el	**clima**	climate
el	**este**	east
el	**frío**	cold
el	**grado**	degree
el	**hielo**	ice
el	**invierno**	winter
el	**norte**	north
el	**oeste**	west
el	**otoño**	autumn
el	**paraguas** (*pl inv*)	umbrella
el	**parte meteorológico**	weather report
el	**pronóstico del tiempo**	(weather) forecast
el	**sol**	sun; sunshine
el	**sur**	south
el	**tiempo**	weather
el	**verano**	summer
el	**viento**	wind

USEFUL PHRASES

¿qué tiempo hace? **what's the weather like?**

hace calor/frío **it's hot/cold**

hace un día estupendo, hace un día precioso **it's a lovely day**

hace un día horrible **it's a horrible day**

al aire libre **in the open air**

hay niebla **it's foggy**

30° a la sombra **30° in the shade**

escuchar el pronóstico del tiempo **to listen to the weather forecast**

llover **to rain**

nevar **to snow**

llueve **it's raining**

nieva **it's snowing**

ESSENTIAL WORDS *(feminine)*

la	**estación** *(pl* estaciones)	season
la	**lluvia**	rain
la	**niebla**	fog
la	**nieve**	snow
la	**nube**	cloud
la	**primavera**	spring
la	**región** *(pl* regiones)	region, area
la	**temperatura**	temperature

USEFUL PHRASES

brilla el sol the sun is shining
sopla el viento the wind is blowing
hace un frío que pela it's freezing
helarse to freeze
ha helado there's been a frost
fundirse to melt
soleado(a) sunny
tormentoso(a) stormy
lluvioso(a) rainy
frío(a) cool
variable changeable
húmedo(a) humid
el cielo está cubierto the sky is overcast

IMPORTANT WORDS (masculine)

el	chaparrón (pl chaparrones)	shower
el	claro	sunny spell
el	humo	smoke
el	polvo	dust

USEFUL WORDS (masculine)

el	aguacero	downpour
el	amanecer	dawn, daybreak
el	anochecer	nightfall, dusk
el	arco iris (pl inv)	rainbow
el	barómetro	barometer
el	cambio	change
el	carámbano	icicle
el	charco	puddle
el	copo de nieve	snowflake
el	crepúsculo	twilight
el	deshielo	thaw
el	granizo	hail
el	huracán (pl huracanes)	hurricane
el	pararrayos (pl inv)	lightning conductor
el	quitanieves (pl inv)	snowplough
el	rayo	lightning
el	rayo de sol	ray of sunshine
el	relámpago	flash of lightning
el	rocío	dew
el	trueno	thunder

IMPORTANT WORDS (feminine)

las	precipitaciones	rainfall
la	previsión meteorológica (pl previsiones ~s)	(weather) forecast
la	sombrilla	parasol
la	tormenta	storm
la	visibilidad	visibility

USEFUL WORDS (feminine)

el	alba (pl f las albas)	dawn
la	atmósfera	atmosphere
la	brisa	breeze
la	bruma	mist
la	corriente (de aire)	draught
la	escarcha	frost (on the ground)
la	gota de lluvia	raindrop
la	helada	frost (weather)
la	inundación (pl inundaciones)	flood
la	luz de la luna	moonlight
la	mejora	improvement
la	nevada	snowfall
la	ola de calor	heatwave
la	oscuridad	darkness
la	puesta de sol	sunset
la	ráfaga de viento	gust of wind
la	sequía	drought
la	tormenta	thunderstorm
la	ventisca	snowdrift

ESSENTIAL WORDS (*masculine*)

el	**albergue juvenil**	youth hostel
los	**baños públicos** (*LAm*)	toilets
el	**bote de la basura** (*Mex*)	dustbin
el	**comedor**	dining room
el	**cuarto de baño**	bathroom
el	**cubo de la basura**	dustbin
el	**desayuno**	breakfast
el	**dormitorio**	dormitory
los	**lavabos**	toilets
el	**mapa**	map
los	**servicios** (*Sp*)	toilets
el	**silencio**	silence
el	**visitante**	visitor

IMPORTANT WORDS (*masculine*)

el	**carnet de socio** (*pl* ~s ~~)	membership card
el	**lavabo**	washbasin; toilet
el	**saco de dormir**	sleeping bag

ESSENTIAL WORDS *(feminine)*

la	**cama**	bed
la	**(cama) litera**	bunk bed
la	**cocina**	kitchen; cooking
la	**comida**	meal
la	**ducha**	shower
la	**estancia**	stay
la	**lista de precios**	price list
la	**noche**	night
la	**oficina**	office
la	**sábana**	sheet
la	**sala de juegos**	games room
la	**tarifa**	rate(s)
las	**vacaciones**	holidays
la	**visitante**	visitor

IMPORTANT WORDS *(feminine)*

la	**caminata**	hike
la	**excursión** (*pl* excursiones)	trip
la	**guía**	guidebook
la	**mochila**	rucksack
las	**normas**	rules
la	**ropa de cama**	bed linen

USEFUL PHRASES

pasar una noche en el albergue juvenil to spend a night at the youth hostel
quisiera alquilar un saco de dormir I would like to hire a sleeping bag
está todo ocupado there's no more room

The vocabulary items on pages 666 to 703 have been grouped under parts of speech rather than topics because they can apply in a wide range of circumstances. Use them just as freely as the vocabulary already given.

ARTICLES AND PRONOUNS

> **What is an article?**
> In English, an **article** is one of the words *the*, *a* and *an* which is given in front of a noun.
>
> **What is a pronoun?**
> A **pronoun** is a word you use instead of a noun, when you do not need or want to name someone or something directly, for example, *it*, *you*, *none*.

algo something; anything
alguien somebody, someone; anybody, anyone
alguno/alguna one; someone, somebody
algunos/algunas some, some of them; some of us, some of you, some of them
ambos/ambas both
aquel/aquella; aquél/aquélla that
aquellos/aquellas; aquéllos/aquéllas those
cada each; every
cual which; who; whom
  lo cual which
cuál what, which one
cualquiera any one; anybody, anyone
  cualquiera de los dos/las dos either (*see also* Adjectives)
cualesquiera (*pl*) any (*see also* Adjectives)
cuanto/cuanta as much as
cuánto/cuánta how much
cuantos/cuantas as many as
cuántos/cuántas how many
cuyo/cuya/cuyos/cuyas whose

en cuyo caso in which case
demasiado/demasiada too much
demasiados too many
dos: los/las dos both
el/la the
él he; him; it
  de él his
ella she; her; it
  de ella hers
ello it
ellos/ellas they; them
  de ellos/ellas theirs
ese/esa; ése/ésa that
esos/esas; ésos/ésas those
este/esta; éste/ésta this
estos/estas; éstos/éstas these
la her; it; you
las them; you
le him; her; it; you
les them; you
lo him; it; you
los/las the
los them; you
me me; myself
mi/mis my
(el)mío/(la) mía/(los) míos/(las) mías mine

mismo/misma/mismos/mismas
same
  mí mismo/misma; yo mismo/
  misma myself; nosotros mismos/
  nosotras mismas ourselves;
  sí misma; ella misma herself;
  sí mismo; él mismo himself;
  sí mismos/sí mismas; ellos
  mismos/ellas mismas themselves;
  ti mismo/ti misma; tú mismo/
  tú misma; usted mismo/usted
  misma yourself; vosotros
  mismos/vosotras mismas;
  ustedes mismos/ustedes
  mismas yourselves; uno
  mismo/una misma oneself
mucho/mucha a lot, lots; much
  (see also Adjectives; Adverbs)
muchos/muchas a lot, lots; many
  (see also Adjectives)
nada nothing
  nada más nothing else
nadie nobody, no one; anybody,
  anyone
  nadie más nobody else
ninguno/ninguna any; neither;
  either; none; no one, nobody
  ninguno de los dos/ninguna de
  las dos neither (see also Adjectives)
ningunos/ningunas any; none
  (see also Adjectives)
nos us; ourselves; each other
nosotros/nosotras we; us
nuestro/nuestra/nuestros/
  nuestras our; ours
  el nuestro/la nuestra/
  los nuestros/las nuestras ours
os you; yourselves; each other
otro/otra another, another one
  (see also Adjectives)
otros/otras others (see also

Adjectives)
poco/poca un poco a bit, a little
  dentro de poco shortly
pocos/pocas not many, few
que who; that
qué what; what a
quien/quienes who; whoever
quién/quiénes who
se him; her; them; you; himself;
  herself; itself; themselves;
  yourself; yourselves; oneself; each
  other
su/sus his; her; its; their; your; one's
(el) suyo/(la) suya /(los) suyos/
  (las) suyas his; her; its; their; your;
  hers; theirs; yours; one's own
tal/tales such
tampoco not…either, neither
te you; yourself
ti you
todo/toda (it) all
  todo el mundo everybody,
  everyone (see also Adjectives)
todos/todas all; every; everybody;
  everyone (see also Adjectives)
tu/tus your
tú you
usted you
ustedes you
(el) tuyo/ (la) tuya/ (los)
  tuyos/(las) tuyas yours
un/una a; an; one
unos/unas some; a few; about,
  around
varios/varias several
vosotros/vosotras you
vuestro/vuestra/vuestros/
  vuestras your; yours
  los vuestros/las vuestras yours
yo I; me

CONJUNCTIONS

What is a conjunction?
A **conjunction** is a word such as *and*, *but*, *or*, *so*, *if* and *because*, that links two words or phrases of a similar type, or two parts of a sentence, for example, *Diane <u>and</u> I have been friends for years*; *I left <u>because</u> I was bored*.

ahora though
  ahora bien however; **ahora que** now that
antes: antes de que before
así: así (es) que so
  así pues so
aunque although, though
como as
conque so, so then
consiguiente: por consiguiente so, therefore
cuando when; whenever; if
cuanto: en cuanto as soon as; as
dar: dado que since
decir: es decir that is to say
desde: desde que since
después: después de que after
e and
embargo: sin embargo still, however
entonces then
fin: a fin de que so that, in order that
forma: de forma que so that
hasta: hasta que until, till
luego therefore
manera: de manera que so that
mas but
más: más que more than
menos: menos que less than
mientras while; as long as
  mientras que whereas; **mientras**

  (tanto) meanwhile
modo: de modo que so that
momento: en el momento en que just as
ni or; nor; even
  ni...ni neither...nor
o or
  o ... o ... either ... or ...
para: para que so that
pero but
porque because
pronto: tan pronto como as soon as
pues then; well; since
puesto: puesto que since
que that
ser: o sea that is
  a no ser que unless
si if; whether
  si no otherwise
siempre: siempre que whenever; as long as, provided that
sino but; except; only
tal: con tal (de) que as long as, provided that
tanto: por (lo) tanto so, therefore
u or
vez: una vez que once
vista: en vista de que seeing that
y and
ya: ya que as, since

ADJECTIVES

> **What is an adjective?**
> An **adjective** is a 'describing' word that tells you more about a person or thing, such as their appearance, colour, size or other qualities, for example, *pretty*, *blue*, *big*.

abierto(a) open
absoluto(a) absolute
absurdo(a) absurd
académico(a) academic
accesible accessible; approachable
aceptable acceptable
acondicionado(a) fitted out
   con aire acondicionado
   air-conditioned
acostumbrado(a) accustomed
activo(a) active
acusado(a) accused; marked
adecuado(a) appropriate
admirable admirable
aéreo(a) aerial
aficionado(a) keen
afilado(a) sharp
afortunado(a) fortunate, lucky
agitado(a) rough; agitated; hectic
agotado(a) exhausted
agradable pleasant, agreeable
agresivo(a) aggressive
agrícola agricultural
agudo(a) sharp; acute
aislado(a) isolated
alegre happy; bright; lively; merry
alguno/alguna (*before masc sing*
   algún) some; any (*see also* Articles
   and Pronouns)
algunos/algunas some; several (*see
   also* Articles and Pronouns)
alternativo(a) alternating; alternative

alto(a) high; tall
amargo(a) bitter
ancho(a) broad; wide
anciano(a) elderly
animado(a) lively; cheerful
anónimo(a) anonymous
anormal abnormal
anterior former
antiguo(a) old; vintage; antique
anual annual
apagado(a) out; off; muffled; dull
aparente apparent
apasionado(a) passionate
apropiado(a) appropriate, suitable
aproximado(a) rough
arriba: de arriba top
asequible affordable
asombrado(a) amazed, astonished
asombroso(a) amazing,
   astonishing
áspero(a) rough
atestado(a) crowded; popular
atento(a) attentive; watchful
atractivo(a) attractive
automático(a) automatic
avanzado(a) advanced
bajo(a) low; short
barba: con barba bearded
barbudo(a) bearded
básico(a) basic
bastante enough; quite a lot of
   (*see also* Adverbs)

bien well-to-do
bienvenido(a) welcome
blando(a) soft
breve brief
brillante shining; bright
brutal brutal
bruto(a) rough; stupid; uncouth; gross
bueno(a) good
cada each; every
caliente hot; warm
callado(a) quiet
cansado(a) tired
capaz capable
cariñoso(a) affectionate
caro(a) expensive, dear
cauteloso(a) cautious
central central
ceñido(a) tight
cercano(a) close; nearby
cerrado(a) closed; off
científico(a) scientific
cierto(a) true; certain
civil civil; civilian
claro(a) clear; light; bright
clásico(a) classical; classic
climatizado(a) air-conditioned
cobarde cowardly
comercial commercial
cómodo(a) comfortable
complejo(a) complex
completo(a) complete
complicado(a) complicated; complex
comprensivo(a) understanding
común common; mutual
concreto(a) specific; concrete
concurrido(a) crowded; popular
conmovedor(a) moving
consciente conscious; aware

conservador(a) conservative
considerable considerable
constante constant
contemporáneo(a) contemporary
contento(a) happy; pleased
continuo(a) continuous
convencional conventional
correcto(a) correct, right
corriente ordinary; common
cortado(a) cut; closed; off; shy
creativo(a) creative
cristiano(a) Christian
crítico(a) critical
crudo(a) raw
cuadrado(a) square
cualquiera (*before masc and fem sing* cualquier) any (*see also* Articles and Pronouns)
cualesquiera any (*see also* Articles and Pronouns)
cuanto/cuanta as much as
cuánto/cuánta how much
cuantos/cuantas as many as
cuántos/cuántas how many
cultural cultural
curioso(a) curious
debido(a) due, proper
decepcionante disappointing
decidido(a) determined
delicado(a) delicate
delicioso(a) delicious
demasiado/demasiada too much
demasiados too many
democrático(a) democratic
derecho(a) right
desafortunado(a) unfortunate
desagradable unpleasant
desconocido(a) unknown
desesperado(a) desperate

desierto(a) deserted
desnudo(a) naked; bare
despejado(a) clear
despierto(a) awake; sharp; alert
despreocupado(a) carefree; careless
destruido(a) destroyed
detallado(a) detailed
diestro(a) skilful
difícil difficult
digno(a) worthy; dignified
diminuto(a) tiny
directo(a) direct
disgustado(a) upset
disponible available
dispuesto(a) arranged; willing
distinguido(a) distinguished
distinto(a) different; various
divertido(a) funny, amusing; fun; entertaining
dividido(a) divided
divino(a) divine
doble double
domesticado(a) tame
doméstico(a) domestic
dos: los/las dos both
dulce sweet
duro(a) hard
económico(a) economic; economical
efectivo(a) effective
eficaz effective; efficient
eficiente efficient
eléctrico(a) electric
electrónico(a) electronic
elemental elementary
emocionante exciting
emotivo(a) emotional; moving
encantador(a) charming; lovely
enmascarado(a) masked
enorme enormous, huge

enterado(a) knowledgeable; well-informed; aware
entero(a) whole
equivalente equivalent
equivocado(a) wrong
escandaloso(a) shocking
esencial essential
especial special
específico(a) specific
espectacular spectacular
espeso(a) thick
espiritual spiritual
estrecho(a) narrow
estricto(a) strict
estropeado(a) broken (off); off
estupendo(a) marvellous, great
estúpido(a) stupid
étnico(a) ethnic
evidente obvious, evident
exacto(a) exact; accurate
excelente excellent
excepcional outstanding
exclusivo(a) exclusive
exigente demanding, exacting
experto(a) experienced
éxito: de éxito successful
exitoso(a) successful
exquisito(a) delicious; exquisite
extra extra; top-quality
extranjero(a) foreign
extraño(a) strange; foreign
extraordinario(a) extraordinary; outstanding; special
extremo(a) extreme
fácil easy
falso(a) false
familiar family; familiar
famoso(a) famous
fatigoso(a) tiring

federal federal
feroz fierce
fijo(a) fixed; permanent
final final
financiero(a) financial
fino(a) fine; smooth; refined
firme firm; steady
físico(a) physical
flexible flexible
fluido(a) fluid; fluent
formal reliable; formal; official
frágil fragile; frail
frecuente frequent
fresco(a) fresh; cool; cheeky
fuerte strong; loud
futuro(a) future
general general
generoso(a) generous
genial brilliant; wonderful
gentil kind
genuino(a) genuine
global global
gordo(a) fat; big
grande (*before masc sing* gran) big; great
grandioso(a) grand; grandiose
habitual usual
herido(a) injured; wounded; hurt
hermoso(a) beautiful
histórico(a) historic; historical
holgado(a) loose
honrado(a) honest; respectable
horrible horrific; hideous; terrible
horroroso(a) dreadful; hideous; terrible
humano(a) human; humane
ideal ideal
idéntico(a) identical
igual equal

ilegal illegal
iluminado(a) illuminated, lit; enlightened
ilustrado(a) illustrated
imaginario(a) imaginary
impar odd
importante important
imposible impossible
imprescindible indispensable
impresionante impressive; moving; shocking
inaguantable unbearable
incapaz (de) incapable (of)
increíble incredible; unbelievable
inculto(a) uncultured
indefenso(a) defenceless
independiente independent
indiferente unconcerned
individual individual; single
industrial industrial
inesperado(a) unexpected
inevitable inevitable
infantil childlike; childish
inflable inflatable
injusto(a) unfair
inmediato(a) immediate
inmenso(a) immense
inmune immune
inquieto(a) anxious; restless
intacto(a) intact
intencionado(a) deliberate
intenso(a) intense; intensive
interior interior; inside; inner; domestic
interminable endless
internacional international
interno(a) internal
interrumpido(a) interrupted
inútil useless

invisible invisible
izquierdo(a) left
junto(a) together
justo(a) just, fair; exact; tight
largo(a) long
legal legal
lento(a) slow
libre free
ligero(a) light; slight; agile
limpio(a) clean
liso(a) smooth; straight; plain
listo(a) ready; bright
llamativo(a) bright; striking
llano(a) flat; straightforward
lleno(a) (de) full (of)
lluvioso(a) rainy, wet
loco(a) mad, crazy
lujo: de lujo luxurious
lujoso(a) luxurious
magnífico(a) magnificent;
  wonderful, superb
maligno(a) malignant; evil, malicious
malo(a) bad
malvado(a) wicked
manso(a) meek; tame
maravilloso(a) marvellous,
  wonderful; magic
marcado(a) marked
más more of a
máximo(a) maximum
mayor bigger; elder
  el/la...mayor the biggest...;
  the eldest...
mecánico(a) mechanical
médico(a) medical
medio(a) half; average
medioambiental environmental
mejor better
  el/la mejor the best

menor smaller; younger
  el/la...menor the smallest;
  the youngest
menos less of a
mental mental
militar military
minucioso(a) thorough; very
  detailed
mismo(a) same
misterioso(a) mysterious
moderado(a) moderate
moderno(a) modern
mojado(a) wet; soaked
molesto(a) annoying; annoyed;
  awkward; uncomfortable
montañoso(a) mountainous
mucho/mucha a lot of, lots of;
  much (see also Pronouns; Adverbs)
muchos/muchas a lot of, lots of;
  many (see also Pronouns)
muerto(a) dead
mundial worldwide, global
mutuo(a) mutual
nacido(a) born
nacional national; domestic
nativo(a) native
natural natural
necesario(a) necessary
negativo(a) negative
ninguno/ninguna (before masc sing
  ningún) no; any (see also Pronouns)
ningunos/ningunas no; any
  (see also Pronouns)
normal normal; standard
nuclear nuclear
nuevo(a) new
numeroso(a) numerous
obediente obedient
objetivo(a) objective

obligatorio(a) compulsory, obligatory
obvio(a) obvious
ocupado(a) busy; taken; engaged; occupied
oficial official
oportuno(a) opportune; appropriate
original original
oscuro(a) dark; obscure
otro/otra another
  a/en otro lugar somewhere else; otra cosa something else; otra persona somebody else; otra vez again (*see also* Pronouns); otros/otras other (*see also* Pronouns)
pacífico(a) peaceful; peaceable
pálido(a) pale
par even
particular special; particular; private
patético(a) pathetic
peligroso(a) dangerous
peor worse
  el peor the worst
perdido(a) lost; stray; remote
perfecto(a) perfect
personal personal
pesado(a) heavy; tedious
picante hot
pie: de pie standing (up)
poco/poca not much, little
pocos/pocas not many, few
poderoso(a) powerful
polémico(a) controversial
polvoriento(a) dusty; powdery
popular popular
portátil portable
posible possible; potential
positivo(a) positive

práctico(a) practical
precioso(a) lovely, beautiful; precious
preciso(a) precise; necessary
preferido(a) favourite
preliminar preliminary
presentable presentable
presunto(a) alleged
previo(a) previous
primario(a) primary
principal main
privado(a) private
privilegiado(a) privileged
profundo(a) deep
prometido(a) promised; engaged
propio(a) own
próximo(a) near, close; next
psicológico(a) psychological
público(a) public
pueril childish
pulcro(a) neat
puntiagudo(a) pointed; sharp
puntual punctual
puro(a) pure
qué what; which; what a
querido(a) dear
químico(a) chemical
racial racial
radical radical
rápido(a) fast, quick
raro(a) strange, odd; rare
razonable reasonable
reacio(a) reluctant
real actual; royal
reciente recent
recto(a) straight; honest
redondo(a) round
refrescante refreshing
regional regional

regular regular
religioso(a) religious
repentino(a) sudden
repuesto: de repuesto spare
reservado(a) reserved
resistente resistant; tough
responsable (de) responsible (for)
revolucionario(a) revolutionary
ridículo(a) ridiculous
rival rival
romántico(a) romantic
rubio(a) fair, blond
ruidoso(a) noisy
rural rural
sabio(a) wise
sagrado(a) sacred
salvaje wild
salvo: a salvo safe
sanitario(a) sanitary; health
sano(a) healthy
  sano(a) y salvo(a) safe and sound
santo(a) holy
satisfecho(a) (de) satisfied (with)
seco(a) dry
secreto(a) secret
secundario(a) secondary
seguro(a) safe; secure; certain; sure
semejante similar
sencillo(a) simple; natural; single
sensacional sensational
sentado(a) sitting, seated
señalado(a) special
separado(a) separate
servicial helpful
severo(a) severe
sexual sexual
significativo(a) significant;
  meaningful
siguiente next, following

silencioso(a) silent; quiet
sincero(a) sincere
singular singular; outstanding
siniestro(a) sinister
situado(a) situated
sobra: de sobra spare
sobrante spare
social social
solemne solemn
sólido(a) solid
solo(a) alone; lonely; black;
  straight, neat
soltero(a) single
sombrío(a) sombre; dim
sonriente smiling
soportable bearable
sorprendente surprising
sospechoso(a) suspicious
suave smooth; gentle; mild; slight
sucio(a) dirty
superior top; upper; superior
supremo(a) supreme
supuesto(a) assumed; supposed
tal/tales such
tanto/tanta so much
tantos/tantas so many
técnico(a) technical
terrible terrible
típico(a) typical
tirante tight; tense
todo/toda all (see also Pronouns)
todos/todas all; every (see also
  Pronouns)
tolerante broad-minded
total total
tradicional traditional
tremendo(a) tremendous
triste sad
último(a) last

el último the latest
ultrajante offensive; outrageous
único(a) only; unique
urgente urgent
útil useful, helpful
vacante vacant
vacío(a) empty
valiente brave, ourageous
valioso(a) valuable
valor: de valor valuable
variado(a) varied

varios/varias several
vecino(a) neighbouring
verdad: de verdad real
verdadero(a) real; true
viejo(a) old
vil villainous; vile
violento(a) violent; awkward
visible visible
vital vital
vivo(a) living; alive; lively
voluntario(a) voluntary

supplementary vocabulary

ADVERBS AND PREPOSITIONS

> **What is an adverb?**
> An **adverb** is a word usually used with verbs, adjectives or other adverbs that gives more Information about when, how, where, or in what circumstances something happens, or to what degree something is true, for example, *quickly*, *happily*, *now*, *extremely*, *very*.
>
> **What is a preposition?**
> A **preposition** is a word such as *at*, *for*, *with*, *into* or *from*, which is usually followed by a noun, pronoun, or, in English, a word ending in -ing. Prepositions show how people or things relate to the rest of the sentence, for example, *She's at home*; *a tool for cutting grass*; *It's from David*.

a to; at; into: onto
abajo down; downstairs; below
  allá abajo down there
absolutamente absolutely
acá here, over here; now
acerca: acerca de about
actualmente at present
acuerdo: de acuerdo OK, okay
adelante forward
  en adelante from now on
  hacia adelante forward
además also; furthermore, moreover, in addition
  además de as well as; besides
admirablemente admirably
afortunadamente fortunately
agradablemente nicely
ahora now; in a minute
  hasta ahora so far
alcance: al alcance within reach
allá there, over there
allí there
alrededor de around
ansiosamente anxiously
ante before; in the face of; faced with

ante todo above all
antemano: de antemano beforehand, in advance
anteriormente previously, before
antes before **antes de** before
  cuanto antes as soon as possible
  lo antes posible as soon as possible
apartado: apartado de away from
aparte: aparte de apart from
apenas hardly, scarcely; only
aproximadamente approximately
aquí here; now
arriba up; upstairs; above
  allá arriba up there
así like that; like this
  así como as well as
atentamente attentively, carefully; kindly
atrás behind; at the back; backwards; ago
  hacia atrás backwards
aun even **aun así** even so
  aun cuando even if
aún still, yet; even
azar: al azar at random

bajo low; quietly; under

básicamente basically

bastante enough; quite a lot; quite (see also Adjectives)

bien well; carefully; very; easily

brevemente briefly

bruscamente abruptly

cambio: a cambio de in exchange for; in return for
  en cambio instead

camino: de camino on the way

casi almost, nearly

caso: en el caso de (que) in the case of
  en todo caso in any case

casualidad: por casualidad by chance

causa: a causa de because of

cerca (de) close (to); near (to)

claramente clearly

cómo how

como like; such as; as; about

completamente completely

con with

concreto: en concreto specifically, in particular

continuamente constantly

contra against

correctamente correctly

cortésmente politely

cuando when

cuándo when

cuanto: en cuanto a as regards, as for

cuánto how much; how far; how

cuenta: a fin de cuentas ultimately
  teniendo en cuenta considering

cuidado: con cuidado carefully

cuidadosamente carefully

curiosamente curiously

curso: en el curso de in the course of

de of; from; about; by; than; in; if

debajo underneath
  debajo de under; por debajo underneath; por debajo de under; below

débilmente faintly; weakly

delante in front; at the front; opposite
  delante de in front of; opposite
  hacia delante forward
  por delante ahead; at the front

demasiado too; too much

dentro inside
  dentro de inside; in; within

deprisa quickly, hurriedly

derecha: a la derecha on the right

desde from; since

desgraciadamente unfortunately

despacio slowly

después later; after(wards); then
  después de after

detrás behind; at the back; on the back; after
  detrás de behind; por detrás from behind; on the back

día: al día per day

diariamente on a daily basis

diario: a diario daily

donde where; wherever

dónde where

dondequiera anywhere

duda: sin duda definitely, undoubtedly

dulcemente sweetly; gently

durante during; for
  durante todo/toda throughout

efecto: en efecto in fact

ejemplo: por ejemplo for example

en in; on; at; into; by

encima on top
  encima de above; on top of; por
  encima over; por encima de over;
  above
enfrente (de) opposite
enseguida right away
entonces then
  desde entonces since then; hasta
  entonces until then
entre among(st); between
especialmente especially,
  particularly; specially
evidentemente obviously, evidently
exactamente exactly
excepción: con la excepción de
  with the exception of
excepto except (for)
extranjero: en el extranjero
  overseas; abroad
extremadamente extremely
fácilmente easily
fielmente faithfully
fin: por fin finally; at last
finalmente eventually
forma: de alguna forma somehow
  de esta forma like that; like this;
  de ninguna forma in no way;
  de otra forma otherwise;
  de todas formas anyway
francamente frankly; really
frecuentemente frequently
frente: frente a opposite, facing;
  against
fuera outside; out
  fuera de outside
gana: de buena gana willingly,
  happily
  de mala gana reluctantly
general: por lo general as a rule

generalmente generally
gracias: gracias a thanks to
gradualmente gradually
hacia towards
hasta to, as far as; up to; down to;
  until
honradamente honestly
igualmente equally; likewise
incluido including
inmediatamente immediately
intensamente intensely
izquierda: a la izquierda on the left
jamás never; ever
junto: junto a close to, near; next
  to; together with
  junto con together with
justamente just; exactly; justly
lado: al lado (de) next door (to); near
  al lado de alongside; al otro lado de
  across; de un lado a otro to and fro;
  por este lado (de) on this side (of)
largo: a lo largo de along
lejos (de) far (from)
ligeramente lightly; slightly
luego then; later, afterwards
  desde luego certainly
mal badly; poorly; ill
manera: de alguna manera
  somehow
  de esta manera like that; like this;
  de ninguna manera in no way; de
  otra manera otherwise; de todas
  maneras anyway
más more; plus
  el/la más the most; más allá de
  beyond; más bien rather; más
  cerca closer; más lejos further;
  más o menos about; más...que
  more...than; no más no more

medio: **en medio de** in the middle of
  por medio de by means of
mejor better
  el mejor the best
menos less; minus
  el/la menos the least;
  menos...que less than; **por lo
  menos** at least
mentalmente mentally
menudo: **a menudo** often
misteriosamente mysteriously
modo: **de algún modo** somehow
  de este modo like that; like this;
  de ningún modo in no way; **de
  otro modo** otherwise; **de todos
  modos** anyway
momento: **en este momento** at
  the moment
  en ese mismo momento at that
  very moment
mucho a lot
  no mucho not much (*see also*
  Pronouns; Adjectives)
muy very
naturalmente naturally
nerviosamente nervously
no no; not
nombre: **en nombre de** on behalf of
normalmente normally; usually
novedad: **sin novedad** safely
nunca never; ever
paciencia: **con paciencia** patiently
para for; to
  para atrás backwards; **para la
  derecha** towards the right; **para
  siempre** forever
parte: **de mi parte** on my behalf
  en cualquier parte anywhere; **en
  gran parte** largely

en otra parte elsewhere
  en parte partly, in part; **en todas
  partes** everywhere; **por otra
  parte** on the other hand
peligrosamente dangerously
peor worse
  el peor the worst
perfectamente perfectly
persona: **por persona** per person
personalmente personally
pesadamente heavily
pesar: **a pesar de** despite; in spite of
  a pesar de que even though
pie: **a pie** on foot
poco not very; not a lot; not much
  poco a poco little by little, bit by bit
por because of; for; by; through
  por qué why
precisamente precisely, exactly
primero first
principalmente mainly
principio: **al principio** at first
probable likely
probablemente probably
profundamente deeply
pronto soon
propósito: **a propósito** deliberately;
  on purpose
qué how
querer: **sin querer** accidentally
quién: **de quién/de quiénes** whose
rápidamente fast, quickly
rápido quickly
realidad: **en realidad** in fact, actually
realmente really
recientemente recently, lately
regularmente regularly, on a
  regular basis
relativamente relatively

repente: de repente suddenly
seguida: en seguida right away
seguido straight on
  todo seguido straight on
según according to; depending on
seguramente probably; surely
sencillamente simply
sentido: en este sentido in this
  respect
separado: por separado separately
ser: a no ser que unless
serio: en serio seriously
sí yes
siempre always
  como siempre as usual
siguiente: al/el día siguiente next
  day
silencio: en silencio quietly; in
  silence
silenciosamente quietly, silently
sin without sin embargo still,
  however, nonetheless
siquiera: ni siquiera not even
sitio: en algún sitio somewhere
  en ningún sitio nowhere
sobre on; over; about
solamente only; solely
sólo only; solely
  tan sólo only, just
suavemente gently; softly; smoothly
suelo: al suelo to the ground
  en el suelo on the ground
sumamente highly, extremely
supuesto: por supuesto of course
tal: tal como just as
  tal y como están las cosas under
  the circumstances; tal vez
  perhaps, maybe
también also, too

tampoco not…either, neither
tan so; such
  tan … como as … as
tanto so much; so often
  tanto más all the more
tarde late
  más tarde later; afterwards
temprano early
  más temprano earlier
tiempo: a tiempo in time; on time
  al mismo tiempo at the same
  time; mucho tiempo long
todavía still; yet; even
todo: en todo/toda throughout
  todo lo más at (the) most
total in short; at the end of the day
  en total altogether, in all
totalmente totally, completely
través: a través de through; across
vano: en vano in vain
velocidad: a toda velocidad at full
  speed, at top speed
ver: por lo visto apparently
vez: algunas veces sometimes
  cada vez más more and more;
  cada vez menos less and less; de
  vez en cuando from time to time,
  now and then; en vez de instead
  of; rara vez rarely, seldom; una vez
  once; una vez más once more
vía: en vías de on its way to
  en vías de desarrollo developing;
  en vías de extinción endangered
vista: de vista by sight
  en vista de in view of
voz: en voz alta aloud; loudly
  en voz baja in a low voice
ya already
  ya mismo at once; ya no not any
  more, no longer

SOME EXTRA NOUNS

> **What is a noun?**
> A **noun** is a 'naming' word for a living being, thing or idea, for example, *woman, desk, happiness, Andrew*.

la **abertura** opening
el **abismo** gulf
el **aburrimiento** boredom
el **abuso** abuse
el **acceso** access
la **acción** (*pl* acciones) action
el **acento** accent
el **ácido** acid
el **acontecimiento** event
la **actitud** attitude
la **actividad** activity
el **acuerdo** agreement; settlement
la **advertencia** warning
la **afirmación** (*pl* afirmaciones) claim
la **agencia** agency
la **agenda** diary
el/la **agente** agent
la **agitación** (*pl* agitaciones) stir
el **agujero** hole
la **alcantarilla** drain
la **alcayata** hook
la **alegría** joy
el **alfabeto** alphabet
el **alfiler** pin
el/la **aliado/a** ally
el **aliento** breath
el **alivio** relief
el **alma** (*f*) soul
el **almacén** (*pl* almacenes) store
el/la **amante** lover
la **ambición** (*pl* ambiciones) ambition
la **amenaza** threat
el/la **amigo(a)** mate

la **amistad** friendship
el **amor** love
el **análisis** (*pl inv*) analysis
la **anchura** breadth; width
el/la **anfitrión(ona)** host
el **ángel** angel
el **ángulo** angle
la **angustia** anguish
el **animal doméstico** pet
la **antigüedad** antique
el **anuncio** announcement
el **anzuelo** hook
el **apoyo** support
la **aprobación** (*pl* aprobaciones) approval
la **apuesta** bet; stake
la **armada** navy
el **arreglo** compromise
la **artesanía** craft
el **artículo** article; item
la **asociación** (*pl* asociaciones) association
el **asombro** astonishment
el **aspecto** aspect
la **astilla** splinter
el **asunto** affair
el **atajo** short-cut
el **ataúd** coffin
la **atención** (*pl* atenciones) attention
el **atentado** attempt
la **atracción**; el **atractivo** attraction
la **ausencia** absence
la **autoridad** authority

supplementary vocabulary 683

la aventura adventure; affair
el aviso notice
la ayuda assistance, help
el/la ayudante assistant
el ayuntamiento council
el azar chance
la bala bullet
la bañera tub
la barandilla rail
la barrera barrier
el barril barrel
la base base
la batalla battle
la batería battery
la beca grant
el beso kiss
la Biblia Bible
la bolsa bag
la bomba bomb
la bondad kindness
el borde edge
la broma joke
el brote outbreak
el bullicio bustle
la burbuja bubble
el cable cable
la caja box
la calcomanía transfer
el cálculo calculation
el caldo stock
la calidad quality
la calma calm
el camino path; way
el campamento camp
la campaña campaign
el camping (pl ~s) site
el canal channel
el/la canguro baby-sitter
la cantidad amount

el caos chaos
la capa layer
la capacidad ability; capacity
el capítulo chapter
la característica characteristic;
  feature
la caridad charity
el/la catedrático(a) professor
el cazo pot
los celos jealousy (sing)
el centro centre; focus; middle
el centro turístico resort
la cesta basket
el chiste joke
el cielo heaven
el cierre closure
la cima top
el círculo circle
las circunstancias circumstances
la cita quote; extract; appointment
el/la civil civilian
la civilización (pl civilizaciones)
  civilization
la clase sort; period
la clasificación (pl clasificaciones)
  classification
la clave code
la codicia greed
la columna column
el columpio swing
la combinación (pl combinaciones)
  combination
el combustible fuel
el comentario comment, remark
el/la comentarista commentator
las comillas: entre comillas
  inverted commas: in quotes
la comisión (pl comisiones)
  commission

el **comité** (*pl* comités) committee
el **compañero** fellow
la **comparación** (*pl* comparaciones) comparison
la **compasión** (*pl* compasiones) sympathy
la **competición** (*pl* competiciones) contest
el/la **competidor(a)** rival
la **comprensión** (*pl* comprensiones) sympathy
el **compromiso** commitment
la **comunicación** (*pl* comunicaciones) communication
la **comunidad** community
la **concentración** (*pl* concentraciones) concentration
la **conciencia** conscience
la **condecoración** (*pl* condecoraciones) honour
la **condición** (*pl* condiciones) condition; status
la **conducta** conduct
la **conexión** (*pl* conexiones) connection
la **conferencia** conference
la **confianza** confidence
el **conflicto** conflict
el **confort** comfort
el **congreso** conference
la **conmoción** (*pl* conmociones) shock; disturbance
el **conocimiento** consciousness; knowledge
la **consecuencia** consequence
el **consejo** advice
la **construcción** (*pl* construcciones) construction; structure
el/la **consumidor(a)** consumer

el **contacto** contact
el **contenido** content
el **contexto** context
el **contorno** outline
el **contraste** contrast
la **contribución** (*pl* contribución) contribution
la **conversación** (*pl* conversaciones) conversation
la **copia** copy
el **corazón** (*pl* corazones) heart; core
la **corona** crown
el/la **corresponsal** correspondent
la **corrupción** (*pl* corrupciones) corruption
la **cortesía** politeness
la **cosa** thing
las **cosas** stuff (*sing*)
la **costumbre** custom
el **crecimiento** growth
el/la **criado(a)** servant
la **crisis** (*pl inv*) crisis
la **crítica** criticism
el **cuadro** picture
la **cuba** tub
el **cubierto** place
el **cuchicheo** whispering
la **cuenta** count
  por su **cuenta** of his own accord
el **cuento** tale
la **cuestión** (*pl* cuestiones) question
la **cueva** cave
el **cuidado** care
la **culpa** blame
la **cultura** culture
la **cuota** fee
la **curiosidad** curiosity
los **datos** data (*pl*)
el **debate** debate

el **deber** duty
la **decepción** (*pl* decepciones) disappointment
la **decisión** (*pl* decisiones) decision
el **defecto** fault
la **definición** (*pl* definiciones) definition
el/la **dependiente(a)** assistant
la **depresión** (*pl* depresiones) depression
el/la **derecho(a)** right
  los **derechos** fee
el **desagüe** drain
el **desarrollo** development
el **desastre** disaster
el **descanso** break
el/la **desconocido(a)** stranger
la **desdicha** unhappiness
el **deseo** desire; wish; urge
el **desgarrón** (*pl* desgarrones) tear
la **desgracia** misfortune
el **desorden** disorder; mess
el **destino** destiny; fate
la **destreza** skill
la **destrucción** (*pl* destrucciones) destruction
la **desventaja** disadvantage
el **detalle** detail
la **devolución** (*pl* devoluciones) refund; return
el **diagrama** diagram
el **diálogo** dialogue
la **diana** target
el **diario** diary; journal
la **diferencia** difference
la **dificultad** difficulty
la **dimensión** (*pl* dimensiones) dimension
el **Dios** God

el/la **diplomático(a)** diplomat
el/la **diputado(a)** deputy
la **dirección** (*pl* direcciones) direction
la **disciplina** discipline
el **discurso** speech
la **discusión** (*pl* discusiones) argument; discussion
el **diseño** design
el **dispositivo** device
la **disputa** dispute
la **distancia** distance
la **división** (*pl* divisiones) division
el **drama** drama
la **duda** doubt
el **eco** echo
la **economía** economics (*sing*); economy
la **edición** (*pl* ediciones) edition
el **efecto** effect
el **ejemplar** copy
el **ejemplo** example
  por **ejemplo** for instance
el/la **elector(a)** elector
la **elegancia** elegance
el **elemento** element
la **encuesta** survey
el/la **enemigo(a)** enemy
la **energía** energy
el **entusiasmo** enthusiasm; excitement
la **envidia** envy
la **época** period
el **equilibrio** balance
el **equipo** equipment
el **error** mistake
el **escándalo** scandal
el **escape** leak
la **escasez** shortage
la **escritura** writing

el esfuerzo effort
el espacio space
la espalda back
la especie species (*sing*)
el espectáculo show; sight
la esperanza hope
el espesor; la espesura thickness
el esquema outline; diagram
la estaca stake
la estancia stay
la estatua statue
el estilo style
la estrategia strategy
el estrés stress
la estructura structure
el estudio studio
la estupidez (*pl* estupideces) stupidity
la etapa stage
la excepción (*pl* excepciones) exception
el exceso excess
la excusa excuse
el/la exiliado(a) exile
el exilio exile
las existencias stock
el éxito success
la experiencia experience
el/la experto(a) expert
la explicación (*pl* explicaciones) explanation
la explosión (*pl* explosiones) explosion
una explosión a bomb blast
las exportaciones exports
la exposición (*pl* exposiciones) exhibition
la expresión (*pl* expresiones) expression

la extensión (*pl* extensiones) extent
el extracto extract
el/la extranjero(a) foreigner
la fabricación (*pl* fabricaciones) manufacture
la facilidad facility
el factor factor
el fallo failure
la falta: absence
falta (de) lack (of)
la fama reputation
el favor favour
la fe faith
la felicidad happiness
la fila row
la filosofía philosophy
el fin end
la flecha arrow
el fondo background; bottom; fund
el/la forastero(a) stranger
la forma form; shape
la fortuna fortune
el fracaso failure
la frase sentence; phrase
la frente front
el frescor, la frescura freshness
la fuente source
la fuerza force; strength
la función (*pl* funciones) function
la ganancia gain
el gancho hook
los gastos expenses
la generación (*pl* generaciones) generation
el gol goal
el golfo gulf
el golpe bang; blow; knock
la gotera leak
el grado degree

el gráfico chart
la grieta crack
el grito cry
el grupo group
la guía guide
el hambre (*f*) hunger
el hecho fact
la higiene hygiene
la hilera row
el honor honour
los honorarios fee
la honra honour
el hueco gap
la huella trace
el humo fumes (*pl*); smoke
el humor humour
la idea idea
   no tengo ni idea I haven't a clue
el idioma language
el/la idiota fool; idiot
la imagen (*pl* imágenes) image
la imaginación (*pl* imaginaciones)
   imagination
el impacto impact
el imperio empire
las importaciones imports
la importancia importance
la impresión (*pl* impresiones)
   impression
el impuesto duty
el impulso urge
la inauguración (*pl* inauguraciones)
   opening
el incidente incident
la independencia independence
el índice index
la indirecta hint
la infancia childhood
el infierno hell

la influencia influence
los ingresos earnings
el/la inspector(a) inspector
el instante instant
la institución (*pl* instituciones)
   institution
el instituto institute
las instrucciones instructions
el instrumento instrument
la intención (*pl* intenciones)
   intention; aim
el interés (*pl* intereses) interest
la interrupción (*pl* interrupciones)
   interruption
el intervalo gap
la investigación (*pl* investigaciones)
   research
la invitación (*pl* invitaciones)
   invitation
la ira anger
el jaleo row
el/la jefe(a) chief
el juego gambling
el juguete toy
la lágrima tear
la lata can
el/la lector(a) reader
la leyenda legend; caption
la libertad freedom
la licenciatura degree
el/la líder leader
la liga league
el límite boundary; limit
la limpieza cleanliness
la línea line
la liquidación (*pl* liquidaciones)
   settlement
la lista list
la literatura literature

el local premises (*pl*)
la locura madness
el logro achievement
la loncha slice
la longitud length
el lugar site
el lujo luxury
la luz (*pl* luces) light
  luz de la luna moonlight
el/la maestro(a) master
la magia magic
la manera manner
la máquina machine
la marca brand; mark
el marco frame
el margen (*pl* márgenes) margin
la máscara mask
la matrícula fee
el máximo maximum
la mayoría majority
el medio (de) means (of)
la mejora, la mejoría improvement
la memoria memory
la mente mind
el método method
la mezcla mixture
el miedo fear
el milagro miracle
la mina mine
el mínimo minimum
el ministerio ministry
la minoría minority
la mirada glance
la misa mass
la misión (*pl* misiones) mission
el misterio mystery
el mitin (*pl* mítines) rally
el mito myth
la moda fashion; trend

la molestia annoyance
el molino mill
el montón (*pl* montones) mass; pile
la moral morals (*pl*)
el mordisco bite
el motivo pattern
el motor motor
el muchacho lad
la muchedumbre crowd
la muestra sample
la muñeca doll
la naturaleza nature
el naufragio wreckage (*sing*)
la negociación (*pl* negociaciones)
  negotiation
el nervio nerve
la niñez childhood
el nivel level
el nombramiento appointment
la nota note
el número number; issue
la objeción (*pl* objeciones) objection
el objetivo objective; purpose;
  target
el objeto object; goal
las obras works
el odio hate
el/la oficial officer
la olla pot
el olor smell
la opción (*pl* opciones) option
la opinión (*pl* opiniones) opinion
la oportunidad chance; opportunity
la oposición (*pl* oposiciones)
  opposition
la orden (*pl* órdenes) order
la organización (*pl* organizaciones)
  organization
  organización benéfica charity

el orgullo pride
el origen (*pl* orígenes) origin
la oscuridad darkness
la paciencia patience
la página page
la paja straw
la palabra word
el palacio palace
el palo stick
el pánico panic
el paquete pack; packet
la pareja pair
la parte part
  parte de arriba top; parte
  delantera front; parte trasera rear;
  de parte de algn on behalf of sb
la partida item
el parto labour
  estar de parto to be in labour
el pasaje; el pasillo passage
la pasión (*pl* pasiones) passion
el paso footstep
el patrón (*pl* patrones) pattern
la pausa pause
el payaso clown
el pedazo piece
el pedido order
la pelea row
el peligro danger
la pena distress; penalty
el penalty (*pl* penalties) penalty
el pensamiento thought
el periódico journal
el periodo period
el/la perito(a) expert
el permiso permission
la persona person
el personal personnel
la perspectiva prospect

la pesadilla nightmare
la picadura bite
la pieza piece; item
la pila battery; pile
la pista clue
el placer delight; pleasure
el plan plan; scheme
el plato dish
la plaza place
el poder power
el poema poem
la política politics (*sing*); policy
la póliza policy
el polvo dust
la pompa bubble
el porcentaje percentage
la porción (*pl* porciones) portion
el portavoz (*pl* portavoces)
  spokesman
la posibilidad possibility
la posición (*pl* posiciones) position
la práctica practice
la preferencia choice
el prefijo code
la pregunta question
el premio award
la preparación (*pl* preparaciones)
  preparation
los preparativos arrangements
la presencia presence
la presión (*pl* presiones) pressure
el presupuesto budget; quote
la princesa princess
el príncipe prince
el principio beginning; principle
la prioridad priority
el problema problem; trouble
el proceso process
el/la profesor(a) master

la profundidad depth
el programa schedule
la prohibición (*pl* prohibiciones) ban
el propósito purpose
  a propósito on purpose
la propuesta proposal
la prosperidad prosperity
la protección (*pl* protecciones)
  protection
la protesta protest
las provisiones provisions
el proyecto plan
la publicidad publicity
la puja bid
la punta point
la puntería aim
el punto item; point
  punto de partida starting point;
  punto de vista point of view
el/la querido(a) darling
la rabia rage
la raja crack
el rato while
la razón (*pl* razones) reason
la reacción (*pl* reacciones) reaction;
  response
la realidad reality
la rebanada slice
el/la rebelde rebel
el recado message
la recepción (*pl* recepciones)
  reception
la recesión (*pl* recesiones) recession
la reclamación (*pl* reclamaciones)
  claim
el recuerdo souvenir
el recurso resource
  como último recurso as a last resort
la red network

la reducción (*pl* reducciones)
  reduction
la reforma reform
la regla period
la reina queen
la relación (*pl* relaciones) relationship
la religión (*pl* religiones) religion
la reputación (*pl* reputaciones) status
el requisito requirement
la reserva fund; stock
la resistencia resistance
la resolución (*pl* resoluciones)
  resolution
el respecto: con respecto a with
  regard to
el respeto respect
la respiración (*pl* respiraciones) breath
la responsabilidad responsibility
la respuesta reply; response
los restos remains; wreckage (*sing*)
el resultado outcome
el reto challenge
el retrato portrait
la reunión (*pl* reuniones) meeting
la revista magazine; journal
el rey (*pl* ~es) king
el riel rail
el ritmo pace
el/la rival rival
la rodaja slice
el ruido noise
la ruina ruin
el rumor rumour
la ruptura break
la rutina routine
el sacrificio sacrifice
el/la santo(a) saint
la sección (*pl* secciones) section
el secreto secret

el sector sector
la sed thirst
la seguridad security; safety
la selección (pl selecciones)
   selection; choice
el sentido sense; way
el sentimiento feeling
la señal sign; mark
el señor lord
el servicio service
la sesión (pl sesiones) session
el significado meaning
el silbato whistle
el silencio silence
el símbolo symbol
el sindicato trade union
el sistema system
el sitio place
la situación (pl situaciones) situation
el/la socio(a) member
la soledad loneliness
el sollozo sob
la solución (pl soluciones) solution
la sombra shadow
el sondeo (de opinión) poll
el sonido sound
la sorpresa surprise
la sospecha suspicion
la subasta auction
el subtítulo caption
la subvención (pl subvenciones)
   grant
la suciedad dirtiness
el sueño sleep
la suerte luck
   buena/mala suerte good/bad luck
la sugerencia suggestion
el suicidio suicide
la suma sum

la superficie surface
la supervisión (pl supervisiones)
   supervision
el/la superviviente survivor
el/la suplente substitute
el surtido choice
la sustancia substance
el/la sustituto(a) substitute
la táctica tactics (pl)
el talento talent
la tapa top
la tapicería, el tapiz (pl tapices)
   tapestry
el tapón (pl tapones) top
la tarea task
la tarifa; la tasa rate
el teatro theatre; drama
la técnica technique
la tecnología technology
el tema theme; issue
la tendencia trend
la tensión (pl tensiones) tension;
   strain
la tentativa attempt; bid
la teoría theory
el territorio territory
el terrón (pl terrones) lump
el texto text
la tienda store
la timidez shyness
el tipo type; kind; fellow, guy
el tío (Sp) guy
la tirada edition
el título title
el tomo volume
la tortura torture
el total total
la tradición (pl tradiciones)
   tradition

la **trampa** trap
la **tranquilidad** calmness
la **transferencia** transfer
el **tratamiento** treatment
el **trato** deal; treatment
la **tristeza** sadness
el **trozo** bit; piece; slice
el **truco** trick
el **tubo** tube
la **tumba** grave
el **tumor** growth
el **turno** turn
la **unidad** unit
la **valentía** bravery, courage
el **valor** value
el **vapor** steam
la **variedad** variety; range
la **vela** candle
el **veneno** poison

la **ventaja** advantage; asset
la **verdad** truth
la **vergüenza** shame
la **versión** (*pl* versiones) version
la **victoria** victory
la **vida** life
el **vínculo** bond
la **violencia** violence
la **visita**; visit; visitor
el/la **visitante** visitor
la **vista** sight
el **volumen** (*pl* volúmenes) volume
el/la **voluntario(a)** volunteer
el/la **votante** voter
la **vuelta** turn; return
  dar una **vuelta** to go for a stroll;
  dar una **vuelta en bicicleta** to go
  for a bike ride

VERBS

> **What is a verb?**
> A **verb** is a 'doing' word which describes what someone or something does, what someone or something is, or what happens to them, for example, *be*, *sing*, *live*.

abandonar to abandon

abrigar(se) to shelter

abrir to turn on
  abrir(se) to open

abrochar to fasten

aburrir to bore
  aburrirse to get bored

acabar de hacer algo to have just done sth

acampar to camp

aceptar to accept

acercarse (a) to approach
  acercarse a to go towards

aclarar(se) to clear

acompañar to accompany; to go with

aconsejar to advise; to suggest

acordarse de to remember

acostarse to lie down

acostumbrarse a algo/algn to get used to sth/sb

actuar to act; to operate

acusar to accuse

adaptar to adapt

adelantar to go forward; to overtake

adivinar to guess

admirar to admire

admitir to admit

adoptar to adopt

adorar to adore

adquirir to acquire; to purchase

afectar to affect

afirmar to assert; to state

agarrar to catch; to grab; to grasp

agradecer to thank (for)

aguantar to bear

ahorrar to save

ahuyentar to chase (off)

alcanzar to reach
  alcanzar a algn to catch up with sb;
  alcanzar a ver to catch sight of

alimentar to nourish

aliviar to relieve

almacenar to store

alojarse to put up
  alojarse con to lodge with

alquilar to hire; to rent: to let

amar to love

amenazar to threaten

amontonar to stack

andar to walk

anhelar to long for

animar to encourage
  animar a algn a hacer algo to urge sb to do sth

anunciar to advertise; to announce

añadir to add

apagar to switch off; to turn off; to put out

apagar to turn off
  apagarse to fade

aparecer to appear

apetecer to fancy
  me apetece un helado I fancy an ice cream

aplastar to crush
aplaudir to applaud; to cheer; to clap
aplazar to postpone; to put back
aplicar a to apply to
apostar (a) to bet (on)
apoyar to support; to endorse
  apoyar(se) to lean
apreciar to appreciate
aprender to learn
apretar to press; to squeeze
aprobar to approve of; to endorse
aprovechar to take advantage (of)
apuntar to take down
arañar to scratch
arrancar to pull out
arrastrar to drag
  arrastrarse to crawl
arreglar to fix (up); to arrange; to settle
  arreglárselas to cope; to manage
arrepentirse de to regret
arriesgar to risk
arrojar to hurl
arruinar to ruin
asar to bake
ascender to promote
asegurar to assure; to ensure;
  to secure
asentir con la cabeza to nod
asfixiar(se) to suffocate
asistir (a) to attend
asombrar to amaze; to astonish
asustar to alarm; to frighten; to
  startle
atacar to attack
atar to attach; to tie
atender to treat
  atender a to attend to
atraer to attract
atrasar to hold up

atreverse (a hacer algo) to dare
  (to do sth)
aumentar to increase; to raise
avanzar to advance
averiarse to break down
averiguar to check
avisar to warn
ayudar to help
azotar to whip
bailar to dance
bajar: to come down; to go down;
  to lower
  bajar (de): to get off; bajar de to
  get out of
balbucir to stammer
barrer to sweep
basar algo en to base sth on
batir to whip; to beat
besar to kiss
bombardear to bomb
brillar to shine; to sparkle
bromear to joke
burlarse de to make fun of
buscar to look for; to search; to seek
caerse to fall (down)
  se me cayó I dropped it
calcular to estimate
calentar(se) to heat (up)
callarse to be quiet
cambiar to alter; to exchange
  cambiar(se) to change
cancelar to cancel
cantar to sing
capturar to capture
carecer de to lack
cargar (de) to load (with)
causar to cause
cavar to dig
celebrar to celebrate

centellear to sparkle
cerrar: to turn off: to close; to fasten
  cerrar(se): to shut; cerrar con
  llave to lock
charlar to chat
chillar to scream
chismear to gossip
chocar con to bump into
chupar to suck
citar to quote
clasificarse to qualify
cobrar to claim; to get
coger to catch; to grab; to seize
colaborar to collaborate
coleccionar to collect
colgar to hang (up)
colocar to place
combinar to combine
comenzar (a) to start (to)
cometer to commit
compaginar to combine
comparar to compare
compartir to share
compensar to compensate (for)
  compensar por to make up for
competir en to compete in
complacer to please
completar to complete; to make up
comprar (a) to buy (from)
comprender to comprise
comunicar to communicate
conceder to grant
concentrarse to concentrate
concertar to arrange
concluir to conclude; to accomplish
condenar to condemn; to sentence
conducir to lead
conectar to connect
confesar to confess

confiar to trust
  confiar en to rely on
confirmar to confirm
confundir (con) to confuse (with)
  confundir a algn con to mistake
  sb for
congelar to freeze
conocer to know
conseguir to achieve; to get; to secure
  conseguir (hacer) to succeed (in
  doing)
considerar to consider; to rate
constar de to consist of
  hacer constar to record
constituir to constitute; to make up
construir to build; to put up
consultar to consult
consumir to consume
contar to count
  contar con to depend on
contemplar to contemplate
contener to contain; to hold
contestar to answer
continuar to continue; to keep;
  to resume
contribuir to contribute
controlar to control
convencer to convince
convenir to suit
convertir to convert
copiar to copy
correr to run
cortar to cut (off); to mow
costar to cost
crear to create
crecer to grow
creer to believe; to reckon
criar to bring up
criticar to criticize

cruzar to cross
cubrir (de) to cover (with)
cuchichear to whisper
cuidar to look after; to take care of;
  to mind
  cuidar de to take care of
cultivar to cultivate
cumplir to accomplish; to carry out
curar to heal
dañar to harm
dar to give:
  dar a to overlook; dar asco a to
  disgust; dar de comer a to feed;
  dar la bienvenida to welcome; dar
  marcha atrás to reverse;
  dar saltitos to hop; dar un paseo
  to go for a stroll; dar un puñetazo a
  to punch; dar una bofetada a to
  slap; dar vergüenza a to embarrass;
  dar vuelta a to turn; darse cuenta
  de algo to become aware of sth;
  darse por vencido to give up;
  darse prisa to hurry;
deber must; to owe
  deber hacer algo to be supposed
  to do sth; debo hacerlo I must do it
decepcionar to disappoint
decidir(se) (a) to decide (to)
decidirse (a) to make up one's mind
  (to)
decir to say; to tell
declarar to declare
  declarar culpable to convict;
  declararse en huelga to (go on)
  strike
decorar to decorate
dedicar to devote
defender to defend
definir to define

dejar to leave
  dejar caer to drop
deletrear to spell
demorar(se) to delay
demostrar to demonstrate
depender de to depend on
derribar to demolish
desanimar to discourage
desaparecer to disappear
desarrollar(se) to develop
descansar to rest
descargar to unload
describir to describe
descubrir to discover; to find out
desear to desire; to wish
deshacerse de to get rid of
deslizar(se) to slip
desnudarse to strip
despedir to dismiss
despegar to take off
despejar(se) to clear
despertar(se) to wake up
desprenderse to come off
desteñirse to fade
destruir to smash
desviar to divert
detener to arrest
determinar to determine
detestar to detest
devolver to bring back; to give back;
  to send back
  devolver a su sitio to put back
dibujar to draw
diferenciarse (de) to differ (from)
dimitir to resign
dirigir to conduct; to direct; to
  manage
disculparse (de) to apologise (for)
discutir to argue; to debate; to discuss

diseñar to design
disfrazar to disguise
disfrutar to enjoy
disminuir to decline; to decrease;
  to diminish
distinguir to distinguish
distribuir to distribute
divertir to divert
  divertirse to enjoy oneself
dividir to divide; to split
doblar to fold
  doblar(se) to double
dominar to dominate; to master
ducharse to shower
dudar to doubt
durar to last
echar to pour:
  echar a algn to throw sb out;
  echar a algn la culpa de algo
  to blame sb for sth; echar al correo
  to post; echar de menos to miss;
  echar una mirada a algo to glance
  at sth; echarse to lie; echarse a
  llorar to burst into tears; echarse
  a reír to burst out laughing
educar to bring up; to educate
ejecutar to execute
elegir to choose; to select; to elect
elogiar to praise
emocionar to excite
empatar to draw, to tie
empezar (a) to begin (to)
emplear to employ
empujar to push
encarcelar to imprison
encender to switch on; to turn on;
  to light
encerrar to shut in
encontrar to find; to meet

enfocar to focus
enjugar to wipe
enseñar to teach; to show
entender to understand
enterarse de to hear about
enterrar to bury
entrar (en) to enter
entregarse to give oneself up;
  to surrender
entrevistar to interview
enviar to send
envolver to wrap up
equivocarse to make a mistake;
  to be mistaken
erigir to erect
escapar (de) to escape (from)
escarbar to dig
escoger to choose; to pick
esconderse to hide
escuchar to listen (to)
especializarse en to specialize in
especular to gamble
esperar to wait (for); to expect;
  to hope
establecer to establish; to set up
  establecerse to settle
estallar to blow up
estar to be
  estar acostumbrado a algo/
  algn to be used to sth/sb; estar de
  acuerdo to agree; estar de pie to
  be standing; estar dispuesto a
  hacer algo to be prepared to do
  sth; to be willing to do sth;
  estar equivocado to be wrong;
  estar involucrado en algo to be
  involved in sth
estirar(se) to stretch (out)
estrecharse la mano to shake hands

estrellar(se) to crash
estropear to ruin
  estropear(se) to spoil
estudiar to study; to investigate
evitar (hacer) to avoid (doing)
exagerar to exaggerate
examinar to examine
  examinarse to sit an exam
excitar to excite
exclamar to exclaim
excluir to exclude; to suspend
existir to exist
experimentar to experience
explicar to explain
explorar to explore
explotar to explode
exponer to display
exportar to export
expresar to express
exprimir to squeeze
expulsar temporalmente to suspend
extender to spread: to extend
  extender(se) to spread out
extrañar (*LAm*) to miss
fabricar to manufacture
faltar to be lacking; to fail
felicitar to congratulate
fiarse de to trust
financiar to finance
fingir to pretend (to)
firmar to sign
flotar to float
fluir to flow
formar(se) to form
forzar a algn a hacer (algo) to force
  sb to do (sth)
fotografiar to photograph
frecuentar to frequent
freír to fry

funcionar to work
  (hacer) funcionar to operate
fustigar to whip
ganar to earn; to gain
garantizar to guarantee
gastar to spend: to waste
  gastar(se) to wear (out)
gemir to groan
golpear to knock; to beat
grabar to record
gritar to shout; to scream; to cry
guardar to keep; to store
guiar to guide
gustar to like
haber to have
hablar to speak; to talk
hacer to do; to make; to bake
  hacer añicos to shatter; hacer
  campaña to campaign; hacer
  comentarios to comment; hacer
  daño a to hurt; hacer las maletas
  to pack; hacer preguntas to ask
  questions; hacer público to issue;
  hacer señas *or* una señal to signal;
  hacer una lista de to list; hacer
  una oferta to bid; hacer una
  pausa to pause; hacer una señal
  con la mano to wave; hacerse
  to become; to get; hacerse adulto
  to grow up; hacer(se) pedazos
  to smash
helarse to freeze
herir to injure
hervir to boil
huir to flee; to run away *or* off
identificar to identify
iluminar(se) to light
imaginar to imagine
impedir to prevent (from)

implicar to imply; to involve
imponer to impose
importar to matter; to mind; to care
  ¡no me importa! I don't care!;
  ¿y a quién le importa? who cares?
impresionar to impress
imprimir to print
inclinar to bend
  inclinarse to bend down
incluir to include
indicar to point out; to indicate
influir to influence
informar to inform
inscribirse to register
insinuar to hint
insinuar to imply
insistir en to insist on
instruir to educate
insultar to insult
intentar to attempt to
interesar to interest
  interesarse por to be interested in
interrogar to question
interrumpir to interrupt
introducir to introduce
invadir to invade
investigar to investigate
invitar to invite
  invitar a algn a algo to treat sb to sth
ir to go
  ir a buscar a algn to fetch sb;
  ir bien a to suit; ir deprisa to dash;
  ir en bicicleta to ride a bike
irse to go away
irritar to irritate; to aggravate
jugar to play; to gamble
juntarse con to join
jurar to swear
justificar to justify

juzgar to judge
lamentarse to moan
lamer to lick
lanzar to throw; to launch
  lanzarse a to rush into
leer to read
levantar to raise; to put up; to lift
  levantarse to get up; to rise
limpiar to clean
llamar to call
  llamar por teléfono: to ring;
  llamarse to be called
llegar to arrive
llenar (de) to fill (with)
llevar: to carry; to bear; to wear
  llevar a cabo to carry out;
  llevarse to take
llorar to cry, weep
llover to rain
  llover a cántaros to pour
luchar to fight; to struggle
maltratar to abuse
manchar to dirty
mandar to command, to order
manifestarse to demonstrate
mantener to maintain; to support
  mantener el equilibrio to balance
marcharse to depart; to leave
medir to measure
mejorar(se) to improve
mencionar to mention
mentir to lie
merecer to deserve
meterse en to get into
mezclar to mix
mimar to spoil
mirar to look (at); to watch
  mirar fijamente to stare at
modificar to adjust

molestar to annoy; to disturb; to trouble

montar a caballo to ride

morder to bite

morir to die

mostrar to hold up
mostrar(se) to show

mover to move

multiplicar to multiply

nacer to be born

necesitar to need

negar to deny
negarse (a) to refuse (to)

negociar to negotiate

notar to note

obedecer to obey

obligar a algn a to oblige sb to

observar to notice; to observe

obstruir to block

obtener to obtain

ocasionar to bring about

ocultar to hide

ocupar to occupy
ocuparse de to deal with

ocurrir to occur

odiar to hate

ofender to offend

ofrecer to offer
ofrecerse a hacer algo to volunteer to do sth

oír to hear

oler to smell

olvidar to forget

operar a algn to operate on sb

oponerse a to oppose; to object to

organizar(se) to organize

otorgar to award

pagar to pay

pararse to come to a halt, to stop

parecer to seem (to); to look
parecerse a to look like, to resemble

participar en to take part in

partir to share
partir(se) to split

pasar to pass; to overtake; to spend

pedir to request; to order
pedir a algn que haga algo to ask sb to do sth; pedir algo a algn to ask sb for sth; pedir algo prestado a algn to borrow sth from sb

pegar to hit; to stick; to strike

pensar to think
pensar en to think about; pensar hacer to intend to do

perder to miss:
perder a algn de vista to lose sight of sb

perdonar a to forgive

perdurar to survive

permitir to allow, to permit, to let
permitirse to afford

perseguir to pursue

persuadir to persuade

pertenecer a to belong to

pesar to weigh

picar to bite

pinchar(se) to burst

planchar to iron

plegar to fold

poder to be able to; can; might
¿puedo llamar por teléfono?: can I use your phone?; el profesor podría venir ahora: the teacher might come now; puede que venga más tarde he might come later

poner to put; to lay
poner de relieve to highlight; poner en duda to question; poner

en el suelo to put down; poner en orden to tidy; ponerse to put on; ponerse de pie to stand up; ponerse en contacto con to contact
portarse to behave
poseer to own, to possess
practicar to practise
precipitarse to rush
predecir to predict
preferir to prefer
preguntar (por) to inquire (about)
  preguntarse to wonder
prender fuego to catch fire
preocupar to trouble; to bother
  preocuparse (por) to worry (about)
preparar(se) to prepare
prescindir de to do without
presentar to present; to introduce
prestar to lend
prevenir to warn
prever to foresee
privar to deprive
probar to prove
producir to produce
prohibir to ban; to forbid
prometer to promise
pronosticar to predict
pronunciar to pronounce
propagarse to spread
proponer to propose
proteger to protect
protestar to protest
proveer to provide
publicar to publish
quedar to remain
  quedarse to stay
quejarse (de) to complain (about)
quemar to burn

querer to want (to); to love; to like
quitar to remove
  quitar algo a algn to take sth from sb; quitarse to take off
reaccionar to react; to respond
realizar to fulfil; to realize
reanudar to resume
recalcar to emphasize; to stress
rechazar to reject
recibir to receive
  recibirse (LAm) to qualify
reclamar to demand; to claim
recoger to pick (up); to collect; to gather
recomendar to recommend
reconocer to recognize
recordar to recall
  recordarle a algn to remind sb of
recuperarse to recover
reducir(se) to reduce
reembolsar to refund
referirse a to refer (to)
  en lo que se refiere a ... as regards ...
reflejar, reflexionar to reflect
reformar to reform
regañar to tell off
regar to water
registrar to register; to examine
reír to laugh
  reírse de to laugh at
relajarse to relax
relatar to report
renovar to renew
reñir to quarrel
reparar to repair, to mend
repartir to deal; to deliver
repetir(se) to repeat
reponer to replace
  reponerse to mend

representar to perform; to represent
requerir to require
resbalar to slide
reservar to book; to reserve
resistir to hold out
  resistir(se) to resist
resolver to solve
respetar to respect
respirar to breathe
responder to reply, to answer;
  to respond
restaurar to restore
resultar to prove
retar to challenge
retirar(se) to withdraw
reunir(se) to collect
  reunirse to gather; reunirse con
  to rejoin
revelar to reveal
rodear (de) to surround (with)
romper(se) to break; to tear;
  to burst
ruborizarse to blush
saber a to taste of
saber to know
  sé nadar I can swim
sacar to bring out; to take out
  sacar brillo to polish; sacarse el
  título to qualify
sacudir to shake
salir to emerge
saltar to leap
saludar to greet
  saludar con la cabeza to nod
salvar to rescue; to save
secar(se) to dry
seguir to follow
  seguir haciendo algo to go on
  doing sth

sentarse to sit (down)
sentir to be sorry
  sentir(se) to feel
señalizar to indicate
ser to be
servir to serve
significar to mean
sobrevivir to survive
solicitar to apply to; to seek
soltar to release
sonar to sound
  (hacer) sonar to ring
sonreír to smile
sorprender to surprise
sospechar to suspect
subir to climb; to come up; to go up
  subir a to board; to get on
suceder to happen
sufrir (de) to suffer (from)
  sufrir un colapso to collapse
sugerir to suggest
sujetar to fix
suministrar to supply
suponer to assume; to suppose;
  to involve
surgir to emerge
suspender to suspend; to fail
suspirar to sigh
sustituir to replace
telefonear to telephone
temblar to shake
temer to fear
tender to hold out
tener to have; to hold
  tener antipatía a to dislike; tener
  cuidado to be careful; tener éxito
  to be successful; tener lugar
  to take place; to come off; tener
  mala suerte to be unlucky; tener

miedo to be afraid; tener que to have to; tener que ver con to concern; tener razón to be right; tener suerte to be lucky; tener tendencia a hacer algo to tend to do sth
terminar to end; to finish
tirar to throw away
  tirar de to pull
tocar to touch; to play; to ring
tomar to take
torcer to twist
trabajar to work
traducir to translate
traer to bring
traicionar to betray
tranquilizar(se) to calm down
trasladar to transfer
tratar to treat
  tratar (de) to try (to); tratar con to deal with
unir to join
  unir(se) to unite

untar to spread
usar to use
vaciar(se) to empty
vacilar to hesitate
valer to be worth
variar to vary
vencer to conquer, to defeat, to overcome
vender to stock
  vender(se) to sell
venir to come
  venirse abajo to collapse
ver to see
visitar to visit
vislumbrar to catch sight of
vivir to live
volar to fly
volcar to overturn
volver to come back; to go back; to return
  volver(se) to turn round; volverse hacia to turn towards
votar to vote

More fantastic titles in the
Collins Easy Learning **range:**